McKee Rankin

AND THE HEYDAY OF THE AMERICAN THEATER

McKee Rankin in his heyday.

McKee Rankin

AND THE HEYDAY OF THE AMERICAN THEATER

David Beasley

Wilfrid Laurier University Press

This book has been published with the help of a grant from the Humanities and Social Sciences Federation of Canada, using funds provided by the Social Sciences and Humanities Research Council of Canada. We acknowledge the support of the Canada Council for the Arts for our publishing program. We acknowledge the financial support of the Government of Canada through the Book Publishing Industry Development Program for our publishing activities.

National Library of Canada Cataloguing in Publication Data

Beasley, David, 1931-
  McKee Rankin and the heyday of the American theater

Includes bibliographical references and index.
ISBN 0-88920-390-3

  1. Rankin, McKee, 1844-1914.　2. Actors—United States—Biography.　3. Theatrical managers—United States—Biography.　4. Theater—United States—History—19th century.　I. Title.

PN2221.B42 2002   792'.028'092   C2002-900013-0

© 2002 David Beasley

Cover photograph: McKee Rankin as Sandy McGee in *The Danites*.
Photograph by Sarony, from the Billy Rose Theatre Collection.
Cover design by Leslie Macredie.

The author and publisher have made every reasonable effort to obtain permission to reproduce the secondary material in this book. Any corrections or omissions brought to the attention of the Press will be incorporated in subsequent printings.

The complete list of Rankin's roles can be found on the WLU Press Web site.

Wilfrid Laurier University Press
Waterloo, Ontario, Canada　N2L 3C5
www.wlupress.wlu.ca

Other books by the author can be found on the Davus Publishing Web site: www.kwic.com/~davus

Printed in Canada

All rights reserved. No part of this work covered by the copyrights hereon may be reproduced or used in any form or by any means—graphic, electronic, or mechanical—without the prior written permission of the publisher. Any request for photocopying, recording, taping, or reproducing in information storage and retrieval systems of any part of this book shall be directed in writing to the Canadian Reprography Collective, 214 King Street West, Suite 312, Toronto, Ontario　M5H 3S6.

I dedicate this book with much love to my dear wife, Professor Violet Beasley, who died in November 1999.

A Villanelle for Violet

Violet—gentle, warm, kind,
Generous friend,
Ever called to mind.

Her fine-wrought hands
Sketched stories
Of hibiscus lands

Taking us rapt
With her
Upon a journey lapped

About with perilous ways,
Scheherazade
Painting deep-felt days

Of struggle and grace
And courage enough
To win the race.

Violet—gentle, generous, kind,
Warm-hearted friend—
I miss you, my dear,
Always in my mind.

—J.M.

The period roughly between 1850 and 1920 was the heyday of popular theater in America. Before 1850, drama had a principally urban, heavily elitist audience; after 1920, movies and radio supplied the popular drama, and the theater returned to its elitist base. But for the seventy years in between, live drama was everywhere in the nation. This period is usually ignored or at best skimmed over in theater histories because it produced few plays that critics judge to be important. But in that period more than any other, drama belonged to the people, the common people. It reflected their desires, needs and tastes. While trying to plot successful careers for themselves, actors and promoters playing to the average American unconsciously discovered basic formulas that continually re-emerged in American popular culture.

—Robert C. Toll, *On with the Show*

Contents

LIST OF ILLUSTRATIONS	xiii
PREFACE	xv
ACKNOWLEDGMENTS	xvii
PROLOGUE	1
Preliminaries	5
1860: The Tyro in Rochester	7
ACT ONE: REPERTORY THEATER	15
1863: Cincinnati	15
1863–1864	
Indianapolis	24
Lexington	31
Kitty Blanchard	33
Rankin on Canadian Stages	38
1864–1865	
Pittsburgh	40
Boston	44

1865–1866
    Leading Man: Philadelphia 49
    Boston and E.L. Davenport 61
1866–1867
    New York City and Light Comedy 63
    Chicago and St Louis 66
    On the Road 67
The Burlesquing of American Drama 69
1867–1868
    Rankin Tours as Actor-Manager 75
1868–1869
    Variety and Chicago's Plaudits 82

ACT TWO: STARDOM 89
New York City in 1869 89
1869–1870
    Pike's Dramatic Company 93
    Acting in Tandem 95
1870–1871: Go West, Young Actor 100
1871–1872: St Louis and Rankin's Comedy Theatre 112
1872–1873: Fame as Rip Van Winkle and Bankruptcy 118
1873–1875
    The Boucicault Interlude 122
    The Union Square Theatre Company 123
    The Two Orphans 129
1875–1876: *The Two Orphans* on Tour 136
1876–1877: Philadelphia 139
1877–1878: The Fabulous *Danites* 149
1878–1879: The Theater Changes 158
1879–1880: England Welcomes the West 164
1881–1882
    Blanchard's Troubles 172
    '49, Successor to *The Danites* 176
1882–1883: Stock and Saxe-Meiningen 181
1883–1884: Rankin's Third Avenue Theatre 185
1884–1885
    Rankin's Cooperative Stock Company 190
1885–1886
    Successful San Francisco Days 198
    Macbeth 211
    The American Theatre Company Continues 218

ACT THREE: OBSESSION 237
1886–1887: The Rise of Mabel Bert 237
1887–1888: Reversals 243

Contents

1888–1889: *The Runaway Wife* versus
   The Golden Giant Mine 247
1889–1890: *The Canuck* 254
1890–1891: Sued for Support 257
1891–1892: *Abraham Lincoln* and Frank Mayo 261
1892–1893: Setback and Reconciliation 266
1893–1894
   The Drew–Barrymore–Rankin Connection 271
   The Great Discovery 274
1894–1895: Lamson Blossoms into O'Neil 279
1895–1896: Interlude with "Gentleman Jim" Corbett 283

ACT FOUR: THE REIGN OF NANCE O'NEIL 285
1896–1897: Creating a Star 285
1897–1898
   The Murray Hill Experience 291
   Nance O'Neil's Star Begins to Rise 294
1898–1899
   Homecoming 299
   London Bound 306
1899: Star Rising 309
1900
   The Australian Experience 312
   Melbourne and Adelaide 317
1901
   Au Revoir Sydney 319
   New Zealand 323
1901–1902: Africa 326
1902
   London 330
   The Syndicate 334
1903
   Retrieving Lost Fortunes 336
   The Debacle in Chicago 346
1904
   Boston: Unimaginable Success 354
   Lizzie Borden Interlude 368
   New York City: The Big Chance 370
1905
   Licking the Wounds 375
   The Great Australasia Return 379
1906: Coming through Disaster 384
1906–1907: The Last Chance 391
1907–1908: Vaudeville—Where the Money Is 395

1908: *Agnes* and the Shubert Imbroglio 400
1909: Larkin Bunce, Belasco, and *The Lily* 408

ACT FIVE: RANKIN ON THE REBOUND 417
1909–1911: Lionel, Doris, and Mac 417
1911–1913: Margaret Drew and the West 422
1914: Death 430

APPENDIXES
Appendix A
  Progeny 435
Appendix B
  Plays by McKee Rankin 439

NOTES 443
SELECT BIBLIOGRAPHY 497
INDEX 501

List of Illustrations

1. McKee Rankin in his heyday .... *frontispiece*
2. Pike's Opera House, Cincinnati, 1863 17
3. Playbill for *The Willow Copse* 18
4. Stage of Pike's Opera House 20
5. E.L. Davenport 21
6. J.W. Wallack 21
7. Mrs John Drew, 1864 50
8. William J. Florence, Irish-American comedian 70
9. Playbill for *Ours* 77
10. Playbill for *Undine* 79
11. Kitty Blanchard as William in *Black-eyed Susan* 90
12. Program for *£100,000*, Rankin's Theatre 115
13. Rankin as Georges de Lesparre 125
14. Kitty Blanchard as Henriette in *The Two Orphans* 131
15. Rankin as Jacques Frochard 133
16. Charles Thorne, Jr, as Chevalier de Vaudrey 136
17. Phyllis and Gladys (Pixie and Dido) in the late 1870s 143

18. Rankin in 1877	146
19. Playbill for *The Danites*, 1878	160
20. Program, New Sadler's Wells	169
21. Poster for one of Haverly's theaters, where Rankin played in 1881	173
22. Playbill for *Macbeth* at the California Theatre	214
23. Playbill for *The Canuck*	259
24. Mabel Bert in *Daddy Long Legs*, 1915	264
25. John, Ethel, and Lionel Barrymore	269
26. Playbill for *The Rivals*	271
27. Phyllis Rankin as Fifi in *The Belle of New York*	295
28. Nance O'Neil as *Magda*	297
29. O'Neil as Leah in *The Jewess*	308
30. Playbill for *Camille*, Sydney	315
31. Agnes Ranken (Rankin)	342
32. Fiske versus O'Neil as Hedda Gabler	373
33. Nance O'Neil as Odette in *The Lily*, with Julia Dean	413
34. Doris Rankin	419
35. Rankin and Margaret Drew in *Magda*	426
36. The last picture, 1914	431

Preface

They say that the deeds of actors are written on water. The experience of watching actors on stage in the milieu of their time cannot be duplicated on the printed page. Reviewers of the day sometimes give one an idea of the effect of a performance on the audience, but, in doing so, they inadvertently say more about the biases prevalent at the time. Just as actor and audience together shape the performance, so must they both be taken into account in any reconstruction of a theatrical experience. Yet, some of the greatest performances have gone unrecorded. Moreover, many of the tens of thousands of actors whose art moved playgoers cannot be recalled, even by name. Alas! poor Yorick!

Actors who write autobiographies can tell us of their childhood, their struggles, and their ideas of stagecraft—and, as in the case of the wonderful actor Clara Morris, they can pull us into the atmosphere of the repertory companies with their jealousies and kindnesses among actors—but to sing the poetry of their performances is quite beyond them. Their biographers often do no better: many emphasize their clandestine love affairs, but actors' importance should be judged by their dedication to their art and their contribution to the development of the theater. McKee Rankin's acting qualities and theatrical contributions cannot be exaggerated; they cry out to be recorded for the light they throw on the American and Canadian theater through the decades of its prime.

This book follows Rankin's career closely on the assumption that a profound and rounded portrayal will entertain and enlighten readers and give historians meat for their grinder. The notes act as a subtext by giving the plots of forgotten plays, the idiosyncrasies of forgotten actors, and references for those who want to look deeper into aspects of the story.

Acknowledgments

I am indebted to many archivists and librarians who helped me to find materials in the Archives of Ontario in Toronto; the Billy Rose Theatre Collection of the New York Public Library; and in university, research, and public libraries in the United States, Canada, England, Australia, and New Zealand. I thank in particular Dr Bell of the Harry Ransom Humanities Research Center at the University of Texas at Austin and Dr Levi Phillips of the Shields Library of the University of California at Davis for their help. Mr Peter Rankin supplied me with important notes and photographs, and especially encouragement, for which I am very grateful. I owe a huge debt to the Drama Department of McMaster University in Hamilton, Ontario, for making it possible for me to obtain newspapers on microfilm through inter-library loan, and I thank the staff of the inter-library loan office in the Mills Library at McMaster University for their courtesy and willingness to help.

I thank my late wife, Dr. Violet Beasley, for editing the manuscript and making suggestions for changes in the text. Her support throughout the long period of research was invaluable.

McKee Rankin

AND THE HEYDAY OF THE AMERICAN THEATER

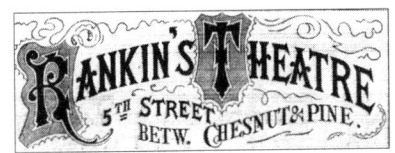

Prologue

Arthur McKee Rankin entered the world on February 6, 1844.[1] His mother, Mary McKee Rankin, lived in Sandwich, Canada West, a village next to Windsor and facing Detroit, Michigan, from across the narrowest section of the Detroit River. She gave the child his father's first name, Arthur, which proved prescient because the son inherited many of his father's qualities. On receiving news of his son's birth, Colonel Arthur Rankin, who was in England promoting a Wild West show with Ojibwa Indians, threw a banquet for the members of his troupe.

Colonel Rankin was an extraordinary man of imaginative individualism and entrepreneurial brilliance. As a young man, he had spent time with Canadian Ojibwa, learning their language, hunting and fishing with them, and living in their lodges in winter. Later, when the Ojibwa chief expressed a wish to meet the British monarch, to whom the tribe had been loyal through the American Revolution and the War of 1812, Colonel Rankin got the idea of showing them in their native costumes and customs to the English and arranged their passage to England. When they arrived in Liverpool, the Native people caused a sensation. George Catlin, the American painter who specialized in portraits of Native people, was then

---

Notes are on pages 443-44.

in London. Since Catlin already had experience in arranging exhibitions of American Indians and lecturing on their customs, Rankin wrote asking for his help in managing his troupe. Rankin and Catlin formed a partnership, bringing large crowds to see the Canadian Ojibwa perform their war dances and rituals at the Egyptian Hall in London. The reception given to the Native people by Queen Victoria was widely reported, contributing to the excitement and adding to the coffers of the two men.

Despite their success, the partners were soon at odds over the marriage of the group's interpreter, Albert Cadotte, to an eighteen-year-old English girl. Cadotte—whose Indian name was Not-een-a-aum or Strong Wind—was the son of an Indian woman and a French Canadian who had served the British government for many years as an interpreter. The *Manchester Guardian* described him as "a very fine specimen of the physical man."[2] Catlin adamantly opposed the marriage and blamed Rankin for arranging a Church wedding which attracted crowds of Londoners. After Catlin broke off their partnership,[3] Rankin made Cadotte his new associate.

Colonel Rankin had showmanship: posing as a Native chief, he drove his troupe in a van hitched to a team of six gorgeously caparisoned cream-colored horses drilled to the quick step of a brass band in attendance. Later, as a Member of Parliament in Ottawa, he walked across the floor of the Commons to tweak the nose of the minister of Finance. He was also a risk-taking entrepreneur. After discovering copper deposits on the north shore of Lake Superior, he sold the mining rights to a Quebec company for a large sum; later, he opened Bruce mine and sold it to the Montreal Mining Company, making himself rich in the process. He invested in real estate in Windsor, with the expectation of the railway passing through that city, and in Chatham, where he built a line of vessels which sailed between Chatham and Montreal.

Colonel Rankin's Scots-Irish, Protestant gentry background had fashioned his independence of mind.[4] Born in Montreal, he attended a Catholic college, but he was restless. He ran away to sea to work as a cabin boy on a New York–Liverpool packet for some years, articled in his brother's surveying office in Owen Sound, in Upper Canada, when he became friendly with the Ojibwa, and joined the Infantry Regiment in Sandwich, where, as second in command, he led the militia to rout invading Americans during the 1837 Upper Canadian Rebellion.

His father's sympathy for and democratic attitude towards the less fortunate strongly influenced the course of Arthur McKee Rankin's life and became a dominant theme in his choice of drama to entertain and educate theatergoers. For example, in August 1837, on a steamer from Windsor bound for Buffalo, New York, Rankin, then a lieutenant, observed a young black man standing on the deck with his hands tied behind his back. He learned that the man had fled slavery in Kentucky to find refuge in Canada, and that the two men guarding him were bounty hunters returning him to his master. Rankin, detesting slavery, remonstrated with the men that they could not steal the man from Canadian soil, but to no avail. Despite the danger to his own life, Rankin was determined to try to rescue the prisoner when the steamer stopped at Cleveland, Ohio. He found allies in an Englishman and two Americans who were passengers and two black crewmen. A plan was hatched whereby one of the crewmen was to jump ship as the steamer entered Cleveland harbor and secure two pistols from a friend, who was a barber near the docks. Once the steamer was in dock, Rankin took the pistols, waited for the prisoner and his two guards to disembark, and advanced with a knife to cut the cord that bound the slave's hands. One of the guards grabbed Rankin by the arm, and drawing a small dagger, threatened him with instant death. But Rankin put one of his pistols at the guard's head and declared he would blow his brains out if he did not immediately drop his dirk. Although the guard dropped his weapon, he also called upon his friend to run to a magistrate for a warrant. Before the second guard could flee, Rankin knocked him down with a blow to the chin. One of Rankin's party had picked up the dirk and cut the prisoner loose, while the others kept the crowd from pressing too closely upon them. Rankin, with a cocked pistol in each hand, rushed through the crowd and threatened to shoot anyone who dared to interfere with them. They ran as hard as they could, closely followed by their friends and a motley crowd of men, women, and children, some encouraging and others hooting derisively, to an adjoining wharf, where a steamer bound for Detroit was taking in wood. The people on board had seen all that had occurred, and they refused to allow the fugitives to come aboard, fearful of consequences. Rankin, followed by the Englishman, the slave, and the barber, jumped into a small boat belonging to a schooner, and pulled across the river in the midst of the threats of the people on board the schooner to shoot them.[5]

Landing in Ohio City, the fugitives made for the woods. The Englishman and the barber went for food while Rankin and the runaway slave hid. Warned by a stranger that a hunting party was in pursuit, they set out through the forest for a settlement twenty miles to the west. Pursued by the sounds of shooting, the two fugitives ran on for hours. They met a black man who took them to an inn kept by an abolitionist, where they hid in a small room just fifteen minutes before two men with rifles came in asking for grog and cursing the fugitives. The innkeeper gave the fugitives supper, which they ate with gusto, having had no food for thirteen hours, and provided beds for them in an upstairs garret.

Early the next morning, the innkeeper went to Cleveland to assess the situation. When he returned, he reported on printed descriptions offering a $500 reward for their apprehension. He proposed a mode of escape: a neighbor would take them by wagon through Cleveland in the dead of night eastward for thirty-five miles to Fairport, where they would catch a steamer for Buffalo. Because their pursuers expected them to continue fleeing westward, the wagon, with Rankin dressed like a farmer on the seat beside the driver and the runaway slave hidden under straw in the bottom, passed safely eastward to reach Fairport an hour before the steamer embarked. At Buffalo, Rankin and the runaway took a small boat across the Niagara River to Fort Erie. Rankin then returned to Buffalo to pick up his luggage where one of his friends on the first steamer had deposited it. Warned that a large reward was posted for his capture, he returned to Fort Erie for the fugitive, recrossed the river to Black Rock, took the train to Lewiston, and caught a Canadian steamer to Toronto, where his mother awaited him. Rankin's handwritten account of this adventure ends thus: "arrived at the capital of Upper Canada (the land of true freedom) the same evening. The Negro (David Miller) is now employed at his trade and receiving liberal wages."

As a politician, Colonel Rankin had a reputation for impulsiveness, a hot temper, and insubordination to party leaders. He allied himself with Sandfield Macdonald, the Ontario premier, who, as a liberal Catholic, opposed separate schools for Catholics. Once, he challenged John A. Macdonald, who became prime minister at Confederation, to a duel, but later they became close friends. Indeed, at the time of the Riel Rebellion, Rankin offered to negotiate secretly on behalf of the Macdonald government with the Metis because he knew the Metis well.

Colonel Rankin bequeathed some of his political combativeness to his elder son, George Cameron Rankin, born in 1841, who became a local politician and entrepreneur. Generally, however, George's temperament owed more to his mother's family, the McKees. In the 1730s, Alexander McKee and his son "Captain" Thomas had come from Ireland to Lancaster County, Pennsylvania. At the time, the territory to the north, east, and west of the Ohio River, including the Great Lakes region and upper St Lawrence River, was a vast forest with little settlement—Montreal on the east, Mackinac on the west, the Detroit River in the centre, and Pittsburgh in the south. "Captain" Thomas had children by either an Indian woman or a woman who had been brought up by Indians and lived in the last white settlement below Shanokin in Ohio.[6] His son, Alexander, became adept in Indian languages, worked as assistant agent for Indian affairs in the Western Territories, and built a large house known as McKee's

Mansion on a grant of 3,439 acres. By the time of the American Revolution, he was the richest man in the Pittsburgh area. As a Loyalist, he was imprisoned, but he escaped to Detroit, was made a colonel in the militia, and, with the famed revolutionary fighters Billy Caldwell and the Girty Brothers, led Aboriginal people on many successful attacks against the rebel forces. Continuing as an Indian agent in the British colonies after the peace, he secured a treaty with the Ottawa, Chippewa, Pottowatomie, and Huron in May 1790 for the purchase of land known now as Essex, Kent, Lambton, and most of Middlesex and Elgin Counties in southwestern Ontario. Alexander married a Shawnee woman—reputedly Tecumapease, an older sister of the great chief Tecumseh—and had three children, the eldest of whom, Thomas, was born in 1770. Thomas's son, Alexander, was the father of Mary Rankin.[7]

McKee Rankin was proud of his Indian background. Early in his stage career, he played numerous Indian roles, giving them individuality that contravened the stereotype.

Preliminaries

Early in 1853, Colonel Rankin took his family to England and enrolled his sons in the University College School in London.[8] It was a classical day-school offering instruction in Latin, Greek, English, French, German, history and geography, writing, ciphering, drawing, dancing, and gymnastics, including fencing. The school was started in 1827 by the founders of London University, Lord Brougham and James Mill, and it was built next door to that liberal institution on Lower Gower Street, a couple of hundred yards from the British Museum. No theology was taught, hence there was no interference in the first-class education that the school derived from its closeness to the university. Corporal punishment was banned; instead, students were punished by losing rank, working at extra tasks, and having recreation time curtailed.[9]

The headmaster, Thomas Hewitt Key, a tall man with restless energy overflowing into innumerable channels, was a human dynamo. He fostered a hard-hitting liberalism, supporting the repeal of the Corn Laws, which made Free Trade possible, and the passage of the Reform Bill, which enfranchised the growing middle class. He taught Latin with the object of getting the boys to write only what was worth reading.

The school's reputation traveled far to reach Colonel Rankin, and the teaching must have been first class for him to keep his sons there for two years. Because its students were expected to pass on to the Latin, Greek, and mathematics classes in the university, the school attracted good students; one who later became famous was the poet Thomas Hood, who edited the school magazine in 1851. McKee Rankin benefited from the study of languages; years later he translated plays from French and German to the American stage. His fencing training prepared him for the many stage fights he was called upon to perform, and critics were to praise his expertise. No doubt the school also provided opportunities for an appreciation of the theater, since the University of London had student productions, and the several professional theaters in London hosted student classes at matinee performances. Thus, when he was nine or ten, McKee would have attended Drury Lane, Covent Garden, and Eliza Vestris's Olympic; perhaps he had roles in his school's productions at Christmas. Yet, the real importance of the school's education was its liberalism, with its emphasis on self-reliance and experimentation, which stayed with McKee Rankin throughout the ups and downs of his life.

Colonel Rankin brought his sons home in 1855, probably because he wanted them to grow up in the family and experience Canadian life. He taught them to hunt and to ride, and McKee was considered an excellent horseman in later life. He sent his sons to Upper Canada College, Toronto, which was considered as providing the best education for the country's future leaders. Again the education was classical: the boys studied Greek, Latin, French, writing, and mathematics, with the addition of divinity. The college's records show that McKee was a boarder in 1856 and 1857.[10] Although he remained at the school until early 1860, the records do not list him, possibly because he was a day scholar living with his aunts in Toronto. McKee was not a good student.[11] He was rambunctious and was thought hard to discipline by the masters, who had quite a different approach to punishment from that of their counterparts in London.

During the summer months in Sandwich, McKee and some friends formed a minstrel band, the Nightingales, in which he played the end man, dancing, singing, and strumming in black face, as was the rage at the time. His family considered this youthful exuberance amusing and entertained no worries that it would lead to the stage, a profession that Mary Rankin considered beneath the family's station.

McKee's experiences in Toronto really began his infatuation with the theater. Toronto had a resident stock company that was visited by stars acting the circuits as far south as New Orleans. Colonel Rankin loved attending the theater and often took his family with him. A Canadian favorite was John Nickinson, a former British army recruit. From 1853 to 1858, Nickinson ran both the Toronto and Hamilton Lyceum Theatres, and his wife and daughters acted in his troupe. His youngest daughter, Virginia, ran the Toronto Lyceum Theatre with her young husband, Owen Marlowe, an Englishman who had made his debut at the Barnum Museum in New York City.

In 1859, McKee surreptitiously joined an amateur dramatic company, the Flower Minstrels, under the name George Henley.[12] At fifteen, he made his debut as the monk in *The Robber of the Rhine*. The actors scrambled to make up their own costumes, which, in McKee's case, led to a number of amusing incidents as he borrowed items from his household while he misled his aunts about his doings. For the role of the duke in the melodrama *Lucretia Borgia*, he sewed a pair of socks to flannel drawers to create theatrical tights, then unobtainable in the city, and took them to a dye-shop. Feeling guilty, he imagined that his aunts and everyone near him were watching him. His furtiveness made the dyer suspect that the extemporized tights were stolen, and Rankin had to explain his intention, which led to his aunts learning of his theatrical escapades. When McKee returned home to Sandwich for the Christmas holidays, his father lectured him several times to concentrate on his studies, which served to reinforce McKee's determination to join the theater.

1860: The Tyro in Rochester

While scheming to run away, McKee completed the school term to the end of February 1860. He wanted to go to the States, where there were more repertory companies than in Canada. It was hard to find a theater to take novices: war was threatening in the United States, and the American economy was in a downturn. Owen and Virginia Marlowe must have helped him, conveying the news that the Metropolitan Theatre in Rochester, New York, where Virginia's father, John Nickinson, was the first old man, would need actors, as Nickinson and some others intended to leave the company.

There was a daily steamship service across Lake Ontario between Toronto and Rochester, so Rankin's physical trip was simple relative to his emotional voyage. Although determined to flee the restrictions of a school whose harshness grew worse commensurate with his poor performance and that became more intolerable when enforced by the implacable will of his father, he feared the effect that his disappearance would have on his family and the tenacity of his father in tracking him down. For the moment, however, he was enthusiastic about his prospects in the theater and the life of freedom that it seemed to offer. He rejoiced to be traveling in the company of professional actors like Owen and Virginia Marlowe, and he entered the growing city of Rochester with confidence.

According to his own account, Rankin tried to impress Wellington Meech, the manager of the Metropolitan Theatre, with his potential talent. Rankin expected a salary of at least $35 a week for playing secondary parts.[13] "I guess I can give you a position as general utility," Meech drawled. "How much do you want for salary?" "I'll leave that to you," Rankin said, deflated by the offer. "Well, I'll give you $5 a week." Rankin accepted. He understood that it was the value that others put on his services that really counted, and, as a runaway, he had no choice.

The stock company comprised lines of business that defined the kinds of roles that an actor could be expected to play, even if he or she might be inappropriate for a particular role. The most important actors after the touring star were the leading man, the leading lady, the first old man, and the first old woman, followed by the first and second juvenile man, the first juvenile lady, the second old man, and the second old woman. In addition, a company had a first and second comedian, a first and second heavy, a first and second singing maid, a first and second walking gentleman, a first and second walking lady, a first and second heavy woman, and a first and second singing walking gentleman. Further down the hierarchy came the respectable utility, general utility, and utility players, and the ballet dancers. The utility men, Rankin's first job, often had the responsibility for the climax of a situation—delivering flying messages with perfect timing, for example. Because they were dealing with stars who, for the most part, had short tempers, such scenes became nerve-wracking ordeals for these novices. The Metropolitan Theatre employed few utilities, so Rankin had to play several small roles in a piece.

The stars received a certain percentage of the house receipts and collected the full receipts on the Friday night benefit. They chose the plays and directed the stock actors to play the roles as they wanted them played. The first visiting star, Rachel Denvil, was a large woman of commanding appearance with a deep, impressive voice. In some plays, women were called upon to play male roles because the tights they wore showed off their legs, which provided the Victorian men in the audience with vicarious pleasure. For instance, Denvil played Hamlet, which, commented the Rochester paper, she did well, seeming "qualified mentally and physically for the difficult undertaking."[14] The second star, John Andrew Jackson Neafie, popularly known as "Mr Neafie," belonged to the robustious school of acting typified by the American actor Edwin Forrest. In contrast to the English star William Charles Macready, who treated the theater as a living museum where an imaginative pictorialization of the past relied as much upon the eye as upon the ear, Forrest sought to show the truth of nature by powerful gestures, leaps, and howls as an underdog battling tyrants. Those Americans who considered Macready's lofty idealism and aloof acting style an affront to Forrest provoked the Astor riots in New York City on May 10, 1849. On cue, part of the audience began to abuse Macready's performance at the Astor Opera House. Street fighting erupted, and the military, which was called out, killed twenty-two rioters and bystanders.

Fortunately, Rankin did not have to choose between the two acting styles. By 1860 the underlying causes of theater riots like the Astor riot began to be understood by the theater professionals and the acting styles were less dogmatic. The early American stage had reflected a paternal society in which a union of fatherly and heavenly justice was played out in fairy-tale melodramas. With the upsurge in industrialization in the 1820s, the lower classes began to challenge a nervous patriciate as new money raised their status and undermined the social position of the old monied classes. The rioters, beginning with Jacksonian audiences in the 1830s, championed democracy against authoritarian rule and protested the paternalistic patron-to-artisan relationship reflected in the plays. The theater reacted to the new charismatic social relations in this era of liberal capitalism, which valued male individualism, by mounting plays with rebellious heroic underdogs to whom workers could bond and feel more like individuals than members of a class or ethnic group. These new melodramas in which workers could revel in apocalyptic visions were helped by the replacement of oil lamps by gas lighting, which, with greater illumination, increased the playing depth of the stage and allowed actors to perform within the scenery, not just in front of it. Weird and startling images were achieved, for which the Bowery Theatre in New York was renowned.

As a result of the social shifts in the theater, the elite deserted it for the class-based rituals of grand opera. At the same time, a new business class emerged under liberal capitalism. It dismissed the beliefs of the patrician and working classes, favored sensational melodrama, and established its own theaters, where the examples set by moral reform plays and sensational action encouraged its audiences to play new social roles without hypocrisy or embarrassment. It was onto the threshold of this new drama that the sixteen-year-old McKee Rankin was stepping. Neafie and the other followers of the dynamic antics of Forrest were destined, like their mentor, to become old-fashioned sooner than they could have believed.

The tall, strong-voiced Neafie began his engagement at the Metropolitan with *The Corsican Brothers*, in which the star plays twins, one of whom in Corsica sees the murder of the other in Paris as if in a dream and avenges his death. Rankin, who would win recognition as the twins later in his career, soaked up the invaluable experience of plays and styles from earlier decades that Neafie now presented at the Metropolitan. In one of them, *Jack Code*, a play set during the Kentish Rebellion of 1450, Neafie played the title role. The play, by depicting the growing hatred of the urban worker for the authoritarian upper classes, deeply stirred American audiences, whose own experiences of revolution and local rebellions reflected such sentiments.[15]

Another Forrest follower, the emotive, scene-chewing, robustious Edward Eddy, the leading star of popular-priced melodrama at the Bowery Theatre in New York City in the 1840s, at six feet tall, manly, handsome, and stentorian-voiced, followed Neafie as the visiting star. He modified his style in his opening piece, Shakespeare's *Richard III*, which the Rochester paper called "intellectual," a description that Forrest would neither have merited nor wanted. His second night, on which he played *Macbeth*, was particularly memorable for Rankin. In the play, Rankin filled the roles of the second witch, the bleeding sergeant, the physician, and the second murderer. As he stirred the witch's brew and recited "Eye of newt, and toe of frog / Wool of bat, and tongue of dog," he looked up to see the gray head and whiskers of his father sitting in front. He continued bravely with his parts, but after the final curtain when the prompter informed him that "a gentleman" wished to see him at the back door, he changed into his street clothes with trepidation. His father met him with kindness but was adamant that he return home. McKee just as strongly refused, but when his father persuaded him that his mother was in an agony of distress, he relented.[16]

His heart near to breaking, McKee dismissed all ambition for the stage, which had seemed to make life meaningful, and prepared to accept a safe career in whatever walk of life his father decided upon. Colonel Rankin, remembering his own runaway youth as a cabin boy, would have had some sympathy and admiration for his son, but Mary Rankin's fears for her son's future and her strong disapproval of the acting profession ruled him. They returned to the Rankin homestead, where a worried Mary Rankin tried to console McKee with the argument that his parents had saved him from a demeaning vocation, which would have ostracized him from decent society. Prevailing wisdom regarded an actor's chance of success as extremely unlikely and the certainty of a miserable life unquestioned. Just prior to McKee's arrival in Rochester, a reporter for the Rochester paper wrote: "Few, very few, attain the degree of eminence which renders them independent of its mortifications and its trials...while the many toil through a long life of thankless servitude, and at last drop into an unhonored grave, the blighted victims of a 'hope deferred.'"[17]

Prologue

The night after Rankin's departure, Edward Eddy was playing Schiller's *The Robbers*. McKee's replacement apparently was inadequate. "Where's Mr Henley?" Eddy inquired furiously. "His father has taken him home," said the prompter. "I wish to God," said Eddy, pointing to the offending young actor, "that his father would come and take him away." His anger may have improved his performance, however, as the Rochester critic reported that the "freshness and vigor" in Eddy's acting as Charles de Moor brought out "the warmest applause and commendations from our proverbially stoic audience...and the thrilling effect he gave to the curse scene in the 4th act was awfully grand."[18]

Through his father's political influence, the unhappy McKee was appointed assistant secretary to the Bureau of Agriculture. He began a trying time as a civil servant in Quebec City, where he developed a strong distaste for official work. When he applied for a clerkship in Windsor, the premier, Sandfield Macdonald, dealt with his application in a humane way. "I wouldn't like to appoint you, Rankin, without consulting your father," he said. "Besides, I don't approve of a young man of your parts becoming a mere official machine. I have heard that you have done well on the stage. You had better stick to that, or any walk of life to which you feel yourself adapted. You will spend your whole life in clerkships and such positions until you find yourself an old man, without having advanced yourself a particle, and then feel yourself incapable of anything except dull, soulless drudgery."[19] McKee threw up his secretaryship and returned to his home in Sandwich.

Meanwhile, Colonel Rankin had been alarming the Canadian political establishment. He had gone to the American president, Abraham Lincoln, to offer his services to the Union in the Civil War. Knowing Rankin's anti-slavery record, Lincoln commissioned him to raise a regiment of Lancers from the Detroit area, but, after Rankin had recruited about 240 men, the Canadian press began criticizing him for fighting in another nation's war. At the same time, questions were raised in the Canadian Parliament about the propriety of a Canadian politician defying the position of neutrality that his government had taken. Moreover, following Great Britain's lead, which favored the South for the sake of the cotton trade, many Canadians supported the Confederacy. When a statement was made in Parliament that Rankin should either give up the Lancer Regiment or his Canadian citizenship, Rankin decided not to continue with his plans. Perhaps a stronger motivation for changing his mind came from the American military, which considered the lance an outmoded weapon for cavalry in a war where cannon and explosives were becoming tools of mass destruction.

Reflecting his father's political beliefs, McKee, now eighteen, applied to the Union Army for a commission and was given a lieutenancy in the 1st Michigan Regiment under Colonel Broadhead, a veteran of the Mexican War and a friend of the Rankin family.[20] No longer a civil servant and still meeting his mother's adamant opposition to a stage career, McKee was paying his respects to his family before joining his regiment at the end of August 1862. He was visiting his grandmother, whose favorite he was, when the news reached them that his regiment had been decimated and Broadhead killed in the Second Battle of Bull Run. It was a shock that brought home the reality of the savagery of this new kind of warfare. Rankin tried to get a commission in another regiment. He seemed bent on suicide, as if life had little meaning for him if he could not be on stage. Seeing the situation clearly, his mother began to weaken in her resolve against an acting career. His grandmother argued that it was preferable for McKee to be on the stage than a corpse in a foreign war. McKee's mother's decision must have been painful, as it took some months of self-examination before she gave in to her son's wishes. Early in 1863, rejuvenated and thankful, Rankin traveled to Chicago, where there was a thriving theater district.

The Chicago theaters were undergoing hard times. Owing to enlistment, there was a shortage of actors, yet because theaters were suffering from depressed economic circumstances, they were not hiring. Finding no work in Chicago, Rankin wrote to all the theater-owners in the country. With immense relief, he received one offer—from Wood's Theatre in Cincinnati, Ohio, as a walking gentleman at $10 a week. He arrived in time to rehearse the role of Count Winterson in Kotzebue's *The Stranger*, starring the handsome Jane Coombs as Mrs Haller, who takes refuge in Winterson's castle. Coombs set a good example for the young actor: she played naturally, used her wonderful eyes, and had excellent elocution.

The play, translated from the German in 1798, remained popular for its air of melancholy and mystery and its theatrical romanticism.[21] It celebrated family feeling over rationality, and, by drawing attention to the pitiable situation of the modern family, it declared benevolent paternalism to be the solution. The anxious rhetoric of the characters revealed the prevailing doubts about the egalitarianism of the new democracy and market capitalism. Its underlying message held true for several decades, but its technique of moving the action through circumstance rather than intrigue had become old-fashioned. "One feels relieved," commented the reviewer, "when the last tear has fallen and the last sob has been wrung out of the unhappy couple."[22]

Jane Coombs followed *The Stranger* with a great favorite, Dion Boucicault's comedy *London Assurance*. In years to come, Rankin would

Prologue

play many of the roles in this play including Dazzle, the breezy parvenu and a precursor of Oscar Wilde's Ernest. Coombs played the determined horsewoman Lady Gay Spanker, who romps in and out of the amorous adventure. This had been Boucicault's first London success. In America, it was notable not only for the first long run in American stage history—thirteen nights—but, as in the London production under Madame Vestris, for introducing the box set: the audience appeared to be watching the action from the fourth wall of a real house and the actors entered through doors rather than from the wings. Prior to this innovation, the apron extended far in front of the proscenium and the scenery comprised wings and flats well to the rear. The box set began an evolution in stagecraft, which was helped on its way by the many technical inventions back stage until in 1900 the apron disappeared. The proscenium arch framed a picture created by painter and costumer, who flooded it with light. Whether symbolic, realistic, or fantastic, the drama became a series of pictures designed with an art and executed with a brilliance that led quite naturally into the motion picture decades later. This period of evolution coincided with McKee Rankin's career.

If Jane Coombs was feted in the local press, no mention was made of A.M. Rankin in the papers, but he was at last on his way. In later years, he recalled the date as March 14, 1863, instead of Friday, March 13, a mistake fashioned by the actor's inbred acknowledgment of superstition.

ACT I

Repertory Theater

1863: Cincinnati

Wood's Theatre in Cincinnati catered to the working classes, which liked broad humor, farce, and sensational melodrama. For the first month, Rankin acted with stars who could milk tears from a stone or bring an audience to a paroxysm of laughter.[1] In a state of continuous excitement from his plunge into the demanding world of professional theater, he was blessed with an easy and engaging personality, which brought him many friends, and a retentive mind, which allowed him to absorb his early stage experiences and use them for inspiration in stage direction years later. Plays in which he performed in 1863, such as Bulwer-Lytton's romantic drama *The Lady of Lyons*, were kept on stage well into the 1880s.

On March 16, 1863, Mr and Mrs William J. Florence arrived in Cincinnati. Billy Florence was to become one of Rankin's best friends; indeed, there were few stars more beloved, both by fellow actors and audiences. The couple opened in Dion Boucicault's *Colleen Bawn*, an Irish melodrama in which Rankin was to act many times in the future. Billy Florence played Miles na Coppaleen, a roguish bootlegger, with his usual

---

Notes are on pages 445-54.

"genial merry spirit."[2] In the afterpiece, *Thrice Married*, Mrs Malvina Florence sang and danced in five separate characters. Farces and comedies often gave stars the opportunity to play several widely different characters to demonstrate their versatility, and Mrs Florence was particularly good as a mimic. She, like her sister, Mrs Barney Williams, was superb as Yankee women, and both the Florence and Williams teams worked the Yankee comedy vein in a set of plays written to exploit the American character. None of this was lost on Rankin, who later developed regional character types previously unknown to the stage. Nor did he forget the showmanship of these actors. In one such instance, Billy Florence hoisted an Irish flag, presented to him by a General Corcoran, over the theater prior to the first performance. Presumably there were numerous Irish theatergoers in Cincinnati.

After the Florences, Wood's brought on Maggie Mitchell, who attracted full houses with her favorite sensational dramas *Little Barefoot* and *Fanchon, or The Cricket*—pieces in which Rankin would play the supporting actor or leading man in the future. Mitchell, a petite, curly-haired gamine, could pluck the hearts of audiences at will and had them in tears for much of the time. *Little Barefoot* might best be described as bucolic. *Fanchon* is the story of a wild, slightly mysterious country girl. Mitchell's Shadow Dance in *Fanchon* and the scene in which she wins over the father of her would-be husband were among the most famous theatrical moments of the era.

Maggie Mitchell's sister, Mary, was also an actor. Mary, who had a personality suited to tragic roles, would star in another theater in the same town and at the same time that her sister was playing, which made for an intense sisterly rivalry. Among other sisters who were stars, such as the Denins, only the Western sisters, Lucille and Helen, were rivals like the Mitchells. In their case, Lucille was the greater, more intense actress, whereas Helen was more beautiful. Rankin would be associated with them all in his climb to stardom.

In contrast to Wood's Theatre, Pike's Opera House, built by Samuel Pike, a successful whiskey manufacturer, attracted the upper classes in Cincinnati with a higher tone of drama and opera. After just over a month in the city, Rankin moved from Wood's to Pike's in circumstances that can be credited to good luck, a raw talent that stars were quick to see and encourage, and the significant fact that John Nickinson became stage manager at Pike's on March 11, 1863. Billy Florence, who had toured Canada in Nickinson's company, may have told Nickinson about Rankin and his promising talent. Nickinson, possibly owing to his friendly association with the Rankin family, took the young Rankin under his wing. He taught him many stage tricks, but, most importantly, he instructed him in the art of make-up, at which Nickinson excelled.³ The skills of acting were only a part of Rankin's education; the ideas, philosophies of life, and the personality of the actors, in particular the famous stars, influenced the young Rankin and subtly encouraged him to fit into the actor's life of tolerance, exhibition, and empathy with those from all walks of life.

Pike's Opera House, Cincinnati, in 1863.

It is likely that Rankin came to Pike's at the same time as Adah Isaacs Menken, or "the Menken," as she was universally known, who began a two-week engagement on March 30, enacting Byron's *Mazeppa* and, for a night, presenting her own adaptation of Fenimore Cooper's *The Last of the Mohicans*, entitled *The White Eagle*. Both dramas focused on her equestrian abilities on the stage and the form-fitting skin-colored garment in which she was lashed to the horse's back. Menken was beautiful and passionate, instinctively a courtesan, the most uninhibited woman of her day; but she was also intelligent, scholarly, poetical, and sensitive. To the public, she seemed strange, obscure, enigmatic, but great, not as an actress but as a theatrical personality. In *Mazeppa* there was a large supporting cast representing Poles and Tartars at war. In later years, Rankin played Abder Khan, the King of Tartary, father to Mazeppa, but probably had a minor role on the occasion of the play's presentation at Pike's.

The first playbill to be found listing Rankin was for a performance at Pike's of Boucicault's *The Willow Copse*, a domestic drama, on Saturday evening, April 18, 1863.[4] The stars—Charles Couldock, an English actor, who exuded integrity as a beau ideal of the wealthy farmer, Luke Fielding, and Rose Fielding, who played his daughter Eliza—brought intense emotion to the stage. Rankin played Arthur Apsley, a small role providing a true-love counterpoint to the troubled relationship between Fielding's daughter and her lover, who is being blackmailed. When first produced about 1850, the play was regarded as "simple and perspicuous," a relief from "the prettiness of turn and tinsel of ornament which give a gaudiness, a glitter and glare to almost all our present play nights."

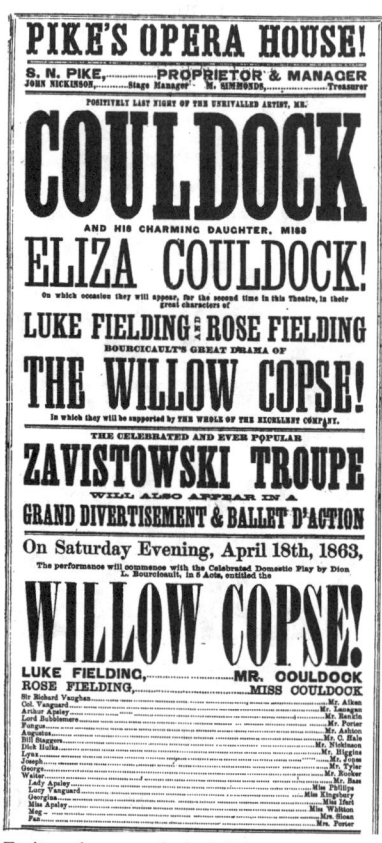

Earliest discovered playbill listing Rankin (as Arthur Apsley in *The Willow Copse*).

Rankin's roles at Pike's went from elementary to challenging. In Samuel Beazley's one-act farce *The Lottery Ticket, or The Lawyer's Clerk,* Rankin played Charles, a valet. In the very popular spectacular *Naiad Queen! or, The Spirit of Lurlie Burg,* Rankin played the wild and liberating Siegfried, a relatively small part. In Douglas Jerrold's domestic drama *The Rent Day,* he played Grantley, the young estate-owner, who makes a visit to the country estate left him by his father and discovers that his steward is terrorizing and defrauding the tenants. The steward was a new type of villain when the play was introduced to the stage in 1832; although he oppresses the poor, his motivation becomes understandable—and the character more sympathetic—when it is revealed that he is avenging the rape of his wife by the old squire, Grantley's father. When audiences began to accept that villains were not unlike other people, classical melodrama began to fade away, but this took time.

Repertory Theater

Some productions, such as *Naiad Queen*, called on all the resources of the Pike's theater company. The Zavistowski troupe of dancers, resident at Pike's, choreographed and danced the scenes featuring the Naiads, nymphs, and demons, such as the duet and dance under the waters, the grand *ballet d'action* in the stalactistic hall of the Naiads, and the grand march of female warriors. The scenic artist had to produce scenery to match the fantasy of mortals meeting immortals in caves and gardens. In the course of every play, the orchestra was called on to provide dramatic music, particularly to help change the mood from one scene to the next and at emotional moments. In *Naiad Queen*, it had to provide original music for the dances, choruses, and individual songs in addition to appropriate music as background to the dramatic scenes. A major reason for the play's popularity was the display of the legs of fifty female warriors, which, it was said by the local critic, "no mortal man could resist the opportunity of seeing." The role of Sir Rupert, the Fearnought, the knight who pursues the beautiful queen of the Naiads into the waters of the Rhine, was taken by the Pike's leading man, G.L. Aiken, who had distinguished himself by adapting Harriet Beecher Stowe's *Uncle Tom's Cabin* to the stage.

There were several experienced actors in the company, such as Matthew Lingham, whose youthful enthusiasm and earnest professionalism would have given Rankin a good model. Lingham began his career in Washington, DC, and, within three months, was greeted with applause on his initial entries on stage. Graceful, with a fine voice, Lingham brought the aura of a cultured gentleman to his roles and the sense of a quick and clear mind. The actors Rankin met in his early repertory years would reappear throughout his career as they struggled to survive as actors or managers; others would never rise beyond a certain line of business and would be swept off the stage by the changes in the theater that would soon be upon them.

When Nickinson introduced Rankin to the traveling stars who opened a long engagement at Pike's, E.L. Davenport and J.W. Wallack, Rankin blessed his good fortune. It was a great honor for a young actor and a sign of Nickinson's confidence in his talent, which he seemed to be recommending to the established actors. Certain characteristics that distinguished both men's acting were adopted by Rankin, and these bear scrutiny at this point.

Davenport was more restless in study, his mental activity "on the stretch." He was precise with every word and intonation. He displayed a painstaking and sensitive ambition in a kind of scrupulousness that compelled every situation to conform to the most careful taste. His delineations of character were subdued yet intense, carefully crafted yet kindled by acute sensibility, and he was master of all passions—a mastery best expressed by a satirically quiet manner. His weapon was the polished rapier, blue and glittering. Said to be the most versatile actor of his day, he surpassed Edwin Booth in range but was inferior to him in subtlety and electrical tragic inspiration. His physique was almost equal to the handsome, perfectly formed Wallack.

The stage of Pike's Opera House, Cincinnati, 1863.

James Wallack, Jr, a born actor, upon whom nature showered its gifts, engaged audiences immediately with an utter freedom from affectation and an inherent pleasantness of manner. His was "the nicety of art which conceals itself...the identity in which he lies merged is the offspring of this art...the outline alone concealed by the execution."[5]

With these great actors as teachers—for the visiting stars often instructed the local players on how to play their parts, and Davenport, in particular, was known for giving advice unasked—Rankin learned quickly. Davenport and Wallack also were engaging and pleasant, without any of the sense of superiority that lesser stars often showed towards the ordinary stock actor. Traveling with them as the third star was Mrs Farren, the widow of an Irish actor. The three opened in Shakespeare's *Othello*. Rankin may have learned from Wallack's sedately devilish Iago, but he took nothing from Davenport's Othello, whom Davenport portrayed as chaste and scholarly. Davenport's interpretation is interesting, however, as it provided a different avenue for Othello's murder of Desdemona—that is, a combination of offended ego and a cold lack of sexuality that Desdemona's supposed infidelity revealed as deficient. Rankin, in contrast, would eventually play a hot-blooded Othello.

The following night, Davenport took the role of Macduff, Wallack that of Macbeth, and Mrs Farren that of Lady Macbeth in Shakespeare's *Macbeth*. Wallack was said to have dimmed the local critic's memory of the other Macbeths, so magnificent was his performance. Rankin played Ross, Scottish nobleman and friend to Macduff, who must tell Macduff of the murder of his wife and children by Macbeth. This important role marks Rankin's progress. Although Colly Cibber's shortened versions of Shakespeare's dramas were commonly used from the eighteenth throughout the nineteenth century, Ross's scenes were too important to the action to be shortened.

Edward L. Davenport, tragedian.

James W. Wallack, tragedian.

These Shakespeare plays attracted immense audiences, and the house was filled the next night for *Hamlet*. Davenport's Hamlet was quiet, meditative, subdued, and "carried his auditors' inmost souls from step to step imperceptibly."[6] His fine physique and rich and sympathetic voice lent the same freshness and finish to his last as to his first speech. He used no mannerism, and, according to the critic, "borrowed little from art save where art added to its intellectual dignity."[7] Wallack played the Ghost of Hamlet's dead father with a solemnity that brought terror and a dreadful awe to the spectators. Nickinson was praised as the best Polonius that the critic had seen. Dressed with sumptuous fidelity as a Danish attaché of state, Nickinson played the interfering old diplomat with the unctuousness and faithfulness of a court favorite. Rankin often played Laertes later in his career, but because he was employed at Pike's as a walking gentleman, he was relegated to a smaller role at this time. Walking gentlemen—like the roles of Guildenstern and Rosencrantz in *Hamlet*—played characters essential to the development of the plot, but their dialogues were not part of the emotional characteristics of the play's language.

The critics of the day applauded lack of mannerisms and "natural" acting to the point where a young actor dared not adopt the robustious style that had been so popular prior to 1860. Some actors, especially in Shakespearean roles, continued to rant and gesticulate in a manner in which Hamlet himself disapproved in his speech to the actors, but, long after they had lost their big-city followers, they were tolerated by audiences in the back country because of a certain tenseness and glory they brought to their roles. Rankin was fortunate that his first serious tutors were Davenport, Wallack, and Nickinson, from whom he learned the value of deep character study, a casual naturalness, and attention to detail. Rankin later became known for studying his portrayals closely to pull out every nuance to bring them alive.[8]

Damon and Pythias, or, The Test of Friendship, was a Greek drama peculiarly fitted to Davenport's style. Davenport played Damon, a senator, while Wallack played a soldier who was Damon's friend. Rankin, who was beginning to get more demanding roles, played the commanding yet thoughtful personage of Proclus, captain of the guard. He wore Grecian armor, a lambrequin, a red mantle, a sword, and sandals, and carried a shield and helmet. He spoke in rather difficult blank verse: "It is his creed that in this flesh of ours / Self even entertains predominance." Davenport and other stars such as John McCullough kept *Damon and Pythias* in their repertoires, so it must have resonated with audiences. Its attractions were the themes of loyalty and friendship. Scenes from the golden age of ancient Greece removed audiences from their own competitive, grubby, and treacherous world of advancing industrialization and urban poverty.

With admiration for the magic of the actors who conjured up different atmospheres night after night, Rankin went from ancient Greece to Lord Byron's *Werner, or, The Inheritance.* Macready had cut the original play by two-thirds and altered Byron's hero from a man burdened with guilt to a pathetic wretch dominated by love for his son, Ulric.[9] Wallack took the role of Werner, and Davenport played Ulric in a way that spurned Macready's diminution of the role from a complex and political man, at once superficial and profound, to a mere "son gone wrong." The program stated that he had made the character "peculiarly his own," which implied that Byron's creation was at least partially restored. Rankin played Rodolph, Ulric's confidant.

In *St Marc! Or, The Soldier of Fortune,* written for Davenport, Rankin experienced the power of tableaux to move audiences. Each of the five acts began with the actors posed in a picture tableau that foretold the story of the act and presented an aesthetically beautiful arrangement enjoyed by the audiences of that day. The play was advertised as "abounding in beautiful sentiments, patriotic inspirations, and soul-stirring pictures and effects."[10] Davenport took the title role of St Marc; Wallack that of his friend, Gismondo, the captain of a disbanded regiment. Rankin played Billafiore, a court noble. Declared "romantically beautiful" by the local critic, *St Marc* was repeated by popular demand on the last night of the engagement.

Davenport's Friday-night benefit was a big occasion, inspiring the company with unusual zeal and animation in Shakespeare's *Julius Caesar*, featuring Davenport as Brutus, Wallack as Cassius, Mrs Farren as Portia, Matt Lingham as Marc Antony, and G.L. Aiken as Caesar. Rankin's role was not noted. For the second play, Davenport chose a long-time favorite, the short nautical drama *Black Eyed Susan*, in which he danced the hornpipe "with dignity and grace."[11] It became a favorite piece for Rankin later in his career.[12] The critic wrote that the next generation would speak of Davenport, Wallack, and Farren reverentially as a "rebuke to the triviality of posterity," which valued "the literary sensations of Boucicault over the glowing sentence of Shakespeare and the crisp and elegant repartee of Sheridan."[13] Unfortunately, the next generation, aside from a few actors, forgot them.

After the departure of Davenport, Wallack, and Farren, Pike's Opera House gave over to Italian opera for the remainder of the season. While leading actors such as Matt Lingham could tour theaters in other cities and find starring roles for a few nights, unknown actors at Rankin's level could not find a place because all of the companies had full rosters until the end of the season. Pike's may have retained its minor actors at lower salaries to complement the singing cast of the opera, or Rankin may have filled in at other Cincinnati venues such as the National Theatre, which opened late in the season with light musicals and comedies, and waited for Nickinson to use him again.[14] Nickinson probably used this time of relative idleness to instruct Rankin in stagecraft.

Remaining in Cincinnati, Rankin likely took the opportunity to attend some of the productions at Wood's Theatre and become acquainted with the visiting stars. Mary Provost, one of the most painstaking of actresses, came to Wood's for a week as Nell Gwynne in *The King's Rival*, Peg Woffington in *Masks and Faces*, and Julia in *The Hunchback*, plays that Rankin would perform in and produce many times in the years to come. At the time, Provost depended on John Albaugh, the leading man who traveled with her. He was a promising young actor who was engaged at Wood's Theatre in Louisville, Kentucky, and was on loan for two weeks. The Cincinnati critic was "delighted by his chaste and correct representation of characters assigned to him" and predicted his popularity. Albaugh did become an important fixture in the theater for decades, but, more importantly, he and Rankin became lifelong friends.

Many years later, Rankin expressed his appreciation for the stock company of his early days, which he contrasted with the stock company late in the century. "As a member of a stock company, one week I was supporting Lotta," he said, "the next Mrs. Drew, the next Chanfrau, the next Booth, or Boucicault or Charles Mathews, Edwin Forrest, Maggie Mitchell or John E. Owens. These people showed us how to play our parts and how they wanted them played, so that we learned our business under the greatest exponents of tragedy, comedy and farce then living or who have lived since for that matter."[15] Actors of a later period had no one to instruct them, not even the stage managers, who knew very little themselves.

Despite his appreciation for the company, Rankin was dissatisfied with the walking gentleman roles that Nickinson had planned for him. Although the Cincinnati papers listed him as a member of Pike's for the fall of 1863,[16] he did not appear there. Rather he went to Indianapolis, Indiana, to the Metropolitan Theatre. That theater was under a new stage manager, W.H. Riley, who had a reputation as one of the best managers and most accomplished actors in American theater. Riley displayed a physical force on stage and a vigorous elocution. Rankin needed such an example before him if he were to progress as an actor.

Rankin was listed first among the men as "A. Rankin."[17] He expected to play major roles, especially as many experienced actors were swept up in the army draft during the summer.[18]

1863–1864

Indianapolis

In Indianapolis, the prolific number of plays, enacted by the most seasoned actors, gave Rankin first-hand experience by which to learn and improve his craft. On September 26, 1863, the town was full of excitement at the start of the dramatic season that night. A competition for the best opening address had produced a winner that was duly read to the audience, followed by Bulwer-Lytton's *Money*, a grand Spanish dance, and the farce *A Kiss in the Dark*. Rankin played the second leading man with the company. W.H. Riley took the most important roles and, according to the papers, was a great favorite.

A fair in town that week brought an overflow crowd to the theater. Many were crowded out of their seats "by the vigilance of our young gentlemen, who, wishing to take their 'cousins' to see the opening performance, had even engaged all the available standing room." Visitors from other parts of the state walked away swearing that the hall should have been made larger while the performance "opened with a yell that would have intimidated the oldest man in the world."[19]

Among the plays that Riley produced that season were Sheridan Knowles's *The Wife*, August von Kotzebue's *Pizarro in Peru, or, The Death of Rolla*, and *The Stranger*, which showed simple people reaching greatness in important situations by being true to themselves. Rankin may not have played in all the main events but rather in the farces at the close of the evening after the ballet or Spanish dance. Plays such as *Poor Pillicoddy, Toodles*, and *A Loan of a Lover* performed in Indianapolis that season gave him needed experience in comedy.

The audiences in Indianapolis participated with great vigor and were not shy at expressing their approval or disapproval. The local critic complained sarcastically that the soldiers and newsboys in the audience were discriminating in their applause of the visiting star, Sallie St Clair, who, in her role as a French lady in *The French Spy*, assumed the disguises of a cadet of the lancers and an Arab boy who indulged in wild Arab dances, sword fights, frenzies of madness, prophetic visions, and silent exaltations. He pointed out that when an actor poses as a hero fighting for the "old flag," the audience "brings down the house" regardless of poor acting, whereas when an actor plays the villain he risks having his throat cut or being otherwise disabled by the whole audience. "They even," said the critic, "interrupt an actor of that kind with some foolish slang which they probably think is sharp, while they do not appreciate good acting." Thus the Indianapolis audience behaved just as the "bhoys" in the famous New York Bowery Theatre who sat in the cheaper gallery seats and howled their approval and disapproval of the stage characters. The more respectable classes tended to avoid such theaters. In the 1820s, it was common practice for members of the audience to get up, talk, and walk around during a performance, and it was not until the 1850s that the lights were turned down because the audience was more interested in the action on stage than in their fellow playgoers. A sense of respectability came to the theater, especially after prostitutes were dissuaded from plying their trade in the upper tier. The Indianapolis audience reflected this respectability in a rather proprietary way. When in a private box filled with officers, a young "sapling" eating popcorn, big apples, and chunks of gingerbread, stretched his legs over the railing as he tried to catch the eye of a young lady, shouts of "boots in the box" resounded throughout the house.[20]

Sallie St Clair traveled with her companion, Charles Barras, who took leading roles opposite her. This practice of traveling with male stars—sometimes husbands, sometimes lovers, sometimes simply business companions—was absolutely necessary for actresses, who needed protection and a male negotiator in the masculine world of the theater. Sometimes these male companions wrote and adapted plays for their stars. Barras, for example, adapted Wilkie Collins's novel *The Woman in White*.[21] Unlike original plays, adaptations could be used by an actor as long as the adaptation was his; moreover, no international copyright applied.

Learning his parts quickly under pressure, Rankin must have been dismayed at how much he had to learn, with rehearsals every morning and performances every night in a different piece. The intellectual demands on the stars in interpreting roles must have impressed him. Playing one of the great roles of the century, Mary Provost starred in *Camille* by Alexandre Dumas *fils*. Marguerite Gautier, also called Camille, a consumptive courtesan, nobly relinquishes marriage to her rich young lover at the plea of his father. Rankin frequently played the role of Camille's lover, and, as he grew older, he played the lover's father; he would, moreover, direct the play countless times. For now, however, he was one of the cast "generously encored" in this and in plays such as *The Hunchback*, *The Lady of Lyons*, *Lucie D'Arville*, *Aurora Floyd's Secret*, and so on.

The next visiting star—the robustious Mr Neafie—was known to Rankin from Rochester. He was to open in *Hamlet* but, when he did not appear, W.H. Riley had to play the title role. It was feared that Neafie, who, as an energetic businessman, kept his engagements, had met with a railroad accident or had been killed by guerrillas. When he failed to appear the second evening for *Damon and Pythias*, the company improvised as best it could, with Riley in the star's role and Rankin in support. Finally, on the third day, Riley received a telegram from Neafie announcing his arrival at 5 PM and his intention to play Damon that night. After the performance, Neafie apologized to the audience and explained that guerrillas had blown up bridges, locomotives had broken down, trains were running behind schedule, and, like so many traveling stars, Neafie had found transport by wagon and other means until he could connect with a train for Indianapolis. Stars often resorted to canal barge and horseback to reach their engagements on time. Understandably, the weary Neafie gave a weaker than usual performance, but the next night in *Jack Cade* he held a large and fashionable audience spellbound by his "wonderful exhibitions of grief and rage."[22]

Rankin's lifelong conviction that melodrama provided the major ingredient in the making of a successful stage play came from his experience with plays like the three-act comic drama *Don Cesar de Bazin*, which Neafie presented the following night. Don Cesar is an engaging, happy-go-lucky, picaresque rogue, who interferes with a brutal captain flogging a young boy from his company. The roustabout becomes a lion, a magnificent moment that "aroused the blood" in the audience. The ensuing action—his death sentence, marriage to a street singer, escape, defense of his wife from the king's designs, and revelation to the king of his councilor's seduction of the queen—is accomplished through disguises, misrepresentation, and derring-do. The play's romantic antics were borrowed by playwrights from Sardou and Gillette to Bernard Shaw in *Arms and the Man*.

Rankin's roles in Neafie's presentations were not recorded except for Neafie's *Macbeth*, in which Rankin played Malcolm, son to King Duncan, a larger role than Ross, whom he had played earlier. As Malcolm, he could give more play to passion and show resolve in leading the army against Macbeth.[23]

The next star to visit Indianapolis was Frank Chanfrau. He was of particular interest to Rankin because of his ability to project American characters on stage with tremendous success. In 1848, he had starred in *A Glance at New York* featuring the character of Mose the fireman, an impudent, cocksure, jaunty, devil-may-care hooligan, and had become the darling of the 12½-cent seats in "the gods" or the uppermost balcony. There followed a series of plays with Mose as the hero, and Chanfrau, a Bowery boy himself, became famous. By the time he came to Indianapolis, he was thirty-nine and experienced in comedic characterizations, as was amply illustrated by his first-night presentation of Lord Dundreary and his brother Sam in *Our American Cousin at Home*. Lord Dundreary was originally a part of about fifty lines spoken by an elderly, crotchety peer, but was transformed into a great role by E.A. Sothern in *Our American Cousin*.[24] Chanfrau gave Lord Dundreary an American brother, Sam, and played both roles to perfection. The quick changes between characters seemed like magic. Despite bad weather, the theater was filled, and everyone wore broad grins. Rankin was listed among those who received their share of "justly merited" applause. In the other plays, too, such as Robert Jones's *The Hidden Hand*, Rankin was reported to have played his role, usually that of Wool the old Negro, in an able manner.[25]

Rankin gained ample experience in playing minor roles in a series of melodramas produced by Riley, including *Nick of the Woods*, *Your Life's in Danger*, *Virginia*, *Jack Cade*, *The Rebel Chief*, *Gio*, and the *Armourer of Tyre*, and in Shakespeare's *Macbeth*, *Othello*, *King Lear*, and *Richard III*. The whole company took part in all these plays, and Rankin was kept busy learning his roles. There was little time for rehearsals: on average, actors had from two to three days to prepare. Those who were not "quick studies" could not last under such conditions.

Stars such as Joseph Proctor, J.B. Roberts, and Emily Thorne left impressions of their particular gifts with the members of the stock company. Roberts, for instance, played King Lear "as few men can, giving a rendering in perfect consonance with the spirit of the play and the highly wrought story."[26] Emily Thorne was primarily a comedian and a singer with whom Rankin would be associated a good deal in later years. Her parents and brothers were actors who traveled the world, including long stints in China. Indianapolis was very excited about her appearance in the city. At her performance as Peg Woffington, the fabled English actress, in Reade's *Masks and Faces*, two hundred people had to be turned away from the theater. Those in attendance found that their high expectations were handily surpassed. The critic reported that no greater enthusiasm "had ever before been manifested in the walls of the theatre."[27] This kind of audience fired Rankin's enthusiasm for a career on the stage as the most satisfactory of professions.

W.H. Riley's company staged benefits for the actors for a few days without the presence of stars. On a benefit night, Riley was called before the curtain for making the theater an artistic and monetary success. Before the advent of the star system, actors and managers would never venture to speak to audiences, but later, following the example of Kean and Forrest, stars often stepped forward to make speeches of appreciation and receive flowers from their admirers.

In early January 1864, the tragedian Emma Waller arrived, later to be joined by her husband, the actor D.M. Waller. She was regarded as the greatest actress of her time. The critics were so excited by Emma Waller that they ignored the performances of her fellow actors, among whom was Rankin, who played Macbeth opposite Waller in a production on January 4, 1864. Rankin was no doubt given the opportunity because Riley, as the resident star, could not be expected to take over such a demanding role when he had other roles to fill. Rankin brought an innovation to the portrayal: by the end of the play Macbeth's hair had turned completely white from guilt and worry.

Reviewing *Naomi, the Deserted*, the critic praised Waller for her womanly tenderness and exquisite pathos in the first two acts and raved over her delivery of the curse scene in the third act. "Human in its passion," he wrote, "superhuman in its pythonic rage and the power and the terrible reality of action and intonation with which it was fulminated. It was an anathema marantha—a bolt from Jupiter Torrens—in a word, it rivetted sense and soul, and the fall of the curtain was a positive relief from the tension and feeling experienced during its delivery."[28] Young Rankin took note of the role's power and effect on audiences and used a version of the play years later as a vehicle to star a tragedienne that he was training. Rankin also observed Emma Waller's acting techniques in male parts such as Iago in *Othello*; although Riley played Othello at this time, Rankin would play the role opposite Emma Waller's Iago in October.

Rankin may have been a poor student in school but, as an actor, he was receiving the best education in character motivation, history, and play construction, all delivered by the great players of his time in an atmosphere of extreme excitement and challenge to his mimetic and analytic talents. When Jane Coombs arrived in Indianapolis, he could compare his progress to months earlier, when he was a walking gentleman with her. He had grown into larger roles in her familiar plays, *The Lady of Lyons, The Hunchback, Ingomar, the Barbarian, The School for Scandal, The Stranger, Fazio, the Italian Wife*, and *The Honey Moon*. This last play, first produced in 1800, remained second in popularity in the US, only to Sheridan's *The School for Scandal*. Like Sheridan's play and Goldsmith's *She Stoops to Conquer*, it attacked the sentimental comedy and false moralizing of eighteenth-century plays and treated human failure more as a matter of folly than of sin.

Rankin was not being mentioned in the papers in the rare times when others of the company were listed; later, he referred in a joking way to Indianapolis playgoers' pejorative comments on his acting. The poor salaries and the hard work to keep up with the nightly change of bill began to tell on him. On average, the actors appeared in twenty plays over two weeks. The leads received $25 to $50 weekly, and the others got $8 to $10, although on a benefit night half of the gross receipts went to the actor. Despite his growing discontent, Rankin had been looking forward with great anticipation to supporting the next star slated to play in Indianapolis.

Edwin Adams arrived on February 1, 1864, for a two-week engagement. Ten years Rankin's senior, he had spent his early acting years in Edwin Forrest's company, as had his close friend John McCullough; unlike McCullough, he avoided picking up Forrest's robust mannerisms. Always interesting, often delightful, sometimes superb, Adams looked like the handsome, dashing sailor of romance and perfectly filled the ideal, at once poetic and popular, of the gay, audacious, always successful hero of breezy adventure. He was not, intrinsically, a tragedian, but rather generally a portrayer of genial emotions. His method was careless, but he was spontaneously dramatic, and, if he did not often excite the intellect, he always touched the heart. Critics understood that Adams was making a heroic effort to rescue the drama from the sensational school that Edmund Kean had visited upon the American theater when he influenced Forrest, who, in turn, left his mark on Joseph Proctor, Edward Eddy, McCullough, and others. Kean's acting had depicted nature at its most raw and free, with deep intensity of power, just on the edge—sometimes over the edge of madness. Indeed, such portrayals had prompted Forrest to study madness and live in the wilderness with Indians to catch the poetic fire at the core of his nervous system. Adams, on the other hand, was called a classic actor in the manner of E.L. Davenport, Edwin Booth, and James Murdoch. He was "a student of nerve, not fearful of discarding the traditions of his art when his judgment disapproved, but not flying to open rebellion." [29]

Deeply impressed, Rankin studied Adams's technique in acting tragedies. Adams opened in Indianapolis with *Hamlet*, of which the local critic wrote: "Every thought and feeling of the young Prince urging him on to avenge his father's death was depicted on his countenance or expressed in his words and actions."[30] He was refreshing in his easy movements and happy disregard of imaginary boundaries.

Adams played the roisterous young Rover in *Wild Oats, or, The Strolling Gentleman*, a raffish comedy set in Hampshire, England, and William, the honest sailor in *Black Eyed Susan*, Douglas Jerrold's nautical comedy. The latter was revolutionary in introducing a domestic story instead of the usual romantic plot and setting humorous scenes with sprightly dialogue, which was meat for Adams's mercurial temperament. But it was in the role of Robert Landry, the selfless hero of *The Dead Heart*, that Adams could not be matched.[31]

Rankin read the *New York Clipper*, the main newspaper for drama, faithfully. In the January 24 issue, he saw an advertisement by the Apollo Theatre in Lexington, Kentucky, for "ladies and gents." He was attracted by the opportunity to play under the veteran actors Barney Macauley, Martin Golden, and H.A. Weaver. Weaver ran the theater, which, reported the *Clipper*, was "highly thought of" and praised for delighting its public with its choice of domestic and military dramas. But he was not able to depart before February 28, when W.H. Riley advertised for "stars and ladies and gentlemen of acknowledged ability" to replace the actors leaving the Metropolitan in Cincinnati.

The old rigid lines of business and devotion to one theater were becoming things of the past. The mobility, not just of the stars but of the company actors, who moved on with each new season, brought actors together frequently and reinforced a sense of one great acting family. The *New York Clipper* reflected the sadness felt in this acting community when it reported John Nickinson's death in Cincinnati on February 9, 1864. The old actor, who had not been well and had had trouble remembering his lines, walked into his local drug store, sat on a sofa, and fell asleep. When the store was closing, the clerk found him dead.[32]

Lexington

In contrast to the Metropolitan Theatre in Indianapolis, the Apollo Theatre in Lexington was a throwback to earlier times before the star system came to dominate in the 1830s and 1840s. There were no visiting stars, fewer performances were given, the actors had time to study for their roles, and, unlike the old stock companies, the company did not classify actors rigidly by line of business; indeed, it strongly encouraged young talent. A correspondent to the *Clipper* remarked that Rankin made "quite a hit amongst us" as Wool, the old servant, in *The Hidden Hand*, which he played soon after his arrival in Kentucky.[33]

Rankin was right to move to Lexington. Here he was given greater opportunities, not only to excel in new roles but also to be noticed by the press and audiences. For instance, at a benefit for Martin Golden, for which the theater was jammed, the paper reported that Rankin "is perfectly at home in every character he assumes—he dresses his characters with taste and precision and acts them with a will and intent which displays the earnest actor."[34]

For Barney Macauley's benefit, Macauley chose *The Corsican Brothers*, in which he played the Franchi twins to a packed house of the "elite and beau monde of the city." Rankin played the cynical duke, Chateau-Renaud, who duels with the first brother, Louis di Franchi, in Paris and kills him. Later, the duke duels Fabian di Franchi on the same spot in the Bois de Boulogne on which he killed his brother. The duke breaks his sword and calls off the duel, but Fabian breaks his sword intentionally and kills the duke. "Mr. Rankin is at home with the sword," wrote the local critic, "and throughout the play he was true and faithful to his character."[35]

For the benefit of Samuel Drake, the company's second old man, the tragedian Mrs Blake—Drake's mother—came out of retirement to play Meg Merrilies in *Guy Mannering* and brought memories of better days in the theater. When the cast omitted songs and cut lines, the critic asked angrily if they did not know that Lexington playgoers were too conversant with the language of the plays to allow them such liberties, which would never have happened in the memorable days when the Duffs, Drakes, and Deanys had played before them. The mention of Mary Duff and her husband, John, was like calling on the gods to be witness. Mary Duff was acclaimed by critics as the greatest tragic actress ever—"refined, yet powerful; not boisterous, yet forcible; graceful in all her motions, and dignified without stiffness."[36] Despite the shortcomings of the company, the local paper claimed that the citizens wanted it to stay and to be permanently established under the present combination. "Our people have never hesitated to support an efficient company with the most liberal encouragement although much abused by a set of strolling incapables, whose dismal efforts have invariably met with deserved contempt."[37] Not only the local population but the throngs of troops, resident and in transit, would make it profitable.

The benefit for the popular new acquisition, Mr Rankin, for Friday evening, May 7, 1864, was called "the truly great event" by the local critic. Rankin chose to play Bob Brierly in *The Ticket-of-Leave Man*, produced in the city for the first time.[38] It protested against injustice and inhumanity, preached charity to those less fortunate, and showed that none was so lost but could be reclaimed by proper influence, sentiments that Rankin wanted to bring to his audiences. The local critic called Rankin one of the most meritorious of the company, with a personal popularity that was irresistible: "We bespeak a favorable hearing for the beneficiary. The young ladies, we know, will delight to honour him with their smiles, and where they are concerned 'there is no such word as fail.'...He has done a great deal toward the success of every piece in which he has appeared. He has a judicious study; a pleasing figure; a voice of some melody and culture, and invariably dresses his parts with good taste. Seldom overstepping the modesty of nature in his deportment, he is but little censurable for that ridiculous distortion of features and lacerations of text which so often disfigures the stage."[39] The critic also praised *The Ticket-of-Leave Man* for its graphic pictures of London life, its fine poetical rhetoric, its ingenuity of plot, and the spectacular scenic effects, which were all subordinate to "a revelation of life but dimly understood."[40]

Rankin would remember his performance because the fight scene had an unexpected ending. He confronted the ringleader of the counterfeiters, Martin Golden, leveling a pistol that was supposed to misfire. Unknown to Rankin, the property man had mistakenly charged it heavily with gunpowder, and it blew up in Golden's face, burning his face and eyes. The curtain came down and Macauley quickly appeared to assure the audience that Golden would be all right. Mooney's minstrels, who entertained between the main play and the afterpiece, speedily went into their act.

Rankin's benefit had called out the best house of the week, and he carried away with him "something more substantial than the good wishes of a host of friends and admirers."[41] The *Clipper* was "astonished" by Rankin's acting: "He fairly surpassed all former efforts."[42] Rankin was not expected to return with the company, which was decamping for the theater in Frankfort, Kentucky, for two weeks. No mention was made of Rankin's destination, but the critic seemed resigned to his passing on to a better place for developing his talent.

Rankin stayed with the company for most of May in Frankfort, where it played to "large and fashionable audiences." When the company returned to Lexington towards the end of the month, he left for Wood's Theatre in

Louisville. J.W. Albaugh, leading man at the Louisville theater, was leaving; hence the theater was in need of Rankin's services. Albaugh took his farewell benefit on Friday, June 3, as Richard, Duke of Gloucester, in Shakespeare's *Richard III*. The *Clipper* reported that the play was well rendered and that McKee Rankin deserved much credit for his rendition of Richmond, "which was really first rate."[43]

While in Louisville, Rankin met Kitty Blanchard and supported her in her benefit. Because she was used only in ingenue roles, the benefit was the theater's way of recognizing her yeoman service during the season. When she met Rankin she was a pretty, vivacious seventeen-year-old dancer. Although they may have had a brief flirtation during this first meeting, neither Rankin nor Blanchard could have divined that they would come to symbolize to Americans the ideal married couple in the theater.

Kitty Blanchard

Kitty Blanchard started dancing professionally at age ten in 1857, when she was hired for the role of a nymph in *The Naiad Queen* at the National Theatre in Philadelphia.[44] Her father, Loring Blanchard True, a professor of mathematics in Bowdoin College, made and lost money through his inventions, notably the rubber gum used extensively in dentistry at one time. He died when she was four, leaving her and her mother penniless. Her mother took in sewing, but her eyesight was becoming too poor to continue. Kitty learned dance steps from a friend and attended a good dance school in Philadelphia, where her natural ability developed into a talent. She answered a newspaper advertisement asking for small children for a play and was invited to audition by John Drew, the elder. She was hired to dance in *The Fireman's Ball* the next night. She rushed home with her cousin and sat up almost the whole night preparing her costume. When she arrived at the stage door, the doorkeeper, thinking she was one of the young children trying to sneak in to see the show, kept her from entering at first. She described her first stage experience movingly:

> The excitement of that first night I shall never forget. When I heard the orchestra play the chord for my entrance in the ballroom scene, my heart gave one frightful bound, and I started to run as though I were being pursued by someone. The stage was so large that it seemed as though my feet would never carry me to the center. After another flourish from the orchestra, I made a low bow and commenced dancing as though it were the last act of my life. I finished all right, bowed with my face to the audience, and started on a foot race back to the

entrance, where my mother stood waiting. I threw myself into her arms, and she wept with joy, while the audience kindly applauded. That night I was engaged at a salary of four dollars a week for the production of "The Naiad Queen."[45]

Kitty had become the family breadwinner, but $4 was a small amount for two people to live on. She and her mother had a small room—nine by twelve feet—up three flights of stairs. Although there was no money for toys, Kitty's childhood was not sad. Her mother was her constant companion and made her happy. Because her mother could not see well enough to read, Kitty delighted in reading to her in every spare moment. She did not have Christmas presents, but at the theater she was called for an encore and presented with a doll and a bouquet by a small boy representing the audience. After the performances, her mother carried her home piggyback through the snow and the dark streets. It was a long walk, and by the time they reached their room, Kitty was sound asleep.

When the run of *The Naiad Queen* was finished, Kitty secured work at small concert saloons in Philadelphia until Frank Rivers hired her as a dancer for his melodeon. Melodeons, which got their name from the portable reed organs that originally supplied most of their music, began in the mid-1850s. The forerunner to vaudeville, they offered cheap, fresh, and impudent entertainment. Customers would drop in for drinks, smoke a cigar, and watch the revue comprising white minstrels in blackface, off-color jokes and songs, farces, dance routines, and tableaux with women in varying states of undress. Kitty improved her dancing and singing and learned to act pantomime. Frank Rivers ran successful melodeons in Philadelphia and on Broadway in New York City. Just as, years later, actors acted in vaudeville when they were unable to find employment in the legitimate theater, so did actresses find roles in the melodeons that lent melodeons a bit of respectability.

From Philadelphia Kitty went to Rivers's Broadway melodeon in 1860 and soon became a favorite with her bobbing blonde hair and saucy, piquant singing. She returned to Philadelphia in 1862 as the main attraction at the Olympic Music Hall and shared top billing with Tony Pastor—later the "Dean of the Vaudeville Stage and prince of all comic singers and jesters"—at the Continental Theatre in the city. In the summer of 1863 at the National Theatre in Cincinnati, she was hailed as "the premier danseuse of America: acknowledged by press and public to be the Queen of the American Stage." Dancing and singing in farces, she was an "immense hit...who was nightly honored with a triple encore."[46] Although she was just sixteen, her name, written in huge letters, topped the names of all the other performers.

A successful summer engagement rarely led to employment in the theater's stock company, but the publicity she received secured her a job as the last member of the resident cast of the Duffield Theatre in Nashville, Tennessee—one of the handsomest theaters in the Southwest. After years of training and struggling, she had made the legitimate theater—not as an actress, but as a dancer, entertaining the public between plays, yet closer to her dream of becoming an actress.[47] Kitty went as first singing chambermaid at Christmas to Wood's Theatre in Louisville, which Duffield also managed. She continued to dance between the plays and to watch the visiting stars such as Maggie Mitchell, whom she studied closely. Kitty was impressed with John Wilkes Booth's swashbuckling ways.[48] He was an inspired actor, with more fire than his brothers Edwin and Junius Brutus, Jr. In the last act of *Richard III*, it was customary for the star as Richard to rush on as if dressed for court while the fighting was taking place, but John Wilkes Booth would dart across the stage as if he meant business and reappear, face covered with blood from slaying men he had thought were Richmond, his beaver or face shield lost in the fray, his hair flying helter-skelter, his clothes mussed; he would pant and fume like a prizefighter in a terribly real impersonation of a man bent on killing his greatest enemy. Once in a fencing scene he pushed E.L. Tilton, who was acting Richmond, so hard that he forced him offstage into the orchestra. He was a magnificent swordsman and used a double-handed heavy broadsword weighing seven pounds. He once cut Barney Macauley's face open with this sword in a dueling scene.[49]

In 1864, when John Albaugh became stage manager in Louisville, he gave Kitty Blanchard a small role with a few lines to speak. She played it earnestly and, when the curtain fell, ran to him to ask how he thought she played. "Very well, my dear," he replied, "if we could only have heard what you said."[50] Gradually he encouraged her with more roles, which she played in addition to her dances. On June 8, while Rankin was with the theater, she was given a benefit and the lead role in *The French Spy*, which was the dancing and pantomime part. She was a hit, and the press reported on her favorably. She was engaged for the next season as first singing chambermaid and danseuse, with the understanding that she would have the privilege of playing star engagements of one week at Nashville and one week in Cincinnati. The *Clipper* proudly reported, "When one of the little people makes advances in the profession, it gives us great pleasure to record the fact, in the hopes that it may induce others to strive hard for promotion."[51]

That summer, in a new company at Lexington with the infant phenomenon Little Alice Hogan, Blanchard began to catch the audiences' attention, and her success induced the manager to extend the company's engagement. She seemed to embody the whole company "in a single specimen of bewitching femininity—song, dance, pantomime, melodrama—dashing belle or devilish boy—in petticoats or pantaloons anywhere and everywhere."[52] She took lead roles and danced during the intermission throughout the summer, which, considering the heat, was proof of her dedication. Reported the paper, "The bewitching Kitty has our theatregoers completely invested and their only escape is an unconditional surrender; hearts is trumps, and she has taken every trick."[53] The critic concluded: "The exquisite grace and poetry developed in every motion truly stamp her as one of the greatest living American dancers. But as an actress we would more particularly speak of her. The astonishing aptitude with which she grasps each phrase of passion in the many characters she portrays make it a matter of wonder to her auditory how one so young can be so gifted....The brilliant display of the higher flights of the drama appear as easy and natural to her as the more facetious roles of the comedienne, possessing all the advantages so essential to a successful actress."[54] The germ of genius in her, he predicted, would rank her some day among the greatest American artists.

This was heady praise for a singing chambermaid, and it made Blanchard more determined to succeed. She returned with her mother to Wood's Theatre in Louisville for the fall season as first singing chambermaid and earnestly hoped that she could break into more significant roles. She had been given the chance to play dramatic roles in Cincinnati for a week such as Tillie Slowboy in *Dot,* and the major role in *The French Spy,* in which her talents in pantomime made her a success. But because opportunities to escape from dancing and singing roles were rare, she transferred from Wood's Theatre to its rival, the Louisville Theatre, in January 1865. Here she proved her acting ability in secondary roles. "Miss Kitty is at present the reigning favorite of Louisville," wrote a critic for the *Clipper,* "and in my humble estimation is destined to become ere long a star in the theatrical galaxy of remarkable luster and magnitude. There is a certain grace and maidenly simplicity in her acting that never fails to please."[55]

Engaged as the star for the summer season of 1865, she began as the Cricket in *Fanchon,* for which she was lauded by the papers as having more power, quite as much vivacity, and more versatility of talent than Maggie Mitchell.[56] For the second night, she rushed to prepare to play Capitola Black in *The Hidden Hand,* buying a new riding habit made to order and finding new songs to sing while the whole company learned an African-American walkaround dance. She went to a music store for an appropriate song to celebrate General Sherman's victory that ended the Civil War, and, after a long search, she came across an unknown new song, "When Sherman Marched Down to the Sea." It was tuneful, catchy, and patriotic. She learned it immediately. The town was filling with Union soldiers returning from victory further south to the welcoming banners and flags that the citizens hung over the streets.

The basket-boy from the theater ran to her boarding-house room with a message from the manager, Colonel Marc Mundy, that the soldiers had been in the theater since six o'clock demanding that it open, hollering and stomping their feet, and it was already 6:30. "You better herry, Miss Kittie, quick as you kin, the theater won't hol' no mo' soldiers." She entered the first act in her street-Arab costume. The soldiers listened to every word and sang with her "We'll rally round the flag, boys." They called and recalled her repeatedly after the curtain fell on the first act.

For the first time in her career she felt a horrible, sickening nervousness, but Colonel Mundy said she looked like a four-time winner. He told her that General Sherman was coming for the next act. The colonel sent her a brief note while she awaited her cue: "General Sherman in right hand box. Came in late through side door." The scene was a plantation with slaves doing the walkaround and the cakewalk. After ten minutes of their dancing, Blanchard rushed on as Capitola. The character Wool asked her to sing her last new song for the slaves. This was to be the song's premier; no one had heard of it. Blanchard felt a cold chill as the orchestra leader tapped the music stand with his baton. During the prelude, her eyes wandered to fall on the respectful face of General Sherman; his inspiration added to the spirit of the song. When she reached the line "Boys, up and be ready, for Sherman will march to the sea," all, as with one voice, shouted, shrieked, applauded, and cheered again and again. All their pent-up feelings over the past hardships and toils and triumphs of the march burst out in such genuine emotion, it was overwhelming. The soldiers tore off their army badges and threw them at her. She dodged them with her arms over her eyes as if she were dodging snowballs, which made them laugh and become more enthusiastic, demanding more verses, until Wool shouted, "Miss Caterpillar's got a long way to ride on horseback and she hopes you'll 'scuse her fur tonight. She'll sing it fur you when she comes back." This brought more cheers and more badges and a bouquet from one of the upper boxes.

After the play, Mundy approached her with a middle-aged gentleman. "Miss Kitty, the general wants to thank you for your song. General Sherman, allow me to present to you Miss Kitty Blanchard." The general offered both his hands, into which she tremblingly put her own. "This great man was smiling down upon me," she wrote, "holding my hands, and he—he was thanking me for the pleasure I had given him and his men. No artistic triumph, however great, has given me more true happiness than that which I experienced then, so early in my career."[57]

After this triumph, Blanchard's starring engagement was extended to three weeks, and she appeared in other roles such as Miami and Madame St Aubert, the wild and civilized personalities in *The Huntress of the Mississippi*, Caroline Morton in *Our Gal*, and the title role in *Pocahontas*. She then went to the Masonic Temple in Louisville, opening in *Jack Sheppard* and *The Rough Diamond*, no doubt bringing her fans from the Louisville Theatre with her. "Her genius and beauty are bearing down on all rivals," reported the *Clipper*. By August she was starring in New Albany, Indiana, as Eily O'Connor in *The Colleen Bawn*, and Zoe in *The Octoroon*.[58]

Decades later, in 1908, a hotelman in Illinois wrote to Blanchard recalling those days when "a silly boy about my size and age squandered his money for valentines and 'sich' and addressed them to Miss Kitty Blanchard during the summer of '65. You and a company played 'The Hidden Hand' at the old Woodyard Hall, New Albany, and, of course, I was in a front seat every night—worshipping the star at a distance. At the age of 62 this would seem silly but I remember those days better than if it had happened a few days ago." She kept the letter with her papers.[59]

Blanchard opened the Opera House in Columbus, Ohio, on September 2, 1865, and remained as "The Star of the West" until the end of that month, playing the lead in *The French Spy* and Nan in *Nan, the Good for Nothing*.[60] In *Fanchon, the Cricket* and *Little Barefoot*, she was declared "superior" to Maggie Mitchell, who had had a firm grip on both roles for some time. More important, business was "splendid" in what was called one of the best theatrical cities in the American West.[61] She remained to star in western theaters until chance brought her together with Rankin again.

Rankin on Canadian Stages

After the close of the season in Louisville, Rankin spent the remainder of June and July 1864 in one of the theaters under George Wood's management that ran short summer engagements. He then headed for Montreal to meet his parents. During most of the year, Colonel and Mrs Rankin enjoyed the theater in Quebec City, but, in the summer, the Quebec company moved to Toronto's Royal Lyceum, which forced the Rankins to go to Montreal for the theater. The generally cooler climate in Canada enabled theaters in cities like Halifax, Montreal, and Toronto to have full summer seasons, in contrast to their counterparts in most American cities. Actors looked forward to supplementing their incomes in Canada, and Canadians looked forward to the productions mounted by first-class actors.

The Theatre Royal in Montreal opened with a good company, comprising, among others, Vining Bowers, one of the best low comedians; Viola Barrett, a first-rate American actress; and an old English actor, T.J. Hind. The visiting stars were John McCullough, Kate Denin, Sam Ryan, and finally Emma and Ada Webb, sisters, who played comedies and farces. For the Webbs' first Friday benefit, on August 5, the theater announced that Arthur McKee Rankin, the eminent Canadian artist, would appear as William in *Black Eyed Susan*, with Emma as Susan. Although he was very young, Rankin's reputation had already been established in the western press. "Handsome, of graceful carriage, his acting is full of thought and study," wrote the Montreal critic.[62] His anticipated debut before a Canadian audience in the exquisite and touching character of William, with his delightful hornpipe dancing, caused much excitement.

After the last rehearsal, T.J. Hind engaged in a conversation with the twenty-year-old Rankin on the plaza of a hotel and mentioned that, twenty years earlier in England, he had known a gentleman who resembled the young Rankin greatly. "I traveled with him in an Indian exhibition," he said, "and he gave a fine banquet when he received news that a boy had been born to him in America." Rankin, seeing his father approach at that moment, replied, "There is the man, and this is the boy." "But," stammered Hind, "this is a young man!"[63]

The review in the *Montreal Herald* called Rankin's performance as William a "most decided success" and commended his acting for being "finished, refined, and full of study." "His rendition of the pathetic is capital and he bids fair to be one of the first actors of the age. The audience was perfectly enraptured, and round upon round of applause was bestowed upon the young Canadian. At the close of the play, he was called before the curtain, and made a very neat little speech thanking the audience and his friends for the flattering manner in which he had been received."[64]

The following Monday, Rankin appeared as Claude Melnotte in *The Lady of Lyons*, in which he gave a credible performance. "The piece is of a very difficult rendition," wrote the local critic, "and we are glad to see that Mr. Rankin is so free from rant so common to all actors who are young in the profession." On Tuesday, Rankin played again in *Black Eyed Susan*. He appeared only once more, at Ada Webb's Friday benefit of *Fanchon, the Cricket* in the part of Fanchon's bourgeois and apprehensive lover, Landry Barbaud.

Invited by John Albaugh and Mary Mitchell, he went to Detroit, where, at the Young Man's Hall, he played William with his salty sailor talk in *Black Eyed Susan* and Bob Brierly in *The Ticket-of-Leave Man*. According to the local critic, the latter was one of the most difficult parts to sustain as the dialect was "particularly embarrassing." Rankin, however, was equal to the task: "He will soon establish himself as a favorite," the local critic predicted.[65] By the end of the week, he enacted the twin brothers di Franchi in *The Corsican Brothers*.[66] The eerie musical score, its evocation of psychic sympathy, and its theme of renunciation suited the romantic actor whose swordsmanship and quality of implacable vengeance during the final dueling scene impressed the audience with a sense of careless masculine superiority. For his appearance in Detroit, perhaps to differentiate himself from his father, he dropped the "Arthur" and the "A" before his name and became McKee Rankin.

That same summer, Rankin opened across the Detroit River at the Windsor Town Hall in *The Stranger*. Rankin played Francis, the servant character most favored by audiences, while John Albaugh took on the title role and Mary Mitchell played Mrs. Haller.[67] The company played to a large and welcoming house for three nights, at which point it was discovered that the business receipts were "in a snarled condition." Consequently, the company cut short the running time of the plays on the next night and was pursued to its ferry at the dockside by the incensed audience, among whom were little boys pleading for the return of their quarters.[68]

Following the debacle in Windsor, Rankin returned to Detroit, fulfilling his obligation to support Albaugh and Mitchell at the Detroit Athenaeum in an adaptation of *Manon Lescaut* and other tragedies. Arrangements had already been made for him to move on to Pittsburgh, and his engagement in Detroit delayed his arrival in Pennsylvania by a week.

1864–1865

Pittsburgh

On September 26, 1864, as "leading man" at the Pittsburgh Theatre, Rankin opened to great fanfare in the role of Bob Brierly in *The Ticket-of-Leave Man*. Although it was a big step upward in his career, Rankin entered a delicate situation. The quotation marks around his position derived from William Henderson, the proprietor of the Pittsburgh Theatre, who needed Rankin to take some of the acting load off his shoulders but was not willing to forego the role of leading man. Although this situation seemed to worsen as his reputation increased, it also worked to his benefit because he did not have to endure the pressure of being the official leading man.

As Bob Brierly, "Mr. Rankin fully sustained the high reputation which preceded his first appearance on our boards and was rewarded by the loudest plaudits from the audience," wrote the local critic.[69] Rankin continued as the twin brothers Franchi in *The Corsican Brothers* and Claude Melnotte in *The Lady of Lyons*.[70] The self-proclaimed great Saturday-night bill featured Rankin as Walter Carwin, the villainous lawyer in *Therese, or, The Orphan of Geneva*, and as William in *Black Eyed Susan*. *Therese*, adapted from the French, was extremely popular on the English-speaking stage. In its New York production in 1829, Forrest had played Carwin, and the future Mrs John Drew, then in her teens, played Therese in a famous triumph. The role of Carwin required the transformation from self-confident defendant to a whimpering creature begging forgiveness, which must have taxed the talents of young Rankin.

The first visiting star at the Pittsburgh Theatre was Edwin Adams. Rankin supported him in every play: *Hamlet*, *The Lady of Lyons*, *Wild Oats*, *The Heretic*, *The Drunkard*, *Macbeth*, and *Richard III*. The two actors attracted the largest houses that ever visited the theater, and Rankin's fame began to spread.[71] "Most certainly a most praiseworthy and painstaking actor," reported the *Clipper*.[72] Adams, who considered Rankin to have arrived, recommended the young actor to the proprietor of the Arch Street Theatre in Philadelphia, Mrs John Drew. The Arch Street Theatre represented the eye of the needle through which actors had to pass to achieve stardom in New York City.

Because the Pittsburgh papers spent most of their space reporting on the Civil War, and scarcely commented on theatrical performances, other than to report crowded houses, the critiques of the actors were verbal, and these quickly made the rounds of the acting profession. In this way, the reputations of Adams and Rankin for raising their plays to theatrical heights raced through the theaters about the country. Indeed, years later, Rankin's support of Adams was still remembered as a great event. At this juncture in Rankin's career, Adams probably helped him to learn that stage techniques developed with the utmost care might have no effect on an audience while quite natural actions might have great appeal. From this Rankin learned to act by listening to the audience and adapting his stage business to what it wanted.

On November 3, Rankin played the role of Othello for the first time, supporting the benefit of visiting star Emma Waller, who played Iago.[73] Rankin's approach was elemental, restoring the barbaric character to the Moor, whom others had played as an unwitting instrument of destiny. George Crichton Miln, a minister who had been famed for his sermons but had lost his faith and turned to acting, recalled years later that Rankin, as Othello, "was a noble figure....Second only to the Othello of all time, Signor Salvini, he need fear comparison with no actor on the English stage."[74]

War hero Pauline Cushman, a major in the Union Army, also lectured on her experiences as a spy behind enemy lines. From roles demanding deep passion opposite Waller, Rankin supported Pauline Cushman in Boucicault's light-mannered *Colleen Bawn* and comedies such as *Peep o' Day*, *The Married Rake*, *His Last Legs*, and *Barney, the Baron*.[75]

The most traveled star on the stage, McKean Buchanan starred for a week with his daughter Virginia. Tall and muscular, with a booming voice and a declarative manner of speaking that classified him in the school of rant, McKean Buchanan had a habit of losing breath between sentences and catching it up again with the exclamation "a!" as in "Tis-a he-a." His agents regularly swindled him of the box office receipts, but he played poker with them after the performance and always won the money back.

After the Buchanans left, Rankin starred again as the Franchi brothers in *The Corsican Brothers* and as Bob Brierly in *The Ticket-of-Leave Man*. His depiction of the innocent young Brierly from the country being duped, betrayed, and wrongfully imprisoned in the big city had a powerful effect on his audiences. He played the role "to better advantage than anything else he has attempted since he has been in the smoky city."[76]

Matilda Heron, who appeared in Pittsburgh for a two-week engagement, was the apostle of naturalism, emoting extravagant displays of temperament, yet using a conversational tone with novel stage movements that seemed like the physical and clinical reactions of someone unconscious of them. She had an irresistible magnetism and a wild passion that she brought to bear on the character of Marguerite Gautier in *Camille*, the role that made her famous and that Rankin could observe from sharing the stage with her as her lover Armand. Heron's limited knowledge of stage traditions, together with an awful earnestness—which came out in her expressive, finely featured face and in her eyes, which were as communicative as speech—allowed her to throw herself into the part. Her abandon amounted to a licentious freedom necessary to the role. In the final scenes, she brought out the pathos, causing the women in the audiences to weep and moan over Camille's sufferings.[77]

At this time, the stars still chose the pieces to be produced, and they used the theater to educate the public aesthetically and factually. The public tended to give the acting style precedence over the play, which could come to a town several times a season in different interpretations. Within a few years, the managers, taking control of the theater, changed all that, emphasizing the play rather than the acting. They repeated the most popular plays in long runs, more for the sake of profit than for instructing the sensibilities of the public.

Playing more and more in a secondary position to Henderson and wanting to move on, Rankin found a better engagement as leading man in Albany, New York, for the new year.[78] His train was delayed in Philadelphia and, having time on his hands, he dropped in at the Arch Street Theatre. He watched a performance and sent his card behind the scenes to his friend Owen Marlowe. When he went round to the stage door, he ran into the business manager, Joe Murphy, in the street. "Is your name McKee Rankin?" Murphy asked. "Yes, sir." "How would you like an engagement in this theater?" "I would be glad to get it—as seconds, I suppose," Rankin replied, knowing that a position in the Arch Street Theatre was a big step upwards in the profession. "Yes, second to the stars," Murphy said, meaning taking the leading role in support of the stars. Rankin was dumbfounded, having had no idea that Edwin Adams had recommended him. To prove to the Arch Street manager that he could take on leading-man roles, Rankin insisted that Murphy see him play a leading role at the Albany theater.[79]

After visiting his parents for a few days over the holidays, he went to the Academy of Music in Albany and began rehearsing the part of the sensitive, self-sacrificing sculptor Robert Landry in *The Dead Heart*, which he had seen Edwin Adams do so well. On the opening night, January 18, 1865, he was extremely nervous. Watching from a private box was Joe Murphy. Murphy had told him that if he filled the bill, he would call on him after the performance, and if he failed, he would leave without seeing him. Rankin knew that his nervousness hurt his performance. He retired to his hotel room with a heavy heart and waited in his room with the thoughts of a condemned prisoner. After two hours, he swallowed his disappointment and rang for dinner. He was eating in a mechanical way when he heard the stage wagon stop. Murphy suddenly appeared. "Excuse me, Mr. Rankin, I met a friend, and that delayed me. It's all right. I leave for Philadelphia in an hour, and when I get there I shall recommend you. You did first rate." Rankin felt such a surge of emotion that he had to excuse himself and leave the room for a few moments to recover.[80]

Despite Murphy's approbation, an Albany newspaper reported that Rankin's debut was "not one of the most flattering nature." The historian of the Albany stage has recorded Rankin's two nights in the role as "a total failure."[81] This failure could not have affected Mrs Drew's decision to employ him; she would have had reports on his progress for the past year from many of the best actors of the day, not just Edwin Adams. His engagement at the Arch Street Theatre in Philadelphia was set for the fall of 1865, and Rankin was determined to rescue his reputation in the meantime. Unemployed for a month and reported by the *Clipper* with *double entendre* as "suffering from an affectation of the heart for the last two weeks," he recovered and became leading man at the Howard Athenaeum in Boston in February 1865.

Boston

Known as the Athens of America, Boston was a great theater town. Its several theaters and its many famous actors were treasured by the citizenry. At the Howard Athenaeum, Rankin played familiar roles with star actors, whom he had come to know.[82] Kate Denin and Sam Ryan were essentially comedians, and the serious side of their plays relied on Rankin to make them credible. In Boucicault's *Octoroon*, Rankin was the Indian chief Wahno-tee, who tracks down the murderer McClosky, while Kate Denin played Zoe, the octoroon. In Boucicault's *Colleen Bawn*, Rankin played Hardress Cregan of the gentry class to Denin's wild Eily O'Connor. Rankin was working so hard that a senior actor, Charles Thorne, Sr, took some of the load and allowed him a night off on occasion. Rankin relished character roles, and to show his versatility he played three parts, Count Walter de Marsdoff, the Spirit of the Night, and the Hooded Stranger, in the melodrama *Demon Student, or, The Headless Man*. Such parts must have been fun and a reprieve from the responsibilities of the serious roles such as Pierre Daubry, which he created in a new play, *The Workmen of Paris*. In late March, he left for Deering Hall in Portland, Maine, to act in a company recently formed by the theatre managers Bidwell and Pike.

The Portland company gave the city its first sustained theatrical season, from January 30 to August 7, 1865. From March 26, Rankin was billed as the star—his first starring venture. He played Bob Brierly, the Franchi brothers, William in *Black Eyed Susan*, Pierre Baudry in *The Workmen of Paris*, and the criminal Jacques Strop in *Robert Macaire*, impressing his audiences and the press with his versatility and his true-to-life quality. Determined to succeed, at the close of his first week he appeared as Robert Landry in *The Dead Heart*, redeeming himself for the Albany performance. A local critic thought Rankin had considerable merit, but that he was "hardly equal to star engagements." He added kindly, however, that "Time and experience will do much for him."[83] The company went to Portsmouth for a few days while Deering Hall was being refurbished. While they were there, they received the shocking news of President Lincoln's assassination.

On the evening of Friday, April 14, at Ford's Theatre in Washington, Lincoln was watching a performance of Laura Keene's company in *Our American Cousin*. During the play, he was shot from behind at close range by John Wilkes Booth. The old lady in the play had just gone offstage, and

Harry Hawk was answering her exit speech when he heard the shot, looked up at the president's box, heard a man exclaim, "Sic temper tyrannis," and saw him jump from the box, seize the flag on the staff, and drop to the stage. The man slipped but was on his feet in a moment and, brandishing a large knife, he shouted, "The South shall be free!" Hawk recognized Booth, who ran at him while brandishing the knife. Hawk, thinking Booth was after him, ran off stage and up a flight of stairs. Booth escaped out of the back door of the theater, mounted a waiting horse, and rode off. All of this took place in a quarter minute.[84]

That evening at the Boston Museum Theatre, Edwin Booth, an older brother to John Wilkes, was taking a farewell benefit in *The Iron Chest* and *Don Caesar de Bazan*. The next night he was to play Hamlet as his farewell performance in Boston. With his particular romantic and poetic sensitivity, it was a role in which he excelled, but when he learned of the assassination that morning, he thought first of his mother and left the city to be by her side. All the theaters in the nation closed indefinitely. Actors became fearful of being slain by mobs, angry that one of them had killed the president just when the Union Army had won the Civil War.

Rankin returned to Boston after the national calamity. By his account, he had no inkling of John Wilkes Booth's intention when, a few weeks earlier, he met him passing through Boston on his way from Montreal to Washington. Booth was known as one of the best pistol shots in the country and demonstrated his ability in a Boston shooting gallery in a splendid throwing shot, firing between his legs and hitting the target so exactly in the center that the proprietors preserved it as a memento. "One morning," Rankin recounted,

> I was going down Tremont Street on my way to a rehearsal with two ladies of the company, Mrs. Octavia Allen and Miss Louise Anderson. As we neared the Tremont Hotel, Mrs. Allen exclaimed, "Hello, there's John Wilkes Booth!" He was standing in the porch of the hotel talking to Bill Pitcher, one of his close friends, and at that time a sort of steward in the hotel. I had a few words with him in passing, and made an engagement for that afternoon at the Parker House where he was staying. I met him at the appointed time and we had quite a chat about mutual friends, the theater, and things in general. He said he had just come from Montreal from which place he had shipped his wardrobe to Havana upon a little blockade runner. He was considerably excited over the state of affairs at the time, the difference between the North and the South. He was dissatisfied with the conditions about him, and said he

expected to cross the line somewhere and get into the South to play. No one at that time thought the war was anywhere near at an end. We talked a while longer of things in general, and of interests we had in common. He told me of his plans and prospects, and while he was in a most unsettled frame of mind, he spoke freely and at length upon the continuance of his work in the theater, in the South, which he considered for him a more congenial field. That night he left for Washington, and it was the last time I ever saw him.[85]

The full story of the conspiracy to assassinate Lincoln has not yet been told, although some have speculated that Booth's base of operations in Montreal linked him to a murky group of prominent Irish nationalists and rich Confederates suspected of assassinating the Canadian politician D'Arcy McGee months later.[86] One of Booth's co-conspirators, Lewis Payne, severely wounded Secretary of State William Seward at the same time the president was shot. In a long letter to his brother Junius, John Wilkes Booth wrote, "This country was formed for the *white*, not for the black man." The letter caused the government to arrest Junius and John S. Clarke, their brother-in-law, with whom Junius was staying at the time, and to detain them for a couple of months in prison. John S. Clarke was so angry at the treatment he received that eventually he left the country and acted on the English stage for many years. Edwin Booth was devastated and planned never to act again, although by September he was co-managing the New Walnut Street Theatre in Philadelphia with Clarke and returned to the stage the following year.[87]

The blockade runner upon which Wilkes Booth shipped his effects was wrecked in the Gulf of St Lawrence on the very night of Lincoln's assassination. Unclaimed, Booth's trunk was taken over by the Canadian Admiralty Court and sold for salvage in July. Rankin's brother, George, then in the Civil Service in Quebec City, bought the things for Rankin, thinking they would be of use to him in his theater work, and shipped them to their home in Windsor. Rankin picked them up when he returned briefly to Windsor after his Boston engagement.

Rankin was appalled by the murder, not only because of the reverence in which he held Lincoln, but because the acting profession, which was struggling for acceptance in society, bore the guilt. A deep gloom settled on the American people. "Everything has been deranged by the atrocious crime," wrote the *Clipper*, "engagements broken, time curtailed, entertainments postponed, speculations ruined, hopes deferred, and aspirations nipped in the bud."[88]

Rankin resumed acting on April 28, when he played Armand Duval, the young lover of Camille, to Helen Western's Marguerite Gautier. The combination of Rankin's manly and thoughtful Armand with Western's florid Camille must have been fascinating to watch. Rankin would have been curious about the next star at the Athenaeum, James Stark, who was born, like him, in Windsor, Upper Canada, worked as a carpenter in Nova Scotia, and migrated to Boston to learn acting. A patron of the drama had sent him to England to study under Macready. He was the first important star to go to San Francisco, where he created a taste for Shakespeare's plays. Tragedians tended to be consumed in the flames of passion, and by 1859 he was fatigued, ill, and in decline as variety and minstrel shows supplanted drama. Stark turned to a series of readings, acted in tawdry dramas, fell into financial difficulties, and began to drink out of frustration and recurring illnesses. In Boston, he was fulfilling the few engagements he could find. His fortune was gone, and, as he had no business sense, he was sliding downhill.

Rankin played the Chevalier de Mauprat to Stark's Cardinal Richelieu in Bulwer-Lytton's *Richelieu*, a drama of a high order of poetry with passages of great beauty. No mention was made of their performances, but Rankin and Stark acted several Shakespeare plays together. Stark enacted his famous Hamlet while Rankin played Laertes, brother to Ophelia and foil to Hamlet. Then to Stark's Othello, Rankin played Cassio and Charles Thorne played Iago. The old fire must have reappeared in Stark's characterizations. Part of his attraction was the great performances for which he was known.

A few years later, his health and morale shattered, Stark played mining camps until stricken with paralysis in Virginia City. Refusing to let him starve, his fellow actors played benefits for him. In 1875 in New York during Edwin Booth's famous hundred-night run in *Hamlet*, Stark had a minor role in the cast. A quarter of a century earlier, he had been one of the greatest Hamlets, and, as he watched Booth being acclaimed in the role, he died.

When the spirited Felicia Vestvali, a Polish Jew, came to the Athenaeum, Rankin supported her in most of her plays. Rankin did not play every night; the practice of occasionally giving the leading players a day or two off was being established as a right. Acting in the old style, Vestvali played to the audience, speaking to them, seeing only the crowd, and ignoring the actors on stage. "Of ponderous proportions," she was considered an Amazon beauty and a tiger. While playing Captain De Lagadere in *The Duke's Motto*, she was annoyed by two men propositioning the girls backstage. When she came offstage in her male costume, one of the men thrust his hand down her bosom and exclaimed, "Bully boy!" She pulled her sword and cried, "Brute, your head comes off! I would run you through the body if it were not a disgrace to the profession." She walloped him over the head and shoulders and drove him hatless and without his overcoat into the street. She returned to confront his companion. "Who are you?" "I'm nobody." "Then, I'll make you less than nobody, sir. Get out of here!" and she drove him out. Enraged, she quarreled with the actor who had allowed his two friends backstage. Just then, her cue came up for a dueling scene between her and the actor with whom she had been quarreling. As they fenced, their faces red with genuine passion, the fire flashing from their eyes equaled the sparks from the clashing steel.[89]

Among Rankin's roles in Boston were parts in the highwaymen or Jack Sheppard plays and spin-offs such as *The Lonely Man of the Ocean*, in which, as Lieutenant Adam Bashford, he displayed his dancing talent by executing a double hornpipe and his athleticism in a terrific sea fight. These plays reflected the tendency, after 1855, towards a melodrama of moral reform, wherein class divisions were ignored in order to concentrate on a working-class hero who saved the deserving poor from petty villains. In the Jack Sheppard pieces, the workers' apocalyptic and vengeful hopes were led into what has been called "the political cul-de-sac of psychological anxiety and sexual release."[90] The gothicism, dark adventure, and sexual desire—the latter expressed by the almost universal casting of actresses as Jack, the bandit, in breeches—underlay much of the popularity of these plays.

Bourgeois culture pervaded and contained the working-class theater as in the short play, *Robert Macaire*. This play represented an advance in the concept of the working-class hero, about whom the audience is ambivalent from the start. Macaire speaks well, and acts like a gentleman, but he is really an escaped prisoner. In the French original, he was the complete representative of the dashing, impudent, but still gentlemanly thief. With his nervous companion, Jacques Strop, a cruder personality, he comes to an inn, where he pretends to be the father of a young man about to come into a fortune. When the real father arrives, Macaire tries to murder him. Macaire is about to flee with the money when the father, who was only wounded, revives and sounds the alarm. Macaire is killed trying to escape. The character hides a menacing disposition under a likable facade—a challenge to any actor. Rankin played this role, in addition to Louis and Fabian di Franchi in *The Corsican Brothers*, on his benefit night. The role of Macaire was excellent preparation for Rankin for similar roles that were to come his way.

The intensity and immediacy with which Rankin had to prepare for roles made him work with an urgency and quickness of mind that stood him in good stead in the years ahead. In *Robert Macaire*, by playing the sidekick, Jacques Strop, months earlier, Rankin learned from the way his fellow actor played Macaire, reflecting on how he would play the role himself.

Being young and full of energy, Rankin loved the wild melodramas and their spectacular battle scenes. When Leo Hudson arrived with her horse Sensation to play in Byron's *Mazeppa, or, The Wild Horse of Tartary*, Rankin as Abder Khan, King of Tartary, the father of Mazeppa, was enthusiastically involved in the final battle between the Poles and Tartars. Leo Hudson, when apprenticed under the chief equestrian at the Hippodrome in New York City, was the first woman to leap with her mount over a canal excavated for this feat. She had a fine form, a pleasing face, and was better than fair as an actress. Her courage was exceptional: onstage, she had to direct her horse, while bound to its back, up narrow scaffolding for the proper effect.

Many of Hudson's roles involved stunts with horses. In *Rookwood, or Dick Turpin*, she played the highwayman of the title. Rankin played Peter Bradley, the old sexton and grandfather to one of the gypsies who helped Hudson drag her horse to a barn and defend herself with pistols over its body. Hudson also played mounted on her horse in *The French Spy*, in which Rankin was Mohammed, an Arab of the desert; in *The Wept of Wish-Ton-Wish*, in which Rankin played Conanchet, chief of the Narragansetts; in *Putnam, or, The Iron Son of '76*, in which Rankin was Oneactah, an Indian loyal to the rebels in the American Revolution; and in *Dick Turpin and Tom King*, a serio-comic, two-act drama, in which Rankin enacted Tom King, Dick Turpin's fellow highwayman. Despite several falls, Hudson continued this dangerous acting until May 1873, when an accident broke her horse's spine and resulted in Hudson's death from internal injuries.[91]

In early July 1865, the Athenaeum closed, and Rankin, excited about taking up his responsibilities as leading man at the prestigious Arch Street Theatre, run by the formidable Mrs John Drew, retired to spend a few weeks at the Sandwich homestead. For someone who was just twenty-one, his theatrical success was remarkable and must have brought a dramatic change to his mother's attitude towards life on the stage.

1865–1866

Leading Man: Philadelphia

Called the "first temple of drama in America," the Arch Street Theatre in Philadelphia was managed by Louisa Lane Drew, a short, imperious woman, who had strong likes and dislikes and had no time for fools. She disliked Macready and liked Forrest; fortunately, she liked Rankin from the start. She took over the management of the theater in 1861, when her last husband, the comedian John Drew, made a world tour. She had two girls and a boy by John Drew: Louisa, John, Jr, and Georgie, two of whom became actors. In 1868, six years after John Drew's death, she had a second son, Sidney, who would become a comedian. Before Sidney was born, Drew left the theater for some months; she then returned from a trip to California with a baby whom, she said, she had adopted. She was very probably the mother, however, and Sidney's father was thought to be Robert Craig, a young but married actor who was in her company and whom she described as "one of the most talented young men I ever met."[92]

Mrs John Drew, 1864, painted by John Sully.

Drew embodied an amazing force without effort, and her supreme rule at the theater crystallized into ceremonials that marked her comings and goings.[93] According to the actors, who called her "the Duchess" when out of her presence, her manner was a blending of kindliness with the imperiousness of Queen Elizabeth I. Good-hearted, just, and strict, she exhibited a chilly authority, sharp sarcasm, self-control, and self-respect. Actors liked her theater because it was the cleanest in the country, and, as a great actress herself, she understood actors.[94]

In the summer before Rankin's arrival, the Arch Street Theatre was refurbished, with newly painted scenery, a superb velvet carpet, and the renovation of everything behind the curtain. Drew emulated Mme Vestris in London by providing for the comfort of the actors. The green room was refitted as a handsome drawing room with mirrors and comfortable furniture, and the dressing rooms were all neatly refashioned. A large room within a short distance of the stage, the green room was the place where actors came for rehearsals and waited when dressed for their parts in the evening. It was from the green room that the callboy would summon them to the stage. While waiting in the green room, the actors kept their conversation subdued and observed the most perfect etiquette. In later years, when theaters became more impersonal, the green room was dispensed with by managers, who regarded space from the viewpoint of profit rather than the actors' comfort.

There were thirty-four actors in the Arch Street company, including Drew. One of them was Rankin's old acquaintance Owen Marlowe, whose low-key acting style earned respect from his fellow actors. Marlowe played with an exquisitely mannered sangfroid, which was regarded as the best artistic representation of the "letting of acting alone" school. Then there was Stuart Robson, a short, innocent-faced comic with a squeaky voice that made audiences laugh.[95] Frank Mackay, E.L. Tilton, and P.A. Fitzgerald, like Rankin, were appearing at the theater for the first time. Mackay was one of the first young actors to "hold the mirror up to Nature"—that is, represent nature or reality without exaggeration. He had a long career, playing a thousand characters from Shylock to Uncle Tom. Tilton was a solid stock actor who could be counted on in secondary roles. P.A. Fitzgerald had been around, and Rankin admired him because he had been to Columbia University. Fitzgerald wrote poetry and plays, acted in other theaters in Philadelphia, and managed theaters in Rochester, New York, and Canada.

Among the women in the company on whom Rankin came to depend were Louise Sylvester, May Howard, and Mrs Charles Henri, later known as Caroline Henri, who was soon to become Rankin's lover. Henri was the daughter of a provincial English theater manager and went on stage as a child. She was twenty when she came to America in 1851, acted at the Arch Street Theatre in Philadelphia, and married Charles Henri, an English actor whose real name was Montague. The couple ran the Athenaeum Theatre in Wheeling, West Virginia, with great ability. Doing more business than expected in that locality, they successfully ran a theater in Memphis, Tennessee, before returning to Mrs Drew. The season was barely a month old when Charles Henri came home from rehearsing a part, complained of tiredness, and fell down dead while talking with his wife.

Caroline Henri had no time for mourning. She carried on in the many roles that had been planned for her that season. How soon it happened that she and Rankin fell in love is a matter of conjecture, but it could not have been long after Charles Henri's death that Rankin moved in with his widow and their young son. Caroline Henri was full of spirit and made an excellent actress. Her advice to the twenty-one-year-old actor as to his responsibilities as lead actor and mainstay of the company must have been indispensable to him.

As leading man, Rankin was paid $50 a week. Utility players made $12 a week, while stars received from $300 to $500 a week. Rehearsals were held every day, including Sundays, for four hours, starting at 10 AM; the afternoons were for study; and performances were at 8 PM (there were no matinees at this theater in the 1860s; matinees did not become fixtures in most theaters until about 1873). A distinction was made in the billings: while other male cast members were listed as "Mr," Rankin was named as McKee Rankin.

The season opened on September 2, 1865, with Sheridan's *A School for Scandal*. Drew played one of her famous roles, Lady Teazle. Caroline Henri was Mrs Candour, Mackay was Sir Peter Teazle, Owen Marlowe was Sir Benjamin Backbite, Rankin was the reformable reprobate Charles Surface, Tilton was the hypocritical Joseph Surface, Stuart Robson played Mr Crabtree, Charles Henri was Trip, and P.A. Fitzgerald played Rowley. For those familiar with the play, the casting illustrates the characterizations the actors would be portraying throughout the season.[96] The critics thought that the new company was not working well and that the actors, except for Drew, were too nervous. As for Rankin, they differed. The *Clipper* preferred to see him again before judging him, but noted that he was young and handsome with a fine figure and easy manner.[97] The *Press* in Philadelphia credited Rankin with playing judiciously, "if not quite with the abandon which brings out the idiosyncrasy of the character."[98]

Drew made the theater interesting by producing new kinds of drama. *Old Heads and Young Hearts*, a new type of comedy by Dion Boucicault, represented the "upholstery school." The decorations and scenic effects were the prominent features, and they were brilliantly supported by the playwright's close observation of contemporary characters, his skill in the management of situations, and his sparkling dialogue. The defect, according to the critics of the day, was the heartlessness pervading his picture of modern manners. Rankin played the lawyer Littleton Coke, a blasé man of fashion, a spendthrift, sneerer, and scoffer, whose professed love for Lady Alice Hawthorne is actually a compound of selfishness and cupidity. All plot and counterplot revolve around Jesse Rural, a simple-hearted clergyman who is baited and ridiculed for five acts. The play was very popu-

Repertory Theater

lar, and Rankin found plenty of scope in acting the senior cynic Coke, especially when he and Lady Anne, disguising their emotions, try to surprise each other into the first admission of love.

Today's critics see the play as superior to *London Assurance* and fit for the living stage. Jesse Rural was kindhearted, and his well-meaning confusion provoked good-natured laughter. The absurd situations, talking at cross purposes, disguises, and mistaken identity avoid the artificiality of an Oscar Wilde comedy by the high quality of dialogue and devices of wit using word-play, parallelisms, metaphor, and image.

In the afterpiece, Rankin, as the young Spanish officer Ruy Gomez in Planche's *Faint Heart Never Won Fair Lady*, had to use wit and ardor to convince the duchess to love him. By acting very different roles on the same night—the self-absorbed lawyer Coke and the love-struck, importunate cavalier Gomez—Rankin demonstrated his versatility. The variety of roles offered him and their significance as exemplars of that time gave him the best training in stagecraft and analytical introspection. They helped him discover his talent and seek the essence of every character such that his reputation for playing certain roles spread throughout the country.

Rankin was given every second or third night off and probably learned and rehearsed his new parts on these days. One of the new roles that brought him fame was Elliot Gray of the Lancers, which he played to Drew's Rosa Leigh in Lester Wallack's *Rosedale*. Drew's patient coaching had much to do with Rankin's success, but at this point, confident in his abilities, she left Rankin responsible for the actors' stage performances and settled into managing the theater.[99]

One day, Rankin informed Drew that he had John Wilkes Booth's costumes, although he had left Booth's swords and other properties with his brother in Windsor. She became greatly excited and begged him to tell no one. If word leaked out, the public fury against actors because of the assassination would turn on Rankin and ruin not only his career but endanger the season at her theater. Since the costumes were sea-stained and useless, Rankin boxed up the trunk to conceal the name "J. Wilkes Booth" on the cover and put it away.[100]

When Edwin Adams arrived at Arch Street as the star, Rankin greeted him with gratitude for recommending him to Drew, but he did not appear in any of his plays. He did support the program by taking the leads in the afterpieces, and he appeared in the two-act afterpiece *The People's Lawyer* as Robert Howard, defending the employee of an unscrupulous merchant who framed him for theft. At the Arch Street Theatre it was customary for the leading man to support all female stars but not the male stars, yet he was expected to fill in should the male star fall ill. Thus,

Rankin supported Mrs F.W. Lander in all the main plays but appeared in just one of the afterpieces.[101] Lander, who was from England, was an infant prodigy, playing Richard III as a child to great success, but when her husband was killed in the Civil War, she left the stage for a half-dozen years to serve as a nurse to the wounded soldiers at the front. Returning to the theater, at Arch Street she played Adrienne Lacouvoeur in *Adrienne, the Actress*, with Rankin as a German nobleman, Maurice, Count de Saxe, who saves her from molesters and expresses his love for her. Adrienne comes to love him, but mistakenly believes that he loves the princess. She takes poison and dies in the count's arms as he swears his love for her. This kind of role made Rankin's already popular stock with the ladies soar to new heights.

One role that Rankin was to return to repeatedly over the course of his life was Sir Charles Pomander in *Masks and Faces, or, Before and Behind the Curtain*, which he now played with Lander as Peg Woffington, an actress during the reign of George III. Forty years later, he was still playing Pomander. The part, in which, said the *Press*, Rankin deserved praise, requires a pervasive sense of suave connivance as a Regency-styled rich gentleman, typified in this speech: "The Green Room, my dear madame, is the bower where fairies put off their wings and goddesses become dowdies, where Lady Macbeth weeps over her lap-dog's indigestion, and Belvedira groans over the amount of her last milliner's bill. In a word, the Green Room is the place where actors and actresses become mere men and women, and the name no doubt is derived from the general character of its unprofessional visitors." The play is a defense of the actor, whom the public of the time perceived as scheming, untrustworthy, and opportunistic. In it, the character Peg says, "Say stage masks may cover honest faces, and hearts beat true beneath a tinseled robe."[102] Although Rankin received praise for the role of Pomander, the mounting of the play at Arch Street was not a great success. This was largely because the star, Lander, failed to attract large houses. Her choice of play suited her classical style of quiet acting when the public wanted startling sensations.[103]

Rankin appeared only occasionally in support of the comedy team of Mr and Mrs Barney Williams. These occasions included the roles of Robert O'Neil in *The Fairy Circle*; Pierce Joyce, a ruined spendthrift, in *All Hallow's Eve*; and Dick Kelly, the Idiot, in *Shandy Maguire*. The last was not a large role, but it required a subtle capacity for disconnected thought expressed in shrill bursts. He took a leading role, Lacey O'Connor, in C. Gayler's *The Connie Soogah*, which means an Irish traveling peddler or "cheap John." Rankin had little to do or say but "efficiently represented" the part. To be the center of attraction and deprived of good reasons for movement and speaking is the most difficult acting task; the role's stage business must appear natural and necessary to dispel the vacuum in which the character has been placed. The play was written for the Williamses, who had tried it out at Niblo's Garden in New York City the previous year with enormous success. It stole liberally from other plays, which may have accounted for its popularity, though the Williamses' stage experience in working it into shape was important. Lacking literary worth, it was full of good situations and had an intelligible story line. The play eventually became the Williamses' main vehicle for many years to come.[104]

For its production at Arch Street, Drew lived up to her reputation for spending liberally: new scenery was created by the resident artist and new music was composed by the resident conductor. The Williamses had chosen the best stage to present their play to the public, for Drew's company was equaled only by Lester Wallack's company at Wallack's Theatre in New York City. Drew was rewarded with crowded houses every night regardless of the inclement weather in late November; it was called the most successful engagement they had ever played in Philadelphia.

Rankin studied the techniques of all the stars who visited for a week or two, not only to improve his own acting but to render them excellent support by entering into their styles and rhythms. His next visitor intrigued him. Madame Celine Celeste, who was born in 1814 in France, developed from a child actress into one of the great pantomimists. At age fifteen, she won instant fame touring the United States. She married a Southern "gentleman" who gambled away her money and abused her until she divorced him and moved to England. In her prime, she had an elegance and symmetry of person, a handsome face, eloquent dark eyes, and an expressiveness of feature beyond any actress of the age. Every movement was full of grace, and every attitude was a picture. The power, pathos, and effect of her pantomimic acting has never been approached, while her assumption of male attire and heroic character were marvelous exhibitions of daring ambition and successful achievement. Unable to learn English until late in her career, and therefore confined to pantomime, she eventually became a melodramatic actress of the first order with an indescribable charm and a pathos in her broken articulation. In comedy, her droll quaintness, imperfect English, and inexhaustible vivacity kept her audiences in continual spasms of laughter; in the pathetic parts of domestic drama, she moved the feelings and excited the tears of the spectators as powerfully as the most fluent speaker on the English stage.

Rankin supported her in nearly all her roles; he played Connor Kennedy in *Green Bushes*, a young Jacobite farmer in W.B. Bernard's *St. Mary's Eve*, Colonel Bernelle in *The French Spy*, and Chevalier de

Torquerelles in *The House on the Bridge of Notre Dame*. The latter role was that of a roué and schemer, which called upon Rankin's talent for portraying earthy and threatening figures.[105]

Trouble arrived with the next visiting star, the veteran James Murdoch. His urbane and scholarly style ranged between the severe requirements of tragedy and the broad lines of comedy, free of mannerisms and imitation. His musical voice, clear and distinct articulation, and easy and natural delivery made him a Shakespearean star. Service as a soldier during the Civil War harmed his health, so he turned to tending the wounded, reading to men in the field, and entertaining all over the country for the aid of the Sanitary Commission to help the wounded. Ill health continued to plague him after the war. Due to open in *Wild Oats* at the Arch Street Theatre, he was too ill to go on stage. Drew had to hurriedly substitute *Rosedale* out of the stock repertoire, and she played Rosa Leigh opposite Rankin's Elliott Gray for a week.

When Murdoch recovered, he again began rehearsals for *Wild Oats*, but soon came down with neuralgia. Rankin had to step into the star role of Rover, the strolling gentleman. Fortunately, Murdoch traveled with Mme Ponisi, a veteran actress, who took the roles Drew would otherwise have had to do. The company put on *The School for Scandal*, in which Ponisi played Lady Teazle and the members of the company took on their usual roles, including Rankin as Charles Surface. Murdoch remained away for the remainder of his engagement; thus, Ponisi became the star and Rankin her chief support.

Ponisi, born of a poor village family in England, was so infatuated with the stage that she walked miles to attend performances and later to act in them. To reach the theater for her first professional performance, she walked twenty-five miles, fainting when she reached her destination. She made her American debut in Philadelphia in 1850 and spent years at the Old Broadway in New York. Forrest sought her as his leading lady, and, as such, she was expected to sleep with him. Her lovely eyes with long lashes, a child-like expression, womanly feeling, and an unrivaled spirit of high comedy, made her a popular performer.

Playing opposite Ponisi in *The Honey Moon*, Rankin took his customary role of the Duke d'Aranza. He also played Claude Melnotte in *The Lady of Lyons*, about a young girl, Pauline, who is tricked into marrying Melnotte, her gardener's son, by the suitor she rejected. Remorseful, Melnotte annuls the marriage and goes to war. He returns, using a pseudonym, and rescues Pauline from having to marry to save her father from bankruptcy. Pauline, who had always loved him, now puts love over social station. The play reflected the changes in society under the new republican capitalism. In her last play, *Macbeth*, Ponisi played Lady Macbeth to E.L. Tilton's Macbeth, and Rankin played Macduff, a role he had come to know well.

In an effort to unify the acting profession against unpaid wages and cavalier treatment by unscrupulous managers, actors from all the Philadelphia theaters combined to benefit the Actor's Art Union of Philadelphia, in a matinee performance of Shakespeare's *The Merry Wives of Windsor* at the New Chestnut Street Theatre. Rankin took the part of Pistol, the follower of Sir John Falstaff, thus showing his allegiance to the actor rather than to the manager.

Worried over finances, Mrs John Drew came back on stage on Christmas Eve, a Sunday, when the theater was usually closed, to present the play *Lost in London* by Watts Phillips. It had failed in Philadelphia before, but with Drew in the part of Nelly Armroyd, it was a huge success, running through January 11, 1866, and restoring the theater's fortunes. Rankin played Job Armroyd, a rough but honest miner.[106] Drew then staged a new comedy, Craven's *The Needful!*, one of the thousands of plays lost from the period, in which Rankin was Captain Feargus Daly to Drew's Kate Harley, an intriguing, matchmaking mother. After two nights, the play was replaced by *Fortunio and His Seven Gifted Servants*, in which Drew had played for two hundred successive nights at the Park Theatre in New York City and which she knew would bring in the crowds. Rankin was not in the cast as he was preparing to support the next visitor, Jean Hosmer, whose beauty was expected to fill the house.

Two years older than Rankin, Hosmer projected a handsome dignity on stage and was regarded as one of the best actors in a range of characters from Lady Macbeth to Lucretia Borgia. On her opening night at the Arch, she played Marguerite Gautier to Rankin's Armand Duval "with a touching tenderness and delicate grace." The critic also liked Rankin as Duval but thought his performance uneven: "One or two portions of McKee Rankin's acting were so excellent as to redeem his connection from the charge of crudity."[107] His "crudity" was actually an attempt to develop a distinctive style. At first, critics could not appreciate his innovations. As Rankin grew in confidence and public acclaim, he brought this impression of roughness, coarseness, and crudity to certain roles, which stamped them in the public memory.[108] In the lead role of Gennaro in *Lucretia Borgia*, he played with the earthy crudity of a thoughtless character who could kill a woman who tried to save his life. Of course, the melodramatic passions of both Lucretia and Gennaro fueled the action and explained their motivations.[109]

Then, as if to tax Rankin's feats of memory at having to learn long, impassioned speeches in blank verse, Jean Hosmer indulged a penchant for serious plays in majestic blank verse such as *Evadne, or, The Statue*, in which Rankin played the Marquis Colonna, a bluff and forthright soldier who was loyal to the king, and Sheridan Knowles's *Love, or, The Countess and the Serf*, in which he played Huon, the serf.[110] In *Ion*, a five-act tragedy in blank verse, capturing the noble sentiments of ancient Greece, Rankin played Ctesiphon, a noble Argive youth who assassinates the king.[111]

When Hosmer left, Rankin supported Emma and D.M. Waller, who by now had become his close friends. He undoubtedly looked forward to acting with Emma, an emotionally powerful actor. Rankin was familiar with her repetoire. It included *The Duchess of Malfi*, in which Rankin played the central role of Antonio, master of the household, while Emma was the duchess and her husband played Ferdinand, Duke of Calabria. Antonio is the central character in the play and his malicious thinking becomes a major force. He supported the Wallers as Macduff in *Macbeth*, Cassio in *Othello*, and Colonel Mannering in *Guy Mannering*. Emma Waller was incredibly talented in both female and male roles. The critic marveled at how a woman could play a character like Iago so magnificently:

> It is pure intellectuality, of a high refined order, that infuses into each performance a breath of such brilliancy and power and which elaborates every portion up to the most exquisite degree of finish. The brief visit of this actress reminds us that all the born tragedians are not dead yet and that some of the oldest theatergoers and most accomplished judges of good acting, who can but seldom be persuaded to leave their homes of nights in this degenerate age, are eager to pay to genius today the same homage they lavished years ago.[112]

Frank Chanfrau, who played "Sam" in his play about Lord Dundreary and his American cousin Sam, intermittently for four weeks in February and March 1866, brought three actors with him. Their presence meant that Rankin was absent from the stage for most of Chanfrau's plays, but he was not idle. Drew was preparing him to run the business side of the theater as well as help with stage direction. He also may have been loaned to other theaters in the city.

Rankin continued to gain invaluable experience supporting visiting stars in a great variety of plays. He supported Charles Dillon in *King Lear*, playing Edgar, son to the Duke of Gloucester, who wanders the wilderness disguised as poor Tom, a mad beggar. He also supported the recovered James Murdoch in *Hamlet*, Lawrence Barrett in *Richard III*, and Celine Celeste again in *The French Spy*. Celeste failed to draw audiences, which was blamed on the inability of the modern generation to appreciate pantomime, she being the most refined of living pantomimists in a school of art that was almost extinct.[113] "Every true lover of acting in Celeste's peculiar school, who could have gone to see her and did not," wrote the *Press*, "has something for conscience's tooth to gnaw over to his last day."[114] On the Saturday of her run, the company put on Boucicault's potboiler *The Streets of New York* and allowed Celeste to leave the city without having to be embarrassed by one more unappreciated performance.[115]

A contributing reason for poor attendance at the Arch Street Theatre was the return of Edwin Booth to the stage at the rival Walnut Street Theatre. His notoriety as the brother of John Wilkes Booth made him a curiosity at the very least. The papers devoted long analyses to his acting in *Hamlet*. Rankin took the opportunity to write Booth a note explaining how his brother's trunk had come into Rankin's possession. Expecting that Booth would be eager to possess his brother's belongings, he offered him possession of the trunk and was surprised that Booth did not reply. When Booth left the city, John Clarke wrote in carefully worded terms that Booth had not responded because he feared any connection with his brother's heinous deed. He had his good name and the good name of the theater to uphold.

The critics, preferring piquante and petite English actresses, frowned on the last star of the season, Lucy Rushton, from the London stage, but the public liked the novelty of a large, fair Englishwoman with blonde hair, soft, sparkling eyes, and a mellow voice. Rankin played Orlando to Rushton's Rosalind in Shakespeare's *As You Like It*.[116] Rushton's *embonpoint* disconcerted the critics, who saw Rosalind as being all coquetry, archness, and airy grace. Rankin played Charles Surface to Rushton's Lady Teazle in *The School for Scandal*, the Duke D'Aranza to her Juliana in the comedy of *The Honey Moon*, Claude Melnotte to her Pauline in *The Lady of Lyons*, and Horace de Massarena to her Domino in *Black Domino*. The critics thought that Rushton should stick to parts like Black Domino, but they lit into Rankin and Louis James, who were supporting her. Rankin "has an indescribable way of running his words together. He ought to take lessons in elocution."[117]

When Drew took the stage as star the next week, she made sure that her young actors shaped up. She began as Kate Harley in *The Needful*. "We have never seen," wrote a critic, "either McKee Rankin or L.L. James act better than they did as Captain Feargus Daly and Ernest Ottway. The spirit and energy with which Mr. Rankin surprised the audience are an earnest of what that gentleman can do if he choose."[118] For his only benefit, Rankin chose to play Robert Landry in *The Dead Heart*, in which he had failed in the Albany Theatre. He wanted to prove his worth in the role to the stage manager, Joe Murphy, and succeeded. Ironically, for the afterpiece, he chose to play Charles Paragon in the comedy *Perfection*.

Theatergoers knew that Rankin was leaving the company when he did not support a company actress in her benefit. Instead, she was supported by a tall, handsome young actor from the Walnut Street Theatre named Frank Mordaunt, whose appearance on the Arch Street stage indicated that he would replace Rankin as the leading man for the next season.[119]

Rankin finished the season playing Charles Surface to Drew's Lady Teazle in *The School for Scandal* and Colonel Freelove to her Lady Eliza Freelove in Marie Kemble's *The Day After the Wedding*. After June 8, 1866, Rankin did not appear at the theater. In his months of training under Drew, Rankin had appeared in nearly a hundred major roles in the main pieces and many roles in the afterpieces. He had passed through the eye of the needle with distinction and could now set his sights on becoming a star. Moreover, throughout these months, Rankin's attachment to Caroline Henri grew stronger, despite their age difference (she was thirty-five and he was twenty-two). In discussing their roles and delving deeper into characterization, the one was invaluable to the other.

In mid-June, the *Clipper* noted that Rankin, late of the Arch Street Theatre, and Mrs Charles Henri were married in Philadelphia. Because he was a romantic young actor, it was beneficial for the public to view Rankin as a bachelor. For this reason, Rankin and Henri may have postponed their wedding until they both left the Arch Street Theatre, limiting knowledge of their relationship to their theatrical family. Henri was immediately engaged by the Conways at the Brooklyn Theatre for the next season. It was the hottest, sultriest summer in memory and insufferable in a theater.[120] Although there is no record of Rankin's whereabouts, the 1912 edition of *Who's Who in the Theater* reported him at the Olympic Theatre in London, England. He did say that he had acted under the guidance of Charles Matthews, its manager. He would have had time to take a steamer to London in mid-June, spend a month in England, and take up his duties at the Continental Theatre in Boston in mid-August. Probably he and Caroline took their honeymoon in England, which she had not visited since she left fourteen years earlier, and he may have played just a few performances in order to receive the blessing of London stage experience, always helpful to the credibility of a would-be star.[121]

Boston and E.L. Davenport

In just three years on stage, Rankin had gathered a kaleidoscope of impressions of great actors and hundreds of dramas. On August 20, 1866, he started an engagement as leading man at Whitman's Continental Theatre in Boston under E.L. Davenport, which demonstrated Davenport's confidence in him. The theater had been renovated to make it one of the most beautiful in the city. Gilt-framed mirrors lined the sides of the parquets, the orchestra section was enlarged, its chairs were more attractive, and new carpets were laid. Whitman chose a company in which new actors would complement the original company in his pursuit of conserving the standard plays. Rankin met James Lewis from New York, who was to become a close associate; H.A. Weaver, who had been stage manager when Rankin had played in Lexington; May Howard, who had played in Chicago and the South, and whom he had met at the Arch Street Theatre; Louise Myers, from the New York theaters, with whom he was to associate on and off throughout the years; Fanny Davenport, E.L. Davenport's beautiful stepdaughter, who was to become one of America's most famous actresses; and Kitty Blanchard, who had been playing in southern and western theaters, and whom he had befriended in Louisville.

Rankin also came to know Frank Mayo, who was the leading man at the Boston Theatre. Having spent the early 1860s in San Francisco acting with the Booth brothers Junius Jr and Edwin, Mayo developed into an accomplished actor. He was expressive without exaggeration. There was nothing forced, hard, or mechanical in his style; it was all free, flowing, and easy, whether in passionate or intimate passages. He was graceful in form and bearing, his voice was clear and expressive, although not rich in tone, and, like Rankin, he made a careful study of his roles. Alike in many ways, Mayo and Rankin developed a close friendship in the course of their careers such that the dramatic press referred to them as "buddies." Although they never shared a stage, they did share many a witty story in the bars and taverns at which they would frequently meet when they played the same towns as they crisscrossed the continent. Rankin was a very social person and always made a point of joining a social club if he stayed in a city for any length of time.

The Continental company began with Shakespeare's *Much Ado about Nothing*. E.L. Davenport took the part of Benedick, a young nobleman of Padua and a friend of Don Pedro, the Prince of Arragon, played by Rankin.[122] Davenport then brought out his favorite, *St Marc! Or, The Soldier of Fortune*, with himself in the title role and Rankin as Gismondo, the captain of a disbanded regiment. The role of Gismondo was originally played by J.W. Wallack opposite Davenport. It was, therefore, a giant step by Rankin into Wallack's shoes and brought home to him his meteoric rise. He and Davenport continued to carry the company in the main plays and often in the afterpieces. Davenport was a thorough teacher; the three weeks that they worked together gave Rankin a final polish. On the third night Rankin played John Dory, an old salt, to Davenport's Rover in *Wild Oats* and in the afterpiece Kitty Blanchard made her first appearance. She took the lead role of Caroline Merton in the protean farce *The Four Sisters!* and also played Caroline's sisters: Diana, the female jockey, Eugenia, the sentimental girl, and Ellen, the little housekeeper.

As Mrs L.B. Perrin had all the leading women roles and Fanny Davenport and Louise Myers took the other prominent parts, Kitty Blanchard continued to sing and dance and await her opportunity to appear in the main plays. In a Saturday matinee, she got her chance in two offerings: the first was *Married Life*, a wry look at five disparate couples, the foremost being Mr and Mrs Dove, which she and James Lewis made a great comedy hit; the second was *Lola Montez, or, Catching a Governor*, in which she played Katherine Kloper. The first time that Rankin acted with Blanchard was in *The Honey Moon*, when he played the Duke d'Aranza to her Volante, a role that Caroline Henri liked to play. Blanchard was winning more prominent roles, which meant that the public was beginning to notice and like her.

On August 31, 1866, the company brought out Shakespeare's *Othello*, featuring Davenport as Othello and Rankin as the evil Iago. It is sad for historians that the Boston newspapers neglected to review these summer plays.[123] When he began his career in Cincinnati at Pike's Opera House, Rankin had watched J.W. Wallack create a sedately devilish Iago to Davenport's chaste and scholarly Othello. A worshipful admirer of Wallack, he would have played Iago in the Wallack manner, but, since he also had Emma Waller's interpretation of Iago as an example, he may have combined elements of both performances.

During the first week in September, Davenport presented a round of his most popular characters, which, reported the *Clipper*, filled the house every night. The paper added that "McKee Rankin is spoken of as a young actor of much ability and promise."[124] Rankin's last night was on Monday, September 10, in *Henry IV, Part I* as Henry (Hotspur) Percy.[125] At that point, Caroline Henri, who had spent these weeks with him, took up her appointment at the Park Street Theatre in Brooklyn, and he accompanied her to New York.

1866–1867

New York City and Light Comedy

In 1866, theatrical life in New York City was exciting and full of promise for a young actor. Joseph Jefferson, returning from a European tour, was opening in the Boucicault version of *Rip Van Winkle*, touted as one of the finest pieces of acting on the modern stage. The great Ristori was playing tragic roles such as Medea at the French Theatre. Caroline Henri soon won praise for her performance in *Antony and Cleopatra* in Brooklyn. New York was becoming the major center for theater, although Boston, Philadelphia, Chicago, and New Orleans were not to concede that distinction for some years yet.

Canal Street was the main business thoroughfare north of which the theater region began. From south to north, the theaters were the Broadway, Barnum's New Museum (Barnum's old Museum near City Hall Park had recently burnt down), Niblo's Garden, the Olympic, the New York, and Wallack's. The Winter Garden was on the west side of Broadway between Amity and Bleecker Streets. The famous Park Theatre near City Hall Park had long ceased to exist. These theaters were all light and commodious, and gave everyone in the audience a view of the stage. The Olympic was profusely decorated with sculptural ornaments; a large fountain erected in the center of the orchestra chairs conveyed a refreshing sense of coolness in the hot summer months. Niblo's Garden was the greatest theater for attracting stars; it was where actors showed themselves before touring other cities.

The city's other theaters were a contrast to these in the theater region. The Old Bowery on the East Side—which was then almost a German colony—hosted sensational melodramas. Its four tiers of boxes rose to the "gods," whose occupants took a noisy interest in the action on stage. Next door was a huge music hall with a convenient restaurant selling cold ham, hot boiled sausages, and lagerbier, and a stage at one end for slight farces. At the Theatre des Varieties, a large space with densely packed chairs, the audience received every pleasantry with hearty laughter and passed the usual bounds of circumspect behavior with reckless hilarity. The wilder the dance, the louder came the shouts for encores from every part of the house. At the French Theatre, the French language and French attitudes were observed. Christy's minstrels were in halls in every district. The game of baseball was new at the time, which gave rise to the minstrel "Ethiopians" tossing a huge plaster ball into the midst of audiences, who were expected to toss it back, the pleasure being derived in direct proportion to the number of heads hit.

An English visitor observed that Americans liked everything large—heavy tragedies, strong sensations, ballets three hours long—but not vulgarity in the mainstream theater where the audiences were sedate and decorous; they appreciated, for instance, the subtle acting of Joseph Jefferson in *Rip Van Winkle*. Unless they were attending opera, audiences in New York tended to dress informally, which gave the theaters an air of social equality. Where the regular English theatergoers roared, the Americans merely smiled, but the Americans, like the Parisians, were resolute playgoers. They considered the drama as a necessary social institution to a degree inconceivable to a Londoner.[126]

After settling a dispute with the government, which was taxing theaters to pay for the recent war, Mark Smith and Lewis Baker reopened the New York Theatre, which had failed under Lucy Rushton, and asked Rankin to join their new company to play comedies and burlesques. Rankin, billed as a "light comedian," made his debut on September 14, 1866, in *A Regular Fix*, as Hugh de Brass, the young libertine in debt. He made a "favorable impression."[127] The subsequent notices Rankin received in the many farces and burlesques were mixed. In any case, the theater was not attracting enough customers, despite the excellent production of and good singing in *The Beauty and the Beast*.

Fanny Young, a burlesque actress just arrived from Australia, played Lady Bell with great spirit opposite Rankin as her lover, Lord Lovell, in the musical burlesque *Rum-ti-foo-zle*. As the title character, Lewis Baker cleverly sang and danced up to the level of his comic acting. The *Clipper* thought it one of the best burlesques in a long time: its rhyming couplets were easy, tripping, and jocund; its dialogue rippled and sparkled with puns, jokes, and parodies. Not only were its new songs very funny, but Fanny Young's dancing created a furor. Rankin also played in the forepiece, the two-act comedy *A Fine Old English Gentleman*, in which he portrayed an English fop "to advantage."[128] This bill, however, failed to fill the house, and, in the middle of its second week, it was replaced by an English opera. Some of the company remained in New York while others, including Rankin, went to Boston to play *Rum-ti-foo-zle* at the Howard Athenaeum. Rankin had left Boston so confidently weeks before as a leading man, and must have been disappointed to be back playing burlesque comedy. Burlesque was not yet the girly show it was soon to become once theater managers took control of their establishments and commercialized entertainment. For the time being, burlesques were still clever satires on current events and wicked impersonations of public figures. They were a higher form of entertainment than the singing and dancing extravaganza *Cinderella*, in which Kitty Blanchard was winning fame as the "pretty, dashing, gay, piquante, bewitching Prince Poppetti and Carline."[129] *Rum-ti-foo-zle*, despite the vivacious Fanny Young, failed to attract Bostonians and closed after a few nights. Rankin, unhappy with his prospects, advertised in the *Clipper*: "Mr. McKee Rankin, the elegant comedian and sensation star having a repertoire embracing all the new and startling plays of the day, would most respectfully beg leave to notify managers of having time that he can be engaged through his only agents Frank Rivers and Company."[130]

The Olympic Theatre of New York responded, hiring him for the role of the sailor Johnny Reilly in a production of Dion Boucicault's *The Long Strike*. Boucicault himself was playing the role in a successful production in London. While Rankin rehearsed *The Long Strike* in the mornings, he continued to play in burlesque pieces at the New York Theatre in the evenings. Leonard Grover, who managed the Olympic Theatre, had managed Grover's Theatre in Washington during the war, and he recounted stories of President Lincoln, who frequently attended productions in the capital. Some of the actors Rankin met in the Olympic Theatre, such as Charles Vandenhoff and James Ward, would become lifelong friends. Charles Vandenhoff had encountered the young Maurice Barrymore in England and persuaded him to become an actor. Soon Barrymore would arrive in the United States and join Rankin's particular circle.

Ironically, given that *The Long Strike* dealt with unions and a workers' strike, the house was half-full on the first night owing to a big political meeting at the Cooper Institute on Fourteenth Street. Although opening night was less than a success, the play quickly became popular and enjoyed a long run. Rankin made all that was possible out of his role of Reilly, the sailor, which prompted a critic to remark that since it was a new line of business for him, he deserved credit. He was fortunate to play with J.H. Stoddart, who was credited with saving the piece by his clever acting as Moneypenny and warming the audience up to a pitch, which kept it in the best of humor throughout the evening. Playing in a nervous, fidgety, and crabbed manner, Stoddart gave the first sympathetic portrait of a lawyer on stage. One of his scenes was the most suspenseful ever presented: at the urging of a young girl, Moneypenny telegraphs to the mouth of the Mersey River to intercept Reilly's ship because Reilly can save her lover from a charge of murder. After the telegraph clerk explains, to their despair, that it is too late to get the message through, the instrument begins to click and the clerk announces that the station is open, thus electrifying the audience. A pilot delivers the message as the ship waits to cross the bar. When the captain refuses to allow Reilly to return, Reilly jumps overboard, swims to shore, and arrives in court in time to exonerate the innocent man. Stoddart's performance stayed in Rankin's memory, and he made the role a vehicle for himself forty years later.[131] The play ran from October 30 to December 8. Rankin's acting brought him to the attention of Lucille Western, a dynamic young actress, who hired him to support her for a run in Chicago.

Chicago and St Louis

Rankin opened in Chicago at the Crosby Opera House on December 10, 1866, with Lucille Western as Lady Isabel in *East Lynn*. With the exception of Western and her two traveling male supports, Rankin and Theodore Hamilton, the cast of *East Lynn* was made up of the stock company of the Crosby Opera House. Western was regarded as the best Lady Isabel on stage, the apotheosis of the snubbed, bullied, and loving figure of the governess in Victorian times. Rankin played Sir Francis Levison, who lures Isabel away from her husband and deserts her. Western had fashioned her own version of the play, which was declared to be entirely different from and to eclipse other versions with its beauty of construction.[132] The Chicago press thought the cast too lightweight, however, and complained that Rankin did not "give satisfaction." Western, on the other hand, received lavish praise although she was criticized by some critics for trying too hard. The theater was crowded every night.

When Western moved to the Olympic Theatre in St Louis, Missouri, Rankin accompanied her, playing Fagin, the ringleader of the purse-snatching boys, in *Oliver Twist*. Theodore Hamilton was the violent Bill Sykes, and Western was Nancy Sykes. The critics considered Lucille's blood-curdling depiction of Nancy as genius of the highest order and praised Rankin and Hamilton as giving "unmistakable evidence of study and talent."[133] The stock company in St Louis was very good; it included the veteran Mrs Farren, and W.E. (Bill) Sheridan, whose stage presence and declamatory power led him into heroic roles. Both Theodore Hamilton, who had grown up in Baltimore with Edwin Booth and served with the Confederate Army during the Civil War, and Sheridan, who had served with the Union Army, became minor stars and were to be associated closely with Rankin in later years.

In St Louis, Rankin shone in two plays: Buckstone's *Cynthia, or, the Gypsy Queen*, and *Leah, the Forsaken*, a version of the German play *Deborah* and a variant on Emma Waller's *Naomi*. In *Leah*, Rankin played Rudolph, the Christian lover of Western's Leah, a role he had filled in the old play opposite Emma Waller. Hamilton was Nathan, the Christianized Jew, whose malicious intervention between the couple causes Leah's heartbreak and the ensuing tragedy. The obvious parallel between the class hatred it depicted in Germany and the racial division threatening to destroy the United States made it significant to Americans. By contrast, *Cynthia* was full of romance, interest, and beauty, according to the St Louis critic. Rankin's portrayal of the light-fingered thief, Knichen, emphasized his remarkable versatility as an actor.[134] Many of the plays Western presented were familiar to Rankin. In *London Assurance*, Rankin played his usual role of Dazzle, the young man of indeterminate background who breezes into the high-bred Courtley social circle.[135] The critics claimed the play had the best cast ever to appear in St Louis.

At this point, Western headed south with only Hamilton in tow. She planned to end her tour in New Orleans, her birthplace, with a three-week stand at the Charles Street Theatre for the latter part of January. Possibly she no longer required Rankin because the stock company with which she planned to play had its own good leading actors. Hence on December 30, 1866, Rankin headed for Brooklyn, New York, to celebrate the New Year with his wife.

On the Road

Rankin's separation from Lucille Western was temporary, as Rankin made clear in a letter dated January 2, 1867, from Brooklyn to D.M. Waller, who was managing a successful repertory theater in Newark, New Jersey: "Can't I go to Newark and play 'Rosedale,' 'Lost in London,' 'Dead Heart,' etc. and fill a week or two for a moderate salary—say fifty dollars a week? I've got nearly four weeks to fill up between this and 'Lucille Western'."[136] Western's agent had expected to get an engagement for her in New York for February 18, and Rankin was expected to join her then. When Western could not secure the engagement, she became resigned to a long stay at her hideaway home, the Glades, outside Boston and did not expect to return to the stage until late spring. Rankin, turned down by Waller and desperate for income, joined the road company of the Olympic Theatre. When, by chance, Western got a six-week engagement in Philadelphia starting in March, Rankin, already committed, was on the road.

All the company actors at the Olympic Theatre had been fired to make room for an English opera company, so they formed their own company—in James Stoddart's phrase, "a kind of commonwealth"—to fill the requests of managers to bring *The Long Strike* to their theaters. Because theatrical papers in the 1860s tended to ignore secondary traveling companies, Rankin's itinerary is obscure, but J.H. Stoddart, in his memoirs, related that Rankin traveled throughout New England with the original cast in *The Long Strike*.

For three days, starting March 1, 1867, the company appeared at the Academy of Music in Brooklyn, with Rankin as the Irish sailor Reilly. Then, starting on March 5, it opened at the Griswold Opera House in Troy, New York, for a week, in plays such as *The Serious Family*, with Rankin playing the forthright Captain Maguire, a role which he knew well, and Boucicault's *Dot*, in which Rankin played the Stranger. A critic, although deploring that the house was just two-thirds full for *Dot*, praised Rankin for being natural in every phase of the character, "impassioned and earnest while restraining himself within the bounds of probability," which, considering the play's cloying sentimentality and broadly grotesque comedy, was high praise.[137]

Rankin was in New York just before a fire destroyed the Winter Garden on March 23, 1867. At the time, Edwin Booth was presenting his magnificent productions of Shakespeare's plays at that theater. Rankin was staying at the House of Lords, an actor's hotel on the corner of Houston and Crosby Streets, and acting in *The Long Strike*. One day, when he happened to be in the Metropolitan House Cafe, an actor's resort at the corner of Prince and Broad Streets, then known as the heart of the Rialto, he was taken aside by Barton Hill, a member of Booth's company, who said he wanted to buy John Wilkes Booth's trunk containing his wardrobe. Astounded that Barton Hill knew he was in possession of Booth's wardrobe, as he had been very careful to keep it secret, Rankin told him that the costumes were sea-stained and of no use. Hill was persistent, offering him $75, and Rankin relinquished the trunk the next morning. Later that evening, the actor Claude Burroughs, another member of Booth's company, greeted Rankin with the words, "Hello Mac! I hear you sold Wilkes Booth's wardrobe to Ned!" He then revealed that Hill had bought the trunk for Edwin Booth. The next day, the Winter Garden Theatre burnt to the ground, and everything inside was consumed, including, Rankin assumed, Booth's trunk.[138]

Through April and May, Rankin continued to tour with the Olympic Theatre Company freelance group, but, at some point, he left it and may have acted in Lotta Crabtree's and Edwin Forrest's companies, since he claimed to have supported them. Rankin recounted a story that Forrest told him to emphasize the importance of being willing to learn regardless of the source. When playing Macbeth, Forrest, like all the great actors before him, used to advance slightly towards Banquo's ghost when he told him to hie himself hence. Forrest noticed that a supernumerary in his company, who used to watch the star's acting closely, appeared displeased at the scene. When Forrest asked him why he turned away with disgust when the lines to Banquo's ghost were read, he replied, "Because sire, I did not think that Macbeth should advance toward an object he feared. He should shrink back—I should say in the direction of his wife, who was his chief." As a result of that super's suggestion, Forrest changed the rendition of the scene.[139]

On June 15, Rankin returned to New York to rejoin the Olympic Theatre Company, which was entering its fifth week in Grover's comedy, *The Treasure Trove*. Rankin acted Mr Haywood, a financier, one of two new characters introduced into the play to sustain the public's interest. Many of his friends, including Stuart Robson, George Clark, J.M. Ward, and Belvil Ryan, were in the production.[140] As is discussed in the next section, the play itself reflected dramatic changes in play production that would have a profound effect on American culture. Rankin saw that change was coming and, although he disliked what he saw, he prepared to meet it.

The Burlesquing of American Drama

The high-class drama represented by Drury Lane and Covent Garden in England was undermined in the 1830s when the British Parliament, believing that the freedom to reproduce higher-class drama in the minor houses would raise the public taste, abolished the monopoly held by those two theaters. Within two years the companies of the great houses disbanded and scattered among the minor houses. Covent Garden became an Italian opera house and Drury Lane a circus. The acting tradition, in which actors aspired to the royal theaters and learned from the great actors the movements and gestures of every scene, and where the grouping of the actors on the stage and their relations to each other were the product of the careful study of two or three centuries, was destroyed. An opening was provided for the entrance of the theater manager, who introduced burlesque, *opéra bouffe*, and the deluge of French plays after 1842.

The actor George Frederick Cooke started the star system in America in 1810, but it eventually caused internal divisions in stock companies, particularly when the star received very high remuneration. By 1819, companies were giving six to seven performances a week, up from three to four. By the 1850s organizational changes were introduced to relieve the pressure on actors, to pay them better, and to give them more leisure time. Managerial duties were divided between one manager for the theater company, called the audience manager, and one for the stage. The latter was initially called an acting manager, but came to be known as the stage manager. Under the combination system, to which Rankin would soon have to adapt, these managers developed different allegiances. The stage manager looked out for the welfare of the actors in the traveling company, and the audience or troupe manager worked for the agency in New York which sent the company on the road by controlling expenses and pressuring the troupe to make a profit.

The combination system came about as a result of the playwrights' struggle to copyright their plays. Early in the century, English actors came to America because plays in England were the property of established stars; the only way new actors could get started was to play in pirated productions in America, where there was no copyright. At first, statutory copyright applied only to published works, but by 1856 it included performing rights. The drawback was that the copyright was limited to a certain number of years, and it was costly and difficult to enforce. Consequently, playwrights did not publish scripts and promptbooks, and actors jealously guarded them should they chance on a complete script. Usually actors were given only the words to their part. Some actors had phenomenal memories. When Billy Florence produced *London Assurance* in New York, he was sued by Lester Wallack, who had the rights from London to produce it in America. Billy proved to the court that he had reproduced the play exactly after the London production, not from a script but from his memory of attending the play several times. He won his case.

The blossoming of the American theater was made possible by the plays adapted from Germany, France, and England. The American theater gave scant encouragement to native playwrights; it was cheaper to adapt foreign plays. Dion Boucicault, who resented having to write adaptations on a manager's whim rather than having his own plays produced, got his revenge with a play he adapted from an American dime novel over a single weekend in New York—*The Colleen Bawn*.[141] When he took it to England, he insisted that theater managers buy the play with the supporting actors. Rather than the poor lump sums authors were paid, he demanded and got half of the gross receipts. Suddenly the author was

William J. Florence, Irish-American comedian, 1867.

the star, and the acting company belonged to the play. By promoting the idea with other playwrights in France and America, Boucicault eventually made it possible for the playwright to gain command over the production of plays. The plays, no longer controlled by actors, were put into the hands of theater agents and entrepreneurs, who paid the playwrights royalties and controlled the companies. Eventually even the theater managers, who formerly used to arrange with the star actors which plays to produce, came to rely on the entrepreneurs in New York for the new plays. In this way they lost control over the stock actors, and stock companies were no longer viable. This gave birth to what is called "the combination company" in America—that is, the traveling company comprising whole casts with scenery and properties. With the new copyrighting efforts of Boucicault, American playwrights began to emerge in the 1870s, just as Americans were tiring of the well-made French plays of Scribe and Sardou.[142]

The Scribean well-made play devised innumerable twists in a plot that became a labyrinth, offering at each turn a clue rather than a key; it differed from traditional melodrama by introducing a rational, detective-like character, who analyzes the situation to bring order to an increasingly unintelligible world, although he rarely explores the underlying causes of the disorder. The plot depended on chance rather than evil intent as motivation and relied on cause and effect, making the result mechanically inevitable. The pleasure came from following the dramatist through this maze. The melodrama, on the other hand, depended on villainy to motivate the plot and relied on intuition to resolve the episodic action, which was no more than the hero restoring what the villain had violated. In melodrama, only the villain concentrated on money, but, with Scribe, money was all-important: high finance divided daughters from fathers and people from their freedom.

Dion Boucicault owed his early livelihood to adapting French plays to the English and American stages, but he introduced into the audience a sense of expectation, suspense, and reflection by eliciting sympathy for the characters and bringing pleasure to the spectator. His trick was to prevent audiences from reflecting on the plot at the beginning by causing them to look forward with curiosity. Moreover, his dramas lent themselves to the aim of bringing the raucous poor into the theater with hopes of elevating their sentiments to the staid bourgeois level, rather than excluding the masses to sanctify the theater. Laura Keene, the statuesque English beauty, typified this effort with her sparkling repartee in comedy and her passion and pathos in melodrama, which was so unlike the thrilling of an audience with the grotesquerie and sublimity of the earlier era of actresses such as Charlotte Cushman.

The weakening of the theater manager's grip over the play allowed native writers to introduce more realism. In England, Tom Robertson's domestic and sentimental comedies, for instance, gave new life to the theater in the 1860s. Robertson's dramas provided relief from the elaborate stage machinery of the French melodrama, which called for speeding trains and giant waterfalls. Robertson introduced a central purpose to the drama, surveyed the moral problem impartially, and constructed the plot with skill. The new realism set serious drama in America and Europe in a different direction from what it had been in the past, which countered but could not overcome the extravagant commercial productions that dominated the theater for some time to come.

A theater manager who had been bringing burlesque and *opéra bouffe* to prominence hit upon an extravaganza that later was regarded as the beginning of the musical comedy. Before 1866, burlesque was witty, topical, and sophisticated, but that changed with the coming of *The Black Crook*. In the spring of that year, the history of modern burlesque in America began when a troupe of ballet dancers and burlesque comics arrived in New York from Europe only to find that their intended theater had burnt down. The manager of Niblo's Garden, having recently bought the sensational melodrama *The Black Crook*, decided to incorporate the visiting dancers into the extremely simple plot. An artist, Rodolph, loves a village girl, Amina. The local lord, Wolfenstein, lusts after Amina and falsely imprisons Rodolph for insanity. A magician named the Black Crook, who had bargained with the devil to save his own soul if he could provide another soul in his place, persuades Rodolph that Amina is false and tells him where to find a lake of silver if he will give up his soul for his freedom. In the course of finding the lake of silver, Rodolph meets Stalacta, queen of the mermaids, who asks her lovely beauties to dance for him. Thus, to quote the critic, "their alarming / Extravagant wardrobe could be with much ease / Reduced to silk tights, puff drawers and chemise"[143] Stalacta guides Rodolph safely home, where he sets up as a prince, later encountering Wolfenstein at a masked ball. Stalacta helps Rodolph win the ensuing duel, defies the Black Crook, who had helped to get Rodolph's soul, and brings Rodolph and Amina back together.

The lines were spoken "straight off without let or hindrance, occupying less than five minutes in aggregate," and the magnificent scenery and the ballet divertissements further distracted attention from the dialogue. A reviewer gave a graphic account of how the work was presented: "Some half-dozen words are uttered before a picture is placed in the front grooves, and when this is drawn aside, the serious work of dancing begins, to be interrupted by similar infinitesimal gaps. New Yorkers consider it not only delightful but astounding." The ballet dancing and the scantily clad women were extraneous to the play, yet they added to its attraction. This was a new experience. The theater was particularly crowded with men who paid no attention to the plot but watched in fascination the movement on stage. As the spectacle went on month after month, women started attending, and soon the houses were filled largely with women. The scenic effects were thought never to have been surpassed in the country: "The Wild Glen in the heart of Brocken is beautiful, as is the Grotto of Stalacta, which is dazzling with stalactic glories and living loveliness; from this rises a bed of coral, falling from which is a perfect cataract of silver water, with nymphs disporting in the bath....The air is freighted with human forms, and everything is enchanting."[144]

Companies began touring the play, establishing its popularity in all parts of the country and signaling the coming ascendancy of the commercial theater over the legitimate drama. Soon there were imitators. Leonard Grover's *The Treasure Trove* was condemned by some and praised by others for emulating *The Black Crook* in emphasizing scenery over content. In *The Treasure Trove*, buried treasure is found near Saratoga, New York, which allowed for scenes of the Union Hotel, the Leland Opera House, and Canagaga Falls; then the treasure is lost on the New York Stock Exchange, which provided for an interior view of the stock exchange; when the treasure is reclaimed on Broadway, it brought on scenes of lower New York and a final tableau of Grace Church on Broadway and East Tenth Street. There were twenty-nine speaking parts and scores of ladies, gentlemen, brokers, messengers, bulls, bears, lame ducks, sharps, flats, convicts, waiters, servants, and so on. Not only were the scenes lifelike, but human activity gave them added interest: on the grounds of the Union Hotel in Saratoga, for example, a band played while ladies, gentlemen, and children walked, played, and sat in the corridors of the hotel; on Wall Street, six newsboys appeared and executed a clog dance.[145]

Critics blasted such extravagance for its sensationalism. "Doubtless," commented the *Clipper*, "'Treasure Trove' is trashy, judged by the highest and purest standard; but who is to blame for its production—the public, who clamor for that sort of thing, or the intelligent manager who gives it? The critics can't fill all the houses. They may write up and puff a play as much as they please; but, unless the people take it, it's a dead cock in the pit in less than a week. 'Fine words butter no parsnips,' nor does fine writing pay actors' salaries, rents or expenses." The paper criticized writers who were constantly talking about the decline of the drama and the superseding of the legitimate by the sensational. It pointed to Wallack's Theatre, the temple of the legitimate, which produced several of the finest English comedies ever written to almost empty benches; finally, seeing the success of *The Black Crook*, it turned to Boucicault's *The Flying Scud* and its sensational scenes of horse racing, a bevy of semi-clad ballet girls, and a fair scene introducing an organ grinder with a live monkey, a gymnast, five minstrel performers, a Punch and Judy show, and others "too numerous to mention."[146] Managers who stuck to the legitimate suffered great losses, concluded the *Clipper*.

Rankin played his role of a villainous Wall Street financier in *The Treasure Trove* from June 15 to June 29, when the play ended. Grover gave up the Olympic, and Rankin returned to serious melodrama. The advent of *The Black Crook*, however, would soon create huge problems for actors, not so much for its crass popularity as for the attraction of such musicals for the new class of profit-hungry entrepreneur. The profiteers from the Civil War were buying up theaters, newspapers, concert halls, and all outlets for the arts. They saw the opportunity to make great sums by pandering to the new tastes of a public tired of the bleak years of the war, and to foster the capitalist mindset in the wake of its victory over the plantation economy and slavery. As the new capital centralized and consolidated business, monopolies became prevalent and, within a number of years, extended their control into all aspects of cultural and social life. Artists began to discover that their work would have to conform to the marketplace in order to be seen and heard.[147] The line of demarcation for the commercialization of the arts can be set in 1870. In the case of the theater, when the transcontinental railway was completed and whole companies could be sent to the West Coast from the base of control in New York City, it effectively ended the star system.

Following Rankin's run in *The Treasure Trove*, Lucille Western opened at the Broadway Theatre, a small house of light and elegant appearance, which was just north of Canal Street in downtown New York, and asked Rankin to play Fagin in *Oliver Twist*. The critics found that Western no longer strained after effect. She had ease, grace, and naturalness in her acting, which was complemented by a voluptuous figure, pure and distinct enunciation, a dignified and graceful walk, and a face alive with expression and mobility. It was generally known that Western's lover-managers had been driving her to pay off their gambling debts and her heroin habit. "Our special pet—our spoiled pet," one critic called her. "The woman who is sacrificed six times every week, fifty-two weeks in the year to an insane desire for money." Her strong, impulsive nature and vigorous physique especially suited her for the part of Nancy Sykes, which she continued to play into her second week.

Rankin's Fagin was declared without exception to be the best of his impersonations. Since J.W. Wallack's acting of Fagin was thought to be "marvelous," Rankin showed courage in attempting it on Broadway, and, despite the unstinting praise, he had to contend with the occasional carping that he was but a faint copy of Wallack. "The prison scene," wrote the *Clipper*, "is rendered terrific by the insane fury of old Fagin, and we question if Mr. Dickens himself ever imagined it capable of being carried by dramatization so far beyond his written description of it. Mr. Rankin deserves great praise for his careful and conscientious interpretation of the role."[148]

After Lucille Western moved on, Rankin became the leading man at the Broadway Theatre. He supported Julia Dean, who was appearing in New York after an absence of twelve years. The daughter of a theater manager in upstate New York, Dean became a star at a young age and had a checkered career spending years pioneering the drama in the western territories. She now faced a new generation in the East, which made her apprehensive. No longer a radiant star, she seemed a saddened woman and a coarsened artist. Rankin felt the heavy responsibility of supporting her. This was his first real test as a major actor in New York. Until now, New Yorkers had seen him in farces and secondary supporting roles but nothing comparable to the classic tragedies and comedies he was to perform with Julia Dean. They began with Knowles's *The Hunchback*, with Rankin as Sir Thomas Clifford. Rankin was so nervous at first that he nearly forgot where he was, but he quickly recovered and got through the role remarkably well. Augustin Daly, theater manager and critic, described him as "one of those actors who love and plot treason with the same shrugs, gripes and scowls intended for fascinating wiles."[149] In *Fazio, or, The Italian Wife*, Rankin, who played the role of Fazio, was much more conscious of the demanding Broadway audience. It was these roles that gave him the reputation of the pantaloon hero of the New York stage because of the form-fitting costumes that these roles required that he wear. In *The Woman in White*, Rankin played Count Fosco, an easy-going, music-loving, smiling scoundrel.[150] Daly reported that, although the play had insipid dialogue and a threadbare narrative style, the perils and dangers were happily surmounted by the aid of numerous sensational tableaux, all of which gave unqualified delight to the large audience. The play's success kept it on the boards for the next three days. Rankin continued to support Julia Dean in several other plays, some of which were done for just a couple of nights each to fill in time before the company's actors were treated to their benefit evenings.[151]

1867–1868

Rankin Tours as Actor-Manager

Preparing to make the most of the changes in the theater, Rankin switched from his agent, Frank Rivers, to a new international agency, Corbyn and Wall, two young men who offered actors a new policy of not charging a booking fee until they procured an engagement. He bought the sole rights to a new play, *Ours*, by Tom Robertson, from them. It had done well in London, very well in New York and Philadelphia, and very badly in Boston. Rankin had the rights to present it in Buffalo, Troy, Rochester, Albany, Newark, Pittsburgh, Richmond, Cincinnati, Cleveland, Louisville, St Louis, Memphis, Detroit, Vicksburg, Indianapolis, Montreal, Halifax, and Saint John until June 1, 1868.[152] At considerable outlay, he imported the uniforms for both the band and the acting company, and the stage scenery of trappings, cuts, etc., and increased his repertoire with Boucicault's *Flying Scud*, Tom Taylor's new comedy *Antipodes*, and *Lost in London*, *Idiot of the Mountain*, *Rag Picker of Paris*, and other plays. Perhaps at this point his ambition was greater than his grasp. Nevertheless, the move demonstrated his impulsive enthusiasm for the new drama and a gambler's instinct that risked all in support of his convictions. On June 15, he advertised that from six to twelve days thereafter he was prepared to negotiate with theater managers.

As an actor-manager, Rankin had to depend on the willingness of the stock company actors to support him well. He was responsible for the shipping of the costumes, stage properties, and scenery for *Ours*. For the other plays in his repertoire, he depended on the local theaters to provide scenery. By July, he had not signed contracts with managers in all the cities in his purlieu and therefore had to advertise twice more. He was twenty-three and must have wondered whether he had enough experience and sufficient reputation to persuade playgoers in the outlying cities that he was a star.

Rankin had his hands full producing *Ours*. Robertson's quest for realism and return to nature meant that he had to show a regard for detail such as the patter of rain on tree leaves in Act I, the sound of bands and marching columns offstage in Act II, and the military and domestic paraphernalia in the hut for the final stage. In addition, Rankin played Hugh Chalcotte, who, through the first act, lounged on a park bench for the most part.[153] *Ours* was not successful on the first stop on Rankin's tour at the National Theatre in Cincinnati. Robertson's drawing-room drama with its humor of understatement was too new to be easily accepted. Moreover, the local critic said that Rankin would make a good leading man but lacked the superior qualities that people expected in a star.[154] More significantly, the manager, fearing that a newcomer like Rankin might not attract a large audience, hiked the admission prices by 25 cents to 75 cents and $1, very steep for those hard economic times and a deterrent to many. The local critic wryly commented that it was better to have a large attendance at low prices than empty benches at high prices.[155] Rankin tried *Lost in London*, in which he played Job Armroyd, for which the manager wisely lowered prices to 50 cents. Both moves came too late, and the house closed in two days. Rankin had lasted only ten days of his three-week engagement—"business being so good he couldn't stand it," quipped the *Clipper*.

Not to be defeated, the resourceful Rankin opened his next engagement a week early at McVicker's Theatre in Chicago to a good house. This time he began with an old favorite, Kotzebue's historical melodrama *Pizarro*, in which he played Alonzo. On the second night, he again produced *Ours*, and again he drew poorly because of high prices. He tried to quicken interest with *The Corsican Brothers*, in which he had always had great success as the Franchi brothers, but it was poorly cast and had to be shelved after two nights in favor of *Ours* again. He closed an admittedly very poor engagement on September 21, 1867.

Since he had sunk his savings and others' investments into his tour, there was no thought of giving up. On September 24, he opened at the Academy of Music in Cleveland with a supporting cast that included the leading lady Clara Morris, whom he would support a few years later on Broadway when she became a great star. Cleveland responded to Rankin. The company, under the tall, black-haired John Ellsler, was a good one. The local critic remarked on the many good scenes worked up in an excellent manner, particularly between the lovers in the first act of *Ours*. Rankin "established himself at once in the minds of the audience as a most pleasing actor...natural and lifelike throughout....Rankin would undoubtedly find more favor with his audience if he were to articulate more distinctly and pronounce his words in full, with less rapidity."[156]

Playbill for *Ours* with Rankin's first appearance as actor-manager, August 24, 1867.

For his Friday-night benefit, Rankin played Job Armroyd in *Lost in London*, and "gave an unexceptionable rendition."[157] After playing *The Corsican Brothers* on Saturday with the farce *Pat o' Blunders*, Rankin tried out another Robertson play, *Caste*, for Monday and Tuesday, in which he acted as the Honorable George McAlroy. The play represented the high point of Robertson's achievements; it was economical in plot and characters and had few artificial contrivances of the French well-made play. Finding that Cleveland audiences were responding to him, Rankin gave a variety of plays the following week to keep them coming to the theater: *Lost in London, The Streets of New York, Rosedale, The Drunkard,* and *Black Eyed Susan.* As Badger in *The Streets of New York,* Rankin impressed the critic with "one of the few faithful and judicious renditions of that character that we have seen in one of the best performances he has given us."[158] As Elliott Gray in *Rosedale,* Rankin gave an artistic and discriminating performance that won the "unqualified approval" of a full house for his farewell benefit.[159]

The following week in Troy, New York, Rankin again encountered poor attendance. He opened in another old favorite, Selby's *The Marble Heart, or, The Sculptor's Dream,* in which he played Raphael Duchalet, a young sculptor. But here again he failed to impress the local critic, who wrote that as Raphael, Rankin "did not appear to any advantage."[160] In *Ours* and *Rosedale,* he "appeared to better advantage and gave more general satisfaction." The whole experience in Troy was a rueful one, and Rankin could not have avoided questioning his own abilities as a star, particularly when the star following him was the popular Fanny Price, his former colleague from the stock company in Indianapolis. In Rochester, where he opened on October 14, he again failed to create any enthusiasm for his role as Eccles in *Caste*.[161] A small audience greeted *Ours,* found it smoothly played, and loudly encored a romantic moonlight scene. For his Friday-benefit, he played Fagin in *Oliver Twist,* which the audience found to be a marvelous piece of character acting. "Had he opened in this part," wrote the critic, "his success would have been assured."[162]

In financial trouble, Rankin called on his wife, Caroline Henri, who took leave from the Park St Theatre in Brooklyn to support him at the Academy in Albany in *Lost in London* as Tilly Dragglethorpe, then as Mary Nettley to Rankin's Chalcotte in *Ours,* and as Nancy Sykes in Rankin's version of *Oliver Twist,* which he now called *Fagin, the Jew,* with a larger part for the title role. Probably he did not have to pay Henri, who did what she could to rescue his reputation as they toured to other cities for which he had contracted. Rankin had to admit that, at present, he lacked the drawing power to be a star, and that his assumption that good acting and good plays would attract audiences was naive.

Chastened, disillusioned, and out of funds, he was rescued by his friend Billy Florence with an offer to play Jack Hawkshaw, the detective, in *The Ticket-of-Leave Man* at the Broadway Theatre. Hawkshaw sees through the counterfeiters' subterfuge of using Bob Brierly as a dupe to cover their own crimes. Florence had played the role of Brierly over a thousand times, and Rankin, who had had success as Brierly, now had to assume a more complex and determined character in what was the first detective role onstage. The reviews, which concentrated on Billy Florence's acting, relegated Rankin's role with the others as "evenly good." Rankin left three weeks before the play terminated to fill a commitment for the week in Detroit starring as Robert Landry in *The Dead Heart* with his old friend from the Arch Street company of Philadelphia and the Boston Athenaeum, May Howard, as Catherine Duval.

To recoup his losses from his sortie into stardom, Rankin bowed to the power of the new musical extravaganzas and appeared at the Crosby Opera House in Chicago from December 2, 1867, in *Undine* as Sir Rupert, a role he "sustained with much spirit."[163] The play's mainstay was a Viennese ballet troupe, comprising four premiere dancers, six soloists, and about thirty coryphées dancing in four ballets. So pleasurable was it that its engagement was extended to January 20, 1868. It went to Pittsburgh for a week and then on to the Williamsburg Opera House in Brooklyn, where it ran throughout February. Rankin became bored with his limited role, for which his reputation as a matinee idol and favorite with the ladies were his chief recommendations. He considered joining the West Coast manager Tom Maguire, who was trying to engage actors for his theaters, but owing to Caroline Henri's objection, he resisted the temptation. A single sentence in the *Clipper* stated: "McKee Rankin did not sail for San Francisco on February

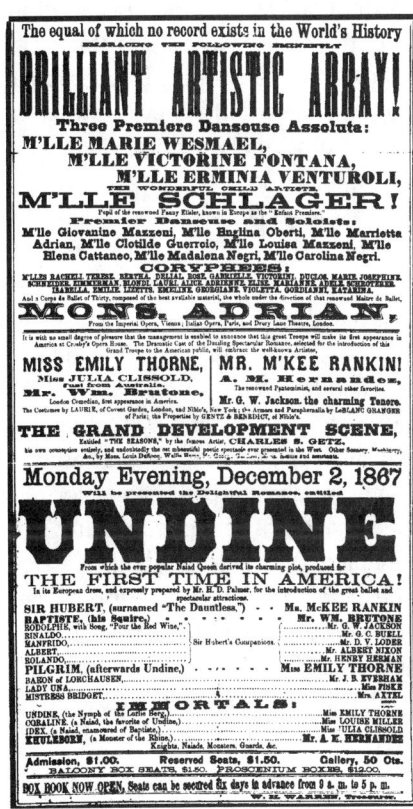

Rankin in the musical *Undine*, Crosby's Opera House, Chicago, December 1867.

29th." Instead, he continued in his unchallenging but lucrative part in *Undine* in Pittsburgh for the month of March. A new dance, the can-can, having just been introduced at Niblo's Garden in New York, was brought into *Undine* as a voluptuous diversion.

Fortunately, in April, Rankin found employment with Augustin Daly, in one of his traveling companies touring with *Under the Gaslight*. Rankin played a one-armed soldier, Snorkey. The play became famous for the railroad scene where Snorkey was tied to the tracks by the villainous Byke in expectation of a train soon to come. The scene, which Daly borrowed from an English play, *The Engineer*, became a sensation and was adopted by countless cheap melodramas and early films such as *The Perils of Pauline*.

Back in New York at the request of his actor friend Fred Maeder, Rankin played in *Lost*, Maeder's adaptation from the French, at Pike's new Opera House in New York. A hit as Count Emil de Rougeville, Rankin enhanced his reputation as the knight of the parlor. The big attraction of this melodrama was the red chamber transformation scene, which occurred in an elaborately crimsoned set built on a platform and wheeled onstage with its characters and furniture out of the view of the audience. By manipulating the platform, the scene was transformed to an exterior view of water, open country, and rustic bridges, and a tableau of Abel pursuing Cain, with an inscription of Cain's oath. Occasionally, ballerinas trespassed on the action and danced while the players stood watching. The scenic wonders of *Lost* kept the play on the boards for two weeks.[164]

Rankin took the part of a villain in the following play, Watts Phillips's *The Poor Stroller*. Watts Phillips was called the gloomiest writer for the stage. He took audiences on paths so close to battlefields that audiences could hear the groans of the wounded in their ears. *The Poor Stroller* had a complicated plot and a collection of skeletal characters made exciting by theft and murder. Daly considered that, when acted "with any dramatic appreciation," the play would be interesting, but not with the present cast, except for McKee Rankin, whom he praised for his "personation of soft-toned villainy."[165]

Daly employed Rankin in his new play, *A Flash of Lightning. A Tale of City Hearthsides and City Heartaches*, which opened the summer season at the Broadway Theatre in June. Rankin played a young man, Chauncy, of the *bon ton*. According to the local critic, he "looked and acted the part to the evident satisfaction of all."[166] Daly assembled good actors from New York and other cities. The play required thirty performers and an army of machinists to work the elaborate physical effects of every scene for five acts and ten tableaux. One of the actors, surprisingly hired to play opposite Rankin in a starring role, was Kitty Blanchard, on loan from Selwyn's Theatre in Boston.

Blanchard had caused such a lasting sensation in Boston in her role as Prince Poppetti and Carline in *Cinderella* that over forty years later a gentleman wrote to a Boston newspaper that: "No man who ever heard Kitty Blanchard sing 'You naughty, naughty men' is likely ever to forget it."[167]

She became a star in comedies with the comical James Lewis, and played opposite Joseph Proctor in a New England summer tour of the Boston Theatre. Immediately afterwards, she was employed as the leading lady at the prestigious Selwyn's Theatre, where she played opposite Stuart Robson, Rankin's friend from the Arch Street Theatre.

Blanchard had learned to flirt from her years in burlesque in Frank Rivers's Melodeon in New York, and she had become the favorite attraction with the "gents" who dropped in for a drink and a smoke and a little excitement. Now she was the idol of Harvard men. When the theater needed supernumeraries for a spectacle, it could always count on students from Harvard lining up at the door. So infatuated were they that they fought to decide to whom Blanchard had given the longest look. She was followed in the streets, and, when she attended a theater, the theatergoers watched her rather than the play. Daly called her "a vivacious and elegant blonde, who is all the rage in Boston."[168] By casting her opposite the handsome Rankin, who was the rage in New York with the opposite sex, Daly was looking at the box office, rather than matchmaking.

Meanwhile Caroline Henri, leading lady in Mobile, Alabama, was being hailed as "a palpable hit" for her singing and acting. Her separation from Rankin, which was out of professional necessity, opened him to temptation. Thrown together for weeks in intimately connected roles during the hot summer, Rankin and Blanchard became very close, and their love scenes were rehearsed with unnecessary frequency. As for the play, it "finished on a dreary waste and knocked a hole in the manager's exchequer." It was an example of Daly's early work, which was play carpentry in comparison with the artistry of his later plays. In it, however, he indicated his scrupulous striving for reality, which he considered essential to combat the unreality and sentimentality of the French adaptations. In the scene of the heroine's detention in a den in the New York slums, for example, he employed people from the real slums. Going home one night, Daly heard a boyish voice of wonderful power flooding the night air with "Garibaldi's Hymn" and "Santa Lucia." Tracing the music to a backstreet, he came upon two little Italian wandering minstrels and added them and their parents to his collection of human documents for the play.[169]

In August, Blanchard returned to Selwyn's in Boston, and Rankin opened in Boucicault's *Foul Play* at the New York Theatre. Their separation seemed to affect Rankin's acting. His performance as the villain Arthur Wardlaw was perfunctory, which led Daly to comment that "McKee Rankin worked through the strange part of Wardlaw as if he felt little interest in his duty. This, however, is nothing new to say of Mr. Rankin and it would perhaps be just as well for his own reputation and the pleasure of his audience if he could now and then utter Cap'n Hudson's boast of 'duty to s'mployers'."[170]

If Rankin appeared indifferent, the situation behind the scenes was tumultuous. The manager, Colonel Lloyd, fought with the leading man, Dan Harkins, over a financial matter that divided the cast, most of whom, including Rankin, removed to the Broadway Theatre with Harkins to play another version of the play. Lloyd sent four deputy sheriffs to arrest Harkins at the Broadway, but, while they threatened the actors with drawn guns and shot the doorman and the boy who lit the gas lamps, Harkins escaped. Two police officers arrested Lloyd's sheriffs under the assumption that they were assassins. Undeterred, Lloyd sent a process-server to jump onstage during a performance, but he was stopped by men in the audience, who feared he was going to kill Harkins. Eventually Harkins's production was stopped by a court injunction.[171]

1868–1869

Variety and Chicago's Plaudits

Although Rankin and a handful of actors such as John Jack and Mrs G.H. Gilbert were hired at the Broadway Theatre for the winter season, Rankin was not in the cast when the theater opened four days later on August 31. Rather, he appeared a week later, on September 7, at the Theatre Comique. Possibly the contretemps over *Foul Play* soured his relations with the Broadway. This may explain his abandoning dramatic roles for the comicalities of a zany group, although he may have relished the change because he loved light-hearted humor. On a deeper level, a wandering spirit appeared to have taken him since his failure as a star, and may have decided him against a long-term contract with a theater. Certainly his confidence had been shaken, and he gravitated to character roles, the more varied the better. Yet he had not given up his dream of becoming a star—a star not in the manner of Booth and Davenport, but rather one to fit the changing requirements of the theater.

A comic from London, William Horace Lingard, had been drawing crowds to the Theatre Comique for weeks. He brought a new style of entertainment that had caught the fancy of the public. Within a framework of light pieces, tableaux, and farces, which were intentionally played poorly to contrast with the artistically arranged tableaux, he added singing, imitations, ventriloquism, and Dutch comicalities or German-accented routines. Lingard brought a novel sense of humor, fair singing, and recognizable imitations of notables. He created all the sketches, including an after-dinner speech given by Mr Fuddlebrain.[172] Alice Dunning, who was later celebrated on London and New York stages, sang and danced, outfitted in a sky-blue silk dress cut low in front to showcase her figure. The most eccentric performer, Joe Emmett, gave performances on a tiny mouth organ, and W.H. Hilton held a comical ventriloquist dialogue with a dummy. Rankin took part in *A Loan of a Lover* and other farces until the next week, when one of the great deadpan comedians of the age, John T. Raymond, joined the company.[173]

Raymond began auspiciously as Toby Twinkle, the easy-going workman of the spinning factory in J.M. Morton's comedy *All That Glitters Is Not Gold*. Rankin played Stephen Plum, an unassuming member of the social-climbing family who owns the factory. He is admonished by his family for his friendship with the low-born Twinkle. Playing comedies and farces, the actors soon made the Theatre Comique the most popular in the city. But Rankin returned to serious drama when the English Opera Bouffe company moved into the theater, obliging the actors to put on their farces and comic sketches before and after the opera.

Rankin appeared as Sir George Medhurst, a forger, in Boucicault's *After Dark, or, London by Night* at Niblo's Garden.[174] The play's production was made possible only after Boucicault agreed to pay Augustin Daly $25 a night for the use of the railway scene. Playwrights then had an automatic common-law copyright on any innovations or novel creations; the rights lasted into perpetuity, but could be lost and deemed to have entered the public domain if action was not taken immediately. Of course, Daly had copied the idea from elsewhere, which is why he agreed readily to a monetary settlement.

Boucicault and Tom Robertson were the first playwrights to stage-manage actors and make the whole ensemble run smoothly instead of allowing actors to work out the movements on their own or at the star's direction. The American producers of *After Dark* copied the instructions that Boucicault used in the London production. They were rewarded with praise for the finished style, in which the scenery, costumes, and mechanical equipment were made to work. Scenes of Victoria Station, Grosvenor Hotel, Little Compton Mews, Black Friars Bridge, the Dry Arches under Victoria Street, the Elysian Music Hall, Westminster, and the Underground Railway with the Flying Express, whetted the appetites of Americans for far-off places, and kept the play running for eleven weeks. The tall, handsome, romantic Charles Thorne Jr took Rankin's place as Sir George Medhurst when Rankin left to play leading roles at Crosby's Opera House in Chicago. Within a few years the two actors would be regarded as the romantic stage heroes of the age.

Because the frivolous New York theater held no promise for him to develop into a star, Rankin went to Chicago to be the leading player in repertory, which was producing serious drama. He was impatient to succeed, and he understood the fleeting nature of time, especially when he reflected on the past year and what had befallen actors he had known: Julia Dean died in childbirth; Adah Isaacs Menken died in Paris from a chill; Helen Western had to be carried from the stage and died of a congestion in the bowels.

The theatrical competition in Chicago was vigorous. Acting in that city taxed an actor's energy: plays were presented seven days a week, and there were matinee performances on Saturdays and sometimes on Wednesdays. Edwin Booth was attracting huge crowds to his classical plays at McVickers' Theatre, which gave hope to lovers of the legitimate theater that sensation drama had had its day, despite the fact that Wood's Museum was doing *After Dark* and fighting an injunction from two other Chicago theaters that claimed the right to produce it.

Rankin appeared as Vyvan in *The Rightful Heir* at Crosby's Opera House.[175] The piece had beautiful and polemical set speeches, but the cast was not well rehearsed and made errors in the text. The critic questioned the wisdom of beginning the new season with an unfamiliar play that had never been done in the city. He liked Rankin's performance, however, as "decidedly the best of the evening and, rather curiously, he was the best in the most trying and difficult passages of the role. His make-up was very neat and correct and his reading fine, especially in the apostrophe to the sea and the narrative of his escape from the pirates which he relates to his mother."[176] The leading lady was May Howard, one of Rankin's particular friends. A year younger than Rankin, she was handsome in face and form and carried herself with grace and elegance. Furthermore, she was noted for her splendid wardrobe, which was a prime consideration with audiences in that day.[177] Rankin supported the popular comedian John E. Owens in the roles he knew, such as Robert Howard, the people's lawyer, in *Solon Shingle* and the Stranger in *Cricket on the Hearth*. He emulated Owens's timing in comedy and, having last seen him in Cincinnati, still marveled how Owens held an audience with his quick little walk and rolling eyes.

Because an exciting melodrama was required to bring out audiences over the Christmas holidays, Crosby's mounted a magnificent production of Alexandre Dumas's *The Three Guardsmen*, which held the stage to January 9, 1869. Rankin had played Athos in another version, *The King's Musketeers*, but as leading man at Crosby's, he probably played D'Artagnan. He also played Corporal Haversack in *Napoleon's Old Guard*, which had been John Nickinson's favorite role. In *Tame Cats*, a critic considered him "very good" as a poet and pseudo-child of nature who, as a scoundrel at heart, makes love to everybody, especially to Mrs Langly (May Howard), a grass widow addicted to poetry.[178]

Rankin, enjoying the variety of his roles and relishing the stage experience, which gave him the chance to study character and bring it alive, continued with the company when an English opera troupe replaced it at the Crosby Opera House. He led the company to Davenport, Iowa, for the week, and to towns near Chicago, such as Lafayette, Indiana. On February 1, the musical side of the company returned to the Crosby Opera House to long-running success in *The Field of the Cloth of Gold*, while the Crosby dramatic acting company kept touring until it could return to Chicago in March 1869. Rankin had to lease Wood's Museum, which was made possible by Fred Aiken, who had recently left it to take a ten-year lease on the newly erected Dearborn Street Theatre. When it was built, Wood's Museum had suffered from the puritanical attitude to theaters: to mask the building's real purpose, it was fronted by a museum of curiosities, while two rooms hidden at the back—innocuously called the lecture room—constituted the theater.

The competition among Chicago theaters was so intense that it was essential for them to find the best actors. Rankin brought Matt Lingham to Wood's Museum to share the leading honors with him. Lingham had progressed steadily since they first met at Pike's in Cincinnati, but not with the brilliance of Rankin. When Rankin opened at Wood's Museum in Robertson's *School*, Fred Aiken produced the same play at the Dearborn and even took the role of the sport, Poyntz, that Rankin played. They differed in such things as costumes; for example, at the Dearborn, Aiken and J.W. Blaisdell, a popular leading man, played in hunting suits, "such as every English gentleman is expected to wear," commented a critic.[179] At Wood's Museum, on the other hand, Rankin and Lingham wore business suits, and Rankin sported an eyeglass. "This gentleman's conception of the character he plays," wrote a critic about Rankin as Poyntz, "is that of a sport and his ideas seem to have been inculcated from witnessing Chanfrau in Dundreary....He affects the accent as well as the manner of a snob. Mr. Aiken conceives the character more properly, I think, and portrays Jack Poyntz as a plain spoken, blunt mannered, yet a gentlemanly young fellow, who has been educated at large and is equally at home everywhere." Another critic, however, rated Rankin's interpretation as the more imaginative. "Rankin's Poyntz was an excellent specimen of the off-hand loose and careless style of acting which the role requires and which Rankin is especially adapted to....His rendition was exceedingly enjoyable, in dress, voice, and action generally."[180] By the end of the week, the consensus was: "We have never known two rival places of amusement before to produce the same play with so little room for preferences."[181]

In the second week, audiences thinned out, and Rankin and May Howard walked through their parts in a listless manner. Their lack of interest reflected their disappointment that the actor Blaisdell had taken over the lease of Wood's Museum from Rankin in the hope that Blaisdell's popularity with the public could revive its fortunes. In *Oliver Twist*, Blaisdell played Bill Sykes. May Howard as Nancy carried the piece with great acting, but Fagin was the chief interest because Rankin played him exceedingly well. A critic wrote: "Without being the equal of J.W. Wallack who has made a reputation in the part, Mr. Rankin certainly may justly lay claim to both strength and originality. He makes Fagin his own creation in every respect, sinking Rankin completely—an achievement which he sometimes fails to accomplish—and in manner and make-up is forcible and striking."[182]

The production played to standing room only. Whether Blaisdell was put off by being outshone or for some other reason, neither Rankin nor May Howard appeared in the bill for the next week. Howard transferred to the Crosby Opera House company, and Rankin went over to the Dearborn. At the same time John Dillon, one of Chicago's great crowd-pleasers, who had recently joined the Dearborn, switched to Wood's Museum.

Rankin began as leading man at the Dearborn in *Knaves of the Pack*, which ran for a week. In this sensational drama, adapted from the French and as involved in plot as all French dramas, Rankin played two roles: Joseph, an impostor, and Rocambols, a murderer.[183] The next week, Rankin again appeared in dual roles: as Betminster Harfthal and his son Rudolph in Robertson's latest play, *My Lady Clara*, adapted from Alfred Lord Tennyson's poem. "Mr. Rankin as Rudolph is in his element," wrote a critic, "and his portrayal admits of no criticism. The change to the father is excellently done, though the portrayal spoils the effect of the younger character to a measure. The interview between Rankin and Miss Cluer [playing Clara] in the second act is as natural a piece of acting as one could conceive."[184]

The Dearborn Street Theatre adopted a policy of presenting old and new plays that had not been seen in Chicago and dressing them up in beautiful scenery and costumes. For Planché's romantic drama *Knights of the Round Table*, for example, Aiken created rooms of the Neapolitan ambassador to London, gypsy encampments, and London slums. Decidedly not about King Arthur and his knights, it concerned card-sharp-ing knights. Rankin played the scheming villain, Leonard d'Arcy, who is blackmailed into becoming a member of the knights. Rankin was unfamiliar with his lines on the first night, but presumably improved on the second. On the last three nights of the week, the company played in *Oliver Twist* with Rankin again as Fagin.

Surf, a new play by Olive Logan, the actress and advocate of women's rights, was a good-humored satire on the nouveau riche who gathered at a fashionable resort. There was hardly a plot, and progress was made up of indiscriminate dialogue. Aiken produced it in fine style: the dresses worn by the women were the most elegant and fashionable ever seen on the Chicago stage; the scenery and properties, the music, and the actors were declared first class and in perfect harmony. A bathing scene was a great success. Rankin played Lothario Smasher, "a swell of the Dundreary order." "Rankin," reported a critic, "had almost nothing to do as the dressy silly fop, and did it."[185] The play ran four weeks and then alternated with *Rosedale*, *Oliver Twist*, and *Flowers of the Forest* for the fifth week.

On benefit week, all the important actors had one night put aside for them, except for Rankin, who had a benefit on two nights, Tuesday and Wednesday, May 25 and 26, and for the matinee on Wednesday. This unusual move showed how valuable the company considered his contribution. For his benefit performances, Rankin chose *Eustache Baudin*, a work that reflected his predilection to play men whose character had been nurtured by the elements of nature. It was the story of an honest and courageous man of low birth who is persecuted by the nobility. The play's message was that real nobility lies in the character of a man rather than in his status. Rankin's choice indicated the direction that he thought modern drama should be going; having imbued the sense, from the great actors under whom he studied, that the theater was an educating force, it was the direction in which he would take it.

The next week Aiken produced *Foul Play*, with Rankin as Arthur Wardlaw. Rankin may have been bored by the role because his sluggishness of manner again came to the fore, although this may have been an intentional characterization misunderstood by the critic. "He continually impresses one," wrote the critic, "with the idea that he is striking an attitude or settling himself down for a good comfortable nap. There is no excuse whatever for such constant carelessness and dullness, both of presence and delivery. 'Reform it altogether.'"[186] This last was written in inverted commas as if the critic were quoting the proverbial headmaster. This critic, however, revised his opinion when the Dearborn tried another new play, *Black and White* by Wilkie Collins. Commenting on Rankin playing the Count de Lagrac, who falls in love with a West Indian heiress, he wrote: "Rankin surpassed himself discovering his dying mother....His acting was very good."[187]

Rankin acted in benefits for other members of the company before leaving for New York in mid-June. "It is the opinion here," wrote a critic, "that he is one of the best leading men we have had in Chicago."[188] Moreover, he was generous to his colleagues, as demonstrated in his note to Colonel Thomas Alston Brown, the dramatic editor of the *Clipper*, introducing May Howard as the greatest favorite of the Chicago stage and a perfect stranger to New York: "Anything you can do such as favorable notice in your newspaper much appreciated."[189]

ACT II

Stardom

New York City in 1869

It was Lucille Western who lured Rankin back to Broadway. Pike's Opera House was leased to Western's manager, James Herne, for a year, and since the Opera House maintained no company of its own, she brought together an excellent cast: J. Newton Gotthold, W.E. Sheridan, E.L. Tilton, S. Vining Bowers, W.A. Donaldson, and Marie Wilkins, actors who had acted with Rankin and upon whom he would rely in his own productions in the future. As a dress rehearsal for New York, Western played in Brooklyn for two nights in *East Lynne* and *Oliver Twist*. She opened at Pike's Opera House on June 21, 1869, in *East Lynne*. Rankin played the villain, Sir Francis Leveson, who lures Lady Isabel away from her husband, deserts her, and commits murder. Rankin, said a critic, "could not have been surpassed. He played the character to a charm."[1] As for Western, she played the dual role of Lady Isabel and the housekeeper, Madame Vine, as well as ever, holding the audience spellbound.

On July 2, Lucille produced Augustin Daly's *Leah, the Forsaken*, and on the 5th, she appeared as Nancy Sykes in *Oliver Twist*. As the hapless

---

Notes are on pages 454-71.

Nancy, she was "the very incarnation of the character, performing it with a naturalness that was painful to witness, particularly in the scene where she is supposed to be dashed to smithereens by Sykes and then crawls across the stage with her hair disheveled and her face covered with blood."[2] The public response was so overwhelming that Western, who had planned for a brief season in New York, remained for months to respond to an insatiable demand for her acting. In contrast, Rankin as Fagin, the ringleader of the young pickpockets, had lost the power he had shown in the role at the Broadway two years before. According to the critic, he was "getting careless…forgetting the character he is representing and appearing as Mr. Rankin off stage."[3]

Rankin's inattention to his stage business could, perhaps, be attributed to his love interests. He and May Howard may well have planned to continue a relationship begun in Chicago, but when he arrived in New York, he encountered another attraction playing at a New York theater. Kitty Blanchard, now head of the Selwyn company from Boston, was on a visit at the Fifth Avenue Theatre for the last two weeks in June, playing in Reade's *Dora* and a burlesque treatment of *Black Eyed Susan*, called *Black-eyed Susan*, in which she played William, "the 'Bill' of the Play." Stuart Robson was Captain Crosstree.[4] A picture of Blanchard as William in sailor garb, the first time an actress had appeared on a memento card, was selling fast in New York as her popularity soared. Although Augustin Daly, as critic for the *New York Times,* cast occasional sarcastic remarks upon Lucille West-

Kitty Blanchard as William in *Black-eyed Susan*, New York, 1869.

ern and her sensationalism, he praised the visiting Selwyn company of Boston. He said that it proved that the public had not yet surrendered all interest in theatrical entertainments of a worthy class, despite that everything that could be done had been done to pervert its instincts and upset its understanding. He praised Blanchard for being the owner of a few original ideas, which differentiated her from the heroines of Broadway, but faulted her for adopting the coarse method of speech, half nasal, half guttural, which first came in with the "Mose" drama, the east-side New York working-class plays that Chanfrau starred in. She abstained from it in *Dora*, in which she played the heroine, Mary Morrison, which showed she could avoid it if she pleased. Blanchard eclipsed May Howard in the eyes of Rankin, and they resumed the romance that they had begun the previous summer.

Rankin's relationships with and attraction to women were complex, yet they were secondary to his passion for the theater. According to the critic Amy Leslie:

> He was constantly in trouble with one woman or another. Not that he ever sought them or let any of them worry him in the least, but he seemed to have a faculty of making grief and mourning and misery for them as well as being an almost heroic helper by some accidental toss of the weird sisters which made it dramatic or sympathetically theatrical for him to be of notable service in a gallant way.[5]

Although still married, Rankin was acting like a gallant bachelor with Kitty. While Kitty played in New York, Rankin continued to support Lucille Western in all her plays, except her last. He bowed out of this one because he wanted to devote his time to writing a stage version of *Rip Van Winkle*. He knew that, if he was ever to escape from being a leading man in never-ending melodramas, he needed a vehicle in which he could star. By taking a proven theme and copying the style of one of the most successful actors of the age, Rankin grasped for a second chance at stardom. He attended the performances of Joseph Jefferson in the Boucicault version of *Rip* at Booth's Theatre during the summer, which were attracting the largest audiences of any star in the city in a long time. Boucicault's script differed from the earlier versions such as that by Charles Burke, Jefferson's half-brother, by having Rip speak to spirits who did not reply and were invisible, thus making the scene more dramatic and real. Rankin included small children in his script because of the added interest they had for audiences.

Jefferson was imbued with the American dramatic spirit yet retained the best of the old English school, whose followers were quiet, modest, learned gentlemen offstage and matchless actors on it. His stage characters were full of simple tranquillity, propriety, and freedom from exaggeration, and he brought all of these qualities to the characterization of Rip. From Rip's first entrance, the audience knew that a descendant of the old players stood before them. "He leans lightly against a table, his disengaged hand holding his gun. Standing there, he is himself the incarnation of the lazy, good-natured, dissipated, good-for-nothing Dutchman that [Washington] Irving drew. Preponderance of humour is expressed in every feature...the kindly, simple, insouciant face...the lounging careless figure, the low, musical voice....The remarkable beauty of the performance arises from nothing so much as its entire repose and equality." The famous scene at the end of the first act when his wife throws him out of his home was beautiful in its tenderness and dignity. "His tones, vibrating with the passion that consumes him, are clear and low and sweet, —full of doubt that he has heard aright the words of banishment,—full of an awful pain and pity and dismay. And so, with one parting farewell to his child, full of nameless agony, he goes out into the storm and darkness."[6]

Yet the real challenge to the actor was Rip's awakening from years of sleep.

> This maundering, almost imbecile old man, out of whose talk come dimly rays of the old quaint humour, would excite only ridicule and laughter in the hands of an artist less gifted than Mr. Jefferson; but his griefs, his old affections, so rise up through the tones of that marvelous voice, his loneliness and homelessness so plead for him, that old Lear, beaten by the winds, deserted and houseless, is not more wrapped about with honour than poor old Rip, wandering through the streets of his native village.

Jefferson's facial expression corresponded to the demands of the text, foretelling the coming bursts of humor or pathos "as surely as the overcharged summer sky presages the lightning's flash." Rankin, therefore, had to emulate that same quality of simplicity that was Jefferson's charm.

The play expressed the unspoken feelings of a population moving rapidly into industrialism. It mourned the carefree days of the past and endorsed the humane values lacking in the new American society. Old Rip, as a passive victim, symbolized a country enmeshed in the incomprehensible forces that were having such a dramatic impact on people's lives. It was this message, underlying the quality of the acting, that kept the play running for years. But, of course, Jefferson and Rankin made it comprehensible and a work of art by their artistry.

1869–1870

Pike's Dramatic Company

When Kitty Blanchard returned with the Selwyn company to Boston, Rankin left for another engagement at Crosby's Opera House in Chicago, this time as stage manager for Pike's Dramatic Company. This was a new experience with great responsibility.[7] He was to open with Boucicault's *Formosa, or, The Railroad to Ruin* on September 20, 1869, but since both Wood's Museum and McVickers Theatre produced *Formosa* on that night, Rankin postponed his opening until the 23rd to see how his competitors designed their sets so he could touch up his own to out-do them. Wood's had a scene with exterior and interior views of a villa, in which an elegant garden was illuminated with gaslight and a mechanical contrivance made streams of water reflect the rays of the moon. Inside the villa, men and women were seen gaming and flirting. Rankin's own scenery brought raves from the critics. His villa scene was "the finest ever seen here," and the boudoir set and boat race spectacle "reached the climax of stage art."[8] Commentators branded the play immoral because it pictured the salon of a professional woman of low birth who used her charms to make money from high society. But the reformation of a high-class courtesan, in whom goodness ultimately prevailed, intrigued audiences, thus influencing decades of unrealistic melodrama and countless Hollywood movies.

Rankin's stage business was perfect down to the most minor detail. His portrayal of Tom Burroughs, the oarsman, was fresh and natural and full of abandon, bringing a very enthusiastic reception from the large opening-night audience. Despite having the best production and forcing the other two theaters to close after a week, Rankin's *Formosa* lost money and closed after two weeks.

Rankin turned to the sure income-providers *Oliver Twist*, in which his Fagin was the chief attraction, and *Camille*. This was followed on October 7 with his first appearance as Rip in *Rip Van Winkle*. His friends and supporters were astounded by the drama and by Rankin's superb characterization of the old man. His real test as a manager, however, came when he took Pike's Dramatic Company on the road.

After touring small towns in Michigan, the company opened in Indianapolis, where it supported visiting stars such as John Collins, whose popularity was restricted to the frontier, where the people were starving for entertainment. Collins fell ill while playing in *Married Life*, and Rankin had to step into the star's part. The three Worrell sisters, Sophia, Irene, and Jennie, arrived on October 25, and, because their singing and dancing group accompanied them, Rankin's company moved for a week to Lafayette, where Rankin tried out his *Rip Van Winkle* among other plays in the company repertoire. The company returned to Indianapolis for two weeks, and in mid-November it opened for a week with *Rip Van Winkle* in Detroit, where Rankin's family and friends in the area came to see him as the rising star of the stage.

In his first stop in a Canadian city, Rankin opened in *Rip Van Winkle* in Hamilton on November 22, 1869, to a citizenry proud that a Canadian actor had won great praises from the American newspapers. The local critic called Rankin a "rare histrionic talent" who recognized that the perfection of acting consisted of "simple naturalness."[9] When Rankin played Fagin in *Oliver Twist*, the audience applauded frequently and rapturously, thus persuading him to extend his stay in the town until the end of the week. On Thursday, he played the title role in *Enoch Arden*, making "one of the finest pieces of acting that has ever been witnessed on the Hamilton boards," wrote the critic. "We have no hesitation in saying that Mr. Rankin holds the first position as a Canadian actor, and doubt if he is excelled in his particular *role* by actors of greater note."[10]

Rankin met with the same success in Toronto, and on opening in Montreal on December 6, 1869, at the Theatre Royal he was hailed as the popular young Canadian *artiste* "pronounced by the entire press of the U.S. one of the Greatest Living Character actors." After the third night of *Rip Van Winkle*, the critic called Rankin "really great" for leaving none of the eccentricities of Rip unnoticed, especially when he portrayed Rip awakening from a twenty-year sleep with rheumatism and wearing a decrepit gray beard, and for getting over the difficulties of German pronunciation, which he "mouthed" with the greatest of ease.[11]

In the midst of this adulation, Rankin received a telegram informing him that Kitty's mother was dying and to come at once to Boston because she wished to see Kitty married to him. Of course, Mrs Blanchard's concern about leaving her young daughter alone and unprotected would have Rankin's sympathy and understanding. In a state of apprehension, he left for Boston on the morning train of December 9.[12] By the 10th, he was in Boston with Kitty Blanchard, preparing himself for a second marriage. Their affair during the summer had blossomed into love, and they became engaged with no thought of marrying soon, before Rankin had prepared the way. Kitty readily accepted her position as second wife. She referred to herself professionally as Kitty Blanchard until a week before Caroline Henri's death several years later, when she appeared in the billings for the first time as Mrs McKee Rankin. Henri raised no complaint, for she was a practical and understanding woman, and, being thirteen years older than

Stardom

Rankin, she might have expected such an eventuality. It is unlikely that the public knew that Rankin was already married; the newspapers stayed quiet about it. Kitty was twenty-two years old, McKee twenty-five when they married on December 11, 1869.[13] The quick wedding was attended by their actor friends in Boston. Mrs Blanchard recovered miraculously, and Kitty, who had taken leave from playing in Shakespeare's *A Midsummer Night's Dream* at Selwyn's, was able to rejoin her company as the joyous Puck a couple of days later. The papers reported humorously that she had been replaced by Mrs McKee Rankin, who was said to be her equal.

In the meantime, Rankin had to live down the bad reports coming from Montreal that he had left his company stranded without funds.[14] The Montreal public gave a benefit for the stranded players, who performed dances and songs and played farces such as *A Regular Fix* and *Toodles*.

Acting in Tandem

Rankin spent the remaining days of December coming to terms with his new status and explaining matters to his parents. As a married woman, Blanchard was sure to lose her popularity with the public and thus lose her value to the theater management, and Rankin could not be expected to set aside his career for hers. They would have to act as a team. For the present, she had to fulfill her contract with Selwyn's while he cast about for employment. Luckily, on January 3, 1870, Lucille Western, opening in Boston in *Oliver Twist*, hired Rankin in his famous role of Fagin for a week before moving on to Worcester, Mass.[15]

John Selwyn planned to bring Rankin into his company with Blanchard and capitalize on the publicity of their marriage. The opportunity arose in mid-January 1870 with *Little Em'ly*, the stage version of Charles Dickens's *David Copperfield*. Charles Vandenhoff appears to have made a sacrifice for his good friend, Rankin. When Selwyn fired Vandenhoff for refusing to play Copperfield's hero, Steerforth, he was replaced by Rankin. Blanchard, after eighty performances as Puck in *A Midsummer Night's Dream*, played Em'ly. To attract larger audiences, Selwyn produced Robertson's *School* as an afterpiece to *Little Em'ly*, with Blanchard as Naomi Tigue opposite Rankin as Lord Arthur Beaufort, the sporting gentleman who rejects the suggestion that he marry Naomi, the orphaned West Indian heiress. Possibly the role of Poyntz, which he had played in Chicago, would not have worked for him here because Poyntz marrying Naomi would have been too close to real life. Helped by *School*, *Little Em'ly* ran for forty-nine nights. These long runs were made possible by regular train service to the theaters from the outlying towns and by arrangements for conveyances to the commuter trains waiting outside the theaters after the performances.

Following the run of *Little Em'ly* came the prospect of a great stage moment for any actor, let alone an actor as young as Rankin. He was offered the role of Horatio in support of Charles Fechter as Hamlet in Fechter's first appearance in America. Charles Dickens prepared Fechter's way to America with an article in the *Atlantic Monthly* touting him as the greatest living actor. For years, Fechter had been the romantic idol of Paris and celebrated widely for his outbursts of passion and his deep understanding of character as he played in both French and German. When he taught himself English and played his great roles of Ruy Blas and Hamlet on the English stage, the American public too clamored to see him. But by the time he arrived in New York, he was already an older, fatter version of the handsome, dynamic young actor he had been in his heyday. He unwisely opened in his famous role of Ruy Blas, which disappointed playgoers who had expected to see the dashing young man of legend. Fechter's advisers then pressed him to do his famous Hamlet, and he began arranging for a quite different version of the play from the productions to which Americans were accustomed. Fechter made his Hamlet blond and bearded, dressed in long robes, and surrounded by courtiers clad in rough, barbarous garb of a primitive age. The scenery was Nordic in all its rude simplicity.

When Fechter opened at Niblo's Garden in *Hamlet* on February 14, 1870, the critics compared him to Edwin Booth, who was playing Hamlet for a record one hundred successive evenings at Booth's Theatre. "Mr. Booth's is the superior in evenness, in repose, in dignity and in general elaboration. Mr. Fechter's is the finer in naturalness, in fire, and in originality. Mr. Booth succeeds by the aid of physical advantages and Mr. Fechter in spite of them....Nature has denied Booth the intellectual grasp and intuition and the prodigious magnetic power which at intervals make Fechter seem almost inspired."[16] Fechter spoke rapidly, avoided cadence in his speech, and never paused to make points as did so many actors. His Hamlet had a realistic grandeur. He conveyed a veiled passion, ineffable tenderness, and splendid scorn "all thrown out by lines with dazzling radiance," wrote Augustin Daly. "We regard Fechter as a revolutionist in art, an iconoclast, who has declined to do vast good by overthrowing unnatural and artificial signet rings."[17]

With such a torrent of words to praise Fechter, there was room only to commend Rankin for a fine Horatio. Yet Fechter's original reading of the play had an effect on the other actors, who had to respond to the meanings that Fechter implied. For example, normally, when meeting the Ghost,

Horatio says "But soft; behold! lo, where it comes again! / I'll cross it, though it blast me. Stay, illusion!" and Horatio moves before Hamlet can cross the Ghost's path, as if to stay its progress, but in Fechter's production, he required Horatio to make the sign of the cross at which the Ghost stopped, as a Catholic ghost should. Furthermore, Hamlet was more open with Horatio, his only valued friend, than with Marcellus and others whom he feared might be spying on him. Hence when Hamlet said, "There are more things in heaven and earth, Horatio, than are dreamt of in your philosophy," he emphasized "philosophy" to indicate that treachery was not in Horatio's character. He thereby avoided the implication of other actors who emphasized "your," implying a superior wisdom on Hamlet's part.[18]

In early March, Rankin returned to Selwyn's in Boston and played Count de Valreas in Daly's adaptation from the French of *Frou-Frou*, to Blanchard as Gilberte. Unfortunately, another version of the play was on at the Boston Museum, which forced Selwyn's to close its version earlier than expected. The *Clipper* observed that the actor playing the Count at the Museum was by no means perfect, but he was "much better than McKee Rankin."[19]

Rankin continued to play his customary roles in the familiar plays, such as the Stranger in *Dot*, while Blanchard, feeling the effects of her pregnancy, either lacked the stamina to be onstage or was too obviously enceinte to play a role. Rankin created the role of Lord Alfred Colebrook, fiancé to a bank owner's daughter in Boucicault and Byron's new melodrama *Lost at Sea* on April 4, when "a very severe cold made his words almost inaudible and seriously hampered the freedom and intelligibility of his performance." The play ran for three weeks, due largely to Boucicault's talent for thrilling scenes like the rescue from a burning building and for the realistic settings of life on the pier at Hungerford Bridge and in the banking rooms.

In late April, management reported that it wanted all the bad points in the company weeded out and the good improved for the next season. At the same time, it announced that Kitty Blanchard and McKee Rankin would be leaving.[20] This was a surprisingly sudden negative view of the newlyweds. Possibly, theatergoers suspected that Blanchard had to marry Rankin because she was pregnant. This suspicion alone would have led to a decline in Blanchard's popularity. Before Rankin left for an engagement in New York City, the Selwyn company played *Ours* for the last week in April, with Rankin as Hugh Chalcotte.

In New York, Rankin appeared in *Mosquito*, which had been written expressly for Lydia Thompson by Alexandre Dumas, Sr, with Lydia and her bevy of beautiful British blondes. These singers and dancers had immense success in burlesque in the wake of *The Black Crook* phenomenon. Lydia was well proportioned and had a pleasing though not a handsome face, which was lit by sweet smiles and merry humor. Her plaintive, pathetic voice thrilled every pulse and gave her audiences a strong feeling of pleasure. The blonde dancers were used to decorate scenes, ranging from the harbor of Puerta da Santa Maria and Quintana's plantation by moonlight to the brilliant fete in France "with a host of maskers in gay costume moving about the fountains and statuary."[21]

To emphasize that this melodrama was not burlesque, Lydia hired good actors, such as Mrs C.M. Walcot (one of the daughters of Rankin's departed mentor, John Nickinson) and John Dunn, who had been absent from the New York stage for years in Australia and New Zealand. Owing to his role in a popular comedy, Dunn was called "That Rascal Jack" and had been unable to shake the nickname, despite his long absence. Rankin confided in him his desire to act in Australia, and Dunn persuaded him to tour the West and then accompany him back to Australia. Rankin saw the change as an escape for Blanchard and himself from the prejudice shown by managers to their marriage. In the United States, actors, who no longer enjoyed the security of the repertory company, found that managers were seizing upon the new commercial relations to extend their power over them.[22] Indications of a hardening attitude came from New York when Pike's Opera House announced the novel policy that it would no longer hire a company of actors for the season but only for individual productions. Moreover, Lester Wallack stopped giving benefits to his actors, with the dubious excuse that it was demeaning for them. The manager at Niblo's Garden stopped giving benefits to the stock actors but had to accede to stars' demands for them. Later, managers argued that benefits to stars were becoming a burden for the supporting cast, who were not paid for such performances, and canceled them.

In Boston, Selwyn insisted that Blanchard continue acting. He cast her in Sardou's *Fernande*, as a courtesan who wants to leave her immoral business and live a married life, but she refused the part, saying she was ill, and the opening had to be postponed several times. There was discord at the theater: the theater-owner discharged John Selwyn, who, given that he had a long-term contract, refused to leave. Rankin rejoined the company to play in *Little Treasure* for the benefit of the company treasurer. Not surprisingly, Selwyn's offered Blanchard no benefit, but instead hosted E.L. Davenport, who began the summer season on the day that actors, led by Stuart Robson, gave Blanchard a farewell benefit at the rival Boston Theatre.

Rankin, back in New York with his new wife and mother-in-law, opened on June 6 at Niblo's in another of Watts Phillips's depictions of the working class, the blood and thunder military drama *Not Guilty*.[23] The strong cast included Charles Walcot and his wife; Frank Mackay, Rankin's colleague from the Arch Street Theatre; C.H. Morton, a low comedian who was to be associated with Rankin in many ventures; and Rankin as Robert Arnold, an honest journeyman locksmith. Despite the strong acting, the play closed a week before expected. Its short run was likely attributable to its premiere the previous November at the lower-class Bowery Theatre, which prejudiced critics and sophisticated playgoers against it. Always in demand at this stage in his career, Rankin used the week to rehearse a number of comedies, farces, and commediettas for Hooley's Theatre in Brooklyn, which the actress Lina Edwin leased for July. Not only did Rankin look forward to a summer of good fun, but the engagement helped him to mark time while waiting for his wife to give birth and for the infant to be old enough to undertake the arduous journey to the West.

Rankin was in an experienced company: Fanny Davenport and George Clark, who had been in Daly's stock company during the winter season; Charles Vandenhoff and Stuart Robson, fleeing from Selwyn's in Boston; Marie Wilkins, an English actress and manager of London theaters, who brought her comedic talents for good to America; and several others whose talents had been proven in song and dance. Billed as a "Star Combination," they opened with *Everybody's Friend* and *Pluto* and followed that bill with the burlesque *Black-eyed Susan*, in which Fanny Davenport, a very beautiful woman, played William, and Robson enacted his famous outrageous caricature of Captain Crosstree. Rankin, the handsome youth George Clark, Marie Wilkins, and Lina Edwin were in *Used Up*, which kept the stage for a week to moderate houses. Burlesque and comic operas such as *Poor Pillicoddy*, *Spitfire*, and *La Sonnambula* were tried in the third week. In the fourth, benefits were played for some of the stars. For Fanny Davenport's benefit, Rankin played Rip in his *Rip Van Winkle*.

Individually, the actors would have made their mark in any stock company; together, they were not financially successful. The excessive heat added to pecuniary failure convinced Miss Edwin to disband the company. But this caused no inconvenience to the actors, many of whom, including Rankin, moved to Brooklyn's Park Street Theatre, which was run by the Conways. Sarah Crocker Conway was just as talented as her sister, the great tragedian Mrs D.P. Bowers, but, after her marriage, Conway had curbed her desire to be a fine artist in order to become a rich star. She was one of the most industrious managers in the country. At her theater, Rankin with Kate Denin, "Rascal Jack" Dunn, and others combined in a series of tragedies and drawing-room comedies such as *The Marble Heart*, *Peep O'Day*, *The Corsican Brothers*, and *School* from August 22 to the end of the month.

This brief period in Brooklyn brought Rankin to the attention of the critic for the *Brooklyn Eagle*, William Hudson. Hudson later recalled that "I was so much impressed by his performance of a part in a frivolous play that I sought his acquaintance to tell him how delighted I was with his work." He claimed that "no young man on the stage at that time seemed to have an equal promise of fame":

> Nature had liberally endowed him with gifts peculiar to his needs as an actor. He was tall and manly in appearance, with a natural and unconscious grace of movement, enhanced by his early training in the formal school of acting. His features, regular and symmetrical and mobile, were quickly responsive to his emotions. His temperament was sympathetic and emotional, but his emotions seemed to be subject to the appeals of his intellect, or of an intellectual comprehension, rather than to those of external causes. His voice, musical, flexible and of wide range, was under perfect control. And over all reigned an intelligence of a grade only rarely dealt out with the mimetic faculty. In those years he was given to study and reflection, though, because of his own magnetism, he was often tempted into the primrose path.[24]

1870–1871: Go West, Young Actor

Rankin was enjoying steady work. Augustin Daly, who was managing Mary Frances Scott-Siddons's American tour, arranged for Rankin to play Bishop Gardiner in a new Tom Taylor play, *'Twixt Axe and Crown*, in September 1870 at Wood's Museum in New York. It portrayed the conflict between the English Catholic Queen Mary and her sister, the Protestant Princess Elizabeth. A reviewer wrote that Rankin was "out of place as a representative of old men. His gray-haired bishop, however, showed imagination to conceive, if not the special capacity to execute."[25] Scott-Siddons, starring as Queen Mary, was the granddaughter of Sarah Siddons, whose majestic performances in tragedy are legendary in the theatrical profession. Also in the cast was Charles Thorne, Jr, six feet tall and entirely possessed by the passion of love. The women called him "My God Thorne." When he acted his romantic roles, delicious creepy chills ran up and down the feminine spines in the audience. This appearance with Rankin marked the start of an intertwining of the two actors' careers that would bring fame to both. In Shakespeare's *As You Like It*, starring Scott-

Siddons as Rosalind, Rankin played Jacques to Thorne's Orlando. Whereas Orlando depicts the mild dejection of self-accusing humility, Jacques displays the humorous sadness of an amiable misanthropy. Thorne was praised for the depth of feeling in his love scenes while Rankin was commended for acting with taste and discretion.

Rankin admired Daly's dedication to producing good theater, in opposition to the commercial fare that the new theater entrepreneurs used to fill entertainment venues. Several times throughout their careers Rankin and Blanchard would ask Daly if they could take roles in his companies, as if he were a touchstone for theatrical art. Daly took over Booth's Fifth Avenue Theatre and devised a new way to organize a good stock company. He freed the actors from lines of business such as first old man, second old man, walking gentleman, and so on. At first dejected at being made to act out of their line, the actors became elated at their successes.[26] When Agnes Ethel refused to play the heroine in Daly's opening play, Daly tried Clara Morris, who arrived in the city from Cleveland with letters to New York managers, all of whom, except Daly, ignored her. Clara Morris was a great success, marking the first time that an actress from what was then the West had been accorded such honor from New Yorkers. Daly wanted ensemble playing, not stars, and cast his actors in major roles in one play and in minor parts in the next. His habits of doing everything himself, checking the minutest details, and setting rules that had to be followed exactly began to annoy the cast. Clara Morris called the tall, thin, and nervous Daly "dictatorial, exploitive and manipulative."[27] For some reason, he expressed his anger at her for having been born in Toronto, as if she were unpatriotic. But for the time being Morris needed this dark, damp theater and this fidgety, imaginative, and ever-busy manager as much as he needed her talent for eliciting emotions in audiences that fused actor and spectator as one in the dramatic moment.

After the close of the Scott-Siddon's engagement, Rankin played in a couple of farces and in *The Honey Moon* for a couple of days while waiting for Kitty to give birth. He signed contracts for his company to appear in western theaters later in the month. Then on the morning of October 8, Blanchard presented him with a twelve-pound daughter. He was seen standing alone wearing a Kossuth hat with a green ribbon and a small feather and looking across a restaurant at J.F. Sheridan, another actor, who was contemplating him. The reporters who witnessed the encounter learned that both men had recently become fathers and, despite suffering the pangs of fatherhood, looked well. This public-relations venture quashed all speculation as to when his daughter was conceived.[28] Colonel Brown, who had become Rankin's manager after retiring from editing the *Clipper*, knew how to use the periodicals for his client's advantage. Brown set up the route to the West for a road company that Rankin was forming and billed John Dunn, McKee Rankin, and Kitty Blanchard as "the Great Triple Alliance."[29]

The Rankin company, along with Rankin's baby daughter, Mary Gladys, and Kitty Blanchard's mother, left on the continental train for Ben De Bar's Opera House in St Louis, Missouri, where it opened on October 24, 1870, in *Rip Van Winkle*. Ben De Bar was brother-in-law to J.B. Booth and had been a good comedian in the Southern theaters. Rankin played Rip every night for the first week. The *Clipper* found him "really creditable. The voice, make-up, expression, and pose are like Mr. Jefferson's, and, I believe, were these two gentlemen to play the part on alternate nights, the public actually would not know which was which."[30] John Dunn played Rip's friend Derek Von Brummell excellently, and the little children, Marie Fairchild as Hendrick Vedder, Carrie McHenry as Rip Junior, and Florence Fairchild as Katchen, "deserve especial mention."

Since business was light, Rankin switched to another play he had written but not yet staged, *Nannie, or, The Dutch Orphans*, with leading roles for Dunn, Blanchard, and himself. It was of the sensational order, with an exciting plot, many humorous and thrilling situations, and a character called Bertha, the belle of Chicago. Rankin and Blanchard developed what they called "the double characteristic melange," comprising songs, dances, solos, instrumental songs, and so forth. The combination of thrilling action and burlesque-like entertainment that seemed to fit perfectly, or, as the critic wrote, "added materially to the effort," caught the fancy of the public. Blanchard was supposed to make her first appearance in the play as Nannie, a German peasant girl, but she was too ill, and Rankin's former colleague from the Arch Street Theatre, Louise Sylvester, stepped into the role with songs, dances, and a solo performance on the banjo that earned her the favor of the house. The critic found the play too closely fashioned after another comedy, *Fritz*. In *Nannie*, the main character, Jacob Van Albersleben, a Dutch immigrant, spoke in the same broken English and used similar Dutch gags, but Rankin's playing of Jacob as a loving brother and warm-hearted friend merited commendation.[31]

Despite closing with the popular *Oliver Twist*, in which Rankin continued to play Fagin, Rankin's two-week engagement was not monetarily successful. However, Rankin did secure further engagements for his young company. Tom Maguire, the West Coast theater magnate, was in St Louis and checked out Rankin and his company's performance. As always, he was on the lookout for actors to fill his theaters in San Francisco and Virginia City. Entrancing Rankin with stories of the beauties of the country and the wealth to be made, he engaged his company for San Francisco.

Rankin improved his company with additional actors, playing *Rip* and *Nannie, or, The Dutch Orphans* in Louisville, Kentucky, and then going north to Buffalo, New York, to open in *Nannie*. By this time, Blanchard was well again and acted Nannie with sparkle and vivacity. Her songs and dances in the beer garden scene were repeatedly encored. By leading with this sensational drama, Rankin made his company popular with the public, who attended in large and excited crowds and returned for his other productions later in the week.[32] The company played the double bill of *Wallace, the Hero of Scotland* (for which Rankin hired a young actor, W.H. Whalley, who was having success in New York and Boston theaters, to play William Wallace) and *Nicholas Nickleby*, with Blanchard as Smike, Rankin as the imperturbable Newman Noggs, and his old friend from Union Square company touring days, Ben Rogers, as the nasty schoolmaster Squeers. Rankin seemed satisfied that he had a good, well-balanced company and that he could invade the West with hopes of success.[33]

The company played Omaha, Nebraska, for the week November 25 to good business and left for the West Coast on December 5, using the new train connection to San Francisco. Because the train lacked dining cars, passengers had to get off three times a day to eat at the stations. "We fell in with all sorts of queer provender at those stations," Rankin recalled. "Bear and antelope steak, coffee without milk served on brown sugar in tin cups and so on. The cheapest meal we encountered was a dollar."[34]

The company, on arriving in San Francisco, stayed at the most fashionable hotel of the day, Lick House, and opened at the Alhambra Theatre on Bush Street on Sunday, December 11, in *Rip Van Winkle*. The company had powerful competition from the California Theatre on Bush Street, which the San Francisco banker Ralston built for John McCullough. Ralston continued to lavish money on it to make it the most popular amusement venue in the city with the best stock company ever gathered in the United States, including the Charles Thornes, Senior and Junior, John T. Raymond, and May Howard. The Rankin company did fairly well, but the theater-owners, deciding to renovate the Alhambra, closed it temporarily, and reopened it with the Rankin company on December 24.[35] "Rascal Jack" Dunn, seeing that Rankin was becoming enamored of the West, sailed for Australia without the Rankins.

The atmosphere of newness and adventure, the unpredictable nature of the society, the almost classless, unassuming people, held a special attraction for Rankin and pulled him back to the West Coast many times throughout his career. Starting with *Nannie, or, The Dutch Orphans*, the Rankin company attracted a sizable audience, which grew during the first week. Rankin changed to the Irish play *Robert Emmett*, starring William H. Powers in his first appearance in San Francisco, and added the burlesque, *The Field of the Cloth of Gold*, in which Blanchard was declared to be "positively charming" as the Earl Darnley and delightful in burlesque. Rankin took roles in both plays.[36]

Rankin presented W.S. Gilbert's *Sweethearts*, the first time it had been performed in the United States, and added *Nicholas Nickleby*, *Oliver Twist*, *Cinderella*, *Fanchon*, and *Little Mother*. The last play concerned an orphaned newsgirl who, while supporting her young brother, bucks her wicked stepfather and a thieving sailor who try to force her into marriage. Despite these efforts, the company's popularity was short-lived; it closed "in gloom" on January 22, 1871. Rankin did not seem to be overly disappointed. He loved the air of risk-taking that permeated the region, and he looked forward to his next opportunity.

On January 25, Tom Maguire gave Blanchard a benefit at the Opera House, in which she danced a Polka Comique with Mme Moriacchi, and both Blanchard and Rankin did a vaudeville routine in the characters of Anthony and Cleopatra.[37] Maguire received an offer from an innkeeper named Pico in Los Angeles to open the Mercred Theatre there, and Rankin became a partner in his enterprise. On the 26th, Maguire and Rankin's company embarked for Los Angeles on a trip that Rankin called "awful in some ways." They went by an old steamer, built for the cattle trade in the Civil War, to Santa Monica, a voyage of three days, took a train the short distance to San Pedro, and rode in mud wagons from there to Los Angeles.[38]

The company arrived on a night of great excitement: the vigilance committee had hanged a man for killing another for "two bits"—a quarter. The next morning, Rankin went to the barbershop and discovered that the ferocious-looking, corpulent Frenchman shaving him was the head of the vigilantes and had placed the noose about the neck of the offending citizen. Although Rankin felt quite uncomfortable at the time, he later found the man to be genial, and they became excellent friends.

In Los Angeles all the buildings were adobe. The only European-styled buildings were the Pico House Inn, which had the only decent accommodations, and the newly built Mercred Hall. The Rankin company opened the Mercred Theatre with *Rip Van Winkle* and played to excellent business for two weeks, presenting *The Dutch Orphans*, *The People's Lawyer*, and other light comedies. Given that theirs was the first acting troupe to visit the area and the old settlers had seen only the puppet shows that came up from Mexico, the settlers drove their rigs from as far away as Santa Ana and stared at the thrilling dramas in open-mouthed amazement. "We had

Greasers, Frenchmen, a few real Spaniards, and as picturesque an array of white folk as I ever saw," Rankin recalled. "A bunch of gamblers who had drifted in from Arizona lent color to the gatherings and prosperity to the box office. They didn't care how much they put in for a seat. Sometimes they were loaded to the guards with both rum and artillery, but they never made any disturbance, and, within the theater, conducted themselves in an eminently respectable manner."[39]

The Franciscan padres of San Gabriel mission, hearing of the actors and curious about their productions, invited them to visit them in their cool patios. The troupe drove in wagons through the present site of Pasadena, then a vast sheep range. A prolonged drought had made the hills desolate and the valleys stark brown and bare, and the sheep were dying by the thousands. The price of a sheep was 10 cents—the value of its pelt on the ground. Herders crowded around the actors and implored them to buy, but they had no use for the animals. At San Gabriel, the padres served them plentifully with food and drink, and they bought wine and olives and saw all that was to be seen in those days before returning to the coast.

After a week, the company sailed back to San Francisco, where it remained idle for a few days. "No one was ever really hungry in the Bay City then," Rankin recalled. "The smallest coin was the 'two-bit' piece, and it cost two bits to get a shine, two bits to get a drink, and even two bits to buy a paper. Anyone out of money could have two bits from the passerby for the asking, and in a saloon where he could buy a glass of beer—same old two bits, the uniform price for everything—was a free lunch that included everything from oysters to black coffee."[40]

A couple of prominent Mormons were in the city, vainly trying to persuade a Mormon actress, Annie Adams, who had fled Salt Lake City with her "gentile" husband, to return. Annie had recently given birth to a daughter, Maude Adams, who was destined to become famous in the theater. Rankin accepted the Mormons' offer to play in Salt Lake City in about six weeks' time for himself, his wife, and William H. Powers, who wished to return east with them. Shortly afterwards, John Piper, who owned Piper's Opera House in Virginia City, Nevada, offered him an engagement for a full company immediately.

With some of the same company who were with him at the Alhambra Theatre and in Los Angeles, Rankin set out on February 21 for Virginia City. John Piper guided them via Reno, which then was a primitive place with a station and one or two buildings.[41]

Transferring to mud wagons, the actors traversed the mountains in stormy winter weather. Rumors of road agents holding up travelers were rife and disconcerting to Rankin, whose mother-in-law, the company treasurer, carried $10,000 in a chamois wallet hidden in her bosom. They arrived safely and put up at the International Hotel. Virginia City, known for its famous gamblers O'Brien, Flood, John Mackay, and others, was then the greatest mining camp in the world. Every saloon in town had a complete gambling outfit attached to it. Miners in rough flannel shirts and boots crowded around the roulette tables; here and there, a woman also played.

The company performed at the Opera House for two weeks to very large business. Everyone had plenty of money and was eager to enjoy the entertainment, from French comedy to sensational drama such as *Oliver Twist*. The company closed on the Thursday of the second week, as it was expected to perform in Carson City on Friday and Saturday nights.

After the performance, Rankin and Powers went to the bar in the gambling rooms attached to the hotel. They were talking to the proprietor when a party of three men entered discussing the Franco-Prussian War that was then being fought in Europe. In a good-natured way, two of them were chaffing a tall young man of possibly German descent about the German navy, which was a farce in those days. A man, standing at the stove, tried to enter into the conversation several times but was rebuffed by them, and retired back to the stove. When drinks were ordered, the man by the stove tried to get into the conversation again but was brushed aside by the tall young man of German descent. Immediately, the man by the stove, who felt he had been snubbed once too often, drew out his gun and shot the young man through the left eye, splattering parts of his brain against the white sleeves of the bartender. He threw up his hands and dropped his revolver while shouting, "My God, gentlemen, I did not mean it!" The gambling room emptied, and a sheriff took the murderer to the town jail. As the gambling room filled up again, several elderly men in groups of three and four entered and began questioning bystanders about the incident. The bar proprietor told Rankin that they were vigilantes.

Rankin went to bed about 2 AM but was awakened by a commotion outside the jail, which was across from his bedroom window. He quickly dressed and joined the crowd, which, being lectured by the sheriff about the need to be a law-abiding community, was jeering and laughing at him. Suddenly, a man from the upper window of the jail shouted out, "He's gone!" Apparently, by riling the crowd, the sheriff had been stalling for time while his deputies smuggled the prisoner, Perkins, in the sheriff's buggy to Carson City, only eleven miles away, where he was locked up in the new penitentiary. Vigilantes pursued the buggy but were unable to catch it.

After returning to Virginia City from a two-day engagement in Carson City, Rankin was awakened early Sunday morning by a great commotion in the street. Looking out the window, he saw that a crowd of vigilantes had captured Perkins when the authorities were bringing him back to Virginia City to be tried on the Comstock, the area of its gold-mining operations.

Rankin quickly dressed and followed the crowd to Piper's Opera House, where men had thrown a rope over the rafters on the stage. Perkins piteously begged to be allowed to take off his boots, but the men pinioned his arms, tied his ankles together, and adjusted the noose. A word was given and, with scores of hands pulling the rope, Perkins went up in the air. As he swung clear, a dozen revolvers emptied lead into his writhing body. Two of the vigilantes stood beside Rankin as he watched. "I have played in Piper's Opera House many times since then," Rankin commented years later, "and no play has ever been able to sweep that picture out of my mind."[42]

Eager to leave Virginia City, Rankin, Blanchard, her mother and her baby, and Powers took the stage for Reno. Their horror at the events that had transpired must have been profound because, in leaving, they were foregoing four weeks of their very profitable contract with John Piper. The rest of the company remained in Virginia City.[43]

The little group had several hours of idle time waiting for the overland train. An enterprising saloonkeeper suggested they give a performance that evening. Rankin obliged by presenting scenes from *Rip Van Winkle* and followed them with songs and dances by Blanchard. To their consternation, they found that the conductor of the small orchestra that had been assembled could not read music but conducted by ear. He managed to accompany most of the songs but threw up his hands at the dance music that followed each verse. Rankin and Powers improvised by whistling the music to the dancing until the absurdity of the situation provoked them to laughter. Trying to whistle when laughing proved impossible, and Blanchard had to sing her own dance music.

After the curtain fell, Rankin asked Powers to go out front and get their take of the receipts, but Powers had been watching the audience through a peephole and was convinced that the men had disliked the improvised performance and were forming a vigilante committee to string them up before the train arrived. Rankin was removing his makeup with trepidation when the saloonkeeper appeared with a sack of money, which, he said, was the actors' share. The audience was delighted with their performance, agreeing that the play "was up to handle and nothing was left out" and considering the whistling orchestra an original stunt.

When the train arrived, everyone showed their concern for the actors, helping them with their baggage and offering vociferous farewells. Like a scene out of a Bret Harte short story, big flannel-shirted miners gathered about baby Gladys, paying her court as if she were the first baby they had seen that year and loading her with fruit, candy, sandwiches, canned vegetables, and everything indigestible by a baby.

On the train to Salt Lake City, Rankin met a man whom he had encountered frequently in New York, Chicago, Washington, and San Francisco and with whom he was on friendly terms. He was always curious about the man's profession. Later, he heard that he was a government detective detailed to ferret out the truth about the Mountain Meadows Massacre, in which migrating settlers were set upon by Mormons disguised as Indians. The situation was still volatile, and it was dangerous to discuss the massacre, but the incident sparked Rankin's curiosity, and, with his experiences of mining camps and the Mormon community, he eventually saw the massacre as a theme for a drama.

When the actors reached Salt Lake City, they had difficulty getting rooms at the best hotel because visitors from all parts of the world had been attracted there by rumors of loads of gold in the Emma mine. Still possessed by the recollection of being driven out of Nauvoo, Missouri, for their religious practices, the Mormons were made exceedingly nervous by the presence of so many "gentiles." Their great organizer, Brigham Young, prepared them to raze the city and, at an hour's notice, destroy their homes and leave their beautiful valley just as they had found it. Owing to their mistrust of the crowds of foreigners, the Mormon leadership had called in their police, known as the Danites or Destroying Angels. The name derived from the Biblical sons of Dan, who were bound together by an oath for revenge.[44] But the foreign presence in the area was temporary: the Emma mine swindle being exposed quickly, and the hopeful newcomers, who had been lured to Utah with fabulous dreams of wealth and who had sacrificed everything they had in the world to get there, left for their old homes, disgusted and heartbroken, cursing the country and everyone in it.

Rankin was delighted to find that the theater was one of the best-constructed in the United States, that the pieces were beautifully presented, and that the resident company, all Mormons, acted wonderfully. The theater's props were as complete as possible and, together with the variety of wardrobe and a good library, were estimated to be worth $1 million. Rankin found the stage manager to be resourceful and particularly adept at lighting effects, considering that he had no gas to modulate them but depended on coal oil, which lighted the front and back of the house. Rankin chose *Fanchon* for the first play, but it did not draw well for the first week. When he tried his version of *Rip Van Winkle*, the theater filled up for the remainder of his visit. Rankin was amused by the interrelationships among the stock company actors. The three children in the first act were the offspring of one man in the cast, but each had a different mother. Rip's wife and his grown-up daughter in the last act were played by two women who were wives of this same man, but neither was mother to any of the three children.

Many of the plays Rankin presented had never been seen in Salt Lake City before, but the stock company was equal to the task and came through with anything needed on a day's notice. Only *Oliver Twist* was cut out of their repertoire because, as Brigham Young explained to Rankin, the scene of a brute killing his mistress was dangerous for prospective mothers to witness. Young sat in a large rocking chair placed almost in the center of what was called the orchestra, and on the right of the dress circle facing the stage was a large space called the royal box, occupied always by about forty of Young's children. Rankin became fascinated by Young's absolute control and his gracious, courteous, and solicitous concern that the actors have a pleasant stay. The Mormons paid in produce such as butter, eggs, and grain, which the theater traded for cash at the cooperative store.

Rankin, who was Roman Catholic at this time, met a Catholic priest, Father Foley, who had a shack of a church that ministered to twenty-five people. Powers, who had been an altar boy in a church in Montreal, assisted the priest in Sunday services, and Rankin could not help being amused by the wig worn by the reverend gentleman, which was the worst he had ever seen. Father Foley cried when they came to say good-bye.

Working their way eastward, the three actors presented their plays with the help of local stock companies in the small towns along the way. As the train wound through the countryside swarming with buffalo, deer, and antelopes, the actors marveled at the thousands of animals and the tall tales told by their companions. Two prominent businessmen invited the troupe to spend a week with them in Cheyenne.[45]

The hall in Cheyenne had a museum of living wonders on the second floor. It comprised eagles, owls, monkeys, coyotes, wolves, and prairie dogs as well as a giant and three dwarfs, one of whom wanted to be an actor. Rankin put the dwarf on in their tabloid or short version of *Rip van Winkle*. He played very well and was a hit with the audience. Since the actors were the best that had ever performed in the town, the officers of the military post and their ladies attended to a body and the musicians of the regimental band augmented the orchestra. The acting was an unqualified success. Owing to a deafening windstorm, the actors could not hear the orchestra and assumed that the audience could not hear them either. They were wrong, however, and the men in the audience responded by stomping their feet and clapping their hands. In a reception given to them later, the actors could not hear the band serenading them. Rankin wrote a note of apology to the bandmaster, and the band serenaded them the next evening when the wind had died down.

They performed for a week in Greely, Colorado, where they experienced the real frontier and bizarre scenes. In the frontier town of Denver, Rankin met Jack Hughes, the fabled "Cattle King of the West," and Wild Bill Hickok, who was quick with his weapons, loved a fight, but never sought a quarrel. Once surrounded by a dozen men intent on killing him, Hickok shot them all with his rifle and revolvers, save for the last, whom he killed with his bowie knife. After a performance, the male actors took in the dance halls and gambling joints, and Rankin saw Hickok attacked by three Mexicans with their knives. Hickok whipped out his revolver and the first two fell across one another like cordwood. The third drew back, and Hickok told him to clear out. Then Hickok went to the bar, swallowed a glass of whisky, and left the bodies where the coroner would pick them up the next morning. The dancing continued in the halls and the gambling went ahead unabated.

Denver was made up of cattlemen and miners who attended the theater regularly. An excellent actor, Jack Langrish, managed the theater. He was called of "the old school," a term Rankin deplored because he thought acting was either an art or nothing. There were a great many bad actors, but Langrish and his competent company were good.

By providing a change of bill two or three times a week for three weeks, Rankin kept the miners hugely entertained. "They laughed and cried and laughed again," Rankin recalled, "and sometimes the place seemed a pandemonium of noise. The love scenes were real to them. They applauded the heroics, and, at times, they cursed and reviled the villain. Sometimes I really felt that a competent villain stood a smart chance of being assaulted right on the stage."[46] The box office had a pair of balances, into the pan of which practically every other man shot a golden stream from a long leather wallet as payment for his ticket.

Here Rankin missed the financial opportunity of a lifetime. "A man in sudden hard luck came to me and offered me six lots for $1000," Rankin recalled decades later. "I liked the location and hurried to the hotel to find banker mother-in-law. But mother-in-law wept when I told her of the great chance. She was an estimable Boston woman, and such nerves of hers as hadn't been stretched beyond repair by sundry and festive lynchings were quite shattered by the hilarious daily gun-play that went on before our doors. Bursting into tears, she sobbed, 'Arthur, this is too much! You have worked hard enough to earn this money without deliberately leaving it in any of these dreadful places!' So I didn't invest, the debtor had to hunt for another source of relief, and the property climbed quietly and steadily to its present valuation—just a million and a half."[47]

In Boulder, Colorado, using the few props they carried with them and turning the miners' boardinghouse attached to the hotel into a makeshift stage, they hung brown army blankets to divide the space into scenes. Coal-oil lamps were used for lighting, and three people served as the orchestra. The place was packed, and those who could not get in surrounded the building, looking through the windows and applauding by drumming on the panes. Occasionally, they discharged firearms into the air to show their approval. The outside audience was largely miners and cowboys, who passed the hat at the conclusion and sent in their money to show that they were not freeloaders.

The actors stopped for a brief acting stint in Central City, Colorado, where they had heard that business was exceptional. Arriving by stage after a long trip through the mountains, they were dismayed to see just a few buildings other than the hotel and the dance hall, where they were to perform. Yet, when the performance began, every seat was taken and droves were turned away; they could have filled the place twice over. Unable to find anyone to care for the baby, Mrs Blanchard took her to the theater and put her to bed in a trunk. Everything went smoothly until the orchestra began to accompany Kitty Blanchard's singing and dancing. The child let out a wailing that the orchestra could not drown out. The audience yelled at the orchestra to shut up and give the child a chance. The child stopped when the orchestra did, and the audience yelled "Bring out the kid!" "The calls were so vociferous," Rankin said, "that I took Miss Mary Gladys Rankin out of her trunk and carried her in my arms to the stage. You never heard such a yell of delight as went up when the little tyke laughed and kissed her hand to them. I tell you we were 'some proud family that night' over our baby and the performance ended in a blaze of glory."[48] They returned to Denver for a farewell week before continuing east.

In Omaha, Nebraska, Rankin felt once again the call of a prosperous future, but the town was a pathetic, desolate mudhole, which his female companions feared would swallow up any investment, and he passed on, "leaving another immense embryotic fortune behind." Crossing the Mississippi River, the Rankin threesome played in Quincy, Illinois, from July 3 to 5, and headed for Chicago, the terminus of their adventurous tour.

Rankin's experience gave him a vision of the unlimited possibilities for drama in North America. Inspired by the grandeur of the scenery and the unique characteristics of the people, he sensed that a new kind of play would emerge that both he and Blanchard, now established partners on the stage, could exploit. All thought of fleeing abroad was banished by his western tour. In America he and Blanchard would find themselves and contribute in their way to the advancement of society. It would take a few years for the profound effects of this tour to take form in his consciousness and create one of the most significant events in theater history.

On his arrival in Chicago, Rankin replaced Charles Wyndham as Hugh Chalcotte in the Wyndham Company's production of *Ours* at the Dearborn Theatre.[49] Attracting large audiences, he was enthusiastically called before the curtain. Soon he formed a company of his own, leased Hooley's Opera House, and opened it on August 7 with Blanchard as co-star.

His company began playing *Dora* and the farcical *Black-eyed Susan*. Although the temperature was in the nineties, the theater was filled. The critics said that Rankin played Farmer Allen in *Dora* with unusual effectiveness and praised Blanchard's characterization of Dora as careful and conscientious and for winning the highest commendation from the audiences. As William in *Black-eyed Susan*, Blanchard gave a happy performance, displaying a bent for burlesque that was thoroughly pleasing. The Chicago actress Katie Mayhew, who was to have a long association with the Rankins, received prolonged applause for her singing and dancing as Susan.

The company honored Sir Walter Scott's birthday by presenting *Rob Roy* on August 14. Rankin played Rob Roy and Blanchard took the role of Di Vernon. All members of the cast were exceptionally fine. The next night, in Scott's *Guy Mannering*, other actors in the company took the lead roles, with Katie Mayhew making a thrilling Meg Merrilies and Rankin enacting his practiced role of Colonel Mannering. On the last night, the company produced Scott's *The Heart of Midlothian*, in which Mayhew had another triumph as Effie. For his benefit on the closing night of the engagement, Rankin played Rip in his *Rip Van Winkle* and brought in a full house. By now he had competitors other than Joseph Jefferson in the role. Some critics considered one of them, Robert McWade, better than Jefferson in the stark realism of his production. In that version, for instance, Rip's dog, Schneider, begins Rip's long sleep tied to a bush, and when, twenty years later, Rip awakens, he finds Schneider a skeleton hanging from a tree.

1871–1872: St Louis and Rankin's Comedy Theatre

While Hooley's Opera House went through a complete refurbishment to make it one of the most beautiful and comfortable theaters in the country, Rankin took his comedy company to Milwaukee to open the new Nunnemacher's Opera House. The company played *Dora* and *Black-eyed Susan* for the first week in September and Robertson's *School* and *Caste* for the second and closing week. The appreciative citizens organized a body of prominent men to present Rankin on his benefit night with a gold watch on which was inscribed "To Arthur McKee Rankin by his Milwaukee friends, September 15, 1871."[50] His fears that he and Blanchard would be ostracized for the circumstances of their marriage seemed groundless. By staying for months in the West, they had prevented it from becoming a subject in the East. The western tour had also indicated that there was no single sense of morality across the vast country, and that what might not play in conservative Boston could be acceptable elsewhere.

It was lucky that Rankin's troupe had other engagements preventing them from being in Chicago early in October. On the eighth of that month, a raging fire destroyed much of the city, killing hundreds of people and leaving thousands homeless. Two small fires had broken out the previous day but were extinguished. The citizens had assumed that the crisis was over. When the alarm bell sounded at 9:45 the next evening, however, the population felt terror strike their hearts. The houses and sidewalks of the city were constructed completely of wood, so the flames advanced like a whirlwind, giving people little chance to escape.[51]

Because the theaters had burned down, many of the actors left the city to join other companies. Annie Campion joined the Rankin troupe, then playing in Louisville. The troupe made its way southward, appearing in Mobile, Alabama, and in New Orleans. A report from Memphis, Tennessee, in early November praised Matt Lingham, who had joined the company for the tour, for his masterly skill in playing the villainous Miles McKenna in *Rosedale*. The Memphis audience called Rankin forth at the end of the third act to applaud his acting of Elliott Gray, for which the critics professed a special admiration. While at the Olympic Theatre in St Louis, Rankin produced *Little Em'ly*. Rankin was "thoroughly good" as Mr Peggoty, and the young actor Charles Stanley, as Uriah Heep, portrayed "cringing mannerisms and a fawning humility artistically." Bevil Ryan won the most applause playing Micawber in an "original" manner.[52] When Rankin presented Robertson's *School*, a local correspondent for the *Clipper* panned it. Rankin, in a letter to the editor, called the critic "a myth whom I have never seen" and enclosed a good review from the local paper by "a gentleman of scholarly and critical attainments." Now that he was an actor-manager, he would encounter hindrances and anonymous criticism.[53]

Divining a need for light entertainment, Rankin and his business partner, A.L. Parkes, leased the Fifth Street Opera House, a minstrel hall in St Louis, and began refurbishing it as a first-class comedy theater. Meanwhile, the McKee Rankin Comedy Company continued touring, opening in Terre Haute, Indiana, on November 27. It stopped for one-night stands at other Midwestern towns before arriving for four nights and a matinee in Peoria, Illinois, on December 13, where the financial returns and the large audiences demonstrated its success. Here, among his standard plays, Rankin produced Tom Robertson's new play, *Home*, about the unmasking of Mrs Pinchbeck's villainous plans to marry the senescent old father of the play's hero, who returns to England after years in America. Peoria liked Rankin and found his acting in *Rosedale* "highly creditable to an already well-earned reputation." Rankin's manner was "so easy and natural that he at once elicits the praise and plaudits of his hearers."[54] For his Rip in *Rip Van Winkle* on his Friday benefit, Rankin received a rousing reception. The company continued touring over the Christmas holidays and into the New Year of 1872.

Rankin's Comedy Theatre in St Louis was being transformed into the coziest little theater in the city, "where one can see and hear everything," owing to the design.[55] Rankin's decision to settle in one place after months of travel, and his hunch that St Louis would respond to a comedy company of high caliber, made him hopeful that he could strike deep roots in the community. St Louis had the reputation of being a good theater-town. "A compromise between rain and snow, harmonizing in slush underfoot, cannot stay the multitudinous throngs assembling nightly at our theaters," reported the *Clipper* on January 27, 1872. Since McKee disliked keeping accounts, George Rankin left his civil-service job in Canada to be his treasurer. George had always been interested in the theater and must have been glad of McKee's offer to help his company. For his part, McKee welcomed his brother, whom he could trust, to take care of finances. George became a favorite with little Gladys, to whom he devoted more attention than the busy McKee could. The wardrobe keeper was Mrs Blanchard. For some reason, perhaps because of bad health, Blanchard was not acting.

During its opening week, Rankin's Theatre, this "pretty bijou of a place," was crowded every night by the beauty and fashion of St Louis. The critic compared it to Mitchell's Olympic of New York, where the actors and audience fraternized, and it seemed as if one were dropping in on old friends to spend a pleasant hour. Rankin opened the season on January 22, 1872, with Robertson's *Play*, in which he took the role of Frank Price, the lover of Rosie Farquhere, played by Katie Mayhew. "Mr. Rankin, a born gentleman, has improved greatly since we saw him seven years ago," wrote the critic, "and our dear little friend, Katie Mayhew, is a jewel."[56] The splendid effects of scenery, sets, and mountings made the play a success. Rankin drove himself at a furious pace: he produced the modern comedy *£100,000*, which declares in the end that a man's worth is in his character rather than in his wealth, and "effectually rendered" the role of

Gerald Goodwin "to much better advantage than heretofore"[57]; he tried another Henry Byron comedy, *Dearer Than Life*, about a father who assumes blame for his son's misdeeds, added a double bill with *Miriam's Crime* and *A Regular Fix* for the Wednesday matinee and Thursday night, and another double bill, *Milky White* and *A Bull in a China Shop*, for Friday and Saturday matinees.

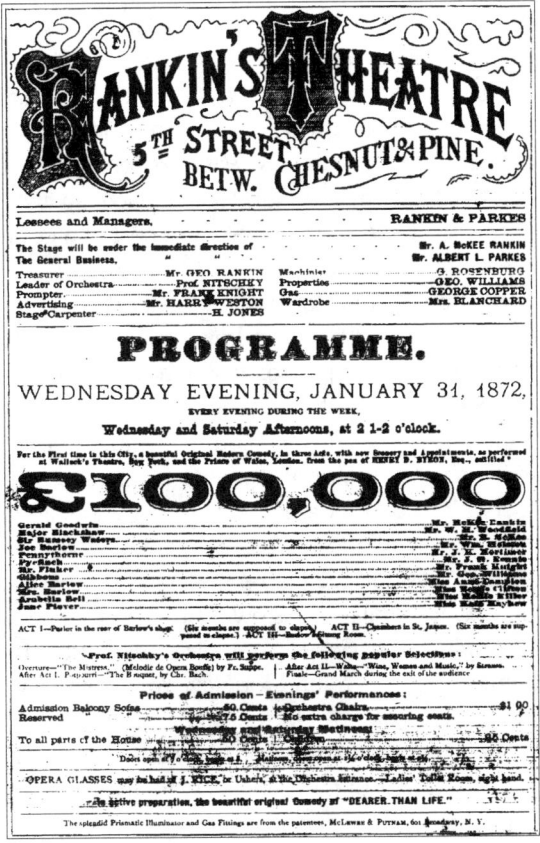

Program from 1869. Rankin's Theatre, St Louis, MO, 1872.

The *Clipper* critic who had recently angered Rankin praised the characters in *Miriam's Crime* for being "well rendered," and noted that Rankin portrayed Scumley well, but "the same scarcely can be said of his Hugh de Brass in 'A Regular Fix.'" Rankin had played this role several times before more-sophisticated audiences, including New Yorkers, and must have been miffed when the critic added that "Rankin is in no wise adapted to light comedy....He would do well to stick to character parts to which he seems most especially adapted."[58]

Although the new theater seemed to be doing well, Rankin's partner became alarmed at a sudden downturn in the economy and a falling off of attendance. Fearing bankruptcy, Parkes withdrew from the partnership. Rankin, as sole lessee, hired a business manager to replace him, but faced the added pressure of being solely responsible for the theater.

In February 1872, Rankin produced Olive Logan's *Surf*, about the nouveau riche in the resort of Long Branch. This unstructured play of contemporary social commentary brought out the playgoers at last. The cast played with buoyancy and created a lively humor, and the scenery and mountings were superb in detail and realism. Indeed, Rankin was beginning to get recognition for the attention to detail in the mountings of the plays in his theater. Rankin presented *Partners for Life* for two evenings and returned to the moneymaking *Surf* for the following week. "This is the only theater," reported the *Clipper*, "that can boast of a good business for the past two weeks."[59]

Rankin's production of Tom Robertson's *Society* also was a success and played to good houses. A middle-class drawing-room comedy, it dealt with politics and the humorous interplay of aristocracy confronted by nouveau-riche social climbers. In Robertson's plays, snobbery and hypocrisy are despised, good fellowship and loyalty count for more than social prestige, and hard cash is no substitute for the generous impulse. Robertson made his serious observations on modern civilization in the realistic settings of a box set, real ceilings, actual doorknobs, and genuine food. This attempt to reflect the realities of life onstage held a fascination for Rankin. Moreover, Robertson's views were similar to his own. Rankin produced more realism in *Wrecked, or, Americans at Sea*. The public turned out in force to see the drama about a pleasure ship bound for New York from New Orleans and wrecked off the coast of Florida. In the third act, the good nature of the passengers in adversity is rewarded with a rescue. Rankin played Proteus, god of the sea and initiator of the shipwreck, in an easy manner.

Blanchard appeared for the first time on the next bill as Victorine in *The Coming Woman, or, The Spirit of '76* and as William in the afterpiece, *Black-eyed Susan*. She was warmly received by the public, but trouble was brewing. As Rankin was about to bring out *Surf* again to replenish the treasury, its star, Anna Campion, suddenly left the company, possibly because she was billed behind Blanchard. Rankin substituted *Partners for Life* and *A Bull in a China Shop* for the first days of the week, while Blanchard learned Campion's role in *Surf*, which was brought out to finish the week. Things began going badly when Rankin played *St Louis As It Is*, adapted from Boucicault's *The Streets of New York* to reflect local conditions. The adaptation destroyed much of the sentiment of the original and was so patched and rewoven that there was no thread to guide the spectator through the action. As Rollingstone, fashioned after the original Badger but a wide departure from that shrewd and lithesome character, Rankin played in a nervous manner, possibly owing to the dissension he was facing in his company. The acrimony seems to have arisen on Blanchard's return and may have resulted from suspicions she harbored about her husband's relations with other actresses. Her part in *St Louis As It Is* required her to adopt a German accent, but, according to the *Clipper*, she "was completely out of place at German interpolations."[60]

The Rankin company seemed to be disintegrating. Bessie Clifton, a faithful member, transferred to De Bar's Theatre to fill in for an ailing actress. Katie Mayhew and her sister, who had become great favorites with the St Louis patrons, disappeared from the company, "a circumstance sincerely to be regretted," said the *Clipper*.[61] Anna Campion was reinstated, however, in time to take part in Robertson's *School*. Although it was reported that the cast was rehearsing a new comedy written for Blanchard, *The American Baron*, it was not produced. Announcing the play may have been a gesture on Rankin's part to appease her and restore a sense of her importance. Instead, Rankin engaged his old friend, veteran comic Mark Smith, who was held in high esteem in St Louis, to star in his company as Dr Pangloss, the pompous, pedantic clergyman in the younger George Colman's classic *The Heir at Law*. Finding receipts to be low, Smith switched at mid-week to Boucicault's *London Assurance*.

Rankin continued to manage everything with great energy: he controlled the company, arranged for the scenery and costuming, trained the actors in their roles, and took parts in the plays. As for attracting audiences, Sheridan's *The Rivals* could always be counted upon, especially when Mark Smith played the volatile Sir Anthony Absolute, and the play brought in good houses for the week of April 22. Rankin called on his friends for help and secured from J.W. Wallack a new play, *The Bells*, which Wallack had recently brought to New York from a successful run in London that had catapulted the young actor Henry Irving from obscurity to stardom.[62] Irving portrayed the protagonist, an Alsatian innkeeper, Mathias, with vitality and passion; Wallack himself made him a subtle study of the morbid, haunted mind but with less success. Rankin, recognizing the predilection for melodrama in his audience, followed Irving's lead.

Despite giving benefits to his most popular actors to capitalize on their popularity with the locals, and despite reprising Robertson's *Society* and Olive Logan's *Surf* and presenting a piece by a local playwright, Rankin's receipts declined. George Rankin resigned as the theater's business manager to become manager of the Phoenix Life Insurance Company of

Missouri. Playing to the end of the season in mid-June, Rankin presented *Rip Van Winkle* for two weeks with fair houses, then *Enoch Arden, The Long Strike,* and *Uncle Tom's Cabin,* and closed Rankin's Theatre on the 15th. Theatre life was rife with disappointment, and, regardless how great the artistic worth, economic forces could always undermine the best efforts.[63]

1872–1873: Fame as *Rip Van Winkle* and Bankruptcy

On July 1, 1872, the McKee Rankin Comedy Company commenced a two-week engagement in St Paul, Minnesota, with Rankin acting his customary roles in every play and filling all the duties of stage direction and management. He did well and then toured to the small towns in the cooler regions of the north. Owing to Blanchard's earlier fame in the West, the company presented the many plays in its large repertoire under the headline of Kitty Blanchard as its main player. By mid-August, it was in Stillwater, Minnesota, and heading west. When it arrived back in St Louis, Blanchard left the company, possibly because she wanted to be with her daughter, and Rankin formed a new company without her to tour with only one play, *Rip Van Winkle*. The arrangement made sense because it saved on production and shipping costs. The St Louis critic acclaimed the production as the best ever seen in the city and praised Annie Waite, who shared the honors with Rankin. George Rankin returned as business manager to the new company. From November 11, the company took the play to Detroit for a week, where Rankin was said to have surprised the audience agreeably with his dialect, which unfortunately disappeared when he got excited in certain scenes. Lizzie Shirley replaced Annie Waite as Rip's wife, Christine, until Blanchard joined the company on February 10, 1873.

The company toured dozens of small towns throughout Canada and the American Midwest, playing one- to three-night stands. It was like a partial combination company, carrying scenery with it and filling the important roles of the play, but depending on the stock companies for the minor roles. Wherever it went, the children, Carrie McHenry and Master Walter, met with encouraging praise in the roles of Rip's children. On November 25, the company surfaced at the Wheeling Opera House in Toledo, Ohio, where the recorded attendance was good, despite the difficulty of conveyance to the theater. The critic called the company supporting Rankin less than mediocre.[64] In Cincinnati, a local critic called Rankin inferior to Jefferson but admitted that audiences applauded Rankin in a manner that would place any actor "on good terms with himself and the rest of mankind."[65] Another critic thought the "unmeasured applause" that Rankin drew from beginning to end was richly merited. "It is a pleasure to record such a success as this where the effort to please has so long been unrequited," he wrote.[66] Rankin was like Jefferson only in that he used his voice to create the character: "Mr. Rankin laughs occasionally, weeps once in a while, gets mad as a Texas steer at intervals, and gallops around like most human beings in ordinary life." Blanchard carried off the difficult role of Rip's neglected wife with great success. His supporting company was stronger than other productions visiting the city and the stage mounting was much better.

Rankin continued playing one-night stands to March 12 in Detroit. There, his well-balanced cast played to a very large house for a week. The local critic noted that his dialect had improved since his visit in November. At his next long stop in Chicago, Rankin drew special praise for his rendition of Rip. His dialect was called "excellent, and, at times, he rises to marked emotional power, particularly so in the last act where he reveals himself to his daughter."[67] Since attendance at the theater was light, Rankin varied the fare: *Oliver Twist*, with his famous role of Fagin, played for half a week; two other plays—*Married Life*, in which Blanchard and the newly arrived Stuart Robson reprised their man-and-wife act of Mr and Mrs Dove from their days in Boston, and *David Copperfield*, a different version of Dickens's novel than *Little Em'ly*—each ran for a couple of days. Rankin, in hopes that he could revive his box office receipts, then brought on the squeaky-voiced Stuart Robson in *Law in New York*, coming from its first New York production. The play attracted a first-class house, something rare for a home-grown work, always considered inferior to European plays. Robson played an absurdly obese policeman who is made jittery by the slightest noise or shadow, in a plot that follows the tricky manipulations of a convict turned alderman, reminiscent of recent scandals about the Boss Tweed ring and the Credit Mobilier bank crash, the one a group of corrupt New York politicians and the other a bank crash caused by a swindle.

Despite his hard work, Rankin had to declare bankruptcy in mid-April. He was $12,000 in debt, largely to actors, hotel keepers, and newspapers in various parts of the country where his company had performed. He owed $3,000 to Dr Pallen of St Louis (probably for Blanchard's illnesses among other costs); $750 to Lavielle and Warner, hotel keepers in St Louis; and $150 to the playwright Olive Logan. His whole property comprised a few articles of clothing not worth $100.[68] At this time, he adopted the philosophy that theater was too important to be hindered by debt, and he became inured to financial calamity, which gave him that calm equilibrium in the face of adversity remarked upon by others. Unburdened of his debts, Rankin continued as manager of his company at Aiken's Theatre in *Little Em'ly* with Stuart Robson as Wilkins Micawber, in which, it was said, he had few equals, and Rankin as the scheming Uriah Heep, making him as devilish as possible in a "most realistic" performance. For Rankin, the attraction in playing Heep, who held the honest Whitfield in his power, was the symbolizing of his creditors, for he seemed to regard himself more as a victim of circumstance than an offender.

At the end of April, Rankin left the legitimate theater for burlesque in a vain attempt to restore his finances. The Kitty Blanchard Burlesque Troupe opened on May 5, 1873, at Myer's Opera House in Chicago with much the same company as Rankin's Comedy Company. Katie Mayhew was back with the troupe, and the comedian Ed Marble joined them as well. In their first presentation, T.J. Langdon of their old company starred in the title role of *Bad Dickey*. After a week and a half this venture failed as well.[69] The public was not spending what little money it had on entertainment. Moreover, attitudes had changed, and the witty types of burlesque in which Blanchard had made her name no longer appealed to the public.

While Rankin was struggling with his finances, he was deeply saddened to learn of the death of James W. Wallack on a sleeping car en route to New York City from South Carolina, where he had been recuperating from tuberculosis. Rankin owed his early success in roles such as Fagin and Elliott Gray to Wallack's initial interpretations. The *Clipper* described Wallack as "somewhat rugged in manner but ever a true and warm-hearted friend."[70]

Misfortune from all quarters continued to dog the Rankins. Rankin secured an engagement in the extravaganza *The Seven Beauties* for Blanchard and himself at the Globe Theatre in Boston, but the theater burnt down on the morning of May 30 just before they were to open. The Globe had once been Selwyn's Theatre, where Blanchard had won acclaim in Boston.

The Rankin family (McKee, Kitty, baby Gladys, George, and Mrs Blanchard) summered in Bois Blanc Island in the Detroit River. Colonel Rankin had acquired the island from the Canadian government for $40, keeping 225 acres for himself and leasing for life the 14 remaining acres at the south end to the lighthouse keeper. The colonel transformed one of the three blockhouses built by the Canadian military during the War of 1812 into the main building of an elaborate estate. McKee bought the island from him in 1869. A small yacht, the *Kitty B.*, ferried Rankin's guests to and from Amherstburg, Ontario.[71] It was an idyllic place to recuperate, but Rankin, forever restless, was soon casting about for theatrical work. He wrote

Augustin Daly asking if he would employ Blanchard in his production of *A Midsummer Night's Dream*, which was to be produced late in August, and hoped that a role could be found for himself.[72] Daly did not oblige; rather, he employed a newcomer, Little May Templeton, as Puck, with the eccentric comedian George Fox, of Humpty-Dumpty fame, as Bottom.

The Boston backers of *The Seven Beauties*, undeterred by losing a theater, opened the play at the Boston Athenaeum in mid-June. Rankin and Blanchard joined with burlesque stars, pantomimists, the clown J.D. Kelly, and others who had made their names in witty burlesques and comedies. The minor roles and supernumeraries were in the hundreds.[73] The seven daughters of Pluto flee from Hell to Earth. They visit Paris in 1870 under the Commune, and later land in Boston, which becomes the setting for romance with an impoverished bohemian author. Blanchard played three roles: Satanella, the first of the daughters; the Goddess of Flowers; and Tom Highboy (in a sex change so beloved by audiences in those days), who becomes Captain Highboy of the Amazons. Rankin played Pluto, King of Hades, "a monarch by no means as black as he is painted."[74] A female impersonator played Pluto's wife. Such fantasies offered the economically depressed citizens a flight into wonderland.

The shift in audience taste to bawdy burlesque was evident in New York, where one of the many revivals of *The Black Crook* was playing to crowded houses at Niblo's Garden. In one week in August it had 45,000 spectators and had to refuse admittance to another 20,000. The promoters seemed justified in expecting *The Seven Beauties* to be a summer-long attraction, but it ran for only two weeks. It was followed by *The Invisible Prince, or, The Fair One with the Blonde Wig* with most of the same actors, except for Rankin. The critic found Blanchard, who played Leander, the rightful heir, "pretty and, except for a somewhat weary manner induced doubtless by the hot weather and nine performances, more than satisfactory."[75] Blanchard choreographed the dances and sang the songs, but even her enthusiasm could not prolong the production more than a week. The manager offered to keep all the actors in the company for playing comedies and farces if they took a salary cut of one-third, which did not interest the Rankins.

Rankin, after trying in vain to obtain work from E.L. Davenport at the Chestnut Street Theatre in Philadelphia, finally arranged for Blanchard and himself to fill the remainder of the summer at the New Orleans Academy of Music Theatre and join the new Park Theatre in Brooklyn in September.[76] When the Park Theatre opened, their fortunes had changed. They had hitched themselves to one of the stars of the stage, the playwright and actor Dion Boucicault, who had just returned to America after an absence of many years.[77]

1873–1875

The Boucicault Interlude

Boucicault was a curious man, with his glittering eyes, scrubby mustache, fringe of hair dyed very black about a bald scalp, and cold, bilious, sarcastic personality. He was a brilliant conversationalist and a charming host, and enjoyed serving tea in his dressing room to his favorite actors.[78] Aware of Rankin's success in the American productions of his plays, he employed the Rankins to act in his company beginning on September 8 in his *The Colleen Bawn*. Owing to a sudden illness, Boucicault had to call upon an Irish actor, Sheil Barry, to replace him as Myles na Coppaleen. Rankin played Danny Mann, a role as meaty as that of Myles. Whereas Myles is the sunny comic servant type, Mann hints at a darker side of the traditional Irish mentality: he knows right from wrong but is overcome by a sense of slavish fidelity to his master. (In this play, Rankin had usually played Hardress Cregan, less satisfying for an actor but challenging in the character's contradictions between his Anglo-Irish background and his love for the Irish Eily.) Blanchard played Ann Chute, who has considerable spirit and vivacity and more wit than most female characters. And as Mrs Cregan, Hardress's mother, there appeared Madame Elizabeth Ponisi, whom Rankin had known when she supported James Murdock at the Arch Street Theatre in 1866. She had been supporting Edwin Forrest in his last tours until Forrest retired to his walled-in garden and great library in Philadelphia with a misanthropic view of his fellow creatures and a distaste for the outside world. The critic for the *New York Times* praised the creditable work of Rankin, Blanchard, and Ponisi as "smooth and satisfying."[79]

Owing to its popularity, *The Colleen Bawn* was kept on for an unexpected second week. Because Rankin had another engagement, which kept him from returning to the Boucicault company for two weeks, Sheil Barry had to play both Myles and Danny Mann. Rankin rejoined the company at the Arch Street Theatre in Philadelphia on September 29 in *Mimi*. By this time, Boucicault was again healthy, and played the role of Maurice O'Donnell. His mistress, Katherine Rogers, played Mimi. Together Rogers and Boucicault had had great success in New York in these roles. Rankin was in the cast as Max and Blanchard as Rigolette, the painter friends of Maurice and his mistress. Their performances were "well-sustained." The play continued for a second week, at the end of which Boucicault took a benefit by playing a double bill: Charles Coldstream with great ease and naturalness in his *Used Up*, and an old servant in an elaborate and finished performance in his short play *Kerry, or, Night and Morning*. Rankin studied his performances closely and played the old Irish servant Kerry for the next week in Jersey City, New Jersey. Boucicault and Rogers, on leaving the company, gave the Rankins permission to produce *Arrah-na-Pogue* in Jersey City.[80] Rankin also played Rip in *Rip Van Winkle*—this time in the Charles Burke version rather than his own, which was too close to Boucicault's version to risk playing when Boucicault was in America.

Theatrical receipts had been down for some time, reflecting a poor economy. People feared that a crash was coming. That fear became reality on September 18, 1873, when the financier of the Northern Pacific Railroad, Jay Cooke, failed and dragged the nation into the deepest, ugliest, and most prolonged of American economic depressions to that time. The massive debt, persistent inflation, and speculation in land, manufacturing, and railways stemming from the aftermath of the Civil War were calling the nation to account. Investment in the theater declined to the point where only those willing to take small profits speculated on plays as theaters felt the economic pinch. The *Clipper* complained that there were too many poor: "Among all classes, a dollar is valued at one hundred cents." Although no major legitimate playhouses closed, some turned to vaudeville or comedies while others skimped along with poor houses and parsimonious managers. Many lesser amusement places throughout the country shut down. Rankin was lucky to be asked to join the Union Square Theatre Company in New York at the end of October. It was managed by Alfred Marshall Palmer, a lawyer who had been hired by the owner to transform it from a rather unsuccessful burlesque house to a legitimate theater.

The Union Square Theatre Company

The Union Square Theatre building was tasteful in design, elegant in furnishings, and ample for the modern plays it was to produce. On the south side of Union Square in the middle of the block between Broadway and Fourth Avenue, it was surrounded by theatrical agencies, costume companies, and other shops connected in some way with the theater. The area became known as the new Rialto.

Marshall Palmer, like Augustin Daly, dispensed with the old stock lines of business and expected the actors to take on any assigned role. His tenure brought in many other changes: he increased rehearsal time, sometimes to as long as six weeks, and kept plays onstage as long as possible; he reduced the annual budget from twelve to four plays; he hired a Scottish comedian, John Parselle, to be stage director; and he picked the actors he wanted for the 1873-74 season. Soon he had the best acting company in the United

States. An actor of that day wrote: "To be a member of the Union Square Company was the ambition of all players in the country."[81] The real genius behind the enterprise, however, was a Bohemian journalist and linguist of wide and curious learning with great practical ability and cosmopolitan experience. A.R. Cazauran read the plays, translated them, adapted them, and acted as supervising stage manager.

Palmer intended alternating Rankin with Charles Thorne, Jr, in plays needing the same type of romantic, matinee idol role. Both actors appeared in W.S. Gilbert's *The Wicked World*, which opened on November 16, 1873, with Clara Morris in the lead role. She had struck a bargain with Daly, who agreed to let her leave his theater if she promised to play in his company for three more months, and if he kept his promise not to run a play in a competing theater opposite her. Daly had already lost one leading lady, Agnes Ethel, to the Union Square Theatre Company when Ethel realized that her place under Daly was being usurped by the brilliant Clara Morris; Daly clearly did not want to lose Morris as well. As the title character in *Alixe*, as produced by Daly, Morris portrayed a count's illegitimate daughter who commits suicide when she sees that the life of a courtesan awaits her. Morris created a moving performance that confirmed her reputation as a powerful emotional actress. Daly, despite his agreement with Morris and possibly to provoke a legal confrontation through which he could bind her to his company, ran *Alixe* in a competing house in Philadelphia while Morris was playing the role there; consequently, she went to Palmer, who was very willing to defend her against Daly. But to get her, Palmer had to agree to her request to play in his *The Wicked World* for only two weeks so that she could be free to fulfill previously scheduled engagements before returning to him. On the opening night of *The Wicked World* she had to foil young men who tried to file injunction papers upon her on behalf of Daly.[82]

In *The Wicked World* Rankin as Phyllan and Thorne as Ethala arouse love in the fairies in fairyland. Queen Selene, played by Morris, desires Ethala. The actors spoke in flowing rhythmical verse and moved through beautifully constructed scenery emanating a harmony rarely seen. The vociferous duo of Thorne and Rankin were declared "admirable" by the local critic despite looking rather ridiculous in costume. The novelty of Gilbert's play was in its literary quality and its moral lesson, a satirizing of the style and substance of the romantic hero. In contrast to the nineteenth-century farce, which relied on mechanical movement from a simple situation to a snowballing of complication on complication, and which made its characters seem unreal, Gilbert undercut the conventions of character parts by combining romantic excesses and mundane Robertsonian realism to create a comedic alternative.

Palmer also cast Rankin and Thorne in his next play, which became one of the most famous productions of the century. *Led Astray* was another adaptation from the French. It so happened that Boucicault, wanting to direct a company favorite, Rose Eytinge, arranged with Palmer to stage *Led Astray* starring Eytinge. Boucicault was thorough in rehearsals. The first performance was as smooth and well-rounded as the last. A dark beauty, Eytinge was called the handsomest and cleverest of actors, the most essentially womanly and the most charming. She credited her success to the enforced repose of the character of Armande. Her voluptuous charm, dramatic power, and artistic skill together with the suggestion of illicit passion glossed over with sentimentality drew crowded houses.[83]

McKee Rankin as Georges de Lesparre in *Led Astray*, December 1873.

Rankin played Georges de Lesparre, the poet, whom he made "extremely handsome and plausible as 'the serpent of the hearth'."[84] But the *New York Times* critic still found the roughness of his ways less becoming than Thorne's vigorous portrayal of the Count of Chandoce. Thorne was having health problems, however, and Frank Mackay was obliged to fill in for him while he recovered. The excellence of the acting, which gave a spirited smoothness to the tautly written script, the elegance and tastefulness of the costuming and scenery, and the believable situations carried *Led Astray* through 161 successive performances and 214 performances in total by the time it closed, an amazing feat in a depressed economy.

Although the play was making $1,000 a night, Palmer closed it when Clara Morris returned from a starring tour. Morris wanted to be in the old *Love's Sacrifice*, but Eytinge claimed it as her property, which she was about to play in another theater, and suggested that Morris play Camille. Eytinge recalled Morris playing in *Camille* in an actors' charity benefit: "I had great faith in her performance of the part, although Harry Palmer, the manager, who had in his experience the measurement of all the great Camilles, sententiously said to me, as he came out, 'She cannot play Camille.' Miss Morris's Camille has since the time of which I speak become as familiar to most of the playgoers of my generation as Edwin Booth's Hamlet."[85] Her Camille was womanly, tender, and yet terrible in her impassioned power, causing her audiences to sit under a spell, look at those pleading eyes, and listen to that heart-penetrating voice.

Rankin played the Baron de Varville, who competes with Armand Duvalle (or Duval), played by Thorne, for Margeurite Gautier's affections. Morris called McKee Rankin "piratically handsome."[86] Halfway through the run, Thorne did not turn up for a Saturday matinee, and Rankin took his part as Armand while F.F. Mackay took over Rankin's role of the baron. Rankin added to his reputation by his correct, earnest, and gentlemanly impersonation of Armand, which he played better than Thorne had done.[87] Thorne, mentally upset by the demands of work, had taken a boat for the Baltic states, telling no one that he was going. His temperament seemed to crave the center of attention both offstage, as when he played practical jokes or had running voluble quarrels with fellow actors, and onstage, as a Chicago critic reported: "He injured the company by 'guying' on stage, and spreading disorganization through his insubordination."[88]

For the summer season at the Union Square Theatre, Rankin wanted to produce Robertson's *Caste*, but since Lester Wallack claimed to have the sole right to produce it, Rankin chose Bartley Campbell's *Peril, or, Love at Long Branch*. He assembled a strong cast, which included actors from the Union Square Company, such as the gorgeous Maude Granger and the spirited Marie Wilkins, and actors who had been in his own companies, such as Bevil Ryan and young Ada Gilman. Rankin as the hero, Dick Rothly, played "with a suavity of manner, easy grace, and, when required, vigorous action."[89] A critic's comments explains the play's New York run of just two weeks: "There is some good dialogue, and the situations are sufficiently inspiring to draw applause from the audience: but there is a want of motive, or rather a lack of dignity of motive in the working out of the plot which prevents any active exercise of sympathy."[90] The play, however, remained popular for many years. Rankin and his company toured with it until he was due back at the Union Square Theatre in September.

While Rankin toured, his wife prepared for the birth of their second child. The baby girl, born on August 31, 1874, was christened Phyllis, but nicknamed Pixie. Gladys, now four, was nicknamed Dido. Several months after the birth, Blanchard wrote to Augustin Daly for a place in his company, and said that a "yes" or "no" was all she required by way of reply.[91] The answer was "no" because she would not have fitted in with Daly's ensemble casting. She did get an engagement, however, at Booth's Theatre and began rehearsing to support the legendary Charlotte Cushman, who was touring the large cities in her great roles before retiring from the stage.

At the Union Square, *The Sphinx*, which had been readied the previous spring and packed away to allow *Camille* to be produced, opened on September 21, 1874, with Clara Morris as Blanche de Chelles and Rankin as Henri de Savigny, with whom Blanche becomes obsessed. *The Sphinx* had a run of five weeks. "Of actual adultery," wrote a critic, "'The Sphinx' manages to steer clear, but almost from the rise of the curtain to its fall, the minds of all the principal actors in the story are occupied by that crime."[92] As Blanche, Morris provided psychological insight into the young woman possessed by gross inconsistencies. Dominated by her passions, Blanche plots to poison her friend and to run away with her friend's husband, Savigny. To prove her innocence of such designs, she agrees to marry a man she detests. Morris's acting was subtle, fascinating, venomous, full of passion and strong-eyed despair. She filled the audience with horror in Blanche's dying scene when she swallows poison. Eyes upturned, face pallid, mouth foaming, and hands clutching her bosom, she tears open the waist of her dress in the agony of the moment.[93] Above all, she made the character believable. The playgoers thronged the theater. The play won the reputation of a minor triumph and could have continued indefinitely except that Morris became upset about the disagreeable character she had to play.[94]

Rankin as Savigny won emphatic praise:

> Mr. Rankin, as Savigny, scored another indisputable triumph....The changes in his manner towards Blanche were made with artistic ease, and when he realized that in his heart burned a wild love for her, the realization was depicted with

remarkable cleverness. There is a manly grace about his acting that commands immediate attention, and he is so good an actor that he maintains his hold upon one throughout the play. We know of no actor at present before the public who could have given a more satisfactory personification of Henri de Savigny.[95]

Rankin began rehearsing for the role of Mr Rochester in Jane Eyre, which was to tour in New Haven and Hartford, Connecticut, in preparation for an opening in New York on November 16.[96] In the evenings, he attended the performances of Charlotte Cushman at Booth's. George Vandenhoff came out of ten years of retirement to play opposite her. The long absence caused him to appear rather formal, but the refinement, the symmetry, and the intellectual character of his acting were delightful. A critic tried to define the strange, nameless quality about Cushman—"like that which hallows the lonesome sea, in the gloaming and on the eve of the tempest. It separates her from her race, and it makes her their type and voice. It is power and it is sorrow; it is revelation and prophecy. Back of everything she does stands this mysterious force."[97]

Cushman's portrayal of Lady Macbeth, whose hold over Macbeth was through the intellect, would have most interested Rankin and doubtless inspired him to create his own interpretation through actresses he would direct in the years to come. She now suffused Lady Macbeth with a glow of mournful gentleness that brought it nearer to Shakespeare and closer to the universal heart.[98]

Rankin was on the road with Jane Eyre when Cushman played her great role of Meg Merrilies in Guy Mannering with Kitty Blanchard as Julia Mannering. After Cushman's last performance, when all the noted lights in the arts and learning and society were present, Cushman entered her carriage opposite the stage door, and amidst the cheers of the populace, and a tumult like that of the old-fashioned Fourth of July, was driven to the Fifth Avenue hotel, where she appeared on the balcony and greeted the populace, while the Ninth Regimental Band performed a serenade, and the spaces and vistas of Madison Square were illumined with fireworks. It was not until long after midnight that the festivities ceased and the vast assemblage of spectators melted away.[99]

Rankin portrayed well Rochester's descent into evil and his salvation through Jane's love. "Rankin's relatively quiet demeanor and more subdued style won him some sincere approval," wrote the New York Times when the play returned to the Union Square Theatre. "It should be stated that he was manfully suffering from a severe cold, a condition of things necessarily unfavorable to dramatic effort."[100] "On the whole," wrote a second critic, "his impersonation is a good one, and if he could only dispense with that slouch of voice and walk, which made him appear somewhat like a high-toned swash-buckler, he would be more satisfactory."[101]

The Union Square Company had expected to produce *The Two Orphans* after *Jane Eyre*, but despite preparations that had taken almost ten months and a month of rehearsals, it was not ready. Rose Eytinge in her successful role of Margaret Elmore in *Love's Sacrifice* appeared in the two-week interim. Rankin as Matthew Elmore, which he had often played outside New York, supported her. The legendary English actor John Vandenhoff had created the best Matthew Elmore in 1842: "a thrilling picture of anguish, remorse, and despair."[102] Rankin had to equal that result but with a different style for the modern taste, which, when one considers the blank verse and the "theeing and thouing," was a tall order. His Matthew Elmore was called "pathetic and always forceful." (Here, "pathetic" was used in the sense of moving or emotional, eliciting pity or sadness.) The cast's acting was so good that it kept the audience's unvarying attention. The handsome settings helped to draw large audiences, which were so important for theaters in transition between major productions.[103]

Blanchard was not idle during this time. She played Meenie van Winkle opposite Joseph Jefferson as Rip van Winkle for three weeks at Booth's; for another week, she took the role of Mabel Vane, the young woman who pleads with Peg Woffington to release her husband from his infatuation for her in *Masks and Faces*. Rankin, sensing the importance of the long-awaited *The Two Orphans*, advised his wife to audition for one of the orphans. Rankin informed his wife that the play was the chance of a lifetime. He claimed that "'The Two Orphans' is the strongest melodrama written in years. It will make a great hit and have a long run. In all the advertising of the play you will share, inasmuch as you are half the title. They cannot bill one alone. It must read 'The Two Orphans'."[104] It was destined to be the play of the century and would run for almost seven months. Since the economic depression had forced the theater managers of New York to call a truce in their competitiveness and lend their actors when needed, Blanchard's transfer from Booth's was easily effected.

The Two Orphans

The opening of *The Two Orphans* on December 21, 1874, was almost its closing. A large and brilliant audience assembled, and the theater seemed "at the outset of a new golden era."[105] The company had rehearsed the play for two months, but the scenery was so complicated and difficult to change that the performance lasted until 1:30 AM, by which time there was but a thin and apathetic audience. A dejected Palmer began planning for another play to succeed it. But the city was in the aftermath of a blizzard, which deterred people from their usual evening amusements, and, although the papers gave the play mixed reviews, the critic for the *New York Times* thought it was destined for a protracted run. This critic argued that its defects—triteness of subject and unbroken gloom of tone—were more than offset by the skillful development of the plot, the variety and contrast of the characters, and its perfect adaptation to the taste of the public. Its great power came from *ficelles*—that is, the tricks of authors who "know the ropes." Added to this *savoir faire* were two facts: one, that tact without genius was more potent than genius without tact, and, two, the unsurpassed liberality and zeal of the managers in Paris and New York to prepare a favorable reception for the play.

The Two Orphans was written by two successful French playwrights, D'Ennery and Cormon, and loved by Parisian audiences. A play reader, adapter, and house manager, Hart Jackson, adapted the piece for the American stage but was unable to raise the $720 that D'Ennery wanted for the American rights. When Jackson read it to J.B. Booth, Jr, at Booth's Theatre, Booth fell asleep. Booth's Theatre recommended it to the theater managers Jarrett and Palmer, but A.M. (Harry) Palmer of the Union Square Theatre got wind of the negotiations, read the play, was reduced to tears, and paid D'Ennery for the right to produce it. Palmer sent his stage manager, John Parselle, to Paris to get the absolutely correct models of scenes and costumes.

In the play, three or four narratives cleverly interweave and augment the symmetry of the whole, but the main incidents grow out of the separation of two sisters, Henriette and the blind Louise, who come to Paris to meet an uncle. A roué nobleman has Henriette carried off to his chateau, and her sightless sibling falls into the clutches of an old hag, Madame Frochard, whose husband has been put to death for murder and who now lives with a favorite son upon the proceeds of mendicancy and theft. The woman treats Louise so badly that death would be a welcome relief were it not for the consolation she occasionally derives from the sympathy and aid of the crippled Pierre, the second son of her torturer. Henriette is rescued from the chateau by another nobleman, who falls in love with her but is imprisoned in the Bastille by his family because he wants to marry her. Meanwhile the brutal son of Madame Frochard, Hercules, otherwise known as Jacques Frochard, drags Louise about the streets and makes her beg. He damages the poor girl with such insult, misery, and anxiety that his crippled brother, Pierre, engages him in a knife fight, which became one of the novelties of the day and one of the best duels ever seen on stage.

Rankin played Hercules with a slouching gait and slovenly manner, and sent consternation into the souls of the audience when he appeared. Frank Mackay was Pierre. In the French version, Pierre kills Hercules, but, in America, the police arrive to intervene. Rose Eytinge took the small but important role of the outcast Marianne. In a particularly moving scene that gave force to the sixth tableau, Marianne, seeing that Henriette was to be banished for loving a nobleman, volunteered to take her place. Seven tableaux were spaced throughout the piece to highlight elements in the action, of which the most beautiful and massive were the courtyard of the orphanage of La Salpetrière, the Place St Sulpice after a storm of snow and sleet, and the illuminated garden and terrace at Bel Air. The stage designer boxed the sets rather than using the drop wing and border style, and dropped the curtain for every scenic change. The role that won the sympathy of the audience and provided a rich vehicle for Kate Claxton for most of her life onstage was Louise, the blind orphan. So popular did the role make her that the public would see her in no other; eventually she had to buy the piece from Palmer and tour in it for decades.

Kitty Blanchard as Henriette in *The Two Orphans*, Union Square Theatre, New York, December 1874.

On the second night, receipts dropped from a "papered" house of $675 to $450. The first full house was on Christmas Eve and netted $1,300, before settling to $1,000 a night despite frightfully cold weather. After 180 performances, the play grossed $192,897. "It is not always that a company in its best strength can be supplied with a fitting play," said Palmer, "but the Union Square Theatre saw this conjunction. 'The Two Orphans' represents a point where the company was instinct with vitality, flushed with success, and pliable from the training together. I began to look on them as my veterans, prompt, eager, obedient, and loyal in the performance of their work. The spirit in the company was admirable."[106]

The drama critic for the New York *Arcadian* attended the matinee on Christmas Day: "We never remember to have seen a piece in which there was such an unlimited use of pocket-handkerchiefs, from the lace-befringed cambrice to the grimy and disreputable red rag. Everybody wept. The actors wept, the actresses wept, and the audience wept. Even the author, we mean Hart Jackson, Esq., wept as he played hide and seek between the stage and his private box, cursing the while at the irritability and intractability of the scenery which wouldn't 'set', no how."[107] This critic found Kitty Blanchard a sweet representative who would have been more effective were there more depth in her. He thought Rankin "was admirable as Hercules. The part fitted him like a glove, and a very handsome glove at that." He "plays the scoundrel, Jacques, with permissible brutality." Thorne had the small role of the Chevalier de Vaudrey in which his fine physique, sympathetic voice, and chivalrous bearing helped him convey his championship of the oppressed in his two good scenes; Mackay won praise for his elaborateness of detail as Pierre Frochard; Robson as Picard, the valet to Vaudrey, made too much unnecessary talk and stage business, but his part was expected to be reduced; Parselle as the Count de Linieres, who kidnaps Henriette for his delectation, was insufficiently severe; Fanny Morant as his wife was "faultless"; Marie Wilkins as La Frochard, the deceitful and cruel tormentor of Louise, had "unqualified commendation...bestowed with justice."

By early January 1875, only standing room was available. The play had been cut to end at twenty minutes before midnight, and a snowstorm had been added to its attractions. For his scenic wizardry, set designer Richard Marston was nightly summoned before the curtain to take the plaudits of the audience. He always wore a heavy overcoat and carried an umbrella so as not to destroy the harmony of the scene.

By February, the play's success was attributed to Thorne's manly impersonation, Rankin's devil-may-care style, Mackay's artistic excellence, Kate Claxton's pathetic portrait of Louise, the interest with which Maude Granger invested Marianne (she replaced Rose Eytinge in mid-January), and the fiendish cruelty of Marie Wilkins's La Frochard.[108] The impresario Robert Grau, in his memoirs thirty-five years later, recalled how Marie Wilkins thrilled her auditors with horror that no actress could duplicate. "No interpretation of the villainous and brutal woman ever approached this masterpiece." He also recalled Rankin's vivid portrayal of the son as one of his memorable performances in a long and varied stage career. "What a volume could be written around this player's life alone!"[109]

Kitty Blanchard regarded the long run as one of her most pleasant experiences in the theater, especially as every cast member made a hit. "Jealousy and envy, as it exists today in some companies," she wrote in 1910, "were absolutely unknown in our midst."[110] Everyone settled down to have a good time, which was helped by their amiable manager and the practical jokes that Thorne played on members of the cast. Thorne, Rankin, and Claude Burroughs, who was not in this play, advertised their combined services as tutors of acting shortly after the play began, which indicated that they knew their stay in New York was to be long.

McKee Rankin as Jacques Frochard ("Hercules") in *The Two Orphans*, Union Square Theatre, New York, December 1874.

The critics credited the managers with extensive and liberal preparations to ensure the play's acceptance by the public. The *Arcadian*, however, enlightened its readers on the amounts of money paid per week by the theaters to the critics of the *New York Times* and the *New York World*. Daly's Fifth Avenue paid $35; Booth's $50; Wallack's $50; the Grand Opera House $25; Union Square $30; Wood's Museum $15; Niblo's Garden $25; and the Olympic $20. These critics received an equal amount from the operatic managers and traveling stars. Such large amounts came about when the critics formed a union, struck in the fall of 1872 for a revised tariff, and got it. Their payoffs amounted to $25,000 annually, which was in addition to the large sums they received from their newspapers.[111] Puffery or exaggerated praise by critics made it difficult for the public to tell truth from fiction in reviews, undermined the public judgment, and eventually shaped public taste to accept inferior entertainment.

In addition to payouts to the critics, Palmer paid his actors well. The leading men received $200 weekly while stars such as Clara Morris received $300. Daly, on the other hand, paid his actors such as Ada Rehan and John Drew only about $35 weekly. Sometimes Daly owed them large sums of money that they could ill afford to lose.

When the theater season ended on June 15, Rankin was hailed as having the potential to rank among the best actors of the stage: "Mr. Rankin has risen rapidly in public estimation since his appearance in this city; to every personation he has brought a careful study and an intelligence of a ripe and high order, and we look to him for some good work next season."[112] Aside from his own benefits, he donated his services to others: for the benefit of the widow of the master carpenter of the theater, he played Matthew Moineau, who falsely accuses a rival in love to be a Prussian spy during the Franco-Prussian War, in *The Geneva Cross*. He repeated the role with Rose Eytinge as Gabrielle, who chooses death over marriage to Moineau, for the benefit of the retiring minstrel and Irish comedian, Dan Bryant.[113]

The closing of *The Two Orphans* was a gala affair. The names of the various plays performed at the theater during the past season were spelled out in white flowers reposing on massive banks of evergreens on the proscenium boxes. Every woman was given a bouquet and a memorial program. Hundreds could not gain admittance.[114]

Given the unprecedented popularity of the play, there were several attempts to remount it. Palmer brought court injunctions against two rival productions in New York and stopped another version from starting in Philadelphia. At the same time, Rankin and Thorne wanted to take *The Two Orphans* to Hooley's Opera House in Chicago. Since most of the performers of the original cast to accompany Rankin to Chicago were still under contract to him, Palmer gave his permission for it to run in Chicago for three weeks.

Before leaving for Chicago, Rankin played opposite Clara Morris at the Brooklyn Theatre for three nights in *Article 47*, which had brought fame to Morris when under Daly's management. She played the Creole, Cora, who had been shot and scarred by her mercurial lover, Georges Duhamel, played by Rankin. Morris's triumph was owing to her dramatic treatment: her subdued appearance for ten minutes in the trial scene, which lasted for the hour-long first act, her absence from the second act, and her sudden emotional crescendo, which dominated the action thereafter. She rejected the Parisian production's nicety whereby the actress wore a large scarf to suggest she was hiding her defacement. Morris had white welts with angry red spaces painted between and attached strong sticking plaster to her eyelid to draw it from its natural position so that the scar was so large and hideous that it horrified playgoers at the rear of the balcony. She depicted Cora's scene of oncoming madness with a rocking figure, staring eyes, and muttered ravings, increasing in intensity until, tearing the covering from her scarred cheek, she let out a maniacal shriek that rang through the house and chilled the audience to the marrow.[115]

Clara Morris followed "the middle ground" style of acting, which used emotional excitement for expression but did not let emotion disturb the actor's awareness that he or she was imagining the character. To help her depict sudden death, she paid a person with heart disease to run upstairs and observed her physical reactions. Similarly, Richard Mansfield, who came to prominence in the 1880s, studied people in the streets, clubs, hospitals, to make his characters as lifelike as possible.[116] Stage manager James Herne advocated the middle ground, asking his actors prior to the production to imagine the life of the characters they played. The middle ground lay between the intellectual school as defined by Constant Coquelin, the great Parisian comedian, and those who lived the role twenty-four hours a day. Coquelin built up his parts systematically by understanding the psychology of the character and his relationship to the action. He would ask an imagined creature to recite the lines to him and then imitate him in his imagination. For him, acting was idealism, not realism. Edwin Booth belonged to this school. He kept within the bounds of nature and held his audiences by a psychic force. A real struggle seemed to take place within him, but he had intellectual control. His Hamlet was so introspective that the character completely absorbed him. As for those who lived the roles they played, William Warren and Junius Brutus Booth were the greatest exponents.[117]

Rankin tended towards the Coquelin school. E.L. Davenport had taught him to prepare for his roles with great study of the character and the times in which that character lived. By studying Joseph Jefferson as Rip Van Winkle, Rankin learned the intellectual conception with which Jefferson built the role. A critic remarked that Rankin was not a great actor but tried to get as close to that mark as a careful use of his ability would permit. He worked to get more out of a part, regardless of its size, than anyone. In contrast to many actors of his day who concentrated on elocution, he made his characters speak from their feelings and stressed the force of character. Rankin feared the elocutionary approach would lead to a mechanical portrayal, which seemed to be the case when the School of Delsarte was introduced to America from France by Steele Mackay in the 1880s. Mackay taught actors to use certain gestures to indicate particular emotions and initiated the quiet, restrained quality of acting on the American stage, which soon took over the New York theaters.

On the other hand, Charles Thorne, Jr, used clear diction and grace of manner in a fine bold style after the fashion of Lester Wallack, although he was more melodramatic and less of a comedian than Wallack. He seemed more suited to the English comedies in the line of Montfort, Elliston, and Charles Kemble. He was different from the types of romantic leading men who came to dominate the American stage in the 1880s. The latter breed were visiting Englishmen who usually pleased by a seductive gentleness, limpidness of articulation, and a carriage and manner that blended with rich furniture and innocuous pretty girls in drawing-room comedies. In contrast, Thorne's pronunciation, movement, dress, and expression were distinctly American, which made his acting more thrilling, with a magnetism that audiences found superior to the beautifully clothed Britons with their mellow voices and fascinating intonations. A degree of nervousness, regarded as an American idiosyncrasy, made Thorne less phlegmatic than Englishmen and more dignified than Frenchmen. This quality was just marked enough to keep him advantageously distrustful of himself; it allowed him to escape all appearance of a depressing conceit, which often ruined the personalities of good leading men.[118] Thorne's constitution was not strong enough, however, to take the demands that Palmer had made upon it. He wrested himself free of the manager's grasp by agreeing to pay back a year's salary for an enforced leave. The effort Thorne expended while playing the Franchi brothers in *The Corsican Brothers* at Booth's Theatre in 1883 was said to have caused his death at age forty-three.

Charles Thorne, Jr, as Chevalier de Vaudret in *The Two Orphans*, Union Square Theatre, New York, December 1874.

Unlike Thorne, Rankin freed himself from the tentacles of managers by creating a new kind of theater and a new kind of hero who departed radically from his roles as the romantic lover in drawing-room plays. He began this road towards independence with *The Two Orphans*.

1875–1876: *The Two Orphans* on Tour

Rankin made changes to the cast before *The Two Orphans* opened in Chicago on July 5, 1875: Charles Vandenhoff replaced Frank Mackay as Pierre, Frank Pierce now played the roué nobleman, and Marian Clifton was La Frochard because Marie Wilkins had commitments in New York.[119] Overflowing houses kept it running for eight weeks, despite the heat, and its forty-eight performances were said to be unprecedented in the annals of the Chicago stage. It made $9,300 the first week.

Rankin's enjoyment of directing an immensely popular and profitable play was undercut on August 5, when Mrs Blanchard died of dropsy one evening at the age of forty-nine. She had had an operation a few days earlier and seemed to be mending well. Her daughter had visited her in the interval between the second and third acts and was assured by the doctors that her mother was in no danger. Learning of her death after the performance, Kitty was devastated and, unable to perform, relinquished her role to another actress for two nights.[120]

Thorne and Rankin each made $15,000 during the Chicago production of *The Two Orphans*. When the play was in its seventh week, Rankin telegraphed Palmer asking to tour it, but Palmer already had sold the U.S. rights to entrepreneur Charles Furbish for $25 a performance. Palmer's move is questionable because he had given Rankin the right and the risk of proving the viability of the play as a touring property, but then secretly bargained the right to another, although he must have known that either Thorne or Rankin would have wanted to continue touring it. Palmer really wanted power in the hands of his entrepreneur-manager class, which had been trying to wrest control from the actor-manager and set a new direction for the theater. Palmer set a dividing line between manager and actor much as that between employer and employee. He wanted Rankin back in the ranks as an actor, not adding to the increasing competition among combination companies. This competition began in the wake of the panic of 1873 and the ensuing depression, when New York managers sent companies westward to recoup their losses. Rankin, undeterred, let it be known that he would tour with the version that had been played at the Olympic Theatre in London and that Samuel French, the printer, had published. Actually, he began touring with Jackson's version and switched to the London version when Palmer's legal pursuers threatened to close the theaters. He was backed by J.H. Wallack, Leonard Grover, and others, most of whom were actor-managers.[121]

Rankin began touring on August 16, 1875, in Aurora, Illinois, and continued with one-night stands through Illinois towns and into Indiana. At Logansport, Indiana, he was enjoined by the Furbish Fifth Avenue combination company in the Indianapolis Circuit Court from performing the Jackson version of the play. The next night, he opened in Fort Wayne in *Led Astray*, as Palmer obtained another injunction. Meanwhile Furbish's company was playing *The Two Orphans* successfully in Philadelphia and moving on to Detroit. Rankin moved into Mississippi and continued brief stands with *The Two Orphans* until reaching Milwaukee, Wisconsin, where he played for two weeks. Palmer was pursuing him, but court action took time, and he was usually too late to stop the show. Rankin opened at the Adelphi in Chicago on September 20 to enthusiastic crowds. His superior company was playing in the same intelligent manner as in its last Chicago appearance. Sam Piercy, a great favorite in Chicago, played the Chevalier de Vaudrey, T.B. Baker was in Robson's role of Picard, the valet, and Madame Ivan Michels was trying to play La

Frochard as well as Wilkins had done. Charles Vandenhoff was good as Pierre Frochard as was Frank Pierce as the roué nobleman. Mary Myers was not up to Kate Claxton as Louise.

Palmer's restraining order was heard on September 24 but was postponed when Rankin gave bonds and promised not to play the version he had played during the week. He "whipped the devil round the stump" by playing the English version by John Oxenford, and, when the case was heard on September 27, the court declared all versions public property except for Jackson's. Palmer moved for an attachment to have the English version held in court to await further judgment and Rankin had to show the court why he should not be attached for violating the injunction. He was again victorious, but, of course, Palmer could bring an action in another state.

When Rankin's company arrived in Pittsburgh, Pennsylvania, Palmer's men were waiting with a temporary injunction, which was to be heard the next morning. The orchestra played the overture, the curtain rose revealing the actors in street clothes, and Charles Vandenhoff stepped forward to inform the audience of the injunction, which won the public to their cause. The hearing took hours the next day, the injunction was dissolved, and the announcement, when read in the theater lobby, brought shouts from the crowd, one of whom was assessed $10 for contempt for exhibiting too much enthusiasm. The house was jammed that night for the London version. More court argument was heard on October 6, but the play was performed without interruption. The court granted a preliminary injunction for October 7. That night Rankin played Rip in *Rip Van Winkle* and continued it for the remainder of the week.

Rankin played *The Two Orphans* in Indianapolis for a couple of weeks and in smaller Indiana towns in October without interference, but just as Charles Vandenhoff as Pierre hobbled in sight with his grinding wheel at De Bar's Opera House in St Louis, Missouri, on November 4, a constable stepped out from the second entrance and read an injunction filed by Furbish. Vandenhoff promised that all would be put right on the morrow and offered refunds or tickets for the next night. Vandenhoff and Piercy were arrested and released on bail, which was later refunded. The next morning, the court dissolved the injunction and set a hearing at a later date. Its decision was made known by dodgers, posters, and handbills. That night, a crowded house enjoyed the English version. A member of the audience remembered watching the cripple's noble defense of the orphans in the last scene: "I felt an almost uncontrollable desire to rise in my seat and shout at the top of my voice."[122]

In Cincinnati, Rankin's company enjoyed a large business for two weeks and returned to St Louis to reopen at De Bar's at the end of

November to reap the benefit from the great excitement it had aroused earlier. Rankin's Jacques was declared "a picturesque performance" and reinforced the *Clipper's* view of him as "a light comedy ruffian." Blanchard was still being criticized for "lacking sympathy." Vandenhoff left the company unexpectedly, causing Sam Piercy to double as the Chevalier and Pierre, playing both well. Mary Myers was now satisfactory as Louise, and Madame Ivan Michels played La Frochard so naturally that she was repeatedly hissed, a great compliment. T. Brougham Baker marred a good performance of Picard by constantly speaking at the audience, which dated his acting style.

His duties of managing and acting becoming onerous, Rankin hired a manager in Memphis, Tennessee. The company drew a slim audience, which became slimmer for the next two nights, and when it failed to appear on the fourth night, the manager departed suddenly, leaving unpaid bills and attachments against it.[123] The company escaped to Little Rock, Arkansas, where it played for a couple of weeks in December and then disappeared into towns in the Southwest. It resurfaced in Detroit, Michigan, in January 1876, playing *Rip Van Winkle*, *The Two Orphans*, *Rosedale*, and Gilbert's *Sweethearts*. Possibly *The Two Orphans* had lost its appeal as a sole offering. After Rankin had won the decision to put all but the Jackson version in the public domain, a flood of companies toured widely with different versions of the play. Palmer's pursuit of Rankin from city to city had cost Palmer $11,500, but he may have considered it worth the expense as it somewhat deterred the pirating of scripts. (Stenographers sold verbatim copies of plays at the front of the house after performances and soon thereafter a published script appeared selling for $10.) Having failed in the courts, Palmer sent a touring company with his version to the cities in which the Rankin company was playing and advertised his play as the "authorized version" at a rival theater.

Rankin's company continued winning acclaim in *The Two Orphans* in Cleveland, then in northern New York State, pursuing a number of one-night stands, adding old favorites to the billing for longer stays. The company moved on to West Virginia, back for a week in Pittsburgh, and finally to Colonel Wood's Museum in Philadelphia for an unlimited season.[124]

1876–1877: Philadelphia

The McKee Rankin Combination Company's success in Philadelphia depended upon its reception by the patrons of Wood's Museum. The company, which was called "full and fairly good" by a local critic, worked hard. Rankin began in a cautious way with John Brougham's blood-and-thunder melodrama, *The Duke's Motto*, for the first week starting April 27, playing every evening and on Wednesday and Saturday matinees. Rankin relished playing Captain Henri de Lagardere, a role full of bravado, with plenty of sword fighting and an escape from ambush by rope through a window while carrying a child. Although suffering from a severe cold, he gave a vigorous and natural performance that elicited frequent applause from the audience.[125] Blanchard played Blanche de Nevers, who loves the captain and wins him at the end. With dialogue spoken in brief and sharp repartee, the play offered the audience an escape into the romantic and adventurous Europe of castles and gypsies of centuries past.[126] On every afternoon of the week except for the Wednesday and Saturday matinees, Rankin produced *School*. This pattern of almost constant presentation of plays set the mode for the following weeks.

For the second week, as the main play the company gave Boucicault's *Led Astray*, which it had been pulling from its repertoire now and then when on the road. Rankin's depiction of the poet Georges de Lesparre was an attraction because his success in the New York production was known to theatergoers throughout the country. For the matinees other than Wednesday and Saturday, the company replaced *School* with the burlesque *Black-eyed Susan*, with Rankin as William and Blanchard as Susan, and *A Regular Fix*, with Rankin as the debtor Hugh de Bras. For the third week, *Black-eyed Susan* became the main play, preceded by Charles Reade's short domestic play *Dora*. The company kept this bill for the Wednesday matinee, but played *School* for the Friday and Saturday matinees and *The Hidden Hand* for the Monday, Tuesday, and Thursday matinees. For the fourth week the company did Boucicault's *The Colleen Bawn* every evening and on Wednesday and Saturday matinees, and Charles Morton's comedy *Whose Child Is It?* and the one-act *The Irish Mesmerizer* for the other matinees. All the plays were presented to fair houses.

On the sixth and last week of the company's engagement, Rankin played Rip in his version of *Rip Van Winkle*. This was the first time that he presented it in Philadelphia. Blanchard played Rip's wife, Christine. Rankin's reliance on the audience's fascination with child actors was evident in this play. The two child roles were billed prominently as "the two most wonderful and beautiful children on the dramatic stage"—Little Mamie playing Hendrick Vedder, age ten, and Baby Elberts as Ketchen Van Winkle, age eight. On Monday, Tuesday, and Thursday afternoons Rankin presented *A Regular Fix* and *Who Killed Cock Robin?* Audiences were still just fair—"medium patronage."[127] After Blanchard's benefit at the close of the week, the company traveled to other Pennsylvania towns.

In mid-June, to the consternation of the actors, who had not been made aware of the theater's financial straits, Wood's Museum closed suddenly and its effects were auctioned. Rankin managed to secure another locale, however, and on June 20, his company returned to Philadelphia and performed *The Two Orphans* for the benefit of the lessees of the Walnut Street Theatre. This display of his company's talent may have brought him the financial backing for his next venture: the forming of a partnership to lease Wood's Museum for the summer season and reopen it under the name the Museum.

Once again, Rankin sought to sink roots into a strong theatrical community and, owing to his former prominence at the city's Arch Street Theatre, he was confident that Philadelphians would welcome him. Constant travel was hard on the children, who needed good schooling and the settled conditions in which they could develop friendships. Opening on July 1, the Museum presented comedies in the first two weeks and began the third with a production of *The Two Orphans*. The play ran for 169 performances with Rankin as Jacques Frochard. For the matinees other than Wednesday and Saturday, Rankin played *Duel in the Snow* for one week and acted Badger in *The Poor of New York* the next week.

The Rankins had been living in a boardinghouse in Philadelphia, but because they were anxious to stay in one place for a time, they listened to the enticements of Patrick Delaney, a frequent visitor, that they buy a house. Patrick Delaney was a relative of Rankin's and doubtless traded on that relationship to work his way into his confidence. He persuaded Rankin to take out a mortgage on a property on Eighteenth Street, which, although worth $10,000, he would sell for $9,000. As is common with very busy people, Rankin made an agreement based more on trust than wisdom. If he was dissatisfied with the property within a year, Delaney would refund his payments, take back the property, and not call upon him to fulfill the mortgage. Rankin paid Delaney $50 per week up to $750 and made improvements to the property in the same amount. Then he discovered that the property was worth much less than Delaney had claimed. The two men had a falling out, and Rankin gave back the property as per agreement. He did not ask for a refund of his payments and made Delaney a present of the improvements in the property. This was an end to the matter as far as Rankin was concerned, but Delaney thought otherwise.[128] The sheriff sold the property for $2,500, which left the balance of the first mortgage of $5,000 and a second mortgage of $3,000 to be paid. Delaney did not charge Rankin in the courts for the time being as Rankin obviously lacked the funds to pay him. Rankin, however, was suspicious of Delaney's intentions and began to put whatever valuables he might have under his wife's name.

To add to Rankin's troubles, disturbing news of his true friends of the stage reached him. Owen Marlowe died of consumption in Boston, leaving his widow and several children in Toronto. George Aiken died of diphtheria a week later in Jersey City Heights, New Jersey. Aiken was known for producing more plays successfully than any man of the same age. Both he and Marlowe were just forty-six years of age. Charlotte Cushman had passed away in Boston in February 1876, marking the end of an era.

A new era had begun, and Rankin sensed it. Bret Harte, the western short-story writer, brought the atmosphere of the West to the theater with *Two Men of Sandy Bar*. Rankin was interested because a play about the West was something he had been dreaming of doing since his trip to the West Coast. He was aware that Harte's play had just opened in Chicago because his friend Stuart Robson invested heavily in its production. As it turned out, in fact, Robson lost all his savings. Harte's play was a picturesque representation of an America with which few were familiar, but it lacked continuity and was crudely adapted to the stage. C.T. Parsloe played the role of the "Heathen Chinee" as the perfect representation of a Chinese coolie, capturing the look with good makeup and walking and talking so that he became a hit with audiences, who instantly recognized the character.[129] When Rankin wrote his play, he worked the role of a Chinese camp cook into it because of the character's popularity with audiences.

As *The Two Orphans* was coasting into a long run, Rankin chanced upon the theme for his play. On the afternoon of July 18, he was chatting about Harte's play to some actor friends and bohemians in a Philadelphia hotel bar when one of them, James "Philadelphia Jim" Ward, said that he had been impressed on reading a story, *The First Families of the Sierras*, by the new western poet Joaquin Miller.[130] Ward described the scenes so vividly that Rankin saw it as the way to achieve his dream. He got a copy of the book the next day from the publisher and began reading it to his wife. He did not stop until it was after three in the morning. The next evening, he began constructing the framework of the play. Rankin asked Joaquin Miller, who lived in Boston, if he had no objection to making a play from his stories and if he would lend his name as the author in return for royalties. Miller wrote back in an indecipherable hand. "I never did really translate it," Rankin said, recalling the sequence of events, "but I made out enough to know that if I saw anything in the story of 'The First Families of the Sierras' that I could help myself."[131]

As he wrote the scenario for his play, Rankin became stuck on the second act because it lacked the ingredients for drama. After a few days, he came across an anonymous short story, *Schoolteacher at Bottle Flat*, in the February 1876 issue of *Frank Leslie's Popular Monthly*.[132] It depicted miners in the Sierras preparing to beat up the schoolteacher expected to arrive in their community and suddenly acting on their best behavior when the teacher turns out to be a pretty young woman. Using the story in his scenario, Rankin was able to finish constructing five acts before he had to break off to concentrate on the rehearsals for the popular new play *Our Boys*. Blanchard had left the Rankin company to help open *Our Boys* in June 1876 at the declining Chestnut Street Theatre, which Frank Mackay and others took over and made succeed by keeping *Our Boys* going during the summer months.[133] Blanchard left the play after its eighty-third performance on August 19, at the same time that Rankin left *The Two Orphans* and took the role of Charles Middlewick in *Our Boys*. Rankin was said by the critic to have shown a greater appreciation for the possibilities of the role than did the actor he replaced. Rankin's stage business was "exceedingly clever."[134]

Phyllis (Pixie) and Gladys (Dido) as children, photographed in the late 1870s.

A few days later, P.A. Fitzgerald, with whom Rankin had acted at the Arch Street Theatre and who had been writing plays for the Philadelphia theaters, dropped round to see if Rankin had work for him. He agreed to write the dialogue to Rankin's scenario about the West for $25 an act. He brought the first two acts to Rankin within four days and the third act four days later. Having his immediate monetary needs satisfied for the moment, Fitzgerald took two weeks more to write the last two acts. Shortly afterwards, on November 3, he hanged himself from the transom in his home.[135] He had been unable to find work as an actor and had become despondent, although he had expressed great interest in seeing the play onstage. Years later, his widow recalled that he had sent their young daughter to deliver the first act to either Rankin or his wife, whom she described as "the lady who died subsequently at the Jewish Hospital, and was known as Caroline Henri."[136] The widow was under the impression that Rankin was married to Mrs Henri and that Blanchard, at that time, was the third member of a ménage à trois. The Fitzgerald daughter found Blanchard behind the counter of the confectionery store above which the Rankin entourage lived. "Her clothes were neglected," the widow said, "and she frightened the child by her manner. Mr. Rankin came in, and, while the child waited, the two grown people looked over the manuscript. The child came quietly away while they were reading and told her father what she had seen." Mrs Fitzgerald obviously believed that Blanchard had married Rankin only after Henri's death in September 1879 of consumption. Blanchard's insecurities about Rankin, which became apparent in later years, must have had their beginnings in this bohemian arrangement because she could not be certain that she was first in his affections.[137]

Rankin was taking a great risk in producing the play and went against all the warnings of his theater friends that it would never work. He read it enthusiastically to many of his friends, who failed to see its value. John McCullough and Stuart Robson thought him crazy and felt sorry that he had bothered with such a piece. Nevertheless, pleased with the script, Rankin began trying to find a theater willing to take the risk of presenting it.

In the meantime, his acting career cast him in a series of demanding roles: Alfred Evelyn, a nouveau riche, who learns who really loves him when he pretends to have squandered his fortune, in Bulwer-Lytton's *Money*; Malvolio in Shakespeare's *Twelfth Night*, giving a "capital performance...lacking nothing in breadth"; Harry Arnold, one of the admirers of the flirtatious type of American woman who entangles her male victims by her thoughtless wiles in *Flirtation*; Sir Charles Pomander in *Masks and Faces*, in which his acting was "quiet and effective"; Matthew Elmore in *Love's Sacrifice*, acting "with nice discrimination and judgment."[138]

Because Rankin knew these roles through his frequent playing of them, he spent rehearsals preparing for a new play, Leonard Grover's *Our Boarding House*. This comedy relied for laughs on its eccentric characters who had little to do with the plot.[139] Rankin played Giuseppi Fioretti, a mean-spirited man who kicks little newsboys. Rankin's makeup as the Italian boarder and his perfect adoption of broken English transformed him completely. The play began with poor houses but soon became a success, playing to the largest houses of the season. In New York, the same play was presented by a cast that included the brash William Crane and the squeaky-voiced, staccato-sounding Stuart Robson. They performed so comically in tandem that they became the most popular comedy team for the next decade. Rankin's production in Philadelphia ran for five weeks; the New York production, because of Crane and Robson, ran for three months.

Rankin as Jacques Frochard again teamed up with Frank Mackay as his crippled brother, Pierre, in the Hart Jackson version of *The Two Orphans* for two weeks. It was a great success, even though it had frequently been revived in and around Philadelphia. Indeed, Rankin's combination company had been playing it throughout the summer at the Museum Theatre. By this time, Palmer had given up on trying to stop its production.

Rankin's familiarity with the play allowed him to devote rehearsal time to a new play, *Lemons*, which had recently been adapted and Americanized from the German by Daly for a long run in New York. To avoid legal problems with Daly, the Philadelphia production used its own translation from the German and did not Americanize the characters' names. Rankin played Julius Hirsche, attorney-at-law, "with special pleadings before Cupid," in which he seemed perfectly at home.[140] The magnificent scenery was artistically arranged and a "tide of mirth" flowed until the curtain dropped.

Four weeks later, when *Lemons* had run dry, the company tried out *Three Days*, a first play by young playwright Franklin File (later Fyles). In the printed script, an eighteen-year-old girl falls in love with her stepfather, Arthur Wentwich, played by Rankin. But in the staged play, Rankin changed the character from the wife's daughter to her sister. According to the critic, Rankin's Arthur Wentwich "excelled in power and pathos."[141]

Rankin played Don Philip in Colly Cibber's classic comedy from 1702, *She Would and She Would Not*. It is a breezy tale with catchy songs. "What matter if the elements be conventional," wrote theater historian Leonard Ashley, "if the ghosts of Shakespeare and Fletcher stalk, if the disguises get so involved as to recall Ben Johnson in his dotage? The play moves quickly, amusingly; criticism is stilled, disarmed. All we can remember is the captivating Hyppolita, a creature of many madcap moods, and the enjoyment of a rattling good yarn told with economy and élan."[142] It delighted the audiences for a week.

Rankin next acted as the Corsican Joseph Marino in John Brougham's *Slander, or, The Iron Cross*. The play was a satisfying modern romance favored by the heroic actors of the day.[143] The critics were unanimous on the fine acting, and the audiences called for Brougham to come before the curtain and receive accolades, which the witty and loquacious Brougham acknowledged with a speech.

While he was restoring his finances and building a fund for his next big venture with this frenetic stage work, Rankin persuaded James C. Duff, who had taken a three-year lease on the Broadway Theatre in New York, to give Rankin's western play, still called *A Romance of the Sierras* but soon to be retitled *The Danites*, a trial run. A few evenings later, Rankin was sitting in the green room of the Chestnut Street Theatre when a tall, bearded man, with long hair, came in. He had on a frock coat and carpet slippers. Extending his hand, he gave his full name as Joaquin Miller. "Of course," Rankin said, "I was delighted to see him and after a little chat he made an appointment to come by my house the next day and hear the play read. We soon came to a bargain, by the terms of which I was to pay him $5000 for the use of his name and the material taken from his story. When the money was paid a few days later, 'The Danites' became my sole property for all time."[144]

McKee Rankin in 1877.

This momentous event happened when Miller was in Philadelphia in mid-April 1877, to give a lecture on literary London in a series called "The Star Course," which featured literary men. "The poet's manner," wrote a critic, "was no better than his matter. The lecture field, evidently, is not his forte."[145] Rankin's memory served him well, except when it came to payment. In the Davis University Library, there is a note from Miller dated March 26, 1878, acknowledging the receipt of $2,200 on account of the drama *The Danites*.[146] This was the initial payment. Rankin stated at another time that he offered to pay Miller $7,000, but then Miller allowed him $1,800 for his trouble and expenses of dramatizing it, which left him to pay $5,200.[147] Unfortunately, the agreement was not by contract but verbal—something Rankin would regret. Blanchard wrote the letter to Miller that informed him of their interest in doing a play, and she copyrighted the play in her name. When it became a valuable property, Rankin's creditors could not seize it.

Miller, satisfied and possibly very pleased with the drama, returned to Boston. Rankin continued in his varying roles such as Captain Conrad Bertram, the idealistic rescuer of a woman being defrauded of her inheritance by a lawyer, in *Quits*, and H.J. Byron's new play *Married in Haste*, in which he played Gibson Greene, a friendly man-about-town, as a *deus ex machina*.[148] *Our Boarding House* was brought back, but, failing to bring out the crowds, was replaced after two days with *Money* for a day. The enormous energy needed to act matinee and evening without a break and to prepare to brilliantly impersonate ever-changing lead roles would have exhausted the average man, but Rankin was preparing for yet another role that required greater dedication. The night after the Chestnut Street Theatre closed, he opened as the lead in Shakespeare's *Macbeth* at the Walnut Street Theatre on the 250th anniversary of Shakespeare's death, May 25, 1877. Rankin had been chosen to play the part weeks in advance and had been given the run of a Shakespearean library belonging to a Philadelphia scholar, Furness, to prepare for it.

The performance was billed as his first try as the thane of Cawdor. His earlier Macbeth, presented in Indianapolis in 1864, would not have been known to the Philadelphia public. The *North American*, "the oldest newspaper in America," reviewed his performance:

> His Macbeth while not stamped with any brilliancy of execution or marked by any broad departures from the beaten track laid down by those eminent as Shakespearean students who have preceded him in the character, was as a whole a very creditable effort and deserving of much praise. The rendition was uneven and faulty at times, giving evidence of careful study having been devoted to certain scenes, whilst others received but slight attention beyond the memorizing of words and situations. The attempt of Mr. Rankin will not detract from his reputation for though not altogether successful as a complete personation, the evidence given of his versatility should and no doubt will lead him to further efforts in the same direction, which, with careful study, cannot fail to improve on each succeeding performance. Mr. Rankin, in his "make-up," was the perfection of art. We cannot call to mind an actor who has given such a close copy of the historic thane of Cawdor as did Mr. Rankin last evening.[149]

As he had in the Indianapolis performance, Rankin wore white hair in the last act to illustrate his sleepless nights over seventeen years since he murdered Duncan.

Another critic thought that Rankin's "fresh creation" possessed so many points of historical accuracy and rational consistency that "we should hail the latest interpretation as the best."[150] Rankin's slight changing of the text for different emphases and his rearrangement of the stage settings to better reflect the spoken words of the protagonists were applauded. "One of the chief excellencies of Mr. Rankin's conception is his representation of Macbeth, on his first appearance, as the noble, valiant soldier he has been depicted, and then adroitly exhibiting the gradual change worked in his being by the combined influences of self love and devotion to an insanely-ambitious wife."[151]

By representing the court scene as a large, open space with stairways and galleries leading to sleeping apartments on either side, Rankin avoided the discrepancy of the murder scene when Macbeth's voice is heard from within, although he says later that he spoke as he descended. "After the soliloquy, Macbeth, extinguishing the only light in the courtyard, and thus leaving the stage in darkness," wrote the critic, "crawled stealthily up the stairway to Duncan's room, and on hearing Lady Macbeth below, returned to the gallery and *whispered* (not called), 'Who's there?—what ho!' After the murder he descended the stairs, and his subsequent reference to his downward journey had some meaning." Rankin's acting ability, according to the newspaper, was widely recognized, and particularly by Philadelphians, who knew him for "some rare bits of fine character acting." He repeated his role for the Saturday matinee and evening performances the next day.[152]

Then he was off to Chicago, where Leonard Grover had engaged him for a production of *Our Boarding House* on the following Monday. At the start of the run, Rankin shared top billing with Crane and Robson from the New York production, but by the end, three weeks later, Rankin was getting sole billing. The critic opined that Rankin's Joseph Fioretti was the best role he ever played in Chicago—"full of passion and marked with a most delicate individuality."[153] The audiences greeted his "artistic performance" with hearty applause.

The Chicago papers announced Rankin's plan to star in *The Bells* for the next season, and to produce a new play by Joaquin Miller, called *The Danites*, named after the Mormon secret police. Furthermore, he was offered a large salary to be the leading man at McVicker's Theatre in Chicago for the next season.[154] Here was a clear choice between risking everything and accepting a sure thing. Rankin chose risk and set about casting *The Danites* and creating the scenery and the musical accompaniment. Joaquin Miller took no part in its preparation. In a note Miller sent to Blanchard in July, he wrote, "If the alterations in the play are of the order of subtractions only, R. can strike out without my help. If it's additions only, of course I ought to see what is going out in my name. I'll meet you in New York if I can."[155]

1877–1878: The Fabulous *Danites*

Rankin spent the remainder of the summer in New York rehearsing the cast for the opening of *The Danites* at the Broadway Theatre on August 20, although renovations to the theater delayed the event until the 22nd. Rankin had instructed Colonel Brown, his agent, to arrange a touring itinerary for the first few months after the opening in New York. Rankin supervised the alterations and the installation of lavish new decorations, including the new drop curtain painted for the occasion, said to be a beautiful specimen of distemper painting in which the colors were mixed in an original way.

About a week before the opening, Rankin was informed that thieves had broken into his home in Philadelphia but were caught by police before they escaped with his valuables, such as they were. Rankin was broke: he had spent literally his last dollar on preparing the play and had to borrow 25 cents to get his wife and daughter on the streetcar to the hotel where he was staying. Two days later, he was locked up in the Ludlow Street jail for debt, but his manager bailed him out in time for him to appear that night onstage.

A large audience turned out for the first performance of *The Danites*, and, despite a review calling it "obscure and tedious," Rankin felt relieved and vindicated as the audiences continued to grow.[156] As the run continued and minor changes were made in the dialogue and stage action, the acting appeared more harmonious. One critic doubted that a young lady could conceal her sex for a long time in the prying community of a mining camp. Another critic, however, noted the new direction into which *The Danites* was taking the drama. The play, he said, held the view that the stage should present literal copies of objects that may be seen in the streets, as against the traditional view that objects should be selected for drama to symbolize on the surface the emotions beneath it. *The Danites* was a photograph of the vulgar, wild, and rough life of California. The spectator, caught by the animated fashion in which the action moves the story forward, leaves the theater with a sense of having seen an abundance of low life.[157] Indeed, the play influenced the writing of such western dramas as that written by Bartley Campbell, in particular *My Partner*. None of the other westerns, though, had the literary quality of *The Danites*, which kept it on the boards long after the western drama was declared dead and gone.

The play opens with Nancy Williams and her seven-year-old brother seeking refuge in a miners' camp at the foot of the Sierras. Nancy confides in a miner, Sandy McGee, that she is fleeing from the Danites, a secret Mormon society bent on avenging the murder of their prophet, Joseph

Smith. Her family is being exterminated. Sandy, vowing to protect her, leaves her for a moment, during which two Danites shoot her brother. Nancy rushes to save him and falls over a precipice, supposedly to her death. She reappears in the second act as a miner, Billy Piper, who is disliked by his fellow miners for his effeminate ways. No one, including the audience, knows that Billy is really Nancy.

The miners, who are preparing a rude reception for a schoolteacher who is arriving by train, are dumbfounded when the teacher turns out to be a pretty widow, Huldah Brown. Billy Piper becomes friendly with the widow and infuriates "the Parson," who, vying with Sandy for the widow's affections, now perceives Billy as another rival.

In the fourth act, a year later, Sandy and the widow are married and have a child. Sandy ignores the rumors about the widow's closeness to Billy until he finds them embracing. In response, he throws Billy off the premises forever. Meanwhile the miners, egged on by the Danites, who have discovered Billy's true identity, prepare to run Billy out of town. Sandy intervenes when he recognizes the Danites, who then are taken away to be hanged, and the widow reveals that Billy is Nancy Williams in disguise.

In real life, among the several murders of westward-migrating "gentiles" by the Mormons, the most notorious was the Mountain Meadows Massacre, in which settlers were attacked by Mormons dressed as Indians. The authorities took years to track down the main killers, the worst being Orin Rockwell. In the end, only John D. Lee, a bishop of the church, was hanged, in an arrangement whereby he would plead guilty if his accomplices went free.[158] Lee's execution took place a few months before the play opened, and the newspapers in the country were full of stories about the Danites, or the Avenging Angels. The New York *Herald* published Lee's papers, including a list of the fifty-four Mormons who perpetrated the massacre and an account of those who had since died. There was also a list of seventeen children among the victims who survived the massacre, and information on their families. Linking the public interest in the massacre to his play, Rankin issued a pamphlet detailing several of the deadly ambushes of settlers by the Danites and setting the background to the play.[159]

Initially, curiosity may have helped build an audience, but it was the strong dramatic writing, the directness of novel characters well played, and the romantic scenery of the mining camp in the Sierra Mountains that determined the play's success. Rankin played Sandy McGee, "a poet, a painter, a sculptor, a mighty moralist, a man who could not write his own name." His role was the foundation stone on which the structure was erected. "Manly and natural," he played with "quiet energy and excellent taste."[160] Critics saw him as straight out of Bret Harte's western stories, the strong man who is animated by the desire to protect the weaker of either sex. With a noble appearance, this rough miner with a heart of gold was tender and affectionate in his love-making and leonine when facing danger.

Blanchard provided a good foil for Sandy in the characters of Nancy Williams and Billy Piper. When she recited the wrongs inflicted on her family in the first act as Nancy Williams, she "caused one's blood to thrill in the veins," and as Billy Piper "she depicted the despair within her heart so effectively as to thoroughly enlist the sympathies of her auditors, and oftentimes caused their throats to clog."[161] Her acting as a man was convincing. Of course, this was not the first time she had played a man. She had appeared in trousers when acting at Selwyn's in Boston in an old farce, *Parents and Guardians*, in which she acted as a real boy from Boyville, not as a bogus affair dressed up in men's clothes. On another occasion when a tenor fell sick, she took his place in a dress suit in the men's quartet. As her voice was like a tenor, she blended in without notice. She had often played male heroic parts such as the highwayman Jack Sheppard. She attributed her success in boy's clothes to her beginnings as a dancer: short skirts, like trousers, did not hamper the limbs.[162] Before the introduction of the Italian school of dancing, she was acknowledged to be the most graceful and skillful dancer in the country, a talent that helped her to adopt a man's walk and a masculine manner of standing and sitting. Rankin was astonished at the ease with which she threw off all suggestion of femininity in appearance and manner when she donned trousers. She even took his walk on the street as a model. She was attentive to detail and retained the male attitude onstage when not participating in the action. Men, she noticed, are always conscious of their legs, crossing them, spreading them, and associating their hands with their knees.[163]

Louis Aldrich, who had been a child actor and had been in companies with Rankin in recent years, filled the role of Charlie Godfrey, amusingly "called the 'Parson' because he could outswear any man in the camp." At one dramatic point, he holds Billy Piper by the neck over a chasm out of jealousy over the schoolteacher. "He was particularly brilliant in his brusque love-making scenes with Huldah; in his sudden encounter with and his defeating the plans of the Danites; in his farewell to Sandy and Huldah when he gives them his cabin; and in the interview in his paralyzed condition with Billy Piper in the last act."[164] After Rankin, he was the highest-paid actor and had a small share of the profit.

In smaller roles were W.H. Lytell, a stock actor who had been in a number of plays with Rankin, and who, in a comical manner, played William Wise, "elected 'Judge' because he was fit for nothing else"; the excellent low comedian G. Vining Bowers, who played Thomas Adolphus Grosvenor, called Limber Tim because he looked it; W.J. Cogswell, who played Stubbs, a miner; B.T. Ringgold as Grasshopper Jake, the cinnamon-haired bartender of the Howling Wilderness; Alex Fitzgerald and G.B. Waldron as the two Danites Bill Hickman and Hezekiah Carter. The Danites had small but important roles: they had to leave an impression on the audience of menace and relentless pursuit to give impetus to the play and carry over the long period of their absence from the stage. Washee Washee, the Chinese character, was played by Harry Pratt.

Huldah Brown, the schoolteacher, christened "the widder" by the miners, was played by Lillie Eldridge, who had been a member of the Union Square Theatre Company. After the New York run, her role was taken by Dora Goldthwaite. The two camp women of ill repute, Sallie Sloan, known as Captain Tommy, and Henrietta Dickson, known as Bunker Hill, were played by Ida Jeffreys and Ada Gilman, both of whom had had roles in Rankin's touring companies. In November, on tour, Mabel Jordan played Captain Tommy. Georgie Williams, the boy who is killed by the Danites, was acted intelligently by Little Mamie. A number of small children filled the role when the Rankins toured with the play, until their daughter, Gladys, grew old enough to play it.

The popular French opera prima donna Mlle Aimée and her troupe, who were expected to take over the Broadway on September 15, had to be put in Booth's in order to allow *The Danites* to continue. Eventually, attendance declined, and the play closed on September 25, 1877. Rankin concluded the week with performances of *Oliver Twist*, which drew large crowds. He again played Fagin, giving the Jewish master of pickpockets a "powerful delineation." The critic remarked that he had changed his makeup since his early days in the role, but not for the better; it was "too original." Rankin made Fagin's death scene painfully real. Blanchard played Nancy Sykes in a strong and artistic performance modeled after that of Lucille Western. The critic remarked that with Charlotte Cushman, Fanny Wallack, Lucille Western, and Matilda Heron dead, with Mrs W.R. Blake retired, and with Rose Eytinge and Fanny Davenport otherwise employed, Blanchard had the role of Nancy all to herself.[165] Blanchard would have been faultless in the role had she put aside a monotonous drawl in moments of pathos. The playbill listed the minor role of Toby Crackit as played by James A. Herne, who was noted for his Bill Sykes; it was a mistake and should have listed his lesser-known brother, John Herne.

Rankin moved *The Danites* and its scenery to the Grand Opera House and opened with the same cast on October 1, except that John Herne replaced Ringgold as Grasshopper Jake. The managers had reduced prices and established a policy that attracted patrons from comfortable families on New York's West Side, ensuring that the theater would provide the best Broadway attractions at half price. Not surprisingly, *The Danites* sustained a two-week run during which Rankin cleared $1,134.92.[166]

For four years, the Rankins played continuously in *The Danites*, one of the most successful plays of all time. Rankin constantly worked to improve and deepen his role as Sandy McGee, the hard-boiled miner with a heart of gold, as Blanchard perfected her role of Billy Piper, the effeminate miner who infuriates the Parson because of Billy's intimacy with the "Widder." The time was ripe for traveling combination companies. Many theaters sent their stock companies on the road to make room for traveling companies with new plays, and a growing number of theaters employed no actors and catered exclusively to traveling companies. Rankin varied his combination to suit the situation. Sometimes, as he had done for years, he traveled with a few actors to fill the major roles and depended on resident stock companies to fill the minor parts. At other times, he took a full supporting cast.

Rankin had to arrange for the shipping of the scenery. Three kinds of pieces had to be moved: the wings or pieces pulled in or pushed out at each side of the stage; the flats or background scenes shoved together in the center of the stage; and the set pieces of furniture, chairs, tables, and so on. Adapting these to the different stage sizes was an art. Because stages had borders running across the top that were on rollers that could raise or lower them to fit the scenery, a problem arose when scenery made for a large stage was put on a small stage. The scenery struck all sides, in the flies, or the space over the stage and against the borders. To remedy this problem, the top of the scenery was fastened with hinges, and the part bent back was called a flipper. First-class theaters averaged eighteen feet from the stage to the borders, while smaller houses went as low as fourteen feet. As the transporting of scenery about the country became more common, country theaters were constructed to fit city scenery, and managers began to expect the adoption of one regulation size.[167]

To simplify transporting scenery, a wagon was invented on which flats could be loaded like packs of cards and then pulled up on skids into the end of a railway freight car. When unloaded, the freight car was sidetracked and the wagon pulled the skids down to the theater.

On the road, Rankin's expenses increased. He had to pay an advance man to represent him in disposing contractual agreements and to secure publicity, and he had to increase his actors' salaries to cover boarding costs. His contracts with theater managers and combination managers were intense affairs that determined his financial success, and they varied considerably. Theatrical managers considered Rankin to be either hopeless or unlucky in business matters, but, all in all, he managed well in these early years of touring, especially for an artist. For his first engagement at Boston's Globe Theatre in mid-October 1877, he made 50 percent of the box office gross, which netted him $3,761 for two weeks.

The poets Henry Wadsworth Longfellow, Oliver Wendell Holmes, Sr, John Greenleaf Whittier, and other distinguished guests attended the play during its run at the Globe. Joaquin Miller acknowledged the audience's calls by coming forward and bowing. Critics had expressed surprise that a poet who had not written for the stage could produce such an effective drama, despite some verbosity and absurdity of plot. Major New York newspapers praised him for the "rich poetic fancy" of the speeches, particularly those by Billy Piper. As the play's success became widely recognized, Miller relished his role as the author and soon began asserting himself as an important playwright. Rankin could not have foreseen the problems that Miller was to give him, and, for the moment, Miller was congenial. At a rehearsal, he presented Rankin and Aldrich each with an old-time bull pup, a type of revolver used by the '49ers during the gold rush in California.[168]

When Rankin took the play on the New England circuit under the auspices of the managers of the Boston Theatre, the managers paid the railway fares and provided three actors to replace those leaving minor roles. Rankin had a net profit of $400 for six one-night stands, which augured well for the play's touring potential. It was an exciting time for Rankin, who as actor-manager had control of a very popular property and began realizing his ambition of being recognized widely as a great star. But his finances were on occasion troublesome. When he took the company to Brooklyn for a week, for example, he recorded a loss of $160: the manager had negotiated to take $300 of the box office returns to pay for the production costs and computed Rankin's share based on the remaining funds. Had the manager shared all returns equally, Rankin would have broken even. Furthermore, the attendance was light and, though it increased during the week, it was not what the play deserved.[169] Despite these occasional difficulties, Rankin had cleared almost $4,200 above expenses so far.

Rankin, gauging his actors' abilities, selected Aldrich as the Parson, Vining Bowers as the Judge, and Dora Goldthwaite as the Widder to travel with Blanchard and him as an abbreviated combination that was dependent on a theater's resident company to fill the other roles. The only flaw was Blanchard's occasional illnesses; on November 7, for example, Mabel Jordan filled in for her at the last moment and gave a smooth performance.

In mid-November, the smaller combination played a week in Detroit followed by a week on the Ohio–Michigan circuit controlled by the Detroit manager. Allowed only 35 percent of the gross, Rankin's profit was small. The critic in Detroit wrote: "Few dramas combine so much of the wildly passionate, the richness of coloring, the variety of startling incidents." He added that the key to its success was the continuous anxiety felt by the spectator for the condition of the unhappy, doomed girl suffering an unrequited and concealed passion for Sandy McGee, all the while subject to the unjust suspicions of the camp while awaiting the bullet of the assassin.[170]

Rankin changed his policy and secured more actors from New York, including Charles Parsloe as the Chinese camp cook, rather than rely on the local ones when he toured Chicago, Milwaukee, Indianapolis, and Terre Haute. Parsloe had become popular as the Chinese Hop Sing in Bret Harte and Mark Twain's short-lived play about a Chinese cook presiding over a camp of miners, whom he outwits. His choice appeared justified when the Thanksgiving week stand in Chicago brought high returns and much praise from the critics for the actors. Milwaukee, however, was not a success, and Rankin realized only a modest profit. In Indianapolis for the next week, the company met with even less success. Blanchard, ill again, did not join the company until mid-week. Rankin took 50 percent on the first $1,000 in gross receipts and 60 percent on whatever was over that amount, netting him just under $70 for the week. In Terre Haute, he tried a new arrangement: he sold the play to the manager for $350, which was the take for the first two nights, and toured under the manager's direction for the remainder of the week. With the expense of salaries, printing, railway fares, and Parsloe's board, which Rankin paid exclusively, Rankin finished with $30.

From Christmas 1877 to early March 1878, Rankin's company toured as a partial combination to eleven cities. Rankin's earnings were substantial on Christmas week in Philadelphia. The New Years' Day evening performance and a special New Years' Day matinee in Baltimore were also very lucrative. Rankin shared the week's receipts with management and netted $1,466.

It was in Baltimore that Patrick Delaney, the deceptive real estate agent from Philadelphia, struck through the courts at Rankin. He had assigned a collection agent to follow Rankin and look for an opportune moment to seize his assets. When the agent attached the receipts of the Holliday Street Theatre, where Rankin was playing in Baltimore, he discovered that Rankin had sold his rights to all the receipts of the week in clever anticipation. But Rankin's legal actions were not always defensive. Late in January 1878, Rankin, learning that a company was presenting *The Danites* for four nights in Buffalo, where he was scheduled to appear later in February, tried to have a restraining order served. A fair house turned out for the first performance by the rival company, a storm canceled the second, and audiences did not show up for the last two evenings. The offending party failed to appear in court and an injunction was granted by default.[171] Rankin discovered that two stenographers had taken notes during one of his performances and sold his play to unsuspecting parties.

When the Rankin company arrived in Chicago, Rankin joined with the actor and theater manager John Blaisdell to track down a man who had been advertising *The Danites* and other new plays in the *Clipper* at low prices. They descended on a little hovel in a backstreet and found a former actor who had been dealing in stolen plays for two years. Rankin advertised the titles of the large number of plays in manuscript that he found and offered to return them to those who had the originals.[172]

Chicago audiences gave the play a "large business" for the first week and only slightly less business the second. The actors had become "mellow" in their impersonations, and the scenery was enhanced by a local artist, who made the cascade of water in the last scene with real water. In Buffalo, Rankin had disappointing box office, and, on a week's tour of New York towns, under the Buffalo management, he did only slightly better. Dora Goldthwaite as the Widder left the cast at this time and was replaced by Fanny Price, a good actress and an old friend active in Philadelphia theaters, who had been playing Captain Tommy since Chicago. In Toronto, the company played at Charlotte (Nickinson) Morrison's Grand Opera House. The arrangement did not work well for Rankin: he had a net profit of only $202. He increased his cast with New York actors for his visit to Cleveland, which allowed him to obtain 70 percent of the gross, for a weekly profit of $237. In Cleveland, the strong cast and sensational order of drama fascinated the audience. The initial suspicion of unnaturalness at the powerful idealization of the scenery was dispelled by a skillful blending of human heroism and human weakness in the characters.[173] In Albany, Rankin met his old friend John Albaugh, manager of the Leland Opera House, who was closing the regular season and sending his company on the road in support of various stars. Still, a few actors remained to fill in the minor roles in *The Danites*. Fanny Price left the company.[174]

Rankin began a month-long arrangement with the managers of the Boston Theatre whereby his partial combination was supplemented by the Boston company for two weeks in Boston, then toured to Providence for a week, and on the New England circuit for a week. If Rankin had had a contract in which he shared the gross equally, he would have had a more profitable run. Management, however, skimmed off $2,800 of the gross in the first week and gave Rankin 50 percent of the remainder, less expenses.

This was the pattern followed for the remainder of the month, which left him with a profit of $1,491, compared to a profit of $4,002 for the first month.[175] Misfortune hit the Rankin company on this tour. The actor Vining Bowers had a hemorrhaging of the lungs in Salem, Massachusetts. He courageously completed the next two performances that ended the tour and returned to New York City a worried man.

Blanchard and Rankin took the train to San Francisco to fill an engagement with Tom Maguire at the Baldwin Theatre. Rankin found that the stage manager was a friend from his days with the Western sisters, James Herne, who had been married to Helen and had been Lillian's lover and manager. The prompter was David Belasco. Blanchard and Rankin used the Baldwin stock company actors, which, the press admitted, made "a powerful company." C.B. Bishop, a veteran comedian, played William Wise, the Judge, "surprising and delighting his friends."[176] With his gross figure and lumpish face, Bishop had the old style of the fun-maker without a trace of natural humor, which appealed to the gallery. Annie Pixley, later to become famous in Bret Harte's play *M'liss*, played the Widder "charmingly." Herne's new wife, Katharine Corcoran, acted Bunker Hill well.

At the opening on May 6, 1878, the house was filled by a brilliant audience, which applauded throughout the play. The literati were there: the poet George Sterling, the novelist Ina Coolbrith, and others. The full houses persuaded Maguire to keep the play for a fourth week. Unaccountably, business fell off dramatically, and Maguire realized that he had made a mistake. According to the local critic, it was the beautiful scenery, not the play, that had attracted theatergoers. In fact, the critics were cool to the play and may have influenced the sudden decline in attendance.

Maguire took $3,000 of the gross receipts for the first week and gave Rankin 50 percent of the remainder. Since gross returns would decline in succeeding weeks, Rankin contracted for a star's share of $1,000 per week rather than a share of the gross. In four weeks at the Baldwin, he netted $3,250. He expected better returns when John Piper asked his company to play *The Danites* and *Two Men at Sandy Bar* at the Virginia City Opera House. Piper assured him that the miners of Virginia City were just as appreciative of entertainment as they had been on Rankin's earlier visit. When Piper learned, however, that Maguire planned to send a weak supporting cast with the Rankins, he argued with Maguire, who cavalierly canceled the contract and arranged with a West Coast manager to take Rankin on the California circuit.[177] The supporting cast that Maguire chose was poor, and may have been the "snide" cast to which Piper had objected. David Belasco went as stage manager.

On the California circuit—San Jose on Monday, Stockton on Tuesday, Sacramento for the next three nights, and Marysville on Saturday—the company failed to draw audiences and was dissolved rather than continue for a scheduled second week in Nevada. The weekly box office gross was the lowest recorded, and Rankin's account ledger was in the red. His share was $50 above expenses. Nevertheless, after the expensive train fares across the continent were deducted from his earnings, Rankin netted $2,543 for his California season, which brought his total for the year to $22,222.

Aware of the popularity and financial success of *The Danites*, the widow of P.A. Fitzgerald, whom Rankin had hired to write the dialogue, thought that her husband should have received more than $125 for writing a drama that was bringing in thousands: "We would not have minded the money so much, but we would like to have had the truth known [that Fitzgerald, not Miller, had written the play]. If it had not been for the play I think my husband would have lived."[178]

The Rankins arrived in New York City in time to take part in a benefit on June 28 for Vining Bowers, who was dying of consumption. Then with their close friend Fanny Janauschek, the heroic tragedian whose superb physique, strong face, deep voice, great vigor, and majestic style had made her Lady Macbeth comparable to Cushman's, they spent the summer in the seaside town of Scituate, Massachusetts. It was Janauschek's pronounced bohemianism that brought her close to the Rankins; they too were bohemians and liked similar company when they rested after a year of performing.

1878–1879: The Theater Changes

As the Rankin family summered on the Massachusetts coast, they could celebrate their good fortune. The *Danites* tour had left Rankin in the black, but in other quarters, the theatrical world was in a crisis. On all sides combinations were "exploding," companies were "bursting," and dramatic organizations were "falling apart." The old stars and veteran companies were no longer drawing audiences. The managers were desperate because, under the star-manager relationship, the managers took all the risk and the star took all there was. Managers were borrowing money from tradesmen to keep going. The situation was leading to a consolidation among managers and the precipitous decline of the star system. Rankin also had to adapt to the rapid changes: the fifty stock companies in 1871 had dwindled to eight by 1880; the combination companies jumped from a half-dozen in 1873 to 138 in 1881 and increased exponentially thereafter.[179] The chief beneficiaries were the theater capitalists of the Rialto and their financial backers, the national industrial bourgeoisie, whose decisions, made in New York, affected the whole country.[180] Every summer, managers conducted as much of their business as possible from Union Square. Sitting in the Charlie Collins Cafe, also called "Dollar Five Charlie," they would arrange tours into the morning hours as they signed contracts for the bigger cities and left the small places for signing on the road.[181] This centralizing of the theatrical business marginalized local pockets of theatrical resistance to the dominant culture. It also hindered the introduction of serious plays that were critical of society's mores, such as those by Henrik Ibsen. Less-controversial playwrights had greater access to the national audience, and, during the 1870s, plays written by Americans began to find acceptance. Bartley Campbell, who had written for theaters in Philadelphia, began experiencing national success. Bronson Howard, considered the best American playwright of the period, had learned his craft traveling with combination companies, in particular Rankin's, and wrote his plays for touring companies when most playwrights were still thinking of the stock-company format. Rankin encouraged actors to write plays and playwrights to travel with his companies to learn stagecraft. Tom Davey, who had theaters in Detroit, Memphis, and Nashville, formed the Theatrical Managers' Association of America in 1876 with other important managers to foster new plays and to purchase for general use the successful works of foreign playwrights. These managers hoped to prevent destructive competition between theater managers and to create friendly arrangements in which stars could be shared and weekly incomes would at least cover costs.

At the same time, most performers became job actors—that is, they were hired for only the run of a play. During the past twenty-five years, as quiet natural acting replaced the old English style, which was still used in tragedy but was unwanted in comedy, theaters were built smaller to accommodate the new sense of quiet realism. Increasingly, the idea developed of unity in a production and the overall control of the director. Augustin Daly had been fostering this idea, and Rankin admired him for it. Rankin exerted directorial control in *The Danites* and had met the touring challenges facing a combination company reasonably well. For the 1878–79 season, however, he made a deal with Colonel Jack Haverly, known as "Colonial Jack," for the several theatrical enterprises that he controlled. Haverly minimized Rankin's financial risk, provided a full supporting cast whose salaries he paid, and took care of traveling and printing costs. Rankin was responsible only for paying the advance agent. Since only New York, Boston, and Philadelphia had resident theater companies any longer, Rankin was glad to accept terms for a full company. For forty weeks, Rankin was guaranteed $40,000, or 25 percent of the gross box office returns under $3,000 and 30 percent of returns over $3,000. The company Haverly provided was said to be "the strongest ever put together in America."[182]

Haverly used the Managers' and Stars' Agency, recently set up by Charles Gardiner in New York, which booked dates at the best rates for several combination managers. Gardiner kept current on theatrical business in every part of the country. He knew when payday was in the coal country and how many attractions it could accommodate and the number of companies in the region. He could take advantage of local conditions to route companies at the best times and avoid competition. This was far superior to the complicated and slow methods formerly used to book companies in isolated theaters competing for attractions. But centralized booking would not have been economically feasible without the buildup of theater circuits. Beginning in the 1870s, circuits comprised from a handful to two dozen theaters in neighboring towns in a geographic region. By booking a circuit, Gardiner exercised control over theaters without owning them or even leasing them. He could book an attraction for one or more weeks in a single transaction. At the same time, he charged combination managers for his services, which eventually made him a fortune.[183]

When Rankin's company opened its tour with *The Danites* at the Grand Opera House in New York on August 26, 1878, the box office gross almost doubled the amount of the engagement at the same theater in the previous year. Audiences filled the house. The critics were impressed by the tightening of portions of the dialogue, the elaboration of bits of stage business, and the improvement in the performances. Rankin's Sandy McGee had become mellowed through repetition; Aldrich displayed his old-time intensity as the Parson; Louis Mestayer showed zeal and unction as the Judge; Bessie Hunter as the Widder was attractive, with the skill of a "cul-

The Danites at the Grand Opera House, New York, 1878.

tured artist"; Parsloe made "many new points" as Washee Washee. For such a small speaking part and for so few appearances on stage, Parsloe had third billing, was paid very well, and seemed valued by actors and public alike for the comical presence he brought to all of his scenes. He was the prime example of the importance of stage business and personal magnetism in creating a major presence out of a small part.[184]

Offstage, there was a contretemps when a theatrical agent, whom Rankin had hired when touring with *The Two Orphans*, sued him for $900 for services rendered. Fortunately the court officer, who was to seize Rankin's effects, served the warrant after midnight after the last performance and when Rankin had finished packing his luggage and his contract with the theater was over. This nullified the attachment order.[185]

The company played one-night stands on the oil circuit in Pennsylvania to lower profits. Flooding and washouts on the railway lines detained it for two days in Erie, Pennsylvania, but it played the third night to a very good house. Profits increased in Pittsburgh, where the critics praised the play for its good acting and effective scenery. The following week in Chicago was so lucrative that Haverly notified the *Clipper* of the box office returns: Monday $1,045; Tuesday $1,232; Wednesday matinee (rainy) $297 and evening $1,237; Thursday $1,302; Friday $1,071; Saturday matinee $767 and evening $1,447; Sunday evening $1,303.[186] A poor turnout in Detroit was offset by a steady increase in returns from stops in Toledo, Indianapolis, Louisville, and St Louis. In the first three months, Rankin cleared $8,584. For the next three months, he toured New York, Rhode Island, Connecticut, Massachusetts, New Hampshire, Maine, and Pennsylvania in a series of one-, two-, and three-night performances.

Rankin found that the occasional festival or holiday celebration brought in unexpected returns. Thus, his earnings were very high during a two-week run in Boston over the Christmas and New Year period. When management used special theater trains to transport patrons to the theater, profits soared. In Worcester, Massachusetts, for example, the audiences were so large that the orchestra was driven from its usual place and forced to play behind the scenes.

Delaney, the real-estate man pursuing Rankin, brought court action against him during his visit at Mrs Drew's Arch Street Theatre in Philadelphia. When charged with secreting his assets, Rankin replied, "I simply have none to secret, except a pair of pantaloons, two flannel shirts, and a pair of old boots that I wear in the drama."[187] As for *The Danites*, that was owned by Mrs Rankin, but the litigants were welcome to it, if they could play it, for that was all the use they could make of it. The judge determined that Rankin was not shown to have concealed his property and that copyright was not concealment. He discharged the action. Unwilling to accept defeat, a man who claimed to have the first mortgage on the property in question sued Rankin the following day. This seemed to give more credence to Rankin's claim that he was being harassed by people who believed that his success in *The Danites* made him vulnerable to their claims. It was at this stage in his career that Rankin adopted an equanimity when confronted with suits, injunctions, and threats of imprisonment. He was to encounter much more litigation as well as attacks in the newspapers that became vicious and unrelenting for the rest of his career. How much at fault he was or how much his adversaries created situations for their own benefits must be judged through a pattern of frequent charges.

Rankin's troupe made its way through Pennsylvania, to Newark, New Jersey, and to the Novelty Theatre in Brooklyn. Business improved considerably and continued through a two-week run at Booth's Theatre in New York, even though the Rankins had caught severe colds, almost incapacitating them. By cutting parts of the play for the first night, they got through their roles with very hoarse voices. The *New York Dramatic Mirror*, a new paper devoted to the stage, supported primarily by Jack Haverly, wrote a review of *The Danites* at Booth's that any advance man would have considered a masterpiece: "The dialogue is the best, probably, of any play of native authorship....It has no set moral beyond what the relations of people, when truthfully stated, are apt to suggest."[188] The troupe closed out this three-month tour in the East with an overall gross of $29,418 and earnings to Rankin of $7,261.

For seven weeks, the company toured the southern states, which Rankin had avoided in his first season, and came back east via Kentucky and Ohio. Box office returns were moderately good. In Louisville, where the resident scenic artist created a "wonderful waterfall mechanism—a cataract of real water showing five distinct falls," the houses were filled.[189] A week in Cincinnati netted Rankin $469; jumping to Brooklyn, the company had very good houses.

Regardless of the grind, the tiresome rail travel, the haphazard hotel living, and other trials and inconveniences, the company stayed together and probably took its energy from the enthusiastic audiences that it encountered and the money it was making. But there were still miles to go—a tour of one- and two-night stands over the New England circuit, weeks in Philadelphia and Chicago, and a tour of the western states. The company finally ended the season on May 28 to 31, 1879, in Milwaukee, Wisconsin. The total net gain of $22,222 for Rankin was the same as the previous season. Rankin's forty-week seasons demonstrated the demand for the play: the average for a combination company was thirty-five weeks. In this second season, however, Haverly had markedly increased the number of one-, two-, and three-night stands and split-week engagements (the splitting of a week in a theater with another combination company). Gardiner's booking agency had made it possible: by eliminating the casual arrangements between theater managers and combination companies, he allowed small-town managers to remain open six nights a week, thus encouraging companies to visit smaller communities.

The frustrations and drawbacks of such touring were bones of contention between Rankin and Haverly. The added effort, inconvenience, and miles of extra travel wore out the company. Rankin accused Haverly of setting out routes to unprofitable small towns when a bigger jump to larger towns would have increased the receipts. Moreover, he criticized Haverly's business dealings and his employment of unsavory actors, adding that he would play in no theater that employed actresses whose character and habits of life were distasteful to Mrs Rankin. An added cause of the antagonism between them was Rankin's loss of Aldrich and Parsloe, both of whom had joined Bartley Campbell's new play *My Partner*. Campbell wrote it with Aldrich in mind and gave Parsloe a good part as a Mongolian laundry man. It was backed by Haverly.[190] This seemed an underhanded blow to Rankin, who would find it difficult to replace such sterling actors. Rankin's displeasure with Gardiner and Haverly also had much to do with the centralized control that entrepreneurs were beginning to exert over the artistic side of the theater, a control that other actors and managers were trying to counteract. For these reasons Rankin did not renew his contract with Haverley. A *New York Dramatic Mirror* reporter, probably at Haverly's instigation, painted Rankin as a dictatorial, disagreeable, and willful personality with a penchant for crusading against all immorality in the theater. The tone of the attack revealed Haverly's acrimony over losing control of *The Danites*.

A further reason for the *Mirror*'s bias against Rankin became clear when it derided him for supporting a new rival paper, the *New York Dramatic News*, owned by Josh Hart and James Meade, who was organizing a minstrel company to compete with Haverly. The *Mirror* called itself the organ of ladies and gentlemen and the *News* an organ for tramps and vagrants. The *News*, it said, charged all reputable managers with leaguing together to crush the acting profession.[191]

For the summer, the Rankins joined McKee's parents on Bois Blanc Island in the Detroit River. With his new wealth, Rankin transformed the island into an elaborate estate. He stocked the grounds with deer, wild turkey, and elk, and he built extensive stables for his horses. He imported an Arabian stallion, which became his favorite riding horse. In this sylvan retreat he planned for his next theatrical season.

1879–1880: England Welcomes the West

By now, it was clear that *The Danites* would remain popular for a long time. The reasons stemmed from Rankin's dramatic structure and themes. Following Boucicault and Robertson, Rankin increased the dramatic realism, but whereas the other two dramatists implied that the working or lower classes were destined not to move into the middle class, despite their aspiration to middle-class comfort and behavior, Rankin described the working-class miners freed of class conventions and portrayed honesty and decency as reflected by Sandy McGee, following in the line of Eustache Baudin and Rip Van Winkle. Sandy's marriage to the schoolteacher, a representative of middle-class refinement, together with the strangeness of a mining camp, made the presentation of the working class acceptable to middle-class audiences. The anarchism of the West undermined the class barriers among audiences and gave human expression to prostitutes and outcasts, initiating a tolerance and even an acceptance of them that has been a staple of dramatic entertainment to this day. Bourgeois hegemony had co-opted the working class through a desire for social respectability and a belief in middle-class professional expertise and leadership; this was reflected in plays after 1850 and into the 1870s to bring about working-class passivity throughout the industrializing world. *The Danites* challenged that middle-class hegemony and became a cultural landmark by influencing playwrights of western themes such as Bartley Campbell and William Vaughn Moody. The latter wrote *The Great Divide*, about a rich girl from the East kidnapped by and falling in love with a rough-edged western desperado, thus bridging the chasm between the classes. Despite the fascination with the apparent classlessness of the frontier, audiences were not ready to accept stage treatment of lower-class life in the familiar environment of cities, as may be seen by the public's rejection of *Step by Step*, about life in a San Francisco slum, which Rankin produced five years later.

For the third season of *The Danites*, Rankin booked through Wall's Dramatic Agency. He made Alexander Fitzgerald his stage manager and gave him his old part as Hickman, the Danite. He hired George Waldron as the Parson, Frank Bodworth as Washee Washee, and Ben Maginly as the Judge. These actors were not equal to the ones who had left, but they were good and soon perfected their roles. Eventually, Bill Sheridan played the Parson, in which role he made a great hit. The *Danites* company opened in Toronto at the Royal Opera House on September 8, 1879, for a week of enormous business. An industrial exhibition and the presence of royalty attracted many visitors to the city at the same time the play was staged. As a sign of their success, the Rankins were invited to a citizens' ball in Toronto given in honor of the visiting Princess Louise, a daughter of Queen Victoria, a few days before the opening. The company split a week in Rochester and Buffalo, then moved on to Detroit, when Rankin got news of Caroline Henri's death on September 20, 1879. For the past several seasons, she had been playing old women roles at the Walnut Street Theatre in Philadelphia.[192] She seemed to be more of a friend than a wife to Rankin throughout the years, although in Philadelphia she was regarded as his wife while Blanchard played a secondary role. Blanchard's relief or triumph at the news of Henri's impending death may be seen in the change of her name in the playbills for *The Danites* from Kitty Blanchard to Mrs McKee Rankin a week before Caroline died. She would now have Rankin to herself alone, she thought, and she could bear his name without fear of contradiction. Possibly she and Rankin entrained to Philadelphia for Henri's funeral on the following Sunday, when they had no performance, and met Mrs Drew and Henri's other close friends.

In Minneapolis, Rankin ran into trouble. A deputy sheriff with orders to attach the box office receipts arrived at the matinee performance on behalf of two creditors: the proprietor of the local newspaper, who claimed that Rankin owed him $98 for printing done for him in 1875 when Rankin took *The Two Orphans* through town, and a local manager, who wanted $225 for scenery he provided for that occasion. Since Rankin's advance man had made a contract with the theater-owners to keep the receipts, the newspaper proprietor issued an attachment for the advance man to compel him to tell if Rankin was the company's proprietor and had the deputy sheriff issue an arrest warrant for Rankin. After the performance, both Rankin and his advance man were arrested and, with their attorneys, had a stormy session with their claimants. Rankin called the claims "unjust." Both men went to jail. Since the arrest papers for the advance man could not be found, he was released. Rankin's lawyer posted bond for Rankin's release, which prompted one of his claimants to issue another arrest warrant. This second time, the deputy could not find Rankin. Because Rankin did not turn up at the theater in the evening, the part of Sandy McGee was played by George Waldron.[193] The fact that the advance man was let go so easily and Rankin became the subject of two arrest warrants makes the affair suspect.

Thereafter, the company played one-night stands through the Middle States. Rankin may have endured more harassment along the way, although, if he did, it was not reported in the general dramatic press. The company took one-, two-, and three-night stands through the South, broken by a week in New Orleans. In Columbus, Georgia, the usually even-tempered Rankin seemed to crack under the pressure, and the press took apparent delight in reporting Rankin's "tantrum." Before the play commenced, he came before the footlights, stated that he had paid for the license to rent the hall, and asked two policemen who had not paid for their seats to leave or the company would not perform. Obviously Rankin thought the police were there to intimidate him. The *Mirror,* claiming the police were there out of custom to protect the performers on stage from disturbances in the gallery, upbraided him for insulting the public.[194]

As the tour continued, the larger cities in the East brought in good returns. Over the holidays, Mrs Drew's Arch Street Theatre was a bonanza. When the company came to New York's Grand Opera House for two weeks, the hostile *Mirror* commented that the only two remarkable features of the company were the badness of the actors and the obesity of Mrs Rankin, who had grown too fat to play a man's part.[195]

From Brooklyn through Pennsylvania, Ohio, and Michigan, the company came to Chicago in McVicker's Theatre, where owing to the splendid mounting on stage and the beautiful pictures, it had good houses. There were some changes in the cast, the best being the hiring of Cora Tanner as the Widow Huldah Brown. Tanner had joined the McVicker stock company at the age of fourteen and trained there for three years before joining *The Danites.* She had much grace and sweetness and a high-minded idea of the theater. "The theatre can clothe ennobling thoughts so that they strike the hearts of even the most crude," she said, "and thus force words into an unwilling listener's ears, which otherwise, perhaps, would never have reached him."[196]

Haverly's *Mirror* continued criticizing the actors, reporting, for instance, that Rankin's acting as Sandy had a "sameness" that made him seem stale and adding that Blanchard seemed indifferent to her characters from constant repetition. Meanwhile Rankin was still pursued by his enemies. The advance agent who had tried to sue Rankin in New York for $500 owed him during the tour of Rankin's *Two Orphans* company, brought him to a Chicago court.[197] Rankin argued that the agent actually owed him the money, as the agent had borrowed various sums from him under the pretext that he had to "fix" the critics of the Chicago *Times,* the *Interocean,* and the *Tribune.* That agent was now the agent for Campbell's *Two Partners* company, rival to *The Danites* on the road, so there was more than money at stake in his pursuit of Rankin. The case against Rankin was not proven.

Rankin quietly planned to take the company to Mrs H.L. Bateman's New Sadler's Wells Theatre in Islington, London, England. Islington's New Sadler's Wells was far out of central London, as Harlem is from midtown Manhattan, but this was not considered a drawback for Rankin's company in the summer months. Although he was uncertain of how the English would react to the low mining types, Rankin knew that if his play was popular with the English, its attraction for Americans would be greatly increased. The English might find the play vulgar and objectionable, yet Rankin believed in the intrinsic power of art to reach the sensitivities of any audience. Before sailing, the company fulfilled short engagements in Wisconsin, Cincinnati, Pittsburgh, and Providence.[198] When news of the London engagement appeared in the *Mirror*, Rankin decided to leave a week earlier than originally scheduled.

The actors who were to travel to England with the Rankins assembled in Providence for rehearsals. Rankin added some veteran actors such as Matt Lingham as Bill Hickman and Harry Hawk as Washee Washee. This was the first time that an entire company of American actors had crossed the Atlantic Ocean. It performed in New Haven, Connecticutt, where it closed on April 1, setting sail for London the next day. Meanwhile a second American company of Rankin's continued to play *The Danites* throughout New England to the end of the contracted season. This company was reported as giving satisfaction and ended its run successfully in Portland, Maine, on May 1, 1880.[199]

Mrs Bateman, who founded the New Sadler's Wells, was the mother of the Bateman sisters, who had been child stars in their parents' acting company touring the western and southern American states.[200] Her judgment about *The Danites* as a play for the English coincided with Rankin's. He saw that its success in England was possible only if all the parts were played by American actors. The play *Arizona* had failed in England because the parts were played by English actors who lacked the aggressiveness and colorfulness of Americans. Rankin sent over models of the scenery so that the English designers would have the correct idea of the vast ranges, mountain passes, giant trees, and rough job cabins. Another advantage in England for *The Danites* was its authorship; Joaquin Miller had visited London when his western poetry was published there and became a popular character with his western clothes and eccentric behavior. A play carrying his name would definitely have a draw.

When the play opened on April 22, 1880, a critic welcomed it as a relief from the customary drama of police court cases and the French Revolution but regretted that "The hand that with such genius guided the intricate threads of the plot to success in the first four acts seemed to have lost its nerve in weaving up the last and most important."[201] He predicted that Rankin's magnificent presence and good voice would make Sandy McGee as popular as Jefferson's Rip Van Winkle. Blanchard was better in quiet pathos than in forcible situations. He praised Sheridan, Hawk, and the actor who played Grasshopper Jake. Little

Belle, who played Georgie Williams, he signaled out for showing "much intelligence," and he said that George Waldron's playing of Carter the Danite gave evidence of higher artistic abilities than any of the others. Waldron's every motion was perfect, and, although he was not often onstage, the audience could not forget him for an instant. "He has a way of rubbing his hands slowly over each other, an action that he makes so expressive that one never sees it without feeling a sickening apprehension of his violence. There is something terrible in the silence of his movements and one might say to him as Victor Hugo said to Baudelaire, 'Vous avez inventé un nouveau frisson.'"[202] What particularly entranced the English were the "strange and fantastic portraits of a peculiar type of humanity."[203]

Rankin could not believe the sensation they were causing. "I had counted on doing a good business," he said,

> but the first reception of the play fairly staggered me. The enthusiasm of the public was so intense and uproarious that at times we asked Mrs. Bateman if it was genuine. We really began to suspect that the audience was guying us. Each night after the performance, when Mrs. Rankin and myself came out to get into our cab, the crowd, gathered to see us, almost made the street impassable. They would follow us to the hotel, wildly cheering and shouting "Good night, Nancy," "Good night, Sandy," "God bless you" and the like. I grew a full beard to fit the part I was playing and that in itself was a novelty in London at the time. Actors were always supposed to be clean shaven.

Because the New Sadler's Wells had been unable to accommodate the crowds waiting to see the play, the company moved on June 28 to the Globe Theatre in central London and celebrated its hundredth performance on August 14, at which

> we had a most fashionable audience. James Russell Lowell, the American Minister to the Court of St. James, occupied the royal box. John A. Macdonald, Mr. Colin and Sir Charles Tupper, all of Canada, were in another one. After the performance Charles Dickens [actor son of the late novelist], Alfred Tennyson, and Mr. Bannock the Scotch poet, together with Grace Greenwood, John Tool, the great English comedian, were our guests. All these people helped to make that night a most memorable one for us.[204]

There were minor changes in the cast. Cora Tanner became homesick; this was her first trip abroad and she was just seventeen. She was replaced by Lillian Clarke as the Widder. Charles Morton, whom Rankin had known in the United States as an actor and stage manager and the main spirit behind *The Black Crook*, took over the role of Stubbs and filled in for Rankin as stage director, now that Rankin was having to meet the commitments of a celebrity. The role of Sam (called the Gopher because he lived underground) was now being played by L. Williams. Henry Lee played Limber Tim. Lee also played Colonel Freelove in the afterpiece *The Day after the Wedding*. The actors with smaller roles in *The Danites* took turns playing in the afterpieces.

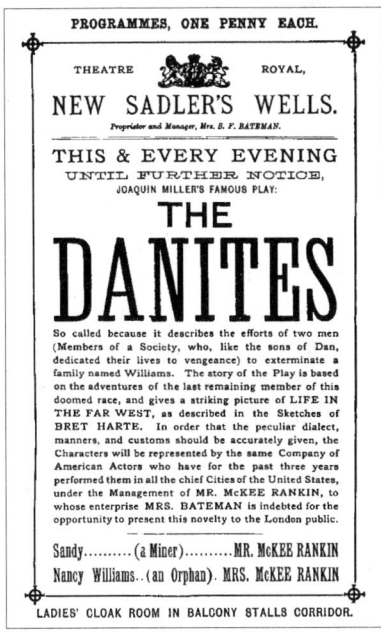

Program of Rankin's *The Danites* at the New Sadler's Wells, London, April 1880.

By August 1, Rankin had become a very great favorite, "not only by his clever and artistic acting but by his hearty manner in private life." His friends Frank Mayo and Daniel Harkins were touring England: Mayo was playing his famous role of Davy Crockett, and Harkins played in a number of Shakespeare's dramas. Rankin's old friend William Florence and his wife were also appearing in London at the time, at the Gaiety Theatre.

Also appearing at the Gaiety that summer was Sarah Bernhardt, and Rankin met the "Divine Sarah" at this time. Henry Abbey, the theater manager who had leased Booth's Theatre in New York, was in England looking for plays and stars to attract audiences. Rankin knew him from the early 1870s when he sold reserved seats for traveling attractions in Akron, Ohio, and played cornet in the local band. Abbey wanted Bernhardt to appear at Booth's for the coming season but had had no success in negotiations with her manager. He told Rankin that if he could meet the unapproachable actress he felt something could be arranged. Rankin made a date with his friend Count Garson, who had told him that he knew Bernhardt quite intimately. He took Abbey with him to meet the count at his London club, and a meeting with Bernhardt was easily arranged for breakfast the next morning.

"I shall never forget the impression this great woman made on me at close range," Rankin recalled. "Beside being the greatest actress the world has ever produced, she has a mentality that stamps her as one of the great women of the century. Her wit, her philosophy, her wonderful analysis of human nature and her wise sayings and quick repartee were something bewildering. She was delighted at the idea of coming to America, and Abby secured her as a result of that breakfast, which lasted several hours."[205] Unknown to Rankin, Bernhardt already had arranged with other managers to tour America for the first time so that her accession to Abbey was not so momentous as it appeared.[206]

On August 18, *The Danites* moved to the Standard Theatre "to more suitable hunting grounds." The box office receipts improved. In a letter to Joaquin Miller, Rankin revealed that he had lost money on his London engagement. Every cent of the $1,750 he brought with him had gone, and Blanchard's diamonds had been pawned for £80 to meet the salaries for the play's last week in London, ending September 10. "This is a God-forsaken country," he wrote, "for making money in our business." His problem was paying his actors American salaries, which were about three times what an English company would cost. The terms he received from English managers were from 10 to 16 percent less than in America while business was about one-third lighter. Rankin's best week in London brought in £577, which was about $2,835; the worst week brought in £161, from which £143 went for expenses. Expenses were paid from the 40 percent of the average receipts coming to Rankin, which left him with a small and sinking fund. He kept the houses looking prosperous, however, by filling them with free passes. As a result, he had less than one pound, he said, and had to depend on current income to meet expenses. His experience with Mrs Bateman of the New Sadler's Wells, he told Miller, was bad, thus revealing another reason for leaving her theater. "I never in my whole life met with a more unmitigated old scoundrel than she is. It's a long story which I'll tell you when we meet."[207]

The Danites played a week in Leicester and twelve nights in Liverpool, where the opening night brought in only £43.15.6. Rankin hoped for better houses in Manchester. Nevertheless, he regarded the English experience as beneficial: Miller and the Rankins were covered with glory, and this would help sustain the play back home.

When he wrote to the agents who were to schedule his next North American tour, Simmonds and Brown in New York, from Liverpool, his tone sounded more successful than when he wrote to the playwright. "Great success in London…am offered time in the Spring season here and also during the pantomime season in London—but best to let well enough alone...and am afraid that I might undo it if I buck the pantomimes as they absorb public attention entirely. Can't afford to be idle during the Christmas season with a company on my hands—so driven to resolve to return home." He intended to open in New York City on December 27 and to play for not longer than fifteen weeks. His terms spelled out to Simmons are interesting: "In Cincinnati, I must play at Heuck's—if they give me the same terms I had last year, viz, 70%. In Philadelphia at Mrs. Drew's, 60%. In Chicago at McVicker's 50% on the first 2000, 60% on the next 1000 and 70% on all over. My usual terms in New York, Boston, Pittsburgh, and Brooklyn is 50%—get more if you can. Cleveland, 60%, St. Louis, 60%. Of course the 'Danites' will be the only piece I play as I intend to reserve our new play for next season."[208] He wrote that business was large in the provinces but would be regarded as ordinary in America.

He mentioned to Simmons, but not to Miller, that he had licensed another company called "Mr. and Mrs. Rankin's 'Danites'" to tour small English cities such as Wolverhampton, Middleborough, Lincoln, and Barrow-on-Furness from September 20 for another two or three years. "We will keep a company going until we have 'squeezed the lunch dry.'" The second company was under the direction of Charles (Black Crook) Morton, who played Sandy McGee, with a new company of supposedly American actors whom Rankin had found in England. In Rankin's own company, Bill Sheridan had left and James Carden now played the Parson.[209]

In Rankin's letter to Miller, there is mention made for the first time of the play '49, which Rankin expected to introduce to American audiences in the coming year. In his tour of the West in 1870, Rankin had accidentally met his maternal uncle, Alexander McKee, in Nevada. Alexander, a gold-rush prospector who was living on rats and toast, provided a colorful character for a play on the western theme. Rankin told Miller the story and suggested it would make a good drama. Miller wrote a story on the theme for the *Californian* magazine and then dramatized it as *California Gold*. Rather than offering it to Rankin, he sold it to Jim Williamson, a character actor, who at that time was starring with his wife, Maggie Moore, in a popular play, *Struck Oil*. After reading the script, Williamson declined it. Miller, who enjoyed following *The Danites* performances when on tour, showed Rankin the play. Since the play was not acceptable to Rankin they agreed that Rankin should write a scenario and that Miller would write the dialogue under Rankin's direction. They settled upon so much per night as a royalty.[210] In his letter to Miller, Rankin mentioned that he paid Williamson the $500 that Williamson had given Miller and intended to pay Miller an additional $300 in New York, where, he wrote, "I hope you will be when we arrive for I have much to talk to you about in regard to the next season." Rankin had been working at a dramatic outline of '49 for the past weeks when he wrote to Miller. "I feel confident that it will prove a better piece than the old 'Danites.'"[211]

Manchester gave the Rankins a good reception. The *Guardian* newspaper, although critical of Blanchard for lacking the subtlety and strangeness that could have made Billy Piper real and moving rather than "a big boy in a fright," found Rankin's undertones and half-asides artfully thrown in, and the byplay excellent, especially the part about wooing and winning the widow, which "deservedly brought down the house."[212]

After playing for one-week stands in Stockton-on-Tees, Glasgow, and Newcastle, the company went to Dublin for two weeks, to "moderate" success. The Irish could not comprehend the play and disliked the characters. When in Glasgow, Rankin wrote to Simmonds that he was delighted with the manner in which he had arranged the tour for the next season and to add another three weeks. "Close the Monday after Cincinnati unless you can fill it on the way and open in Milwaukee for five nights on the 12th April. London, Canada for 2 nights, Hamilton 4, with Toronto and Montreal to follow taking in Ottawa for a couple of nights on the way. *Don't touch Detroit.* I don't think it worth it."[213] He wanted three minor parts filled for a total salary of $80 or at the most $85. He was willing to take Lin Harris back for his old part at $35 *"but not one cent more."*

After leaving Dublin, the company played for a week in Sheffield and closed its tour in Edinburgh on December 4. The company set sail on December 11 and arrived in New York on December 22, 1880.[214] *The Danites*, having been blessed by the English, was assured of lasting success in America, but unlike other stars who exploited popular roles for years to the detriment of their acting abilities—as in the famous case of James O'Neil in *The Count of Monte Cristo*—Rankin was well on his way to replacing his "cash cow" with another gamble.

1881–1882

Blanchard's Troubles

When the Rankins landed in New York, Stuart Robson met them, and Charlie Thorne, Jr, gave a dinner for them.[215] Their friends in the theater were invited to celebrate their successful tour. New York audiences received the Rankins in *The Danites* enthusiastically, and their stay was not only profitable but thoroughly enjoyable. The Rankins loved the city and found the sleigh riding in Central Park better than it had been in years. The *Mirror* reported that Rankin was as ruggedly handsome as ever and that his beard had doubled in length.

Rankin contacted Miller: "My dear Joaquin—Have been with Haverly all afternoon and arranged to produce ''49' next September. Have received my settlement for week in a check, so please draw on me at sight for $550 which will close our bargain for the 'Danites'—draw on me through your bank here, at any bank in Philadelphia. In great haste, please tell bearer if I am to have the pleasure of your company this evening."[216] This note is significant for two reasons: Miller, who, as Rankin said, "was plainly entitled to a rake-off," had been paid in full, and Rankin had mended his relations with Haverly and was willing to try him again as a manager.

Poster for Colonial Jack Haverly's Brooklyn Theatre with Rankin as Sandy in *The Danites*, January 1881.

Rankin replaced some of *The Danites* cast. Charles Chapelle played the Parson, W.C. Donaldson was Grasshopper Jake, Eva Randolph acted the Widder, and some of the minor characters had new faces. They played at the Grand Opera House for two weeks and at the Windsor Theatre for another week before moving to Jersey City, Brooklyn, and Philadelphia.

In Philadelphia on February 11, 1881, the Rankins celebrated the thousandth performance of *The Danites*, printing satin programs for the female patrons. Making one-night stands through Pennsylvania to Boston, where the play was called the "notable event of the season," with new scenery picturing the rugged mountains contributing to its success, the company split a week between Buffalo, New York, and Erie, Pennsylvania, and continued to large profits for a week each in Cleveland, Chicago, Milwaukee, and St Louis, thus giving Rankin and his cast a much-improved schedule over Haverly and Gardiner's routing of the previous year.[217] On the outside, all seemed to be working smoothly. But in St Louis, a storm that had been brewing backstage burst into the public arena to embarrass Blanchard. The *St Louis Post-Dispatch* for April 9, 1881, headlined an article "Kitty's Temper" and gave an account that must have shocked her admirers.[218]

The newspaper explained that it was revealing the truth about Blanchard's absences from the stage because the programs continued to list her, thus deceiving the public that she was just temporarily indisposed.

Blanchard had become excessively jealous of Rankin's love scenes with the Widder. Whenever Hulda and Sandy had scenes together, Blanchard prowled about backstage watching them with "feline acuteness." According to the paper, these jealous fits first appeared when the company was playing in Edinburgh, then at Newcastle and other places, which led to her demanding that the actresses playing the Widder be replaced. When Eva Randolph took over the role for the American tour, quiet was established for a couple of weeks until Blanchard began to suspect her. She broke into a terrible temper when the company was playing in Cleveland, as she thought Rankin was playing his scenes with Randolph with too much gusto. She complained to Randolph's husband, E.M. Holland, who was playing the Judge, and Holland told his wife, who told Rankin. The quartet held an angry meeting that almost broke up the company. A compromise was reached, which held until the first night in St Louis, when Blanchard excitedly upbraided Rankin for his conduct as he was coming off in the third act.

When Rankin indignantly refused to listen, she became more vociferous and stormed into her dressing room. She demanded that Eva Randolph be fired. Rankin refused because there were no grounds for the action. Finally, Rankin called several of the cast into the dressing room and declared that he intended never to appear on the stage with Mrs Rankin again.

The curtain was rung up, and Blanchard barely had time to wipe her tears before she went on for the next act. The newspaper claimed that the cast's sympathy was with Rankin and Eva Randolph, the former for doing all that was possible to placate his wife's insane jealousy and the latter for behaving in a proper fashion. Rankin replaced Blanchard with Isabel Waldron, who had played Sallie Sloan (Captain Tommy) on the English tour. According to the cast, Waldron was as good a Billy Piper as anyone who played the role.

Blanchard remained in her hotel room for the week and appeared only for meals. "She occupies a separate room from her husband," wrote the reporter, "scarcely recognizes him even when she meets him in public, and in every way shows her marked displeasure." In the past, Rankin had made threats to never again appear with his wife and was expected to reconsider if he found a change in Blanchard's behavior.

Displeased by the negative publicity, Rankin went to see the paper's editor to find the source of his information, but the editor could not be found before the company left town that evening. At the performance—in a much-needed public-relations gesture—the women in the audience were given satin programs to celebrate the 1,070th performance of the play.

Blanchard wrote to a family friend about to leave for England and asked for his support in countering "the wicked falsehood." She was writing from Cincinnati, where she was still too ill to act, she said, but expected to have confirmed from Joseph Pulitzer, the paper's publisher, that the informant was the man she suspected. If she did not get satisfaction, she intended to file suit against the paper. "You cannot imagine how this malicious, disgraceful falsehood has preyed upon my mind. I can think of nothing else. It is the first time I have ever figured in anything of the kind and if I thought it was to continue I should leave a profession where one's name is to be handled as commonly as the lowest of God's creatures." Her claim of being victimized appears disingenuous; there was no retraction by the paper and no suit by Blanchard.[219]

Avoiding Detroit, the company swung into Ontario, arriving two days late for a three-day stop in Toronto, which indicated more trouble. Blanchard appeared in the play for the afternoon and evening performances in Toronto, where the company played to small houses. Ending the tour in Montreal on May 7, 1881, the Rankins retreated to Bois Blanc Island, where they were shut away from the world, and tried to regain both mental and physical health after a grueling nonstop tour of two continents in twenty months. They had made 98 one-night stands, 31 two-night stands, 12 three-night stands, and 6 four-night stands in North America alone, in addition to which they had spent 33 weeks in England.

Bois Blanc certainly provided the peace and beauty that the tired couple needed. From Rankin's doorway on his island, one saw to the south Lake Erie stretching as far as the eye could reach; to the westward, across the river, a distance of two miles, the green-wooded islands of Elbe, Sugar, Hickory, and Fox; to the north, up the river to Grosse Isle, Stony Island, and the Canadian Southern Railway bridges and ferries; to the east, over the fields of corn and grain to the spires of Amherstburg and the masts of the vessels that were constantly passing up and down the east side of Bois Blanc.[220] The grounds were laid out tastefully and the lawn stretched to the river. Rankin had a sailboat, a rowboat, and a boat for fishing. He raised cattle and Shetland ponies and had a number of handsome horses, in particular a Percheron stallion from Normandy. His activities of milking cows and harvesting his lands gave the impression of a hard-worked farm, but inside his home there was a sense of luxury and ease. His guests from New York, Philadelphia, and Chicago came from the theater, and often the Rankins gave weekend parties with friends, known as the Delmonico crowd.[221] Here he began planning his tour for the next season, and having patched up his quarrel with Haverly, he transferred his business from Simmonds and Brown back to Haverly.

'49, Successor to The Danites

While in England, Rankin had bought from the Kendals, the foremost acting couple of the day, a modernized version of *Black Eyed Susan*, entitled *William and Susan*. Now he engaged J.H. Barnes from the London stage to play Captain Crosstree and to stage-manage the production, and J.J. Holland, the youngest son of the great comedian George Holland, to play the Admiral. Rankin played William Bowlin and Blanchard was Susan. Just before the play opened at Haverly's Fourteenth Street Theatre in New York on September 19, 1881, Rankin fired his manager, Haverly, over a disagreement. He signed a contract with the New York firm of Brook and Dickson, management agents, whose expertise was with minstrel companies and who thus could provide a variety of established routes. He had to make a hasty decision, which was a bad omen.

The critics thought the play tailor-made for the Rankins but not a breadwinner in America. Tinkering with old plays, while acceptable in England was sacrilege in America, where they were venerated.[222] Moreover, *Black Eyed Susan* had been burlesqued as *Black-eyed Susan* so often for the past decade that a new version could not be taken seriously. Unluckily, Rankin was suffering from hoarseness, which undermined his role.[223] All the male cast "whiskered up" to resemble Rankin, who "ripped and roared through the three acts, and the few people who saw him bitterly regretted that he was saved from the yard-arm." As for Blanchard, she adopted "a French-Irish-Scotch-Dutch accent, which rendered her words unintelligible." Most of the audience left after the second act.[224]

The event that killed the play began on July 2, 1881, when President Garfield was shot by an assassin. Hope for his recovery faded when blood poisoning set in, and the news of his death on the evening of September 19 reached the theater as the play was ending. All the theaters had finished their performances except the Fifth Avenue, where the curtain was abruptly dropped on the star as she was doing her last scenes. The theaters remained closed until Garfield's burial on the morning of Saturday, October 1. That afternoon the Rankins gave the last performance of *William and Susan* to light attendance. In the evening, confident of success, they presented *'49* for the first time.

Rankin had asked Miller to do the dialogue to the detailed scenario that he had drawn up for *'49*, but when the script arrived, it was, according to J.H. Barnes, "in a terribly chaotic state...and we had to use all our wits and experience to get it into acting shape." They agreed that Miller would receive royalties of $20 a performance. Later Miller demanded $75 per week for large cities and $50 a week in smaller ones. Rankin offered $60 in large cities and $10 a night for any single performance and $30 a week for the rest of the country. Miller refused and hostilities began.[225] Because Rankin had replaced all of Miller's ideas with his own, he billed the play with himself as co-author. Miller took exception to this and wrote that Rankin had stolen his play. A.C. Wheeler, a popular drama critic, printed Miller's charges, which led Rankin to sue both of them for libel.[226]

Rankin gave the first rewriting task to Archibald Gordon, a journalist from Ceylon. Gordon's wit and humor, classical learning, mastery of several languages, and potent gift of satire that never became invective, made him a valuable collaborator whom Rankin would call upon in future. Through Gordon's efforts, the dialogue and stage business were constantly being improved but not enough to bring out the play's potential. Rankin called on Leonard Grover, who wrote *Our Boarding House* and other popular plays, to rewrite it once again.

Blanchard wrote a prologue dramatizing the attack on the migrants by Mormons under Bishop Lee in the Mountain Meadows Massacre of 1857. The father of a family is killed and his wife mortally wounded, but before she dies she entrusts her daughter to her black manservant, Old Ned. Just as Lee is about to dash out the brains of the little child, an Indian asks to be given custody of her. Ned escapes with his life and seeks refuge with the Indians.

In the first act, Colonel James, a lawyer, has in his trust a will bequeathing $500,000 to the missing daughter. He hires a bank clerk, Arthur Dennison, to find the girl in the Indian camps along the Pacific coast. Colonel James's clerk, Bradshaw, however, copies out the documents, keeps them, and gives Arthur Dennison blanks. Bradshaw intends to find the girl, marry her, and inherit her fortune. The second act opens in a Nevada mining camp, specifically in a gorgeously frescoed hotel, bar, and office, where miners in red shirts and cowboy boots provide local color. Bradshaw has become intimate with Belle, whom he mistakenly believes is the lost heiress, and marries her to get her money. Both Belle and Carrots, a wild gamin and companion of an old miner named '49, were rescued from the Indians and brought up by Mississippi, the hotel owner. When Arthur Dennison arrives, he and Bradshaw quarrel. Bradshaw draws a bowie knife, but '49 realizes that the girl they want is Carrots, declares he has not seen a bowie knife since 1849, and knocks it out of Bradshaw's hand. The curtain falls.

In the third act, Carrots falls in love with Dennison, and old '49 learns that Dennison is his son. Borrowing Dennison's coat to hunt for game, '49 accidentally leaves the coat in the bush near the location of a stagecoach robbery. When Bradshaw recognizes the coat, Dennison is suspected, but '49, to save his son, claims that he robbed the coach. In the fourth act, the vigilantes prepare '49 for hanging, but Bradshaw's pocketbook and papers are found along the road, pointing to him as the real robber. Carrots, for Belle's sake, begs the vigilantes to release Bradshaw on the condition that he leave the state. Old Ned is brought from St Louis by Colonel James to identify the real heiress. He sings a ditty "Coal-black Rose" that he used to sing to the girl, which Belle does not know but which Carrots recognizes. Bradshaw understands that he has married the wrong woman and that Dennison will get the half-million after all.

Reviewers, although recognizing the play's faults, were encouraging:

> We have seldom seen every part in a play so capitally cast. Mrs. Rankin looked charming as Carrots, and acted the character to the life. Not in "The Two Orphans" or "The Danites" has she appeared to such advantage. Her singing is just what a girl like Carrots would do; her humor and her pathos were equally unforced and delightful. Mr. Rankin, as the grizzled and bent old miner, '49, played with quiet force, dignity, and reserve, and made the artistic hit of his career. It was no small sacrifice to disguise his good looks under a gray wig and whiskers, and the stoop of age; but he did it artistically, and he has his reward....We have had many a quiet laugh since the coon dinner which old '49 gives to Dennison, in the mountains, and the mingled fun and pathos of that incident would make the fortune of a much less effective melodrama.[227]

Meanwhile, in court for libeling Rankin, Miller and Andrew Wheeler, a drama critic, had to answer for using these words: "Our respect is due to eminence and originality, and you cannot refuse it to this new worker when I tell you that he is the most colossal liar and the most impudent thief that ever made use of the practices of both without having necessary skill in either."[228] Miller, his hair and beard auburn and shaggy, sat back of the lawyers and talked with a policeman. Rankin, wearing a flaming red neck scarf and speaking in a hoarse voice, said that he paid Archibald Gordon $50 an act to write the play's dialogue and that some incidents were taken from Miller's version but differently used and the characters were reconstructed. Offended, Miller had rewritten the play from memory and showed it to Rankin, who demanded that he turn it over to him because it was written in violation of their agreement. In a seemingly capricious ruling the judge saw no connection between the play and Miller's abusive words. He regarded "colossal liar and impudent thief" as equivalent to literary liar and literary thief, which did not attack Rankin's character, and hence were not libelous.[229]

After the play terminated at Haverly's, and as Rankin and Blanchard were getting into a carriage in front of the Union Square Hotel late on Saturday night to go to Wheeling, West Virginia, Miller served them with an order restraining Rankin from playing the litigated play. Rankin swore softly but started on his journey.[230] Miller's restraint was not successful.

Rankin's company played '49 the first week and *The Danites* for the second in the cities it visited. In Chicago in November, *The Danites* drew the larger patronage —'49 was not a success. "Too much of a good thing nauseates," said a critic, meaning that the western theme in both plays when played together seemed repetitious.[231] At the same time, J.H. Barnes parted with the company to join an English company touring in a popular Drury Lane drama. He had been criticized for his Regent Street accent: "an exceedingly disagreeable intonation of voice which becomes very monotonous."[232] "Obviously I could not be expected to rival a fine actor like W. E. Sheridan in a purely American part that fitted him superbly in 'The Danites'," Barnes wrote, "and in a thousand little unpleasant ways I was made to feel it."[233]

While in Chicago, Rankin was embroiled in another court case brought by the agents managing his company. By their agreement Brook and Dickson allowed the Rankins $100 a week for personal expenses, paid theater rents, the salaries of the actors, and traveling expenses. After the expenses were deducted from the receipts, Rankin was to receive two-thirds of the profits. Since Rankin ran out of money, the firm lent him $700, then $150, and finally endorsed a note for $1,000, which he needed as a consequence of the failure of *William and Susan* and the poor business he did at Haverly's. Haverly closed the engagement early, which the contract allowed if receipts fell below a certain mark. To get their loans to Rankin back, the firm instructed their man, whom they sent on the road with the company, to withhold receipts until Rankin started repayments, which caused Rankin to cancel their agreement. The firm considered his action a deliberate attempt to defraud it and argued that one bill in particular came to $3,500 for lithographs for '49 and *The Danites*, for which the firm had to guarantee payment as the printing houses feared Rankin would swindle them. The firm's total loss on the road was $900, and, with the borrowed money and liabilities, it amounted to $6,000. "I have met many deadbeats in this world," said one of the partners, "but Rankin is the biggest of the lot."[234]

A reviewer wrote: "The handsome, amiable, popular heroic actor, over whom the ladies rave, may be in real life an arrant rascal and thorough cad;…but in "'49" he made a decided hit." Rankin's habit of avoiding his obligations began to give the public a puzzling look at his character. For the moment, these charges were still doubtful and not widely publicized outside of the professional journals. The *Chicago Tribune*, however, reported that Rankin refused to have any more business with the firm after it tried to withhold profits from him. "If the firm knew me, they would know that I would pay it," he said. When the firm served an injunction on Hooley, preventing him from turning over box office receipts to Rankin, Rankin claimed that his contract with Hooley was made in the previous season and had nothing to do with the firm. Likewise, he had engaged his company before the firm took over as manager. "If the company had been theirs," he said, "they would have had me in a box, and I would have been compelled to do as they said." The disagreement from his viewpoint was not over money but control. His predicament underlined the ongoing conflict between actor-manager and the new entrepreneurial managers, reflecting the change from an actors' theater to a commercial theater. "They have treated myself and wife as mere dependents since we have been with them and I have not been consulted at all about anything. These theatrical middlemen are something new in the theatrical business, and, from the brief experience I have had with them, I cannot say that they are an astonishing success. They are arrogant and unscrupulous, and treat those who are filling their pockets with money as mere menials."[235]

After playing in Indianapolis, the company took three days off to rehearse Grover's new version of '49 with an added fifth act. Rankin tried it out in Detroit and it proved to be infinitely better than the earlier version. In Cleveland, where '49 ran for the week of December 5, 1881, the local critic described it as "a gem which will become brighter by wear."[236] The play's simplicity, depth, genuineness, humor, and slight plot were "essential to the strength and beauty wrought from the development, the underlying thread upon which all hangs is never hidden from the auditor who follows the winding with ease and is thus in a position to sympathize with the joys or sorrows of the *dramatis personae*." Between Christmas and New Years in Philadelphia, *The Danites* met with greater success than ever. For the second week, Rankin played '49, which also had full houses. He announced that he would be playing '49 to the end of the season.

In New York in January 1882, the company played only '49 to crowded houses for two weeks. After a week of "good-sized audiences" at Brooklyn's Park Theatre, the company took the Mischler circuit of one-week stands through major eastern and midwestern cities and several one-night stands in Ohio. Still harried, Rankin had trouble with the firm of agents in Louisville, who attached his box office receipts on two successive evenings to pay their lithographic costs, but Rankin telegraphed his backers to bring pressure on them to back off. The company returned to New

York for a week at Niblo's Garden, where it closed the season on April 22, 1882. For most of its stops, it had large and appreciative audiences.

To terminate a season as early as April was unusual for the hard-driving Rankins. An explanation was Blanchard's ill health. She was diagnosed as having Bright's disease, a degeneration of the kidneys, which eventually leads to dropsy. But it seemed to attack her only spasmodically, after which she was as vigorous as ever. The Rankins retired to Bois Blanc Island, where they hosted their friends from the theatrical world. Leonard Grover joined them on the island in May to write his play *The Metropolis*, which they hoped to use in the next season.[237]

1882–1883: Stock and Saxe-Meiningen

Opening the fall season earlier than usual, on August 14, 1882, at the Windsor Theatre in New York, Rankin experimented with a shortened version of *The Danites* that left out the role of the Parson, possibly to save on a large salary.[238] It was well mounted, well acted, and gave great pleasure to large audiences during the week. Rankin as Sandy McGee did "a good healthy piece of acting which does one good to see," and Blanchard was excellent, although "grown too round and rosy to evoke much sympathy in her expression of the camp girl's woes."[239]

The company "rested" for the last week in August before touring with *'49* and *The Danites*. Rankin restored the play to its original size with the Parson's role intact and used the time to make changes in the cast, most notably recasting Blanchard as Nancy Williams and Huldah Brown, while a slimmer actress, Bessie Justice, took the role of Billy Piper.[240] This change, in response to the critics, was either a rebuke to Blanchard, who had to slim down to win back her role, or a concession to her jealousy of whoever played the widow.

Starting in Baltimore on September 4, the company did moderate to good business in stands of one week in larger cities such as Washington, Cleveland, Milwaukee, and St Louis, and shorter stands through Minnesota, Nebraska, Missouri, Kansas, and Ohio. Shortly after setting out, a slimmer Blanchard took back her role as Billy Piper and gave up the widow's role to another actress, who was careful not to appear too loving with Rankin. Chicago turned out to see both plays for a profitable two weeks in November.

Opening again in New York, this time in the smaller Niblo's Garden, the company played *'49* for two weeks to good business. The orchestra and the first balcony were crammed, and the family circle was almost filled, but the second balcony was only moderately represented. From this, it appeared that the play appealed to the middle classes more than to the lower classes, who, at one time, had mobbed the theaters.[241]

Over the Christmas holiday season, the Rankins played their usual stand at the Arch Street Theatre in Philadelphia, although, in the second week, Blanchard fell ill and was replaced as Billy Piper by Lizzie May Ulmer. The great success of both plays was as beneficial to Mrs Drew as to the Rankins, who easily drew the holiday crowds. Drew had been having difficulty maintaining a profitable theater, and, after several public arguments with her trustees, she turned it into a combination house, thus bowing to the inevitable. She herself began touring with Joseph Jefferson, often playing Mrs Malaprop to Jefferson's Bob Acres in Sheridan's *The Rivals*.

By the next engagements, in Boston, Brooklyn, and Providence, Blanchard had returned, but she again had to be replaced in '49 in Williamsburgh. She remained ill through weeks of touring to the company's closing in New York City in the last week of April. From early February to early July, during which time Blanchard remained in New York, her illness, which lay behind her irritations and jealousies, worried Rankin, and he decided to strike out in a different direction. He believed that the combination system was on the wane; it brought the public the same old stars and attractions once or twice in a season, while the public, wanting a more stable theater, demanded that stock theaters be established in the larger cities. Moreover, he was convinced that the western border dramas like "'49" that he was playing were losing favor with the public.[242] But primarily, he was eager to develop the new ideas of the German director the Duke of Saxe-Meiningen.

George II of the principality of Saxe-Meiningen, referred to as the Duke of Saxe-Meiningen, broke onto the theatrical scene in Berlin in 1874 with remarkable productions acted by the group of actors he had trained. He emphasized ensemble playing, which required historical accuracy in costuming and artistic and vital interrelationships between the movements of the actors and the decor. Traditionally directors emphasized the movements of the characters without considering them as elements in developing meaning within the scenes. The Saxe-Meiningen company inspired theatrical reform when it performed in the cities of Europe. The duke insisted on stage movement, and he brought the crowds of supernumeraries to life through stage direction. "Special reminders must be given the supers not to stare at the audience," he wrote. "They do this naturally, since for many of them acting is a new and unusual experience, and their aroused curiosity makes them look around the dark auditorium." He taught that each performer in the crowd had a separate identity.[243]

The duke's innovations paved the way for the stage naturalism of the plays of Emile Zola, as opposed to the mechanical banalities of the well-made plays of Scribe, Sardou, and Augier in which bourgeois morality and sentiment played into a formulaic denouement, happily resolving all complexities. Zola emphasized the double influence of characters on action and action on characters. The fluid stage of Saxe-Meiningen, providing separate acting areas on different levels to serve the actors' movements, gave the new drama a distinctive thematic complement to the action.

Frank Mayo had experimented with ensemble playing in the Providence Opera House in October 1881 with a series of Shakespearean plays. The critics called the performances thoroughly intelligent. They praised Mayo's stage management, noting a series of beautiful groupings and stage pictures with attention to detail and with every actor acting after the manner of Saxe-Meiningen. Mayo's interpretation was unconventional, bold, and masterly, and was full of new thoughts and new business. The costumes were called models of accuracy and elegance.[244] Rankin learned from his friend's experience.

Rankin contracted for Hooley's Theatre in Chicago to house a stock company from June through early August 1883. The actors he tried to engage were superb. Caroline Hill was ranked second only to Mrs Kendal in England. J.D. Beveridge had played many West End successes in the English provinces. Herbert Kelsey was a handsome young actor in Wallack's New York company. Rankin wanted to revive the Robertsonian comedies, as he was convinced that the public was tired of trashy melodrama and comic opera. Rankin said that he would establish a permanent stock company in Chicago if his summer theater proved successful.[245] Yet, other demands distracted him from his Chicago project. He was constructing a new theater in New York, and he accepted the position of the leading man at the Union Square Theatre for the next season, replacing Charles Thorne, Jr, who had died suddenly in February. Rankin, hoping to get out of his contract in Chicago, asked Daly to take his place at Hooley's, but Daly could not get out of his contract to play in San Francisco. Owing to the uncertainty of his project, Rankin did not hire the leading English stars he had hoped to get, except for J.T. Beveridge. Nor did he acquire the New York stars such as Kelsey, Howard, and Howell, who wanted a more secure arrangement. He depended on some good American actors such as Lewis Morrison and Percy Rede, and his old standbys John Jack and Luke Martin. Emily Rigle, who had been in Daly's company, took the roles that Blanchard would have filled.

Rankin's first production at Hooley's in Chicago on July 2, 1883, was *The Corsican Brothers*, which had been revived the previous season at

Booth's in New York after lying on the shelf since its best interpreter, Charles Fechter, had died some years before. Rankin used the Booth's production, with its elaborate scenery, and played his old roles of the Franchis. The critic found the acting good and the action zestful and smooth, but the play was too "talky." Rankin succeeded "wonderfully well" in transforming himself from a backwoodsman, which he had been playing for years, into the proud Corsican gentlemen. Unfortunately, he had too much "adipose" to appear well in a dress suit.[246]

Rankin's mother and his brother George visited him at this time. Colonel Rankin had come down earlier in April to see his son perform in *'49*. The family may have been concerned about Blanchard, but she was with Rankin now and rapidly regaining her health.

After two weeks, Rankin replaced *The Corsican Brothers* with Robertson's *School*, in which Blanchard played the part of Naomi Tighe, which she had originated in Boston and set the mold for all who followed her. Rankin's portrayal of the sportsman Poyntz was contrasted negatively to his acting in the part years before. Now his assumed nonchalance and lazy drawl seemed exaggerated, and his speech was almost unintelligible. Some of the actors did not know their lines. *School* lasted a week. Beveridge departed for England to take a starring role in a West End production, as Rankin's next play would not have suited him.

Rankin mapped out a play which he entitled *The Americans* and gave the scenario to Lydia Coyne Fletcher, a young woman who worked in a government department in Washington, to work out the dialogue. She was the niece of a playwright, and presumably had met Rankin through her uncle. *The Americans*, produced for the week of July 22, 1883, concerned a young Indian captured in battle, adopted by General Sterling, and named Rex Sterling.[247] The success of the play was due more to its acting than dialogue, however, particularly Lewis Morrison as the brothers Rex Sterling and Red Feather. The play needed some alterations and rewriting but was expected to be brought to the Union Square Theatre for the next season, when Rankin planned to star in it with Blanchard.

In assessing Rankin's effort to revive repertory theater, a Chicago critic used *The Americans* as a point of departure.

> Never have the disadvantages of the combination system been more plainly demonstrated than last evening. The present custom of learning and playing one part through an entire season and of giving a play weeks of careful rehearsal has made it impossible for actors and actresses to learn their parts at comparatively short notice and present plays satisfactorily after a

few rehearsals. The memory is a machine which becomes rusty through disuse and the uneasiness of the members of the cast last evening in their lines fully demonstrated this much-to-be-regretted fact.[248]

1883–1884: Rankin's Third Avenue Theatre

Rankin's boldest investment was the construction of his new theater upon the site of an old variety theater on Third Avenue between Thirtieth and Thirty-First Streets. He said that it was needed to bring the enlightening spirit of the theater to people on the East Side and he hoped to use it to experiment with ensemble acting. To build the theater the Rankins mortgaged it for $15,000 at 5 percent for two years.[249] The woodwork was California redwood, and the decorations had a Moorish pattern in chocolate and red browns, blue, and gold. The stage had no grooves, the scenes being either boxed or set with braces. The proscenium opening was like a circle with the lower part cut off by the stage line, giving the idea of a heavy picture frame. Its opening was $33 \frac{1}{2}'$ by $35'$. The house was lit by electricity, the electroliers being of burnished brass, and the smaller ones representing bunches of lilies. A large lantern of colored glass and brass of Moorish design, containing 120 electric lights, hung in the center of the house. Unfortunately, the lights were not yet adapted to all dramatic demands: they could be on full or not at all. The theater allowed for 650 seats in the parquet, 630 in the balcony circle, and 600 in the gallery. Four boxes placed one on either side of the parquet and the gallery held five seats each. Before opening night, every other row of seats in the balcony had to be removed because the seating was too close. The seats in the lower house also seemed too close together. The seating was soon remodeled, which lessened the total to 1,100 seats. This compared to 2,060 seats for Niblo's Garden, 2,113 for the Grand Opera House, 1,184 for the Union Square Theatre, and 627 for Haverly's Comedy Theatre. Ticket prices were $1 for parlor chairs, 75 cents for orchestra chairs and the dress circle, 50 cents for the orchestra circle and the family circle, 35 cents for the balcony, and 25 cents for the gallery. Rankin hired a competent staff including an electrician, master machinist, scenic designer, doorkeeper, orchestra leader, janitor, advertising agent, treasurers, and so on. He asked Fred Maeder to be stage manager and Frank Curtis to be manager. The theater opened to full houses with Joseph Jefferson in *Rip Van Winkle* on September 3, 1883.

If novelty was enough to attract audiences, then Rankin's Third Avenue Theatre made a good beginning. Electric lighting was novel. So, too, was Jefferson's playing on the East Side. He had not played east of Fifth Avenue since he preceded George Fox as low comedian at the old Chatham Theatre thirty years earlier. But come October, when the West Side dramatic houses would be in full operation, Rankin feared that the crowds would be lured away. By November 1, there would be twenty-six theaters running in New York. Moreover, the problem with the Third Avenue Theatre was its location upon the line of elevated railway. Whereas the Standard and Booth Theatres on the West Side had trains stop noiselessly in front of them, bringing commuters to see their productions, the trains dashed by the Third Avenue Theatre at full speed and often carried cattle to supply the slaughterhouses above Forty-Second Street.[250]

The Third Avenue Theatre was not Rankin's only concern. He had contracted his Chicago company to open the reconstructed Grand Opera House in Milwaukee on August 27, for which he employed Frederick Bryton, a handsome young leading man, a new manager, and a new treasurer. He produced Robertson's *Caste*, the play with which he had opened the same theater twelve years before. Rankin revived his role as Captain Hawtree and Blanchard again played Esther Eccles. Isabelle Evesson played Polly Eccles. *Caste* was followed by Robertson's *School* and Boucicault's *The Corsican Brothers*. The city's elite packed the house for the first night and encouraged good houses for the company's visit.

When Rankin took the Chicago company to St Louis, Blanchard fell ill again and Isabelle Evesson took her roles. The company played *'49* and *The Corsican Brothers* to fair business for a week. The Rankins caught the train for New York to check into their new theater, which Frank Curtis was managing. They were in time to see Jefferson close and Clara Morris succeed him in *Camille*. Morris had everyone talking about her performance because she dragged it out to the point where she was unable to dismiss the audience until a few minutes before midnight. It was good for the box office.

Jumping back to Chicago, the Rankins rejoined their company to play *'49* at Hooley's for a week to good houses. They were called "the only true exponents of truly American drama." Blanchard was commended for her fine acting, despite being so ill that her dressing room had to be built onstage for her accommodation and her understudy stood ready to step onstage at every performance. Yet, when the Rankins came to their Third Avenue Theatre in *'49* on October 1, 1883, they encountered scarcely half a house in attendance. Theatre patrons on the East Side had not been exposed to the frontier drama and had not known what to expect. Moreover, some critics declared the frontier drama dead. Blanchard had got back her old vivacity and mimetic talent and looked young and fresh. Rankin was still good as Old '49, but the critic commented that he should take on some new roles: he was too good an actor to remain in such western character parts. The actor playing Colonel James, the brusque lawyer, brought down the house by his clever mannerisms. By the following week, audiences were crowding the house to see *The Danites*. The papers reported continuous applause and laughter. But Blanchard was ill again, and Cora Tanner took her roles. Frank Curtis, the theater manager, played the Parson with humor. The play lasted for two weeks and could have gone on, but Rankin had to keep his engagement with the Union Square Company, which, it was reported, at a weekly salary of $500, would bring him $14,000 a season.

Another concern requiring Rankin's attention was his management of the company of Mr and Mrs George S. Knight, who played comic roles with German accents, and who toured widely and usually successfully in popular comedies. Employing casts, arranging the route, making the theater arrangements, and promoting companies took time and effort, but Rankin was frequently involved in the management of musicals and dramas while touring with his own companies and seemed to relish the challenge.

The Union Square company had been playing in San Francisco but was in Chicago when Rankin joined it on October 22, the day after he closed in New York. He immediately began rehearsing during the day for the new drama *Storm Beaten* with the company at Haverly's Theatre while opening the next evening in his own production of '49 at the Criterion Theatre. The cast in '49 was excellent, and Rankin did a good business for two weeks while the Union Square Company continued playing at Haverly's. On November 9, rehearsals of *Storm Beaten* ended, and, rather than try out the play in Chicago as planned, the company moved on to Philadelphia to perform *A Parisian Romance* and *The Rantzaus* for a week. The star was the young Richard Mansfield, who was regarded as heir to the classical and heroic schools of acting. In *A Parisian Romance*, Mansfield played a decrepit old roué, Baron Chevral, with a realism that was unique. His success in this play required it be extended for a week. Mansfield was on a short contract to the company, but he liked the plays he was doing and canceled his other engagements in order to stay with the company when it moved to Philadelphia and then to Brooklyn. Rankin continued with the company during this time and opened at the Union Square Theatre in *Storm Beaten* on November 26, 1883.[251]

Rankin's performance as the rugged Christianson was applauded by some, although his voice showed traces of recent bronchial troubles. Others complained that Rankin neither looked the part nor played it well.

In physique he was too fat and in method he was too heavy. "With the habit of the stage at his fingers' end," wrote a critic, "there is always an uncertainty about him which grows probably out of his identification with Nevada miners who talk bad English."[252] It was an easy and superficial criticism to tie him with western characters and a more severe one to complain about his weight. Actually, he was fatter before he went to Chicago and had lost weight so that he could play the role. A critic convinced that he had become too abdominal to play heroic roles met him on the street on his return and found him minus forty pounds and looking ten years younger. "Dumb bells and diet have combined to make this change," he wrote. "He looks now just about as he did when he went to playing Sandy McGee, and I presume he won't change anymore for years to come."[253] Rankin was back with actors E.L. Tilton, John Parselle, and J.H. Stoddart, who had remained with the Union Square company since he left it years before.

Meanwhile, Blanchard managed their Third Avenue Theatre with Frank Curtis. Kate Claxton and her husband, Charles Stevenson, were starring in the melodrama *Sea of Ice* there. Following them were the Florences playing their classic *The Mighty Dollar* to an audience that filled the upper parts of the house. This meant that the cheaper seats were bringing in the income—a losing proposition. Illustrious stars visited for a week at a time: Richard Mansfield in *A Parisian Romance*, Madame Janauschek in *Mary Stuart*, *Bleak House*, and other melodramas, the Yiddish star M.B. Curtis in *Sam'l of Posen*, the Salisbury Troubadors, and Emily Rigle in *The Planter's Wife*.

The criticisms of Rankin at the Union Square Theatre continued. He was said to rant, which he had never done earlier. The notion that a cheaper actor could do the role as well and that Rankin would better earn his $500 weekly salary on the road appeared in the papers. Regardless of the critics' warnings, the public liked *Storm Beaten* and gave it a long run. The criticisms may have prompted Rankin to relinquish his secure position on January 20, 1884, and open at his own theater on the 21st in a new play, another western, *Gabriel Conroy*, to which he and Blanchard had purchased the rights.

Gabriel Conroy was an adaptation of Bret Harte's novel of the same name. Rankin had supervised its dramatization by a Boston writer, and, despite his expressed concerns for the waning popularity of westerns, he hoped that it would replace *'49* as a crowd-pleaser. The fact that he rehearsed the play with a first-rate company at the Theatre Comique from early January demonstrated his determination to have a success. It remained a week at his theater. The critics thought it dragged through a prologue and four acts and lacked dramatic episodes. The story about miners and lost deeds to valuable claims had been told too often, and both Blanchard and Rankin were replaying their old western roles under new names. Rankin received the brunt of the criticism. "In girth he suggested a sort of blood-pudding Sandy. Being the passive and not the active member of the cast throughout, he might have yielded his part to a utility man with the assurance that it would have been done as well."[254] Since Harte's novel had a meandering plot, any play that tried to be faithful to it would come to grief. Rankin, however, had hopes for it. He took the cast to Baltimore for a week and returned to New York claiming that he was delighted with the play. At both his Third Avenue Theatre and in Baltimore, the audiences were small at first but increased at each performance.

At this point, another family emergency affected his plans. With both of his daughters very ill, he canceled a week's engagement in Philadelphia and stayed with them in New York while he revised the play and leased the Third Avenue Theatre to C.A. Stevenson, the actor husband of Kate Claxton. Kate Claxton rearranged the auditorium and the seating over a weekend to make it more comfortable.

As his daughters convalesced, Rankin played *Gabriel Conroy* at the Opera House in Brooklyn for a week to a fair business, but the play still was not right. He cut the characters from eleven to six and restructured the play.[255] When he took it to Pittsburgh at the end of February 1884, a critic declared that it was free from the rubbish that generally abounds in Western drama and had thrilling situations. Frederick Bryton, as the gambler Jack Mason, was the hit of the evening. The cast was superior to the ordinary traveling combination. Yet the reports from the towns where they played one-night stands all suggested that the play needed work. It was reported that a fifth act, showing the married life of Gabriel Conroy, was to be added. In Richmond, the play failed to draw, but, in Milwaukee, large and enthusiastic crowds filled the theater. Chicago gave Rankin a good-sized audience for a week. Here he made some changes in the cast. In Indianapolis, the company did good business in early April.

On his last stop of the season, the week of April 7, an opera troupe wanted the venue, and the manager canceled Rankin. The opera troupe then decided not to appear, and a frustrated manager asked Rankin to fill the time, which Rankin obdurately refused to do. Finally, Rankin agreed on condition that he receive a guarantee of $2,000 for the week. As a result, he came away with a nice profit for this Holy Week; had he played under his original contract, he barely would have made expenses.

Soon, however, his impulsive nature brought him another loss. Rankin had leased the Union Square Theatre for a month from April 12 to present a new society play, *Wife and Child*, which he had written with Fred

Maeder. Rankin had done most of the work, while Maeder wrote a few comic scenes. Rankin had initially hoped to sweep New York with it, but he had to acknowledge that the play was not a good enough draw and shelved it. The company disbanded. To pay for the $7,200 rent for four unused weeks, the Rankins assigned to Shook and Collier of the Union Square Theatre a mortgage held by them on Stevenson's lease of the Third Avenue Theatre.[256]

Rankin retreated to Bois Blanc Island, where he entertained young Frederick Bryton while Blanchard collected their daughters in New York and joined him on the island. On Rankin's recommendation, Bryton became leading man in Clara Morris's company for the next season.

By the end of July 1884, Rankin was back in New York and negotiating with Kate Claxton over the Third Avenue Theatre. She discovered that she had lost $20,000 in the theater over the past season and would have to pay another $7,000 to resume its management. Rankin reluctantly agreed to take it back, but it was a white elephant and he fell into a depressed state. He still owed the contractors and other workmen. Frank Curtis remained as acting manager. One of the dramatic journals remarked that Curtis shared the profits but avoided sharing in the losses.

Returning to Bois Blanc Island for August, Rankin had to consider how he was to finance his theater, but his financial troubles were forgotten in the face of a more serious blow—the death of his mother. While Colonel and Mary Rankin were visiting him, Mary died from a stroke. The unexpectedness of her passing, coming amidst the hopes and celebrations of McKee's theatrical success, cast a pall over the remainder of the summer and served as a presentiment that the good times were over.

1884–1885

Rankin's Cooperative Stock Company

Rankin opened his Third Avenue Theatre for a new season on September 1, 1884, with a stock company, one of a handful in the country, in the conviction that this was the only way to bring good drama to the public. He started well. He employed Edgar Davenport, one of the acting sons of the late E.L. Davenport, as his leading man and introduced an innovation— female ushers. Neat young women, uniformed in black dresses with white collars, cuffs, caps, and aprons, showed patrons to their seats with dispatch and courtesy. He and Blanchard played the major roles in '49 with verve, but their support was nervous. By the end of the week, Rankin had to release some of his company because business did not warrant him continuing the season in stock. He brought in a combination company to play *Nobody's Claim*, but their bad acting caused turbulence in the audience, which guyed the actors unmercifully. Three small boys were arrested by police at the close of the performance to "vindicate metropolitan law and order." The play was denounced as a "mass of stupid sensational claptrap."[257] Rankin lowered his prices.

The next week, Rankin brought in *Storm Beaten*. Audiences were large, but the actors were indifferent and the play was tedious. The following week, a touring star, Joseph Murphy, had a popular reception in *The Kerry Gow*, and then Clara Morris arrived with Bryton in support for an uneven performance in *Miss Multon*. The audiences were immense, but Clara Morris was not strong enough to play all the performances. Katharine Rogers, one-time mistress of Boucicault, took her role for the Saturday matinee.

Frank Chanfrau was expected to play his famous *Kit, the Arkansas Traveler* and to reprise his much beloved Mose in *A Glance at New York in 1848*, but he died suddenly two days before he was scheduled to appear. Rankin scrambled to piece together a company, which put on *A Child of the State* in his stead. The audience again was small, but the play was enjoyable.

Rankin decided to gamble on involving the audience in the play as a way of attracting patrons. He announced *A Play—A Plot*, in which members of the audience were to suggest a better title, the winner receiving $1,000. The Rankins had leading parts, and Frank Mordaunt, now an experienced actor from the Philadelphia and New York theaters, took a major role. The plot was called "silly," and the play's three acts comprised some music and a smattering of scenic and choral effects. Blanchard enlivened it with the dances and burlesque of a quarter-century earlier. She frightened the audience when she tripped making an entrance, but, fortunately, she damaged only her dress. The play drew badly, but with the assurance of a born gambler, Rankin tested it for another week. With his next production, *The Silent Man* by Joaquin Miller, he seemed to hope that some mystic success might arise from the old Miller–Rankin combination. Miller's play was panned as a jumble of border dramas devoid of plot and originality. Mordaunt's imitation of a drunken landowner suffering from *mania-a-potu* was the best bit of acting. Rankin was devoting all his time to every aspect of his theater and was doing all the jobs—taking tickets, keeping the door, and so on. One benefit came from his unconquerable and innovative spirit: he started developing the cast that was to form his stock company along Saxe-Meiningen lines.

Rankin closed his theater for a few days in mid-November and opened in '49 in Williamsburg with a company that included some of the great supporting actors of the day: Theodore Hamilton, with whom he had acted in Lucille Western's company; Frank Mordaunt; J.J. Wallace, who had acted in some of his companies in the recent past; Richard Halley, who was also the scenic designer; and Dan Harkins, with whom he had acted in the 1860s. These actors, with the Rankins, were the core of his new stock company and were bound by articles of cooperation for three years, at the termination of which a majority of the seven could bind all of them to another three years. They received no salary but divided the profits or shared the losses after paying the rent and salaries of the few hired members of the company. Rankin, as the stage manager, had supreme power in casting, and no member of the starring stock could refuse to play a part assigned to him or her.[258]

For their first play at the Third Avenue Theatre, Rankin chose *Notice to Quit*, which had failed in England but which, he thought, might be successful in the United States as it was considered to be a powerful play. Two brothers and a third villainous character scheme to get certain estates from the rightful heir, whose resistance was rewarded by his ingeniously locating the all-important page in the church register. Rankin played John Rivers, a nasty villain. Bijou Heron, the daughter of the late Matilda Heron, took the role of the heroine. The play closed after an unprofitable run of three weeks. Rankin tried another British play, a heavy melodrama, *Brought to Justice*, introduced, like *Notice to Quit*, for the first time in America. The company acted it with an excellence hardly justified by the script, which told of the wickedness and downfall of a villain who wreaked havoc on a decent farmer, played by Rankin, and on the wife of a weak husband, played by Blanchard. The play failed to draw, which finally persuaded Rankin to sell his theater.[259] To fill his last week as manager, Rankin brought James Herne in his popular play *Hearts of Oak*.

M.B. Leavitt, who started in the theatrical profession as a minstrel singer, and Tony Pastor, Kitty Blanchard's friend from her early years in burlesque, took over the Third Avenue Theatre and rechristened it as a combination house—"a combination of legs, beauty and high art, commencing with 'An Adamless Eden'." Leavitt commented: "Had Rankin been anything like as clever a business man as he was an actor, he would have amassed a great fortune."[260] In a gesture of solidarity, Rankin's fellow theater managers arranged a benefit for him at Lester Wallack's Theatre on January 15, 1885, but it rained heavily and the small attendance brought in only $700. The Rankins with their strong stock company set out to play *Notice to Quit* at a theater in Harlem two days later, then stopped for a week in Toronto.

The company and the play were declared good, but business was only fair. It opened in Chicago on February 2, 1885, but failed to draw. The local critic ridiculed Rankin: "Playgoers may see with pain the stalwart Sandy, the hero of the Sierras, playing the villain and committing robbery in the first act, arson in the second, and murder in the third. When they observe his walk, however—that slow, rolling, seaman-like walk—they will admit that it at least is villainous, however little the remainder of the part may suit the actor's abilities."[261] Rankin was disappointed with the play's reception when everyone agreed that the company was first rate. Instead of the scheduled three weeks, the company stayed for one week and left for a number of one-night stands. Under the auspices of Leavitt, it intended to tour from Chicago to the West Coast and back.

Leavitt had bought Rankin's *The Danites* some months previously when Rankin badly needed money, and now he proposed that the play be part of the company's repertoire. Leavitt booked the company to play it at the Salt Lake City theater because of the great publicity that this anti-Mormon play, when performed in the heart of Mormonism, would generate. Rankin protested vigorously, but Leavitt assured him that he had told the Mormons that all elements offensive to them would be eliminated from the production, and they had left the matter in Rankin's hands.

In trying to develop a profitable company, Rankin was fighting the business climate, which was regarded as the worst of the nineteenth century to that point.[262] Bank failures and business suspensions took place in unprecedented numbers. The country had just gone through a fierce political campaign, which was unparalleled for its bitterness and which elected Grover Cleveland as the first Democratic president since the Civil War. Numerous acting companies were collapsing. The *Mirror* claimed that the theater world was populated by too many vampires—that is, sharp and unscrupulous managers, bringing it into disrepute. It advocated the uniting of actors into the American Dramatic Protective Association to help actors stranded in small western towns by managers without means to pay for food and lodging. Traveling in a series of one-night stands meant rising at three in the morning to catch a train, waiting in cold, dreary stations, and playing in shabby halls with no conveniences in the dressing rooms. Actresses came on stage with teeth chattering, hardly able to speak their lines, and often playing opposite actors who were disgusting in manner and person. But the sorry fact was that acting was one of the few ways in which young women could distinguish themselves and become economically independent. The women stars made the profession seem glamorous, and many young debutantes paid for the privilege of appearing on stage in the hope that they could make a career. Rankin sometimes gave debutantes roles for a night or two, which was long enough to help them discover their inadequacies as actors.

On the coldest day of the winter on the way to its first stop, about twenty-five miles from St Joseph, Missouri, the company was marooned when its train was stuck in a snowdrift for ten hours. Some actors, who had planned to eat in St Joseph, had not got up in time to eat breakfast at the regular eating station. By the time they arrived in town, they had gone for thirty hours without food. The company played to a small but very appreciative audience.[263]

The following night in Leavenworth, Kansas, the company was told that there had not been a more striking performance in that town in many years. In Topeka the next night, the local critic declared it the best troupe ever to visit the town. Theodore Hamilton and Alma Stanley were hailed as important to the play's success. On the next stop, Kansas City, Missouri, the audience gave the company an enthusiastic welcome and filled the theater for the three nights it played there. Anticipating the next engagement, however, Rankin feared for the safety of his company. He was to play *The Danites* from February 18 to 20 in Salt Lake City. Providentially, a great snowstorm made the railway impassable, and a relieved Rankin canceled the engagement with a promise to play there for three nights on the company's return from the West Coast. The company headed straight for San Francisco, arriving in time to open in *'49* at the Bush Street Theatre on February 23, 1885. The theater manager had awakened the public to Rankin's arrival, which brought out a crowded house on the first night and contributed to the play's success.

Critics and the public both loved the production. Rankin was considered a better actor than Jefferson. Another critic called him the American Salvini, at the time considered the world's best actor: "His rich mellow voice, his figure, and his actions all recall the great Italian."[264] Rankin was said to have played Old '49 "with such sustained power, such unexaggerated truth that it rivets the attention." He was "the ideal pioneer that makes you feel all his poetry and grace of heart."[265] "The humor which brightens the character a little is never forced or overdone," said the *San Francisco Examiner*. "It is a twinkle of the eye rather than a broad laugh, and it is a fine contrast to the hearty bluff jokes, shrewd slang, and unconscious, ingenuous humor of Carrots."[266] Blanchard was praised for playing with great abandon and with touches of human nature that made her performance as Carrots "little short of genius." The play was variously called "a gem," "far above any of the kindred plays," and a work of "furious realism" reminiscent of Emile Zola.[267]

Rankin's achievement was to tell the story of '49's broken and desolate life without a touch of staginess or claptrap. He had modeled his mannerisms and his makeup after his uncle, Alexander (Sandy) McKee, the real '49, which made his characterization so realistic. His cast of stars were successful: Theodore Hamilton, J.J. Wallace, Frank Mordaunt, Dan Harkins, Charles Edmunds, and Alma Stuart Stanley.[268] A talented comedian and a famous male impersonator, Stanley soon quit to go on the road with her own company. Rankin continued with '49 for a second week.

Large audiences came to the theater despite the strong counter attraction of the opera, for which ticket scalpers were out in force. Two scalpers, one of whom was Ike Belasco, one of David Belasco's actor brothers, squared off in a spectacular fight that the deputy sheriff had to stop. Rankin countered with his own brand of publicity. He gave a box seat to Baldy Hamilton, a well-known stage driver of the Sierras, who had been a long-time friend of his uncle, Sandy McKee. Baldy found that the stage character of Old '49 was a facsimile of his friend Sandy, and the episode in the play of the coon dinner was so familiar a tale that he was shaken in doubt concerning the accepted rumor that Sandy had "passed in his checks."[269] That is, died. Actually, Sandy McKee worked as the caretaker of Rankin's property on Bois Blanc Island.

Rankin produced *The Danites* for the third week. Leavitt advertised *The Danites* as having done as much as all the sermons of all the ministers "to arouse and intensify the bitter Anti-Mormon sentiment."[270] Since the company planned to take the play to Salt Lake City, such publicity, regardless of its draw in San Francisco, seemed foolhardy. The play was called as absorbing as when first produced in San Francisco, and the star company was considered better than the first cast.[271]

A novelty was the introduction of a Chinese-American actor for the first time on the mainstream American stage. Ah Gow, better know as Alphonso, a local Chinese celebrity whose paintings were popular with San Franciscans, played Washee Washee with the self-possession of a veteran. The *Examiner* wrote that a more successful debut in the city had seldom been seen.[272] Alphonso took advantage of his sudden prominence on the stage to advertise himself as a guide through Chinatown who spoke German and English and as the only Chinese artist in the country to understand perspective in painting.

The Danites played a week, after which Rankin put on *Notice to Quit*, but it was no competition for the opera. Rankin tried an old favorite, *Uncle Tom's Cabin*, and cast himself as Uncle Tom rather than in his usual role of George Harris, and Blanchard played Topsy. The audience was dismally small. To make matters worse, the chief drawing card, Blanchard, fell ill and was replaced with Ida Aubrey. The play ran four nights. On Friday, March 20, rather than the old-style benefit, which had been long out of favor, a testimonial was given the Rankins for presenting a program of "rare Ideal Representation." The company played '49 and repeated it for the Saturday matinee. On Saturday and Sunday evenings, it again tried *Notice to Quit*. On the Monday, it moved to the Baldwin Theatre and opened in *Storm Beaten*. The Baldwin had become a fashionable theater since the English actress and beauty Lily Langtry attracted crowds to it the year before. The move restored Rankin's fortunes. Leavitt said later that he agreed to the move to the Baldwin, which was under Al Hayman, and to whom he had provided the capital to buy it, only because the company was so popular and its receipts so large. In fact, Leavitt, aware that his contract with Rankin was to expire during the Baldwin engagement, gave his consent only when Rankin endorsed on its back that he would continue under Leavitt's management until the complete circuit of Leavitt's theaters had been covered, which would bring Rankin back to the Missouri River.[273]

With new and picturesque scenery, the vivid and brilliant dialogue of *Storm Beaten* drew crowded houses. Lewis Morrison joined the company with some other actors from the East, which contributed to the play's success. Blanchard made a demure and tender little Quaker as Priscilla Sefton. Rankin was the most notable as Christianson, the alert, graceful, and impassioned young hero of romance. The versatility proved by his transformation to this character from the conventional Uncle Tom and the rough but tenderhearted old '49 impressed San Franciscans. As stage manager, he also received plaudits for creating the best-balanced and strongest organization in the country. Every production was admirable for its attention to detail.[274]

The economy on the West Coast was coming out of the long recession induced by the Panic of 1873, the effects of which did not reach the West until 1878 but were deep until an economic upsurge in the mid-eighties. Rankin rejoiced in the recovery and saw it as creating an opportunity to bring great theater to the people. Leavitt, who was visiting San Francisco, learned from an agent of the Union Pacific Railway that Rankin had applied for the redemption of his return tickets from San Francisco to the East; he also discovered that Rankin was negotiating for a three-year lease of the California Theatre, which John McCullough and Lawrence Barrett had made so prominent in the early seventies. Rankin needed the $1,300 from the value of the railway tickets to make the first payment. When Leavitt refused to sanction the redemption of the rail tickets, Rankin came to his hotel in a high state of indignation. "The interview between us was both long and heated," Leavitt remembered, "but when, at its conclusion,

Rankin appealed to my good nature, and recounted his own misfortunes, I yielded the point at issue, upon consideration of a new contract that at any time I might call upon him to do so, no matter how great his current success in San Francisco might be, he would take up the tour where it had been broken off."[275]

Leavitt's reluctance was probably owing to Al Hayman's growing influence in San Francisco theaters. By leasing the California Theatre to Jay Rial, his business manager, and Rankin, Hayman was presenting Leavitt's Bush Street Theatre with strong competition. Hayman typified the new breed of unscrupulous theater manager. Having learned his trade from Charles Frohman and Colonial Jack Haverly, Hayman worked under Leavitt until, with Leavitt's help, he took over the Baldwin Theatre and entered into a fierce rivalry with Fred Bert, who ran the California Theatre. While Bert was in New York City booking productions for the California, three of Hayman's men gained access to the theater with a duplicate key obtained from a stagehand. Led by a former police officer, they posted themselves outside the box office, where three of Bert's men had barricaded themselves. They shouted "fire," and when the door opened, the men barged in brandishing pistols. Lawsuits followed, and by a legal ploy Hayman gained control of the California Theatre. Hayman, however, used it only on occasion and preferred to lease it because his aim was to form a powerful western monopoly and a national syndicate. The great Ristori was presently playing in the theater with her own company in Giacommetti's *Queen Elizabeth*. Rankin, who procured an interest in the financial department of the California Theatre, was to open there after his tour of the West.

On his road trip, which had been arranged earlier, Rankin maintained the fiction that this superb company soon would be returning east and implied that now was the only chance to see it. The first stop was Oakland, California, for three nights followed by Portland, Oregon, for two weeks, where they played in the New Market Frye's Opera House, renovated and newly frescoed to make it the handsomest theater in the northwest. Tickets for Rankin's engagement were sold far in advance. When the company put on *'49*, *The Danites*, and *Storm Beaten*, it met with one long continuous success, and *Storm Beaten* was a hit. "It serves to show," wrote a critic, "how theatergoers respond when a good company comes this way."[276]

Rankin's company did one-night stands in towns such as Tacoma, Salem, and Astoria, and spent three nights in Victoria, British Columbia, at the Victoria Theatre, where Thomas Ward and his troupe had played for years and where the young David Belasco fell in love with theater. It traveled through the Sound country circuit of Oregon and Northern California, enjoying success all the way to Los Angeles, where it opened for two weeks in mid-May. At the close of a performance of '49, Blanchard was called before the curtain and a woman tore off her corsage bouquet and threw it upon the stage. This acted as a signal to other women, who did the same, and soon the astonished but delighted Blanchard was up to her knees in roses.

1885–1886

Successful San Francisco Days

San Francisco was the largest city in the West, with a population of about 670,000 in the mid-eighties. It had elegant shops, excellent restaurants, and a hotel system unrivaled in the world, according to a theater historian. The most luxurious accommodation at the Palace and Grand Hotels was $5 a day. At respectable hotels, room and board was $1 a day. Kearney Street was fashionable, and Market Street on the north side, with its new hotels, the Baldwin Theatre and Hotel, was beginning to rival it. The South Side housed the working people and was characterized by small restaurants, open markets, tintype galleries selling cheap ironware, dime museums, inexpensive theaters, and panoramas. Bush Street housed the older shops and the main theater district, in which was found the California Theatre. The streets teemed with vehicles such as advertising wagons from which venders would sing out loudly and ring bells noisily. Sidewalks were crowded with a leisurely moving throng. A telephone system was put in place in 1880. There were electric streetlights and street railways. Hackney carriages would take one to the theater from one's home for $3. Ferries traveled at all times to the neighboring towns. A special theater train left for outlying towns every night at 11:45 PM.

In the 1880s, the middle class became the theatergoers, and, unlike the upper class of preceding decades, it did not feel that it was mandatory to attend the Baldwin Theatre on Monday evenings. It was a more intelligent audience and sampled the fare at all the theaters. The first-class theaters, in order of importance, were the Baldwin, the California, the Opera House, the Bush Street, and the Standard. They all had to endure the ear-splitting noises from the "gamins" in the gallery, and some actors such as C.B. Bishop played to the gallery patrons with old-style fun-making. The most disruptive gallery patrons were from the hoodlum class that came to prominence in the 1880s. Theatres employed special police to control them. These rough and rowdy gangs of boys and girls roamed the streets at night and attacked citizens. They were a phenomenon in the West; the East had its own long-standing problems with homeless children, called street Arabs, who swarmed the eastern cities throughout the century. Gallery patrons in San Francisco were also from the lower economic brackets, including many Italians and Irish who were visibly and audibly demonstrative. In contrast, in the dress circle and orchestra was the fashionable class, including rows of wealthy women in handsome outfits.[277]

In early June, Rankin returned to San Francisco from Los Angeles and rehearsed his troupe in new plays that he had obtained from theaters on the East Coast. His troupe melded with the actors who were in the California Theatre Company, which brought him additional talent, including most importantly the great comedian Charles Bishop and the young actress Isabelle Morris. Alma Stuart Stanley came back, finding employment in Rankin's company preferable to the uncertain returns of touring. Rankin was still pursuing his stock company share plan for his core actors and paying the others salaries. Theodore Hamilton and Charles Edmunds intended to return to New York, presumably being released from their contract of three years by finding substitutes. Hamilton, however, soon began starring in the rival San Francisco Grand Opera House.

Dion Boucicault, who had arrived to produce a play, expressed doubt that the Rankins could revive the California Theatre; it was like "an empty lot where the ruined tomb lies sacred to the memory of McCullough," he said.[278] In response, Rankin immediately had signs printed reading "Standing Room Only." The Rankins and Boucicault could agree that the New York theaters had deteriorated because their managers, aside from Daly, were all showmen. Both thought that the number of stock companies would increase in large cities as a result.

Rankin had known his partner, Jay Rial, since meeting him in a little theater in St Louis fifteen years earlier. He was Leonard Grover's brother-in-law. Rial was gentle in manner and honorable in business with a stage knowledge that would discipline the company and create good results behind the curtain. Rankin was likewise confident in his business manager, E.D. Price, whom he had known for years as a journalist. Price had unbounded energy and plenty of ambition.

Rankin opened at the California Theatre on June 15, 1885, in an adaptation from the French, *The Pavements of Paris*, which he had secured from Hayman. Rankin hired a mechanical engineer to construct an engine to be propelled across the stage by steam. He hired additional actors, including Jean Clara Walters, because the play had thirty-two speaking parts. The play had quick and stirring action, melodramatic situations, a great variety of incidents, and strongly marked characters. Rankin played the Vicomte de Flachon with a look of jaunty dilapidation and airiness of manner that belied an eager watchfulness for every chance of an advantage.[279]

Flachon was acclaimed as Rankin's best role. The critics said that Rankin was one of the few actors worthy to be called an artist because, with each new role he played, he deepened audiences' appreciation of him. "His penetration extends to the most widely differing types of character and he presents each with the smoothness and faithfulness of a good portrait and the detailed clearness of a photograph."[280] The third act particularly illustrated his complete grasp of character: "His bitter brooding when he is alone and does not need the disguise of an assumed gayety; his involuntary return, when he first meets the Countess, to something like the gentlemanly bearing that was his right by birth and education; his fierce denunciation of his villainous associate; his cool contempt for the latter's plan to use him as a cat's paw; and his final lapse into the low merriment of the degraded creatures who are his only friends—all these show how exhaustively he has studied the art."[281]

The attraction of the elaborate mechanical effects, a railway scene, and the beautiful tableaux were secondary to Rankin's mastery at staging: the symmetrically arranged network of scenes, characters, and incidents; the bustle of life; the variety of character; and the constant and picturesque changing of scenery. One of the most popular scenes, especially with the gallery, was the ragpicker's wedding, at which a wedding dance filled the ragpicker's paradise with color and boisterous gaiety. In the last act, Flachon's descent from the garret to the cellar in the murder scene required a thoroughness of illustration that Rankin worked out in detail with the scenic artist.

The scenic painter was coming into greater prominence than in the past, particularly in America. Traditionally in America, up to the beginning of the nineteenth century, theaters stocked ready-mixed colors—brickwall color, tree color, kitchen color, sky color. Scenery at different theaters was all based on the same conventional model. In England, the famous English landscapist and architect Inigo Jones began designing stage decorations of a superior character in the seventeenth century, as did Sir John Vanbrugh at Covent Garden in the early 1700s. These early efforts inspired the actor Charles Kean after 1850 to create modern scenery at the Princess Theatre in London with the costumes and architecture of the periods in which the plays were set. The actor Samuel Phelps followed suit at Sadler's Wells and encouraged a growing class of painters such as Clarkson Stanfield. Then David Roberts elevated the scenic art to a sense of grandeur and reliance on detail. British artists such as Beverly, Grieves, and Talbin brought a flow of artistic talent to the British theater about 1860. In the late 1860s, when *The Black Crook* opened in New York, it gave an impetus to the art in America by introducing a scale of magnificence unsurpassed at the time. Its ballroom scene, for instance, had three vistas of columns, thirty-two in number, each being in a group of three detached shafts that were arranged so as to be seen through. The columns and capitals were in dead or dull silver, the latter profusely perforated and lighted from behind, while at the foot of each column were three lifelike figures holding up branches of lights. The borders of the scene were in dull gold and perfected in patterns so that when the whole was lit up with many hundreds of small gas lights, the effect was that of glass columns supporting a roof of golden lace.[282]

The artist who created these scenes in the New York production, Richard Marston, later went to the Union Square Theatre, where Rankin knew him for his work in *The Two Orphans*. Marston achieved a distinction that placed his work beyond adverse criticism and began teaching the public the art of distemper painting, where pigment is mixed with an element that is soluble in water like egg yoke or glue, with astonishing success. This artistic education of the American public led to an appreciation for art and decoration that was brought into the home, fostering individual tastes and encouraging an independent approach among upholsterers and decorators. A sense of the beautiful pervaded the popular mind and grew with the progress of scenic stage art.[283]

William Voegtlin had been scenic painter at the California Theatre for some years. His scenery helped Rankin's production of *The Pavements of Paris* take the public by storm. In its second week, it grossed $6,000, which equaled the combined revenue of any other two houses. No one was more surprised than Rankin that for every performance he had to use the "Standing Room Only" signs that he had had printed simply to rebuke Boucicault. The play could have had a very long run, but Rankin replaced it after two weeks on the principle that the public deserved new plays and should not be abused by the worst commercial instincts.

Rankin produced one of his favorites, Lester Wallack's *The Veteran*, a stirring military drama set in France and Algeria at the time of the Algerian War. It was gorgeously costumed, and its six tableaux were breathtaking views of the sultan's palace, a ruined mosque on the edge of the desert, the French villa of the veteran, Colonel Delmar, the Zouave camp in Algiers, the Princess of Gulnare's boudoir, and a battle scene ending in the torching of the city. Rankin hired scenic artist William Porter to replace Voegtlin, who had done the early scenes. There were twenty-two speaking parts and one hundred supernumeraries as Nautch dancers, Zouaves, Arabs, fan bearers, and so on. Each character was marked by a substantial individuality and the whole was an astonishingly varied and picturesque assemblage. "Everywhere," wrote a critic, "there were signs of intelligent stage management evident."[284]

Frank Mordaunt acted as Colonel Delmar, the veteran, a fine, soldierly, hot-tempered, warmhearted, loyal old gentleman. Rankin, who had trained down to slender proportions, played his son, Leon Delmar, the role that Lester Wallack had made famous. Although his individuality was less distinct than usual, Rankin brought out all that was in the character—manly lover, gallant soldier. One critic was gratified that he had grown back his mustache, which he had shaved off with his beard for *The Pavements of Paris*: "That happy, corn-fed-boy look has vanished and as Leon he is his handsome self once more." Charles B. Bishop played Ofl-an-agan, the grand vizier, bringing immediate laughter to his comic exploits in the first two acts. Dan Harkins as Emir Mohammed took on an exotic stateliness in robe and turban, with his robust arms and strongly marked face stained to Arab darkness. "The two stalwart figures," remarked the critic of the Emir and Colonel Delmar, "make a picture for an artist when they stand together in the Sultan's hall, the one the living expression of barbaric pride, the other the personification of civilized courage."[285] The beautiful face and supple figure of Alma Stuart Stanley as Gulnare, Chief Sultana, suited the graceful draperies "perfectly," and her remarkably good acting carried off the strange effect of her bare feet with rings on her toes. The bare-footed Nautch dancers with shapely brown legs and coquettish adornments also were made credible by Stanley's presence.

Rankin brought Adele Waters into the company to play the pretty Blanche d'Ivry. Her bright and animated comedy joined with Frank Wright's as Oglou to keep the audience amused. The last three acts gave the play its reputation for suspense and melodramatic spectacle. The scenic artist's ingenuity and Rankin's skill in setting the battle scenes contributed to the excitement and strangeness. The play was kept for a second week by audience demand, and it could have continued, but Rankin wanted to produce another grand spectacle, *The King of Diamonds*.

The best theatergoing public returned to Rankin's theater regardless of the bill because they knew that regardless of what play was presented, it would be well done. Rankin's management had a good reputation throughout the area, attributable to his policy of no forced runs, constant new plays, fresh staging, and good acting. Rankin and Rial had an agent in Paris on the lookout for new plays. Rankin read a half-dozen plays weekly in the search for good drama.

This policy was Rankin's reply to the great slump in theater attendance across the country. A slew of reasons were put forward for the decline: actors blamed the popularity of dime museums and skating rinks; managers blamed the increasing salaries of the actors at a time when business was not increasing; outsiders blamed the deterioration in the quality of amusement; critics blamed the traveling combination system; still other observers saw the extravagance expended on all kinds of accessories to the drama—scenery, costumes, bric-a-brac, and expensive lithographing—as becoming more important than the acting and the plays and thus driving away the intelligent people. The practice of "billing a town" had been transformed: a dozen years earlier, posters and lithographs were placed in show windows; now, expensive pictorial printing of lithographs, photographs, engravings, and life-sized crayon portraits preceded traveling combinations to make faces and scenes familiar long before the company arrived. Dude-headed canes, terra-cotta statuettes, nickel-plated plaques, cigarettes, and even soap were used to arouse public curiosity about the coming show. The commercialization of the theater was compared to the new Christmas-card craze, in which the simple interchange between friends of flower pictures had become a huge business employing thousands of illustrators and tens of thousands of workers, and which multiplied into an extension of souvenirs for every kind of anniversary known to the calendar. The costs of "the expensive monstrosities" of life-sized portraits of actors in cardboard and beautiful lithography provoked managers to call for a mutual agreement to abolish them, but such an agreement was impossible in a profit-driven economy.[286]

The Duke of Saxe-Meiningen would have approved of Rankin's ability to bring about an interaction of actors and scenery, imbued with detail of the period of the action. Rankin again used his talent to advantage in *The King of Diamonds*, a stirring military drama set in the Transvaal, South Africa. A love story is played out against the struggle between the English and Boers, including a battle scene with seventy-five combatants onstage and a confrontation between the English commander and Shoulders, a drover, whom the English wronged in a former life. Shoulders has a deformed back and Herculean strength. He kills his enemies by crushing them in his arms. Rankin became huge by putting on weight for the part and played it with "hideous realism."[287] As the drunken criminal, who has drowned every generous impulse in gin, Shoulders is willing to sacrifice a young girl's life and honor to shield himself from the consequences of theft, and he accepts money from her after slandering her. But when he repairs this behavior on learning that she is his child, the audience melts into tears and forgets not only his crimes but his contemptible meanness. The play attracted large houses, made the galleries wild with delight, and brought in a profit after a week.

For the weeks that these plays ran in San Francisco, Blanchard was recuperating from illness. She took the air in the Golden Gate Park with one of her daughters and later met with a mishap while boating on the bay. Two rowboats were lashed together and anchored while the parties in them ate lunch. Winds came up, and signs of a squall appeared. The boats separated and headed for shore. The first, with Rankin, his children, Isabel Morris, and Rial, reached the shore, but the second, with Blanchard, Emma Marble, Joe Holland, Hank Johnson, and the Rankins' Chinese servant, was carried out to sea. When they tried to cast anchor, the line broke, and just as it looked as if they would be swept out into the ocean and certain death, a passing yacht stopped to lower boats and bring them aboard. Blanchard had been announced to appear in *A Prisoner for Life*, but the production of the play was indefinitely postponed after this misadventure.[288]

For *Separation*, a society play, Rankin hired Ellie Wilton to play the lead, Dora Blair. She had the rights from the author, Bartley Campbell, to play it. Wilton had not appeared in San Francisco for eight years. A large audience greeted her, and she won back her popularity, making this actionless but emotion-filled play a success. The scene painter, Voegtlin, deserted the company for a better offer from the Union Square Company in New York, and left some scenery to be finished by his apprentice. At this point, Rankin brought in a young man who was called the finest interior painter in the country and perhaps the world—John Mazzanovich. He had apprenticed under Voegtlin, made his name at Wallack's Theatre in New York, and worked at some of the other theaters. In New York, enthusiastic audiences called him out night after night. Thus, it was not surprising that Rankin took the first opportunity to hire him. Mazzanovich had an original style without the slightest conventionalism. He was bold in the handling of his subjects but delicate in his use of color.[289] His geniality endeared him to those who knew him, and socially he was a great favorite, qualities that Rankin prized in his efforts to run his company.

Confident that the company could do society plays, Rankin produced *Led Astray* in August, with Ellie Wilton as Armande Chandoce. Wilton had played Susanne O'Hara, the other woman, in the Union Square production back in the spring of 1874. No actor had equaled her performance. Rankin had played the poet Georges de Lesparre in that production, but this time Harkins took the part, and Rankin played Randolph Chandoce in a manly, earnest manner. Critics were delightfully surprised by his performance: they had thought that his fame as Georges de Lesparre precluded his acting any other part in the play. Ellie Wilton touched a responsive chord in the audience with her gently emotional and sympathetic acting. The cast was excellent and the theater was filled every night as Rankin continued his reputation for matchless productions at half the price of comparable theaters. A critic did deign to criticize him for speaking his lines too quickly, which was noticeable in an actor who took the major roles, although Rankin gave the requisite lightness, proper earnestness, and warm feeling to Randolph. Rankin, who had gained ten pounds while playing Shoulders in *The King of Diamonds*, lost it all playing in *Led Astray*.

Although Rankin's theater seemed to be a success, he was beginning to lose some of his best actors. Ellie Wilton intended to end her engagement at the California Theatre after the last performance of *Led Astray*. Adele Waters, who played Susanne O'Hara, left for Chicago and was replaced by a young actress of promise, Helen Rand, who had come to the city in Madame Janauschek's company. Because Alma Stuart Stanley and a couple of minor members of the company intended to join another company in Portland and work their way overland back east, Rankin replaced her with Louise Rial in mid-week. In addition to his other problems, Rankin was reported to have severely beaten Theodore Hamilton for making disparaging remarks about an actress friend. Such violent behavior was out of character for the genial "Mac."[290] On the bright side, Mordaunt resisted efforts to lure him away to star in another theater, and Frank Wright was rapidly winning fame as a character actor in the company.[291]

Rankin produced the older plays at his theater despite the warnings of people experienced in stage management. *Led Astray* had been played so often that he was warned that there was no freshness left in it, but the audiences continued to grow during the week. "Nothing fails now at the theater where of late years so many promising ventures have come to grief," wrote a critic.[292] One of Rankin's revivals, *The Power of Money*, was full of the stereotyped scenes, characters, and incidents of the old-style melodramas, but its magnificent scenery, especially on the Mississippi River, was so realistic that it attracted those past the point of being entertained by melodrama.[293] Rankin was a hit as General Wordsley, an old millionaire, whose death scene he played extremely well. His makeup for the general was modeled after his own father, the colonel. The execution was so correct that his little girls cried with delight thinking it was their grandfather.

Since the play could not sustain a second week, Rankin hurriedly produced *William and Susan* with himself and his wife in the title roles. This was Blanchard's first appearance at the California Theatre and she was greeted with enthusiasm. In contrast to its disappointing New York premiere, the play was an instant success. Its theme of true love and the pathos of unmerited suffering brought audiences to tears. Patrons drifted as if in a trance out of the theater after the final curtain. The Rankins were the magicians whose beautiful acting generated the enthusiasm. A critic wrote: "True love in trouble never gained greater sympathy than theirs; and in all the delicate little strokes that make both personations works of art, there is not a line too deep, nor a touch too light. It is the modesty of nature itself, in which nothing is obstructed and nothing concealed. Mrs. Rankin is one of the most sympathetic of actresses. The tender cadences of her voice put one in harmony with her at once, and there is not a suggestion of affectation in any place of her acting."[294]

No one had forgotten that as William in the burlesque *Black-eyed Susan* at Selwyn's in Boston sixteen years before, Blanchard had captured the hearts of all the Boston youth. That performance, beside Stuart Robson's Captain Crosstree, was remembered with "enthusiastic, retrospective, smiling sighs," so exasperating to those who did not see it.[295] Moreover, it was reported that, as Susan in this new production, she knit upon the same stocking that Mrs Kendall had used in London and had given to her with the words: "Take up my work where I leave off."

Joe Holland, who played Captain Crosstree in the San Francisco production, was said to have given the best rendition of the character ever seen in the country, which was enormous praise. The adapter of the play, W.G. Wills, had strengthened the characters and beautified the language, which undoubtedly helped Holland in his portrayal. Holland's success as an actor came despite his being stone deaf. He memorized all parts in a play and the length of time to speak each speech. It was said that he could commit to memory a play in a shorter time than any living actor. When he was not facing the speaker onstage, he counted one for each word of the speech so as to pick up his cue at the right time. He blossomed under Rankin's tutelage, particularly in stage pronunciation.

The farce *Wanted—1000 Milliners* preceded the main play. This short piece allowed C.B. Bishop to introduce his comedian son, C.J. Bishop, as a new member of the company and assistant stage manager under Rankin.

The Rankins took minor roles in Daly's *P-I-Q-U-E*, a society play about a woman who, in love with one man, marries another, and after unhappiness and temptation learns to love her husband. Blanchard played Raitch, a hoydenish waif. "While the tender tones of her voice in 'William and Susan' are still haunting one's memory," wrote a critic, "it is something of a shock to hear her first, childishly high-pitched, unmodulated utterances when Raitch is discovered polishing up the fender."[296] Rankin played the tramp Ragmoney Jim, looking villainous in "a wonderfully good sketch." The play was a huge success, and, more than any other play that Rankin had produced, likened to the old-time California Theatre triumphs. Indeed, John McCullough, whose mind was rapidly deteriorating, gave his gladiator's sword to E.D. Price, the manager, who showed it to visitors and spoke about the fallen genius, who, in his lucid moments, rejoiced in the resurrection of his old theater to its former glory.

The continent-wide recognition of Rankin's talent and energies was strongly felt and those hopeful of the revival of stock companies rejoiced in his success. Locally, too, Rankin was popular. He did countless tasks for the local theater community such as becoming an usher at a benefit performance for Charles Thorne, Sr, and playing Fagin at a Sunday benefit for a young actress playing Nancy Sykes.

When David Belasco, the assistant manager at the Baldwin Theatre, was leaving for a post in a New York City theater, Rankin and Maurice Barrymore gave a number of recitations at a testimonial benefit for him. Barrymore, a handsome and athletic young actor with a quick wit, had become a matinee idol on the American stage since his arrival from England and his training in the Daly stock company. Through his colleague in the Daly company, John Drew, Jr, he met John's sister, Georgie, an actress. Barrymore married her and they had three children. Owing to Mrs John Drew and her fondness for Rankin, there developed a closeness between the Rankin and Drew families. Barrymore, therefore, became an intimate friend of the Rankins. He was playing at the Baldwin in support of Madame Janauschek.

The Drew-Rankin relationship typified the close relationships maintained by America's top theatrical families. Joseph Jefferson and his family were close to the Drews and the Rankins and to the great comedian George Holland.[297] Rankin's employment of Holland's sons, especially the disadvantaged Joe, was a token of the family's connections. Similarly, the Rankins' early connections with both the Davenport family and the Mayo family remained strong throughout their acting lives. The Rankins also maintained their early connection to the Boston acting families through Emma Marble, a long-time member of their companies. Marble was the granddaughter of William Warren, doyen of the Boston theater. Among the Rankins' papers is a note, dated January 24, 1882, from Warren to Marble thanking her for a picture of the Rankin children and sending his congratulations to the Rankins for their success in '49.[298] The Rankins often met Warren at the home of Amelia Fisher in Boston, where the actors would gather when they came to that city, eating their supper in the old kitchen, and making merry with wit and song.[299]

Blanchard gave a terrapin stag party for some close friends. Joseph Redding, who was composing music for Rankin's next play, *A Prisoner for Life*, surprised the party by his excellent singing. John Drew was among the guests. Presently, another Drew, John's younger brother, Sidney, played in Louis Aldrich's company in San Francisco for a spell. He was quite different from the dependable John, who was to become the first gentleman of the American stage. Sidney was a pool shark and a ladies' man, who although he did not meet Blanchard's measure for a man was destined to play a large role in the life of her daughter Gladys.

All the actors in the city attended the great masquerade ball at the San Francisco Pavilion. Among the ten thousand guests, a reporter saw George Osbourne and Zoe Tuttle from Rankin's company waltzing, and Charley Ray with an actress from another company doing the can-can to the same music. John T. Raymond was wandering around, and Sam Sothern, son of E.A. Sothern, the original Lord Dundreary, and David Belasco, well disguised, were filling up on milk punches. Behind the bandstand, Carrie Swain, an actress friend of Mabel Bert and like her a good swimmer, was teaching Rankin in full dress costume to turn a back handspring. Mabel Bert was dressed as Ophelia and selling flowers. Clay Greene appeared as Orlando. Two actors from another company were throwing "torpedoes" or paper darts, and shot off firecrackers in the gallery. Some played ball on the floor between dances. Others who were leapfrogging were arrested by police, who turned out to be actors dressed in black tights, red wigs, and policemen's caps. Those being arrested threw spitballs at them. They all locked arms and marched down the floor singing the "Conspirator's Chorus."[300]

A Prisoner for Life, adapted from a forgotten French drama, had been produced at the Union Square Theatre the previous season to great acclaim. Despite their worry over their younger daughter, Phyllis, who had malaria, the Rankins took the lead roles. Blanchard played Mignonne, the child of a secret marriage between a French noble and a beautiful ward of King Louis XIV. During the child's infancy, her father, Count de Valnay, played by Rankin, is charged with treason, tried, and condemned through the false evidence of the villain of the play, General Montreuil, played by Dan Harkins.[301]

John Mazzanovich proved his superior artistry in the scenery. For his mechanical and artistic work in an avalanche scene, in which an avalanche sweeps over a mountainside and destroys all in its path, he was called twice before the curtain. It was a relief to see a dramatic romance of one of the most brilliant periods of history done in authentic costumes and background after plays of paupers and London slums, according to the critic. "One prefers to see a noble-minded gentleman, even after sixteen years imprisonment," he wrote,

> in something besides the repulsive rags and dirt of Monte Cristo and the rest. In McKee Rankin's appearance as the Count there is forlorn dilapidation enough and all the physical evidences of his long martyrdom, but there is nothing that a

sweet young daughter might not clasp and pity and love without a tinge of disgust....It is always easy to forget that these two are acting, for there is never artificiality in anything they do. They are natural in even so extreme a situation as that in which the Count escapes through his wife's apartments, when he would naturally have been caught before he had time to attach his rope ladder. Mr. Rankin has—perhaps for this part only—adopted a slower and more distinct enunciation which it is hoped he will not abandon afterward.[302]

During the three-week run of *A Prisoner for Life*, the theater was crowded night after night and people were turned away. Although it was the best moneymaker of the season, Rankin refused to force a run; he had too many good plays waiting in the wings. Despite strong competition from the other playhouses, Rankin's was continuously appealing. At the Grand Opera House, where Theodore Hamilton was starring, there appeared a young and pretty actress, Mabel Bert, who began to attract attention by her beauty and stage presence. She was being courted by theaters in the East and had turned down an invitation to support Madame Janauschek. The critics hoped she would find better employment in the West. She starred in *Undine*, which, according to a critic, gave her the opportunity for rich dressing. "To my mind," he wrote, "this was all the lady required to establish a claim for being one of the prettiest women on the American stage."[303] Rankin hired her for his next play, *Step by Step*.

By staging *Step by Step*, Rankin seemed to reaffirm his belief that the theater should be striving for realism. Two young girls—one a seamstress, the other a pretty young shop girl, who craves pleasure—descend the downward path to a realistic dive in the slums. Here the minstrel Bert Haverly, the singer and dancer Helen Conklin, and the acrobats the Healy brothers entertain the assorted scum of toughs, rounders, waiter girls, country visitors, and confidence men. Rankin as a poor but honest paperhanger was the lover of the seamstress, and C.B. Bishop as a hoodlum was the lover of the shop girl, played by Mabel Bert. Mordaunt was a beer-soaked German, Harkins played the captain of the San Francisco police, Wallace was an amusing old black woman, Ray was the underground dive-keeper. All of them acted well, but, according to the critic, were unhappy because the public objected to casting popular actors in degrading roles.

Although Mazzanovich outdid himself in creating the scenery for San Francisco lowlife, he was called before the curtain only for his Nob Hill scene of a luxurious home with a view of the city through its wide bay windows. The public refused to be interested in the lives of the urban lower classes, and the play had to be replaced by *Dark Days*, a murder mystery with a simple narrative that held the audience's interest until the secret of the murder was revealed at the end. Rankin had reconstructed the play and rewritten the first and second acts to sustain the dramatic interest.

By bringing Mabel Bert into his company to share the starring honors with Isabelle Morris, he lost Morris, who left abruptly with the excuse that the parts she was being offered were not good enough for her talents. Ellie Wilton, returning to fill in for the departing star, made a hit in *Dark Days*. Thinking that her acting career was finished, Wilton had been about to marry a millionaire suitor who had been pursuing her for years when she had this reprieve. Mabel Bert made a pretty and pleasing impression and began confirming the critics' claim that she was an excellent acquisition. The best performance was by J.J. Wallace as a murderer who suffered from ghastly, conscience-stricken fear. Neither of the Rankins appeared in it, possibly because Blanchard was not well enough to perform on a continuous basis and because Rankin was preparing for a new production of Shakespeare's *Macbeth*. Although Mazzanovich created more scenic marvels, it closed after a week, to be replaced by Daly's *Divorce*.

For *Divorce*, Mazzanovich adopted a Saxe-Meiningen innovation by using a special drop curtain for different stage levels to make a quick transfer of action throughout the play. Rankin's choice, however, was ill-advised and influenced by his admiration for Daly, who had produced the play in San Francisco that summer; it had been played widely and so often in the city throughout the years that it no longer attracted patrons. The poor houses it garnered for Monday and Tuesday persuaded Rankin to replace it with *'49* on Wednesday. Unfortunately, *'49* failed to attract as expected and the company limped with it to the end of the week. Such a brief decline in financial returns threatened the whole enterprise. At this time, Blanchard applied to the courts to become the sole trader and manager in the theater in order to protect her husband's interest against creditors.[304]

On October 1, 1885, the cast celebrated its first one hundred nights as a stock company, which, by not having a losing attraction, had established an exceptionally fine managerial record. The core of the stock company, those who shared the profit and loss, were both Rankins, Dan Harkins, Frank Mordaunt, C.B. Bishop, J.J. Wallace, and Joe Holland. The company was stable and dedicated; Emma Marble and Mrs F.M. Bates, who seemed to be attached personally to the Rankins, Charles G. Ray, Charles Green, E.N. Thayer, H.Z. Bosworth, and the comical Frank Wright remained with the company throughout the season. Rankin improved the supporting music by replacing the orchestra conductor with W.S. Mullaly, who brought in an entire new orchestra and began establishing a reputation with his superb arrangements and musical scoring for the plays.[305]

Rankin brought *Storm Beaten* back for a week, with Blanchard as Priscilla Sefton, whose gentle womanly ways had a hint of Quakerish preciseness that, in turn, blended well with the benign manner assumed by her blind father, acted by Mordaunt. Rankin again played Christian Christianson, who did battle on the ice floes with J.J. Wallace as Richard Orchardson, his rival for Kate Christianson. Mabel Bert as Kate Christianson had her first chance to demonstrate her real abilities; she acted with unaffected gentleness and pathos that won over the audience. She demonstrated, wrote a critic, that a beautiful woman can be a good actress. Her emotional power was unmistakable, although "it was only half-developed." As for the play's drawing power: "A good melodrama with this company is never a mere sensation. It gets an air of truth from the natural, earnest manner of the actors, no matter how startling its situations may be."[306]

Glad to prove that the sensational was profitable, Rankin introduced *Brought to Justice* for the first time to San Francisco. Although the company played it well and brought forth frequent applause, the audiences were moderate. The role of Nell Forrest, the wife of a weak husband, usually filled by Blanchard, was taken by Mabel Bert, which indicated Rankin's growing confidence in his new acquisition. The play ran for a week to a modest profit, but the excitement was all for Rankin's promised fabulous production of *Macbeth*, which had been advertised throughout the state as opening next on November 2, 1885.

Macbeth

Rankin's production of *Macbeth* became one of the great events of the theater, not only for his Saxe-Meiningen approach of uniform strength to the whole cast but for the authenticity of the costumes and scenery.[307] Rankin's inspiration to present the play came from special *Macbeth* music that a young American composer had been writing. Edgar Stillman Kelley became known as the American Wagner because he adopted Richard Wagner's new principle of intensifying the spoken word by musical heightening while defining the emotional significance of the music through the juxtaposition of words and themes in his operas. In *Macbeth*, for instance, Kelley defined fifteen themes in his music. These included the theme of ambition, when Lady Macbeth in three strong speeches fortifies her husband's courage to murder Duncan. A theme from the overture, marked by deep brooding and a climbing progression, accompanied each speech. It was said that of the scores of young Americans who studied in Germany, Kelley was the only one who had within him something worth expressing. In Stuttgart, he had told his teacher of composition and orchestration of his intention to set *Macbeth* to music, following Felix Mendelssohn, who had already composed a musical treatment for *A Midsummer Night's Dream*. He was told that actors disliked such music because it distracted attention from the text. By coincidence, however, Kelley had seen a play in which the Rankins had leading parts and where music combined with the text. This gave him the determination to carry out his project.

Kelley had had his *Macbeth* music exposed to the public as he wrote it. In September 1882, "The Defeat of Macbeth" was performed as a symphonic poem: it became the prelude to Act V of the play. In August 1883, his "Overture to *Macbeth*" was performed in Chicago at a Summer Garden concert for 6,000 people. In October 1884, his "Gaelic March" was given a hearing. At this point, a rich young man, John Parrott, Jr, used his money and influence to help Kelley, sponsoring a performance in San Francisco on February 1, 1885, of the entire music for *Macbeth* with a fifty-piece orchestra, a chorus, and a dramatic reader.[308] Rankin was traveling in the Midwest at the time, but, when he arrived in San Francisco, he heard of the event and began mulling over the possibility of using the music in a production that marked a departure from all that had been done before. He advised Kelley from the viewpoint of stagecraft when the composer was making additions to the music. Kelley's music was an instrumental rather than a vocal addition to the play, which differentiated it from the two songs and a dance that Matthew Lock composed for the performance of 1672 under Sir William Davenant. Kelley wrote just one number for voices—the chorus for spirits—and cut out the other vocals and dance scene that Lock had included. His emphasis was on the preludes to certain acts and the orchestral accompaniments to the spoken text in ten scenes, the last being the great battle scene, in which the music accompanied the action rather than the words.

Because Shakespeare's plays were proven money-losers, and the public had such a particular aversion to the somber *Macbeth,* which neither Kean nor Booth nor Irving had been able to overcome, Rankin was warned by all and sundry that he was courting disaster. Not surprisingly, Rankin's instinct for gambling asserted itself, and, along with his acting and stage-managerial duties, he set about carefully planning the production. As early as August, hoping to produce a couple of Shakespeare's plays, he advertised the play widely as "The Great Shakespearean Festival," and arranged for the railway company to run special trains from

Stardom

neighboring towns at reduced fares. An excursion party of 300 was coming from San Jose, and parties were expected to arrive from other cities. "He who caters to 'the thirst that from the soul doth rise,'" wrote a critic, "is far less sure of his reward than the man who provides entertainment for the unthinking. It is in every way creditable to the California Theatre management that the most lavish expenditure of the season has been made upon 'Macbeth.'"[309] A sixty-voice choir was being organized. A lithographer was working on a representation of Macbeth's first interview with the witches. John Sherman, the former proprietor of Phainosidon, a popular show of trick lighting, was retained to create the ghost effects in the banquet scene with Banquo and to use his technique with lighting. The cauldron scene with the witches would have bats flying through the air, serpents slithering from rock to rock, huge dragons, and owls. Apparitions would arise from the fumes of the cauldron. The supernatural scenes would be sublime rather than ridiculous, as had usually been the case. Since the belief in witchcraft and the powers of darkness is the first link on which the whole chain of the tragedy depends, Rankin was justified in employing every device to deceive the viewer into believing the scene was real. The witches' prophecy is believed by the Macbeths and must be acted upon if Macbeth is to gain his rightful place. Rankin claimed that his production, though a departure from the traditional stagings of *Macbeth,* was more authentic. The costumes, armor, and weaponry resembled those used by Scots barbarians 800 years earlier. Rankin had the trumpets used in the "Royal Gaelic March," which introduced the banquet scene, manufactured locally. The catapult was an elaborate and costly mechanism that was solid enough for real service. Mazzanovich and his assistants created extraordinary scenery such that a critic suggested that Mazzanovich had "surprised himself."[310] He used a tableaux drop curtain to hide the shifts of scenery and to keep the action moving quickly. Sherman's mechanical appliance for lights and shadows gave a cold, weird look to the sudden appearance and gradual dissolution of Banquo's ghost.

As for the actors, Rankin hired a rising young and handsome lead to play Banquo. He was Frederic de Belleville, who agreed to take the part on the condition that he play the lead in the next two plays that Rankin was to produce after *Macbeth*. The roles of Macbeth, Macduff, and King Duncan were played on alternate nights by the three main players: Rankin playing Macbeth on Monday, Tuesday, and Friday; Harkins on Wednesday, Thursday, and Saturday matinee; and Mordaunt on Saturday evening and Sunday. Ellie Wilton was Lady Macbeth; she had played the role well in support of Edwin Booth as Macbeth some years before. Mabel Bert played Lady Macduff. Just before the opening, Bert was offered the post of leading lady at the Clunie Opera House in Sacramento, but she declined. C.B. Bishop took the roles of the drunken porter and the first witch.

Many of Rankin's company were well experienced in the play, but all agreed that convention would have no influence over this fresh and novel presentation. J.J. Wallace, for instance, had played every male part in the play between 1853 and 1859 with most of the great stars. Bishop also had played every male part and was considered without equal in the low comedy parts of Shakespeare. Harkins had played the major roles opposite the great stars and had starred in the title role in the British Isles and Australia.

Playbill for Rankin's *Macbeth* at the California Theatre, San Francisco, November 1885.

On opening night, the most select, demonstrative, critical, and thoroughly appreciative audience ever assembled in the California Theatre gave overwhelming approval to the play, thus confounding Rankin's critics. The music was declared far superior to that which usually accompanied plays. "Kelley takes the most pertinent phrases in the text for illustration," wrote a critic, "and offered another medium through which the most striking portions of this terrible triumph of an accepted destiny over a human soul may reach and impress the imagination.[311] Kelley himself conducted the orchestra in the final "Defeat of Macbeth."

Rankin employed one hundred supernumeraries for the last battle scene, thirty of whom were over six feet tall. The movement of large crowds of people and the various details of actions going on simultaneously reflected Rankin's great abilities as stage director. The thought, study, and research that he devoted to every detail was credited to his taste, intelligence, and artistic feeling in his overall direction. "Everyone in the cast devoted himself with enthusiastic earnestness," wrote a critic. "It is this sympathetic appreciation of the theme which has produced so impressive a representation of 'Macbeth.' All united in it: manager and orchestral leaders, actors and musicians, scenic artists, costumers and even the usually inert supernumeraries."[312] Rankin's intelligent and generous manner in accepting the suggestions of the music inspired everyone. Acclaiming the production as the most splendid Shakespearean revival within the memory of the younger generation, the critics marveled at the carefulness of detail, all of which could be supported by historical scholarship. The fight on the drawbridge with the steep approaches to Macbeth's castle on the height was only one of the fine scenes. The only scene that failed, the incantation scene, for which elaborate preparations were made, did so because the person in charge left the production during rehearsals. These scenes, however, were memorable, as Andrew Wheeler, the critic who had sided with Joaquin Miller against Rankin at one time, described them in an article praising the production. Wheeler cited the "uncommon power" of the rousing of the castle when the murder is discovered, the banquet scene, and the final battle scene in which hand-to-hand fights took place on three levels at once. His description of the banquet scene revealed its obvious debt to the maxims of the Duke of Saxe-Meiningen:

> In the third act the banquet scene was a succession of admirable pictures. The scenery gave a compact setting to them all. An immense stone arch sprang from the walls across the entire foreground; in the middle distance, two lesser arches rested on a stone pillar in the centre of the floor; the vaulting of other arches filled up the back. A banquet table, with antique drinking horns at every place, was spread across the foreground on the right, with stools (not chairs) that enabled the outlines of the seated figures to make their full effect; and on the left, two similar tables extended lengthwise towards the rear. Curious archaic lamps hung from the ceiling, and torches flared from links on the walls. The space between the foremost tables and in front of the central pillar was filled during the scene by Macbeth, Lady Macbeth, and the ghost of Banquo. Some idea will thus be obtained by the reader of the concentration of effect, by which the eye was insensibly brought to focus on the central figures; but only one who saw the guests enter and take their places, who marked the felicitous ease of their grouping, who noted in the subdued tone of their garments, as contrasted with the brighter apparel of the royal pair, a distribution of color corresponding most happily with the distribution of dramatic values, who felt the subtle heightening of the picture as the startled guests rose in answer to Macbeth's

cry of wonder that they could sit unmoved,—only one who was witness to all this will be able to recall to his imagination the truly admirable qualities that crowned this great scene with success.[313]

The performers were closely scrutinized. The opening-night critic gave a balanced picture of Rankin's Macbeth. Rankin's nervousness "visibly weighed upon him," which accounted for sometimes indistinct speech. "He was a Macbeth," wrote the critic, "in whom all the weaker qualities of the man were prominent and little appeared of that courage that 'dared do all that might become a man.' Vacillating, spiritually cowardly, infirm of purpose as Macbeth was, there was yet something of native nobleness in him, and this Mr. Rankin did not suggest. His reading of the lines was always intelligent and significant when it could be heard, but his bearing lacked dignity."[314] Later in the week, the critic saw a material improvement from the first performance, when Rankin's responsibilities as a manager had robbed him of his ease as an actor. His fault, however, was still his manner and enunciation. He was the best and worst of the three Macbeths. He made Macbeth's mental anguish so vivid and his "horrible imaginings" so real "that one gives him the palm for his conception of the part," though he lacked dignity, "which, oddly enough, he was able to make a permanent characteristic of Macduff."[315] Andrew Wheeler, on the other hand, praised Rankin for the original characteristics of his interpretation, which was very human and able to enlist the audience deeply in Macbeth's fortunes. "More frequent delivery of Shakespearean verse will give Mr. Rankin's colloquial style a distinctness of enunciation which is now its greatest want; but it was, nevertheless, a pleasant contrast to the mock-heroics of Mr. Harkins' delivery of the same lines."[316]

Wheeler's dislike of the elocutionary style of Harkins reflected Rankin's early disagreement with that approach. It had worked for Harkins in the 1860s when he was closer to the time of the older actors such as McCullough, whose style it resembled. But in the 1880s, many agreed with Wheeler that "his antique method of declamation, in which vowels are drawled and consonants are held until the last vocal quality in them has been extracted, is a sensuous style that deserves to be buried or cremated beyond the power of resurrection. Its stilted effects blunt the sharpness of thought, and are too far removed from nature to hold any place on the modern stage."[317] A San Francisco critic, however, considered Harkins's delivery the chief enjoyment of his performance. Harkins made Macbeth's physical courage and martial qualities predominant, but, in so doing, his portrayal lacked the human side of the characterizations of both Rankin and Mordaunt, which drew on the sympathies of the audience.[318] The Macbeth of Mordaunt had many excellent features, but his interpretation emphasized the hesitancy of the thane's character, which, in the opinion of some, marred the performance.

Ellie Wilton gave an original interpretation to her character, Lady Macbeth. She was "full of true womanliness." Rather than Charlotte Cushman's iron-nerved woman of more than masculine callousness unvarying in her complexion, Wilton assumed a phase of sternness to help her vacillating husband. She gave the character a sweet womanly grace, making her attractive rather than unsympathetic. Despite her lack of vocal power on the opening night, she was a success, and her sleepwalking scene had many recalls from the audience. Because Rankin followed the Saxe-Meiningen method of blending the characters to reflect the parts in a unified composition, his emphasis on the weakness of Macbeth's character seems to have complemented Wilton's accent on Lady Macbeth's human qualities. The critics, unused to such methods, would not have been able to comprehend what he was doing. The public, however, crammed the theater night after night for twenty-five performances, which was the most the play had done successively in the years since its first recorded performance. Rankin's art had reached the average citizen and stirred up an enthusiasm that the managers had not anticipated. "Few spectators," commented Wheeler, "left the theater without feeling that they had witnessed the terrible episodes of a man's real life."[319]

The whole company came in for praise. De Belleville, a manly and imposing figure, was a sensation as Banquo and gave the character an importance that had always been hidden in the passive renditions given in the past. Joe Holland was distinctive as Duncan's son, Malcolm, and looked like a Gustave Doré illustration of Tennyson's *Idylls* when, in the last act, he bounded up the steep approach to Macbeth's castle with his white drapery floating behind him and his sword uplifted. C.B. Bishop, the rotund low comedian, played the first witch "time out of mind," which is to say, wildly memorably. There were some casualties: Mordaunt received an ugly sword gash over the eye, and two of Holland's fingers were disabled in fencing; Mabel Bert fell ill for the second week, and her part had to be eliminated while she was absent; and Mordaunt and Mazzanovich were ill for the third week.

Although the second week began with full houses, management considered it unwise to continue for a third week, but, by the end of the week, the demand was so insistent that management decided it was unwise not to continue. The third week suffered temporarily from lower attendance, but the production, which had to have full houses to pay the expenses, concluded with a good balance in the black, helped by a large house for a testimonial given on Friday night to Rankin and Kelley for their brilliant innovations. An enthusiastic patronage continued despite the arrival of the rainy season, when it rained every night.

Rankin, in addition, was given a benefit on Thursday night. Playing Macduff, he was returning from the battle in the last act with Macbeth's head—that is, Harkins's head—on a pole when two actors dressed as an Indian chief and princess from another theater rushed onstage, took the pole from Rankin, and clapped Macbeth's head on Joe Holland's head with the words, "All hail, Malcolm, King of Scotland" as the curtain fell. The audience thought that Rankin had introduced another innovation. "I don't know whether I wish it hadn't happened or to wish I was dead," Rankin said, "but if anyone else than Nate Salisbury [the Indian chief] had done it, I would have first dispatched him and then died happily myself."[320]

The profitable three weeks in San Francisco, remarked a critic, would have been as many months in New York. It was a distinction to celebrate when the Rankins invited to their home the original members of the American Theatre Company on November 24, the first anniversary of the company's founding. Harkins, Mordaunt, Wallace, and the two Rankins had met with a success beyond their dreams.

During the run of *Macbeth,* news of McCullough's death reached San Francisco. Manager Price draped the actor's portrait in the theater's foyer in black.

The American Theatre Company Continues

By keeping *Macbeth* going for a third week, Rankin gave the company time to rehearse their next play, *A Wall Street Bandit,* based on recent events in New York City. In the prologue, Rankin as a plain everyday farmer dies brokenhearted at his financial ruin in the panic of 1857. His orphaned children are separated. The boy grows up among workers, and the girl grows up on Fifth Avenue as one of the Upper Ten Thousand, the name by which the rich in New York City were known and which derived from the ten dollar bill. Seedy characters were taken from life and introduced in the prologue. Steven Crawley, for example, in real life kept an asylum for orphaned children named the Shepherd's Fold to obtain a state appropriation. He became rich by depriving the unprotected children of food and medical care, and, when exposed by the Society for the Prevention of Cruelty to Children, his atrocities caused a sensation in New York. In the prologue, his character is called Mawley and is played by J.J. Wallace true to the real person. In the main play, Wallace became

J. Edison Shocks, the walking electricity doctor, another character from real life, who was arrested for paralyzing children in the Bowery for five cents a shock.[321]

Rankin's talent for directing children was evident. All of the children were astonishingly well up in their stage business. From the little toddler to the oldest waif, they all looked and acted half-starved and wholly miserable. They were without a hint of unpleasant precocity. One little girl made such an impression as a sharp little graduate of a street education that the critic wanted to see her appear again later in the play, perhaps as a Macy's shop girl. One wistful-faced little girl asks for a kiss from the first friendly human being she has ever known, adding, "I never was kissed in my whole life." The applause was enthusiastic, and the playwright A.C. Gunter was called before the curtain after all the children had answered a recall.

In the main play, the two orphans who were robbed of their inheritance, now adults, meet by chance and recognize one another. The crime that caused their separation is exposed, and the man who committed it is ruined. Mabel Bert played the grown-up sister who loves being considered the prettiest girl on Sixth Avenue. "Her methods are a little abrupt now," commented a critic, "but they are improving and mellowing all the time. She is a very attractive woman, and gives something of her own personality to each congenial part in which she appears."[322] The play made a handsome profit. On a Thursday night, the receipts were $1,422.50, the largest ever taken in at the current prices, and nearly enough people were turned away to fill the theater again.[323]

Rankin followed *A Wall Street Bandit* with an adaptation of *Allan Dare,* a novel written by Admiral Porter. Rankin had purchased the rights months earlier and had adapted the play for the stage amidst all his other activities at the California Theatre. The play was another melodrama but lacking in the humor that had pervaded *A Wall Street Bandit*. It was called "a poor play well played." The action had hairsbreadth escapes and dramatic situations, but, said a critic, the play was extravagant, disjointed, and uneven, and needed copious notes from the novel to explain the situations and make intelligible the relations among the characters.[324]

De Belleville as Robert Diable was the main attraction. He was a superb representative of the picturesque, athletic, dashing thief. A virile and vigorous actor, he conveyed the impression of power without waste or misapplication of force. Rankin, as Allan Dare, the detective, looked nearly as handsome and made almost as good use of his opportunities. The play was superbly mounted. Picturesque costumes from early in the century and the excellent stage effects and mechanisms, which created dissolving views and highlighted an original revolving prison scene, contributed to its success. Rankin, however, knowing that he had to attract the dress-circle crowd as well as the balcony boys to make a profit, used a theater trick that impresarios would call a touch of genius. He hired a society debutante, Susie Williams, to play the small role of Flossy Carollton. From a southern family, Susie made a runaway marriage to the son of General Williams, a California millionaire, but separated when her husband tried to shoot her. Her family disowned her, but she was well-known and liked in San Francisco society and she brought a very large and fashionable crowd to the theater to see her play. She was badly frightened at first but recovered to make a creditable showing. At the end of the play's run, she was handed a basket of flowers to which was attached a diamond ring, containing twenty stones, from twenty gentlemen admirers.

Joseph Redding composed incidental music for the play, including music to a minuet. The combination of local interest with fine-looking actors in picturesque costumes in sketchily written but excellently rendered characters drew tremendously large houses for two weeks. Three times crowds had to be turned away. About this time the Bishops, father and son, resigned from the company to form their own.[325]

The problem with success is that one is tempted to improve upon it. After his success with *Macbeth*, Rankin decided to stage Shakespeare's *A Midsummer Night's Dream* with Mendelssohn's musical accompaniment and additional Mendelssohn fugitive pieces arranged by Kelley. By now, Rankin was confident in his abilities, but he was not prepared for the unanticipated exigencies that often upset the best of plans. Al Hayman insisted on renting the California Theatre for eight weeks to house the Kiralfy Ballet, which began its run in the spectacle *Eighty Days around the World*. Rankin was obliged to rent Hayman's Baldwin Theatre for six weeks. It was dangerous to shift one's base of operations, especially when the theater one was leaving had a reputation for attracting large audiences to one that was not associated with the company's productions. It was made worse when the Kiralfys put on a dazzling spectacle in the California Theatre of beautiful coryphées, ballerinas, elegant costumes, and wonderful stage effects: in effect, they stole Rankin's audience.

A Midsummer Night's Dream opened at the Baldwin on December 21, 1885; Rankin, who did all the stage directing, took no role. Seven artists from other theaters worked on creating the scenery with Mazzanovich for two weeks. Mazzanovich's prettiest scene in the play was the background of Athens shown between the columns of the hall where Theseus received his clients. A critic thought that the music, action, and scenery were unusually well harmonized. Blanchard, who had been considered the best Puck on the American stage in her youth, trained young Ruby Illidge for the part.

Blanchard took the part of Oberon, King of Fairy Land, and, wearing a golden beard, gave an artistic performance "from the tip of her wings to the tip of her wand." The critic claimed the play appealed especially to the eye, although Shakespeare's poetry clothed it. "The manner and appearance of the people who interpret it counts frequently for more than their dramatic ability," he wrote.[326] Mendelssohn's music as played by a thirty-five-piece orchestra under W.S. Mullaly was one of the enjoyable features.

The audiences were small for Christmas week and just slightly larger for the second week. The company showed its appreciation for Rankin's managerial energy and taste with a congratulatory Christmas letter and a cat's-eye scarfpin set in diamonds. Rankin's daughters, Pixie and Dido, gave a Christmas tree to the little children who played the elves in *A Midsummer Night's Dream* and a present to each child. (No doubt, Blanchard was remembering the Christmas present she received as a child dancer.) After working so hard to make the scenery fit the music, Mazzanovich fell ill and was ordered to rest in Paso Robles Springs, Los Angeles. Rankin paid him a full salary and expenses for as long as he was absent.

On January 4, 1886, Rankin brought out *Wife and Child*, the play he had written with Fred Maeder and had decided not to try out in New York. It featured a double scene in which a blind artist who was deserted by his wife many years ago tells the story of that desertion to the young girl whom his son loves. He describes the yearnings that the wife and mother must feel for the love of the son she left behind. At the same time, this very wife and mother is sitting for her portrait in the next room with the artist son who has no idea of her identity. She suffers every pang of maternal love and longing that her husband has imagined. Blanchard made this scene vividly real. Her talent was to make the audience believe that a very sweet nature underlay the sympathetic naturalness of her acting. The role also gave her the opportunity to dress up that rarely came her way. She wore a series of handsome costumes; one, a purple and mauve combination, with a garniture of duchesse lace, was considered handsomer than many of the much-advertised Paris dresses. The play kept the audience's attention, but it was felt generally that it needed more work to be a financial success. It was not long, but it gave the impression of too much in it, especially of aimless talking. "Its faults," wrote a critic, "are those of an unpracticed hand at dramatic writing and do not betray any lack of invention or of constructive talent," at which Rankin and Maeder, as experienced playwrights, must have been amused.[327]

Rankin intended to produce an English version of *Notre Dame*, from Victor Hugo's novel, *The Hunchback of Notre Dame*, which had been staged in 1850 in France but then forbidden by imperial decree until 1879.

It was currently playing successfully at the Théâtre des Nations in Paris and gave promise of theatrical power. When the manuscript did not arrive in time, Rankin brought back *The Danites* for a week.[328] Both Mabel Bert as the Widder and Blanchard as Billy Piper received recalls after two curtains. The audiences seemed to be putting them on an equal footing. If Blanchard had been jealous of the women portraying the Widder in the past, she had good reason to be jealous of the beautiful Mabel Bert, who, under Rankin's tutelage, was making great strides in the profession.

Notre Dame opened on January 18, 1886, at the Baldwin Theatre. Rankin appeared as Quasimodo, the deformed bell-ringer, who is secretly in love with the beautiful gypsy girl, Esmeralda, played by Mabel Bert. Harkins played Frollo, Arch-Deacon of Notre Dame, who lusts after Esmeralda. This spectacular production had nine sets of scenery by the theater's designer, M. Strauss, and new music composed by Mullaly. In the cathedral scene, a choir sang to an organ accompaniment and a male ballet was choreographed for the Paris street scenes at the Festival of Fools. At first, the stage effects and picturesque accessories seemed too much, but they were soon brought into harmony. "The procession of chanting priests, acolytes with incense-breathing censers, the songs of the gypsies and the dance of the fools are all potent parts of the vivid effect the drama leaves on the mind," wrote a critic.[329] The low, agitated undercurrent of Mullaly's music heightened the general effectiveness of the acting.

The play's story was grounded in a dramatic intensity that raised the performances of the whole cast. Esmeralda's defense of the hunchback against the mob; Frollo's plot against Esmeralda; the reveling of the gypsy thieves in the Cour de Miracles; the compulsory marriage of Esmeralda to the half witted poet, Gringoire, her arrest upon killing Captain Phoebus; her pathetic scenes with Frollo and with her mother in prison; her rescue by the hunchback, who hides her in the tower of Notre Dame; the hunchback's struggle with Frollo, whom he throws from the tower—all culminated in a less terrible ending than in Hugo's novel, with the hunchback's pardon by Louis XI. Mabel Bert in the role of Esmeralda, beautiful with her raven hair, flashing eye, and bewitching smile, was the central figure and object of praise from all the critics. For the past two years, she had risen slowly but surely to her present fame. When Frollo gazed intently on her matchless figure and said, "Thine image has drawn slumber from mine eyes," his words, according to a critic, seemed to impress themselves upon the audience as deeply as the subject.[330]

Frollo's frenzied desire for Esmeralda burns and destroys every good instinct in his nature, whereas Quasimodo's fidelity to the lovely girl, who makes his heart ache at every turn, burns out all the dross in his character. Of almost equal intensity, their loves work to ends that are widely separated. Harkins, however, was too cold and measured to convey Frollo's passion; his agony was declamation, his love an effort of elocution, skillful and well calculated but empty of feeling.[331] By contrast, Rankin's deep love and patient despair were touchingly conveyed in his every tone and gesture. His character was strangely attractive at first and then became repellent.[332] As for Esmeralda's goat, time was too short to introduce a trained goat, so a small boy was sent on with an ordinary white goat. Seized with stage fright, it trembled and wanted to get off, but the boy was firm until it was time to leave, when the goat refused to budge. After a week, however, it became a fair actor.

The greatest actor of the age, Tommaso Salvini, was due to displace Rankin's company from the Baldwin on the following Monday, so Rankin had to take his company on the road. Salvini, whose mental supremacy was as obvious as his great physical superiority, riveted his audiences by the perfection of his acting, by harmonizing every detail of it with his ideal representation of the character.[333] Meanwhile, Rankin, complimented by being called the "American Salvini," opened to a tremendous house in Sacramento, where the company played *Notre Dame*, *Wife and Child*, and *Prisoner for Life*. Rankin took the lead in all three. Owing to rains and severe floods, the attendance dropped off during the week, which ended barely in the black. The company opened to very large business in Oakland with much better prospects during the week.

Mazzanovich returned to start painting the scenes for *Hoodman Blind*, Rankin's first production when the company reopened at the California Theatre on February 16, 1886. The actors were delighted to get back and play before a familiar audience that completely filled the theater. News of *Hoodman Blind*'s long-running success at Wallack's Theatre in New York may have stimulated the initial good response. The play concerns the London poor, and the plot is one of mistaken identity. The close resemblance of one woman to another causes an honest farmer, Jack Yeulett, to believe that his faithful wife was untrue. He drives her from home and realizes his mistake only after saving her look-alike from drowning in the Thames. The three principal characters—the husband, the wife, and the destroyer of their peace, Mark Lizzard—were played by Rankin, Bert, and Holland. Rankin's simple, truthful, forcible portrayal of the farmer was marred when his voice gave out, but otherwise he absorbed the audience's attention. His scenes with little Kit, his child, as well as with Tomtit, a little waif of the London wharves, were tender and touching, and that with poor Nance, at their bitter parting, was full of dramatic power. A critic considered the part of Jack Yeulett to be one of Rankin's best, one that would be associated with his name for a long time. As a big, stalwart, fair-haired Saxon, he wrote, Rankin fitted the English place and names so well that one smelt the clover upon him as he came in from the flies. Mabel Bert's double role was well carried off and sufficiently different to set the women apart. "There is in all her emotion and pathos," wrote the critic, "an element of poetry that is less personal than intellectual, and it is this fact that warrants a belief in her future."[334] Elsewhere, she was reported as the handsomest woman on the San Franciscan stage, a crack rifle shot, expert swimmer, and accomplished billiardist.[335] "Who would recognize in the Mabel Bert of last week, in 'Hoodman Blind,' the shallow-minded, artificial, merely pretty girl, who came from the Grand Opera House not so many months ago, half-spoiled, with little else than her pretty presence to recommend her?" wrote another critic. "Yet here is she, with an awakened intelligence—of which she gave the first glimpse in the frankness and sincerity of her Esmeralda—playing a dual role with a delicate dividing line of difference which is positively artistic....And since this Mabel Bert has dropped the airy indifference which was her sometime manner, she has taken on an honest earnestness which is infinitely charming."[336] The remainder of the cast had an all-around excellence that seldom favored a first production on any stage.[337]

For a large cast with thirty speaking parts to have so much praise, Rankin must have been close to perfecting his idea of a repertory company playing uniformly and in harmony with scenery and music. The company had achieved an excellence recognized and commented upon all over the country. Mazzanovich's scenery was the talk of the town. The woods, lanes, and meadows of rural England, and the view of the little town with the wrinkles of age upon it, as if it were a human face, set the environment out of which the actors formed their characterizations. When the curtain revealed the Thames embankment with moonlight gleaming on the river, Cleopatra's needle, and London Bridge, the audience stopped the play until Mazzanovich appeared and bowed his acknowledgment.

Despite the general agreement that the company was eminently suited to this play of strong character parts, the audience abruptly declined on the Tuesday of the second week. It was inexplicable. The weather was good and there was no strong competing attraction. Possibly playgoers were surfeited with melodrama, or they might have resented the slight increase in ticket prices, which was necessary to cover the costs of such detailed productions. By the end of the week, however, the audiences increased to give the play a modest profit. Rankin followed *Hoodman Blind* with another melodrama, *Second Sight*, written expressly for the California Theatre by an English dramatist, Charles Chiltrain.

Second Sight tells how three criminals use a young girl with clairvoyance for their criminal schemes. Although the scenic effects were brilliant and the star, Mabel Bert, was declared a hit, a critic called it hopelessly poor melodrama, and the majority of the small audience went away confused. Rankin replaced it after three nights with *Oliver Twist*, which was insufficiently rehearsed and injudiciously cast. Aside from the sterling performance of Blanchard as Nancy Sykes, the acting was mediocre. Blanchard was a revelation as Nancy. While other actresses who played Nancy made the audience shudder, she played her to make them weep by making them feel the remnant of the angel still in poor Nancy's breast. Rankin was criticized as Fagin for kneeling to pray when the Jewish faith called for a standing prayer.[338] The play garnered modest houses for the three remaining nights of the week.

Rankin was now in trouble. Ever since the company had moved to the Baldwin Theatre and raised its prices, it found its reception disheartening. On its return to the California Theatre it discovered that it had lost its sustaining audience in the interim. During the run of *Hoodman Blind*, Rankin had been aware that he needed a change, and wrote to a theater manager in Chicago:

> Of course you know how successful we have been here and, while our lease continues for two years more and we have a sure thing in this city, still I am inclined to think we could, with the same amount of careful work, do a great deal better in Chicago where the field is so much wider. We have a great deal of material of our own that has been tried and tested here. I would like you to see if there is an opening in any of the first class theatres for the strongest company in the world. See what you can do for an extended engagement.[339]

Another source of bad news was the retirement of Mazzanovich, whose health was declining. The company gave him a benefit and regretfully watched him and his family leave for Mexico. Rankin finally realized that it was useless to keep striving for success unless a radical change of policy was instituted.[340] In an effort to rescue his company, he decided to star Blanchard in a number of standard comedies. She was revered by the women in San Francisco and had what could be termed a "cult following." She worked very hard and was plucky and versatile. Every day of her playing life she spent from 10 AM to 4 PM in rehearsal, then played at night and returned home to study until 4 AM. One of the most experienced actors of the day, she was best in gamin roles and, of course, was superb in burlesque. Yet all her efforts could not give her that which her personality lacked in sophistication, just as Rankin, despite all his intellectual study, could not capture the effervescent gaiety that some roles demanded.

Rankin began his comedy week with Bulwer-Lytton's *Money* for two nights only, in which Harkins played Alfred Evelyn and Mabel Bert was Clara Douglas; neither he nor Blanchard was in the cast. "The resurrection of 'Money' was a perfect treat," wrote a critic. "The rich, sweet, wholesome meat of its text left a good taste in the mouth, tingled the ear with the pleasant, unfamiliar sound of good English, startled the intellect pleasantly out of its lethargy, and sent one away with a new thrill of engagement."[341] Rankin followed it with Boucicault's *London Assurance*, in which Blanchard was a dashing, winning Lady Gay Spanker, for two nights. Robertson's *School*, in which Blanchard shone again as Naomi Tighe, stayed for two nights. A matinee and evening of Taylor's *Ticket-of-Leave Man*, in which Rankin played Detective Hawkshaw, increased the attendance. One critic considered the plays of this week the most enjoyable performances that the company had done in San Francisco. He praised Blanchard: "Her presence in a cast does more to give brightness and 'go' to a performance than the united efforts of all the others in the distribution."[342] Attendance picked up during the week to keep the company from losing money. The old-timers did what was expected of them, and the younger members "covered themselves in glory" by learning so many parts in a short time.

Although Rankin had indicated a shift in direction for his theater, he intended to keep his commitment to J.J. Wallace to produce his play *Erin A'Chorra*, regardless of how reckless his loyalty might seem. The play was a mishmash of all the Irish dramas. It had the impoverished Irish gentleman, Maurice Macarthy, played by Rankin in a manly way with a very bad brogue, who was unjustly imprisoned. There was his sweetheart, Norah Delaney, played by Mabel Bert with an equally bad brogue. There were Fenians, redcoats, informers, vagabonds—only the priest was missing. Bert and Adele Waters were considered the pleasant elements. Quite a fund of humor was provided by an American character who proposed to regulate the entire business of Ireland. The play lasted for a week.

Rankin's former co-manager, Jay Rial, brought from New York his protégée, Genevieve Ward, who had been acting recently to acclaim in Australia with her supporting man, W.H. Vernon. By giving them the leads in his next production, *Guy Mannering*, Rankin temporarily suspended his experiment with Saxe-Meiningen ensemble to allow the star system back. Ward made a powerful impression, giving a weird picture of the gypsy hag Meg Merrilies, which was different from any other actress. She had a compelling manner, a fine aquiline nose, and blazing eyes that with rags, wrinkles, and gray hairs did justice to Scott's character. Mabel Bert as Julia Mannering was discovered to have a sweet, musical voice decidedly better than the other actors. Attendance was good, so the receipts improved, possibly because the opera had returned to town and awakened San Franciscans to entertainment. It looked as if the palmy days had returned.[343]

Despite the signs of better business, Rankin reduced ticket prices in a bid to win back the theater's clientele. Originally, tickets had cost 25¢, 50¢, and 75¢ but had been raised to 50¢, 75¢, and $1.00. Now the cheaper seats were reduced to 25¢ and 50¢, while the most expensive seats remained at $1.00. The problem faced by Rankin was that the balcony crowd loved sensationalism and melodrama but refused to pay above a certain amount, which was not sufficient to cover costs. The orchestra and dress-circle crowd had grown bored with melodrama and demanded more sophisticated drama. W.S. Gilbert's plays attracted the latter, and owing to his fame with Arthur Sullivan for their comic operas, his plays tended to bring in balcony spectators out of curiosity, if not for their wit. By bringing down the balcony and family-circle prices and keeping up the orchestra prices, Rankin hoped to make his theater viable. The company met the challenge of Gilbert's light comedy *Engaged*, whose keen satire and wit attracted large houses.

In April, Rankin, in hopes of making money to meet his costs, decided to split his company for a week, sending players to open a new opera house in Los Angeles and keeping a part at the California Theatre playing the old favorite *Rob Roy*. Rankin led the Los Angeles contingent, which included Mabel Bert, Adele Waters, Susie Williams, Dan Harkins, George Osbourne and his wife, Charles Bishop, Jr, and Hardie Kirkland, a young actor who had been doing good work with the company. The houses, however, were undeservedly small.[344] Meanwhile, back at the California Theatre, the stirring Scottish operatic play *Rob Roy* did much better. With a full chorus, enlarged orchestra, new scenery, and picturesque Highland costumes, the play attracted excellent houses all week.[345]

Jack Sheppard followed *Rob Roy*, with Blanchard as the idle apprentice and young housebreaker. This had been one of her outstanding roles in her youth, and she still enthralled audiences with her versatility. The actors J.J. Wallace and Adele Waters, who had accompanied Rankin to Los Angeles, returned to the California Theatre and joined the performance despite their tiredness from the journey. Because the company included the first act, which was rarely played, there were twenty-six scenes and sixty speaking parts. It required one hundred costumes of the period. Rankin's dedication to historical reality and extensive detail was *de trop*. A palpable staginess, an interminable feel to the many scenes, and a heap of artificial detail was relieved only by Jack Sheppard's glimmer of nature. Fifty years earlier, audiences glowed and wept over the play, but at the California only near the end, when Jack dragged himself painfully across the stage as shouts of his pursuers were heard from the wings, did the natural human sympathy for a helpless, hunted creature express itself. Blanchard's acting in whatever period and character was always personally and vividly interesting, according to the critic.[346] As Jack, her boyish swagger, wicked gleam in her eye, and rough quality to her voice caught the young thief exactly.

Sensing a modicum of success with musical revivals, and anxious to keep his theater out of the red, Rankin produced the burlesque *The Field of the Cloth of Gold*. He hired Charley Reed, end man for the Standard Minstrels, to play the role of Francis I of France. C.B. Bishop took the other comic lead as Henry VIII of England. The spectacle was lengthened to a full evening's entertainment by new songs, new business, and new specialties with Mullaly's music and sundry writers of lyrics. Actresses played men, and actors played women. Blanchard played the banished English peer Earl Darnley as a well-dressed, dashing, handsome young man. She had originated the role years before and must have relished resuming it. George Osbourne, superbly made up, was Queen Catharine, wife to Henry. Two new members of the company with burlesque experience, Edith Woodthorpe and Helen Conklin, played the Duke of Suffolk and Le Sieur de Boisy, the latter doing a sensational hoop dance. The prettiest women, Adele Waters and Mabel Bert, had to play women: Waters was Anne Boleyn and Bert was Lady Constance de Grey. Charles Ray as Tête de Veau, High Constable of Calais, opened the night with an expression of thorough fright in his eye and the ring of intense misery in his voice as he began to sing badly and was carried along by a chorus intervening every so often. Charley Reed, playing without blackface for the first time, made the transition from minstrel work well with his queer, shrill, twangy little voice. At one point, the balcony boys compelled him to sing a popular song not in the play by holding up the proceedings until he complied. Blanchard had a low, deep, rich, and singularly strong voice, and one of her songs seemed destined for popularity outside the theater. Bert's voice was a sweet mezzo-soprano, but Waters's voice was tiny. Unlike Blanchard, they knew little about burlesque, and their dancing looked so untrained it had the attraction of childlike ingenuousness. But Bert's dark brunette beauty was admirably foiled by Waters's fairness in her Nile-green dress with pink roses. To be successful in burlesque, said a critic, the actor needed a certain carriage, a certain tone of voice, a certain specialized swagger. Reed had this quality and had the ability to seize every passing event on its comic side, such as giving King Francis a brogue. He was criticized for bringing the fun of the minstrel laugh into burlesque because with it came a sense of inappropriateness that was unpleasing: "burlesque has its limits which cannot be passed without a fatal lapse from fun to foolishness." As for Blanchard, "a cherub should warn actresses when they become too fat to appear in tights with either propriety or attractiveness."[347] But as the San Francisco *Argonaut* put it: "The California Theatre people have been trying a long time to find out what the public want. The question is solved at last. It is burlesque, good old-fashioned burlesque. Not farce, comedies, and whimsical satires, and humorous extravaganzas, and the other unclassifiable nonsense. But a burlesque full of the most execrable puns that the mind of man can conceive—the worse they are the better they go—and a lot of disconnected singing, dancing, and walk-arounds."[348]

Rankin continued with another burlesque: *Ali Baba, or the 39 Thieves*. Early in the century, it was a musical romance that had been sketched by Richard Brinsley Sheridan from *The Arabian Nights* with dialogue by his brother-in-law and music added. Henry Byron modernized it with pithy, topical commentary, new songs, dances, and various minstrel and tumbling acts.[349] The specialty acts included Edith Woodthorpe and Helen Conklin leading forty young women in an Amazon march; Bishop and Blanchard on the ends in a minstrel scene with Reed in the middle; a dancing elephant; aerial gymnasts; a chorus of District Telegraph messengers; and a popular tenor. The whole, however, failed to live up to expectations and ran only eight nights.

Rankin then introduced Daudet's *Sappho* for the first time in the United States. He had eliminated enough French naughtiness to make it presentable to American audiences but not enough to take away all its interest. Unfortunately the company was not suited to the play, which required a light sophistication, and it lost money. Blanchard took the part of Sappho, an experienced Parisian woman who has her way with an inexperienced provincial. Although she made the role enjoyable, it was really beyond her.[350]

Rankin must have sensed in some subtle way that the playgoers, who had supported him so overwhelmingly for many months, had been lost by his enforced change of theaters and that Al Hayman had known it would happen. Competition from the other theaters was not strong. *The Black Crook* had just a fair run at the Baldwin. Salvini, an artistic but not a financial success, had left for New York to star with Edwin Booth.[351]

Rankin, distressed by the negative turn his prospects had taken, made a quick visit to Chicago to gauge the prospects for his company there and to see what moneys could be raised from the auctioning of Bois Blanc Island to the highest bidder.[352] To have had to surrender this island where his family had enjoyed happier summers and where he had spent a great deal on improvements must have been too painful to organize, and he returned to California still owning the island and without an offer to move his company to Chicago.

The California Theatre management tried two classic short comedies, *Your Life's in Danger*, with C.B. Bishop as John Strong and Adele Waters as the Countess Lansfeldt (Lola Montez), and *Everybody's Friend*, with Charley Reed in his first straight comedy role as Major Wellington de Boots and Mabel Bert as Mrs Featherly. Again the house was crowded on opening night, but, although Reed's performance was viewed favorably, the audiences dwindled to the point where it was financially advisable to resurrect *The Field of a Cloth of Gold* for the three remaining nights of the week. Charley Reed resigned from the company because it could no longer afford his salary. In another blow, Mazzanovich, sick with tuberculosis, left for New York City; he died a week after his arrival.

Rankin, with his back to the wall, decided that a good old western frontier drama would save him. First, however, he honored a commitment to produce Shakespeare's *Julius Caesar*. He expected to supervise rehearsals over the weekend for the production to commence on the next Monday, but Al Hayman, at the last moment, refused to let Lawrence Barrett, who was playing under contract to him at the Baldwin Theatre, take part. He did this even though Barrett and his fellow actors were being replaced at the theater by an array of eastern stars starting on May 31, 1886, the very day that Rankin wanted to produce *Julius Caesar*. Barrett was to play Cassius and was essential to the success of the production. Not only was Barrett renowned in the role, but his appearance in the theater where he and McCullough had brought their company to nationwide fame years earlier would have brought out San Franciscans en masse. Hayman, however, did not want the competition. Quickly, Rankin brought to the fore a complete revision of *Gabriel Conroy*, called *The Golden Giant*, which Rankin had entrusted to a young San Franciscan playwright, Clay Greene, when Greene was in the East writing plays for eastern theaters.[353]

The Golden Giant had complicated scenes of mining life in Idaho in 1878. The first act was full of life and vigorous action, developing in the audience an appreciative humor that continued to the final curtain. The plot was torturous, and the villains, like the vigilantes of the earlier plays, were implacable, but the characters were colorful and the action was entertaining. Rankin played Alexander Fairfax, the Golden Giant, and Mabel Bert played Ethel Wayne, who flees from her husband and seeks refuge in the West and accidentally finds it in the brawny arms of Fairfax. They fall in love and marry, despite a complicated set of circumstances. There were echoes of Sandy McGee's character from *The Danites* in Rankin's impersonation of Alex Fairfax, but the latter had a character of his own. Blanchard played Alex's sister, Bessie, with touches of the gamin Carrots she had played in '49, but again it was a completely original characterization. From the moment Blanchard made her entrance with a fishing rod and a huge trout, she captivated the audience with her "go" and uninhibited sense of freedom.[354]

A large critical audience witnessed the opening night and was unstinting in its applause, recalling the actors after every act. Unfortunately, the enthusiasm could not be sustained into the second week, and the house began to draw smaller audiences. The play ran through Thursday night, June 10, 1886. On Friday, the theater gave a farewell benefit to Blanchard. San Franciscans turned out in force to pay tribute. Although many citizens had gone to their summer resorts, the house was full.[355] On Saturday, a thirty-piece orchestra serenaded Blanchard at her home. According to a reporter, the house was a gathering place for the best families in the city because Blanchard had been accorded a position second to none.[356]

Blanchard was taking the two children with her back east. Although no report appeared in print, the Rankins' friends knew that McKee had fallen in love with Mabel Bert. He had raised her to become one of the finished ornaments on the San Francisco stage. She must have been overwhelmed by his attentions and grateful for her new prominence. Blanchard had decided to remove herself from the situation and sued for separation. She nevertheless expected to secure engagements for the American Theatre stock company when it moved east, as Rankin was eager to try out the plays that the company had in its repertoire. Manager Price traveled with her.

To meet Blanchard's demands for separation money, Rankin had to surrender Bois Blanc Island to her. Blanchard conveyed the title for $13,000 to a Detroit comptroller, who divided the island into 317 lots that he advertised at $250 each to the leading citizens of nearby cities as a summer residence property.[357] The Rankin house, stable, and five acres went as one parcel. Two Detroiters, however, stepped in to purchase the island for $40,000 before it could be subdivided.

Years later, a commentator in a San Franciscan newspaper remembered the breakup as tragic. Rankin, at the zenith of his fame and with the promise of becoming one of the great actors in the United States, was devoted to his handsome, talented wife and two daughters in a domestic life that was always cited as an example of the perfectly happy couple on- and off-stage. Then along came Mabel Bert, a tall, strikingly handsome young woman, and a young and rising actress regarded as a marvel in the city. Her dash and magnetism brought great praise from the press and theater-goers and produced many worshippers, including Rankin, who was blindly, madly infatuated with her.

Blanchard, whose jealousy at one time had made headlines in St Louis, decided that Rankin's philandering was becoming an embarrassment to her. Everyone could see his attraction for Bert, and she was helpless to prevent it. It was because she loved him that she could no longer endure the situation. Possibly as a gesture to recall the success of their youth together, Rankin produced *The Two Orphans* on the Saturday night after Blanchard's benefit. Mabel Bert played the blind sister, Louise, and Adele Waters played Blanchard's old role of Henriette. Rankin was in his role as Jacques Frochard, the bully. The piece was considered far superior to many other plays with which the company experimented.[358] After a couple of nights, Rankin produced *The Pavements of Paris* for a night, and *Led Astray* for another. Then, he starred Susie Williams as Gilberte in *Frou-Frou* for the remainder of the week to bring out her society friends.

Falling back on the western, Rankin hired Clay Greene as house dramatist and mounted Greene's new play *Falsely Accused, or, The Deadwood Stage*, which was written and rehearsed in two weeks. Rankin played the double role of Harry Devoy, a mining engineer, and Joe Stark, an escaped convict, whose close resemblance to Harry Devoy casts a cloud of suspicion over Devoy for a murder Stark committed. Mabel Bert played an ignorant maid of the border, Pix, as "a nugget of gold, concealed beneath the dust of ignorance." A stage robbery was realistically done, with a border vehicle drawn by four horses. Despite good performances, it closed after a week.[359]

Rankin almost lost his theater at this time. He owed $435 on the June rent and took an extension of a few days to pay.[360] When the time expired, Hayman sent representatives to claim the theater and refused the money when Rankin offered it to them. Armed with legal authority, Rankin's men threw out Hayman's representatives and made the issues so legally complex they would have had to be argued in court all summer. The issue was resolved by a judge, who threw out a charge of perjury against Rankin brought by the Hayman party.

In the midst of his personal and professional turmoil, Rankin was able to stage a successful play that helped to alleviate his financial pressures. Greene and David Belasco, now stage manager at the Baldwin Theatre, wrote *Under the Polar Star*, a tender love story that takes place aboard a ship on an exploratory voyage in the Arctic. Although the play was full of pathos and self-sacrifice, its sober scenes were balanced by strong comedy. Material for the play came from the journals of explorers and incidents from Jules Verne's writings.[361] The scene painter, Wilkins, excelled in the magnificent scenery of the Arctic and reproduced the aurora borealis in all its phantasmal splendor with the arctic perihelion, when the earth is closest to the sun. The naval pageant of officers, marines, sailors, and a full brass band who welcomed the heroes back to terra firma was brilliantly staged. Rankin played Harry Carleton, the ship's surgeon, Harkins was the ship's commander, and Mordaunt the first officer. The three prime comedians were Wallace, Holland, and Bishop as a scientist, historiographer, and boatswain. Mabel Bert provided the romance for the ship's surgeon, but she spent much of the play in disguise as a cabin boy named Joe, much to the disgust of a critic who complained that her clothes did not fit her. The play was a hit and the talk of the town. People went to see it a second time. It did good business through a second week, and the company donated one night as a benefit for St Luke's Hospital.

Rankin, desperate to keep his great company alive, tried another innovation. He closed the California Theatre for a week for cleaning and to install the Eden Musée waxworks and the Edison incandescent system of electricity—the first theater to use it on the West Coast.[362] By displaying wax figures of local, national, and foreign celebrities for a charge during the day and without charge during the evening performances, he expected to bring added receipts to the theater.[363] The Musée opened on July 19, 1886, simultaneously with *The Last Days of Pompeii*,[364] and the introduction of another debutante, Adelaide Emerson, whose friends helped fill the theater.[365] Susie Williams, having experienced the difficult life of the actor, submitted to the urging of her family and retired to her mother's home. Before the curtain, the fashionable audience wandered in the Eden Musée past the wax figures of royalty, American political and financial figures, tableaux of Pasteur inoculating children, and other scenes, lit brilliantly with minimal heat by the Edison incandescent method. The Musée was such a success that sixty more figures were ordered from New York.

Mabel Bert played a blind girl of Thessaly in *The Last Days of Pompeii* while Mordaunt took the role of a false Egyptian priest. To provide the humor, Charles Ray played Stratonice, a female gladiator and wife of Burbo, a retired gladiator, played by C.B. Bishop. The flamboyant style of the production and the beautiful scenery, including an assassination, a battle in the arena, and the spectacular eruption of Mount Vesuvius, were reminiscent of the palmy days of the theater when times were flush. Adelaide Emerson betrayed the timidity and incertitude of the novice, but her interpretation was good and her actions graceful, if somewhat restrained. The play attracted good houses for a week but had to be replaced in the middle of the second week by a good modern play, *John Hardy*, in which the company acted the roles well. Unfortunately, after three performances, it had drawn less than $250, and Rankin realized it was time to close the theater for good.[366]

Audiences were uninterested in problem drama; they wanted either sensation or ribald entertainment. The great repertory experiment was over. The venture in the end had been disastrous for management. "Homilies might be preached on extravagance after profitable runs at the theater," wrote a critic implying that Rankin had spent recklessly. He added that it would be a long time before San Francisco would see another such stock company "as the one now forced into temporary retirement through a lack of appreciation on the part of the people."[367] Hayman took over the theater. The Eden Musée stayed open all day and in the evening but there was no acting company for some time.

Amy Leslie, sometime actress and longtime theater critic, saw the demise of Rankin's stock company in terms of Rankin's psychological makeup:

> Rankin was then one of the handsomest men in the world. With a kind of western bravado of carriage, a dash and somber virility, his splendid physical advantages made him at once a desirable accession to the stage and a goodly thing to see any day on the corner of Kearney and Market. He played every sort of part and played with superb intelligence, a dramatic acumen which promised much more sterling achievements than were ever demonstrated by his largest endeavors. Rankin was talented, superbly equipped for his work and a courageous gambler of the theater. Indeed, it was that instinct, accompanied by an overweening cunning which sometimes accompanies the habit, that kept McKee from his biggest earnings as an actor of great attractions and gifts. He would rather turn a neat trick in arriving at a desired goal than easily to move into an eminence waiting for him. He was always parlaying his bets and taking a long chance. That was the wild, wonderfully fascinating and unreliable nature of the man.[368]

By confronting the overwhelming commercialization of the theater, Rankin had brought back the excellence, integrity, excitement, and artistry of the true theater, but the great energy that he and his actors devoted to the cause could not sustain its success without an equally energetic response from the public. After the high point of the *Macbeth* production and the manipulation by the profit-obsessed Hayman, Rankin's enterprise began to slide as the audience weakened and affected the actors, whose energies faltered, revived, and collapsed in the face of worsening receipts. The behemoth of commercial theater seemed unrelenting and indomitable.

In August, when benefits were held for the players, Al Hayman and Palmer paid $100 each for a box seat at Rankin's on the 15th. Attendance was not as large as expected; possibly the public blamed Rankin for the failure of his marriage, which must have been the subject of rumors. Mordaunt stayed in San Francisco and starred in *Uncle Tom's Cabin* and in Joaquin Miller's *Oregon* at the new Alcazar Theatre. Mordaunt's absence from the company made it difficult for Rankin to keep his commitment to play *Macbeth* in the East, but it was really his lack of finances that caused him to cancel the scheduled productions at the Chestnut Street Theatre in Philadelphia and elsewhere. Price had resigned as his manager, so Rankin sent his former treasurer at the California Theatre in advance to contract for eastern theaters. Rankin left immediately afterward with a company of twelve, including Mabel Bert and Adele Waters, to tour eastward.

Rankin's spirit was as buoyant as ever. He came away from San Francisco with the satisfaction that his ensemble company had been an enormous artistic success. Although it seemed that he had lived several lifetimes, so numerous were his activities, he was just forty-two and in love with a beautiful and talented young actress, whom he could train to become a star. With a lucky roll of the die, he could do even greater things in the theater, despite his enemies, who already were looking for ways to use his indiscretion with Bert to undermine him.

ACT III

Obsession

1886–1887: The Rise of Mabel Bert

As it proceeded eastward from Virginia City with three plays—*The Danites*, *'49*, and *The Golden Giant*—in its repertoire, the company played at towns along the route. Mabel Bert took Kitty Blanchard's roles in the plays. Because Alphonso had resigned from the company, Rankin hired an actor from the San Franciscan Chinese Theatre, Ali Tookh, to play Washee Washee.

At first, the company found that the western towns were profitable one-night stands. Actors, however, had to be careful of arrest by Law and Order Leagues formed to stop performances on Sundays. They risked the penalties, while the theater managers who insisted that actors perform on Sundays in all towns west of Chicago went untouched. Actors hoped that the league would be successful in Chicago, where playing on Sunday had been initiated; if the practice were stopped there, the rest of the western theater centers would follow suit.

The ups and downs of touring required equanimity in an actor. In Denver for the week of August 23, 1886, the company met with poor

---

Notes are on pages 471-77.

houses and began touring the state in a series of one-night stands in towns like Pueblo and Colorado Springs. In Leadville, Colorado, poor Ali Tookh, who had gone for a walk, had a narrow escape from a hostile mob. The police, learning that he was with Rankin's company, had to protect him.[1] The company did poorly in Topeka, Kansas, and when it arrived late in Atchison, Kansas, a false report of a cancellation had been put out, which reduced attendance for *The Danites*. The advance sale for *The Golden Giant* the next night, however, was reassuring. Three evenings and a matinee in Kansas City brought in some much-needed cash. The local critic praised *The Golden Giant*, and in particular Mabel Bert, who played the hoyendish Bessie Fairfax with much force and spirit. There followed a very prosperous week in Chicago, where Rankin's Sandy McGee was as popular as a decade before. In fact, all the theaters in that city were doing good business.[2] By contrast, Detroit brought in miserable business, despite Rankin's billing as "World Renowned" and the presence of a "real live celestial," a Chinese, as Washee Washee. The company, which had been losing players and taking on others, was called "good," but Rankin did only *The Danites* for the week, possibly because the new members had to learn their roles. He was served with an attachment for $250 by a decorator, who wanted to collect for work done on Rankin's former home on Bois Blanc Island. But as Rankin had no money, the decorator could not collect. Kitty Blanchard was domiciled in Detroit for the winter months, where she intended to set up a business to prepare women for the stage and superintend amateur theatricals.[3]

George Cameron Rankin, McKee's brother, made an unexpected appearance in the dramatic papers during this week. George had had a tragic life in some ways. His first wife died in childbirth, and his second wife died not long after he married her. He was attracted to the theater but did not have the staying power of his brother. Since the time when he had guided the business affairs of McKee's company back in the seventies, he had stints of managing traveling companies. The previous summer, he managed a company playing Gilbert and Sullivan's *The Mikado*, which was compelled, owing to licensing problems, to stop its performances in Canada. He had also dabbled in politics but without much success. He broke into the news after he knocked down his uncle, Thomas McKee, a customs collector, when he met him on a street. The two had been quarreling over property and had not spoken for years. Thomas McKee took out a warrant for George's arrest, but George barricaded himself in his home, and, standing guard with an ax, threatened to kill the four constables sent to collect him. George said that he was an English gentleman and no officer was going to lay hands on him. Because he was large and powerful, the officers were intimidated. The

Clipper reported that he cooked his own meals and was "otherwise acting strangely" and called him "well-off and dissipated."[4] Fortunately, McKee Rankin was on hand to resolve the confrontation peaceably.

Rankin's company presented *The Danites* to a large audience in Chatham, Ontario, on October 18, and played to a good house in London as well. At that point, Adele Waters, who was playing Huldah Brown, joined a touring company, and Rankin had to cancel several dates while he organized a new company. On November 22, it opened in Toronto for a week and two matinees to full houses. A critic described the favorable impression that Mabel Bert, "this dark-eyed girl, with a strikingly pretty baby face and lithe willowy form," made as Billy Piper; he claimed that as the romping, tomboyish Carrots, she achieved a triumph because she seemed to belong to the camp in the wilds:

> Every word, look, gesture seemed to bring with it the odour of the pines. She was the very ideal of the pet of the mining camp. With a great mane of raven blackness falling to her waist and clustering in masses of tangled curls above the handsome face, with big, dark eyes that one moment flashed saucy defiance at Mississippi or outspoken hatred for Belle, and the next spoke immeasurable tenderness for the grizzly old miner, she made one of the brightest, strongest, and withal most winsome pictures of real life that has been seen for many a day.[5]

The company worked through the small towns along the St Lawrence River, detouring north to Ottawa in early December 1886, where it did good business, then moving on to Montreal. From there, it returned to the United States, stopping at the towns en route to Chicago, where it played over the Christmas holidays at a small house on the west side of the city. A critic commented, "to what a pass has Mr. Rankin come that he cannot find an opening at a higher class theater?"[6] After playing in Grand Rapids, Michigan, for a week to mid-January 1887, the company came to New York City for a brief rest, possibly enforced because Rankin was having trouble finding suitable theaters. His agent had run into the monopoly control over theaters that Charles Frohman had built up; the closer a company came to the East, the fewer independent theater owners there were.

Not one to waste time, Rankin used the rest period to write a play with Fred Maeder, who was in his company, and copyrighted it in April as "Old London; a drama, embodying incidents from Ainsworth's novels and other sources with original effects and situations."[7] He appears not to have had the opportunity to produce it.

Rankin wanted to introduce Mabel Bert to New York audiences, but he sensed that his difficulties arose from theater people sympathetic to Kitty Blanchard. He gave an interview to the *Mirror* in late January: "I am again in the East from California after an interesting and eventful absence of over two years, but after a deal of hard work I am no richer financially. Still, I am equipped with a line of attractions that I think are latent fortunes, and I have a special few that I am arranging for reproduction in New York." There is a tinge of disappointment over his financial failure in these words, but it is followed quickly by optimism. He planned to produce his San Francisco version of *Macbeth*, but on a grander scale, then do *Allan Dare* and other works such as *Notre Dame* and *The Golden Giant*. "I contemplate introducing Mrs. Rankin in her original roles," he added, "and appearing myself."[8]

Obviously, Rankin was having difficulty interesting managers without Blanchard as a star. He persuaded Charles Frohman to finance *The Golden Giant*, but Frohman, ignoring Mabel, selected a new actress to play the leading part. Rankin had assured Clay Greene that he would find a producer for it in the East and had paid Greene $5,000 for the play instead of a royalty. Although Greene later complained that a royalty would have given him many times that amount, he may not have had a choice about the mode of payment.[9] As Greene conveniently forgot, Rankin had done much of the preliminary work in constructing the play in its form as *Gabriel Conroy* and had hired him only to improve upon it.[10]

After a quick trip to Boston to read *Allan Dare* to the manager of the Boston Museum Theatre, who was considering it favorably, Rankin opened with his new company in *The Danites* and *'49* for a week in Wilmington, Delaware, to good business. Hoping to introduce Mabel Bert to New York audiences, Rankin could secure only the Theatre Comique in Harlem, which was too far away from the theater center in Manhattan for the newspapers to review its productions.[11] The company was unusually good and the house was well filled. Rankin complained to the *Mirror* that the papers for the past two months had fostered a rumor that Blanchard was forced to take in drama students to support herself and their two children. Actually, she lived in a large house in Detroit's fashionable district with two servants and a governess for the children. She was devoting herself to their daughters' education and welfare when they were at an age when most in need of a mother's love.[12] Rankin seemed to suggest that a subtle bias against Mabel and him was being built up rather slyly.

In Philadelphia in *The Danites*, Rankin hoped to win some critical acclaim for Mabel, but she received no special attention. In New Haven, Connecticut, on February 28, 1887, they played, for the first time in the

East, *The Golden Giant* and *Wife and Child*. In the latter, Rankin played the blind artist and Mabel Bert was Lady Alice, the wife who deserted him years before. A critic called it a "well-knitted story of a pretty love tale that keeps it moving merrily along."[13] As for *The Golden Giant*, it drew lightly, with Rankin laboring under a cold so severe for the entire week that his articulation on stage was barely audible.

In Jersey City, he attracted big houses with *The Danites* and *The Golden Giant*. At Ford's Opera House in Baltimore, he presented only *The Golden Giant* for the next week and was rewarded with good-sized houses. Suddenly in trouble financially, possibly because of making bad investments in plays and musical companies that habitually he supported, Rankin canceled the next stop in Brooklyn, went to Detroit, sold his home, and brought his family to New York City. He needed Blanchard to play Bessie Fairfax, the hoydenish role that Mabel had been acting, for the New York opening of *The Golden Giant*. The company's sudden call for Blanchard could be explained only by Mabel's being unable to act. On April 18, 1887, just at the moment when her appearances in New York would bring her attention, Mabel Bert, in the company of her mother, departed for Europe, where she expected to stay until September.[14] Mabel was pregnant. Because she had been born in England, where she lived until she was sixteen, it can be assumed that she was going to relatives in England to have Rankin's child. Blanchard's readiness to help and apparent lack of resentment demonstrated her devotion to her husband and an acceptance of her position in his life, an acceptance that perhaps was fostered through all those years when she was the second Mrs Rankin.

She romped with abandon through the part of Bessie in *The Golden Giant*, opposite Rankin as the flaxen-haired Alex Fairfax. Rankin had revised the play and added another character, a Chinese, Jim Lung, played by the twenty-nine-year-old Ah Wung Sing, from San Francisco. Ah Wung Sing provided much merriment, especially in stage business with a small boy. He was the first Chinese to play at a New York theater. Rankin had been obliged to add his part to the play because it had become obligatory for western drama to have a Chinese character. The restrictions against and the unjust taxation of Chinese miners were the reality but not in the dramas, where they were objects of merriment and comicality.

The new leading man, Robert Hilliard, played the gambler, Jack Mason, as a transplanted Boweryite with a shiny hat and "split locks," with his hair parted down the middle. He made a quiet, easy, manly blending of the serious and comic in his work, moving the audience to applause and laughter. Charles Stanley, as a besotted old lawyer, with his cringing attitude, his fumbling of his well-worn hat, his quiet, unobtrusive, but very marked byplay, thrilled the audience. In the throes of alcoholic addiction in the last act when he betrays his confederates, he wrought the audience to a high pitch, and it exploded into spontaneous applause. Luke Martin, Rankin's old dependable, played an amusing Irish miner, and Little Ollie Berkeley was a remarkably intelligent child actress, who spoke her lines with meaning instead of parroting them like so many children. Rankin explained that young girls were more intelligent than young boys and hence were hired to play boys' parts.

During the two-week run, a police officer from Boston entered Rankin's dressing room after a performance and tried to haul him off to Boston on the charge that he owed the Boston managers John Schoeffel and Isaac Rich $350. The reason for this drastic action stemmed from two years earlier, when an actress obtained a judgment on Rankin for $60 in unpaid salary. Schoeffel and Rich, the managers of the theater at which the company was performing, provided a bond of $350 to effect Rankin's release from debtor's jail. Rankin did not return to Boston to challenge the judgment. When Schoeffel later tried to collect on the $350 loan, Rankin claimed he had no money. While waiting under arrest at the New York train station for the Boston train, Rankin notified his manager, Charles Frohman, who immediately dispatched his lawyer to the station. The lawyer persuaded the officer to telegram Boston that the bond had not been forfeited and that Schoeffel was likely to lose his case if he used force against Rankin. The immediate reply from Boston ordered the officer to bring Rankin to Boston regardless of the consequences. Rankin offered to go, give a poor debtor's oath, and return to New York, but after his lawyer insisted that a jury would never convict him of shooting the constable in self-defense, the constable went back to Boston alone. Rankin commented that since the sum was so small, he thought the real motive was to disrupt the phenomenal success of *The Golden Giant* in New York. Since the play was successful he must have been able to repay Schoeffel and Rich. He seemed unable to accept the justness of the original judgment against him, which implies that he thought that Schoeffel and Rich were responsible for paying the actress's salary. When the event appeared in the newspapers, John Schoeffel blamed his partner Rich for initiating the action, which he said that he himself would not do when Rankin was in "bad luck."[15]

The action seemed to be timed to interfere with Rankin's attempts to raise funds for a production of *Macbeth*. Because he had to be with his company in Philadelphia on April 27, 1887, Rankin arranged for Dan Harkins to read *Macbeth* at Chickering Hall, below Fourteenth Street, with a chorus, and a fifty-piece orchestra playing Kelley's music.[16] As a result of this reading, his old business associate Harry Miner negotiated for control of all of Rankin's enterprises for a number of years, including *Macbeth* and its music, *Wife and Child*, *The Golden Giant*, *Allan Dare*, *Old London*, and so on, and kept Rankin as stage manager and actor. Both Kitty and McKee Rankin could not associate with any other than a Miner production. Immediately, other managers claimed the right to the Rankins' services, but Miner's control, which began the next season, superseded all other arrangements. Rankin's contract with Frohman terminated in June. To agree to such terms, Rankin must have had a firm commitment from Miner that he would produce *Macbeth*.

In Philadelphia, *The Golden Giant* had a good critical reception, which considered it superior to other western drama because it was not so intensely heroic and had more humor and pathos. The company played at the Brooklyn Theatre for the first week in May, where *The Golden Giant* drew fairly well, then passed a two-week hiatus in New York before returning to Philadelphia for the final week in May. This time, it played to very light houses, and Rankin realized that he had made a mistake in bringing it back so soon after the initial production. By contrast, in New York, to which the Rankins now returned, the company enjoyed three profitable weeks at Niblo's in *The Golden Giant*—"coining ducats at Niblo's" reported the *Mirror*.[17]

Blanchard's return to the stage did not mean that she and Rankin had reconciled. Harry Miner intended to use both stars in separate venues to bring in the wealth that he expected from his investment. Rankin, no longer independent, had to accept his new status as job director and actor.

1887–1888: Reversals

Miner booked Blanchard and the *Golden Giant* company with Ralph Delmore as Alex Fairfax for forty-six weeks starting on August 29, 1887, in Bradford, Pennsylvania. The company was to play the oil circuit, then into the West, and back to New York City in October for a week before setting out again. Blanchard's role of Bessie Fairfax, now called Bet, was greatly enhanced. Miner arranged for Rankin to open in *Allan Dare* in New York, playing the detective, until mid-October. Then he would open in *Macbeth* at Niblo's Garden and tour the principal cities to the end of February 1888. Only theaters in the larger cities were booked because large stages were required with a touring cast of over two hundred, plus sixty musicians, and two carloads of scenery traveling by private rail.

Rankin rehearsed *Allan Dare* in New York in August, but the script was not the one that he had prepared for the California Theatre. Admiral Porter, the author of the novel, asked an unknown playwright to rewrite it.

The play, in which Rankin had no role, opened two weeks behind schedule on September 5. It was prolix in plot, complicated in incident, vague in language, and insufferably dull and stupid. Admiral Porter, whose authority came from Miner, who now owned the play, gave Rankin little say in its production, and relegated him to directing the actors on stage. "The dramatist," wrote the local critic, "in endeavoring to retain the bulk of Admiral Porter's book, has tangled things to a perplexing extent."

After the first night, Rankin pruned the dialogue hastily and made some changes in the cast, which improved the play considerably, and, as he continued working at the script, the criticism became less severe. But he was working against time: in Philadelphia, the criticism threatened the production's life in this new era of instant profit-taking. In Cleveland, at the end of September 1887, the play was reported to be pruned into conventional shape, with characters lopped off and incidents compressed. It had become an absorbing detective story, in which the tone was elevated because the majority of the characters were from the high life. A critic called it a shrewd mixture of *The Streets of New York* and *The Ticket-of-Leave Man*: "no more handsomely staged and finely acted drama has been seen here for a long time."[18] When it reached Cincinnati, where it was well received and made money, Mabel Bert appeared in the cast for the first time. She had returned from England with a baby girl, Doris.

Miner, however, brought Rankin to New York for he needed Rankin in tandem with Blanchard to pull in the crowds for his New York production of *The Golden Giant* at the Grand Opera House starting October 10. Blanchard's knowledge of the birth of Bert's child could not have made her offstage relationship with Rankin pleasant. The play had large houses for a week before the company went back on tour with Ralph Delmore as Alex.

Adelaide Emerson, the debutante-actress from San Francisco who was acting with the *Allan Dare* company, had to quit because of an eye infection that threatened her sight. Her presence in the company was an illustration of Rankin's loyalty to actors whom he had trained for the stage. It was a side of him that endeared him to many and that was to play an increasingly important part later in his life. Rankin returned to the *Allan Dare* company, which was greeted with large houses in Indianapolis and Columbus, but Miner, influenced by the early reports, declared he would close the play in Brooklyn on October 30, 1887, where houses, affected by his decision, again were poor. Miner then visited a greater calamity on Rankin when he pulled out of his agreement to finance *Macbeth* at Niblo's Garden.

For some time, Rankin had been planning his production of *Macbeth* at Niblo's. During the four months spent preparing for the San Francisco production, he advertised daily for large-framed, muscular, brawny men to play

Scottish barbarians in the combating armies, but it had taken him four weeks to get fifty men. For his forthcoming production at Niblo's, he had picked up twenty by stopping them on the street as he passed along at all hours. The real problem, he explained, was to get big men who were intelligent enough to act as barbarians, which seemed particularly difficult with big men. Four hundred people were engaged for the production, seventy musicians were in the orchestra, and one hundred voices were in the chorus on stage. The scenery had occupied the artists all summer, and advance agents had been busy selling tickets. When Miner claimed that the risk was too high, Rankin, relieved of his agreement with Miner, resolved to finance the production on his own and arranged with Niblo's to mount the play in February 1888.

Meanwhile, he reconstructed *The New Danites* from the old play and toured it in New England briefly in early November 1887. He expanded the role of Billy Piper to suit Mabel's talents. The reaction of the audiences was enthusiastic. He closed the tour in New Haven on November 12 and headed for New York with some money to finance a production of *Macbeth* in Brooklyn on November 28. He arranged to play it for a week in hopes that a success there would win him backers for a longer run at Niblo's. Perhaps hampered by financing, he hurried the preparations and had to postpone the opening for a night. A critic wrote: "The performance of 'Macbeth' last night was in some regards the best that has been seen on the American stage, but was in some respects not far from the worst."[19] He cited a lack of rehearsal, which caused fitful jerks, and long delays between scenes, which carried the play beyond midnight. Macbeth's castle tumbled over with noise and dust, a curtain cord broke, several players tripped over their lines, the orchestra played too loudly, and Rankin was too portly, lacked nobility, and had a throaty, bad delivery, as if his voice was full of whiskers.

With long red hair, mustache, and bare arms, Rankin depicted Macbeth as a frontiersman ready to react with weapons. John Burleigh, in acting Macduff, stirred up a whirl of action that lifted the auditor out of any lethargy induced by the slow going of previous scenes. Mabel Bert as Lady Macbeth had the rare merit of losing her identity in the part. "She is fair to look on," wrote the critic. "Her voice, although not quite deep enough for tragedy, has a range and is modulated in tones of music....She does not wear bustles or corsets—in this last respect she has made a daring departure in the direction of sense and historical truth." She was the first actress to represent a natural woman since Charlotte Cushman, and the role gained in grace, beauty, and freedom in a striking manner. "The craft, valor, and the resolution that make Lady Macbeth one of the most difficult parts were forcibly suggested," he added.[20] There was enough shown of her abilities to give promise of an important future.

The rest of the cast was excellent; the costuming, the brawny, shaghaired soldiers, and the wild scenery contributed to a realistic portrayal of the times. The sights and sounds were conveyed to the audience, even to the smell of burning meat as the soldiers roasted oxen at their fires. When Duncan arrived at the castle of Macbeth, the drawbridge was lowered, the portcullis raised, and trumpeters blew on real trumpets and read the music from slips held in the hand. Kelley conducted, looking like a priestly novitiate. The week was profitable. Rankin continued to work on the production for its presentation at Niblo's, set for February 13, 1888.

Bert was living in New York with Rankin and caring for their baby. But their relatively sedentary life ended when Rankin's hopes for his *Macbeth* at Niblo's were dashed in mid-January 1888; his backers, considering it unprofitable, backed away. *Macbeth* represented his greatest achievement as an actor and director; its success in the East would have brought him great pleasure and fame. Suppressing his disappointment, he looked ahead and, needing money, immediately arranged to take *The New Danites* on the road with Mabel Bert and a new cast. He called on his cousin Thomas McKee, who had experience running theaters in the Detroit area, to be his business manager.

The company opened in the Williamsburg section of Brooklyn on January 30, 1888, for a week to good business and continued on the Jacobs and Proctor circuit, skipping from one large city to another to play at houses owned by either Jacobs or Proctor. The new version of *The Danites* met with success everywhere, Mabel Bert won plaudits from critics and audiences, and Rankin made a good profit.[21] Rankin had to replace cast members from time to time. His New York agents always seemed to find satisfactory players, who entrained from New York to wherever the company was playing.

In Milwaukee on May 10, 1888, Rankin produced *Wife and Child* as a test.[22] Much of it was tiresome and the dialogue was redundant, but it could be improved, wrote the local critic. Rankin began working it over after analyzing the audience's reactions. He finished the season with *The New Danites* in Chicago on May 19, 1888. Two days later, he was in New York City for the ailing Lester Wallack's benefit, at which he played a supernumerary in Edwin Booth's production of *Hamlet*.

Rankin, recognizing that all the good new plays were controlled by theater entrepreneurs, realized that his survival depended on his producing his own plays. He therefore decided to spend some effort on making *Wife and Child* into a more effective dramatic instrument. Rankin with Mabel headed for San Francisco, met Fred Maeder, and persuaded him to help revise the play, which was retitled *The Runaway Wife*. Rankin also had a serio-comic drama in four acts called *The Kanuck*, written, he said, by an author who wished to stay in the background because he was new to writing plays.²³ The author was his brother, George, and the playscript would become a contentious matter between them. The central character was a French Canadian such as could be found in Quebec and the northeastern states. Rankin said he had played such a character once a number of years past in Chicago in a three-act farce, *The First Night,* and made an emphatic hit. He hoped to produce it soon and was sanguine of its success.

At the same time, Kitty Blanchard was doing well. When her company of *The Golden Giant* returned to New York City late in November 1887, she bought the Knolls, a large property in Riverdale, just north of New York City, on the Hudson River, with a mortgage of $72,000. She toured in the New England area, acted in Montreal between Christmas and New Year's, in Toronto in early January 1888, and wound her way through southern Ontario and upper New York State to a series of one-night stands in Ohio and to the south. At one of these stands in Lima, North Carolina, she carried a "real live baby" on stage in *The Golden Giant Mine*, the play's new name, which completely captured the audience. The baby probably belonged to a member of her company and was used as a prop to enhance the extended role of Bet as wife and mother in the play's revised form. The baby also may have reflected Blanchard's determination not to be outdone by Mabel Bert. She disbanded her company in Pittsburgh at the end of March 1888, saying it was not a financial success. This was hard to believe and may have been a defensive measure against creditors. She took the children to their Riverdale house for the summer and prepared for another season without Rankin.

1888–1889: *The Runaway Wife* versus *The Golden Giant Mine*

Because San Francisco and areas north of it enjoyed temperate weather during the summers, the theaters in the area played year-round. Rankin's company began touring on July 16 in Portland, Oregon, possibly because there was no available theater in San Francisco. It filled a week with the plays in its repertoire: *The New Danites,* '49, *The Runaway Wife, The Skirmish Line,* which Rankin and Maeder also wrote in San Francisco, and *The Canuck,* of which Rankin and Maeder now claimed authorship, with dialogue for its French-Canadian character written by George Rankin. Although called "brilliant," the company drew poor business owing to the unexpected extremely hot weather. It moved to Astoria and then took the train eastward, making brief stops in towns along the way towards Chicago.

These towns usually turned out in great numbers to see a company as good as Rankin's. A report to the drama newspapers from Duluth, Minnesota, where the company played on August 7 and 8 in *The New Danites* and *'49*, claimed that not for a long time had the town enjoyed performances as much as it did Rankin's company.[24] In Chicago, the company opened at the Grand Opera House for a week in *The Runaway Wife*, in which it did well, although a critic described it as "a monstrous morbidity....McKee Rankin plays in the old demonstrative style, and his work, judged by that standard is good. The part, however, should be played concentratively. The fashion of today in acting is to suggest rather than express....His roaring and groaning were entirely out of keeping with the few good scenes which were strong enough to play themselves. His bad style, however, tended to vitiate the acting of some of the younger members of his company."[25] This was severe criticism and served as a warning that Rankin had to adapt to the fast-changing modern stage if he were to survive. He kept altering the play throughout the week, which indicated that he was listening to the critics.

Rankin gave the plot more depth than it had as *Wife and Child*. Albert Eastman, an American artist, goes blind and lives in poverty. His wife, abandoning him and their infant son, goes to England, where, after some years, Sir Lancelot Travers, who wishes to marry her, tells her falsely that Eastman is dead. In the meantime, her son becomes a famous portrait artist, and together with his father meets his mother, now Lady Alice, at a soirée in England. The mother recognizes them both and faints but she does not reveal herself to them. The father comes to recognize her by her voice as she sits in the next room for her portrait by their son, who uses the sittings to expose Sir Lancelot's villainy and to effect Lady Alice's reconciliation and reunion with his father. On the family's voyage back to America, the elder Eastman regains his sight.

The Runaway Wife still needed work when it played in Cincinnati. In Louisville at the end of September, it ran smoothly and had a popular reception. This was Rankin's first appearance in six years in a city where he had always been a favorite. The company took another week in Chicago with *The Runaway Wife* to fair profits. Hearing that the South was rife with yellow fever, Rankin changed his route and circled about in one-night stands in Michigan and for one-week and one-night stands about the Midwest. In these places, the theaters often had standing room only. Toledo was a disappointment and hurt his profits, but in Owensboro, Kentucky, he opened a new theater seating 1,100 and played to capacity every night. In Cleveland, the drawing power of *The Runaway Wife* was demonstrated: attracting poor houses at the start, by the end of the week the play was drawing large houses. After another prosperous week in Chicago in early November, Rankin took the company south through St Louis, Kansas City, and one-night stands in smaller stops like Chattanooga, Tennessee. The disappearance from his company of actors who were winning praise for their performances reflected upon Rankin's ability to train them so well that he lost them to the competition. Yet they were replaced with relative ease; in Kansas City, for example, Rankin hired two young actors, Herbert Fortier from Toronto and Townsend Russell from Milwaukee, the latter playing the artist son in *The Runaway Wife*. Rankin also hired a prominent society woman, Future Gayle, to play small parts. The houses continued to be large and enthusiastic in the towns going south. Rome, Georgia, vowed to treat Rankin like royalty the next time that he visited; Birmingham, Alabama, called the company the most evenly balanced to visit in years. Here, Rankin hired Becky Levy, soprano and youngest prima donna on the American stage, for singing roles.

In New Orleans, the company played *The Runaway Wife* to enthusiastic houses. Rankin as the blind Eastman acted with undeniable power in the stronger scenes and was equally good in scenes calling for tenderness and emotion. The great welcome given *The Runaway Wife* prompted Rankin to produce *The Skirmish Line* near the close of the second week. Of the large audience, a majority were delighted with the play and its mounting. The consensus was that it would be a "go" after some judicious pruning was applied.[26]

In this new production, as in their other collaborations, Rankin constructed *The Skirmish Line*, delineated the characters, and, for the most part, left the "literary work" or the dialogue to Maeder. A lovely Southern girl, Ada, married to a Northern merchant, Willard Loring, on a Southern plantation in Kentucky on the eve of the Civil War, sends her husband, whom she tenderly loves, away, saying: "You go to the North, I to the South." The appearance of Free Joe introduces a vivid and realistic depiction of slave life, new to the stage. After a lapse of four years, Owen Averill, a brutal overseer, a Northerner, and an officer in the Confederate Army, tells Ada that Loring was killed in battle and demonstrates his passion for her to no avail. Loring returns, detailed to a special command of foragers by which he hopes to protect his family on the plantation. Ada, nerved still by her loyalty to the South, receives her husband coldly. He learns that he is a father, although his child thinks her father is dead. Loring is in command of the plantation, while Ada has arranged a signal light to bring the advancing columns of the Southern Army upon the Union force, thus imperiling her husband. Ultimately, wifely love and instinct assert themselves, and she begs Loring to save his life. When he is wounded, she drags him into a recess by a secret door. Compelled to receive the unwelcome attentions of Averill, she fends off suspicions that she harbors a spy until the play concludes happily with Lee's surrender. "The plot has much freshness and originality," said the *Clipper*. "It abounds in powerful and artistic situations, and it is developed in dialogue that is always graceful and natural, and at times eloquent in passionate expression, whether of love and confidence or bitterness."[27] Mabel Bert as Ada demonstrated power, intensity, and facility for lightning-like changes of facial expression. Rankin, as Willard Loring, acted in the intelligent manner that audiences had come to expect.

Rankin showed originality and courage in probing the relationships of North and South, breaking stereotypes, and introducing a realistic portrayal of slave life on a plantation. By producing the play for a New Orleans audience, he expected and got sympathy for his theme of loyalty to the Southern cause and understanding for the slaves from a Southern woman, who, nevertheless, put faithfulness to her husband above all else, at a time when no plays about the South were produced. But he shelved it because of advice that the time was not ready for the exploration of this emotionally inflammatory core of the national psyche, regardless of the comedy and quartet of singers he introduced to lighten the message. Quite simply, the play was thirty years before its time.

On its way north, the company stopped in Wilmington, North Carolina, where a critic declared that the cast was the best seen there all season. Jumping to New Britain, Connecticut, to play *The Runaway Wife* for Christmas Day and large profits, the company toured in the area for a few nights before starting the New Year in Philadelphia. Rankin's company opened on December 31, 1888, in *The Runaway Wife* at a small, out-of-the-way theater, the Academy of Music, where "very few saw it outside of the newspaper people and deadheads." By coincidence, Blanchard's company was also playing in Philadelphia for the Christmas holidays, but to splendid business at a good theater, which implied her superior social status in contrast to the declining influence of her husband. Blanchard, who had changed her billing from Mrs McKee Rankin to Kate Rankin as a sign of independence from her husband, had begun touring on September 10, 1888, in *The Golden Giant Mine*. Her company covered the East in one-week stands of excellent business, then three-night stands in Pennsylvania, followed by a series of one-night stands, at one point stopping in New York City at her old Third Avenue Theatre. When Blanchard appeared onstage in New York, she was handed a stand of flowers with the motto "Welcome" across the front. "The lady," reported the local critic, "seemed in exuberant form and certainly never assumed the transposition from rollicking and untutored hoydenness to wifely devotion and matronly cares with better success than on this occasion."[28] The critic remarked on "the bright-eyed baby but a few months old who appeared in the last act." Blanchard continued profitably for the rest of the season touring the larger cities of the Midwest and the Northeast and closing on May 25, 1889, in Philadelphia. Her company remained the same throughout, and she managed to avoid absences by staying in good health. Her role of Bet Fairfax, said a critic, gave her magnetic qualities a chance to be felt. "Her subtle methods elevated the role above the soubrette, imbued it with her personality, and made her acting hard to describe."[29] Audiences were kept interested or in a laughing mood nearly all the time. It appeared that Blanchard was rich enough not to have to take money from Rankin, and she was determined not to give him the divorce that he wanted.

Rankin's spring season had not been so profitable for him. Business was good in short stands in Connecticut. For a week at Niblo's in New York, from January 14 to 19, 1889, *The Runaway Wife* made a favorable impression but no great profit. The play tended to drag until Lady Alice deserted her husband in the second act, after which it moved briskly. The company played in towns in Connecticut, Massachusetts, Maine, New Hampshire, and again in Massachusetts in January and February, to uneven business. In Brockton, Massachusetts, Thomas McKee as the company's advance man made a hit at the hotel with his piano solos.

Back in Williamsburg, Brooklyn, for the week of February 25, the company did very good business, but, as an incident in a New York courthouse made clear, little or no profit was being made. Rankin was charged with contempt of court because he failed to show up as a third party at a trial in which a medical doctor was suing Fred Maeder for unpaid services of $465. Rankin's excuse was that the envelope containing his summons was stamped with the names of the first two parties and he thought it was not meant for him. The *Mirror* wrote: "It remains to be seen how he will wiggle out of this one."[30] Rankin went through a three-and-a-half-hour examination in the New York Supreme Court to determine Maeder's profit from *The Runaway Wife*. Maeder's interest in the play was $60 per week out of the profits until $3,000 was paid. But, Rankin testified, no payments had been made to him because the profits were not sufficient to warrant them. Moreover, Maeder was not interested in managing the company. Rankin was excused from the contempt charge, and the *Mirror* was disappointed once more.

In New York State, the company ran into a spate of poor business. While at the Hotel Bennett in Binghamton, where the company had small but enthusiastic houses, Rankin wrote to a manager in Boston about his hopes of bringing his new play to the Globe Theatre in Boston and about some "Vandenhoff affair" from which he expected some money. "If you get the money would you kindly pay yourself," he wrote, "and send me the balance as soon as possible as I am in a chronic state of bust....My domestic affairs are still as they were when I saw you last."[31]

When Rankin brought the play back to New York City on April 1, 1889, he introduced Gladys ("Dido") Rankin to the stage. She had appeared as a child in *The Danites*, but now she was seventeen and was expected to support herself. She made her debut as Lillian Haye, fiancée to the blind man's son, and acquitted herself well.

Elements in the press spasmodically hinted at Rankin's ill-treatment of his wife and children. The previous fall, Rankin had defended himself in a letter to the *Mirror* "against attacks by Giddy Gusher," who wrote a gossip column in the paper and commiserated with poor, hard-working Blanchard, who was getting "no retributive justice." Rankin said that he bought the Knolls and that his daughters were educated and refined because he surrounded them with refined influences. "If anybody," he wrote, "through either malice or mistaken friendship, continues to attack me, I shall be compelled to go into a most uninteresting exhibit of facts, dates, and figures to show who planned out the enterprises and sustained them, by which the 'Knolls' now remains as a home to my children. No 'retributive justice' will ever impel me to accept it as a shelter, if force of circumstances should make it impossible to be a home for me as well, in every sense of the word."[32]

His sharp rebuke through the public press was rare and must have been in defense of Mabel rather than himself. When others were hurt indirectly through him or when he had to defend his art, he responded to criticism. Otherwise he preferred silence. As Amy Leslie wrote, he scorned the emotional sensationalism of private life, the boasting in the barroom, and the refuge of the cheap curtain speechmaker. "He was simply unaware of his own theatricalism because he never had a single moment either to himself or to the world at large or an individual."[33]

Rankin continued in one-week runs mixed with one-night stands through the Midwest and New England. The business of entraining for so many miles each day, playing in the evening, traveling all the next day, week after week, month after month, year after year, and arranging for the packing of the scenery and costumes, made powerful physical and mental demands on him. Fortunately, he had a strong physique and great energy, which could withstand the demands that travel made upon the body.

Even with age and fame, the acting life did not get any easier. Many actors in whose companies the novice Rankin had had minor roles were still traveling. Actors such as Maggie Mitchell and Jane Combs were still playing their old roles in *Little Barefoot* and *The Lady of Lyons*—they had no choice if they wished to survive. They were strong, but even strength could fail, as was the case with Lucille Western and many more. Many actors relied on alcohol to keep them going, but this killed them, including McCullough, Sothern, and Adams.

The short stops of Rankin's company were interspersed with longer runs in the bigger cities in the East, which was a luxury denied actors who traveled in the Midwest. Rankin's company stayed a week in Providence, Rhode Island, where it had a good reception and good business. The long jumps that Rankin was having to make between stands throughout the past two years was owing to his choice of independent managers, whose theaters were spread over large territories. The more powerful managers owned more theaters in more towns and did not require their traveling combinations to spend so much of their time on trains. But Rankin's experience with Colonial Jack Haverly and other dictatorial managers made him value his independence, even if he paid for it through a grueling schedule.

Rankin's company played in Brooklyn for a week to fair attendance. The company was praised for being good, in particular Mabel Bert and "Miss Dido," whose first appearance in Brooklyn was "favorably recognized." A critic commented that Rankin was a diminishing figure in popularity "but a greatly increasing figure in avoirdupois" as he restored *The New Danites*.[34] The company closed the season on June 15, 1889, in Hartford, Connecticut, where, despite the hot weather, it attracted appreciative audiences. For the first time, a critic mentioned that the emotional *Runaway Wife* was popular with the ladies.[35] It was a sign of the awakening desire for independence among women, which was to become a major issue in the plays of the near future.

Such a desire was unexpectedly expressed by Dido Rankin. She returned to the Knolls for the summer, where the charming rascal Sidney Drew persuaded her to elope with him on July 22. Blanchard had discouraged Dido, who was a very pretty woman, from having anything to do with Sidney, whom she considered rightly to be an incurable philanderer. But seventeen-year-olds are wont to rebel, and Blanchard had to accept the inevitable. She may have consoled herself with the thought that, if Dido had not married into riches, she had at least married into a prominent stage family. None of the family were at the wedding.[36] Dido joined Sidney in the cast of *The Burglar*, which was being sent on a nationwide tour by the Madison Square Theatre Company. Rankin, whose own indiscretions left him no ground to criticize Dido, spent the summer with Mabel and baby Doris.

1889–1890: *The Canuck*

By late August 1889, Rankin was in Cincinnati organizing a new company and preparing to open on September 2 for a week. Mabel, wanting a less demanding role, played Lillian Haye, Dido's role, in *The Runaway Wife*. The Cincinnati Opera House had been redecorated in bronze and gold and the gas jets had all been replaced with electric lighting. Opera glasses were now placed on chairs, thus doing away with the boys who paraded the aisles singing out their wares. Despite the dry torrid heat unrelieved by a breath of cool air or a drop of rain, the company did a good business.[37] It went on to Milwaukee for a week where it "scored big." At this point, Rankin took Mabel and Fred Maeder with him to San Francisco. He arranged for the rest of the company to play through the Northwest circuit and join them in Portland, Oregon, in a few weeks.[38]

Rankin opened at the Alcazar Theatre in San Francisco in his new play, *The Kanuck*.[39] He played the blunt French-Canadian farmer Jean-Baptiste with the dialect, speech inflections, deportment, manner, and idioms to bring the character to life. In his sorrow, he sings: "Fee I was die, den I would be happy so long what I live." Mabel Bert had the role of a New York adventuress. The play had originated in George Rankin's forty-minute sketch to raise money for the organ fund of a local church at Sault Ste Marie, Ontario, in the winter of 1884-85. George had played Jean-Baptiste.[40] The next summer, under the stage name George Cameron, he had presented the work, renamed *L'Habitant*, assisted by professional actors in Montreal, and then toured several Ontario towns. During the winter, he elaborated the play into a five-act drama and copyrighted it as *Jean-Baptiste*. He left the manuscripts of the earlier and later versions with a theatrical acquaintance in Detroit and pursued other interests in the Soo for the next three years. In the meanwhile, the wife of the theatrical acquaintance either gave or sold the manuscripts to McKee Rankin. After producing the play in San Francisco, Rankin wrote to George offering to pay him $300 to strengthen the play by writing a child's part. McKee claimed that rumors that he had stolen George's play were "too absurd to reply to." A feud between the brothers did not come to a head until Rankin's company reached Detroit.

Playing *The Kanuck*, *The Runaway Wife*, and *'49*, the company toured northward through Oakland, Sacramento, and a few one-night stands to Portland, Oregon, where it reunited with Rankin's company. This augmented company, minus several actors wishing to remain on the West Coast, began the long journey eastward through the Oregon circuit.[41] At Helena, Montana, after the third act of *The Kanuck*, Rankin appeared on the stage apron complaining that the theater manager was abusing him.[42] At the company's previous stop, Marysville, Montana, the company's baggage was to be hauled from the rail depot to the theater and back to the depot for $1, but the baggage man refused to take the trunks from the wagon on the return trip unless he was paid $6. Rankin placed the bags from the wagon on the rail car himself but was arrested for it on arriving in Helena because only baggage handlers were allowed to move baggage. His box office receipts were attached for $6 and costs. Because the manager would not return the box office receipts to him, Rankin informed the audience that he would not proceed with the show and that ticket holders must seek reimbursement at the box office. Yet, by now, the receipts were in the hands of the sheriff, and the theater manager could not return the money. An exasperated member of the audience wrote a check for the amount of the attachment, and the show continued, after which Rankin was again arrested for breaching the peace at Marysville. Because he was not going back to Marysville, Rankin received lenient treatment from the judge, who accepted a guilty plea, levying a $1 fine and costs of $22. The suit for $6, however, was still pending. Such inconveniences were doubtless commonly encountered by acting companies, but Rankin's public condemnation of the theater manager and his stopping a performance over such an issue were signs that he was heading for a mental breakdown.

His manager stepped in to demand that Rankin take a rest from performing. The theatrical profession was very aware of the mental effects of overwork. Two years earlier, the playwright Bartley Campbell had died in the Bloomsbury Asylum for the Insane, where he had played emperor to the inmates. He was there as a result of financial difficulties, which had plunged him into despair and delusions of grandeur.

The company dashed to Salt Lake City to open in *The Runaway Wife* on December 12, and *The Canuck*, the title newly spelled, on the 13th. W.C. Crosbie, a veteran actor who understudied Rankin, took over Rankin's roles. Crosbie lacked the ability to sustain the role of the blind artist Eastman in *The Runaway Wife*, but, surprisingly, he was a hit as Jean-Baptiste Cadeaux in the new play. Mabel Bert, who was remembered by Salt Lake City theatergoers as a schoolgirl on her last visit, had developed into a graceful and handsome actor. Both plays were successful.

In Denver, the Metropolitan Theatre, where the company played, was in financial difficulties. Luckily, *The Runaway Wife* was a popular draw, which enabled Rankin's manager to take over responsibility for the theater for four weeks. The long stay in one place gave Rankin the time he needed to recover his mental equilibrium. The houses were variously reported as excellent and good. When the company left the Metropolitan, creditors of the theater formed a stock company of $100,000 to restore the theater because Rankin had shown that it could be profitable.[43]

The company opened in Chicago on January 13, 1890, for a long stay. Rankin's manager did not want to expose him to the pressures of shepherding the company on the road and had arranged for the owner of theaters in Milwaukee and St Paul to take over the Standard Theatre of Chicago, in which the company was playing in order to give Rankin's company a long run while he recuperated. For *The Canuck*, Rankin engaged new actors, including Charles Cowles in the role of Cyrus Stebbins, the Vermont farmer and friend of Cadeaux. Cowles became very popular and eventually outshone Rankin in the play. When the company played '*49* for the second week and *The Danites* for the third and last week, Rankin was back in his customary roles.

From Minneapolis, Rankin wrote to his brother, George, admitting that he had a copy of *L'Habitant*. George considered this an admission of guilt since McKee had claimed not to have "stolen" his play. McKee considered that his and Maeder's rewriting of the script meant that it was a completely new play and took it for granted that George understood this. Probably McKee felt that he was doing justice to his brother by asking George to add some scenes and by crediting the creation of the character of the French-Canadian farmer to him. The brothers, however, had lived very different lives and now easily misunderstood one another.

When the company reached Detroit, McKee and George met for the first time in some years. George handed McKee the child's part, which he had written into the play, and McKee handed George his copy of *L'Habitant*—"nonchalantly," in George's estimation. George came to an understanding with McKee that if the piece were successful in New York City, George would receive a $10 royalty per performance up to $5,000. All seemed well until the last day between the matinee and evening performances, when McKee, in George's words, "surreptitiously took an objectionable woman companion down to lunch at Thornfield, our homestead, a mile below Windsor, thus desecrating our dead mother's home."[44] George had to be restrained from harming McKee. This incident, being a factor in the cause of the long quarrel between the brothers over the play, was really symbolic of a deeper resentment. Later when Colonel Rankin was dead, George could express his long-repressed envy for McKee's success in contrast to his own failure.

The "objectionable woman" was, of course, Mabel Bert, whom old Colonel Rankin would have looked forward to meeting, especially since she probably brought his grandchild with them. McKee would have strongly objected to the aspersions that George cast upon her. It later appeared that Colonel Rankin also was offended by George's behavior.

Soon on the road again, McKee had a profitable week in *The Runaway Wife* in Chicago, big business for a week in Toledo, average business in a number of one-night stands through Ontario and New York State, followed by a week in Williamsburg, Brooklyn, to excellent business. Then it was into New England for two- and one-night stops to close the season earlier than planned in Mystic, Connecticut, on April 30. Poor houses may have convinced him to quit before he lost whatever money he had earned. He also would have been upset to learn the news of the sudden death that day of Charles Vandenhoff of typhoid pneumonia in a hospital in Seattle, Washington.

During May and June 1890, Rankin revised *The Canuck* to the kind of play that he thought audiences wanted while he worked on other plays. His contract with Miner fulfilled, he arranged with independent theater managers to make time for his tour in *The Canuck*, which he assured them would be a success.

That summer, Blanchard introduced her fifteen-year-old daughter Phyllis ("Pixie") to the New York stage in the small part of Felice in *Sara*, a play recently written for Blanchard and in which Blanchard played the title role. Pixie was a success.[45] Her first appearance onstage was at the age of two when her father carried her on in *Rip Van Winkle*, and she had played children's roles in Rankin's *Storm Beaten, School,* and *Wife and Child*. In New York on other business, Rankin was able to see the play before it closed and would have been pleased that Pixie was talented. At the time, Rankin was appearing in Manhattan City Court in answer to a summons to pay $500 to a stage carpenter at Niblo's. In the fall of 1887, the carpenter had built the set for *Macbeth* and had not been paid. Rankin said the play was a failure in the East and that the carpenter should contact Fred Maeder in San Francisco for a settlement. Having wriggled out of yet another debt, he began rehearsing the cast of *The Canuck* for opening on July 28, 1890. The late date reflected that the pressures of the commercial theater had forced managers to extend their seasons.

1890–1891: Sued for Support

The Canuck ran for six weeks at the Bijou Theatre, a combination house in New York. The *New York Times* critic gave it a bad review, predicted that although it was like a moneymaker there would be no money in it, and wondered that Rankin would risk his reputation in it unless he believed that sound artistic standards no longer existed to measure him against. Full of slang and puerile sentiment, the play was unconvincing. Nevertheless, the theater was jammed on the hottest night of the year, and the play was "lustily applauded." "Spectators," wrote the critic, "in the back seats and the gallery yelled and cheered enthusiastically, while those in the front viewed the play listlessly."[46] Rankin sensed a big moneymaker in the new theatrical climate.

Before closing, Rankin gave an afternoon benefit performance in memory of a theatrical photographer, which resulted in a large sum for the man's widow. This beneficence stood in contrast to the treatment he accorded his wife. While on the road, Rankin was served a summons from Blanchard by a deputy sheriff. Blanchard wanted a legal separation and alimony to support herself and Pixie. Blanchard was living in the Knolls, her Riverdale home, but was struggling to pay the mortgage. Too ill to return to the stage, she claimed that Rankin made between $300 and $700 a week out of *The Canuck* and that the play was worth $30,000. Rankin was agreeable to paying over a part of his earnings and hoped to settle the issue out of court.[47] On October 1, however, he was in the New York Supreme Court denying that he had abandoned Blanchard but rather that she deserted him. He was not prosperous, he said. He was $4,000 in debt and did not own $10,000 worth of real estate in Spokane Falls, as Blanchard claimed, or indeed real estate anywhere worth anything. The court reserved its decision.[48]

However difficult Rankin's personal life, he had to be pleased with the reception of *The Canuck*. Audiences responded well to the play wherever it went. Rankin's character acting was called "exquisite."

> The manner, the look of the man, the slippery quaintness of his accent, all suggest the Frenchman. Every word that he utters, his stories of his old horse, of his dead wife, his gayety, his tenderness, his revelry—all seem equally spontaneous and true, equally the outpouring of a strong true nature. Admirably simple and direct is his expression of heart-breaking grief over the flight of his daughter; not less true and sweet his final forgiveness, after persistent threats of obduracy, when she returns a penitent. There is much tenderness, much lovableness in the role as he depicts it, and scarcely once does he offer an exaggerated or inartistic touch....The old rustic giant is a picturesque figure, with his grizzled moustachios, his swallow tail coat, gay waistcoat, and trousers more than ample.[49]

This was a period in the American drama when the kind of detailed realism called naturalism was finding favor. It was before the serious social drama of Ibsen, and before Shaw and others ushered in the revolt against melodrama and the exaggerated portrayal of eccentricity, which the influence of Charles Dickens, among others, had made pervasive. The old plays were still popular in much of the country, and playgoers still kept a sentimental attachment to the old stars, but a change was coming, and the recent death of Dion Boucicault, who had effected so many changes on the stage, symbolized it.

Rankin kept revising *The Canuck* as the company did one-week stands, usually to good business. In St Louis, a critic thought that Rankin was playing second fiddle to Charles Cowles, whose portrayal of the Vermont farmer was "touched with crudeness, not always sustained, but on the whole one of the best and most comical presentations of this kind that our stage has seen."[50] In Cleveland, in mid-December 1890, the audience was treated to what the critic called "an unusual episode." Rankin, who was playing Jean-Baptiste Cadeaux, stepped before the curtain between the first and second acts dressed as Jim Hogan, the New York sport. He announced that the actor in that role, W. Currie, had suddenly left his post, and rather than close the theater Rankin intended to play both Hogan and Jean-Baptiste. "It was a decided novelty," wrote the critic, "to see him during the balance of the play impersonating a New York 'swell' as well as the old Canuck."[51] Currie, intimidated by the criticisms he had been getting, must have developed stagefright.

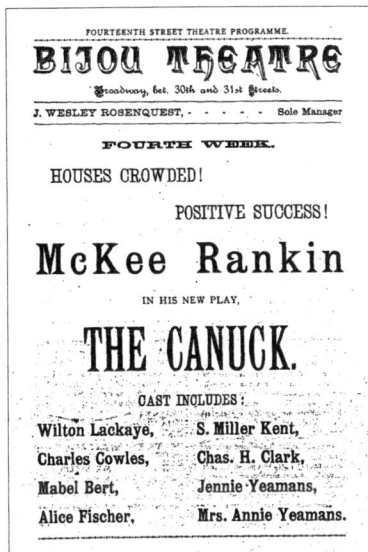

Playbill for Rankin's *The Canuck*, Bijou Theatre, New York, July 1890.

The company jumped from one city to another with "excellent prospects" through to mid-January 1891 and made one-night stands in Nebraska, Iowa, Kansas, and Texas. It played a week in New Orleans in mid-February before heading north. Rankin wrote from Albany, Georgia, to his agent, Colonel Brown, in March that Mabel Bert was about to withdraw from the company because her part had been whittled down, and she wanted experience with other companies. This was the first indication that all was not well between Bert and Rankin. It appears that she had been asking for smaller roles to make her departure from the company easier when it came. Rankin sang her praises to Brown:

the very best all round leading woman in America having had a most remarkable experience in this age of combination so devoid of anything like a school for the young of our profession. Miss Bert was my leading woman during my stock season of eighteen months in San Francisco and played everything from lightest juvenile to "Lady Macbeth." She can sing also. I am sure you will find her a most valuable woman to have on your books. Please let me know what your fee is and I will remit it at once. Think you saw Miss Bert in *The Canuck* while we were playing at the Bijou. P. S. Miss Bert is a very beautiful woman and a gorgeous dresser. Mr. Miner paid her $100 per week and she has been getting this and more with me. She won't take less than 75.[52]

Years later, a commentator suggested, with moral righteousness, that Bert had a crisis of conscience over the wrong she did Blanchard and that the noble part of her nature showed itself by leaving Rankin. This was unlikely, but the years of Bert's and Rankin's theatrical struggles for recognition of her talent must have taken a toll on their relationship. Rankin, according to the commentator, "lost money and caste," after he teamed with Bert, and she might have endured resentment from Blanchard's many friends over the years.[53] Love and "duty" fought within her, but love won for the time being because she stayed with Rankin's company, his letter to Brown notwithstanding. Rankin, as a result, altered *The Canuck* to enlarge Mabel's stage presence and tried it in Boston to "splendid business." Confident of success, he opened at Niblo's on March 30, 1891.[54] As rewritten, *The Canuck* was barely recognizable to the New York critics.[55] It had become stronger and more interesting. The second act was entirely new. Mabel Bert sustained the French-Canadian dialect in a very creditable manner in a new character, Bissonette, a niece to Jean-Baptiste Cadeaux, which she played in addition to Angelique, his daughter. Even her singing was encored. Rankin portrayed the rugged farmer more vividly, and Cowles was next to Rankin in his personation. Unaccountably, the houses were not large, profits dwindled, and the company had to curtail a two-week engagement. Moreover, Cowles fell ill during the week, and Rankin, catching the flu, was absent for the last two performances. Worst of all, Rankin had guaranteed management the first $1,000 taken in the week. With receipts totaling less than that, Rankin received nothing for the week and had to pay his cast from his own pocket. Niblo's Garden, complained a critic, should be replaced by a warehouse because the town had "grown away from this section."[56]

Served to appear before an arbitrator at the request of a lithographer, who wanted to collect on three promissory notes for $120 each to pay for lithographs done in 1888, Rankin ignored the summons, was cited for contempt of court, and had to appear in city court on April 16.[57] Probably he wriggled out of this charge again, with the valid excuse that he was broke. Desperate for money, he canceled his next engagement in Jersey City in order to play *The Danites* in the more prosperous Philadelphia for a week, which brought him medium business.

Between engagements, he attended the funeral in New York of Fred Maeder, who had died of pneumonia. Maeder, his closest friend and collaborator in recent years, had written many plays, including the popular *Buffalo Bill*, which had brought Bill Cody to the stage and to fame.[58] Possibly reminded of the shortness of life, Rankin announced that he intended to devote a portion of his time in the next season to "the arduous task of writing plays." After meeting with houses from slim to fair touring New England, he took *The Canuck* to the Windsor Theatre in New York from May 18 to 23, 1891, and did well financially. In Lynn, Massachusetts, the company closed for the season. Charles Cowles, having won considerable recognition as a brilliant actor under Rankin's guidance, joined another company because it was becoming obvious that *The Canuck* had run out its string.

1891–1892: *Abraham Lincoln* and Frank Mayo

True to his word, Rankin had written a scenario for a new play that was a departure from anything he had done to that point. Archibald Gordon, who had helped Rankin revise '49, wrote the dialogue for Rankin's *Abraham Lincoln*. He seemed the right man to bring the dignity and understanding to the characters that a realistic drama demanded.[59] Rankin had to overcome a bias to produce the play. The *New York Dramatic Mirror* attacked it based on hearsay and called the introduction of Wilkes Booth into a play a "gross impropriety." It deplored the shock it would give the sensitive Edwin Booth, who had been tortured enough by unscrupulous persons, who manufactured fictitious stories on the assassination for the newspapers. "Will it not be ingratitude to a great and beloved leader of our profession, if the stage that he had illuminated so long is made to insult him and degrade his name?"[60]

Rankin cast Elmer Grandin to play Lincoln. Grandin combined great height and size with a strong personality and exceptional acting ability, which suited him for the role, and, incidentally, for other momentous roles such as Ursus, the giant barbarian who twists the neck of a bull in *Quo Vadis,* which he played on Broadway in 1911. Rankin had difficulty casting the role of Wilkes Booth. He tried two actors in the role during rehearsals before calling in Myron Leffingwell, the son of an actor he had known in the 1860s, at the last rehearsal. He hired a number of solid veteran actors to play members of Lincoln's cabinet, including Robert McWade, his old rival as Rip Van Winkle. Mabel Bert had a small role as one of the young women in love with Booth.

Rankin with little financing helped to raise money from the play's early success to keep it going. He assembled the company at the Erie ferry to cross the Hudson and board a train for Indianapolis, Indiana, but, lacking rail fare, he had to delay for another day until he found some money.[61] The opening night in Indianapolis on September 7, 1891, was a marked success. The audience recalled the actors frequently and finally brought out Archibald Gordon, who responded with a speech. It was said to be the first time that Lincoln had been portrayed on stage, although there were numerous short plays, depicting Lincoln as a monster or devil, written by Southerners during the Civil War. When it opened in Chicago, Rankin's play was greeted by an immense audience. No other new play had excited as much interest and comment in the city. Many greeted it favorably, despite the wholesale attacks on it by the press. Grandin's quiet and dignified portrayal helped make it acceptable. Enough people were attracted out of curiosity to make the two-week engagement profitable, although there was a falling off in the second week.

Rankin, of course, was hoping to educate the public about the assassination as well as write a truly realistic piece. "Every scene and act was taken from historical records and photographs," said the program. "Everything true to nature. No exaggeration or eliminations."[62] Several pages of the dialogue from *Our American Cousin* precede the assassination of Lincoln.[63] The effect must have been to involve the audience intimately with the action of the play-within-the-play and cause it to experience the alarming disturbance of gunshots and death as they actually happened. "Nothing in the history of the American stage has ever been produced so realistic," reported the *New York Herald.*[64] Certain critics, however, called the dramatic work poor, a patchwork of history and newspaper anecdotes, slenderly united scenes, and a general incoherence.[65] Rather than a drama, it was a series of historical events and tableaux loosely strung together. It made history "pictorial."[66] In other words, it seemed to have been like the modern-day documentary and indicated that Rankin was years ahead of his time.

In Pittsburgh for a week, the play reportedly bored the audience, which was a good size because it had come out of curiosity. In Columbus, it did fairly well for a week. There was a strong division of opinion about its merits, but the virulent criticism from much of the press eventually forced the play to close. At the Chestnut Street Theatre in Philadelphia when another company canceled, the play was given a chance for two weeks. But by now the press was fulminating against it, and Robert Lincoln, the president's son, whose character appeared in the play, was quoted as saying that it was too soon after the assassination for it to be dramatized. It began to lose money and closed after one week on October 17, 1891.[67]

Shortly after its demise, Rankin and Frank Mayo joined forces in a partnership. Since the fortunes of both had been declining, they hoped that together they could revive them. Mayo began the season in Buffalo on November 2 with a first-class company, which included Elmer Grandin, Charles Parsloe (the former Washee Washee of *The Danites*), and Harry Lee (also formerly of *The Danites*), while Rankin, Bert, and Pixie led a company playing the West Coast. After touring for fifteen weeks, they planned to combine their companies and stage *The Two Friends*, an old play Rankin had recently revised.[68] Rankin opened in *The Danites* at the Bush Street Theatre in San Francisco to good business on November 8, 1891, with a company formed from West Coast players who had been in his earlier productions.

Back on home ground, Mabel Bert broke with Rankin. This was not just because he would never be able to win a divorce from Blanchard: she had become restless and wanted a wider acting experience. Rankin had taught her a lot of stagecraft, and she was regarded as one of the best leading ladies. It seemed, however, that either she lacked the particular magnetism and the unique personality to become anything more than a good leading lady or her association with Rankin prevented her from finding a manager who could bring her to stardom. She asked Rankin not to seek her out. Rankin loved her, but having somewhat desperately delayed her departure for some time, he must have understood that she loved him no longer.

Rankin put his company under M.B. Leavitt's management again, and Leavitt reminded him that he still owed him for the railway tickets, which he had cashed in back in 1884. Whether Leavitt pressured him or not, Rankin gave Bert's leading roles to one of Leavitt's promising young actresses. She was Amelia Bingham, who would become a star one day. She had a fine stage presence, more than average comeliness, and an excellent voice, and she was intelligent and versatile. Her husband was taken into the company with her. The company did three one-night stands down the coast to play three days in Los Angeles to good business. Then, in a series of three-, two-, and one-night stands, it toured north through California and the Northwest, enjoying handsome returns in *The Danites* and *The Canuck* in the New Year. In Denver in late January 1892, the company drew large audiences for a week. But despite the fair success of his tour, Rankin disbanded the company in Kansas City, Missouri. Leavitt wrote that the takings of the tour were large but that Rankin was in difficulties, "so that before the season had expired he again had liabilities with my treasury."[69]

At this point, Rankin was supposed to join forces with Frank Mayo. Instead, Henry Lee, who had been acting in Mayo's company, paid for the use of *The Runaway Wife* for the remainder of the season and hired most of Rankin's company to play it. Moreover, after Bert left him, Rankin was "frenzied," and, according to a commentator, "followed her everywhere and made her life unhappy."[70] He returned precipitously to San Francisco to be near her, which contributed to his failure to link up with Mayo. Frank Mayo, for his part, fell into a profound depression. He had lost money playing classical and Shakespearean roles, and no new piece worked for long. He reverted to playing Davy Crocket to make ends meet, much like Rankin kept falling back on *The Danites* and his other old plays, but the crowds no longer came.

Mabel Bert in *Daddy Long Legs*, New York, 1915.

Rankin found a position in the Alcazar Theatre stock company in San Francisco. L.R. Stockwell, its manager, proprietor, and main actor, was moving to another theater, and George Osbourne took over the management. Both had acted in Rankin's companies and now welcomed Rankin as the star for a four-week season.[71] Rankin began in *The Danites* on February 22, 1892, and followed it on March 14 with *The Runaway Wife*. "His engagement at this house," reported the *Clipper*, "has been highly satisfactory to all concerned."[72] *The Runaway Wife* was so popular that Rankin continued it in April at the Morosco Theatre when the Alcazar engagement was terminated. After Henry Lee's tour with the play closed in July, however, Rankin sold it and negotiated with the Grand Opera House to present Eleanor Barry, a new equestrian star, in *Mazeppa* for a

Obsession

week.[73] He was trying to raise money to spend on a theatrical project and make a break with his past by selling off the plays in which he had starred with Bert. This kind of juggling kept him in debt, but he apparently could not resist. He adapted a novel, *The Kentucky Colonel*, to the stage with a fat character role of a Southern gentleman for himself, which he thought could win him a fortune.

Blanchard filed an affidavit in the San Francisco court requesting that Rankin pay $150 per month alimony and $1,500 in lawyers' fees. Her house in Riverdale was foreclosed, and she and her daughter were living in a boarding house while, she complained, Rankin was making a high salary.[74] To add to his woes, Rankin was brought before a justice of the peace to pay a judgment for $210 brought against him by seven musicians whom he had failed to pay in 1886 for their services. Presumably the musicians got their money at last. As for Blanchard, the court awarded her $500 a month in alimony. She moved back into the Knolls.[75] Blanchard had been doing well onstage, having a successful run in a New York production of *The Junior Partner* and directing a production of *The Golden Giant* in Philadelphia. She called herself Kate Blanchard-Rankin, joined a repertory company in Boston, and became a hit in *The Family Circle*.

Sidney and Gladys Drew arrived in April 1892 at the Bush Street Theatre in San Francisco to play Archibald Gordon's *That Girl from Mexico*. It was quaintly original, high class, and full of humor and satire. The Drews had started their tour in Buffalo on December 14, 1891, played New York City over Christmas, and then set out across the nation. With this play, they seemed to jump to stardom and fame overnight, converting the scoffers. They brought the four-month-old Sidney, Jr, to meet his grandfather. Rankin joined their company for the second week of their San Francisco engagement and played a role in their new curtain-raiser, *A Summer Storm*. On leaving San Francisco, the Drew-Rankin company, as it was now called, played one-night stands throughout the Northwest, reaching St Louis for the week of May 8, after which they closed. Phyllis Rankin, who played a novel-devouring tough girl in *That Girl from Mexico* for two months, joined her mother in plays under Charles Frohman's management for the next season.

Some of Rankin's older colleagues were dying or retiring. The news of Billy Florence's death brought back to him the delightful, carefree days in Billy's company, especially the weeks they had enjoyed fishing together in the semi-wilds of Muskoka, that district of lakes and rivers in central Ontario. Mrs John Drew officially retired at a farewell benefit in Philadelphia, in which the Kendals, who were touring America, participated. Her Arch Street Theatre was almost bankrupt, even as a combination house. She herself had toured with Jefferson in *The Rivals* for the past twelve years, traveling 19,000 miles a season. Now she was going to live in New York with her son, John, and make occasional appearances in productions in neighboring cities.

In mid-July, Rankin returned to New York, boasting that he weigh less than when he left.[76] Mabel Bert had to leave Doris in his care, but he had little time to devote to the child. He was casting for *The Kentucky Colonel*, which was to open at the Union Square Theatre on August 22, 1892.

1892–1893: Setback and Reconciliation

In *The Kentucky Colonel*, Rankin played a generous colonel of the old school, Pemberton (later Remington) Osbury, who mediates a feud between two families. Gladys Drew played his daughter, and was "painstaking but inelastic" in her role.[77] The roles were based on the types to be found living around Louisville. The character acting was all first-rate with the exception of Sidney Drew as Philip Burwood, who, it was said, had to assume this role for which he was not suited because Gladys refused to lavish endearments on the man originally billed for it.

The play seemed destined to fail. It was prolix and, since everyone spoke the same Southern dialect, it became tiresome. It played a month in New York, during which Rankin made changes in the cast and worked on the script. It played a week in Buffalo and set out for the Midwest and South through numerous one-night stands in October and November. The Drews took the brunt of the criticism, returned to New York, formed their own company, and played Sidney Grundy's comedy *Arabian Nights*, with Mrs John Drew as a theatrical mother-in-law. *The Kentucky Colonel* did well in New Orleans, but business began to slacken when it came back into Illinois. When the company became stranded in Springfield, Rankin sent his manager to Chicago to find a capitalist who would reorganize it for its scheduled appearance in Chicago.[78] Under a new backer, the company toured as far north as Winnipeg, Manitoba, then back to St Paul, Minnesota, and on to Chicago. The Chicago Press Club attended in a body. The reporters were hard on the play, although Rankin's addition of the beautiful Belle Stoddart mollified them somewhat.[79] Unnoticed was the role of a small girl, Little Sally, played by Doris Rankin. Doris was five years old.

Rankin's backer withdrew, and Rankin borrowed $250 from the manager of the Detroit Theatre to get his company to that city. There, *The Kentucky Colonel* played for a week, earning less than $835 and bringing a loss to the management and an end to itself.[80] Rankin's prospects looked grimmer than at any time in his career. Moreover, his father was dying in the Windsor hospital.

The colonel, now seventy-seven, decided to settle his affairs. He made an agreement with McKee whereby he gave him his goods and chattels, pictures, furniture, silverware, and jewelry, packed away variously in the vaults of the Windsor Merchant Bank and with a merchant of Windsor who held some property as security for moneys advanced to the colonel. The colonel also transferred to McKee his equitable right of redemption in Fitzwilliam Island, which was between Georgian Bay and Lake Huron in the vicinity of Manitoulin Island. In return, McKee was to pay off all liens, charges, mortgages, and encumbrances, and pay one dollar to the colonel.[81]

A notice appeared in all the papers that Rankin had inherited a large sum of money and would be retiring from the stage. George Cameron Rankin took a jaundiced view of it all. "In this state of collapse," George commented about McKee's theatrical failure, "he hears of his father's serious illness over in Windsor for the first time. He thereupon goes over to see him and tell him of his sorry plight—and the poor old gentlemen offers to do what he can to help him out....Then the stranded actor seeks out the newspaper people and gives them the material for an Associated Press dispatch headed 'McKee Rankin in Luck!'...He is at least an utilitarian who will make the most of his father's death bed for the purpose of lightening the consequences of a theatrical failure."[82]

George had been left out of his father's consideration, which, he explained, was owing to a disagreement between them two years earlier to the effect that the colonel's creditors insisted that either Thornfield or a tract of 6,400 acres in Algoma near Sault Ste Marie be sold to pay them. George argued that the colonel was morally bound to keep the homestead because Mary Rankin wanted it to remain in the family. The colonel, in reaction, sold the homestead. George and his father "became wandering strangers" and estranged from one another. Meanwhile, George complained wistfully, the Algoma lands sank by $15,000 in value and the homestead was worth $30,000 over what it sold for.

George was an executor of his father's estate and vowed that if any money remained after all their father's debts were paid, it would come to him. He may not have known about the arrangement with McKee for the furniture, silverware, and jewelry, which was worth the several thousand dollars that McKee claimed to have inherited. George did know that Fitzwilliam Island was bought by the colonel in 1888 for $15,000 and had 8,000 acres of timber ready to be cut, worth $830,000. The value of the island plus its fisheries was set at $50,000.

McKee attended Colonel Rankin's funeral on March 15, 1893, but George was absent. The next day, George sued McKee for $10,000, "the price of 'The Canuck'," and told reporters the history of the play's composition and the failure of McKee to pay him royalties. McKee countersued for the same amount.[83] Nothing came of it. All the spite seemed to be an expression of George's frustrations and disappointments.

Rankin went to New York in late March with a play he wrote during his stay in Detroit, *The Baxters*. He claimed it was the best that he had done and hoped, with his usual confidence at overcoming reversals, for a new career as a playwright.[84] He must have wondered, like Frank Mayo, whether he was a has-been. The stage seemed to belong to the younger actors, such as John Drew, Jr, who made $1,000 a day in one-night stands and over $10,000 on one-week stands. Recently in Boston, Drew grossed $14,000 at a Saturday matinee and $15,000 in the evening, which, considering that he employed only eight people and used only two interior sets of scenery in his production, left a considerable profit margin.

John Drew, Jr, however, was nearing middle age and had had years of good training in Daly's companies. The young actors coming into the profession were now university graduates, not from the poorer classes as was the case when Rankin started. To work onstage, the young actor needed a good intellect, a good education, good looks, a graceful bearing, a pleasing voice, and a tremendous capacity for hard work. Despite these advantages, many fell short because they lacked true artistic instinct. Rankin knew that their major stumbling block was the paucity of stage experience in repertory companies. On the other hand, Mrs John Drew, Sr, inspired the older actors as she was in her late sixties and made a hit in whatever she appeared. She joined with Julia Marlowe in a number of Shakespeare plays and Sheridan Knowles's *The Love Chase*.[85] She brought Blanchard and Rankin together by arranging for them to meet in a private box at the theater, with their daughters in attendance. A reconciliation, which Drew helped to achieve, was not hard for Blanchard, who never stopped loving Rankin. Rankin, however, may have accepted the inevitable. His daughter Doris needed a mother, and Blanchard was willing to care for her. Moreover, he probably hoped that some of the old magic, which he and Blanchard had had with audiences over the decades, would return and restore their fortunes. Throughout their separation they had maintained a distant friendship, and Blanchard seemed to understand that a part of Rankin's attraction for Mabel Bert was his desire to create a great actress to rival the actresses he had known in his youth.

Mrs Drew conceived a scheme that would keep them together: a revival of Sheridan's *The Rivals*, in which her family and its close adherents would play in the major theaters in the East. She scheduled the production to open on May 1, 1893, at the Grand Opera House in Philadelphia: Mrs Drew as Mrs Malaprop; Rankin as Sir Anthony Absolute; Eben Plympton, the temperamental but highly skilled romantic actor, as the dashing Captain Absolute; Sidney Drew as the comical Bob Acres; Gladys as Lydia Languish; Phyllis as the scheming maid, Lucy; R. Germaine as Faulkland (taking the place of James Herne, who had to renege); Blanchard as Julia Melville, Lydia's cousin; H.D. Gibbs as the servant Fag (H.D. Gibbs bears watching); Edson Dixon as Sir Lucius O'Trigger; John Ince, who played in Shakespeare's comedies and in comic opera, as the servant, David.[86] Aside from reviving their sagging acting careers, Mrs Drew hoped to bring in some money to pay off debts still owing from her Arch Street Theatre days. Also, she needed money for her daughter, Georgie, who returned from six weeks in Bermuda where she had tried to shake off a mysterious debilitating illness. The doctors diagnosed it as acute bronchitis and recommended that she see a specialist in Santa Barbara, California. Georgie would have made a superb Lydia Languish, better than Gladys.

John, Ethel, and Lionel Barrymore as photographed by Kate Rankin.
Courtesy of Peter Rankin.

The advance sale for *The Rivals* was heavy, and people came from all over the city to attend the performances. Houses were crowded for two weeks until the production moved to the Park Theatre in Philadelphia on May 15. The following night, Maurice Barrymore replaced Plympton as Captain Absolute.[87] The minor roles were upgraded with better actors. Herbert Ayling, a first-rate light comedian, played Fag, while H.D. Gibbs became acting manager. Fred Ross, who had been in many Shakespearean productions with Edwin Booth, took over the role of the jealous Faulkland.

At this time, Georgie Drew Barrymore, accompanied by her daughter Ethel, then thirteen, was seen off at the New York docks by the family. Georgie had lost her wonderful spirits and feared for the worst as she prepared to sail to Panama and go by train to California. Her sons had come from Seton Hall to say good-bye. Maurice bade her a tearful farewell. Sidney, whom the Barrymore children called Uncle Googan and saw as gay, naughty, and beguiling, and Aunt Gladys, whom they saw as beautiful and haughty, were there, as were Mrs John Drew and some close family friends.[88]

The following week, the *Rivals* company played in Montreal and then opened at the Hammerstein Opera House in Harlem. The *New York Times* thought it was the best production of the play for some time. The cast was like a family party, acting their parts "with spirit, taste, and force."[89] Except for the sentimental subplot involving the exasperating Faulkland and the patient Julia, no portion of the play had aged. The audience was the largest of the season and called Mrs Drew forward several times.

Buoyed by their success, Mrs Drew and Rankin began planning for a tour to the West. Aside from *The Rivals*, they would play Thomas Holcroft's classic *The Road to Ruin*. It had not been seen in a quarter-century, except for a brief revival at McVicker's Theatre in Chicago. It told of Harry Dornton, who, after his spendthrift habits have imperiled his father's banks, is prepared to sacrifice himself by marrying the odious rich widow Mrs Warren in place of the girl he loves. The sacrifice, however, is made unnecessary by the fidelity of the bank's head clerk, the grim old Mr Sulky. Mrs Drew reduced it from five to four acts and worked up to the climax in scenes according to the idea of modern stagecraft without losing the charm of the comedy.[90] In the meantime Rankin contracted his play *The Baxters* to Charles Cowles and announced that he and Mrs Rankin were producing it. The first performance would be on August 7 at Bartley McCullum's beautiful Summer Theatre on Peake's Island, just off Portland, Maine, built by a rich lover of theater.[91]

Terrible news came from Ethel Barrymore about the sudden death from tuberculosis of her mother, Georgie, in Santa Barbara on July 2, 1893. The body was shipped to Philadelphia, where the funeral was held later in the month. Rankin was a pallbearer, with Clay Greene, Joseph Holland, Eben Plympton, and others. Ethel returned to the convent school. She never forgot her mother's cries to herself: "My children! What will become of my children?" Lionel, the eldest boy, was engaged with the company to play Thomas, the coachman in *The Rivals*, his first stage experience. John, the youngest, returned to school.

Maurice Barrymore, Georgie's husband, did not go with the Drew-Rankin combination. He had to make money, which he was sure to do in the *Aristocracy* combination, which left for California right after the funeral. Blanchard did not accompany the troupe either. Her role of Julia Melville, which was becoming a bit of an anachronism and tiresome, was cut.

Rankin had to leave off supervising the rehearsals of *The Baxters* and join *The Rivals* troupe opening in Omaha on August 14. Blanchard remained in Maine to fulfill the production duties.

1893–1894

The Drew–Barrymore–Rankin Connection

The Drew-Rankin troupe, under the direction of Al Hayman, set out for California with the firm intention of returning to New York City by January 8, 1894.[92] The dramatic attraction between Rankin and the West Coast, however, made it dubious that the company could stay together. A week in Omaha playing *The Rivals* followed by a week in Denver gave the company a chance to meld before playing in California in early September. The Denver audiences filled the house and declared the production fine. In San Diego on September 7, and Los Angeles for September 8 and 9, the company garnered large houses. Nevertheless, Rankin was restless and discontented acting out these old pieces. He wrote from Los Angeles to Augustus Thomas, the playwright, asking permission to produce his play *Arizona* on the West Coast for January, February, and March, and thence in England, where he would open in London at Easter. Thomas either could or would not give him permission.[93]

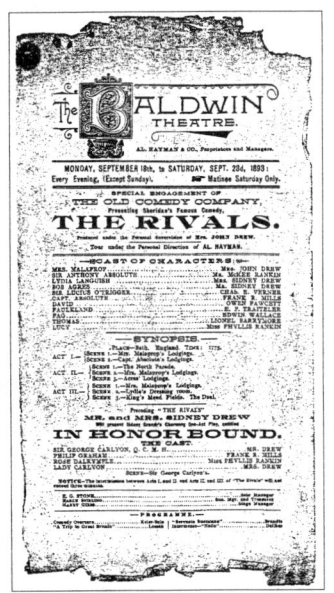

Playbill for Sheridan's *The Rivals* at the Baldwin Theatre, San Francisco, 1893.

The Drew-Rankin company played a few nights along the coast and opened at the Baldwin in San Francisco on September 18. The critics differed over who acted well in *The Rivals*, but seemed to agree that Gladys had too shrewd a countenance, and too decided a voice and manner, for sentimental, lackadaisical romantic roles.[94] In *The Road to Ruin,* Mrs Drew played the Widow Warren, a designing and artful yet woefully simple-minded woman, delightfully. Coquettish and selfish, she was irresistible to the audiences. The young man prepared to marry her to get out of debt, Harry Dornton, played by Clarence Holt, was letter perfect in his lines and played up to Mrs Drew with an unctuousness that cast the rest of the company in the shade. His performance gave him a permanent place in the company. By contrast, Rankin as Dornton, the banker, whose spendthrift son was ruining him, seemed indifferent in his acting and was sorely at a loss for his lines.[95]

The Drew-Rankin company, full of relatives, had developed serious tensions as to who should get top billing. Rankin decided to split at that moment and form his own company. San Francisco, the scene of so many of his triumphs, might bring him salvation again. Moreover, he could see no future teemed with the aged Mrs Drew in old plays, which could hardly last for more than a few months. He leased the Alcazar Theatre, which was a popular house at one time but had been ruined by bad management and lain vacant. It was too far from the city center for night travel, so Rankin took a large risk and had to keep expenses at a minimum. A San Francisco critic called him an accomplished stage manager, who was free from a "big head" and always ready for suggestions.[96] He sent for Blanchard, whose reputation on the West Coast as a mother and model wife was very high and whose acting had given her a permanent place in the affections of San Franciscans.

Mrs Drew hired George Osbourne, now one of the most accomplished character actors in the country, to replace Rankin, and Rankin hired Clay Clement, a handsome novice, to act the leading man in his new company. Phyllis and Doris stayed with the Rankins while Gladys went with the Drews. A San Francisco critic saw the reunion of the Rankins as "a coincidence because it was here that brought about their separation." So now "husband and wife were taking up the broken chord where it was broken."[97]

Rankin opened with *Nancy,* his version of *Oliver Twist,* on October 9, 1893, at the Alcazar with Blanchard as Nancy Sykes, himself as Bill Sykes, Clement as Fagin, and Phyllis as the Artful Dodger. His version eliminated the pathetic parts and emphasized the brutal side with more strength. Blanchard had not lost her capacity to play upon the sentiments of the audiences in the role; after her scene with Fagin and Bill, the audiences gave her enthusiastic applause and huge quantities of flowers "sufficient to delight any actress." Rankin, as Bill, was more of a terror in the part than he was when last seen by San Franciscans some years before. "He was savage to a degree beyond conception," wrote a critic, "and in the murder scene his looks and acting were terrific exhibitions of the brute as Dickens pictured him and as the people don't want to see him."[98] It was a mistake to bring such "coarseness" to an Alcazar audience, the critic thought, especially when the theater was an experiment to see if the management could provide the plays wanted by the public at reasonable prices. The surprise of the evening was Phyllis's performance of the Artful Dodger, which, the critic admitted, was "clever acting." Rankin, the expert with makeup, applied her makeup with fatherly pride.

A week later, Rankin presented *Sara*, the play that Blanchard had tried out one summer in New York City. Rankin played the banker, Marcus Geldheimer, Blanchard was Sara Lyons, and Phyllis was Felice, the adopted daughter of the Duc de Courval. A critic considered the cast rather poor, save for Blanchard and a newcomer to the stage, a recent debutante, Blanche Bates. The daughter of Mrs F.M. Bates, who often acted in Rankin's companies, Blanche Bates was destined for stardom, and the critic spotted her potential right away, calling her "the most promising actress to make her debut in this city in a very long time."[99] A small role was given to Gertrude Lamson, a tall, lanky, eighteen-year-old girl of a certain beauty who had been introduced to Rankin by a local critic as desirous of getting onstage. She was a free spirit, and a determined young lady. Her older sister, Lillian, had been on the stage in San Francisco and Los Angeles for over three years. Rankin gave Gertrude a try as one of two nuns because of her height. Her first line spoken on stage was: "Narren Beaudet, you are dismissed from St. Lazarre." The local critic wrote encouragingly: "a winning Miss Gertrude Lamson as 'Sister Elsie' had a capital scene in the prison which she carried very well."[100] At that time, no one had the slightest idea that this girl was to become one of the most powerful tragedians to walk the American stage. And Blanchard had no idea that she would soon be making room for her in her husband's life.

News came of Mabel Bert's marriage to actor Forrest Robinson, whose stage work was distinguished by earnestness, vigor, and intelligence. Few were more widely liked by other actors for their personal qualities, and no other stock actor had more far-reaching professional popularity than Robinson. Charles Frohman had hired him for the leading male character in his production of *Lost Paradise*, in which company he also hired Mabel Bert. Rankin had to give up all thought of her now. Undoubtedly, his disappointment subconsciously helped direct his ambitions into developing a new talent for the stage in the person of Gertrude Lamson.[101]

The Great Discovery

Rankin mounted Olive Logan's comedy *Long Branch* at the Alcazar. Surprisingly, it had never been played in San Francisco. The large cast made room for two of Rankin's daughters: Phyllis played Miss Euphrosyne Noble, stepdaughter to Mrs Madison Noble, a leader of the New York society, and little Doris played Miss Tootsey Noble, with a distaste for spelling books. Mrs Madison Noble was played with excellence by Blanche Bates, whose name would be associated with David Belasco in years to come. Belasco had been hired into the theater by her parents as their basket boy just a decade earlier. Mrs F.M. Bates played a silly old woman. Rankin, showing "much versatility," played George Washington Smith, an American of African descent.[102]

Clay Clement was Simon Schweinfleisch of St Louis, whose name betrayed his interest in pork. The character was originally supposed to be a low comic Dutchman, but Clement confessed he was having trouble mastering the part; Rankin suggested that he create a German character for himself. Clement created what became known as the "Alphabet" scene, which was a great hit with audiences. Encouraged, Clement expanded the scene into a play, which he called *The New Dominion*, and in which he played Baron von Hoenstauffen. It became a popular play, and Hoenstauffen was his best character, famous for his "flower speech." Clement was a creature of moods—fierce in love, in jealousy, and in anger, but tempered by kindness. When he had his own companies, he employed old and out-of-work actors, and, being generous, it was not unusual for him to come home from a day's work with empty pockets.[103]

Long Branch ran smoothly, with a vim and snap that was refreshing.[104] The biggest ovation came after a love scene between Phyllis Rankin and Clay Clement in the last act in which Clement recited a German poem. Gertrude Lamson played a soldier's widow, but gave a poor performance because of stagefright. Rankin still regarded her as an awkward teenager who could be given only small parts. The play had to be extended to a second week to meet the demand, although the success of the run was threatened by a dispute between Rankin and the musicians' union. The conflict went back to Rankin's failure to pay some musicians when he ran the California Theatre Company. Although a temporary truce had been called, he had been late in his payments in recent weeks. Consequently, the musicians struck and initiated a boycott of his theater.[105]

Rankin tried the perennially popular *The Danites*, but it failed to draw. Blanchard did not appear in the cast because she was sick. Rankin played Sandy McGee, but not as in the old days. "At one time a conscientious and painstaking actor," wrote the critic, "Rankin has fallen into an indifferent mood, which spoils every character he attempts to play."[106] It was while rehearsing *The Danites* that Rankin remarked on Gertrude Lamson's acting. In the role of Bunker Hill, the camp prostitute, she delivered a speech that startled him, and, looking at her closely, he saw that tears were running down her face. Phyllis came to him and said, "Papa, you've got an actress there!"

Rankin began to watch her carefully but could do little about her at this time because he became very ill. He did not appear in the next two melodramatic pieces, although he managed to return to play in a spirited performance in *'49*. Attendance was poor. Rankin fell ill again. A critic warned that the Alcazar was catching at straws to stay afloat. Phyllis, who took over as paymaster, doled out "toothsome bits" of money to the "poor unfortunate players and the attachés." She became the manager de facto. The Alcazar tried to reopen on December 23 in *The Kentucky Colonel*, but "succumbed under the directorship of McKee Rankin."[107]

Broke and stranded, Rankin's deliverance was owing to a theatrical manager named Billy Smith, who lent Rankin $500, which was enough to allow him to proceed with his company. Many in the profession had sympathy for Rankin. They saw that failure after failure had been his lot for years but that he continued on, working with enormous energy and devotion, not allowing creditors to shake his unerring nerve. Years later, Smith booked Rankin at his St Louis theater and asked for the return of his loan. "Five hundred," mused Rankin. "There are so many of these five hundreds, you know, Billy. Oh yes, I remember. But you know Billy, old chap, you can't collect that debt from me because it's outlawed. Statutes of limitation and all that, don't you know. Billy, you remember Mr. Harold Skimpole, that ingenious chap of Dickens who was always owing somebody and who was so ingeniously dependent, just like a little child? Well, that's about my case. I'm so wrapt in my art that filthy lucre is my last thought." Rankin then proceeded to wipe out the debt with a cold bottle of beer.[108]

On Christmas Day, the Rankin company played in San Diego to light business and continued in brief stops down the California coast. It was while Gertrude Lamson was playing Bunker Hill in one of these mining towns that she went for a walk and noticed a woman coming out of a saloon. She was reminded of Bunker Hill and tried to imagine how she would feel and speak if she were that woman. Rankin's admonishment to her when she replied to his urgings to improve, "I was trying my best to act," came to haunt her all night: "My dear little girl, never do it again. Don't you *ever* try to act." She kept his words in her mind as she went onstage the next night and thought of the woman she had seen. She forgot about the audience, forgot about herself, forgot she had to act, and the next thing she knew the audience was applauding and shouting its pleasure. Rankin came running back of the scene with tears streaming down his face. "That was great, great, great!" he cried. "What?" she asked with wonder. "Your acting in that last scene." "But I didn't try to act," she insisted, and then she saw what he had meant, and she began to realize the secret of good acting.[109] The deep chasm between knowing *how to act* and actually *acting* required work and more work. Rankin inspired her with a goal and had no other motive than her success, she said. "But I really think he took as much, if not more pleasure and pride in that than I did."[110]

The Rankin company opened at the Los Angeles Theatre in '49 on January 4, 1894. Although Rankin and Blanchard were praised, the cast was considered poor. At the Pasadena Opera House the following week, Phyllis charged the company's agent with embezzlement because he had taken $49 meant for the company from the theater's booking agent. The agent persuaded the judge, however, that he had advanced Rankin $500 to get the company out of San Francisco and considered the $49 a partial repayment. Rankin, angered by his release, said the man's every utterance was a lie, and that he was continuously drunk, which kept him from attending to business and resulted in the failure of the company. He dismissed the agent in mid-week only to discover that the man walked away with the receipts. Rankin took over the management from Phyllis and reorganized the company.[111]

At this time, Rankin's career as a playwright was tested when his play *The Baxters* opened at the Bijou Theatre in Brooklyn in Charles Cowles's company. As Cyrus Stebbins in *The Canuck*, Charles Cowles had been celebrated as one of the country's most admirable character actors; now Rankin gave him a perfect fit in the New Englander Eben Baxter, a country postmaster. Cowles acted the eccentric, bighearted old man, evoking tears and laughter at the Yankee character, and dancing with a nimbleness that "brought down the house."[112] He carried the play but was hampered by poor support from the company. When he went on tour with the piece, which he retitled *A Country Merchant*, he obtained a stronger supporting cast, including Adele Waters, probably on Rankin's recommendation.

Waters fell ill in March and was hospitalized in Jersey City. While under the influence of morphine, she wandered from the hospital in a daze and fell into the hands of a gang of "roughs," who took her to a shanty and sexually assaulted her. Police rescued her and caught three of her assailants. A month later, Waters registered at the Continental Hotel in New York City as Belle Kingsley and went to the American Theatre Exchange to find work. She looked so ill that the agent recommended she go to the hospital. There, within days, she died of alcoholic hysteria at the age of thirty-two.

Considered as one of the handsomest women on the stage, she was remembered mainly for her work with Rankin's repertory company. When no friend or relative claimed her body, she was buried by the Actors' Fund.[113]

The economic recession that was plaguing the country meant light attendance at all theaters and financial devastation for Rankin. Because his company and a company under Leonard Grover were stranded, the players' troupes in Los Angeles organized a joint jubilee benefit, which, being well-attended, revived them.[114] Rankin, taking his company on a tour of California towns, became stranded in Pasadena briefly. Fortunately, he received an offer to manage the Burbank Theatre in Los Angeles. He and Blanchard decided to try to prosper alone rather than starve together. Or perhaps after watching Rankin's enthusiasm for another young actress consume his time, Blanchard tactfully beat a retreat to her own career, appearing in a New York theater in *Sweet Will* in April.

Rankin reorganized his company without her and opened with *The Danites* the week of February 19. Most of the actors were from the theater's stock company under the direction of Fred Cooper, who played Washee Washee with superb makeup and amusing antics. Georgia Woodthorpe, the female lead, played Billy Piper well. Gertrude Lamson played Hulda Brown, the widow, which was an upgrading for her.[115]

Blanchard took Doris with her while Phyllis joined the company of her sister, Dido, and Sidney Drew, who were touring again in *That Man from Mexico*. Blanchard must have thought that Phyllis was safe under the watchful eye of Dido, but she was in for a shock. When the company was playing in Atlanta in March, Phyllis eloped with the company's property man, Henry D. Gibbs.[116]

When Mrs Drew split with Rankin, Gibbs had remained in Mrs John Drew's company and came east with the troupe. The family regarded Gibbs as a trusted employee, who could find work in any of the Drews' ventures, but he was not considered to be on their social level. As the news wire report of the elopement expressed it, Phyllis "brought sorrow to her friends."[117] She brought fury to her family, although perhaps not to Rankin. The couple fled to New York City.

While Phyllis caused emotional storms in her family in the East, Rankin had found smooth sailing in the West. Business was good at the Burbank. Rankin played *The Canuck* for a week in early March 1894, and Christianson in *Storm Beaten* for the week following, which filled the house. In *The Canuck*, his French-Canadian character was called a work of art and an inspiration to the rest of the cast. Gertrude Lamson played demanding roles as second to the leading lady Georgia Woodthorpe. When Rankin took his company to Pasadena, he starred Gertrude

Lamson in *The Banker's Daughter*. Lamson recalled later that she "bore the brunt of these emotional plays" by taking the most demanding parts.[118] Away from the pressure of the big-city theater, Rankin was able to focus on developing her acting ability.

When Rankin returned to the Burbank playing in *'49* and *Uncle Tom's Cabin* to good business, the owners of the Lyceum Theatre in Denver, Colorado, which was slated to close the season on May 5, asked him to manage the theater for a supplementary season starting May 7. Although he had planned to tour northwards when his season at the Burbank ended, he agreed and asked George Osbourne, who had been acting in the East in Mrs Drew's company, to take his place as leading man and stage director in the Burbank stock company. Osbourne and Gertrude Lamson starred in *The Great Metropolis*, which Rankin had written with Leonard Grover fourteen years earlier and never produced. He had finished stage-directing it before he left for Denver. The scenery and stage mechanisms for this sensational melodrama were excellent and the performances were up to the standard expected from the company.[119]

Arriving in Denver, Rankin kept some of the resident stock and presented *The Canuck* and *'49* with Maud Harrison as leading lady.[120] In mid-June, Lamson joined him in Denver and played Bunker Hill in *The Danites*.[121] She got her chance to play the lead in *Storm Beaten* when Maud Harrison fell ill. She did well, but Rankin was not willing to bill her as the lead of the company just yet.

Meanwhile, Blanchard kept acting to bring in an income. Her troupe, which included Gladys and Sidney Drew, Phyllis and Henry Gibbs, and Doris, as well as Ethel Barrymore, toured the cities of the Maritime provinces and New England in the summer of 1894. Ethel Barrymore, who became a celebrated actress in the late 1890s and remained so through decades of stage work and movie roles until her death in 1959, described the experience in an autobiography. She had just finished her last school term and was brought along to play minor roles. The others did not consider her as having the talent to become an actress. She gave a picture of a loosely structured bohemian troupe, sometimes missing engagements because of travel difficulties, whose business dealings were handled by the somewhat inconsistent "Uncle Googan" Drew. "One unforgettable Saturday night in St. John [New Brunswick]," she wrote, "we stayed in the theater in the dark until after midnight. Then, as it was Sunday, we strolled out and onto a train for other parts. All our luggage had to be left in the hotel and my trunk containing all my worldly possessions—not many really—I didn't see for years. I remember Aunt Gladys leaving the theatre that night looking very proud and grand, also rather fat. She had on five dresses."[122] For the fall season, Ethel found a spot in the company of her uncle John Drew, a decidedly more stable organization.[123]

At the end of June, Rankin closed his engagement in Denver with *Storm Beaten*, intending to summer in Denver, but an opportunity arose that he could not resist. Jeffreys Lewis, an English actress whose special Spanish-type beauty had made her a favorite in America, ran into trouble over a division within her company. She suggested that Rankin join forces with her for a tour over the Montana circuit, where plenty of money was to be made in the small towns thirsty for drama.[124] She had the rights to David Belasco's *La Belle Russe* and included *Forget-Me-Not* and *Shattered Idols* in her repertoire. She and Rankin rehearsed their companies in one another's plays to mid-July, which served also as a resting period for Rankin.

1894–1895: Lamson Blossoms into O'Neil

In the week commencing July 18, 1894, the Rankin-Lewis company opened in Butte, Montana, in *La Belle Russe*, following it during the week with *The Canuck*, *Forget-Me-Not*, *The Danites*, and *Rip Van Winkle*.[125] The Montana circuit included Helena, Missoula, Great Falls, and Anaconda. Dramatic newspapers had no correspondents in this part of the country, so combinations were lost track of for weeks at a time. In mid-July, there were great floods throughout the Northwest and a railroad strike in the area, both of which caused hardship to touring theatrical companies. Many of them were forced to cancel their dates. The Rankin-Lewis company persevered, however. In mid-August, it was reported to be appearing in small towns in British Columbia.[126] At some point after this, probably early in September, Rankin and Lewis had a violent quarrel, and she departed from the company, taking some of the troupe with her. The fact that Rankin promoted Lamson to the leading roles indicated the probable cause of the quarrel—that Rankin favored Lamson over Lewis, the star, in casting roles. He added to the repertory more of his plays such as *Oliver Twist*, in which Lamson played Nancy to his Bill, and presented Lewis's plays, such as *La Belle Russe*, with Lamson in the main role.

Rankin, who had trained so many young actors in his companies, saw something very special in Lamson that he could mold into greatness. He not only seemed to find fulfillment in her achievements, as she suggested, but he lived through her. Gertrude Lamson was a handsome, tall, willowy blonde woman with blue-gray eyes. She tended to like being on her own and was introspective. She considered that her nature was formed from her contradictory heritage of her New England Puritan father, who had come to California to find gold in 1849, and her Southern mother, who loved form and color. Her sense of drama was developed when she and her sister listened to the weird fantasy stories told them by their mother. She spent her vacations at her aunt's ranch in Calaveras County in central California near the big tree line, where rising shrub land meets the forest, where she lived with nature and drew peace and strength from the mountains. She learned to ride astride a horse and spent much of her time outdoors in this Bret Harte country. She left the seminary a year before graduating because she was restless and wanted a stage career like that of her sister's. While she waited in the wings with McKee and Phyllis Rankin to make her first appearance before an audience, McKee had said, "This is the end of your freedom." At the time, a deadly feeling came over her. Her dedication to her art from that moment proved how right he was.[127]

Rankin guided her with the firm, kind hand of a father in small towns in the West and Northwest in every kind of theater from barns to first-class houses and in plays from *Uncle Tom's Cabin* to *Hamlet*. The Rankin company appeared briefly in the news when it opened in *The Canuck* in Seattle in September 1894 to large houses. According to the *Clipper*, the production was a failure owing to poor management and an indifferent company. Shortly thereafter, the company played at the Ninth Street Theatre in Tacoma, Washington, for several weeks in *The Danites* and *The Canuck*. M.B. Leavitt, who owned the theater, gave Rankin the time and space to sort out his organization and revive his prospects.[128]

Rankin's months-long tour in "the wilderness" allowed him to give Lamson the stage experience she needed before facing the more critical audiences in the East. Lamson described her touring of small pioneer settlements as one of the best experiences in her acting life. She found the audiences just as knowledgeable about the theater as elsewhere and very enthusiastic and grateful to companies bringing them good acting and the new ideas in modern plays.[129] It was from the audiences that actors learned to act, Rankin told her. By this time, Rankin had changed Gertrude Lamson to Beatrice O'Neil as a more appropriate stage name because of its association with the great Irish actress Eliza O'Neil, who had become a success in London in the early nineteenth century and for whom the poet Shelley wrote *The Cenci*.[130]

Rankin's company did fair business at a theater in Portland, Oregon, over Christmas 1894, and thereafter wandered through Idaho, Wyoming, and Nebraska. In Kansas City, Missouri, the company arrived late for a booking.[131] Thus with no income that week, Rankin delayed paying the hotel proprietor, who promptly arrested Rankin, his leading lady, O'Neil, his leading man, Barney Fuller, and his property man for obtaining room and board through "deceit and trickery." The theater manager provided bail, and, on the following day, Rankin conducted his own defense, leading to the dismissal of the charges. Rankin now sued the hotel proprietor for $12,000 in damages and left his western tour in order to remain in the city to prosecute the case.[132]

The company played in Denver on March 4, 1895, doing *The Danites*, and *The Two Orphans* and continued to nearby small towns to the east while Rankin argued his case. In mid-March, the case was settled out of court, and Rankin was back on tour. He accepted an offer to manage the stock company at the Lyceum Theatre in Denver again, adding actors to the company, including Ernest Walcott and Frank Sheridan. The company also included a Patrice O'Neil—clearly he was having trouble deciding on a first name for Lamson. The old plays *The Two Orphans* and *The Long Strike* proved popular, and Gladys and Sidney Drew arrived to play their current successes, *A Legal Wreck* and *The Arabian Nights*, but Rankin wanted a new vehicle in which he could feature his protégée O'Neil.[133] To that purpose he and Ernest Walcott adapted the popular George Du Maurier novel *Trilby* to the stage. Rankin brought out the play on April 30, with Patrice O'Neil in the title role, while he played the mesmerizing villainous Svengali, who hypnotizes Trilby and through his energy makes her a great singer.[134] Through its Denver lawyers, a New York publishing house, Harper Brothers, put a restraining order on the play, saying it was fashioned after Du Maurier's novel, to which it had copyright in the United States. In reply, the Lyceum Theatre claimed that the story was not original with Du Maurier but was founded on Charles Nodier's *Trilby: Fairy of Argyle*, written in 1820. As for the play adapted from Du Maurier's novel by Paul Potter, the Rankin version was quite different.

While the case was in court, Rankin hurriedly replaced the play with Robertson's *Ours*, which drew fair houses for a couple of evenings. The judge told Rankin to proceed with *Trilby*, pending a hearing for a temporary injunction, which was being delayed as the lawyers gathered evidence. The houses were packed for *Trilby*, and the acting was good. Rankin was called too heavy for the ideal portrayal of Svengali, but he showed thoughtful study and his makeup was true to the author's characterization. The judge stopped the play after the matinee performance on May 11 by a temporary injunction.[135] The whole matter would now have to be fought in the courts. Rankin presented *The Danites*, *The Canuck*, and *A Legal Wreck* for the last week of the company's engagement and immediately set out as the Rankin-Drew combination on an extensive tour through the Southern states.

During this tour Rankin finally settled upon a first name for Gertrude Lamson. The inspiration came from a short play by Charles Reade featuring Nance Oldfield, the nimble-witted actress from the time of Queen Anne, which was then being played in America by the English actress Ellen Terry. Henceforth Gertrude Lamson was to be known as Nance O'Neil.

In Houston, Texas, O'Neil played a series of leading roles: Mrs Younghusband in *Married Life*, Ethel Granger in *Snowballed*, Rose Dalwimple in *Honor Bound*, Edith Marson in *The Private Secretary*, and so on. The company drew good business doing comedies in Austin, Waco, and Dallas, where it produced *Trilby* despite the injunction.[136] In Little Rock, Arkansas, in August, the company put on *Trilby* for its final Saturday evening. An effort was made by Harper Brothers to stop the performance but, because there was no federal judge in the city, an injunction could not be obtained.[137] There seemed to be no way to predict how these towns would receive the company: Hot Springs brought good business, Pine Bluff poor business. In Helena, Arkansas, the company opened with *The Arabian Nights* to excellent business, which indicated that new plays drew better than the older ones, an observation that prompted Rankin to bring out *The Bachelor's Baby* for the night of September 6 in Birmingham, Alabama. A very large audience declared it a success.

Coyne Fletcher, who had written *The Indians* with Rankin, set this new play in a western army post. The plot concerned a telegram addressed to Colonel D'Arcy from Geraldine, the colonel's ward, which reads: "Baby is on the way." She used the term "Baby" for herself and meant that she was coming home to marry the colonel's son. It is received by mistake by D'Arcy, Jr, who, engaged to Geraldine, cannot explain the baby and hides the news, especially from Mrs Ponsonby, the social scavenger. "The struggle between conscience and duty on one side," wrote a critic, "and the reception and disposition of the coming infant on the other afford Mr. Sidney Drew an excellent opportunity to display his talents as an exponent of light comedy."[138] The significance of the production, however, was that O'Neil created her first original role as Geraldine. Rankin played Colonel D'Arcy, "fulfilling all expectations." Gladys Drew departed from her usual line by playing the comedy role of Billie Breeze and shared the honors of the night with Sidney.

When the play reached Washington, DC, late in the month, O'Neil played one week and left the company. Her departure can be explained by her need for rest. She had been on the go for a year and a half, memorizing dozens of new roles and carrying the responsibility of leading parts in Rankin's companies. Also, disagreements she had with the Drews over Rankin's attachment to her played a part. Moreover, she and Rankin felt that she needed to experience other acting troupes. Rankin had given her a good grounding and expected that she would learn more from other

Obsession

managers. He had spent so many months training her that it is difficult to imagine his separating from her; he must have thought that eventually he would direct her affairs again: the shaping of young talent had become a major compulsion with him.

1895–1896: Interlude with "Gentleman Jim" Corbett

While Rankin continued touring in the Rankin-Drew company in *The Bachelor's Baby* into New England, O'Neil spent five weeks in New York "gaining impressions of the city" and taking in the museums, parks, and theaters. She began to teach herself about art and life, which, she realized, was essential if she hoped to be a good actress. She was just twenty-one. Rankin had taught her to be a natural actress and to stay away from the elocutionary school.[139] She joined *The Land of the Living* Company, an exciting melodrama concerning two business partners, one of whom covets the other's wife and eventually leaves his rival for dead in the diamond fields of South Africa. The leading man was W.S. Harkins, a brother of Daniel, and formerly a member of Rankin's companies. But the member of the cast who would have been asked to keep an eye on Nance was Mrs Owen Marlowe, the former Virginia Nickinson, who played Nurse Bubbles. Nance played the young wife Kate, over whom the men come to a murderous quarrel. In Harlem it had standing room only and would have had the largest business in theater history if the fire marshals had not intervened to stop ticket sales.[140] It began an extensive and grueling tour, playing every evening and several matinees each week.

At the Park Theatre in Boston, *The Bachelor's Baby* company included Junius Brutus Booth and Sidney Booth, nephews of Edwin, acting in the Boston Museum stock company, Lionel Barrymore, and Julia Ring, granddaughter of the comedian Jimmy Ring. It was like "an interesting family party," commented a critic in the *New York Transcript*, and the leader of the company was "our old friend McKee Rankin, a bigger actor (physically speaking) than ever."[141]

Rankin left the company in Baltimore when William Brady, the impresario, asked him to act in and stage-manage his troupe in *A Naval Cadet*. Jim Corbett, the heavyweight boxing champion, was playing a major role; in fact, Corbett, not the play, was the drawing card. The cast was in rehearsal, but things were going badly. Brady had been planning for *A Naval Cadet* for over a year, ever since he had taken Corbett to Europe and starred him with phenomenal success in *Gentleman Jack* in Paris and London. With a genial, well-spoken, well-mannered, and rather handsome celebrity, whose prowess in the boxing ring was admired around the world, Brady had a gold mine. Corbett had wanted to be onstage since his youth when he was close friends with the actor Eddie Foy in San Francisco. He was the first pugilist to become a successful actor, but he needed more training. Rankin's job was to teach him to act and to make the play work dramatically.

Rankin assembled the cast at the Grand Opera House in New York for three weeks of rehearsals. When Corbett fought a burly ruffian who smashed a chair over his head, drew a knife on him, and clinched with him hand-to-hand, a reporter saw it as the most realistic fight ever seen onstage. Rankin agreed: "I have been on the stage a good many years and I have never seen anything like it. They go at it like mad bulls, and you think one of them is surely coming out of it with a smashed head and two black eyes. The best stage fight I ever remember to equal it was in Billy Florence's revival of 'The Ticket-of-Leave Man' in 1868. I played Hawkshaw and Florence was, of course, Bob Brierly. When we got together we used to pummel each other till the gallery went wild. But that fight wasn't in it, so to speak, with Corbett's realistic struggle in this play." Rankin added that Corbett's acting would carry the play. "Let me tell you that in the whole course of my experience I never saw anyone who had accomplished so much in a short time, who was so quick to learn, who had so much natural ease and instinctive stage sense as Mr. Corbett....He will open the eyes of those who sneer at the pugilist's being able to act."[142]

A Naval Cadet opened in Lynn, Massachusetts, on November 25, 1895, with Corbett as Ned Cornell. The plot revolved around the theft of the patent for a gun that cadet Ned Cornell invented and that would make him a millionaire. The excellent supporting cast was headed by Rankin as Fillipi Bonivari in an "admirable performance."[143] As the villain, Rankin was almost killed with a chair by the cadet. The play went on a three-year tour, from which Brady made a fortune. Rankin left at the close of the first season. For a time, Lizzie Lamson, Nance O'Neil's sister, was Corbett's leading lady. After the season's last performance on May 2, 1896, Rankin hurried to Nance O'Neil, who was lying friendless and near death in a New York hospital.

ACT IV

The Reign of Nance O'Neil

1896–1897: Creating a Star

In early February, while in Minneapolis, Minnesota, Nance O'Neil, worn out by the constant travel and frequent performances demanded by *The Land of Living* company, suffered a nervous breakdown after twelve weeks on the road. The press did not report her departure from the company, but it did report Mrs Marlowe as leaving at this time, which indicated that she had elected to accompany O'Neil back to New York, where treatment was available. O'Neil was in hospital for fifteen weeks. Abandoned by her family and with no prospects for a career before her, she was greatly in debt to Rankin because he provided her with the professional care she needed to recover her health. Indeed, Rankin spent the summer with O'Neil until she recovered. This was one reason for her faithfulness to him through the difficult years they were to go through together. "It was while she was convalescing," said a friend later, "that the attachment which never has been shaken was formed."[1]

At the same time as he was preoccupied with O'Neil's health, Rankin had bad news of his close friend Frank Mayo, who, having completed a big

---

Notes are on pages 477-91.

engagement in Denver, was on the train to Omaha on a hot evening in early June. The comedian Roland Reed sat opposite him, and they talked far into the night. Reed retired, but Mayo stayed by the open window with his head resting on his hand. Reed found him the next morning in the same position; he had died of a heart attack.[2]

Rankin was not idle during the weeks he remained in New York with the convalescing O'Neil. Although he had canceled engagements in Albany, New York, and in Fall River, Massachusetts, he was directing two new plays in New York City. The first, *A Woman in Black*, concerned a corrupt millionaire who hires a mesmerist to make his ward marry his son when she wants to marry a political opponent of her guardian. Mesmerism was an extremely popular fad and many were the exhibitions of hypnotism at theaters throughout the country. Belief in its powers was behind public acceptance of the power of Svengali in *Trilby*. Rankin's stage direction was challenged by several scenes in the new play, including a music hall; a thieves' den where the mesmerist, Madame Zenda, reigns; and Madison Square in New York, where crowds watch a huge calcium-lit sign projecting election returns. When the play opened in Milwaukee on September 20, it was a success owing to the strong cast, which, in turn, was owing to Rankin's direction.

The second play, *Straight from the Heart*, offered scenery from a stately English conservatory and a rocky pass in the Algerian desert to Paris streets. Blanche Walsh, a rising star, played the heroine as well as the heroine's brother as a trouser role. Both characters and the heroine's lover are persecuted by anarchists, and when the lover is brought to the guillotine through treachery, the heroine rides up on horseback waving a pardon from the French president.

Rankin with a new company opened on September 14, 1896, in Albany, playing *The Danites* and *Oliver Twist* for a week to large houses. He may have been bringing O'Neil back to the stage and helping her regain her confidence, although the papers mentioned only Rankin as the star, calling him "one of Albany's few favorites," especially as Bill Sykes, which was a far cry from his first appearance in Albany in 1865 when, as the new leading man, he played in *The Dead Heart* and had to retire after two nights. The company gave two performances of *The Danites* on the opening day, a sign that Rankin was raising funds for a new venture.[3] His next actions were calculated to prepare O'Neil for a starring role. He returned to New York City to rehearse a company in *Judge Not*, which he adapted from a German novel.[4] Philip Garth, played by Rankin, comes out of prison after serving twenty-four years for a crime he did not commit and searches for his wife, who is a famous opera singer. His wife had abandoned their daughter, who has grown up, married, has been widowed, and supports a son by working as a typist, thus introducing the woman in a business role to the stage. Garth recognizes her as his daughter because she has a photograph of himself on her bureau. He is arrested as a thief when trying to gain entrance to his wife's house, and he refuses to defend himself lest he bring disgrace to his daughter. But his little grandson appeals to his heart in a touching manner, and he acknowledges his daughter. All are reunited in a happy climax.

When *Judge Not* opened on October 19, 1896, for a week at Forepaugh's Theatre in Philadelphia, Nance O'Neil took the role of Mrs Anna Demming, Garth's daughter. Although the play was considered an unqualified success, Rankin discontinued the tour and returned to New York to work on it. When he opened in St Paul, Minnesota, on November 8, it was called *New York As It Is*, and emphasized the final triumph of filial affection and the lesson of self-sacrifice. Much of the cast had been replaced. At the company's next stop, in Minneapolis, the play was running so smoothly that Rankin had to answer several curtain calls. Playing to big business, the company concluded its run in Pittsburgh.

It was then that Rankin tried vaudeville for the first time. Although it paid very well and required only fifteen or so minutes of acting, the presentation had to be intense and grip the audience from the first seconds. Many performers were failures in this venue. Rankin was either courageous or desperate to risk his acting reputation in a scene wedged between slapstick comedy and dog tricks. He took the famous scene from Boucicault's *The Long Strike* in which the lawyer, Moneypenny, tries to telegraph the ship on which Reilly was going to sea. Rankin rewrote it as *Counsel for the Defense,* using the telephone and including two women in the cast, with himself as Moneypenny, renamed Brooks. Nance O'Neil played a desperate young woman from the East Side tenements who pleads with the lawyer to help her lover, who has been charged with murder. The act was a great success. "His by-play was splendid," wrote a critic, "and he moved his audience to alternate tears and smiles."[5] Weber and Fields had a chain of vaudeville houses, in which an act could be continued for months. Rankin stayed for just two weeks. Most performers were between twenty and thirty years old; when over forty, they were "out of the game" unless they had a good record. Under such circumstances, Rankin's vaudeville success, after age fifty-two, was phenomenal.[6]

Now with sufficient funding, Rankin opened on December 21 with a new company at the newly built Murray Hill Theatre in New York City. *Judge Not*, retitled *New York As It Is*, now became *True to Life*, and Nance

O'Neil became an overnight sensation. The New York critics raved about her as a young actress with great potential for stardom. Critics such as Alan Dale, who later turned against her, hailed her as an important discovery for the stage. She needed polishing and refining, but she had tremendous power and an emotional hold over audiences. As for Rankin, his role as Philip Garth was played with true tenderness and pathos, and "realized to fullness the possibilities of his part."[7]

O'Neil said that she was frightened by this New York debut and that she always had stagefright in a new part. Her success surprised her and delighted Rankin, who henceforth gave her co-star billing with himself. But before continuing to tour the play, Rankin had to direct and take part as Major Hannibal Bugg in a new play, *Captain Impudence*, opening on January 4, 1897, at the American Theatre. Airily played, with flippant epigrammatic speeches, the comedy remained three weeks in New York before setting out for a long tour without Rankin.[8] Rankin, wrote the critic, "was the bluff old soldier to the life, courteous in affairs of the heart, brave in the discharge of even those duties that threatened the happiness of the daughter he loved so tenderly, and chivalrous in the extreme. The character fitted him and he fitted the character of Major Hannibal Bugg."[9]

Rankin used his salary to finance his forthcoming tour with O'Neil. He had to accept that he would receive no more royalties from *A Country Merchant* because Charles Cowles, after three years of touring New England and Canada, not only hurt his foot in Brooklyn but had to disband his company because fire destroyed the theater at which he was to play in New Jersey. Better news came from Rankin's family. Phyllis Rankin Gibbs, after giving birth to a daughter, appeared in vaudeville at the Weber and Fields Theatre in New York in December 1896, a week after Rankin and O'Neil tested the vaudeville waters. She did an imitation of a popular French chanteuse and actress, Anna Held, which gave her the reputation of "a remarkably clever mimic."[10] She had a long run in this sketch. Her mother forgave her for her injudicious marriage and looked after the baby, named Kate, as well as still raising Doris. For this reason Blanchard played the season only in New York City and not continuously. She was with the Holland brothers, E.M. and Joseph, in a series of plays under Richard Mansfield's management, joined Mansfield for the New York revival of Bernard Shaw's *Arms and the Man*, and made a hit in *Piney Ridge* as Dagmar, an octoroon who secretly exchanges her child with the child of a rich family.

Blanchard's thoughts about Rankin were strong, as demonstrated by her sketch issuing in the New Year, which her friends enacted in her New

York apartment. A stuffed figure, closely resembling Rankin and typifying the dying year, was propped up in the prisoner's box. Sidney Drew was the judge and Marshall Wilder was an advocate. The guests were called one by one to testify as to what the old year had done and not done for them. The one-time stage actress Mrs Chamberlain (Emily Thorne), the Holland brothers, Phyllis Rankin, and Ethel Barrymore were among those giving witty testimony. The verdict was that the old year should be thrown out, and, at midnight, the stuffed figure was tossed into the courtyard just as Gladys Drew entered carrying a baby girl.[11]

On February 1, 1897, Rankin and O'Neil opened in *True to Life* in Washington, DC. Their company was first-rate and "gave more than ordinary satisfaction."[12] For "an unknown who captured at one bound the press and public of the metropolis," O'Neil was a hot property.[13] The company had a very lucrative season touring through New York State, Quebec, Ontario, the Midwest, and back, to close on May 8 in Buffalo. Rankin gave his opinions on acting to a reporter.

> You see, I have thoroughly impressed upon Miss Nance the great factor of realism....After all, I think the balance by which we must weigh genius is the judgment which adjusts perfectly the value of time. This great essential to the artistic qualities is perfectly mastered by Coquelin and Jefferson. Each knows to a second just how long the thought that they are picturing with the most delicate touches will take to diffuse itself through and permeate the brains of their audiences. Not one minute too soon, not one second too late, do these admirable comedians use their admirable finesse.[14]

To such expressions, O'Neil added: "It is like feeling among the strings of a harp for the chords that are playing themselves in your heart. The touch of one alien string will bring a discord into the melody that you are trying so hard to make. Leave out one note and the harmony is spoiled."[15] She worked very hard in study and in rehearsals. She found it difficult to rehearse alone in her room and so depended on Rankin to coach her over her lines in stage rehearsals, one hundred times if necessary until she had the right effect. A critic insisted that Rankin take O'Neil to New York City, where only Ada Rehan offered competition. "We could endure Rankin," he wrote, "even without Miss O'Neil. But the two of them should be very valuable in these singularly arid times."[16]

Rankin obliged and gave his company only a week's rest before opening at the Murray Hill Theatre in New York for the week of May 17, 1897, in *True to Life*. Many of the theater's patrons had seen the play at Christmas, but many more who missed their chance then could see it now. For the week of May 24, the company played *The Danites* to a large audience. Billed as co-star in the role of Billy Piper, O'Neil, according to a critic, "indicated by her work in this production that her rapid rise was due entirely to her superior ability and the excellence of her acting which contributed much to the success of the present revival."[17]

Rankin and O'Neil returned to vaudeville in the Keith Theatre circuit in their twenty-minute *Counsel for the Defense*, which was being called "a comic interlude." They played the cities of New England, and enjoyed popular success throughout the summer, particularly in Boston in June. "Mr. Rankin, as the gruff old lawyer who concealed a kindly nature under a forbidding exterior," wrote the critic for the *Boston Transcript*, "played with here and there a touch of farce, as if he considered that now and then he must raise a laugh from an audience that had come to see a variety show. But no such consideration moved his fellow player. She was thoroughly in earnest, and never for a moment forgot the intensity of the situation as she pleaded with her lawyer to save her lover." Rather than seeking applause by emphasizing the Bowery girl side of her character, O'Neil "was effective through her very artlessness, speaking her lines, full of the slang of the streets, in a most natural way, with a little note of surprise in her tone, when the lawyer did not catch her meaning, that was very convincing."[18]

A "Memo" from McKee's brother, George, told him of George's gaining control of their late father's $650 mortgage on 665 acres of iron-mining land at Desert Lake in the Algoma District near Sault Ste Marie, Ontario. George invested $5,000 in prospecting the land with a diamond drill and built a log house to accommodate a dozen people. When the drilling proved unsatisfactory, Sandy McKee, their uncle, the same whom McKee had found prospecting in the Sierras and brought to Bois Blanc Island, took over the log house. Yet George had suffered other financial setbacks and could no longer afford to support his uncle. George wrote to ask his brother for $100 to tide the feeble old man over until the following spring. "Of one thing you can be assured," George concluded, "this communication should never have been sent you but for the fact that you have an interest in common with myself both as to Zan and retaining possession of the Desert Lake mining location, which will be worth considerable money some day or other and which if we lose possession of we shall probably lose altogether."[19] There is no record of any response.

1897–1898

The Murray Hill Experience

Ever the gambler, and ever ready to press his case when he saw a good opening, McKee Rankin returned to the Murray Hill Theatre to star Nance O'Neil in a series of plays for the fall 1897 season. At the same time, he set up the McKee Rankin School of Acting. For years he had lamented the loss of repertory as a training ground for actors and deplored the extra onus that directors had to shoulder when confronted with young members of the cast who had had no training. The pupils in his school would be cast in the same plays that he did in the theater. Rehearsals were held every morning, after which the students would watch the rehearsals of the same play by the regular stock company of professionals. The school was used as the permanent understudy for the stock company, and students would be placed in groups to study each of the plays during the six-month season. The best students were cast in minor parts of the regular company.[20]

Rankin did not teach elocution, but rather acting, pantomime, dancing, and the use of the sword. He was assisted by a corps of teachers and gave private instruction in addition to the regular work of the school. For admission, a student had to read in front of Rankin. The full course cost $300. Graduates were promised positions in many companies. For testimonials, Rankin quoted from several of the leading men of the day such as Wilton Lackaye, Joseph Holland, and Robert Hilliard.

This enterprise emulated Augustin Daly's efforts to use stock to produce good drama, uncorrupted by sensationalism, and it gave Rankin another opportunity to develop ensemble playing and to experiment with stagecraft. Although he intended to produce classic plays from earlier in the century, ones unfamiliar to the new generation of playgoer, he chose *The Bachelor's Baby* for his first production, in which he was Colonel D'Arcy and O'Neil was Geraldine Drew. "O'Neil's presence," wrote a critic, "assumes a clever and enjoyable handling of the principal feminine characters in whatever plays the stock company may present for she possesses both emotional and comedy abilities to a pronounced degree, and, though her work in the current production was not of so satisfactory a nature as were her last season's efforts on this stage, this result was largely due to the limitations of her role."[21]

Rankin had not intended to act in his next offering, *Confusion*, but, having discharged the regular comedian at the last moment, he took the demanding part of Christopher Blizzard and played it with brilliance. His direction of the play was also praised. "In the profession since the death of Frank Mayo," wrote the critic Alan Dale, "Rankin is credited with being among the first stage managers in the country. This he showed last night by handling the complicated comedy scenes like a master."[22]

In the title role of *Leah, the Forsaken*, O'Neil demonstrated her histrionic talent in the curse scene. In response, a critic noted that "Emotional roles are unquestionably her forte."[23] Audiences jammed the house and kept the play running another week. Nevertheless, Alan Dale detected the fatal hand of the tutor on O'Neil and claimed that Rankin was teaching her tricks and filling her mind with "the wretched 'business' of the common or garden star."[24] With such comments, he began a strain of criticism of O'Neil that took various forms over the years.

For *Leah* and *East Lynne*, O'Neil used Lucille Western's promptbooks, which had been given to her by Jane English, Lucille Western's mother. Although she had not seen her act—Western died before she was born—O'Neil most wanted to emulate Lucille Western. Rankin's stories about Western stimulated O'Neil's imagination, especially in her approach to audiences, with whom she had immediate rapport. "I feel the house the moment I enter the stage," she said. "Its chilliness oppresses me; its sympathies encourage."[25]

In Rankin's revival of *Led Astray*, Rankin was good as Rudolph Chandoce as was O'Neil as Armande Chandoce. The poet, Georges de Lesparre, the part Rankin used to play, was taken by a young Canadian actor from Hamilton, Ontario, Andrew Robson, who was soon to become O'Neil's supporting lead. "The clever situations and effective lines of this old comedy were handled in a capital manner by the stock players," wrote the *Clipper*.[26] Their success was owing to Rankin's great efforts, as he devoted his attention to every detail of stage business, acting out the roles as he thought they should be played, and harmonizing the whole in a well-balanced ensemble. Rankin played every part at rehearsals so naturally that the actors grasped the idea and followed it out to the end without feeling that they were being taught something difficult.

Rankin's staging of *Camille* as his next offering was a bold move. O'Neil had just a week to learn the role, and her lack of depth was noted by a critic, who thought that she bore the burden of responsibility very creditably, "although the character seems not to have been fully grasped by her." O'Neil improved so that the play had to be kept over for another week.[27]

With *East Lynne*, his next production, Rankin gave O'Neil as Lady Isabel full power to display her emotions. "One cannot turn one's eye from her when she is on stage," wrote a critic, "her voice in all its varied cadences touches a responsive chord, and one feels as she feels without the desire to feel otherwise."[28] O'Neil said that to move an audience the actor had to feel the emotions of the character. In order to concentrate on real emotions, she kept as far as she could from the artificial atmosphere of the stage and spent her time walking, riding, and playing tennis. On Sundays when the theater was closed, Rankin asked O'Neil to join him in giving special concerts—dramatic readings to music in concert houses. His hard-driving energy affected all those about him and soon tired O'Neil, who took a week's rest while Andrew Robson played the main role in *Jim the Penman*.

Rankin continued to revive his popular plays as well as staging new ones to showcase O'Neil. She played Nancy in Rankin's adaptation of *Oliver Twist*, in which Rankin played the scarifying Bill Sykes. He then staged *The Magdalene*, written by a local playwright in the old temperance tradition, in which the heroine is turned out by her drunken father, whom she had supported for years, because she refuses to marry her father's choice. O'Neil played the girl, Kate Morrison, with great effect. Rankin, as the drunken father, contributed another interesting character study to the stage. Robson was forceful as the clergyman. The somber nature and lack of action, however, made the play unpopular. Rankin brought back *East Lynne* for a week to restore the coffers. According to O'Neil, thousands had to be turned away. During its run, the company celebrated its hundredth performance, a singular achievement when Rankin's detractors had predicted that his company would not last half that time.[29]

Rankin revived *The Ticket-of-Leave Man*, with Robson as Bob Brierly, himself as Detective Hawkshaw, and O'Neil as Bob's girl. *Hoodman Blind* came next, to the delight of the large audiences. These melodramas and well-made plays not only attracted a new generation of playgoers, who wanted to see the plays that their parents had talked about, but they were full of marvelous character parts, which served as good models for the acting students in Rankin's school. There was, however, just so much old-time revivalism that Rankin could depend upon before audiences began to tire of the fare. As a last call to the past, Rankin brought Rose Eytinge into the cast to play the role that she created in *Rose Michel* those many years ago at the Union Square Theatre. What a treat for the students! What encouragement for the professional cast! The company was badly disciplined, however, and it became apparent during the run of *Rose Michel* that its loose organization was bringing it to an end. The theater closed on December 18, 1897. A disagreement over taxes between the theater manager and the estate that owned the land contributed to the company's demise and was settled just after the stock company disbanded.[30] Rankin carried on his school to the end of the year.

Nance O'Neil's Star Begins to Rise

Rankin's restlessness and his innovative mind propelled him onward. He must have been pleased to have provided the young with an opportunity to learn acting, and he was excited about O'Neil's star potential, but the repertory experiment was behind him. He presented a condensed *Oliver Twist*, featuring scenes such as Bill Sykes beating Nancy, for vaudeville at Proctor's Theatre in New York as the holiday bill; for the second week, they played a condensed *Leah*. The acts were performed twice daily between 10 AM and 10:30 PM. Rehearsals were held from 8 to 10 AM every Monday. O'Neil, Rankin, and their four colleagues so pleased the audiences that their manager arranged for them to extend their stay for two weeks. Their salary was $450 as a group a week.[31]

Rankin had been startled by the tremendous attraction of *East Lynne* for the modern theatergoer when he produced it at the Murray Hill Theatre, and he decided to tour in it. He gave it a new form by entirely rewriting the first act, inserting several comedy scenes to relieve the seriousness of the text, and revising the scenic effects. To a very strong company—Nance O'Neil, Andrew Robson, Wilton Lackaye, Rose Eytinge, Burwell Cutler, Harriet Sterling, Mrs John T. Raymond, and himself—he added those who had acted in vaudeville with him and a few new actresses from his school. Ricca Allen, an actress appearing in Rankin's company for the first time, was to stay with him for years.[32]

Rankin opened with *The New East Lynne* at the Park Theatre in Philadelphia on February 7, 1898, to great success. The "leavening of excellent vaudeville acts," as the *Clipper* called the insertion of comic scenes, proved an added attraction. The house was crowded at every performance; many were turned away, unable to get seats.[33] At the Bijou in Brooklyn the play was said to have never been presented by so able a company with so many distinguished actors. By presenting this old tear-jerker in the face of the modern problem plays then predominating, Rankin seemed to have read the people's needs in entertainment. "This is the only place in town that appeals to one's sympathies," wrote a critic.[34] The company met with the same response in Pittsburgh and in Chicago. Rankin added to the bill the authorized version of *Trilby*, the rights for which he had obtained from A.M. Palmer. O'Neil brought innovations to the role of Trilby O'Ferrall, such as appearing in bare feet.[35] In New York City in late March, the company still had full houses for *The New East Lynne*.

At the same time as Rankin's success in *The New East Lynne*, one of his daughters was having her own success on the stage. The musical comedy *The Belle of New York* had established Phyllis Rankin as a popular comedian. Now, after a long run in New York, she was leaving for London,

England, to continue her role in the play. She played a French tart, Fifi Fricot. Phyllis left her baby son, Arthur, along with her daughter in her mother's care. Young John Barrymore wrote to Blanchard: "I saw Pix off! She was all broken up! Loud and deep were my execrations when I realized I couldn't go on that steamer! But I'll see her in about two weeks and there!! You intend to come over don't you. I'd have a fit if you didn't!"[36]

Rankin added Lionel Barrymore to his company and continued to Baltimore, Boston, and Brooklyn in *The New East Lynne* to universal praise for the play and some unkind criticism of Rankin as a fat Lord Mountsevern. Wrote one critic: "I'm going to advise him not to button his frock coat any more, for there is a naughty little wrinkle running around his waist which has the effect of making him look like a sack of something with a string tied round the middle....When he cries I wish he wouldn't wink so hard to call our attention to the fact. We can see that he is not feeling jolly, and a fat man crying is funny enough anyway without the blinking thrown in."[37]

Phyllis Rankin as Fifi in *The Belle of New York*, 1898.

Always ready to experiment, Rankin tried out Rose Eytinge's new play, *That Lass o' Lowrie*, at Albaugh's Lafayette Square Opera House in Washington, DC. The play "served one good purpose," wrote a critic, "that of bringing into prominent notice Nance O'Neil, who though young to the stage is one of the most charming and yet powerful actresses that has been seen here in many a year, and with proper management her future cannot be otherwise than a brilliant one."[38] While she was in Washington, Rankin's old friend John Albaugh promised to give O'Neil his promptbooks of old plays, of which she later reminded him by a disingenuous threat when she had not received them: "If I may take the liberty of using your name I am going to write to a press friend of mine in New York about the prompt books for I am very proud of their having been given me by you." As for the time spent in Washington, she wrote, "I have the pleasantest recollections—in spite of disagreeables."[39]

In Buffalo, Rankin was so immensely popular that the company could have remained several weeks longer to good business. When the company attracted light houses in its second week in Philadelphia, Rankin cut short what was expected to be a season of several weeks and moved on to Minneapolis, where he opened the supplementary summer season on June 12.[40] Here the company settled down for hard work, presenting *East Lynne* the first week and surprising the managers of the Metropolitan Theatre, who expected it to bring in less than half of what it did. Horace McVicker became Rankin's road manager, and his wife and daughter joined the company. Mrs McVicker's father, the veteran actor Henry A. Weaver, was already in the company.[41]

In the second week in Minneapolis, Rankin revived *Oliver Twist*. The local critic said that it had rarely been done more effectively, which was due to Rankin, who went over its seventeen parts in detail with the actors to achieve the effect he wanted. Nevertheless, mistakes could happen. To save money, Rankin gave Lionel Barrymore two minor roles and did not discover that they had a scene together until Lionel was onstage in one character when his second character was to enter. Barrymore looked helplessly around for Rankin, who was preoccupied with O'Neil, and coolly went to a window in the set to carry on the conversation with the second character, who was out of sight. "It was a ventriloquist act, pure and simple," Lionel wrote.[42] Rankin, pleased with the arrangement, kept Barrymore in both roles. Lionel was grateful to Rankin for giving him parts and making it possible for him to eat. "During this time," he said, "some of McKee Rankin's precepts and instructions apparently rubbed off on me, or were assimilated by osmosis, because I gradually got better parts and began to feel more at home on stage."[43]

Along with the standard plays tailored to bring out O'Neil's emotional talents, Rankin kept her busy in new pieces, such as Sardou's *A Wife's Peril*, with a large role for Lionel Barrymore. *A Wife's Peril* pleased the audiences with its clever situations and excellent acting. Lionel Barrymore received his first critical mention for playing Maurice acceptably. For the following four weeks, the company continued a weekly pattern of four days for the first play and three days for the next, while performing all the plays in its repertoire. Business remained good despite the sultry weather. O'Neil wrote to Albaugh: "This summer we did the balcony scene from 'Juliet' as a curtain raiser and we also did 'Katherine'—of course very hurriedly but Mr. Rankin encouraged me very much—and I know I shall like both parts when I have time to study them properly."[44]

In St Paul, Rankin was an old-time favorite and his polished performance as Lord Mountsevern in *The New East Lynne* gave much pleasure. In Minneapolis, for the week of August 7, Rankin presented five different plays, in eleven performances. Among the plays was Hermann Sudermann's *Magda*. For months, O'Neil had been studying the role of the successful actress returning home. She was an instant success, giving a "thoroughly artistic" interpretation. *Magda* showed the tragic conflict ensuing when cobwebbed notions of honor, duty, and caste seek to subordinate the cosmopolitan conceptions of the cultured mind. As a follower of Henrik Ibsen, Sudermann used the struggle of diverse social forces to unearth the skeletons concealed in the human heart. Magda, a renowned actress, comes to perform in her hometown after an absence of many years. Her family, who had ostracized her for her association with Dr von Kellner, now welcomes her home, although her father, Lieutenant-Colonel Leopold Schwartze, wants to subdue her spirit. Confronted with the persuasive force of Pastor Hefferdingt, Magda almost submits to marriage with von Kellner, who had disgraced and deserted her years before. But when von Kellner wants to disguise the fact that they have a son, she repels and refuses him. The enraged Schwartze, in attempting to shoot her, dies of a stroke.

Nance O'Neil as Magda in Sudermann's *Magda*, 1898.

Magda has to confront her feelings of guilt. When she initially ran away to escape from her father's tyranny, Schwartze suffered a stroke and had to retire from the army. On her return she must bear more guilt, when her father dies of a stroke. Mrs Patrick Campbell, a popular English actress, made her Magda kneel and cry contritely, "My God! What have I done?" whereas Sarah Bernhardt made the heroine stand forth by remaining solitary, "in lugubrious magnificence."[45] Critics tended to think that Magda becomes great through her sin: "Her personality is developed, and her life made richer, broader, more humanizing and interesting because of it."[46]

Magda's antagonist in the play, the old father whom she wants to please but who is so cruelly misunderstanding, was played by Rankin with great skill. His characterization thrilled audiences as much as did O'Neil as Magda, and they combined to make the best week of drama ever seen in Minneapolis.

Lionel Barrymore, who played Max, a young lieutenant and Magda's nephew, wrote: "My wardrobe in this production was more important than I was, it being absolutely authentic. We obtained it from a costume company which had got hold of it from a Minneapolis lieutenant, who had been an officer of the precise regiment I was alleged to represent. If I did nothing else right, I modeled that officer correctly. I am certain it was the only correct costume in the play."[47]

The role of Magda was made for O'Neil. She was, however, constantly being compared to the great actors who played the part before her. Eleanora Duse had taken New York by storm when she played the role in 1893. It would have been suicidal for young O'Neil to try it in New York. A critic noted that O'Neil's interpretation seemed patterned after Madame Modjeska's, who revealed a cold, selfish, and spoiled Magda who is chastened by her re-entering her home after twelve years. O'Neil's Magda was thought more impressive than Mrs Campbell's, although coarser than both Campbell's and Modjeska's. "I have been viewing it as a character," she said, "looking at it in its own surroundings, working on it, taking it slowly. That is what I prefer, but I cannot often give that time. Often I never study a part at all, merely learn it in rehearsals as I did Camille, which we took up on a Tuesday and played the following Sunday. That is the kind of quick work we have to do."[48]

O'Neil wrote to Albaugh during a week of rest in Pittsburgh to thank him for the promptbooks. She had been ill from overwork and a severe cold. "I am sure you will understand what a tax it has been for me under the circumstances—haven't had time to read plays—hope to this week—books beautifully marked."[49] Following her rest, she scored an immense hit in the city as Magda. "She is one of the most able emotional actresses ever seen here," wrote the local critic.[50]

Because business was only fair in Cincinnati, the company did only *Camille*, giving O'Neil time to write again to Albaugh:

> Glad you think "Magda" is good to have done. "Mr. Mac" thought so. We will open with it in California most likely....I should like to do "Romeo," in fact intended to try it this summer out west but I had no "Juliet"....I know you will be glad to hear that I am going to try "Meg Merrilies" our third week in California. I will send you the notices if you don't mind. Luke Martin sent me Miss Cushman's marked book to make a copy of my own—which of course will help me greatly, and then Mr. Rankin and Mr. Preaner remember so much of her business too. We have gotten the song—"Oh hush then babe" and I am

sure we will also have the Bishop music—I have not been so interested in any part for a long time except "Magda" as much as I am in "Meg." A friend of mine Mr. Brunell sent me two pictures of Miss Cushman in the part which will help me also. Sorry you suffered with the heat. It has been a strain both physically and financially in the last two or three weeks. But I think all that will end in a few days now when we get to California. My father writes me that there is a great deal of interest in my homecoming and that many articles have been written about me. I think if we make a hit our opening night we will have a big engagement.[51]

The older actors who had seen Cushman act believed that it would be many a day before the old gypsy queen Meg would produce that indescribable effect upon an audience that Cushman had achieved—that is, of a character excited by hope and fear into whom the actress breathed the life and the spirit of the wild. Perhaps, with the coming of O'Neil, the day was at hand. In the meantime, Rankin carefully plotted the next stage in her ascent to stardom: a glorious homecoming.

1898–1899

Homecoming

The company opened at the Columbia Theatre, San Francisco, on September 19, 1898. A large and fashionable audience gave O'Neil a friendly and noisy welcome. But the éclat she hoped to make with *Magda* was prevented by an injunction, brought by a theatrical agent, Emanuel Lederer, who claimed to have the rights to it. O'Neil was disappointed, because she liked to start an engagement with *Magda* for good luck's sake. Rankin presently discovered a defect in the copyright. Unwilling to contest his claim in court because, if O'Neil won, then anyone could produce the play, Lederer let Rankin produce it in return for a stipulated sum and gave him a contract copyright license, which allowed O'Neil to maintain *Magda* in her repertoire. Meanwhile, Rankin opened with *The Jewess*, his version of *Leah*.[52]

Although San Franciscans had heard of O'Neil's achievements in the East, the audience was unprepared for the whirlwind that hit it. "She ran upon the stage as the weird, wild, impassioned, scornful Leah, the Jewess," wrote a critic. "The people sat breathless, watching her wonderfully tragic figure and listening to her baritone voice that is so full of expression."[53] "She caught her audience and carried it with her," wrote another critic. "From the first word she was Leah. Her second entrance was watched for eagerly; her presence received respectful attention. To the curse scene they capitulated."[54] Rankin played Nathan, the Christianized Jew, whose misrepresentations turn Leah's Christian lover against her.

For the first three evenings of the second week, the company presented *Ingomar, the Barbarian*. O'Neil was Parthenia—"dewey, radiant, spring-like, of tender youth and exquisite purity, a lovely maiden, warmly human."[55] Her interview with Polidor is transformed from quaint bantering to despair when she learns that her father has been captured by the ruthless Alemanni. She begs for her father's life and, gaining a subtle influence over the chief, leads him in bands of love back to civilization. "The gentle faith of the girl in her wild lover, the coquetry at her command, and the pleasing acts by which she bends him to her will, were pictured with charming grace."[56]

Rankin finished the week with *Oliver Twist*. The critic Ashton Stevens, whose career covering the theater lasted for several decades, was a particular fan of Rankin. He thought that his playing of Bill Sykes brought the actor into his "melodramatic own" and found that O'Neil was a superlative Nancy:

> All the roughness of voice and method and the Vesuvian personality that have been more or less too much for the other roles that she has played here were given full vent, and she played the part as it has never been played here before. Nancy is a character that demands of an actress strength, health and frank brutality. There is no mincing matters; no delicate compromises. The part will stand for no feminine blandishments. It is hard and terrible; in these qualities lie its spell and grim pathos. Miss O'Neil did not spare an atom of her vanity in playing it for all that it was worth. She was large, husky, dark, and unpretty to gaze upon, and she moved like a ship in a storm; but she was the Nancy Sykes of Dickens and we all were in a goose-flesh of appreciation.[57]

When the company gave *Camille*, Stevens took it for granted that the consumptive heroine in O'Neil's hands would be strapping and that her tempestuous declamation would mar the brilliancy of the lighter scenes. "But from the opening of the third act," he wrote,

> her impersonation was genuinely emotional and surprisingly vivid in its physical expression. The big scene with Armand's father she acted with what for Nance O'Neil was admirable

repression. She let her feelings bore in rather than boil out, and realized a great deal of the emotional value of the lines; and in the scene where she writes the letter to Armand her grief did not find vent in a fury of sobs. She controlled herself as would Camille who was capable of the sacrifice. Her farewell to Armand was louder and fuller of pose and not so convincing, but on the whole this third act was played in a warm human key, and there was scarcely a dry eye to be seen in the house when the lights went up after it.[58]

Rankin as Gustave, Armand Duval's friend, dressed as "a perfect devil of flaneur and he too played in a quieter and happier vein."[59]

O'Neil met a tremendous challenge in the fourth week. She played Queen Elizabeth I of England in Paolo Giacommetti's *Elizabeth, Queen of England*, a blank-verse drama that only the great Ristori and Mrs D.P. Bowers had done successfully.[60] O'Neil physically suited these great roles and at the same time presented a new interpretation of them. By breaking old rules and upsetting traditions, she alarmed traditionalists, but her fires could not be tamed. "To form an estimate of Miss O'Neil's great ability," wrote the *San Francisco Bulletin*, "it is only necessary to remember the difficulties of portraying in one character the iron will of the born commander with the tender fascination of the woman, the tantrums of a jealous woman and the supreme egotism of a sovereign."[61] A San Francisco critic was one of the first to try to describe her voice: "Sometimes a whisper, sometimes a guttural, harsh growl, and again it is vocal velvet, while in climaxes it is like a great organ. Yet every variation of tone compels you to listen, and there is no escape. She uses it in so many ways that one fancies that she has exhausted every variety, and then a new tone will come that will show there is evidently no end to its variations."[62]

In contrast to his very young but emotional powerful protégée, Rankin received more gratuitous criticism: "He grows grayer and more abdominal and guttural voiced as he goes swiftly down the artistic toboggan slide of advancing years."[63]

The company played to packed houses down the coast, heading to Los Angeles, where they were scheduled to play the week of October 24 at the Burbank Theatre. O'Neil impressed critics and patrons there as well. "She is elemental," wrote a critic. "Gusts of passion shake her as a strong young sapling is shaken in the storm. She strides fearlessly through all the canons of art: tramples down all dramatic traditions; ignores all the subtleties of delicate light and shade; —but she compels attention. At times it is easy to watch her without approval of her method of expression; it is impossible to watch her without being thrilled by the emotion she expresses."[64] Of the plays, the audiences liked best *Oliver Twist*, in which Rankin as Bill Sykes "is less melodramatic than his usual style of acting and does an exceedingly realistic and powerful piece of work."[65] Because several hundred people had to be turned away from the house packed to suffocation, the management arranged to play *Oliver Twist* on the next and last night in place of the scheduled but unpopular *True to Life*.

After its run in Los Angeles, Rankin's company took ship for Hawaii and opened in the Opera House in Honolulu on Thursday, November 10, 1898, in *Magda*, since Lederer had no longer grounds for an injunction.[66] The company's sojourn in Hawaii was doubtless in response to its backer, the wealthy sugar baron Adolphe Spreckels, whose family owned many of the banks and industries in Hawaii. The Honolulu newspapers made it clear that mainland drama was followed closely on the island. Their criticism confirmed what had been written about O'Neil but added a significant touch: "Tall, she has a grace like a surf play...."[67] Playing *Camille* and *Ingomar*, the company began to build up an excitement for its productions. In Pinero's *The Magistrate*, L.R. Stockwell, the San Francisco actor, as the droll judge, carried the play. O'Neil as his wife was beautifully dressed and struck her comedy notes clearly. Rankin was excellent as the French landlord with a patois reminding the theatergoers of old times, and he was at home in a scene in which he handled several people at the same time in a mix-up in a restaurant.[68]

The audiences, who were being attracted by curiosity and the desire to see the new tragedian, were in for a shock with the company's *Oliver Twist*. Rankin's version differed from the common one in two major scenes. In most stage productions, Nancy is killed by being beaten to death with the butt of a revolver in front of the audience, but Rankin's play shows Nancy beaten with a club in the stage room while she struggles and begs and shrieks and finally runs into another room out of sight of the audience. There is heard further beating, groans, and gasps, and almost a death rattle. Bill Sykes reappears to prepare for flight. In a moment, Nancy drags herself into view after him as she moans and implores Bill for her life, for a caress, for a word, then rises to her knees and reveals the face that has been shredded with the club, the loosened teeth, the matted and tangled hair, and the blood. Then with a final prayer to the brute, Nancy dies. Such a graphic sight shocked and fascinated the audience. The other major difference was the ending. Other productions followed the novel, in which Fagin is executed, but Rankin has Fagin expiring of terror at the prospect of paying the penalty for his crimes.

The critic considered the production "simply an animated chamber of horrors. The two scenes of that last act will haunt many of the people who saw them for a long time. The very zenith of stage realism was reached. The audience was stupefied. A number of people left their seats before the acting that was piled upon the climax was reached." Rankin's portrayal of Sykes was ideal, and "his scene with his dog that keeps away from its sinning master was a story in itself."[69]

All the remaining plays in the repertoire won enthusiastic receptions. The company, planning to leave on November 28, found that the ship was late in arriving and that certain financial interests guaranteed Rankin a profit if he kept playing for a few more nights until the ship docked and departed. After portraying a fragile and emotional Camille, O'Neil received a magnificent floral tribute. The company was feted royally. An admirer gave O'Neil a dinner plate that Napoleon III had given to Kamekamela III, the Hawaiian monarch, and which he had purchased for a large sum. The royal family gave O'Neil beautiful presents, including plate and silver. Prince David Kawananakoa, a dashing young man with a handlebar mustache, serenaded her at her hotel one evening.[70] The people were gracious, warm, and welcoming.

Sailing for San Francisco on December 8, Rankin's company was scheduled to open at the California Theatre on December 25, 1898. For three nights, they presented *Magda*. The house was crowded and the play was a hit. "We waited a long time for Nance O'Neil's Magda," wrote a critic, "and when it came it did not wholly satisfy. There is too much of it—the criticism that applies to others of this young genius's interpretations. Her Magda is nothing like Modjeska's; not one little gesture even is imitated. All is original conception, a big stormy characterization."[71] O'Neil again made a sensation as Meg Merrilies in *Guy Mannering*. Not everyone was impressed by the offerings. "As Nancy Sykes is perhaps the best of her roles," remarked the critic, "it seems a pity a full week of Nance O'Neil in 'Oliver Twist' could not have been given."[72]

Part of the reason for the enthusiasm for O'Neil was the paucity of good drama in San Francisco. Al Hayman had a monopoly on western theaters and a partnership with the Frohman Syndicate in the East, which gave him the control of plays and touring companies. Since the Frohmans controlled all the first-class plays and rationed them out as they saw fit, the theater public turned to vaudeville, to which the California Theatre, among others, was devoted. Hayman kept the Baldwin Theatre as a "society theater" where the best plays were done, but in December 1898 the Baldwin theater burnt down, leaving San Francisco bereft of good drama. O'Neil's appearance slaked the thirst for legitimate drama, crammed as it was into one week between vaudeville shows. After she left, there was a chronic let-down.[73]

Throughout the 1880s, the change in theatrical business had been dramatic in itself. Whereas Haverly had built his theatrical empire through consolidation, Gustave Frohman gained control of the road operations of traveling companies by arrangements with theater owners. His brother Charles arranged and booked the tours for their companies while another brother, Daniel, selected the casts and rehearsed the companies in New York before sending them on the road. When Haverly's gambling appetites led him to ruination in wildcat mining, his empire crumbled and the Frohmans gained wide control. They directed operations nationwide from New York and, with others, in 1896, formed the Theatrical Syndicate, with which Rankin was to have problems.[74]

After her initial success in New York, Rankin had asked Charles Frohman to manage O'Neil, but Frohman turned him down because he had too many "green" actresses in his employ. If a manager had agreed to take on O'Neil, he would have to include Rankin, as the two were by now inseparable. The same moralistic claque who could not forgive Rankin for sundering his "perfect marriage" to Blanchard began sniping at him in the press and trying to break O'Neil away from him.

On January 3, 1899, O'Neil played in Woodland, California, and two nights in Oakland. She then moved on to Los Angeles, where she was set to play a week at the Burbank, but, owing to public pressure, the run had to be extended to three weeks, from January 8 to 29. The company did the important plays in its repertoire, including *The Danites*, *Led Astray*, and *Guy Mannering*. Again, while playing up the coast, the company had to extend a one-week stop in San Jose to two weeks when *Magda* was the main attraction.

An embarrassing confirmation of O'Neil's closeness to Rankin was reported, allegedly by a woman journalist, who witnessed on January 2, 1899, in the Grand Hotel of San Francisco, "the maiden of 24 and the Falstaffian Don Juan of 54...dressed in a little too much of the altogether."[75] Rankin was said to have explained that he and O'Neil were married but had kept it secret for business reasons. The secret of the marriage kept until February 23, when the *San Francisco Evening Post* revealed it to coincide with O'Neil's return to the California Theatre by public demand on February 27. A reporter in New York wrote that Kate Blanchard denied that she and Rankin were divorced: "It has long been an open secret to those who know the ins and outs of the theatrical profession, that Miss O'Neil has ruined what might have been a glorious stage career by her infatuation with McKee Rankin, who has daughters older than she is."[76]

The story must have been an amusing conversation piece that lasted longer than it should have; in mid-March, Rankin fired his manager, Frank Curtis, the same man who had co-managed his Third Avenue Theatre and acted in his companies, for giving out the story. Curtis accused Rankin of making him a scapegoat. O'Neil called the story malicious and claimed that the editor of the San Francisco paper admitted that Curtis had brought it to him for publication. As for her continuation under Rankin's management, O'Neil said: "Why should I not remain with him? Look what he has done for me, and what he has taught me. He has brought me to my present place. If I had gone with Frohman or any of the other New York managers, I should probably today be playing seconds to some other actress. Remember, it is only five years since I started out. You say Mr. Rankin represents the older school of actors. Granted, but I would not disregard the old school. I would have it allied with the modern school to obtain the best results. I do not override stage traditions, but appreciate the value of just the kind of stage training I have received from Mr. Rankin. Natural ability in an actor must be coupled with rigid practice."[77]

In the face of the scandal, the return engagement at the California Theatre began with an augmented company in *Magda*, followed by the great dramatic roles that San Francisco audiences wanted to see. O'Neil met such acclaim that to answer public demand she had to give repeat performances of *Magda* and *The New East Lynne*. The public went wild over her.

The company continued north through Oregon for a two-week run in Portland, the most successful in the eleven-year history of the Cordray Theatre in that city. O'Neil presented *Magda* four times; each time the house was sold out. In an interview in that city, she compared herself to the actress who seemed to be her most serious competitor in America—Minnie Fiske. Known primarily for her intellectual approach to roles, Minnie Maddern had married Harrison Grey Fiske, owner of the *New York Dramatic Mirror*. O'Neil said that Mrs Fiske represented Magda as heartless and malicious, a veritable cat filled with anger and avarice. But to O'Neil, Magda was not at all heartless; rather she showed love for her sister, her father, and her child. She acted in pity rather than in anger.[78]

O'Neil seemed to be challenging a force in the theater that, aside from the Theater Syndicate, she and Rankin thought was making trouble for her. Harrison Fiske had formed an alliance with independent theater producers against the Theater Syndicate, which was promoting the more unthinking drama in contrast to the serious drama in which Minnie Fiske could best shine. But at the same time, the attacks on Rankin (and by extension on O'Neil) claiming that his bad management would damage O'Neil's career seemed to originate from the Harrison Fiske camp of influence, which was extensive, including the Hearst newspaper chain. An actress who challenged Mrs Fiske's superiority in serious drama could expect to be attacked. As for the syndicate, it simply blocked actors who were not in its employ from access to the major theaters.

Rankin realized that O'Neil was not going to be easily accepted in the major theater centers such as New York City unless she won acclaim from abroad. His old friend J.C. Williamson, who had become the most important theater producer and manager in Australia, suggested that he bring O'Neil to Australia, where he was certain that the people would admire her acting style. But Williamson added that she needed a London imprimatur before touring Australia to make her more acceptable; hence Rankin agreed to take her to England and present her in *Magda* to the West End theater audiences. It was a huge risk, but Rankin was sure O'Neil would be successful.

While these plans were taking shape, the company moved on to Spokane to good business, and to towns like Anaconda and Missoula in Montana to critical acclaim. In Butte, the local critic wrote about O'Neil: "No one in years has won such encomiums or such a lasting place in the favor of our theater patrons."[79] The company had very big business in St Paul, Minneapolis, and Milwaukee, where O'Neil's second week taxed the capacity of the house when she played the lead roles in *Camille*, *Oliver Twist*, *Elizabeth*, *Peg Woffington*, *Guy Mannering*, and *Magda*. The play *Peg Woffington* was a version of *Masks and Faces*, retitled to emphasize O'Neil's role as the famous actress. She played the role for the first time on this tour. Of course, Rankin's promotional talents were exceptional: "What he did not know about expert gratuitous advertising was not in the book," said a critic admiringly, who had seen him in action "pervading the Lake City in open victorias, wearing violent clothing of gray tweed, smoking immense (but expensive) cigars, purchasing champagne and impressing it upon Erie County that Nance O'Neil was a great actress."[80]

London Bound

The company finally reached New York to embark for England. The actors gathered for two days at the Erie depot on West Twenty-Third Street only to be told that the departure was delayed. The problem was financing.

While waiting for financing to come through, the company played in Philadelphia in *East Lynne*. There, a deputy sheriff took Rankin to the police station on a charge of the illegal retention of a manuscript, which had been given him for production. Rankin was always looking for new plays for O'Neil and liked to encourage young playwrights, who had no other way of developing their talents in the commercialized theater of the day. He may have impressed them with the great possibilities of their scripts, but he often found that it was too risky to produce them and subsequently had to defend himself against these disappointed young playwrights. Unperturbed, Rankin jovially settled the matter with the magistrate and returned to the theater in time to play Lord Mountsevern that evening. In the end, the company was left behind. Just Rankin and O'Neil sailed for England, where a cast of American actors was already assembled.

As Rankin negotiated for a theater and a time to put on a play, he and O'Neil went for walks about London. "The ponderous figure of Mr. McKee Rankin takes pleasure in occupying one side of the Strand almost every afternoon," announced a London reporter. "It is generally accompanied on its strolls by the pliant figure of Miss Nance O'Neil."[81] O'Neil's plans to act in *Magda* were thwarted by another actress. By the terms of the copyright on *Magda*, Mrs Patrick Campbell had the rights to the play in England, and she was unwilling to give her rival O'Neil permission to perform in it before English audiences. Rankin announced that O'Neil would act in *The Jewess* at the Shaftesbury Theatre for only one matinee performance, on June 27, 1899.

The audience at the performance comprised American actors and English critics. O'Neil was a hit with the audience and received a great ovation after the curse scene. London critics agreed that she had genius but needed developing. As the persecuted Jewess, O'Neil had overcome the memory of Kate Bateman, who had been considered the ideal exponent. "The play is dull in the extreme," wrote the *Morning Telegraph*, "and nothing but the tragic force of the actress can possibly awaken interest.... There are so few actresses who have the physical, vocal, or nervous strength to play such parts. Her whole performance was remarkably even and excellent."[82] The critics, who had come to scoff, remained to admire.

Coincidentally, at the Shaftesbury, playing every evening and for two matinees a week was *The Belle of New York*, starring Phyllis Rankin as Fifi Fricot. Phyllis was the toast of London. "She can suggest all sorts of humour but she never smiles," wrote a London critic. "Her method is such that her audiences do not know whether she is laughing in her sleeve at them all the time or whether she is deadly serious in her work."[83] The day of O'Neil's matinee marked the 484th performance of *The Belle of New York*; ultimately, the play would run for twenty-two months. Phyllis, homesick for her babies, wanted to leave the company. She also had tired of her husband, Harry Gibbs, and saw her marriage the way others had, as a youthful indiscretion. "Her husband is a modest personage seldom introduced in evidence," wrote a reporter, who called him "her brother-in-law's property man." Her family "ostracized" her from the time of her marriage until her triumph in London, "when the family found members of the British nobility, like chiropodists, at her feet."[84] She was granted a divorce and custody of her children in July. There was another influence on her. In *The Belle of New York*, Phyllis sang "When We Are Married" with Harry Davenport, youngest son of E.L. Davenport; the song proved prophetic: he divorced his wife and married Phyllis. Henry Gibbs disappeared from view until he made an unexpected reappearance decades later.

Idle in London, O'Neil saw her contemporaries on the stage—Sarah Bernhardt in *Camille*, Herbert Beerbohm Tree in *The Musketeers*, and Constant Coquelin in *Cyrano*. She wandered about old London soaking up the atmosphere. She visited Peg Woffington's birthplace and Nance Oldfield's grave at Poets' Corner No. 24 in Westminster Abbey. Oldfield was the only woman to lay in state in the Jerusalem Chamber of the Abbey. The door of the chamber stood open, and O'Neil, thrilled to be standing in the sacred place, took the opportunity to peak in.[85]

O'Neil's reception in her one performance of *The Jewess* prompted Rankin to contemplate producing *Oliver Twist* and other plays after mid-July, and he announced that O'Neil would be touring the provinces. Her Australian tour was assured. J.C. Williamson's partner in a chain of theaters in Australia, who saw her London performance, booked her for their chain and guaranteed good business in every city.

Negative comments began appearing in the American press about O'Neil's London "success," suggesting that an American claque had supported her in London and the critics really thought she was bad. A local manager, just returned from Europe, claimed that O'Neil's performance in *The Jewess* was "the funniest thing of the waning season."[86] He may have been giving his view of her demonstrative acting style, and, no doubt, some in London thought like him, although to have expressed it in that manner to the press indicates a wish to humiliate her which appears

Nance O'Neil in her role as Leah in *The Jewess*.

to align him with one of the factions opposing her. In any case, her performance had served its purpose of setting her up for an Australian tour.

Rankin gave up the idea of touring in England, probably because he lacked the finances and knew from his previous experience that the

English provinces were likely not to be profitable. He returned to New York City with O'Neil in mid-August. An item appeared in the press suggesting that O'Neil wash herself—implying that Rankin contaminated her and a reporter asserted that O'Neil was disturbing her neighbors at night "with passionate declarations, languorous sighs, and the soft murmur of loving protestations mingled with the pleading entreaty, 'Tell me that you love me!'" This was followed with a tumult of strife and altercation, clamorous with contention—"probably O'Neil was rehearsing under the able tuition of her abdominal sponsor, McKee Rankin."[87] The meanness of this attack was probably in proportion to the alarm of her enemies at the prestige that her London performance gave her.

1899: Star Rising

Rankin gathered a company together and entrained for Portland, Oregon, where he began the next stage in O'Neil's career, a thorough preparation for the Australian tour. "Barton Hill was of the company, as was old man Becks, one of the greatest Shakespearean actors of Forrest's day," reported a playwright who met them on the train. "Barton Hill played juvenile parts forty-nine years ago.…There were reminiscences, of course, and many were the stories told of Booth—both the junior and the elder—of Charlotte Cushman, of Joseph Jefferson and his famous foster brother, Charles Burke, of Edwin Forrest, whom they all admired, and even of Macready, in whose company Barton Hill, if I mistake not, appeared. A marvelous man is that McKee Rankin."[88]

The contemporaries of these illustrious actors were disappearing. Recently, Mrs D.P. Bowers, Emma Waller, and Augustin Daly had passed away. Mrs Owen Marlowe was ill and had retired from the stage after the sudden death of her daughter. Who of the greats were left? Just the odd supporting actor, of whom Barton Hill and George Becks were among the best. Becks was running a jewelry store in New York when Rankin persuaded him to return to the stage. Becks could fill the old men roles well. He was admired for his lofty mind, generosity, and fine character, traits that were needed in a company on a very long road trip.

For the week beginning September 10, 1899, Rankin's company opened at Cordray's Theatre in Portland with *Peg Woffington* to the biggest house in the theater's history. The orchestra had to be put under the stage to make room for the playgoers.[89] O'Neil's success in London had raised her value. The company played Sheridan's *The School for Scandal*, with Rankin as Sir Peter Teazle, *The Jewess*, *Elizabeth, Queen of England*, and *Oliver Twist* to very large business. The fourth week the company played Barton Hill's version of *Camille* with costumes from the 1840s; because the play was usually done in modern dress, the period costumes gave it a quaintness and curiosity. The company closed its engagement with *Magda*.

A Portland critic saw Nance O'Neil's Magda as a protest against the tyranny of convention. "Such splendid force is almost solitary," he wrote.

> The salient notes of Miss O'Neil's interpretation are those of a soul that yearns passionately for its freedom and a heart that longs to be loved and understood. Throughout the play these yearnings and passions alternately flamed and smouldered. Her voice was often full of suppressed and affecting emotion. Her eyes flashed with the fire of assertion and indignation, or were swimming with tenderness. The superb figure of Magda—the most powerful figure in recent dramatic literature—was realized completely. Such breathing and throbbing life, so tragic a story, cannot but compel all to pause, consider and pity. This is the genius of plenary inspiration.[90]

The company went to San Francisco and opened at a refurbished California Theatre on October 10, 1899, in *Peg Woffington*. O'Neil idealized Peg Woffington, wrote a critic: "She knows what she does." A week later, after he had seen *Camille*, *The Jewess*, and *Magda*, he added that O'Neil was great as Peg, greater in *The Jewess*, and greatest in *Magda*—"an overpowering natural force."[91] She had improved as Camille since seeing Bernhardt play the role in London. Most actresses fail in *Camille*, explained a critic, because in their anxiety to appear natural they become unnatural and look consumptive from the start. Yet, Duval falls in love with a healthy woman, who wanes only in the final act. O'Neil, unaffected, graceful, and handsome, met all the requirements of a lovable woman. She was never too vulgar in rage, nor too simpering in sorrow. Indeed, according to a critic, she "nears the pinnacle of dramatic art."[92]

O'Neil's success made it impossible for her to leave the city. She extended her stay to the first two weeks of November, presenting the eleven plays in her repertoire. In the space of a few months, the company had gone from the McKee Rankin Company to the O'Neil-Rankin Company to the Nance O'Neil Company. Thereafter, Nance O'Neil was the name under which it traveled.

At the end of the San Francisco run, Rankin replaced Edwin Mordaunt with Clay Clement, who arrived opportunely from Hawaii, where he had starred in a mélange of plays from *Hamlet* to *London Assurance*. Clement was glad to disband his company and join Rankin because, despite having some commercial success, he was gradually losing money. By 1901, he had to declare bankruptcy: he had thirty-seven creditors, most of whom were former members of his companies.

In contrast to Clement's straits, Rankin seemed to be doing well financially. A sign of Rankin's new prosperity was his willingness to settle long-standing debts. Internal revenue officers had been after him for failing to pay his theater license in San Jose for the years 1898 and 1899 and were holding him for trial when he wrote an apology and agreed to pay for his license not only in California, but for those in Idaho, Montana, and other states and territories. His attorney advised him that he could beat the case, but, said Rankin, "I have my doubts about that, and I am tired of the whole affair and am willing to settle with the Government, penalties, costs and all, for my sins against it."[93]

The company played a week in Spokane and a week in Oakland, and opened in Los Angeles on December 3, 1899, at the Morosco-Burbank Theatre for the month. *Magda* gave the local critic a chance to reflect on the changes in the playgoers' attitudes to the problem plays, which at first were thought damaging to young minds. Now the right of dramatists to express their thoughts regardless of their character and the bald references to things formerly considered unspeakable were no longer questioned in the realm of morals. A *fin de siècle* worldliness had overtaken the theater community. The insights into human nature and the dramatist's skill were what mattered. It was as if audiences were witnessing through an open window the working out of a tragedy of the heart in a real home rather than a mere simulation of such a tragedy. O'Neil, for instance, seemed to work out before audiences the tragedy of her own life. As an actress, her crudities of manner were falling away with experience, and her voice was losing its rasping quality so trying to the auditory nerves. Because her interpretation was severe and unyielding, she lacked the gentle womanliness of a Modjeska as Magda, but where the whirlwind in the heart was required, she swept all before her, displaying the divine spark that negated all blemishes in the enthusiasm she generated in the audience. Rankin was still "vitally impressive" as Schwartze, and Clay Clement was earnest, dignified, and deliberate as the parson. The rich costumes worn by O'Neil and the handsome settings created a picture play by themselves.[94] The critic's remarks revealed the refinements that Rankin was making in the plays for the Australian tour, which, he felt, would either make or break O'Neil.

In *Peg Woffington*, O'Neil showed a high order of intelligence and evidence of genius as she accented the tragedy over the comedy. Real tears welled in her eyes when she held to her bosom the naive country wife who was far too good for her dissolute husband. Barton Hill as the impecunious playwright, artist, and verse monger, Triplet, showed the delicate niceties of touch of the old school, which was rapidly passing away. It was an education, said the critic, to see how carefully he brought out every point as clearly as a note struck upon a piano string. Again, the play was beautifully costumed, reflecting the quality of the investments in these productions.[95] *The School for Scandal* demonstrated poise, expertness, skill, and intelligence; O'Neil's Lady Teazle convinced the critic that her real future lay in the drama of the subdued, as she gave a masterful and bewitching performance. "Albeit at times her laugh is a bit strident...she is yet a most charming and graciously satisfying heroine of this rare play."[96]

For O'Neil's last week in Los Angeles, over the Christmas holidays, Rankin produced his version of *Macbeth* with Kelley's music. As Lady Macbeth for the first time, O'Neil, with exquisite poise and sure-footedness, played adroitly upon the spirit of her ambitious but weak-willed husband. Elevated, dignified, potential in command, and purposeful in her general tone, O'Neil shone with a luster unmatched by her company. "If she does not reach the highest rung," ventured the critic, "it's because she's been ill-advised and badly coached."[97] Clement lacked confidence as Macbeth, but Barton Hill's Macduff was good, at least until the final sword fight when his strength appeared visibly taxed. The production used one hundred actors and twenty-five musicians. Billed as the event of the season, it attracted crowds. Business was good, but it may have been owing to the choice of theater, the popular Morosco-Burbank, which Rankin obtained only at the last minute for *Macbeth* and at the expense of the smaller Wyatt Theatre. Henry Wyatt sued Rankin for $2,000 in damages for failing to appear at his theater, but there is no indication that the case went to court.[98]

By January 20, 1900, Rankin's company was playing in Salt Lake City. The company stayed two weeks, doing six plays to standing room only for every performance. It made its last appearance in Portland, Oregon, before leaving for Australia.

1900

The Australian Experience

On February 9, 1900, Rankin and his troupe shipped out of Vancouver for Hawaii. Although the ship arrived at its destination, the passengers did not disembark because a plague was ravaging the islands. O'Neil's many admirers came down to the dock and threw flowers, covering the ship's deck around her. As her ship embarked, they threw long garlands and ropes made of roses from the dock to the ship and paid them out as the ship moved along. A golden sun sank into the azure blue of the ocean making the experience unforgettable. O'Neil and her companions, following the custom, gathered the best of the flowers and threw them into the water to watch them float away.

The ship stopped at Apia on the island of Upolu, Western Samoa, where O'Neil and Rankin visited the late Robert Louis Stevenson's home. After a calm and pleasant voyage, the ship arrived in Sydney, Australia, on March 5. The press noted that O'Neil spoke with perception about Shakespearean characters and was well read in playwrights as analytical in method as Ibsen. Australians called her a woman of culture and reported that offstage she was free of any trace of American accent. They celebrated Rankin as the most widely famous artist in the company and recalled that he and J.C. Williamson once had been the youngest members in Daly's *A Flash of Lightning* production. Barton Hill also had links to J.C. Williamson because Hill directed the original San Francisco production of *Struck Oil*, in which Williamson and his wife became famous, which was just prior to Williamson's coming to Australia. George Becks was reported merely as a veteran actor. The young Charles Canfield was distinguished for having visited Australia in the cast of *Trilby*. Ricca Allen, and Cora Kenwyn, the actress wife of Clay Clement, were the last mentioned in Rankin's company, which Williamson would augment with actors from his stock companies. Foremost among the Australian actors at first were the young George Majeroni, whose father had played romantic roles opposite Madame Ristori, and Mrs Henry Bracy, later known as Clara Bracy, who was the youngest sister of Lydia Thompson, with whom Rankin had shared the New York stage in 1870.[99]

The business arrangements differed from those in America. No traveling company worked on a percentage basis. It had to rent the theater in which it appeared and hire the staff, orchestra, and stagehands to travel with the company. All bookings had to be made through Williamson's firm, which also had control over all plays—a traveling company had to pay from $2,000 to $3,000 for the Australian rights.[100] Rankin considered the customs in the Australian theater to be as fine then as they were in the United States in the days of Lester Wallack.

The Australians tended to sit back and not prejudge: they had a "show-me" attitude. As the company opened on March 10, 1900, in *Magda* in Sydney's Theatre Royale, O'Neil went through her usual first-night jitters. When the performance was over, the men were on their feet clapping and shouting "brava" and the stage was covered in flowers. "When you first look over the footlights at that sea of calm, critical faces you realize that you are at the ends of the earth, thousands of miles from home," O'Neil said, "and that that night's performance is make or break with you. I shall never forget my opening night; it was so wonderfully, so unbelievably successful! The stage covered with flowers! The men on their feet cheering! It was all so wonderful to me. I was utterly unknown to them; unborn, so far as they knew, except for the usual preliminary press notices—it was so wonderful it didn't seem real!"[101]

O'Neil's conception of Magda, wrote the critic, "skillfully enforces the contrast between the surface of the character, hardened by contact with pain, sorrow, and injustice, and the warmly emotional nature underneath." Rankin as Schwartze provided the most pathetic moment when the palsied hand refuses to grasp the weapon and the wounded lion sheds tears of helpless rage.[102]

The Jewess, by contrast, was stagy, unreal, and boring. Not even O'Neil could save it. The curse brought her many recalls, yet, artistically, her best work was in the tender reflective soliloquy preceding the curse scene. Rankin as the burly Bloemfontein burgher, Father Lorenz, exuded genial bonhomie and charmingly carried off a comedy scene with a young boy. Williamson's productions were liberally funded so that the scenery was well done, the last being a widespread view of fruitful hills and valleys ripe with corn.

In some instances, owing to copyright and the licensing agreements, Rankin could not produce versions of some plays that his company had played in America. For this reason, he presented the Bancroft version of *Masks and Faces*, in which the English actress Mrs Bancroft added a third act to the original Reade version of 1852. As Peg Woffington, O'Neil did not force her points and gave a charming impersonation.[103]

The company left Sydney after the Saturday matinee to open in Newcastle in the evening. Here it stayed for two weeks until Williamson refurbished Her Majesty's Theatre in Sydney for the company's return on Easter Saturday. Because she had the style of acting that Australians loved, Williamson was sanguine that O'Neil had embarked on a long career of popularity in Australia. He persuaded Rankin to extend his stay of several weeks to an extensive tour. He improved the company radically. Clay Clement was replaced by the English actor Thomas Kingston. A New Zealand actor named Harry Plimmer replaced Majeroni. Three good actresses were added. The productions were going to be big.

Although Barton Hill's version of *Camille* restored the character of the Comte de Giray, Marguerite's friend, and strengthened the part of Marguerite Gautier, and Rankin's company had become accustomed to playing it, Rankin opened in a rarely played version. This version included the character of the Duke de Maurice, whose dying daughter resembles Marguerite, and Rankin took this role. Barton Hill was the elder Duval, a role he had been playing for years in the companies of a long list of actresses. Thomas Kingston was Armand Duval. The critic found O'Neil to be essentially different from all others who essayed the role. "Her individuality," he wrote, "is so marked that she stamps herself with varying results upon the surface of every fresh character she undertakes, and she attains to an originality of conception which will always be the occasion of criticism and dispute."[104] He thought her interpretation was northern rather than southern because her temperament lacked the gaiety and elasticity of the Latin races. Her Camille makes a bid for sympathy by her air of secret suffering. "The reckless gaiety of the French courtesan which in the earlier scenes represents the golden veil above the grey life is wholly suppressed, and, from the outset, the new Camille stands within the shadow of a great repentance and an early death."[105] O'Neil's powerful and somber characterization delighted the audience, which followed her to the highest level in her scene of anguish with the elder Duval. In her despair, O'Neil sits upon the floor and delivers the great speech upon the hard lot of erring women, an audacity of movement that left the old playgoers "breathless." She was thought to be a follower of the natural school of acting advocated in Paris by Antoine at the Théâtre Libre, but it was Rankin's teaching that had given her the courage of her convictions. Instead of poor surroundings, Camille dies in a palatial room, and she lies recumbent on a luxuriously gilded bed after the manner of Marie Duplessis, the real-life prototype for Marguerite Gautier. O'Neil "reveals with infinite pathos and poetry of feeling the gentle decay of nature."[106]

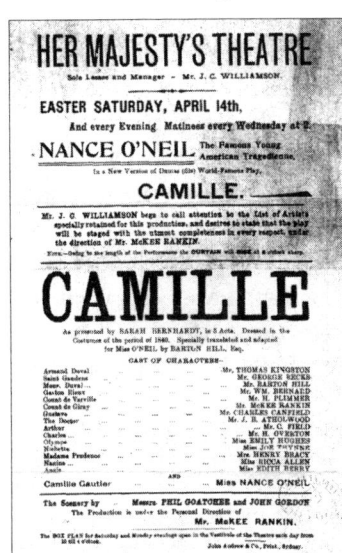

Playbill of *Camille*, with Nance O'Neil in the title role and Rankin as the Count de Giray, Her Majesty's Theatre, Sydney, Australia, 1900.

Rankin presented his version of *Elizabeth, Queen of England*, which cut out the attempt on Elizabeth's life in Giacommetti's play and consequently left out Maria Lambouro, whom Elizabeth pardoned. O'Neil was a decided triumph as the complex, contradictory queen and displayed "astonishing amounts of mental and physical power."[107] Thomas Kingston as Essex created immense excitement. The scenery and costumes were sumptuous, in particular in the throne-room scene, where beefeaters in scarlet and men-at-arms in armor added to the pageantry as the queen entered to a fanfare of trumpets with train-bearers carrying her ermine-bordered robe of state.

The School for Scandal added to O'Neil's triumphs. Her Lady Teazle delighted audiences with her rapid transition from quarrel to coquetry and assumed affection to scorn. Mrs Clara Bracy, whose husband was stage manager of the comic opera company in Adelaide, always merited praise for her character roles, in this case in the trying character of Mrs Candour.

Oliver Twist had not been seen for twenty years in Sydney. The disconnected scenes in Rankin's version gave a great deal of Dickens's dialogue and introduced a score of characters who were so vivid in the novel. But it was O'Neil that the Australians came to see. It had been years since an actress had risen to such high favor. Her fine sense of character and the difference in her roles contributed to her popularity. The local critic warned that audiences would not recognize her as the coarse Nancy Sykes, with her dark hair and makeup. She gave life to the role with a large simplicity of movement and heroic gesture. Rankin's Bill Sykes was warmly applauded as he appeared in the traditional coster's dress—crimson waistcoat, velveteens, gray stockings, high white hat with a prodigious black band—unshaven and exchanging growls with his bull dog. "The sight of the ungracious Sykes," wrote the critic, "eating Fagin's rabbit pie with the devoted Nancy at his feet, was one of the few truly comic passages in the play."[108] The murder scene, he felt, although true to nature, was indefensible on artistic grounds.

For the final week, Rankin reintroduced *Magda* until the company left for Melbourne. O'Neil's speeches carried a thrilling power, and Rankin's Schwartze was beautiful and touching. Schwartze's anguished yearning cry over Magda's head, "Oh, my child, I have loved you with my whole heart and soul," deeply moved the audience.[109]

The theater was densely crowded on the farewell night. Enthusiasm was at a fever heat. Laurel wreaths, flowers, and a cage of pretty Australian lovebirds were given to O'Neil. Rankin expressed the cast's appreciation at the overpowering reception, O'Neil said a few words of thanks, and Kingston informed the gathering that Williamson had renewed his contract so that he was not leaving for England as the newspapers had reported. Rankin and O'Neil remained under Williamson's management until December.

Melbourne and Adelaide

Williamson and his partner Musgrove had parted company, and the separation deal awarded all the theaters in Melbourne to Musgrove. Nevertheless, Williamson secured an old playhouse in the poorest section of the city, renamed it Her Majesty's Theatre, and hired scores of workmen to improve the stage and auditorium for the coming of O'Neil's company. Once shunned by the better classes, it soon was patronized by the first-class families wanting to see O'Neil. There was an advance rush for seats because O'Neil's fame had preceded her. Sydney's enthusiasm seemed unsurpassable, but Melbourne was ecstatic. After the company opened on June 2 in *Magda*, the *Melbourne Age* wrote: "She was born to the imperial purple of the stage."[110] The crowded house watched her with hushed interest as she unfolded the character, making its varying phases readable until it stood out clear-cut in warped nobility. "Real flesh," wrote the *Melbourne Argus* of O'Neil's Magda, "a soul born active, windbeaten, but ascending."[111]

As the company did the other plays in its repertoire, O'Neil developed a tremendous following, especially among women. Her season in Melbourne had to be extended. By July 22, Rankin began presenting new plays. Ibsen's *Hedda Gabler* was hailed as a remarkable pathological study in O'Neil's hands—that is, under Rankin's direction. O'Neil displayed the fine qualities of Hedda's intellect "that had thrashed it out, rounded it, and gave it forth; art was so completely hidden in the process it was forgotten."[112] The Australians thought her interpretation was allied to genius because "her success was gained in the face of colonial difficulties," by which was meant provincial attitudes which frowned on the exposure of the hypocrisy of society's values. Hedda, disagreeable but fascinating, mischievously wicked and eaten up with self-love, was carefully developed by O'Neil, who played with extreme care. She never forced a note as she showed the haughtiness of the character, but "it was in the spirit of malevolence that she touched greatness." Certain passages showed the actress at her most inspired moments, the local critic explained:

> In the scene in which Hedda tempts Lovberg to drink and sows evil between him and Thea, O'Neil's pose, as she leant her head upon her hand and gazed in devilish derision at the pair, had just such an air of sinister power and weird intellectuality as may be noted in the famous painting of Satan playing chess with a man for his soul. The scene of mad wickedness at the stove, and again the look of rapt exultation, in which a touch of madness was apparent at the words, "The great art! That

over which the sense of beauty fails. That he had force and will enough to break away from the banquet of life so early!"[113]

Having given a performance of *Hedda Gabler* for charity in the afternoon, the company played Sardou's *Fedora* for the first time in the evening. It was a catastrophe that would have finished most stars but it seemed to hurt O'Neil hardly at all. Just before the climax in the third act, the curtain was unexpectedly lowered, disconcerting the players. Later, the dying scene was ruined when the curtain dropped, leaving O'Neil's head and shoulders in full view. The play was offered again the next day in a performance improved beyond recognition. O'Neil was powerful and impressive, lacking in subtlety at times, not entirely "en princess" but always theatrically imposing and to the point.[114]

Her interpretation was different from that of other actors, in particular from Bernhardt, who had created the role. Bernhardt came from the exquisitely polished histrionic school of Molière. By contrast, Italian actor Eleanora Duse was a naturalist in art and could not assume the "grande dame" that Bernhardt could. It seemed that O'Neil, being of Rankin's creation, gave Fedora a mental edge that was evident in her entrapment of Loris Ipanoff into a confession of love and in the air of wrapt amazement with which she repeated the final words of Ipanoff's explanation: "I killed him for a woman, my wife." The curtain had to be raised several times in each of the four acts, so great was the applause.

O'Neil had been studying for the next production, which was an adaptation of Thomas Hardy's novel *Tess of the d'Urbervilles*. As in all she did, she was a success in the role of Tess, but, possibly owing to her failing to obtain rights to produce the play, this was the only time she presented it. The Melbourne engagement ended on August 29 with *Ingomar*.

The company went to Adelaide, South Australia, where it opened September 2 at the Theatre Royale in *Magda*. "Rarely," wrote the local critic, "has there been so much excitement."[115] The three hours of the play overwhelmed the audience. The governor general and his wife came to meet O'Neil backstage and invited her and Rankin to Government House. He was Lord Hallam Tennyson, son of the poet, and he gave O'Neil an autographed set of his father's writings and permission to produce any of his plays.

The company set aside three nights for each of the plays—*School for Scandal, Elizabeth, Peg Woffington, Ingomar, Camille, Fedora, Hedda Gabler*, and, for the first time, *La Tosca*. After *Camille*, a critic wrote that O'Neil left "a great and lasting influence—pregnant with pathos, true and illimitable."[116] Her interpretation of Tosca, a role new to her, was awaited with thrilling expectation. The question as to whether physical suffering could be employed as a vehicle for dramatic art was about to be answered by this young actress.

O'Neil met a great reception when she swept on as Floria Tosca in sky-blue silks and with a long silver-tipped rod of ebony in her hand. With her smiling eyes and the impact of her fair-haired presence, she illuminated the marvelously "talky" scene with which Sardou opened his thrilling tragedy. O'Neil gave a charming new reading to the passages of jealous love that distinguished Cimarosa's convent pupil. She was not so much the spoilt child, nor so petulant, as others played the character; rather she gave a playful undercurrent to her earnestness of voice that won all the laughter demanded by such arch remarks as "I pray to God with all my soul for the salvation of yours!" O'Neil's tragic scenes were especially impressive. "Her passionate volubility and rising alarm during the torture scene touched an audience whose attention was otherwise mistakenly distracted by this artist's favorite device of dragging herself along the ground; and, in the fourth act, the look of petrified horror and tearless anguish was well assumed."[117]

Rankin gave an original touch to the murder scene, when O'Neil with a burst of hysterical laughter plunged in the knife with an exultant exclamation of "Die!" and savagely berated the dying Scarpia for his villainy. He excluded the romantic effect of the break of day flooding the scene. And, rather than have Tosca end her life by leaping between the battlements of St Angelo into the void with Rome outstretched below, he had Spoletta shoot Tosca. Rankin received recognition from the audience for his direction, especially for the throne-room scene at the Palais Farnese, which was "brilliantly staged."[118]

1901

Au Revoir Sydney

On September 29, 1900, the company opened in Her Majesty's in Sydney with *Fedora*. The production, hastily mounted in Melbourne, had been ripened by repeated performances into success with an "absolute smoothness."[119] Rankin deserved all the credit for directing the twenty-one characters into a harmonious whole that kept the house crowded and enthusiastic.

Rankin had not been appearing onstage for most of the plays, but now Williamson announced that he would be playing the title role in the company's next production of *Ingomar*. Perhaps Rankin, who had played the role opposite O'Neil in California, thought he could still do it justice, but the first rehearsals must have persuaded Williamson to replace him with Harry Plimmer. Perhaps Rankin's fatness and age no longer fitted him for the role of a barbaric chieftain, or his alcohol consumption may have persuaded Williamson not to trust him with the role. Years of social drinking had brought him to abuse alcohol at times, although not to the point that it had affected his work. Since O'Neil had built her reputation in Australia with her talent for theatrical effect, Australians were curious whether she could give Parthenia the simplicity that alone could make her rational and convincing. More than one-half of the audience at the Saturday evening opening were old playgoers who had seen the play done years before and wanted to see how O'Neil would overcome the obvious difficulties. "Her reply," wrote the local critic, "was simple and transparent."[120] With an unaffected archness, she drew a sweet and girlish portrait of a Grecian maiden. She had changed her style. Her air of unaffected nature was her charm, and her dress enhanced that impression as she appeared with pure white draperies flowing from her tall figure, with just one touch of color in the "glorious blossom" of pink hydrangeas. Her tender scenes with her captor, Ingomar, when the fearless and unprotected girl sets out with confidence in her powers to win his love, were "truly poetic and inexpressibly touching."[121]

Plimmer did not hide the uncouthness of Ingomar; yet despite the rough and petulant nature, he excelled in the tender moments. Again Rankin was praised for the beautiful staging of the piece.

La Tosca, the next production, was received with great enthusiasm by the audience, although the Sydney critic complained that it was not as good as the Mrs Potter-Kyrle Bellew production of past years, but "it will do." Rankin's production had a long run, perhaps because it had not been done on the company's previous visit and had to accommodate the many who wanted to see it.

With *Hedda Gabler*, which also had not been done in Sydney, the Sydney playgoers, hearing claims from Melbourne that O'Neil's Hedda was as masterful as her Magda, reached a pinnacle of excitement. With its many scenes of brilliant comedy, the play was expected to be the great artistic event of the season. After the "tragically poetic situation," when Hedda burns the "child"—that is, Lovborg's manuscript—the audience gave O'Neil four enthusiastic recalls and Kingston the fifth recall. This production made Australians aware that Ibsen had been neglected by them—of Ibsen's plays only *A Doll's House* had been produced and that ten years earlier, when his plays had "caught the ears of Europe."[122]

When the company gave the plays in its repertoire in a series of farewell performances, the second appearance of *A School for Scandal* had changed for the better. Rankin played Sir Peter Teazle with much feeling, which allowed the pathos to heighten the general laughter when the screen scene was reached. His chuckling determination "to have a good laugh at Joseph" by embarrassing Joseph with revealing a girl hiding behind the screen, who, unbeknownst to him, is his own wife, Lady Teazle, told strongly with the audience. Rankin was at home in the atmosphere of old comedy, but he was slow with the text on the opening night, a defect that the critic expected to disappear in the repeat performances.[123] The critic's observation possibly provides an explanation for Rankin's absence from many of the plays. His memory was failing, a not uncommon occurrence with older actors. Maurice Barrymore at the time, and his son John in years to come, had tragic difficulty remembering lines in their later years. The problem was caused by syphilis with the former and alcohol with the latter. In Rankin's case, the problem was alcohol, but it was not yet as debilitating as it would become.

For weeks the company had been preparing its production of *Macbeth*. Williamson published a souvenir edition of the text as revised by Rankin with marginal notes and interspersed with bars of music indicative of Kelly's themes. Three scenic artists painted a series of elaborate tableaux. An extra stage manager was hired, as was a forty-piece orchestra. Williamson gave Rankin carte blanche with regard to costuming and the number of supernumeraries.

The audiences showed unqualified admiration for the "magnificence and artistic picturesqueness" of the piece.[124] The general scheme of color—particolored woolens, royal trumpeters in scarlet—of one hundred figures equipped with eagles' feathers and circular shields of hide was offset by the stately Lady Macbeth dressed in white and the blue gowns of her women. The sixteen changes of scenery were done smoothly and swiftly. The tableau of Macbeth's courtyard was particularly fine: a semi-circular gallery of gray stone raised on arches gave access by a rough-hewn staircase to Duncan's chamber. At the far end of the gallery, a seemingly interminable flight of stairs led to higher portions of the fortress, whose gray round tower rose towards the blue vault of the moonlit sky. In contrast to the grim majesty of the old keep was the rosy glow of the banqueting chamber, where Banquo's shade reflected off the back of an empty chair. Finally, the great battle scene at the end, with bowmen, soldiers in chain-mail robes, and standard-bearers, was ample testimony to the audience of the painstaking care with which Rankin and his assistant had created the spectacle.

Rankin's acting as Macbeth, however, was a disappointment, largely owing to Rankin's fitful grasp of Macbeth's character and his obvious oppression by the weight of managerial cares. Together, these problems sank this colossal mise-en-scène for long periods to "the zero of the commonplace." There were fugitive moments when Rankin came out of himself, most frequently in the last act, but he lacked declamatory power and was often inaudible. "This departure from his usual method," commented the critic, "encourages the belief that he will better justify the high reputation he has won here and elsewhere during the coming week."[125]

O'Neil, whose Lady Macbeth required more elaboration of detail and an aspect less smoothly guileless in the earlier passages than in the later ones, triumphed by her thrilling suggestion of all the horrors that lay behind the sleepwalking of her restless, haunted soul in the fifth act. Her vacant stare betrayed mental desolation. She gave voice to the burden of a broken heart in poignant anguish, for which she received a tempest of prolonged applause. As Macduff, Kingston so moved the audience that he was recalled four times, and to silence the prevailing clamor he had to climb through a stage box to make his fifth appearance before the curtain. A surprise was C.B. Bishop in his great role of the porter. Probably Bishop had been brought to Australia especially to fill the role, although it appeared that the critics were unaware of his background and the significance of his appearance. Large audiences continued to crowd the theater until the local critic admitted that, from the spectacular viewpoint, no Shakespearean revival had been more satisfying, and that O'Neil's impersonation added to the interest.

For the company's last week in Sydney, it put on much of its repertoire, and on the last evening, December 8, Rankin staged the most dramatic scenes from a number of plays. It was an outpouring of affection, a catharsis of tearful farewell comprising a heroic and artistically successful exertion of the star, the cordial cooperation of the company, and the exuberant recognition of every dramatic point by the crowded audience. Beginning with the third act of *Hedda Gabler*, wherein Hedda places a gun in Lovberg's hand with the words, "Do it beautifully," passing to the fourth act of *A School for Scandal*, in which Joseph Surface is unmasked, then to the third act of *The Jewess*, in which O'Neil electrified the audience by the power and music of her voice in the curse scene, which set the whole house cheering and applauding until O'Neil took six recalls. In *Counsel for the Defense*, "the sight of the irascible counsellor wrestling with the telephone," wrote the critic, "caused roars of laughter, and the responsive 'ring up' which finally forwarded the news that the vessel would be stopped delighted everybody."[126] The evening closed with the third act of *Magda*, in which Magda makes her beautiful speech of maternal anguish. It was delivered superbly by O'Neil so as to bring tears to the eyes. Of all the memorable moments, wrote the critic, Rankin's portrayal of the "choleric, self-willed and affectionate veteran" Schwartze would always be remembered by Australians.

The stage was covered with flowers, and at 11:30 PM the audience was still seated and many insisted on a speech. The curtain rose, revealing the company. Rankin addressed the audience briefly, saying that it was the most enthusiastic reception the company had had in any part of the world, and he thanked it for generously supporting his enterprise in bringing O'Neil to Australia. After the cheers, O'Neil said that she would always remember the cities where she was given the warmest welcome that her fondest hopes had dared to anticipate. Kingston said that, after fifteen months in Australia, he realized that night that he had not outstayed his welcome. "You're an actor, that's what you are!" cried a voice, followed by laughter and cheers. Kingston said that he had just signed a two-year contract with Rankin, and hoped to accompany O'Neil around the world and back to Sydney.

O'Neil had a special chemistry with Australians. Rankin attributed her success to her acting and his stage management, which was partially true, but great talent was not always appreciated without that special connection between actors and audience. By signing long contracts with the cast and dreaming of conquering the capitals of Europe, Rankin overlooked the pitfalls in his path.

New Zealand

After resting at Katoomba, a small town in New South Wales, and visiting the Jenolan Caves and other places, the company embarked on December 19 for Auckland, New Zealand, where it intended to spend Christmas. With time to enjoy a few days in New Zealand before taking up the theatrical tour, O'Neil and her party went deep into the interior, a day's journey through rich, tropical jungles into the Hot Lake District at Roturua. The government provided two Maori guides, Alfred Warbrick and Maggie Papakura, to take O'Neil to the Hotte at Waka to see the poi-poi dance of the Native peoples, given in her honor. O'Neil was allowed to activate the great geyser in a ceremony of dropping soap into it, thus creating a fan-shaped body of water and mist rising 500 feet and reflecting the colors of the rainbow. Papakura, a Maori princess who later married an Englishman and earned a degree at Oxford University with a treatise on Maori customs, led the scattering of garlands in O'Neil's path as she left. O'Neil and Papakura kept up a correspondence for many years.[127]

O'Neil opened in Auckland in *Magda* on December 26, 1900, for three nights and followed with three nights of *Peg Woffington*. From January 1, 1901, she played *Elizabeth, Camille, La Tosca, Fedora, A School for Scandal, Ingomar, Hedda Gabler*, and *The Jewess*. The Auckland audiences rated *Elizabeth* as one of the finest plays seen in the city in a long time, and it was remounted, by popular demand, on the company's last night. "In patriotic spirit, in fire, and in energy Miss O'Neil's impersonation lacked nothing," wrote the local critic.[128]

The company played in Wellington at the south end of the North Island, in Christchurch on the South Island, and in Dunedin till March 6. It embarked from Dunedin for North Queensland, Australia, toured North Queensland to Brisbane on the coast, and went to the other side of the Australian continent to play at Perth. It toured the small towns of the Gold Fields, more out of curiosity and a desire to compare them to the American mining towns than for remuneration. Then it took ship for Sydney, where Rankin found a cablegram from William A. Brady in New York offering to undertake the management of O'Neil for an extensive tour of the United States.[129] Her fame had seized the attention of the very powerful manager, but, for all Rankin's complaints about American managers ignoring O'Neil, he appears to have ignored Brady. "I have always thought there was money in her," Brady said in his letter. Rankin was not about to share the wealth with his commercially exploitive friend.

The company entrained for Melbourne and opened at Her Majesty's Theatre in *La Tosca* for Easter Week to begin twenty-one weeks of what was called O'Neil's "farewell season." Melbourne gave promise of exceeding the large business the troupe had done in Sydney; the opening night in Melbourne brought in $1,994. Here, O'Neil extended her repertoire, most notably with Ibsen's *Lady Inger of Ostrat*. This was Ibsen's first play, and its long wearying incoherent first few acts, according to a critic, were sufficient to turn his admirers into Philistines. The characters were unreal. O'Neil was a ranting, shrieking, blasphemous tornado of storm and stress. Rankin as "Father Christmas" unburdened himself of nothing in particular but seemed to get an "inkling" of the plot and took the mystified audience into his confidence.[130]

O'Neil's opinion of the play was very different. The role of Lady Inger bore out the truth of her philosophy more than any other. O'Neil believed that all humans are unwilling agents of higher powers; they are born with dispositions, temperaments, and tricks of heredity not of their choosing. They must be responsible for the life thrust upon them, however, and live it in their own way. The character of Lady Inger, when seen through O'Neil's philosophy, was terrifying. "I play Lady Inger, the mother," she said:

> She goes mad in the last act. I have felt myself going mad with her in that scene where she finds that she has been the means of killing her son, the child born out of wedlock for whom she

has already sacrificed her two legitimate daughters. She hears the blow and the fall of the body, and all the time believes it is her boy's counterpart, a half-brother, that is being killed—until she is brought the ring from his corpse, the ring by which she is to recognize her own. Then she is entirely mad. I am the only woman who has acted Lady Inger in English. I had to stop playing her in Australia. Lady Inger obsessed me. I should have gone mad. There were times that I thought that I should die before the curtain fell.[131]

While in Melbourne, O'Neil met the niece of Ristori, the actress who was the first to play Elizabeth, and bought from her the jewels that Ristori had worn for the role. They comprised crowns, earrings, jeweled orders, and so on. She also acquired a ring formerly worn by Marie Antoinette. The medallion that Charles Dickens had given his good friend Charles Fechter to wear in his role as Hamlet had been purchased by George Becks at an auction of Fechter's effects. Becks now gave it to O'Neil, along with Fechter's Hamlet dress with the hope that she would play Hamlet.[132]

The O'Neil company did all of its repertoire in Melbourne, playing well into July. In early June, festivities for the Duke and Duchess of Cornwall and York were being set in motion and were expected to upset the theatrical business for a few nights, so the company took time for a brief engagement in Adelaide before returning to Melbourne.

Rankin's enthusiasm over their Australian success was apparent in the grandiose plan he described to a friend. The company would leave on August 1 to play an extended engagement in South Africa, then in Egypt, Japan, China, and Australasia, followed by another tour of Australia, and finally an appearance in London, England. By the time the Nance O'Neil Company returned to Broadway, four years would have been "consumed." Rankin's use of the word implied his desire to spend as much time as possible away from the United States, away from the criticism and free of any threat that might take O'Neil away from him.[133]

His vigilance over O'Neil, which extended to his being beside her on all social occasions, annoyed others and revealed a certain insecurity in Rankin. O'Neil was kept too busy and too dependent on his instructions to find fault with the arrangement. She loved pets and kept a Persian cat called Magda, a parrot, and small dogs that traveled with her. Ricca Allen remained a close companion, and O'Neil felt close to Clara Bracy, as if she were her second mother. Bracy wished to accompany O'Neil whenever the company went back to the US.

1901–1902: Africa

In June, an advance man was sent ahead to South Africa to prepare for the company's next season. The company, which had thirty members, many of whom were new, was carried on two ships.[134] The first with three hundred tons of scenery, costly wardrobes, twenty-four actors, and the company's business manager arrived at Cape Town, South Africa, on August 25, 1901.[135] The tour managers immediately began raising the roof of the theater to accommodate the scenery. Rankin, O'Neil, and the leading actors on the second ship, which left Melbourne on August 1, were expected to arrive on September 10 after touching at Hong Kong and Singapore. O'Neil stated that the company had hoped to play in Calcutta, but Rankin could not get the theater and management he wanted.[136] It seems from a remark of O'Neil's, however, that the actors did perform for the great lover of the theater of the time, the Gaekwar of Baroda, perhaps in his castle's theater. O'Neil mentioned the presents that the Gaekwar gave her: an elephant, fifty yards of silk, and other exotic gifts.

In Cape Town, Rankin whetted the citizens' appetites in a local interview: "Miss O'Neil possesses the capacity of taking old characters; by that I mean characters that have been played over and over again, and she gives them new life. She's too young to copy the methods of others; that's her success; that's what you call individuality."[137]

The company opened in Cape Town on September 16, 1901, in *Magda*. Immediately, Rankin was confronted with an injunction against his presenting it. Emanuel Lederer had given him the right to produce the play in the United States and the British colonies, for which he paid Lederer £250 for Australia and New Zealand and £150 for South Africa. George Alexander of the St James's Theatre held the rights for the British Isles, including, he thought, the right to produce *Magda* in South Africa; this he had sold to an actor who intended to play it in Cape Town in October.[138] The court, learning that Rankin had presented the play for over fifty performances in Australia, decided in his favor.

Perhaps more than in any other place, Cape Town came under O'Neil's spell. She was called a revelation to South Africa. Her playing in nearly every point was daringly original, the critics thought. "From beginning to end," wrote a critic, "her study of the part [of Magda] was almost unimpeachable; a study that must be seen more than once to be thoroughly appreciated."[139]

For *Elizabeth, Queen of England*, the *Cape Times* reported: "The house was full and the audience was intensely enthusiastic…and it is doubtful if any study in emotions has ever so thrilled a Cape Town audience."[140] The crowd scenes, which called for large numbers of supernumeraries, were filled by actual soldiers—Englishmen, Canadians, and Australians—who marched on stage to create an impressive effect. Wherever O'Neil played *Elizabeth* in South Africa, the soldiers readily obliged. As for O'Neil, who was almost continuously onstage for five acts, it must have been fatiguing.

> Miss O'Neil presents the popular idea of Queen Elizabeth to the very life—her red hair, her great frill...capricious, handsome, dangerous, hiding a great love in her heart. She signs her lover's death warrant with all the misery of pride and hesitation; she ages at once when the news of his execution arrives; and she appears fifteen years afterwards, a miserable woman, eaten with gnawing remorse and spectre-haunted, yet vain to the end, denying her own feebleness, proud to the end, asserting her throne's dignity. And, above all, bowed down and heartbroken at every thought of the lover whom she cut down in the fullness of his youth and hers. There can be not the slightest question that Miss O'Neil's performance last night must rank as one of the very best and most convincing pieces of "passion-acting" that the modern stage has witnessed.[141]

The other plays in O'Neil's repertoire were equally successful. *Camille* was "a veritable triumph of emotional flexibility," in which Rankin as Duval, Sr, was quiet but forceful. Rankin played Gretch, the chief of police in *Fedora*, which raised O'Neil's fame higher with plaudits such as "a success attained by few...superb...rises to the height of her powers."[142] In *The School for Scandal*, O'Neil colored her Lady Teazle with a natural joyousness that "entirely separated her from the others of the set."[143] *La Tosca* kept the audience as "still as death."[144] O'Neil used the atmosphere of early-nineteenth-century Rome to realize her genius to the full. "Miss O'Neil gave by far the finest and most powerful performance that she has yet afforded to a Cape Town audience," wrote a critic.[145] By leaving at the height of her popularity with no plans to return, O'Neil created a yearning amongst the citizens to see her again. She said that she was obliged to return to Cape Town three times to play the roles of Nance Oldfield, Nell Gwyn, Tosca, Camille, and Lady Macbeth—which she could have done when she played later in Durban. South Africa, at the time, was in the throes of the Boer War, the mementos of which were oblong patches enclosed in white fences scattered over the monochrome of the veldt. The deplorable condition of the soldiers gave Rankin the idea of giving matinee performances for the Soldiers' Christmas Comforts Fund. The company presented *Magda* at the first matinee performance ever done in

South Africa. The governor, mayor, and other officials were present, and, after the performance, the governor presented O'Neil with a bouquet tied with the colors of the city. The benefit was so successful that the company agreed to perform one benefit for the fund in every town it visited.[146]

The company's itinerary took it inland to Kimberly, the center of the diamond fields. The company traveled in an armored train, dispensing books, soap, matches, and other comforts to the soldiers in the blockhouses along the line. The company opened with *Magda*, followed by *Elizabeth*. By the time the company produced *Camille*, the *Diamond Fields Advertiser* was calling O'Neil a revelation, an actress unequaled in method, style, and technique, whose "remarkable personality held you there, and the audience sat like petrified rabbits."[147] When the company presented as its closing play *Peg Woffington*, the critic admitted that the theatergoers "were hardly prepared for the humour and pungency" in O'Neil's playing.[148]

The actors made visits to the refugee camps and attended native barbecues. They visited the blockhouses and entertained the troops. Lord Baden Powell, the hero of Mafeking, entertained O'Neil and her party with native dances performed by the Kaffirs, which O'Neil found terrifying. She was given a raw diamond from the mines. She visited Cecil Rhodes's great estate.

Before leaving for Port Elizabeth, Rankin wrote a note to George Becks, which indicated that he expected a decline in the company's profits, owing to the failure to secure a European tour, which he had eagerly awaited:

> Circumstances before me compel me to lessen my expenses as much as possible. I am sorry therefore to inform you that your present engagement with Miss O'Neil must close on December 7th next in Port Elizabeth. I will contribute £25 towards your expenses home, which is the best I can do. Both Miss O'Neil and myself regret exceedingly that we could not have all gone back home together—but you know that I will not accept your services for any less than you came for—and I can no longer afford the salary for the parts you play outside "Sir Peter" and we have decided to cut that out of the repertoire. Wishing you all sorts of good luck I remain, Always your friend, McKee Rankin.[149]

Rankin's bookings for Cairo, Athens, Constantinople, Rome, St Petersburg, Berlin, and Paris were in jeopardy. Europe was plunged into an economic crisis, and Rankin's backers had retrenched, withdrawing from their commitments. The disappointment among the actors was great, as they had been inspired by Rankin's dreams of international adventure, but it did not affect their performances. In Port Elizabeth, the audiences at the Opera House were stirred to the core by O'Neil and Rankin's acting in *Magda*. When the company did *Camille*, Rankin played the Count de Giray for a change, as it was his philosophy to have the actors play different minor roles to keep them sharp. True to his word, Rankin presented *The School for Scandal* from December 3 to 6 for the last time on the tour. The ship that was to take the company to Natal was late so the company remained to play a few days longer.

Rankin's offer to play in Johannesburg was politely declined by Lord Kitchener, who had placed the town under martial law because the Boers threatened it with a siege. Thus, the company opened in Durban on December 16 and, changing the bill every three nights, continued to perform every night into January 1902. As Nathan in *The Jewess*, the critic wrote, "Rankin is a finished actor, and every word he said, every move he made was full of dramatic effect, but his powerful performance only seemed the more fully to reveal the weakness of other members of the cast."[150] From Durban, the company went south to play briefly in East London, Pietermarietsburg, and possibly again in Cape Town.

The length and pace of the tour was taking its toll on the company. O'Neil's voice was getting husky: when she played Magda, her hoarseness was most noticeable. Thomas Kingston had been laid low with enteric. Despite these setbacks, the company concluded its long and successful stay in Durban with *Fedora* during the penultimate week of January 1902 and embarked on February 2 "with regret."

On the way to Egypt, the O'Neil company stopped for a night at Lourenço Marques, Delgoa Bay, along the East African coast, where it gave a performance of *Magda* in a theater of corrugated iron about the size of a boathouse.[151] The ship stopped at Moçambique town, where the people were holding a festival to celebrate the birthday of the Crown Prince of Portugal. Rows of candles were lit along the streets as there was no other form of power. O'Neil was entranced by the colorful uniforms, the happy crowd, the strangeness, almost madness, of that beautiful night, which, she said later, "remains and forms a part of my subconscious."[152]

At Madagascar, the ship stopped at Majunga and Nossi-Be before continuing to Dar-es-Salaam in Tanganyika (now Tanzania). At some coastal towns, there would be low tide, and the native men would wade out to greet the visitors and carry them on their backs to land. During the remainder of March and early April, the company sailed along the Red Sea to dock at Suez. From there, it took a train to Cairo. The Khedive of Egypt invited the company to play for one week in one of the world's great theaters, the Khedival Opera House, a magnificent building.

The company was allowed to use its own scenery only for *Magda*; the theater used its scenery for *Camille* and *Tosca* as it was marvelously equipped. The hundreds of women of the harem occupied the dress circle, which was shut in by a great gauze partition. The rustle of fans and murmuring from behind the gauze added to the strangeness of the experience. The performances were hugely successful. As a sign of his approval, the Khedive, who attended with his entourage, asked O'Neil to come to his royal box and commanded that she and her party, which included Rankin, be a guest of his household. The English governor and his wife, Lord and Lady Cromer, who attended the theater frequently, entertained O'Neil.[153] The English colony in Cairo was large and wealthy. O'Neil said that she had never played to more intelligent or appreciative audiences. She fell in love with Cairo. She attended a native wedding in the desert and sat on mats and watched the dervishes dance.

At this point, Rankin dismissed the cast and arranged for O'Neil to spend the summer outside Cairo at Gizeh on the edge of the desert. The Egyptian government provided her with a servant, who looked after her with great care. She came to love the quiet and beautiful colors of the desert, calling that time the happiest of her life. A famous archaeologist, Mauriette Bey, taught her the intricate art of riding a camel, and she and Ricca Allen ascended the pyramid at Gizeh, Kheops, to the apex. "We were carried up by the Arabs," O'Neil said. "We stood in the entrance of the Tomb Chamber. It is a wonderful experience, but, if one of the Arabs had made a single slip there would have been no Nance O'Neil."[154] The sense of freedom and eternal peace of the desert wiped away her cares and the petty worries of life. The air, like wine, restored her in mind and body. Rankin, no doubt, was with her and benefited from the restorative powers of the desert. His responsibilities of directing, acting, and keeping the enterprise going must have worn him out, and his disappointment at foregoing O'Neil's prospective European tour needed assuaging.

1902

London

In August, Rankin, O'Neil, Ricca Allen, Mrs Clara Bracy, and any other actors of the company who remained in Egypt sailed for London. The ship stopped at Athens, where the actors watched a classical Greek play in a Greek open-air theater. O'Neil thought it the best kind of theater because she could hear every stage whisper and felt uplifted with "the buoyancy of a bird."[155] O'Neil stopped over in Paris to purchase jewelry and dresses for her roles. Her dressmaker, Madame Duclos, made her a beautiful dress out of the silk that the Gaekwar of Baroda had given her. She arrived at London at the end of August 1902.

Rankin, however great his welcome by some, had walked into a dubious situation. His advance man was at fault for not knowing the theatrical political games played in London. Rankin had paid $10,000 in advance to rent Henry Irving's Lyceum Theatre for several weeks, but, just before his troupe arrived, the London County Council closed the theater, declaring it a safety hazard because certain repairs had not been made. Rankin was directed to the Princess Theatre, which was far away from the theater district and disastrous for O'Neil. Fortunately, he managed to rent the Adelphi Theatre for three months from September 1, 1902, but, with $10,000 tied up, he was running short of funds and depended on the receipts of the day to keep going.[156] Rankin had his old belief confirmed that American companies could not make money in England and that all the so-called American successes there were not true. He sensed a deep-seated English prejudice against Americans.

The Adelphi's fortunes had suffered since a popular actor was found dead at its back door, and it had been unable to record a success for some years. Rankin did not know that a theatrical clique was putting pressure on the Adelphi management to wrest the theater away from the Gatti Theatrical Syndicate.[157] How this pressure was made manifest, Rankin did not say, but presumably the opponents used the press to criticize the Adelphi's plays and performers and used business methods to undermine its dealings with suppliers. Rankin admitted that he had made a mistake playing at the Adelphi: "I did not know the condition of things there, or, that Mr. George Edwards [a critic] was hostile to the American invasion and inspired an influential portion of the London press."[158]

Another mistake, according to some critics, was his decision to open with *Magda*, which O'Neil considered equivalent to a good-luck charm. J.C. Williamson and other expert advisers warned him not to open with *Magda*, *Camille*, or any other old favorites that would prompt the London critics to compare O'Neil to Eleanora Duse, Sarah Bernhardt, or Mrs Patrick Campbell. Rankin was half-inclined to put an Ibsen play in the forefront, but his London friends told him that Ibsen and other foreign masters spelled ruin with the English public. "He hesitated and was lost."[159]

By daringly throwing the house open to ticket buyers and reserving some places for journalist-critics, Rankin broke with the custom of inviting special guests for a first night. Generally, the gallery and pittites, or standees, were provoked into loud booing by the excessive applause from the stalls on first nights, but with O'Neil the audience was on its best behavior, and the applause from all over the building was sincere.[160]

The cast, which included O'Neil as Magda and Rankin as Schwartze, was praised as first-rate. Rankin made a positive impression—he was "absolutely flawless...the trembling, semi-palsied right hand, the quick, hesitating tones, the imperious gestures are splendidly set forth."[161] "He walked off with all the best notices," remarked an American observer.[162] The critics compared O'Neil to Duse and Bernhardt every third or fourth line but said that O'Neil had advantages in point of individuality—a handsome presence and a finely modulated voice. In the acting between Magda and her old lover, O'Neil showed pathos and power but could not compare with Duse's overpowering scorn, said one critic.[163] O'Neil divided the critics: some considered her greater than her predecessors; some thought she was equal to them; some thought she was worse. One claimed that she held the audience "breathless." Another felt that critics should not be comparing O'Neil at the start of her career with Bernhardt at the end of hers. He found her stage presence splendid, with a freedom and naturalness of gesture rarely equaled; in addition to a perfect physique, brains to conceive a character in depth, and a rich voice, she had the divine spark.[164] Rankin's old friend from the American stage, George Crichton Miln, praised O'Neil in a periodical he ran with his novelist wife and gave Rankin as much publicity as he could: "A man of splendid brain power, wide information, of a sweet and convincing humour, his stage performances are chiefly delightful for their intense fidelity to nature, and for swift, but unforced alternations of humour and pathos."[165] Herman Vezin, a prominent American actor who passed his life on the English stage, wrote Rankin to express his admiration for O'Neil: "It is a rare treat to see an actress whose art is so unstagey, natural and true. I have no doubt of her future. On that the British Public must make up their minds." Vezin added that he admired Rankin's interpretation of Schwartze but recommended he make him more autocratic.[166]

For the next week, O'Neil played Marguerite Gautier in *Camille*. O'Neil had improved, but her support was worse. There were moments, however, when her playing went to the heart. "First, and unmistakably, she has intelligence of a very high order indeed," wrote a critic. "One sees this first of all in the evidence of the keen psychological analysis to which she has subjected her stage work. She has thought her way into the corners of her characters."[167] Audiences agreed with him: the theater had to keep *Camille* on the boards for an extra two nights to satisfy the public demand for seats. Rankin as Duval, Sr, was weighty but gave an uncertain performance. The renowned critic William Archer wrote that O'Neil's real and remarkable talent suffered from the habit of playing impossible translations of foreign plays: "Her version of 'La Dame aux Camelias' is full of the most flagrant Gallicisms and cumbrous absurdities of phrase: for example, 'Be what we may—we have all—known—an infancy!'...Never having natural English to speak Miss O'Neil has lost or failed to acquire the habit of speaking naturally."[168] He concluded that no actress on her merits could have been successful in London with O'Neil's repertory. Half a dozen English actresses made large incomes posing as great *artistes* but could not approach O'Neil in strongly emotional parts.

During the third week in September, Rankin chose *Elizabeth, Queen of England*. "It is in parts like Elizabeth, when much breadth and not too much delicacy is required that she will find her forte," wrote a critic.[19] The end came on Saturday evening, September 20, when stagehands, complaining of not being paid, prevented the curtain from rising for the third act of *Elizabeth*. Rankin, who was in another part of the house, promised them through a deputy that the men could have the night's box office receipts, upon which they raised the curtain after twenty-five minutes. Then about sixty supernumeraries refused to perform their parts unless they were also paid. When O'Neil came onstage with Lord Howard and Lord Essex and called "Guards! Guards!" to summon the Scottish soldiers to rally round her, the guards were taking off their Highland uniforms. Since the remaining two acts of the play did not depend on "supers," the play proceeded without further interruption. The majority of the supers agreed to act on Monday provided they were paid, but Rankin decided to close.[170]

The super-master negotiated with Rankin for the money owed his men during the next day while Rankin, ensconced in his hotel, sent cables to America asking for £300. He received no response. Rankin removed all his property from the theater before the supers stopped him. He paid the members of the National Union of Theatrical Employees in full, right away, to prevent their union from advancing them the money due and starting legal proceedings against Rankin to secure payment, thus keeping Rankin in the country.

Rankin received an offer from the Palace Music Hall to engage O'Neil for a month. After consideration, he rejected it as possibly hurtful to her reputation, even though it would have helped him recoup his losses.

O'Neil had to raise the money for their return to America by leaving all her jewels with a pawnbroker. Rankin said that he lost $20,000 and sued the Lyceum Theatre for the return of his $10,000. W.H. Leavitt, who was Rankin's business partner in the English venture, was among those who disbelieved Rankin's losses. "O'Neil is all right," Leavitt said. "But she flew a little high. London is pretty wise when it comes to top-notch acting. I don't think Rankin lost much. He quit too early. He came to London with a bundle of money, and, if you ask me, he has got it yet."[171]

The Syndicate

Some American papers began to call O'Neil a failed actress in London, but put the real blame on Rankin. The *New York Evening Post* headlined "Fiasco in London: End of Oakland Girl's Fond Dream of World Wide Triumph," and reported that rows of empty benches in the Adelphi faced O'Neil every night of the three-week season. The reasons for her failure were traceable to Rankin, who should be replaced by "a modern, hustling fellow of the right sort."[172] But Rankin had made some money for her and a lot for himself and would not let her go. "If Dave Belasco would put her through a course of sprints, then you would see an actress," said a manager.[173] Rankin was to hear a chorus of demands that he give up control of O'Neil. Possibly the idea began innocently enough with the critic Ashton Stevens, who in September 1898 wrote:

> With all credit to McKee Rankin for discovering Miss O'Neil and developing her to her present proportions, I cannot but think that in his zeal to make a great actress he has over-Belascoed his pupil. Mr. Rankin is a master in the good old melodramatic school—elaborate, complicated, twice the size of life. As a tutor-actor he would be a joy at Morosco's, but he is not the model for a rushing emotional gift like Miss O'Neil's. You can read Rankin written all over everything she does. She is under-trained in the subtle work of repression and suggestion, and overtrained in voice, gesture, by-play and all the physical notions of the craft. Often she carries you away by the force of her passion, but oftener she carries herself beyond the credible. She is today a sensation when she might be a success.[174]

The references to Belasco concerned his training of Mrs Leslie Carter to become a great emotional actress. In a court trial in which he sued Mrs Carter's financial backer for withdrawing his support, Belasco told of the rough methods he used with Mrs Carter—dragging her by the hair, verbal abuse—that, to his way of thinking, helped to bring out her unusual talent and emotional power.[175] Rankin's failure in London was easily contrasted with Belasco's success, especially by those who wanted to undermine Rankin's connection with O'Neil. Much of the animosity came from the Theatrical Syndicate, which wanted to eliminate any competition that the independent Rankin presented to its theaters. Belasco was under the syndicate's direction at this time and wrote plays for it.

Rankin had used whatever independent management group he could in order to tour. From the fall of 1895, when McVicker of Chicago and

Miner of New York formed a syndicate to operate east of the Mississippi River, he had used their syndicate. When in the West, he used Al Hayman's theaters, which, in 1895, came under the control of the Frohmans, who claimed three hundred theaters across the continent. There were about forty other booking offices of minor importance, but many of these succumbed to the Theatrical Syndicate of Hayman, Frohman, Nixon, and Zimmerman, who combined with two hundred Southern theaters under Klaw and Erlanger.

Marc Klaw, who began in the theatrical business as a young lawyer hired by the Frohmans to stop play pirates, explained that when he was in Texas a theater manager would book two or three companies for the same night and leave it to the first agent to arrive and display his paper to get the theater, thus obliging the others to look elsewhere.[176] He and Erlanger bought out Thompson's Theatrical Exchange in New York for $2,200, booked companies throughout the country, and ensured that their contracts were made good. Not only did they stop the clashing of dates, but they prevented resident managers in the West from declaring the contract terms too high when companies arrived and from cutting down on the percentage, to which the company manager was forced to consent. Klaw came to be regarded as a safe and sane balance wheel to his aggressive partner, Erlanger, but others saw him as an underling to Erlanger's Napoleon complex. Erlanger's one talent was to know where every company was playing and to rearrange the schedule skillfully to meet unexpected changes. This penchant for detail made him indispensable and allowed him to force his six partners into insignificance.

The syndicate's practices were ruthless as it gained control of all the first-class theaters. It sent out the most popular type of entertainment with the greatest hype, which undermined serious plays and actors who were not willing to go along with it. It rewarded journalists such as Franklyn Fyles of the *New York Sun* who supported it and destroyed journalists who exposed it. By describing its methods, a journalist for the *Commercial Advertiser* caused it to withdraw all advertising from the paper and permanently deny the journalist tickets to any of its theaters. The syndicate compelled producing managers to pay for the houses to play in and, at the same time, charged house managers for the attractions they played, thus earning from both ends.[177]

Culturally, the local pockets of theatrical resistance to the dominant culture were marginalized, and the better type of play fell victim to the business-class ideology after the 1890s. The outraged response to American productions of Ibsen's plays indicated the pervasiveness of the new ideology. Some stock companies appeared in the 1890s and again in the 1920s as actors tried to fight back, but they were local in influence and varied in the theatrical fare they offered. Both when under Rankin's management and afterwards, Nance O'Neil took full advantage to star in those stock companies that produced the classics and the better modern plays.

At the same time that the O'Neil company was sailing for the United States, Harry Plimmer, the New Zealand actor, who had left her company after the end of her Australian tour, arrived back in Australia after eleven months in the United States. Plimmer spoke of the syndicate as a gigantic Jewish financial corporation "who reach out for the dollars with marvelous energy and surprising talent in gauging the public opinion and taste."[178] It presented the best and worst of everything. The actor-manager as known in Britain and Australia no longer existed in the United States. But Plimmer thought the stock theaters were even more horrific for the actor because they presented no less than twelve performances a week, with a change of bill every Monday. The five stock theaters in Chicago played twice a day, including Sundays. Although the actors' salaries were high, actors had to provide their own costumes and take an enforced vacation during the summer in an economy where the cost of living was high. The actor's life was pleasanter in Australia, Plimmer concluded.

The O'Neil company docked in New York on October 13, 1902. A newspaper printed a welcome:

> R is for Rankin he's back from the East
> And through the wide city his troubles are least
> Here's luck to O'Neil and a bumper to Mac
> His friends in the Alley all welcome them back.[179]

1903

Retrieving Lost Fortunes

While Rankin cast about for the best way to retrieve their lost fortunes, O'Neil remained idle and somewhat frustrated for five weeks in the city. Two theatrical events in New York at the time may have caused her to question her failure to conquer the city. Lionel Barrymore had just made an unqualified success as Giuseppi, the Italian organ grinder, in his uncle John Drew's company playing *The Mummy and the Humming Bird* at the Empire Theatre. The play was destined for a long run. Ethel Barrymore opened on October 6 at the Savoy Theatre in *A Country Mouse*. She was supported by Harry Davenport. New Yorkers welcomed the Barrymores' intimate, personable acting styles whereas Nance, the tragedian, could not find a theater manager willing to give her a stage.

Moreover, Blanchard, who now called herself Kate Rankin, had not lacked for dramatic roles in New York. She retained her keen sense of humor, her talent for the apt characterization, and her considerable charm, which gave her personal success whether the play was bad or good. When Rankin and O'Neil left for Australia, Blanchard was playing the Jewish mother in *The Ghetto* at the Broadway Theatre. The next season, she played Mrs Snuffles in *Mam'selle Hawkins* at the Victoria Theatre and had roles in other plays. In the summer of 1901, she felt her memory was worsening; she announced that, after completing the comedy role in her present play, *The Marriage Game*, she would retire from the stage and open a photography studio in Manhattan. Recognized as one of the best amateur photographers in the country, she hoped to make a living at it. She made some memorable photos—one being of the three Barrymore children as young adults. After a few months, however, she returned to the stage, where she could make a better income. She made a hit as Mrs Brown in *The Girl and the Judge*. Mrs Brown was a boardinghouse-keeper who boasted about her high family connections and insisted that she had a lily-white character. At the time of O'Neil and Rankin's return to New York, Blanchard was considering playing a good-natured parvenu in Clyde Fitch's *The Girl with the Green Eyes*. By Christmas 1902, she was declared a great success in the role.

Mabel Bert also had done well. In the spring of 1898, she played the lead in *Heartsease*, and in the summer she played in *Arizona*. It was then that Frohman cast her as the mother in *Ben Hur*, which was still touring and would do so for years to come.

Rankin began negotiating with Charles Frohman to manage O'Neil and feature her in *Macbeth* at the Herald Square Theatre the following year, but first he had to make some money. Because O'Neil had never been to New Orleans, they took the train south on their way to San Francisco and stayed over a couple of days. O'Neil likened it to Port Said, Egypt, which she called the wickedest city in the world.

San Francisco welcomed O'Neil with open arms as a great actress who had won international fame and dazzled the difficult critics in London. She opened in *Magda* on December 8, 1902, with the support of the California Theatre stock company. The cast Rankin used was experienced. E.J. Ratcliffe had come from England to the United States in Mary Anderson's company and played in stock at the Lyceum Theatre in New York for years.[180] Charles Millward also was from England and had come to America with Wilson Barrett in 1901. He was good-looking with a cold, dignified personality. An uneven actor, he played exceptionally well in some parts and very poorly in others. Blanche Stoddard from Minneapolis worked her way up through bit parts to leading woman at the Grand Opera House in San Francisco. She studied O'Neil's methods, which became apparent in her work. She considered O'Neil the best Hedda Gabler and, in the third act, the greatest Camille. Stoddard, Ratcliffe, and Millward remained in O'Neil's company for some time. L.R. Stockwell and Herschel Mayall, excellent as a comedian and romantic lead, respectively, preferred to remain on the West Coast once the company moved on.

The critics found O'Neil more polished and acting with her intellect now. She had art as well as heart.[181] In *Camille*, she was called greater than Bernhardt. It was as if the San Francisco critics were responding to the London critics:

> Bernhardt's performance is made up almost entirely of her marvelous technique, the manipulation of a voice as sensitive as a violin, the control of a thousand arts of gesture and expression, climaxes born of a genius that is all fire. In Miss O'Neil's performance the artifice is less apparent—her superb temperament completely identifies itself with the role. Her audience is swept under, compelled to sit absorbed and intent until the last moment. One of the most powerful factors of Miss O'Neil's genius is her capacity for enflamed emphasis. She never rants or even approaches ranting, yet every line is spoken with an intensity that burns itself on her hearer's brains.[182]

Despite the critical success of *Camille*, O'Neil as Leah in *The Jewess* became the best moneymaker. There was standing room only every night, and the musicians were pushed under the stage to get more room. Rankin took in $8,261 during the week. "All of those monarchs with the artless habit of extracting the teeth of their Jewish subjects in order to compel them to fork out their hard-earned shekels, all Jew-baiters of royal or whatsoever persuasion would better go to the Grand Opera-house this week, and they won't do it again," wrote a reviewer.[183]

The company presented the usual plays in its repertoire. As Nancy in *Oliver Twist*, O'Neil absorbed the personality, and Rankin, as the brutal Bill Sykes, had no equal. "The final two acts were almost too intense and left the audience sitting in a sort of stunned and dazed condition."[184] O'Neil was triumphant as Lady Macbeth, being the only American able to play the role at that time. For the principals, Ratcliffe played Macbeth "commendably," Charles Millward was a "gentlemanly" Banquo, and Herschel

Mayall played Macduff with "intelligence and vim." "Reverence, dignity, sincerity are in every line of it, and a splendor and correctness of production that reflects the highest credit on the management."[185] Business was so good the play had to be kept on the boards until January 23, 1903.

In Giacommetti's *Judith,* which had not been done in English and not been on an English stage since Ristori did it in Italian, O'Neil showed her powerful genius. Although the play needed cutting, O'Neil received nine curtain calls. Judith, the widow of Manasseh, saves her people from the Assyrian general Holofernes and his army besieging her city. In a strong fourth act, Judith, richly gowned and bejeweled, goes into Holofernes's camp, captivates him, and then decapitates him. O'Neil led up to this scene gradually and made the climax fitting.[186] The play did show its age, however, and the first night was disastrous. The audience laughed and guyed the play and some of the players in a way that was truly pathetic. O'Neil as Judith and Herbert Carr as the high priest Eliakim were good, but the rest of the cast seemed "a sordid and saddening mediocrity."[187]

As Hedda Gabler, "Nance O'Neil set the key," wrote a critic,

> with her pallid, cynical face, crowned with her own blonde hair drawn in bored, desperate line from the brow, looking utterly the woman's deadly weariness. The others of the awful sextet—the day's Tesman, Brack, Lovberg, Mrs. Elvsted, Julia—fell also immediately into the Ibsen tone, that would seem to impose itself on every one with its grim reach. More than ever one feels the sheer truth of these creatures, as one feels a portrait's likeness without knowing the original. Ibsen simply takes down the shutters, and there are your half-dozen people of every day, the very body of tragedy in their commonplace circumstance. One has the feeling of eavesdropping, so inescapably real, so intimate the view the dramatist permits.[188]

O'Neil continued as Meg Merrilies in *Guy Mannering,* and, for her last week, she presented five plays she had done earlier so as to give people a chance to see them. A testimonial to her was held by the leaders of the city, honoring her ten weeks at the Grand Opera House. This was the longest run by any star in San Francisco in twenty-five years. O'Neil's maid came onstage with a big jewel box, which, when opened in the presence of the mayor, revealed a perfect crown of laurel leaves done in gold and engraved "To Nance O'Neil from Mayor Eugene Schmitz and the Citizens of San Francisco." "Neck-high" in flowers, O'Neil, deeply touched, heard the mayor say how proud her friends were of her success. She thanked him, the governor for his presence, and the audience for their demonstration honoring her, but they would not let her go. She had to respond to ten curtain raisings before the audience was content. In her dressing room, O'Neil donned the wreath while the mayor with his wife, Rankin, Stockwell, and Charles Bishop toasted O'Neil. It was "a particularly brilliant O'Neillean engagement," reported the *New York Dramatic Mirror*.[189]

When O'Neil gave a final performance of Lady Inger in *Lady Inger of Ostrat*, Ashton Stevens wrote:

> Before what was perhaps the largest audience that had ever attended an Ibsen play in this country, or any other, Nance O'Neil at the Grand Opera House last night duelled her life and reason against *Lady Inger of Ostrat*. The player won but a few of the audience...had a night of exquisite suffering. They thought that there on stage, before their eyes, Nance O'Neil would either die or go mad....Lady Inger is, to my notion, the best part that Miss O'Neil has found for her tremendous but limited personality....Miss O'Neil's handling of the final act is a terrible, thrilling remembrance. It was relentless to the last cry. It was cruel and it hurt.[190]

Just as the Australians had failed to understand it, so too did the Americans. "It has all the splendor of gloom of the later work [of Ibsen] without its clarity, logic, consistency and brilliant cleverness of building dramatically," said a critic.[191]

O'Neil broke all financial records for playing in San Francisco. Weekly receipts averaged $10,000, and, after eight weeks, her profit was $40,000. Rankin, through a San Francisco bank, paid British moneylenders to relinquish O'Neil's jewels, which he had left with them for £10,000.[192]

Finally, Rankin signed a contract with the syndicate to have O'Neil play Lady Macbeth in New York. Rankin, who had been unable to obtain Frohman's services and maintain his own management position, was making his peace with a monopoly organization that had shut him out of the better theaters for years. He dealt directly with Abe Erlanger, whose growing power over his partners' objections made the deal possible. There were those, however, who still wanted to wrest O'Neil away from Rankin, so no agreement was absolutely certain. O'Neil was scheduled to play in *Macbeth*, *Judith*, *Elizabeth*, and possibly *Magda* at the Herald Square Theatre in New York from September 7, 1903. "I have been spoken for Macbeth," Rankin said, "but will devote myself to managerial duties."[193]

Although celebrated in her home state, O'Neil did not feel secure. After nine years on stage, she wondered at her temerity in undertaking the task. "The longer I am in the theatrical business, the harder it becomes," she said.[194] Her allegiance to Rankin was still strong. "Except for Mac, the stage is my only teacher," she said.

> A thousand times since [my first appearance] I should have been crushed and in despair, I think, but for the power and confidence he was able to transfer to me during the years. What I am artistically, it seems to me, he has made me, though he insists that he has merely 'pumiced down my angles.'...Often he would rush back during a performance and criticize my faults by doing it the *better* way—always most considerately and kindly, for at such times a harsh criticism, I think, would have crushed me like an eggshell.[195]

This was said, no doubt, to contrast with Belasco's famously rough treatment of his protégée, Mrs Leslie Carter. All the stress and moil of rehearsals, of course, made her wonder if acting was worth it. "But that within drives me forward in spite of myself. My art is my world. I love it." And as for her method: "I do what I feel to be true because I feel it; and yet I must always have a reason for doing it just that way. Art is suspended by a hair. The difference between the intensely tragic, the true and the ridiculous and false is too slight sometimes for a cobweb to float upon." Again, echoing Rankin's thoughts, she criticized actors of the day for assuming a hollowness and affectation that was in modern society. They had lost the old-time classical sense and become insipid. Then she spoke from her own heart: "An actress must know the despair of her heroines. She could have experienced those passions in other lives, thousands of years ago. Acting lifts [the actor] out of the sordid, narrow life, and thrusts him into a bigger world where he stands in mute handclasp with the larger, cosmic emotions of the gods."[196]

Starting from Los Angeles, Rankin took the company touring. He added an attractive young lady from the Alcazar Theatre stock company by the name of Agnes Ranken.[197] Often her name was spelt "Rankin," and a Salt Lake City newspaper reported that she was McKee Rankin's daughter.[198] Nothing outside of her stage work of a few years is known of her. She may have been born when Rankin was acting at the California Theatre in the mid-eighties. As Amy Leslie wrote: "He was constantly in trouble with one woman or another."[199] Rankin always included her in O'Neil's companies when O'Neil toured the West Coast.

Because the Nance O'Neil Company carried its scenery, Rankin limited its repertoire to three plays: *Magda*, *The Jewess*, and *Elizabeth*. The cast was fair, and the houses were crowded in Stockton, Frisco, San Jose, Oakland, and in Sacramento, where there was standing room only for the three nights.[200]

Rankin's object in touring was more than filling the time until O'Neil's New York appearance; he believed in the efficacy of the theater to influence people's lives and that the actor was in partnership with the great playwrights to make people think and to refine their sensibilities through art. He enjoyed sweeping into cities and towns with a company and creating excitement for the drama for two or three nights. By March, the company was playing in Seattle and Tacoma, Washington, where theatergoers had not seen O'Neil for nine years. In Vancouver, British Columbia, Agnes Ranken in *Magda*, was called "altogether a lovable little girl who carries the ingenue role of the winsome Marie with sweetness, delicacy and grace."[201] O'Neil rested during the days and never spoke above a whisper to save herself for her performances. Traveling eastward, the company began to find business falling off. It was early April 1903, and an economic recession was underway. Rankin must have feared more losses, but in Ogden, Utah, on April 6, an audience filled the Opera House and cheered enthusiastically. In Salt Lake City, Rankin was buoyed by the enthusiasm of the packed houses during a four-day stop.

Agnes Ranken (Rankin) at the Central Theatre, San Francisco, 1905.

Owing to a rockslide that covered the main rail line of the Union Pacific in Wyoming, the company arrived in Denver ten hours late and only half-filled the house the following night. The critic remarked that O'Neil's art had grown in the nine years since her last visit: "Once ungainly in height and lack of figure, she is now commandingly handsome, and in the possession of a figure that would delight the heart of the sculptor. Her whole style is leonine and she has a voice whose depth and power is unknown in any other present-day star."[202] In Kansas City, the houses were small at the beginning of the week—O'Neil was largely unknown there, and the advertising came too late—but they increased during the week and were large at the end. St Louis gave the company a warm welcome for the week of May 4, but the turnout was lighter than the local theatrical men had anticipated.

As Rankin came further into the East, critics began commenting upon the insufficiency of the scenery, especially in a historical play like *Elizabeth, Queen of England*. Obviously Rankin was losing money again. In Milwaukee, the critic, speaking on behalf of the many German immigrants there, complained that the staging of *Magda* was deficient in the German home atmosphere and that everything, even to the serving of coffee, was quite American.[203] "Mr. Rankin must invest his offerings more satisfactorily, or he must retire to cheaper houses. And Miss O'Neil must see to it that she cuts out unsuitable plays from her repertoire. As it is, she stands in her own way of obtaining the largest recognition for her really great talents."[204] The audiences here were just fair-sized. But in Minneapolis, people found *The Jewess* "strangely apropos" because of the recent massacre at Kishinef in Russia that "horrified the civilized world."[205] The four nights in that city were so successful that the company was scheduled for a return engagement of a week after a stint in St Paul. This extra week at the end of May in Minneapolis brought in sufficient money for Rankin to cancel the upcoming engagement in Duluth and return with O'Neil to San Francisco.

O'Neil's New York engagement under Erlanger was still tentatively scheduled for September, but Rankin wanted to take advantage of the temperate climate in San Francisco, where the theaters stayed open all summer, to keep his financial position strong. Moreover, he had negotiated a contract with Frank Perley, one of the best-known managers in the theater and in close touch with the syndicate. Approval came from Erlanger in late June, and the way seemed clear for Rankin to give over his management responsibilities to Perley in New York in the fall. Syndicate approval could mean that O'Neil would have her choice of the powerful plays written by American and English authors. Rankin could concentrate henceforth on stage directing.

On June 6, 1903, O'Neil opened at the Theatre Republic in San Francisco in *The Jewess*. The play went with "a snap."[206] Rankin, as Father Lorenz, made the most of his part, as did Agnes Rankin as Lena. L.R. Stockwell had subleased the theater for three months and was its actor-manager. Not long after the audience left the theater, the assistant-treasurer reported to Stockwell and the stage manager that he smelt smoke in the gallery. With an electrician and stage carpenter, they detected an odor like that from a bakeshop and decided it came from a bakery across the street. Actually, it came from crossed wires that had started a smoldering fire before the electricity was turned off.[207]

During the early morning, fire destroyed the interior and was thought to have destroyed from $20,000 to $25,000 worth of O'Neil's wardrobe, which had been insured by a New York firm until March 18. O'Neil wired the company and, finding that the insurance had not been renewed, she was eager to have her sixty trunks and cases recovered and Ristori's jewels found. None of her trunks was waterproof. The firemen, however, had spread tarpaulins over her wardrobe, which protected it from the water. They took the script she had been using and dried it at the firehouse before returning it to her.

Fortunately, all of her company's wardrobe and scenery for *The Jewess* was recovered from the ruin, and Stockwell arranged for O'Neil to play at the Alhambra Theatre the next evening. "I am glad, you know, not so much for myself as for the ladies and gentlemen of my company," she said. "It is quick work losing one theater and signing for another within a few hours of the disaster." But after the scenery for *The Jewess* was hauled to the Alhambra, the theater association refused to lease the theater for more than two nights, which was not profitable for O'Neil, and she declined to play there.

Undeterred, Rankin contracted with L.R. Stockwell, who provided the financing and gave his undivided attention to managing the O'Neil company. The company received 75 percent of the net proceeds, Stockwell 25 percent. O'Neil was given expenses of $175 dollars a week. Rankin was to give his service free of charge to the company. The contract was for eight weeks starting at the California Theatre on June 15, 1903.[208]

The O'Neil company opened in an excellently mounted *La Tosca*, for which Stockwell had to advance the company $700 to pay for the American rights to the script and production.[209] A critic thought that O'Neil's comedy work in the first act was lighter in touch and tone than anything she had done, thus providing a counterbalance to the dire ending. "An absolute abandon is not only needful, but imperative, if the emotional climaxes of the torture scene and the death of Scarpia are to be carried to conviction," he wrote.[210] It was in just such scenes that O'Neil showed growth. "No one has better expressed La Tosca's mingled horror and joy as she realizes that the knife at her hand will save her honor....The hurried, gasping breath after the singer has stabbed the tyrant is an innovation and is almost wholly effective."[211]

O'Neil then headlined her company's production of Sardou's *Fedora*. This was the first time O'Neil had presented the role in the United States. Fanny Davenport had made the character her own back in the 1880s. In those days, handsome, long-limbed, nervous blonde women like Fanny had taken the place of the raven-haired, black-eyed woman in literature.

Everything from brilliant wickedness to heroic passion was attributed to blondes, and the blonde Fedora united good and evil in herself. O'Neil made a striking dramatic figure of the society woman, with her fine figure and expressive face. She kept the tragic spirit under control and drew out the gradations of Fedora's character to rouse the audience to emotional "demonstrations."[212]

O'Neil had waited a long time to play her next role, Juliet, in Shakespeare's *Romeo and Juliet*, and must have been dismayed and greatly disappointed at her failure. A critic wrote: "She touches the ingenuous, girlish side lightly, and she does the heavier scenes with considerable discretion,...although her heavy voice breaks out once in a while and mars the effect....She is fitted for work of greater caliber, and she cannot complain if she cannot do what nobody before her may be said to have done, play Juliet and Lady Macbeth and Queen Elizabeth all to perfection at one time in her life."[213] O'Neil took the criticism to heart and never again attempted to play Juliet. When she played Lady Macbeth for the latter part of the week, Ashton Stevens considered her to be in the school of acting of Mrs D.P. Bowers of thirty years earlier, which, although out of vogue, had force enough to make O'Neil one of the prominent actresses of the early years of the twentieth century.[214]

Rankin took roles in these productions. As Colonel Schwartze in *Magda*, he had come to symbolize not only the older generation in its misunderstanding of the younger but also patriarchal society confronted with the new, strong-willed woman struggling for her liberation. His minor roles such as the Marquis de Mendoza in *Elizabeth, Queen of England* were distinctive.

Surprisingly, the company closed on July 19, 1903, lasting for only half of the intended engagement. "When Miss O'Neil surrounds herself with more competent support," wrote a critic, trying to explain the company's failure, "there will be no danger of any of her plays becoming obsolescent, if not obsolete."[215] Rankin again had gambled, as he skimped by on minor players to save funds for his New York project.

O'Neil, having fulfilled her dream to play Juliet, now got the opportunity to realize another: to play Rosalind in Shakespeare's *As You Like It*. The open-air performances at Sutro Heights, on the outskirts of San Francisco, for the matinees and evenings on August 1 and 2, took advantage of the beautiful lawns and old trees just below the Sutro residence, the Ocean Cliffhouse. The first day was beautiful. O'Neil as Rosalind and Blanche Stoddard as Celia made their way gracefully through the trees to the sweet refrain of "Celia's Arbor," the beams of the western sun lighting the path before them. Rosalind, wearing light blue and silver, and Celia, wearing white and yellow, cast the spell over their audience to take it back through the years to the Usurper's Court. The wrestling match between Charles, the duke's wrestler, played by James J. Corbett, and Orlando, played by E J. Ratcliffe, was "a most picturesque tussle."[216] Corbett was getting ready to battle James J. Jeffries on August 14 to regain his title of champion pugilist of the world.

As Rosalind, O'Neil was a "hearty success," although it was noted that she lacked the arch and dainty sportiveness with which Rosalind was often played. Ratcliffe, as usual, "rang with virility" as Orlando. His problem was that the roles he had to play as leading man were too big for him; consequently, he lacked the last touches that could have given them distinction. L.R. Stockwell, as the clown Touchstone, was "delightfully human and humorous." He benefited from Rankin's long study of the role and secret wish to play it. The hunting chorus caught the fancy of the audience and called forth unlimited applause.[217]

The remaining performances were "fog-enwrapped and picnicable." The last performance was a testimonial to O'Neil before she left to meet the challenge of New York City.[218]

The Debacle in Chicago

When Rankin arrived in New York, he had to postpone O'Neil's long-awaited appearance as Lady Macbeth at a New York theater because the promised financial backing was not forthcoming. It appeared that the syndicate had been leading him on and then reverted to its former practice of keeping O'Neil out of its theaters. Perley reneged on becoming her manager. Rankin, concealing his disappointment, gave out the excuse that New York City was a poor venue during the month of September and said that he would return with her in February, but actually he was desperate to find a manager for O'Neil. O'Neil, too, tried to find someone; she wrote to Frank McKee, a well-known manager who was an adherent of the syndicate, "I don't care what the salary is, provided I can get enough to live on. You can have all the profits, if there are any, and I believe there will be. Mr. Rankin, who has taught me all that I know, need not figure in the contract, except as stage director. Now, please manage me."[219] McKee declined.

Rankin, hinting that managers rejected O'Neil for her strong acting style, remarked that New York theaters were given over to musical farce and spoken buffoonery. Occasionally, a good actor could be encountered out of town, but he would receive a cold shoulder in New York for not being polite enough. "Some day," he hoped, "the public will rebel at the effeminacy that masquerades as manhood growing over us for a long time past." The best effects were always reached by the quietest methods—with a sense of subdued, concentrated strength behind them. English actors, he said, were imported to fill a hole that the Americans had dug for themselves. As a result the acting in New York was not only repressed but wondrously artificial.

> Even in the walk and manner of shaking hands actors ape the most profound faults of society. This decadence began with the comedies of Robertson that taught the "natural" acting. But a man who has been long at this sort of thing loses all aptitude for what is known as the sock and buskin. If you ask him to play Shakespeare or old comedy he is utterly lost.
>
> To such an extent does this false view of the stage exist, particularly in New York, that critics fall into the errors themselves. I read a notice the other day that spoke reproachfully of some acting in a soul-stirring play as bordering on the melodrama. In Heaven's name what else should it border on? What is finer than good melodramatic acting? Is not Shakespeare full of it? But, alas! where now are our Shakespearean actors? Most of them dead—the others pretty old. The breed will soon be extinct, for there is no school in which to learn any more. Some people speak of the stock company as being a good school. It is the worst of all. The people simply learn a lot of parts, one after the other, parrot-like, but their stage managers of today can give them no instructions in them, because they know so very little themselves.[220]

Nothing, he insisted, was comparable to the experience of learning to act from the great actors, in whose company he first took the stage. "Mind you, I am not of the old fogy sort that goes back to the past to discover every criterion of excellence, but you may see for yourself that under present conditions the birth of a good actor is in the nature of a miracle, and one of the most noticeable results is the paucity of good plays."[221] Rankin's remarks were read by New York managers and critics, who found an opportunity to take their revenge upon him within the year.

Theatrical entrepreneur W.S. Cleveland had been trying to persuade Rankin to cancel all O'Neil's West Coast engagements and open his new theater in Chicago. In desperation, Rankin signed a contract for O'Neil, Ratcliffe, and himself to perform in Cleveland's stock company in Chicago for the month of November. Cleveland, long known as a hustler in the theater business, transformed the armory of the 7th Regiment of Illinois

Volunteers into a theater in short time. He gave his plans to architects, who prepared them in a few days and had contractors working in three shifts continuously for sixty days. It was one of the handsomest and largest theaters in the country.

In the meantime, Rankin, needing money, turned to vaudeville. He joined the Orpheum circuit and began a week on September 28, 1903, in Brooklyn, playing *Counsel for the Defense*, which he retitled *The Lawyer*, because he had sold the rights of the playlet to Mr and Mrs William Robyns, who had been performing it successfully for many seasons. He was assisted by Phyllis Rankin, who made the character of the East Side girl stand out as strongly as O'Neil had done, and Ricca Allen, who was excellent as the housekeeper. Rankin kept O'Neil out of vaudeville at this time because it would have hurt her reputation just as he was planning for her superstardom in Chicago. As if to bolster O'Neil's spirit, he began comparing her publicly to Mary Anderson, who had risen to stardom from nowhere. He explained that the reason people onstage are so variable in performance, so good one night and so indifferent the next, was not the result of their own physical and mental condition, but that of the audience. A cold audience will kill the best actor in the world, whereas an enthusiastic audience will lift him or her up to a transcendental state of exaltation where sometimes great results can be wrought. "Nance would begin to really act," he said, "only when she began to be conscious of the existence of that subtle fluid that runs between audience and performer, and that means sympathy."[222]

Rankin and Pixie continued in vaudeville at Proctor's 23rd Street Theatre in New York, where he made a hit in his portrayal of the softhearted, old lawyer with a gruff exterior. They played two weeks in New York and for a week at Proctor's Theatre in Newark, New Jersey. With some money in his pocket, he opened with *Magda* at Cleveland's Theatre on October 31, 1903. As the audience entered the front door, the workmen were leaving from the back door. The audience was large, but conditions were not promising. The acoustics were bad and the noise from elevated trains running on both sides of the building was disconcerting. Moreover, during the confusion of the opening, the plush backs of about two hundred chairs were slashed and ruined. Cleveland promised to have all the problems remedied.

O'Neil was a success as Magda, and the rest of the cast was good. Unnoticed by almost everyone was the actor who played Max, the nephew. Amy Leslie spotted him, however, and wrote what became a memorable quotation: "The part of Max was essayed by a young actor who calls himself Mr. John Barrymore. He walked about the stage as if he had been all dressed up and forgotten."[223] This was the first notice of the actor who was to become one of the best stage and film stars of the age and whose portrayal of Hamlet caused a young actor of a succeeding generation, Laurence Olivier, to compare him to the rising sun. Barrymore later wrote that Rankin was a good stage manager, "but he had too much to contend with and there never was any money in the theater. He had always to worry about bills."[224]

The company next intended to present *Elizabeth, Queen of England*, in which Barrymore was expected to play Sir Francis Bacon. As Barrymore explained: "A Denver creditor of McKee Rankin with little feeling for the drama, attached the scenery and properties because he had not been paid some trifling bill, and there never was money enough in the Chicago box office to send on to redeem this production." Rankin mounted *The Jewess* in its stead, but more trouble, in the shape of a streetcar strike, kept audiences small.

When the strike ended, good business returned to the theaters, except for the Cleveland, which, being new, had no body of loyal patrons to help it over difficult periods. There was more trouble between the actors and Cleveland. Ratcliffe had agreed to play for $200 a week—$100 from Cleveland and $100 from Rankin—but Cleveland protested that, since Rankin was not playing the pieces he had agreed to play, he would not pay his share of Ratcliffe's salary. Eventually, he relented when Ratcliffe was needed to play Bill Sykes in *Oliver Twist*. Before the Sunday-night performance Ratcliffe told Cleveland he would not play unless Cleveland guaranteed him another week's employment. O'Neil, in support, declared that she would not play unless Ratcliffe was playing Bill Sykes. Hard-fisted stagehands carrying clubs forced Ratcliffe to perform that night. Cleveland kept both actors out of the cast for Monday and Tuesday and would take them back only when they "promised to be good."[225]

This attitude upset Rankin. For an actor who perfected an air of ease that pervaded his performances and his productions, the chaos at the Cleveland Theatre cracked his imperturbable demeanor. The man who had endured all sorts of insults, misconstrued motives, and petty law suits must have finally given way to his feelings. Rankin criticized the lack of quality in the current production—both in terms of the abilities of the stock-company cast and the financial commitment of those engaging the plays. He observed that, "It is the great difficulty of mastering the intricacies of a character comedy like 'Oliver Twist' that prevents the play from being presented by the ordinary stock company. The length and strength is another obstacle for not only are seventeen people required, but the seventeen parts are all character parts that must be intelligently played by experienced people if an artistic performance is to be given."[226] As if this were not enough, theater owners utterly failed to understand the expenses of the touring company mounting the play. The Drury Lane pantomimes had set the standard for the modern stage by spending $125,000 to $150,000 on productions annually. A naturalist perfectionist, Belasco spent $70,000 hunting down articles in France to be used in his *Du Barry* production. Costuming and furniture in this period of naturalism had to be close to the real thing. Comic operas and musicals, with their extravagantly dressed large choruses and frequent changes of costume, sent the cost up to $40,000 a production and more. Complex lighting also added to the costs.

Beset by all these troubles, Rankin appeared before the curtain one evening and berated the audience and the press for not recognizing O'Neil's genius. He was doubtless in his cups. His position as O'Neil's protector against the dictates of management was being undermined by Cleveland. O'Neil, at least, had the courage to defy Cleveland on behalf of Ratcliffe. Moreover, Rankin, grown "sleek, fat and satisfied," may have been conscience-stricken at not fighting for O'Neil's career as strongly as he could have. The situation could not continue. Cleveland informed the press that he in no way countenanced Rankin's attack. "There will be no more speechmaking from the stage," Cleveland said.[227] He lowered ticket prices to five cents for some gallery seats and to twenty-five cents for the orchestra, thus curtailing Rankin's earnings, which were on a percentage basis. In retaliation, Rankin cut short the final week.

Charging that O'Neil and Rankin were going to skip town when they owed him money, Cleveland seized all the properties of the O'Neil company and took Rankin to court to retrieve the advance of $10,000 for costumes and scenery for ten plays. Rankin retorted that Cleveland owed him more than the advance he made to the company.[228]

The ensuing court battle brought out sensational charges that were reported in newspapers all over the nation. Cleveland cast Rankin in the real-life role of Svengali, who hypnotized O'Neil to make her act. "It is a second case of Trilby and Svengali," Cleveland testified. "I have seen Rankin exert his influence over Miss O'Neil. When he looked at her, she forgot her lines, and when he snapped his fingers at her she would act. He has an undue influence over her and has kept her segregated from other actors and managers."[229] Cleveland was said to be repeating what theater people had whispered for years. O'Neil was an utterly incompetent girl, who was hypnotized into giving great performances. O'Neil would come to the theater looking slovenly, her eyes lusterless, indifferent to her surroundings. She would ask the cast advice as to her entrances and exits.

Her queries sounded ridiculous. Then Rankin would appear and immediately O'Neil would be transformed. She began remembering her lines as if reading them, her eyes sparkled, her words rang with feeling, her acting thrilled even the jaded professionals onstage with her. Cleveland claimed that Rankin put her under a spell about a half-hour before the performances and released her after the curtain came down. Then suddenly she became the antithesis of the great actress. As her manager, Rankin was blamed for blighting her early promise.[230] Although O'Neil was lauded by the conservative critics on three continents, she could find only second-rate houses to perform in.

Rankin scoffed at such nonsense. He said that Cleveland was the most foolish person he had met in the theater. He pointed out the inconsistency in Cleveland's argument: it could not be claimed that O'Neil would become the world's greatest actress if released from Rankin's influence and, at the same time, that she was hopeless without him. O'Neil denied the allegations and stated firmly that Rankin had no hypnotic power over her.

Others confirmed that Rankin had a strong effect on O'Neil. He was said to have a hypnotic eye. Lionel Barrymore remarked that Rankin was constantly watching O'Neil but more in the sense that he was enjoying her beauty than controlling her. A stage manager who worked with Rankin said that much abuse had been heaped on him unjustifiably: there was not a more agreeable or genial companion. But he admitted that Rankin's eye could be hypnotic. His large gray eyes were set deep beneath heavy eyebrows, which seemed to stare through a person. "There is not a man living who can resist its [his eye's] power," wrote the manager, "no matter what the distance might be." Rankin had a peculiar searching look and great personal magnetism. He gave all the directions in the theater. "Frequently O'Neil would complain to me about something," said the manager, "but under Rankin's orders I did not consider her suggestions. 'Pay no attention to her,' he would say."[231]

A paper as far removed as the *Hawaiian Star* commented on O'Neil as Trilby and gave an uncomplimentary picture of Rankin. With O'Neil he had become enriched, his diamonds were larger, and his appetite had increased his girth, it reported. The article continued: "Rankin was not a romantic figure. He was an old man, fond of his bottle. As an actor his ability had declined, and his career had not had a refining influence on his personality. He was not the man to be loved by a young, beautiful woman, who might compel admiration where she would. Her infatuation for him, however, seemed complete. She scarcely moved without him and in her social life accepted no invitation that did not include Rankin."[232] Was this a case of hypnotism?

A temporary retreat into the vaudeville circuit away from innuendo and court charges and into ready cash seemed the only way open. He and O'Neil, as they had planned on doing after the Chicago engagement, opened in Detroit for the last week of November in a sketch called *A Long Strike*—yet another title for *Counsel for the Defense*.

The unrelenting attacks on his character, his finances, and O'Neil's abilities were an attempt to derail his independence as manager of O'Neil. Most men would have sunk under the pressure, yet his resilient spirit came again to the fore as he arranged for the O'Neil company to open in Boston after the New Year in 1904.

Sam Shubert of the Shubert Brothers, theater impresarios, happened to be in Chicago and drew up a contract with Rankin to play at the Shuberts' one theater in Boston, the Columbia, for three weeks from January 8, 1904. The terms for Rankin were 50 percent on $5,000 profit, and 60 percent on everything above that.[233] This agreement was a saving grace at a very low point. The Shuberts were a part of the Theater Syndicate but functioned on their own at times. Their theater in Boston had not hosted drama for years. It was used for farces and musical comedies. Its patronage was not likely to be attracted to O'Neil's fare of heavy drama, but the Shuberts may have felt that Rankin deserved a chance. Sam Shubert wrote to Rankin: "We will do everything in our power to try and help business." Actually the Shuberts were becoming less friendly with the syndicate's leaders and would break away in July 1905, much as Belasco was doing in 1904. Belasco had discovered that Erlanger was withholding money that he should have received for his productions that the syndicate controlled. When he found that he could arrange for his productions to tour the West in independent theaters, he sued to break up his relationship with the syndicate and prepared to join Harrison Fiske in partnership.

At this time in 1904, the syndicate finished off Weber and Fields, who had relied on touring its productions through the Stair and Havlin chain of theaters. In return for control over the popular-priced entertainments in the important cities, the syndicate lured Stair and Havlin to join them. Weber and Fields, having no other light-entertainment houses for their productions, had to turn over their three theaters and their business to Stair and Havlin. Other independent managers were forced to give up their independence at the same time.

Belasco was in despair at the state of the theater and echoed Rankin in his verdict. The theater had never been so degraded. High dramatic art no longer existed because the actor had no guidance. The present-day stage managers were worthless. In England, the once great Charles Wyndham was no more than a theater janitor. Theatrical managers assumed the audiences knew nothing, and since art could never compete with business, business ruled the day.

Belasco had a different concept of the stage from Rankin, however, and, although they were regarded as the two best stage directors of their day, Belasco mistrusted intellect in art as much as Rankin developed it. Belasco, who thought that literary drama was not actable, dismissed Ibsen, Hauptmann, and the new intellectual drama as unable to "get beneath the vest." Belasco followed the dramatic traditions set by Shakespeare and the French romantics. Sentiment was the pabulum of his plays. He dealt with mood and situations, not with moral, social, and ethical questions. His *The Heart of Maryland* brought him the success that allowed him to become an independent producer. The play's heroine, Maryland Calvert, was in the words of Mrs Carter, "the crucible into which I put my whole being; my art, my emotions, my life."[234] Charles Frohman called the spectacular scene of Mrs Carter climbing up a tower to stop the clapper of the great bell from sounding the alarm the most thrilling in the theater. George Bernard Shaw, however, castigated the play's romanticization of the American Civil War as "despicable, puerile, and blackguardly." Clearly Belasco was in another realm from Rankin, with Rankin's emphasis on modern European-thinking playwrights such as Henrik Ibsen.[235]

Rankin's early reliance on naturalism or photographic realism, which Belasco had observed in Rankin's western dramas, was taken further by Belasco into an overriding emphasis on period detail to set a basic tone and evoke an atmosphere. Belasco thought that actors were psychologically influenced by stage lighting. He used psychology to bring out good performances, cajoling, coaxing, or tormenting actors, according to what he considered their temperament required. He aimed for harmonious balance between inner truths and character and demonstrated it through stage movement; thus he cast an actor with a deep voice with one having a high-pitched voice, and he hired foreigners to play the roles of foreigners. This led him to reject the concept of stardom and develop the ensemble as Saxe-Meininger and Rankin had done. Rankin, nevertheless, starred O'Neil while working with each cast member to bring the acting of the whole up to a standard that would make the star less noticeable. His financial uncertainties often precluded his attaining this goal. Belasco, who owed his ascendancy to the stars he created, such as the tigerish Carter, the girlishly innocent Blanche Bates, the sophisticated Frances Starr, and the leonine Lenore Ulrich, set down a policy of no stars as soon as he was in a position to run his own theaters.

While critics did not accuse Belasco of hypnotizing his actresses, it was clear that they were dominated by him. When Carter secretly married an actor in 1906 against Belasco's instructions that she never marry, Belasco refused to speak to her again. "Take down the sign," he said. Twenty-five years later, in 1932, Carter met Belasco by chance in Los Angeles when he was ailing. She sent him a note before he died. Repentant, he replied that the long feud was all his fault.

Rankin too had a long personal feud end with death, although there probably was no reconciliation in his case. George Cameron Rankin had died in Sault Ste Marie almost a year earlier, on January 6, 1903. George's body had been brought for burial to Windsor from the log cabin in Algoma where he had spent his last years. A reporter had tracked him down some time before his death and gave a portrait of this "prodigious and auroralike intellect" who had "made several fortunes and washed them away with cocktails and Canadian Club."[236] George had buried himself in the mountains between the Bruce Mines and Desbarats to shake off alcoholism. He lived as a hermit, immersed in the classics, communing with his only friends, a tomcat, and the wildlife of wolves, beaver, and owls, holding communion "with the great trees and everlasting rocks." Aside from his plays *L'Habitant* and *Going to the Fair*, and his novel, *The Border Canuck*, George was known for his verse, which seems not to have been preserved. The claims of critics that he was the first to put the French-Canadian habitant lingo into print was challenged by the supporters of the Quebec poet W.H. Drummond. A dispute arose over who was the true author of "The Wreck of the 'Julie Plante'," which may be found in Drummond's *Complete Poems*. Those who claimed that George was the author may have been dismayed by George's assertion just before his death that his friend Frank Morton, a railway clerk in Detroit, really wrote it.[237] George had a wry sense of humor.

Back in Chicago, because O'Neil and Rankin had been given a rough ride by Cleveland, who was now suing them for breach of contract, the Chicago theater managers and actors gave them a benefit on December 24. It was organized by Otis Skinner, the actor, at the Garrick Theatre. Rankin and O'Neil did scenes from *Magda*. However much was raised, it was still not sufficient to pay their debts in Chicago, and Rankin had to borrow money to pay their railway fares to Boston. He arrived with O'Neil on January 3, 1904, gathered a cast, and rehearsed for a week.

1904

Boston: Unimaginable Success

Bad omens preceded O'Neil opening in Boston on January 11, 1904. There was a recession in the theatrical business, and the country's worst theater fire had just taken place in Chicago, which had put fear into the

The Reign of Nance O'Neil **355**

hearts of theatergoers everywhere.[238] In Boston, there was a systematic investigation of every theater. The Columbia was declared safe. Aside from the weather, which was far below zero throughout New England, Rankin had to contend with patrons unfamiliar with serious drama. His competition was the popular elongated comedian De Wolf Hopper in the musical *Mr. Pickwick*.

Rankin relied on his old company, actors who, in some cases, had been with him for years. He opened with *Magda*. "Miss O'Neil's support was not ideal," wrote a Boston observer, criticizing Rankin for spending valuable time "in his too deliberative methods" and for his over-vehemence, which "tended to give the character of Colonel Schwartze an element of trivial comedy decidedly out of harmony with the past."[239] Another wrote: "His impersonation of the stern uncompromising and narrow-minded old father is rarely seen on the stage today, but it is a fine illustration of what used to be done by the best actors in that more or less distant past now fondly referred to by the older generation as the palmy days of the stage."[240] Rankin had heard such criticisms of late and had criticized the modern style in return, but they must have had an effect on him, especially because he had preached the building of the new on the old to O'Neil.

Despite the press's less than generous words for Rankin, the audience, fair-sized and "of more popular character than has been seen at a performance of 'Magda'" thrilled to the realistic action, called O'Neil before the curtain three to six times after each of the four acts, and repeatedly called "brava," which was rare for English-speaking theatergoers. "Looking back over the history of the Boston stage for over twenty-five years," gushed a critic, "it can be truthfully said that no female star, not even Mary Anderson, Clara Morris, or Julia Marlowe, has during that period made so unequivocal a hit upon an opening night in Boston as did Miss O'Neil last evening."[241] Her beauty, grace, and magnetic stage presence, the emotional intensity in her facial expressions, and her every movement and gesture were lauded. "Even when her face is turned toward the back of the stage, the muscles of her back, her shoulders, her arms and even her fingers betray the emotion that is supposed to be wringing her heart and appeal to the hearts of the auditors scarcely less effectual than the pathos of her voice."[242] Rankin could scarcely believe it. At last Americans were beginning to see what he had seen for years. But then, perhaps by working so closely with her, he had been too close to see the improvement in her.

As the week advanced, the audiences grew larger. The profits were small, however, and it was not until O'Neil did *Hedda Gabler* that they increased. To present an Ibsen play at this theater was an innovation, but it proved to be a revelation to the lovers of musical comedy, who flocked to the theater and established O'Neil as a tremendous favorite.[243] O'Neil, who lay awake at night going over her roles and exploring ways to build up her characters, had by now developed an outstanding Hedda Gabler. "The subtleties of the piece, the epigrams, without which the sense would be ruined and which in less careful hands would have been hopelessly overemphasized, were with her distinctly, yet not too energetically, delivered," wrote a critic. "She splendidly portrayed the desires of an unsatisfied longing for a hand in somebody's destiny, and showed how a woman with unholy secrets, in which a husband may not, perhaps could not, share, could delude herself into a belief that all kinds of things were right for her if wrong for others."[244]

As if to tempt the fates, Rankin now presented a Sudermann play that had not been done in English, *The Fires of St John*. He probably thought that he would have been prevented from producing it in a better theater, and, with the sudden interest in O'Neil, it might go at this time. On the eve of the feast of St John in Germany, country people build bonfires on the hillsides and in the frenzy of celebration let their emotions go back to the spirit of the paganism of their ancestors. Marie, the daughter of a thieving gypsy woman, and George Von Harton are brought up by the Brauer family. George is supposed to marry Brauer's young daughter, Gertrude, but George and Marie love one another. They feel obliged to Brauer to suppress their love until on Johannis night they can hide their true feelings no longer and make love. As Marie's gypsy mother is dragged off to prison again for theft, Marie persuades George to marry Gertrude while she pursues her own way in the world. Marie feels unworthy of George, and, like her mother, is a thief. Critics thought the play too suggestive of animal passion and an unwelcome addition to the American stage. Marie's forcing of herself on George was a bit of daring sensationalism. "The effect of turning out the lights as the woman throws herself into her lover's arms leaves little to the imagination," wrote a critic. "Had Miss O'Neil been one whit less of an artist the scene would have been morally disastrous. Her impersonation of the strangely complex character drawn by Sudermann was really a triumph of dramatic art. It was as unaffectedly natural and as convincingly real as such an abnormal character could possibly be made to appear."[245]

O'Neil's success with audiences was fueling a mania for her. In the third act of *Fires*, she roused the audience to a great pitch of enthusiasm, "something remarkable for a house heretofore exclusively devoted to musical comedy." She had a gift of concentrating attention upon herself when naturally subordinate to her surroundings. This power of holding attention in moments of inaction she possessed "to a greater degree than any other English-speaking actress."[246]

Ricca Allen's acting of the gypsy woman garnered praise from the press and public alike. She was a remarkably talented actress whose long association under Rankin's direction obviously developed her, but she lacked the talent of a leading lady or star. Blanche Stoddard, on the other hand, who played the girlish Gertrude in *Fires*, did become a leading lady, and rather quickly, although not a star on the plane of Nance O'Neil.

Popular demand led to the cancellation of the company's third week at the Columbia and its transfer to another theater. Society people could no longer bear to be kept away from O'Neil, although they could not in all propriety be seen attending the third-rate Columbia. The Shuberts, who soon sold the theater, released the Columbia's manager, Charles Salisbury, to allow him to manage the O'Neil company, which now transferred to the first-class Tremont Theatre to play matinee performances. Dockstader's Minstrels were booked for the evening and regular matinees there. O'Neil did not mind the change because in the evening she could attend social functions, at which she was now a celebrated guest, and she could play in nearby towns on the weekends.

Rankin hoped that the switch in theaters would bring in some profits to his impoverished organization. He was deeply in debt: actors' salaries were overdue; Salisbury had been promised a share of the profits; Rankin had contracted with Ratcliffe to share the profits with him as well if Ratcliffe could raise $1,000 to keep the company going. The bankrupt Rankin was reported to have $100 to meet a demand for over $27,000. For O'Neil's first week at the Columbia, the gross receipts had been $619, and, for the second week, $690.[247]

Rankin's sometime friend, John Schoeffel, was manager of the Tremont. His wife was Agnes Booth, formerly the widow of Junius Brutus Booth. Agnes Booth, whose voice in her heyday as an actress was not unlike O'Neil's, declared that O'Neil had the most beautiful voice she had ever heard and had earned the right to be called "the American Bernhardt." The rich, half-nasal quality of O'Neil's voice lent itself particularly to the expression of the tenderest pathos and drew tears to eyes unused to weep over "mimic woes."[248] Once heard for five minutes, her voice haunted the memory.

The cream of the devotees of high-class drama flocked to see O'Neil at the Tremont. Largely women at the matinees, "they gave vent to their emotions and to their enthusiastic admiration for the wonderful acting of the gifted young star by a copious flow of tears at various times during the performances and by repeated curtain calls."[249] The artistic and literary set opened its arms to her when she began with *Magda*. Men and women were unable to control their tears when swayed by the pathos in her voice.

A critic compared her with Mary Anderson on her first appearance in Boston twenty-seven years before. Like Anderson, O'Neil could charm her own sex, which was always a sure road to dramatic success. Anderson came from the West, unheralded and unknown, and played to thoroughly unprofitable business for about two weeks, after which she suddenly attracted great patronage and became a permanent professional and financial success. "But here is this difference in the two young women," the critic continued.

> While Miss Anderson's sudden popularity, notwithstanding her native talent, was largely the result of "social pull," exercised to an extent that it has never been before or since, mainly through the agency of the literary set, headed by Longfellow, Lowell and others, the triumph of Miss O'Neil which reached its climax yesterday has been attained entirely without the aid of social influence, but solely by the demonstration of a dramatic genius that could not fail of recognition in a community where there is a capacity to appreciate good acting.[250]

Although most of her reviews praised her in general terms, some journalists tried to be more specific: "From her beautiful arm and hand and most exquisite use of wrist and the open fingers in gesture—nobody since Edwin Booth has displayed such hand play—one could reconstruct all the figures of the traditional poses as given in Delsarte and the old French works for the expression and heightening of all the various passions and emotions."[251] Now that she was becoming a model of thespian art, O'Neil gave tickets to actors to attend her matinees.

O'Neil did five matinees a week at the Tremont. For the last two of her second week and for the first two of her third week she presented *Camille*. This was the Barton Hill version, which she had played in Australia. Certain scenes were cut, especially Armand's dialogue and the comedy between Prudence, the milliner, and Gaston, the playboy. The story was made clearer and more forceful. Whereas O'Neil originated the role of Marie in *The Fires of St John*,—and the roles of Hedda in *Hedda Gabler*, and Magda in *Magda*, were relatively new in which few stars had been recognized—by playing *Camille*, on the other hand, O'Neil brought to mind the performances of the great actresses over several decades. Boston critics quickly pointed to the best among them. Sarah Bernhardt was superior in fluency of expression, lightness of touch, power, pathos, and comprehension. Several actresses, notably Helene Modjeska, detracted from Camille's true character by a noble and delicate portrayal of pure womanly attributes. Clara Morris won sympathy for Camille by depicting her physical sufferings with painful realism. Eleanora Duse made her morbid and world weary, accentuating her mental rather than physical suffering and suggesting few of the feminine charms and graces, which seemed a necessary part of the equipment of so prosperous a courtesan. Ogle Nethersole made sensual seductiveness the dominating feature of the character. O'Neil now presented a woman of refinement and naturalness, who, by force of circumstance, has been placed amid surroundings abhorrent to her. Although her lovers and her jewels have been necessary for her existence, she loathes them all and longs for purity. When Armand Duval arrives, he does not change her character so much as bring to life what had been stifled and suppressed by her surroundings. Critics saw that O'Neil captured the refinement of Modjeska and the naturalism of Duse, though she had none of Bernhardt's gaiety and little of Nethersole's sensuality. Comedy was practically eliminated from the play.[252]

Rankin played the elder Duval with thorough sincerity. Ratcliffe gave Armand a thrilling dramatic intensity and was especially effective in the denunciation scene. All the cast was very good. The audience reacted with tremendous enthusiasm, causing nine curtain calls after the third act. O'Neil made a modest speech expressing her gratitude for their favor. Rankin had been scrupulous with costuming in the period of the play, and, when some of the costumes did not arrive owing to a snowstorm, there was concern for the production. The performances were so intense, however, that the audience did not notice any discrepancy in costuming.

There was standing room only for O'Neil's performances, and she became the toast of Boston. Society showered her with invitations, most of which she had to decline because she rehearsed hard every morning and had to reserve her strength for performances. Literary figures such as Thomas Aldrich and Henry James became her friends, and, by extension, friends of Rankin. Everyone was asking the question posed by the *Boston Post*: "What sort of woman is Nance O'Neil, this new tragedienne, who, with the figure of Minerva, the facial expression of Medea, and the halo of a luxuriant growth of golden hair about her intellectual head has within two weeks achieved a hitherto unprecedented feat of giving daily matinees with the classic drama as an attraction and filling the house with the very cream of Boston's most intellectual and cultural society?"[253]

People came to her dressing-room door to pay her sincere compliments, almost always with tears in their eyes. She received two hundred letters a day. Many admirers expressed their appreciation in verse, some of which were quite beautiful. "Such kindness, I think, is the most beautiful thing in the world," she said. "But I can't understand how I can possibly deserve it all."[254]

The editor of *The Literary World* wrote that O'Neil was

> easily the finest English speaking actress I have ever seen, and I've seen all the good ones who have appeared in this country. Physically, she is splendid, a superb figure, a handsome face, a wonderful voice, and every movement is grace itself. She is the most graceful woman I have ever seen. Bernhardt has surely grace, but she had no backbone to hold it up. She is too lithe, too willowy, as the word goes; she bends and sways too much. This woman can stand up, can be rigid and dignified, while at the same time she has every pliant and supple movement. Therefore, I hold that she is superior in this respect to Bernhardt. Her chief characteristic—self-restraint, a reserve so extraordinary that I've never seen the like, and great naturalness. You feel all the time that she is the character she's playing, that she is not acting, that she is restrained by conventional decencies, as we all are in real life; she seems to be trying all the time, as Hedda, not to give way to her passions, and you feel in seeing her that this is so, and you dread lest she should give way as you do in real life when you are in the midst of some emotional crisis with an emotional person.[255]

The company played in Portland, Maine, over the first weekend in February. The local critic called *The Fires of St John* one of the best plays seen there in many months and continued comparing O'Neil to Mary Anderson: "same cold beauty, same clear cut features, same magnetism."[256]

Back in Boston, O'Neil played *Peg Woffington* to some disapproval; by this time, O'Neil was regarded as a tragedian, not a comedian. A critic said that she was "not at home in the part."[257] The playgoers thought otherwise, and the houses were sold out in advance. Rankin made amends to the critics by presenting *The Jewess*. O'Neil, in the famous curse scene, toyed with the sympathies of her spellbound audience and gradually brought the emotions to a crescendo when Joseph sinks helpless at her feet while the forsaken and heartbroken Leah towers above him with her arms and trembling hands uplifted to heaven. The denunciation seemed more mental than physical, said a critic, meaning that she emphasized the consequences of Joseph's betrayal over the act itself.[258] It brought audiences to their feet, shouting. "It was worth going one hundred miles and paying grand opera prices to see Nance O'Neil for about fifteen minutes in the curse scene," said a theatergoer.[259] Critics considered O'Neil as not yielding to a temptation to be theatrical but also avoiding the severe repression of Minnie Fiske. More varied and brilliant in her roles than others, O'Neil reached heights inaccessible to Fiske or any other actress.

Convinced by her critical and popular success, John Schoeffel now took over the management of O'Neil. He kept Rankin as stage manager but did not give Ratcliffe and Salisbury shares in the company because they contributed no capital. Rankin had already called off his deal with Ratcliffe because the latter had been unable to raise $1,000. Schoeffel, however, advanced O'Neil and Rankin $4,000. He arranged for a first-class company to support her and provided new scenery and costumes. He had studied her, he said, and decided she should have better opportunities than had fallen to her.[260] O'Neil's successes at the Tremont were bringing in good profits at last. Rankin's hectic pursuit of funds, when he played the company in the afternoons at the Tremont and in nearby towns in the evenings, was over. Moreover, Jim Williamson, visiting from Australia, stopped by to see O'Neil's performances and offered her another tour of that country.

O'Neil did two performances of Ibsen's *Lady Inger of Ostrat*, revealing another powerful aspect of her artistry when she seemed to go mad on stage. Despite O'Neil's heroic efforts, the play was not liked. For O'Neil's farewell performances of *Magda* and *Camille* at the Tremont, before she moved to the Colonial Theatre on February 22, hundreds were turned away. Audiences could not separate the actress from the characters she enacted. A commentator who had seen her in Chicago as Leah when she seemed a conventional melodramatic actress with a hoarse voice could not explain her transformation in Boston. Her Leah had become another creature, a woman of vibrant sensibility, insidiously diabolical in face and bearing, refined, in spite of occasional lapses in speech, and absolutely faithful to the dramatist's intention. Her Magda carried no suggestion of the conscious woe that Fiske and less gifted actresses created.

> In the earlier and more colloquial scenes Miss O'Neil did not once depart from an easy conversational tone, which her clear diction made perfectly intelligible. There was still to be observed the hoarseness that I had noticed in Chicago, but it had ceased to be disagreeable; at times it seemed to disappear altogether. It was a quality of voice that some people would call "haunting" and it was easily recognized as the "veiled voice" frequently found among players of Irish extraction. It is Miss O'Neil's correct use of it that keeps it from being an inadequate vehicle of speech.[261]

She did not express emotion in a refined way as a refined actress; she spoke with the broken voice of real grief "and she employed tones almost never heard in the theater, agonizing tones of human suffering."[262] Rankin could have told him the reason for the transformation, just as he had told O'Neil that enthusiastic audiences would lift her to a transcendental state of exaltation when "O'Neil would begin to really act." Her practical difficulty, the commentator added, was that she was associated with a manager, Schoeffel, who was in opposition to the syndicate; but, since the syndicate barred her from its theaters, which it kept for the inferior actresses whom it controlled, there was no other manager to whom Rankin could turn.

Matinees at the Colonial Theatre continued to bring out the Boston elite en masse to see O'Neil. Rankin presented a new play every week, including classics like *Guy Mannering*.[263] At the close of the second week at the Colonial, Schoeffel brought the company back to the Tremont rather than have them tour in New England. O'Neil continued to play four matinees a week in Boston and visited nearby towns for evening performances. Her popularity kept increasing in Boston. She revived the plays in her repertoire by popular demand throughout the month of March. On weekends the company played such places as Springfield, Waltham, and Northampton.

There was an unexpected change in the cast in mid-March. Blanche Stoddard was given two weeks' notice. Shortly thereafter, Ratcliffe was given notice. Ratcliffe tried to gain admittance to the theater to play in *Judith* but was stopped. Blanche Stoddard remarked that she, as leading woman, and Ratcliffe, as leading man, in the company "aroused feelings in the star that were not conducive to the happiness of both players."[264] What those feelings were one can imagine. The intimation is that they came from O'Neil's jealousy of their romantic attraction. O'Neil demonstrated an attachment to Ratcliffe when she supported him against Cleveland in Chicago and would not have liked his sudden attentions to her leading woman. There was a report in a Chicago newspaper over a year later, when Ratcliffe played the thief in *In the Bishop's Carriage*, that may bear on this point. Before the fall of the curtain ending the third act, Ratcliffe's character says: "I want to tell you that Nance was more to me: she was my mistress."[265] These words "set up a howl" among Chicago critics, and the theater sold out night after night as the Chicago public, more aware of the peccadilloes of their actors than was reported in the newsprint, wanted to see the play.

It is also probable that Schoeffel wanted new leading players. Ratcliffe must have been difficult to deal with at times. He was charged with violently confronting his hotel bellboy in Boston. By contrast, according to an actor in O'Neil's company, all, from curtain boy to leading man, had the warmest regard for O'Neil's unvarying kindness, patience, and gentleness: "No matter what happens to disturb the scene or mar an effect, Miss O'Neil never utters an impatient word."[266] Blanche Stoddard was too good an actor to lose, however. She joined the stock company at the Castle Square Garden in Boston and quickly became its leading actress. Later, she played *Camille* at the same time as O'Neil presented the play, thus begging comparison with a completely different interpretation.

The loss of these actors affected the company. Rankin's production of Giacommetti's *Judith*, for example, was criticized for an inadequate company and production. O'Neil was the saving grace. She was called a revelation as Judith. Her costume accentuated her height to make her "the most majestic figure on the modern stage."[267] For the rest of March, Schoeffel obtained the English star Charles Dalton as leading man, but Dalton soon decamped for the West. On April 1, O'Neil gave her farewell matinee performance at the Tremont Theatre with scenes from four plays: *Camille*, *The Jewess*, *Magda*, and *Judith*. Her success in a feat that few actresses could accomplish earned her recognition "as the most forceful, most appealing, and most convincing tragedienne known to the English-speaking stage since the days of Charlotte Cushman."[268] She displayed her extraordinary mental concentration by quickly and completely changing from one character to another with apparent ease. "This remarkable woman," wrote a critic, "seems to have the temperament of Bernhardt, the emotional intensity of Mrs Leslie Carter, the intellectual power of Duse, the art of Mrs Patrick Campbell, and the youth and beauty possessed by none of these ladies."[269]

O'Neil left on a tour of Massachusetts with immense gratitude to Bostonians. The many gifts and flowers—including a diamond ring in an apple at Easter—and her acceptance by the literati had overwhelmed her. She had also made large sums of money. After her first week, her receipts were over $40,000, and she had by now played fifteen weeks. Her success she credited to McKee Rankin, who had been her "professional father" and "the most wonderful manager in the country with the exception of David Belasco."[270] Her mention of Belasco may seem odd, but his reputation was such that she may have felt obliged to mention him. Springfield, Hartford, and Worcester welcomed her with praise, although their critics added some negative comment, calling *The Fires of St John* "elaborated dullness."

During the company's week in Providence, Rhode Island, it successfully put on *Elizabeth, Queen of England*. The magnificent stage settings, particularly of the throne scene, when Elizabeth received her officers after the fall of Cadiz, contributed to its appeal. Back in Boston, O'Neil opened at the Hollis Theatre in the same play, commencing a two-week engagement of evening performances, which meant that the men were able to see her. They were as enthusiastic and as moved as the women had been. O'Neil's sudden alteration of moods in the role was praised, but her unpleasant screaming was criticized for lacking the element of culture that a queen would have had. Her success was nonetheless acclaimed—"the simulation of her paradoxical dual-nature was a notable histrionic feat, intelligently conceived and powerfully and convincingly executed."[271] Rankin presented the tragedies in the company's repertoire and added *Macbeth* for April 24, 29, and 30.

Rankin engaged a popular Boston actor, Frank Keenan, to play Macbeth. O'Neil interpreted Lady Macbeth as she had done on the West Coast and in Australia as appealing to Macbeth by feminine magnetism rather than by forcing Macbeth to his crimes by a willpower that cannot be resisted. But now she had refined the character. Her Lady Macbeth in the early scenes was bold, resolute, fearless, and ambitious for her husband, comprehending the slow scrupulousness of his nature as only an obstacle. When Macbeth faltered in the slaying of Duncan, she despised him and showed the coldness of execution when "came the stroke of genius. From that moment she was a woman demoralizing under a strain of fear and terror until her nature lost its firmness, and its purpose shrivelled into a mere ecstasy of causeless terror," wrote Robert Sullivan, who was assisting Rankin in the stage management. With weariness and regret in her voice, her head against the wall, weeping, she sees something in Macbeth's face that terrifies her. She falters, "How now?" "It was all done by moving an exclamation point back to words," Sullivan continued. "What a little thing genius is." Lady Macbeth was now struggling against forces she could no longer control. Horror began piling on horror.

Sullivan called O'Neil's sleepwalking scene a "stupendous piece of acting." With sightless staring eyes and a voice that ranged between a whisper and the babbling of a child's rhyme to a ghastly wail, she mesmerized the audience. Backing into a wall, she awakened in hysterics. When the curtains closed, it seemed that the audience would never stop applauding. "We were afraid of her when we had to run on after that curtain," Sullivan wrote. "She was still screaming, rent by great, big, terror-stricken sobs. Then, when the people were through with making her bow, she stood quite worn and spent in the middle of the stage pitiably asking for her shoes. The poor woman had actually played that scene barefoot and was cold, tired, and worn out."[272]

The version of *Macbeth*, played in five acts and sixteen scenes, was Rankin's. His innovations, such as the gallery as a sleeping quadrangle in Macbeth's castle in the second act and the drawbridge scene in the fifth act, later adopted by Henry Irving, were kept. There were scenes of great beauty in a completeness of detail in accord with historical accuracy. Every seat was taken for the four performances in advance, and hundreds stood until the final curtain, which, given long delays between scenes on opening night, fell just before midnight. Rankin was not in the cast.

O'Neil made apparent that the old-school training was essential for the creation of classical characters. "The contemporaneous modern drama, no matter how valuable in many instances, does not invite those semi-classical methods so essential to the great poetic tragedies," suggested a critic, "and the traditions of the Shakespearean school are only preserved by rare artists whose experience runs back to another decade....O'Neil stands alone today the one woman capable of realizing the ideals of classic tragedy. Her appearance among us may almost be looked on as establishing a new era that had become so nearly obsolete, so well-nigh forgotten by, or absolutely unknown to, the present generation of theatergoers, that it may be regarded as something absolutely new."[273]

Nevertheless, it was O'Neil's *Camille* that attracted the largest crowd of the season and forced the orchestra under the stage to provide extra standing room. O'Neil's impersonation was called the most interesting, the most intelligent in conception, and the most generally convincing in execution ever given in Boston.

O'Neil's value as an actress had skyrocketed as a result of her notices, so that she was fortunate in having John Schoeffel manage her. Schoeffel, who had twenty-five years' experience as a manager, had been called "Bismarck" by Sarah Bernhardt, whom he had managed. The sobriquet had been earned by his diplomatic abilities, swift decision-making, refusal to accept defeat, and a marked personal resemblance to the German statesman. He now set out to defend himself against Charles Salisbury's injunction to turn over the profits as damages for breach of contract. It appeared that Salisbury was fronting for the syndicate, because his court action was merely a nuisance. Edward Ratcliffe's case was more serious. Ratcliffe asked the superior court to uphold his contract as leading man with O'Neil. He claimed that six actors had replaced him but none of them was of leading man caliber. He noted that he had sacrificed for the company. In Chicago he had borrowed $200 for Rankin, O'Neil, and himself and paid $50 interest on it over thirty days.

A surviving piece of notepaper from the Commonwealth Hotel in Boston reveals O'Neil's anger at Ratcliffe. "Miss O'Neil as the most important member of the proposed partnership of O'Neil, Rankin and Ratcliffe, was never consulted, and has never in any way acknowledged the right of Ratcliffe and Rankin to destroy the said document," stated a paragraph. "Therefore

Ratcliffe, in trying through lies and misrepresentations to his lawyer to enforce the validity of the conditional contract, is perpetrating a criminal fraud against her, that she will never forget or forgive, and rather than act with him again she will leave the country forever."[274] This note implies that Ratcliffe replaced the original contract of employment in the O'Neil company with another, more favorable one.

When Ratcliffe said in court that O'Neil could say anything when wrought up to a high pitch, O'Neil looked scornfully at him and muttered to herself. Ratcliffe's contract was found to be invalid, but there was hope that some out-of-court consideration might be given him for his abrupt termination.

O'Neil was beginning to find that her fame could be also a liability. On returning by train from her matinees in Boston to a cottage she had bought just outside Lowell, she had to walk a long street, which was lined with the "blue-nosed" inhabitants by the hundreds to see "that actress woman" pass. Some of their comments she found offensive, and so she gathered up her pets and maids and moved to a hotel in Boston. No doubt, she was better able to afford living in Boston as her profits increased.

Schoeffel planned to tour O'Neil through New England to Montreal, but the demand for her return to Boston was so great that he had to curtail her to one week in New England and reschedule her other dates to a later time. He and Rankin had to hold regular receptions in the foyer of the Hollis Street Theatre every evening to take the congratulations of hosts of friends on their success with O'Neil. Schoeffel claimed that he received fifty playscripts for O'Neil, which he had to read over the summer. He was planning to build a special touring rail car for O'Neil; he rejected offers of the Langtry and Bernhardt cars. O'Neil was having a touring automobile built, which was to be delivered to her after her performance in Montreal, whence she and her friends would drive through Quebec into Maine for ten days. But this also had to be postponed.

After playing at Lynn, Lawrence, and Lowell to capacity houses, the O'Neil company returned to Boston to open at the Colonial Theatre on May 9, 1904, in *Macbeth*. The rush for seats was as great as ever, but, as the week progressed, the audiences fell off somewhat, even though the production was better than that done at the Hollis. Since Rankin received more requests for *Camille* than any other play, he presented it on Thursday. The theater was packed once more and remained so for the other plays throughout the two-week engagement.

Despite being a somber, old-fashioned melodrama full of long speeches, *Judith* was the most popular play of O'Neil's farewell week. It revealed O'Neil's strengths as a tragedian better than the other plays.

O'Neil asked Thomas Bailey Aldrich, a popular Boston novelist, to write a modern version. She admired his poem "Judith and Holoferness" and hoped that he could make the story of Judith, a book in the Apocrypha, into a poetic drama. Aldrich, who had made a study of the Apocrypha, worked on the script throughout the summer.

For O'Neil's farewell performance, Bostonians chose their favorite scenes: the third act of *Camille*, the curse scene from *The Jewess*, the sleepwalking scene from *Macbeth*, the fourth act of *Judith*, and the third act of *Magda*. The largest crowd of the season turned out to see her and went frantic when, after the final curtain, a laurel wreath marked "Queen of Tragedy" was handed over the footlights.

Rather than keep her Montreal engagement, O'Neil retired with Rankin, Ricca Allen, her servants, and her collection of pets for the summer to an eighteenth-century mansion at Tyngsboro, which overlooked a bend in the Merrimac River. The mansion had twenty-two rooms, five bathrooms, numerous outbuildings, a trotting park, golf links, and trout pond. Rankin used the nearby railway to travel frequently to Boston, where he gave a dramatic course of twenty-five lectures on dramatic art and the ethics of drama during June and July.

O'Neil's dazzling success in Boston coincided with increasing prominence for several young members of the extended Rankin clan. Sidney and Gladys Drew were "emphatic hits" in Gladys's sketch, *The Yellow Dragon*, in vaudeville. The comedy was "brimful of bright lines and good comedy situations."[275] It was the start of Gladys's successful career as a playwright, which she pursued under the name of her late uncle, George Cameron. John Barrymore was playing in Clyde Fitch's new play, *Glad of It*, in which his cousin Georgie Mendum had a comedy part. Lionel Barrymore was acting in *The Other Girl*, and Ethel Barrymore was starring in *Cousin Kate*.

A surprising event took place in the Rankin family at this juncture. Lionel Barrymore, on a visit to Phyllis Rankin and her husband, Harry Davenport, at their farm in upstate New York, met the sixteen-year-old Doris Rankin. He had known her from the age of three but had not seen her in some time. They fell in love and were married. Lionel was twenty-six. Lionel, like John Barrymore, detested acting and yearned to be an artist. With a young wife to encourage him, Lionel dreamt of studying painting in Paris. Possibly his disillusionment with acting stemmed from his experience playing in the cast under James A. Herne in Herne's *Sag Harbor* in 1900. Lionel had played Frank, a selfish young sailor and the young brother to Ben Turner, played by Forrest Robinson, Mabel Bert's husband. Herne was kind in firing Lionel and blamed himself for casting Lionel "in an impossible part." His kindness deeply impressed the philosophical Lionel, who accepted the verdict with humor. Acting was the only work for which Lionel could find payment, which served to reinforce his dislike for it, a state of mind that Herne's understated judgment subtly confirmed.[276]

Lionel, of course, did play with distinction in a number of plays up through 1904, but, after starring in James Barrie's *Pantaloon* in 1905, he retired to Paris in the spring with the financial help of his sister, Ethel. His father, Maurice, died insane from syphilis in an asylum on Staten Island in March 1905, at fifty-seven, thus releasing Lionel in a sense. For twenty-five years, Maurice had been a matinee idol to New York theatergoers, and a hero as a father because of his reputation as an amateur boxer and pungent wit, but his long illness left John Drew, Jr, and McKee Rankin to take over a father's role in introducing the Barrymore children to a profession.

Lizzie Borden Interlude

The strangest minor event of the season of 1904 was O'Neil's friendship with Lizzie Borden, who had been acquitted of murdering her father and stepmother with an ax in Fall River, Massachusetts, twelve years earlier. The encounter between the shunned spinster and the glamorous actress fueled speculation among the Fall River puritans that it was a lesbian relationship. This supposition was expanded in the late twentieth century into a book and a couple of plays, reflecting a latter-day interest in same-sex relationships by a movement seeking public acceptance.[277] Lizzie Borden's biographer, Victoria Lincoln, who was from the Fall River area, considered Lizzie sentimental and sexually immature. Lizzie had had crushes on her schoolteachers, but she was not capable of a love affair, opined Lincoln.[278]

Lizzie was a short and, by this time, rather stout woman, with a sizable inheritance. She was ostracized by her community, and, whether she murdered her parents or not—and it would seem that she did—she was forced to live a circumscribed life with her older sister, Emma, as a companion. She had a curious and fun-loving spirit, however, and took pleasure in traveling to Boston to visit the theaters. When she saw O'Neil in *Macbeth*, she became entranced by her. It was suggested that Lady Macbeth's horror of blood stains on her hands affected Lizzie, but this may have been rather sensationalist speculation. Lizzie contrived to meet O'Neil at a large summer hotel frequented by the rich. She made friends with Ricca Allen first and, through her, met O'Neil.

Actors, a bohemian lot for the most part, tended not to sit in judgment on Lizzie but rather accepted her at face value and enjoyed the entertainment she offered. Lizzie threw a large party for O'Neil and her company at her home, Maplecroft, in Fall River. She had palm trees landscaped into her grounds as a romantic notion. She hired an orchestra. The grand party disgusted her sister, Emma, who disliked the free-living actors. Emma moved out the day of the party and never returned. Emma's character closely resembled the penny-pinching, Calvinist soul of her father, which had made him expendable in Lizzie's eyes.

Shortly after the party, Lizzie hired a house in Tyngsboro to be close to O'Neil for the summer and hosted week-long parties for the actors, who offered the glamour and the sophisticated fun that Lizzie yearned for and had been deprived of for years in her dour community. Doubtless Lizzie, like many ardent fans of celebrities, yearned to be close to O'Neil and experience some of her glamour in her own poor and lonely soul. Also, O'Neil had become an icon to women. She represented "the unloved woman" in the roles she played. Women's fascination with her was evident for years. Boston women had brought her fame once more because mainly women attended the matinee performances. O'Neil was aware of her appeal and was responsive to fans, but she remained reclusive and devoted to improving her art. She recognized Lizzie's devotion to her when Lizzie sat in court in support of her during the proceedings that first Salisbury and then Ratcliffe brought against her. Lizzie showered her with gifts, which O'Neil used to pay off creditors. Her subsequent cavalier treatment of Lizzie, however, showed that Lizzie's admiration was not reciprocated.

A year later, in 1905, the newspapers carried a story that Lizzie Borden was writing a play for O'Neil. Whether it was ever written is not clear; certainly O'Neil did not produce it. Some observers thought that O'Neil was using Lizzie, but Lizzie kept accounts of her loans to O'Neil. A year and a half later, she referred to them in a letter to Ricca Allen, asking for the return of the money. Allen, unaware of the loans, simply passed Lizzie's letter on to O'Neil. Allen herself was owed $225 by O'Neil and had had to pawn her rings to raise that amount; she included in her demand for repayment the sum of $50, which she had borrowed from Lizzie Borden on behalf of McKee Rankin.[279] All O'Neil's money went to Rankin. She had signed a contract in March 1898 giving Rankin power of attorney over her affairs, which meant that he decided all her business, took in all receipts, invested her moneys however he wished, kept her bank accounts, and took half of whatever she earned—a power she renewed in 1904 for ten years. It is clear that Rankin took advantage of Lizzie's infatuation with O'Neil in the same way he sought financial help from anyone, even their closest colleagues and friends, who was willing to help the cause of "art."

Rankin's most glaring fault was his penchant for borrowing money with no intention of repayment. He may have used the excuse that the rich could afford to give to the artist, which was a theme in that "art for art's sake" era, which Bernard Shaw exposed in the character of the artist Dudevant in *The Doctor's Dilemma*. Eventually, it hurt his reputation and came to affect his character.

New York City: The Big Chance

Early in September 1904, Rankin recommended changes to Thomas Aldrich for his playscript *The Tents of Asshur*, which he was writing for O'Neil. He suggested taking a scene from the second act between the spearmen and the people and beginning the play with it in a much longer version to inform the audience of the desperate situation of the besieged town. "People can live so much longer without food than without water," Rankin wrote, "that I think the poisoning of the wells and the shortness of the water should be emphasized—also the cruelty of Holofernes—all this would make a very strong scene if properly directed and acted. Then after the people are dispersed, take up your first act as it is now, beginning with Achior's speech. It will give your central figure a much better entrance because, as it is now, the audience would not be settled down to the play before Judith would be on—and that is bad for all concerned."[280] Rankin continued to suggest changes, lengthening or emphasizing certain speeches, and concluded: "I hope you will not misunderstand these practical suggestions or think for one moment that I do not thoroughly appreciate the grand work you have done in this play. Miss O'Neil and myself are delighted with it, and she is most ambitious to produce it, but we must think of the 'great unwashed,' the Public. As soon as you have made the alterations you speak of, I would like to have sketches of these scenes made to submit to you."[281] He had the costumes and scenery made from drawings taken from historical collections. Since the drama was in blank verse, a form that had lost its popularity decades ago, Rankin's concern for the public's attention seems incongruous, yet he was appealing to the Olympian poet to increase dramatic emphasis in the play. Although the verse was highly praised by critics who saw the play, the dramatic element was not strong. Its success with the public was owing to O'Neil's great acting and Rankin's staging.[282]

In the several revisions of the script of *The Tents of Asshur*, the title became *Judith of Bethulia*. Aldrich sent memoranda to O'Neil such as "Bagoas, a native of Koordistan, is not a negro, but a man of dark complection—the light mulatto tint of Booth's face in *Othello*," and "The sacred music in Act IV should not be organ music."[283] On a personal note, O'Neil announced that the falchion Judith would use to cut off

Holofernes's head had been given to her by a friend in Cairo. It had belonged to an Assyrian chief.

Schoeffel had hoped to open in Boston at the Tremont with *Judith of Bethulia* on October 10, but, the costumes not being ready, O'Neil began with *Magda*, added *Hedda Gabler*, and presented *Judith of Bethulia* from October 12. The papers commented on O'Neil's improved health in "the full flush of her young strength and genius."[284] She made a superb Judith, not only in her statuesque physique but in evincing the dread at her intended deed to save her people that she gradually surmounts by religious fervor and a fanatically inflexible purpose.[285]

Throughout the four acts and seven scenes, there appeared the supporting cast of dancing girls, Assyrian lords, soldiers of both armies, and musicians. The role of Naomie, an old woman of the people, was taken by Clara Thompson (Mrs Henry Bracy), who had played in O'Neil's company in Australia and England, and who now came to the United States at O'Neil's bidding to share in her success.

"Miss O'Neil is a young woman with a gift of genuine passionate tragedy," wrote Aldrich proudly to a New York friend, "and has a large following here....As the box office receipts were just doubled the nights she played my drama, I may claim a share in the matter. The house was packed on each occasion, even the third gallery. At the last performance, the box-office was obliged to refuse admission tickets, as there was no legal standing room left. In reading the Boston papers, one would never have suspected all this."[286]

The company toured New England in mostly one-night stands, playing only *Magda* and *The Fires of St John*, and attracting in every town large and fashionable audiences. "No player for a generation at least," wrote the Fall River critic, "has won such a personal triumph."[287] In Rockland, Maine, the town's upper four hundred or elite gave O'Neil an enthusiastic reception in a capacity house for "the event of the season." Rankin kept his own talents before the public as Marie's foster father, Brauer, in *The Fires of St John* and old Schwartze in *Magda* and worked on his roles to rid them of the appearance of an "old style" of acting. In doing so, he had to contend with his reputation as an actor who was, according to the paper in Lewiston, Maine, "famous a generation ago...[and] of profound intellectual acumen, thorough dramatic training and wide experience."

A warning shot fired by a New York newspaper a month before O'Neil's New York opening must have made Rankin apprehensive. Rankin, it said, was a millstone around O'Neil's neck, giving her nothing but years of one-night stands, miserable companies, and miserable productions. Other managers would take her on but her insistence that Rankin remain with her proved the stumbling block. "Why does she not cut the Gordian knot that ties her still a young, handsome and attractive woman to the old man who is despised even by his own family?" it asked.[288] Rankin, of course, was not despised by his family.

Schoeffel had engaged the Herald Square Theatre in New York, which had a large stage to accommodate Aldrich's play, but, through interference from the syndicate, it was no longer available. Schoeffel had to engage the smaller Daly's Theatre on Broadway at Thirtieth Street for O'Neil's much expected New York appearance. Excited and expectant, buoyed by her success in Boston, O'Neil came like a lamb to slaughter. She opened on November 21, 1904, in *Magda*, at Daly's Theatre to a corps of critics lying in wait. The attack began in the first reviews of *Magda*: "as vain and vacuous as the pampered beauties in the music hall next door and just about as dramatic. If she had been facing a photographer instead of an audience she could not have posed more"; "her delivery, although clear, is defective, both as regards flexibility and emphasis...her face does not reflect the passing shades of feeling or sentiment. Her eyes do not light up easily. As Magda she did not suggest a woman of any extraordinary capacity...her manner had not the grace, the ease, or the polish supposed to be associated with the fanciful queen of song. Her intonations were scarcely in accord with good breeding."[289]

The critics then condemned O'Neil's Hedda Gabler for misdirected energy, incompetent training, and unwarranted ambitions. By contrast, they praised Mrs Fiske's Hedda, playing half a dozen blocks away at the Manhattan Theatre. They disliked even O'Neil's stage business: "She didn't, like Mrs Fiske, leave the shooting to a marksman in the wings, but armed with a huge pistol and the nerve which brought her to Broadway, she fired a perfect fusillade in full view of the audience, and, like the leading lady of a Wild West show, rang the bell at the first crack."[290]

The two influential critics who had hailed O'Neil as the great future actress of America when she first appeared at the Murray Hill Theatre in 1896, Alan Dale of the *New York American* and Acton Davies of the *New York Evening Sun*, now panned her. "O'Neil's strenuous life on the road has changed her, in this play at least, into a pronounced barnstormer," wrote Davies.[291] After Alan Dale devoted a full-page review in his newspaper to O'Neil's acting, which can be summed up in his phrase "display of crudity, amateurishness and raw ability that seemed dazzlingly incredible," Rankin lost his temper and barred Dale and Davies from seeing O'Neil's productions.[292] Davies responded in another publication: "*The Stage* is interested in knowing what Mr. John Schoeffel, under whose management Miss O'Neil is appearing, thinks of Mr. Rankin. It would also be interesting to know just what courtesies and attention Mr. Rankin can expect to get from the *Evening Sun* or from Mr. Hearst's string of newspapers throughout the country for himself, for his star, or for anything else with which his name may evermore be connected....For just how much longer will Miss Nance O'Neil permit Mr. McKee Rankin to spoil whatever chance she may have, or even will have, as an artistic and financial feature of the American drama."[293] Davies thought that his threat to have William Randolph Hearst blackball Rankin would be enough to bring Rankin to heel.[294] O'Neil, it seemed, could do nothing right as long as she remained loyal to Rankin.

In *The Fires of St John*, O'Neil eked out a bit of praise from the *Evening Mail*, which likened her to the impressionist school of painters—"of bad art, yet of truth and beauty in the picture despite its errant trickery." This critic wondered at her being worshipped in Boston. "We in New York must feel our isolation more keenly than ever. There is a curious and inexplicable divergence in artistic sense which separates two noble communities as if by ramparts of untranslated speech."[295] The unbiased *Theater Magazine* unwittingly pointed to this divergence: "At times Miss O'Neil struck the right note of simplicity in her acting. If her performance had been free of classical influences her success would have been pronounced."[296] It was, of course, the classical drama that Rankin and O'Neil hoped to revive.

Minnie Fiske versus Nance O'Neil as Hedda Gabler in their opposing productions of Ibsen's *Hedda Gabler* in New York, November 1904.

Given the savagery of this reception, it must have been with dread that Rankin presented *Judith of Bethulia* on December 5. The play's reception was generally good, however, as exemplified by the *Evening Post,* which shied away from criticizing Aldrich. According to that paper, the play was "full of good literary workmanship, smooth, expressive, melodious, compact and admirably clear....From the literary point of view it is one of the most important contributions to the American theater made in a generation."[297] *Theater Magazine* was less impressed: "It lacks sustained interest because of dramatic defects."[298]

Although the papers attacked Rankin for his staging ("The straight crossings and 'trimming of the stage' of the old fashioned director showed his narrow limitations and made the play mechanical and totally unlike life"), they praised his acting: "Art is built up in the heart and he had art of the highest kind. He gave a death scene which made any one who has seen death grip his chair arms."[299]

Thomas Aldrich, writing to a New York friend, deplored the critics' attacks on O'Neil.

> She ran up against the Syndicate; against a clique of ill-spoken critics in the interest of Mrs Fiske, who saw a dangerous rival in the new woman; against that provincial spirit which in New York will forgive anything on earth excepting a first success in Boston—just as Chicago will praise anything New York condemns. During the last ten days or so Miss O'Neil has suffered such persecution as would have crushed any literary man I know. She has borne it all uncomplainingly, doubtless with bitter tears in secret. As I wrote to Winter, I love her for her modesty, her sincerity, and her nerve. Miss O'Neil has a hundred faults but she has genius. She is the only woman on the English speaking stage who possesses the gift of tragedy.[300]

Rankin terminated O'Neil's engagement at Daly's Theatre because Charles Dalton, who was to play Macbeth in the next production, demanded four weeks of steady preparation.[301] Dalton, who had been blasted for his acting by some critics, must have been unwilling to have his reputation shredded in such a major part as Macbeth simply because he was acting in support of O'Neil. Moreover, the audiences, affected by the adverse criticism, had stopped coming. The company took the last week of its scheduled run to lick its wounds and to rehearse *Macbeth* and other plays. The financial loss must have hurt, particularly because it occurred during the normally profitable Christmas week.

If O'Neil read her notices, she may well have fallen into despondency; everything she had learned, all her artistic instincts, all her days and nights of sacrifice for over ten years, amounted to absolute failure. Only after she closed her New York engagement did she respond to her critics. Her first concern was to please the public, she said. "By intelligent audiences I don't mean those whom the first night critic recognizes by the hundreds composed of wine agents, divorce specialists, criminal attorneys, husbands of well-known actresses, young men about town, bookmakers, gamblers and the habitués of all-night cafes. These people are, I know, the shrewdest and keenest judges of musical entertainments, but I do not admit them to be judges of tragedy." Rather, she played for those who loved the dignified and scholarly upon the stage, those who wrote to her in gratitude at variance with the critics. "They came to rend me in New York," she said.

> I was attacked like a ferocious beast of the stage, and the attack was premeditated. Long before I came here, the hostile spirit of a certain element was apparent. I do not understand it except on the ground that the seasoned old campaigners of tragedy and classical drama have adopted the methods of the astute industrial manager, and instead of meeting competition, seek to destroy it. Well, they cannot destroy me, and I have the supreme satisfaction of knowing I am on the ascending side of life's curve, while some others are on the declining.

She seemed to be taking a shot at the older Mrs Fiske. She emphasized her preference for classical drama: "I love that sense of the inevitable and of finality in fate, which breathes such a serene and splendid spirit through Greek drama. I love, too, the struggles for adequate soul expression of Hauptman, Sudermann, and Ibsen and their followers."[302]

Theater Magazine wrote that the New York criticism "has been so virulent, personally, and so shallow, critically, that persons of insight in artistic matters or of wisdom in worldly affairs, as they are manipulated behind the scenes, cannot help but see that it is not genuine or fair criticism at all, but the rotten outgrowth of a condition of things the American public is feared to be on the eve of overthrowing utterly." It was an attempt to run down O'Neil's stock and get control of her. "Her genius is neither flawless, equal to all its tasks, nor fully developed, but so beyond the common in fire and force that it threatens the emergence of more usual talents and personalities. Moreover, it promises a wide choice of plays to a drama-loving public now kept on a starvation allowance."[303] Rankin's view of the criticism was that the supporters of Minnie Fiske and Mrs Leslie Carter combined with syndicate forces to hurt O'Neil.

1905

Licking the Wounds

O'Neil's publicity in New York awakened the public to her plight. Sympathy, curiosity, and attraction for a celebrity motivated large audiences outside the city to attend her plays. On New Years' Eve, the Nance

O'Neil Company opened with *Magda* in New Rochelle, a suburb of New York City, to a full house, and the following evening 1,500 came out to see *The Jewess*. On January 4, 1905, O'Neil began touring the two plays through Massachusetts, New York State, Vermont, New Hampshire, and Maine. Her receptions were invariably large and enthusiastic, and her company was considered excellent. In Burlington, Vermont, there was standing room only for *Magda,* which the critic called "one of the most finished and enjoyable entertainments of the season."[304] Other towns called *Magda* "the best play of the season" and the O'Neil company "above criticism." Such support aside from an appreciation for O'Neil's acting, was a reaction to the hostility shown the actors in New York City. The company was grateful for the crowds.

At the same time, O'Neil's renewed confidence was shaken by a reminder of Rankin's perennial money troubles. In February, a judgment was brought against O'Neil and Rankin in New York City for the money they borrowed when they left Chicago in December. They claimed not to have received legal papers. The case was referred to the New York Supreme Court. Rankin probably invested O'Neil's money in musicals and stage plays, as he did his own. By tying it up in risky ventures, he left little for ready cash—that is, what was left over after paying their extravagant living expenses.

In Rockland, Maine, O'Neil was interviewed by the local paper, which commented that the reception for *The Jewess* was larger than for her appearance in November. O'Neil said she liked the old towns and was fascinated by the town crier. She had a thrill when she heard him calling her name, even under her window. Regardless of how fond she was of towns like Rockland, however, she was beginning to hate the one-night performances with their cold, uncomfortable hotels, poor food, late trains, and thousand other discomforts. She swore never to tour like that again and to finish with Leah after the tour because she was capable of better things. Her problem, of course, was that Schoeffel had to schedule her on such a tour because the syndicate would not let him into the good theaters in the larger cities. O'Neil was kept going by promises of a new play, *Medea,* being written for her, and thoughts of touring Australia with *Judith of Bethulia* in the spring.[305] When she took her plays to large eastern cities like Philadelphia, the local playgoers disliked them, which indicated to Rankin that he would have to find modern vehicles for O'Neil. The gap in preferences between big city and town was growing and became apparent when she played through Virginia and again in Massachusetts. The Bostonians, however, gave O'Neil a heroine's welcome and supported her with their usual enthusiasm, perhaps tinged with anger at the New York critics.

Rankin continued to play Farmer Lorenz in *The Jewess*, the elder Duval in *Camille*, Brauer in *The Fires of St John*, and Schwartze in *Magda*. O'Neil, of course, carried the heavier acting load, but Rankin had to handle the many business problems as well as direct rehearsals and worry about finances. Clara Thompson took roles in every play such as Julia Tesman in *Hedda Gabler* and Mrs Brauer in *The Fires of St John*. Ricca Allen, too, had important roles in most of the plays, some of which met with acclaim, such as the gypsy mother in *The Fires of St John* and the maiden aunt Franziska in *Magda*. O'Neil was given a farewell reception by the wife of the drama editor of the *Boston Post*, at which some of the best-known players in town were present. This was a confidence booster needed for once again facing the New York critics at their next engagement.

At the Grand Opera House on the West Side of Manhattan on April 24, 1905, the company opened with *Macbeth*. The critics were chastened. The *Clipper* wrote: "Nothing but the highest praise can be bestowed on the star and her management for the handsome staging, costuming, drilling of supernumeraries and dignity of the entire performance." [306] The unfair attacks on O'Neil had embarrassed New Yorkers and brought about a strong public reaction against her theatrical enemies and their mouthpieces in the press. The *New York Dramatic Mirror* sounded apologetically awkward: "When she has explored the resources of her art more thoroughly, Miss O'Neil will be willing to employ with more discrimination and artistic consciousness the abilities that her ambition and strenuous perseverance have brought into such prominence," and added that her efforts as Lady Macbeth and Elizabeth "gave the unmistakable impression of actual genius."[307] The *New York Times*, however, was unrepentant and called O'Neil the most striking example of a great talent gone to waste: "as crude and uninformed technically and as lacking in trained resource as were her previous efforts."[308] Rankin responded in a letter to the paper:

> Wherein is the lady "crude and uninformed technically?"...I have been on the stage for forty-four years, and I think it is generally conceded that I know something about the technique and trick of the actor's art. I have imparted all I know about the stage to Miss O'Neil. With this knowledge, backed up by an intelligence far surpassing that of any woman I have ever met, together with a most liberal education, it seems a pity not to "save so great a figure to the theater." Won't these gentlemen please tell the lady wherein she is "crude" so that it might not yet be too late?[309]

Rankin made similar remarks to a reporter for *Theater Magazine*. Rankin, "big, florid, and with little brown eyes like smouldering coals," enunciated: "Crude she is not!"[310]

The syndicate was experiencing a change in attitude towards O'Neil and now agreed with Rankin to open its theaters to her. It was a hard-headed business decision: the syndicate was in trouble. It had limited so severely the presenting of plays by foreign authors that play production was down by one-half. It had three hundred vacant theaters. Its policies left many good actors unemployed and many companies poorly staffed. For example, Mrs Patrick Campbell's company, on tour in America in Sardou's *The Sorceress*, had seventy-two roles to fill. Outside of the star, only four actors were paid well; the remainder were paid next to nothing and acted for the privilege of appearing on stage. The producing managers, forced to grant an increasing percentage of their box office receipts to the syndicate, faced bankruptcy. The syndicate partners were at one another's throats. Zimmerman and Nixon of Philadelphia were feuding with Klaw and Erlanger. Charles Frohman and Abe Erlanger hated one another—a feeling that crystallized when Frohman kept Erlanger waiting at his door for hours. The dramatic theater was declared dead by drama critics generally. Musical comedies were being forced down the throats of the public. The syndicate's attempt to produce Shakespeare's plays amounted to "a muddle of operetta, horse play and gorgeous scenery, flooded with the glare of electricity and calcium."[311] Moreover, David Belasco was doing very well as an independent, and the Shubert Brothers were breaking away from the syndicate to form an alliance with Fiske and Belasco.

The Nance O'Neil Company returned to Massachusetts satisfied with its foray into New York City and jubilant that the syndicate agreed to manage the O'Neil company after all. While the company completed the remaining one-nighters, Rankin wrote to Abe Erlanger reminding him of the suggested itinerary for the next season, which he had sent him, and hinting that he would like an early reply because he would not be in this part of the world for some months to come.[312]

Rankin was obliged to make a second tour of Australia to fulfill a contract with Jim Williamson, made when O'Neil was enjoying her popularity in Boston. Since it took place during North America's summer season, it would not interfere with the momentum that O'Neil was building in the United States, and it gave the syndicate time to arrange her American tour for the winter season. All seemed to be going better than he could have expected.

The Great Australasia Return

When the new O'Neil company set out for Australia from San Francisco on May 18, 1905, the company's luggage, including costumes and scenery, was seized while being transported from the hotel to the ship on the demand of a creditor wanting $299.99. Rankin wired Schoeffel in Boston, who wired back: "Tell the sheriff 'Hands off! All stuff my property.'" The sheriff told the creditor that he would have to file a bond, and, while the man was looking for a bondsman, the luggage was set on board, and sailed away with the company.[313]

At the last moment, Charles Dalton, O'Neil's leading man, and Charles Millward, who had become a close friend of Dalton, suddenly decided not to go to Australia. Rankin, left with only Andrew Robson and George Friend as male actors, quickly hired John Glendinning, a veteran of the English stage, to replace Dalton. Ricca Allen and Clara Thompson, who took the name Mrs Henry Bracy, by which she was well known in Australia, sailed with the company, as did Margaret Bloodgood and Jane Marbury, who joined in San Francisco.[314]

The company performed in Honolulu for one evening; stopped at Samoa, where O'Neil gave umbrellas to two little girls who caused a sensation when they walked through their village; stayed a night in Auckland, New Zealand, where it attended a theater performance; and landed on June 10 in Sydney, after a month at sea. A crowd was waiting for O'Neil on the Sydney pier to welcome her back. The company played first in Melbourne, the city that had showered O'Neil with the greatest love on her previous tour.[315] "The house was packed," reported the newspaper,

> and the audience cheered the young actress for many minutes on her first entrance, and at the end stood in their places and applauded vociferously while the curtain was repeatedly raised. At length Miss O'Neil came forward, and, evidently under the stress of strong emotion, thanked them most gratefully for the whole-heartedness of the reception they had accorded her. The impression made by Miss O'Neil was evidently a favorable one. She has, it is said, added much polish to her art of five years ago, is even more compelling of attention, and her personal magnetism and power of moving her audiences have materially increased.[316]

There may have been a sense of encouragement to O'Neil in the "avalanche of applause" from the Australians, who would have read of O'Neil's troubles in New York City. "It is simply absurd," wrote a columnist, "to deny the claims of Nance O'Neil to great genius. They assert themselves in the most positive and convincing manner, and it looks as if San Francisco is to have the glory of giving the world its greatest living actress."[317] As if in reply to the New York critics that O'Neil made Magda too hard, the Melbourne critic felt that Magda had to be reckless and imperious to constantly fight for her rights. "Nothing could be more tender, more motherly in its tolerance than O'Neil's attitude to Marie—well and girlishly played by Jane Marbury—and properly examined, it will be found that her power with the audience arises from the adroit contrast between the surface of her character, hardened by contact with pain and sorrow and injustice, and the warmly emotional nature which lies beneath."[318]

To the Australians, O'Neil seemed slighter in figure than she had been on her earlier tour but still possessed the splendor of physique so helpful in enabling her to dominate scenes, which she shook with a whirlwind of emotion. She brought a matured method to control her fresh and vigorous conception. Rankin as Colonel Schwartze represented the old military officer as more broken down by ill health: "he melts into tears at every crisis, even moans in helpless rage and weakness," wrote the critic. "Indeed, the character study has become vastly elaborated in its details, but it still remains a performance masterly in its pathos and in all those appeals to the sympathy—the senile chuckle, strange snorts and gasps, palsied hand, weird contortions of the face—which the extreme invalidism of the aged must always make."[319]

In *The Fires of St John*, O'Neil's Marie rivaled her Magda and would vibrate in the memory of Australians. As for Rankin, his portrayal of the farmer Brauer "in velveteen corduroys with pearl buttons, the ruddy face as formidably be-whiskered as that of some old walrus," was "a fine piece of acting." "Hot-tempered, good-hearted, a tyrannical 'papa' and so piously parental with his little Gertrude, Old Brauer had an unsuspecting way of wandering into some scene of secret tragedy between the lovers that was comically true to life." Most of the actors were praised for their roles, and Ricca Allen's gypsy woman won particular notice.[320] *Elizabeth, Queen of England* revived the triumph of O'Neil on her first visit; her Lady Teazle in *The School for Scandal* was as popular as formerly. Rankin appeared as Sir Peter Teazle. O'Neil won acceptance in the role of the ingenue Trilby. Although her acting was too heavy in tone to rank with the best, her success came with the spellbound powerlessness of the hypnotized victim, especially as the beautifully statuesque figure in the courtroom scene. But the honors went to her leading man, Gaston Mervale, as Svengali, whose acting as the weird and squalid Polish musician was the best he had done in Australia. He used a French accent, played the piano well, and laughed in a smooth guttural manner like oil flowing from a bottle. O'Neil and Mervale were warmly recalled.[321]

Because Jim Williamson had the rights in Australia to most plays, O'Neil prepared to appear in *Justice*, a satire upon justice as pronounced by the law, from the French; Sardou's *The Sorceress*; *Medea of Corinth*; *Judith of Bethulia*; and for the seventh and last week, Maeterlinck's poetic drama *Monna Vanna*.[322] For its closing night on August 3, the company presented Giacommetti's *Marie Antoinette*, which was staged under Rankin's direction with careful attention to detail and historical accuracy of costumes and scenery. From the second act, O'Neil developed a tragic intensity that affected the audience deeply. "Whether in the scene where Marie Antoinette faces Santerre and his wolfish sans-culottes and pleads for her children," wrote a critic, "or in the painful and final interview between Marie and her husband, O'Neil met all the requirements of the position." O'Neil maintained the same dramatic fire in the last act and held the tense interest of the audience "when the poor, half-demented Austrian, deprived of husband and children and subjected to the ribaldry of Santerre, Simon, and the armed attendants, welcomes the hour of her death and firmly mounts the scaffold." The play "plunged the spectators into the deepest depths of tearful misery." Its enthusiastic reception convinced Rankin to play it more frequently on the company's next stops.[323]

The company played Brisbane for three weeks and opened in Sydney with *Marie Antoinette* on Saturday, August 26, 1905. "The marked enthusiasm with which the production was received was an emphatic evidence of the success achieved by the star in the title role," wrote a critic.[324] But first, the audience welcomed O'Neil with such prolonged applause and with such "genuine heartiness" that O'Neil was overcome for the first few minutes. There were frequent recalls after every act, as well as continued applause, cheering, and floral tributes at the close. Although the audience did not recognize Mrs Bracy as Madame de Campan at first, it eventually gave her a cordial reception as a welcome back to Sydney.

As the company presented its plays, O'Neil's popularity became greater than on her first visit. On her fifth and last week, O'Neil gave several plays, including *Hedda Gabler* and *The Fires of St John* both for the first time in Sydney. The local critic remarked: "Nothing could have been finer than her indication of mental distress and disquietude whilst her bursts of anguish expressed all the desolation of the bereaved heart."[325] On her farewell night, O'Neil came forward as Magda and thanked the large audience for its friendship and loyalty and said she would try to visit again, at which there were loud cheers. She would always think of them with affection in their beautiful land of the Southern Cross, she said.

The company sailed for Wellington, New Zealand, to continue its tour, opening at the Wellington Opera House on October 5. It stayed for ten nights doing its repertoire, but the engagement was not the financial success anticipated by the management, although all the plays were presented in a first-class style. Rankin was corresponding with Abe Erlanger about O'Neil's upcoming tour of North America and sketched the route up to St Paul and Minneapolis to the end of March 1906.[326] From Wellington, he telegraphed Erlanger to secure *The Sorceress,* a Sardou play that Sarah Bernhardt had made famous and in which Mrs Patrick Campbell had been touring the United States. He was conscious that O'Neil badly needed good new plays, and, of course, the syndicate had control of them. After the company played at Christchurch and returned to Auckland on the North Island, Rankin steamed for San Francisco to sign contracts, sent by Erlanger, with theater managers throughout the country for O'Neil's tour.

Abe Erlanger was a short, bald-headed man. He fancied himself a boxer, and Jim Corbett, knowing this and wanting a better route for his own tour, let him win a couple of rounds. Erlanger carried a gun and surrounded himself with bodyguards, fearing some rash act by an angry actor or manager. He was personable, however, and a high-liver, traits that would have recommended him to Rankin as good company.

On arriving in San Francisco on November 14, Rankin signed a slew of contracts; through January, he continued to receive, sign, and return contracts to Klaw and Erlanger every few days. Klaw and Erlanger had fixed O'Neil's take at 70 percent. Only in the case of the theater manager at Fresno, California, did Rankin have trouble. Since O'Neil had played there before for 60 percent, the manager would pay no more. Rankin expostulated that the costs of her productions required that she make 70 percent, and finally Klaw and Erlanger had to intervene to ensure that the manager paid the fixed amount.

Rankin was concerned about getting a good theater in Boston because he expected to have three new plays ready for that city and was counting on at least four weeks of good business. On New Year's Day, 1906, he returned a signed contract for the Hollis Street Theatre in Boston scheduled for mid-May. "Many thanks for pulling it off," he wrote to Erlanger. "If it is possible will you please fill the weeks of April 30 and May 7 in the surrounding New England towns nearest Boston. Is there any chance of getting into Milwaukee the week of April 2nd? I could then use Holy Week to jump East to whatever point you put us. Wishing you a prosperous and Happy New Year, I am, Yours truly, McKee Rankin."[327] His suggestions for scheduling were detailed, and Erlanger readily obliged him. At last Rankin had brought O'Neil to the pinnacle of theatrical success. There were no more barriers; nothing stood between her and the public recognition of her genius.

O'Neil, writing from Auckland, addressed Rankin by an affectionate nickname.

> My dear Tony, I have just this moment learned that I can send you a letter by the Canadian boat rotating the mail at Sigri— and it is now half past eleven and the mail closes at twelve. I was so glad to get your letter when I got here. I was very lonely after you left but I am very busy with the manuscripts now and go for a walk each day. So the time passes quickly. We had a vile trip. Was ill on coal steamer. The performance went very well. Of course you are terribly missed. You could hardly believe yourself what a difference it makes. It was so strange for you to be out of the cast everyone felt it. I am sending the receipts to you. The company are behaving very nicely. There are a number of little things I wish I had the time to write to you about. Mr. S [Sheehan, the company manager] and Ricca are very annoying but very marked. Harold Ashton met me at the boat and we drove into town instead of waiting for the train. He has been very courteous. This Sunday Mrs. Bracy and I went for a long drive. The country is beautiful. Rob [Andrew Robson] is going today to see Cook. I wish you could be with us. I am sure you would be flattered if you knew how much everyone misses you. I am going on board the "Sonoma" today to select my cabin. I hope the voyage is good. Please forgive the scribbling letter but I am writing against time as it were. Thanks for the enclosed clippings. Please don't imagine I shall forget you for a moment. I hope all will be serene in Frisco.[328]

On its return voyage to the United States, the O'Neil company stopped over in Hawaii, where, by popular demand and in order to meet the schedule set by the departing steamer, it gave a performance at 10 AM, which was called a matinee. It arrived in San Francisco on Monday December 4. Rankin promoted her arrival in his usual grand style, declaring that O'Neil was being hailed as the greatest dramatic success ever known in Australia.

A reporter for the *San Francisco Call* met him at this time:

> He is a man with a presence; with a face of fine, plutocratic purples, majestic mustache (white), thunder, black brows—split

with three fierce white hairs, and thatched stiffly and shortly in uncompromising black and white—said thatch starting rather lowly on the brow in a funny, pompous little avenue. Power, again, lies in the enormous jowl, in the eyes, still black, still burning, and if there be those who have cast Mr. Rankin as Svengali to Nance O'Neil's Trilby, he had probably his eyes, still black, still burning, to thank. Silk-hatted, black-garbed, beringed—with a royal emerald set in silver and a lion's head in gold, Mr. Rankin greeted me the other day.[329]

Rankin discoursed on the poor acting of the present day, when young people could be plucked off the street and asked to act themselves on the stage. "Same with your little girls like Ethel Barrymore—charming personality, I grant," he said, "same with your Maxine Elliott—most beautiful woman I ever saw. But acting is another story." He then listed O'Neil's attributes. "Then, to back her skill she has genius—which I haven't." Rankin admitted that Margaret Anglin was an accomplished actress, and she had studied O'Neil's methods, even writing to thank O'Neil for what she learned watching her. He ended on a defiant note: O'Neil would return to New York City and fight it out with the critics.[330]

1906: Coming through Disaster

During the first week at the Grand Opera House in San Francisco, beginning December 11, 1905, O'Neil became the theatrical sensation of the city. *The Fires of St John* was the main topic of interest, because a San Francisco court issued an injunction against further performances.[331] According to Rankin, Charles Swickard, a singer in one of his musical enterprises, had seen the English version of Sudermann's play called *Bonfire Nights* in London and had a rough translation in manuscript. Rankin rewrote the play and called it *The Fires of St John*. When Rankin refused to hire Swickard to play a role in it because he was a singer, not an actor, Swickard sold the version to the Boston publishers John W. Luce and Company. Schoeffel arranged to pay Luce 2 percent royalties for use of the book, but recently, when Rankin replaced Schoeffel as O'Neil's manager, the publisher asked for a higher percentage. Rankin refused, and the injunction was sought.[332] The case was to pursue Rankin for some time as a nuisance factor, or "out of spite" to quote O'Neil.

The actors that the company brought from Australia appeared in her plays: Mario Majeroni and his brother, Georgio, Paul Scardon, and others. Rankin had to hire some American actors. One of them was Lawrence

Griffith, who had begun acting in 1895 but was often out of work and had to beg, ride freights, sleep in flophouses, and do "slob labor" between acting jobs. While picking hops in Ukiah, California, Griffith was recalled for a role in Los Angeles, then drifted to San Francisco, where he answered Rankin's call for actors. Rankin hired him to play Sir Francis Drake in *Elizabeth, Queen of England*.[333] Griffith's luck changed with O'Neil. Rankin was a great teacher to those willing to learn, and Griffith learned much about stagecraft and direction from him. Both he and Paul Scardon eventually put their training under Rankin to good use in the young movie industry; both would become among the best film directors in the early years of the industry. Scardon directed over two hundred films; Griffith, under his real name, David Wark Griffith, made such classics as *The Birth of a Nation* and *Orphans of the Storm*. Another of his films, *Judith of Bethulia*, clearly reflected his time spent apprenticing under Rankin in O'Neil's company.[334]

At the Christmas Day matinee, Rankin presented Maeterlinck's *Monna Vanna* for the first time in the West. It was billed as "the greatest problem play of the age."[335] Among the cast was William Horace Lingard as the secretary to the captain of the soldiery of Florence. Lingard was like a ghost from the past. This ingenious comedian, into whose company Rankin was fitted at the Theatre Comique in 1868 in the only truly comic theater he had experienced, had surfaced looking for work. Rankin did not forget his friends.

Set at the close of the fifteenth century, the play opens with a long argument over whether to fight to the death to save Pisa from Florentine forces. The heroine, Vanna, despite being married, gives herself as a lover to save her city.[336] This act caused moralists to condemn the play. Ashton Stevens, the critic, faulted the production for lacking the sensitivity and poetic distinction it required. O'Neil was not equal to the part and the play was too hastily done.[337] On the other hand, he said that O'Neil's greatness in *Macbeth*, the next production, was unquestionable. "Throughout the whole world, critics are unanimous that there is no living actress who can portray the role of Lady Macbeth with greater tragic intensity than does Nance O'Neil."[338] The public clamored for *Hedda Gabler* until O'Neil, despite the heavy load of rehearsals, agreed to play it for a special matinee. Rankin gave a massive production of *Judith of Bethulia*, with the scenery and costumes from the Boston production. During the last week, the company did *Macbeth* for two nights in succession on the very evenings that Hélène Modjeska was performing Lady Macbeth at a rival theater. The houses were packed every night, and the company had a very successful season.

Then, precipitously, Rankin left for Boston via Chicago. He had learned that Tyngsboro might be taken from O'Neil, who had bought the 146-acre estate in May 1904 from the Adamant Plaster Company for $15,000. But it now became evident that Adamant did not have a clear title to the property. A Boston resident had a mortgage on the property for $7,500 and had foreclosed in August.[339] The issue was coming to court in early February, which required Rankin's presence.

In Rankin's absence, the O'Neil company played the towns southward along the coast. A note to O'Neil from a fan in San Jose indicated the extent of her popularity: "You are so loved here in San Jose. Lots and lots of we schoolgirls are just dying to see you. Won't you please give us a 'matinee.'"[340] O'Neil had to manage the company and send the accounts on to Rankin. "This is the first time I have comprehended what business really means," she wrote from Los Angeles, "and all my responsibilities, and I can assure you that it truly made my heart ache making up the amount due some of the people who are so utterly unworthy."[341] She was beset by problems, such as the high ticket prices being asked in Oakland and what to do about them, especially as college students would be attending the theater on the final night. When Jane Marbury wanted to leave the company and go east with Ricca Allen, O'Neil tried to delay her until Rankin returned. The actress rehearsing Marbury's roles of Gertrude in *Fires* and Marie in *Magda* did not know her lines. O'Neil wired to Stockwell in Oakland to have Agnes Ranken ready to assume the roles. "Dear Tony, I miss you so much—and the responsibility under such circumstances is very great. I have tried to think of everything. My love and all good sincere wishes always. I do hope you are well and not too distressed....Isn't Ricca living up to her general conduct lately. She apparently has too much pride to think of anything I may have done for her including her sealskin coat....Lovingly, Nance." Rankin's failure to find the money to repay Ricca Allen for her loans was leading to a parting of the ways.

Since the reviews were good, O'Neil wrote that she expected receipts to improve in Los Angeles. "The power and the passion, the strength and the reserve of Miss O'Neil's playing are simply marvelous in one so young," wrote a critic. He continued in a vein already mined by so many—that O'Neil would be among the greatest actresses of the twentieth century because of her superior attributes, "above all a fine and true intellectual grasp of the character she portrays."[342] Yet some familiar negative criticism appeared in The *Los Angeles Examiner*, a Hearst newspaper, which wrote that O'Neil was unable to drop the tricks of old-time stage unreality, that she impressed one with her acting of emotion rather than real feeling: "Under the McKee Rankin 'personal direction' 'Macbeth' is melodrama.

The native force of Nance O'Neil as Lady Macbeth makes it melodrama of an exalted kind. In her white robes and flaming braids, her long, nervous arms and fingers, never still; with glaring eyes and tremulous tones, the whole actuated by a fierce and obvious potency, Nance O'Neil as Lady Macbeth takes her stand as high priestess of melodrama."[343]

During Rankin's absence Lawrence Griffith substituted in his roles. O'Neil, taken by his ability as Colonel Schwartze, henceforth gave him major roles in the other plays. Rankin rejoined the company in Oakland with the good news that O'Neil still owned Tyngsboro. The old mansion was O'Neil's pride and a token of her success. To have it taken away would have hurt her greatly. The assessor's records of 1905 show that she was co-owner of the estate, called the Brinley Farm, with a Benjamin A. Levy, whose identity is obscure. By May 1, 1906, her name was crossed out but Levy's remained.[344]

While helping to plan her American tour, Rankin was also making arrangements for O'Neil to tour Japan, China, the Strait Settlements of Southeast Asia, India, Egypt, and Europe after she concluded the present American tour. She was to take a cast of thirty-six actors, a repertoire of thirty classic plays, and six hundred tons of equipment. A steamship was chartered to leave from San Francisco, in which city O'Neil would store the costumes and scenery required for such a huge undertaking. A world tour, aside from the excitement of seeing new places that it provided, gave her relief from the opposition she encountered in America. A reporter, interviewing O'Neil in Sacramento, caught her sense of indignation at the theater world in the United States as she charged that both trust and independents wanted no rival actors to interfere with the exploitation of their own stars. The independents under Harrison Grey Fiske were as unjust to O'Neil as the syndicate once was: "That Klaw and Erlanger of the Theatrical Trust will hereafter manage this tragedienne; that after a year's tour of the Orient and India, she will again appear in New York, this time as a great Trust star—all this is not particularly to the credit of that Trust. It did not throw its doors open to this woman. She battered them down by the sheer force of her genius, combined with a pluck that nothing could discourage."[345] This championing of O'Neil, however well-meant, was certain to bring the resentment of the syndicate down upon her—not right away, but when she was weakest. The reporter, made aware of his insensitivity, sent O'Neil a note of apology.

In the Northwest and the towns en route eastward, O'Neil drew crowded houses. In Buffalo, the company added Ibsen's *Rosmersholm* to its customary productions. It had not been done in the United States, and Rankin feared that it might be badly received. The ruthlessness O'Neil showed in *Hedda Gabler*, she recreated as Rebekka West, companion to the well-meaning, retired clergyman, Rosmer, played by Griffith. During the course of the play, Rebekka confesses to having driven Rosmer's wife to commit suicide so that she could have Rosmer to herself. To atone for this act, she and Rosmer intend to jump from the same bridge from which Rosmer's wife had jumped. The verbal sparring and philosophizing were too much for the local critic, who disliked O'Neil's cold, unsympathetic portrayal of West. Rankin, and others in the company who were not in the cast, watched the play from a private box to observe its effect.[346] In Toronto, O'Neil drew poor houses because the public had a distaste for Ibsen and Sudermann. According to a Toronto critic, *Monna Vanna* was "indecent in idea and materialization," while *Rosmersholm* was full of "obscure symbolism."[347]

It was while playing in Toronto that the O'Neil company received news that rendered all else insignificant. On April 18, 1906, the San Francisco earthquake destroyed much of that city. O'Neil was playing in Rochester at the time of the quake, but, owing to the slowness of communication, the extent of the disaster reached the company only in Toronto. Although the quake had reduced many buildings to rubble, the uncontrollable fires that followed caused the greatest damage. In San Francisco, the devastation coincided with rumors that other large cities in the United States had been hit with similar disasters, and many San Franciscans believed that the world had come to an end. In the city, the actor Herschel Mayall reported seeing thousands of people on a hillside "indulge in an orgie the like of which probably has never been equaled." Pianos, harps, banjos, guitars, mandolins were played while people sang, drank, shrieked, and made merry on what they believed was their last day. When martial law was declared, the soldiers led in the plundering. They ransacked stores, abused women and children, and committed other offenses until the general in charge arrived. The soldiers forbade many thousands of alcoholics access to alcohol; this drove hundreds insane, many of whom were confined to mental asylums for years afterwards.[348] A couple of actors were killed by falling beams and many others suffered injuries, both physical and mental. Rankin had many friends in the city, but he would have been concerned most about the fate of Agnes Rankin, particularly if she were his daughter. The Alhambra Theatre, where Agnes was employed, was totally destroyed, as were all the other theaters and amusement places. She had been taking the leads in plays like *The Fatal Wedding* and had played Ophelia in *Hamlet*. Fortunately, she survived the quake, although no further reference to her acting career can be found. O'Neil pasted a Christmas greeting card undated into her scrapbook with theater reviews from 1906. The card was from "Agnes" and explained that she had been ill all year but that her thoughts were with O'Neil.[349]

Rankin and O'Neil's second concern was for their properties. About four days before the quake Rankin had shipped the equipment for *Macbeth* to San Francisco, where costumes and scenery for *Elizabeth, Queen of England, Monna Vanna, Judith of Bethulia, Lady Inger of Ostrat,* and *Peg Woffington* were stored. There was no assessment of the extent of the damage for some time; all efforts were bent towards helping the fifty thousand living in the Golden Gate Park and the many other homeless. Ricca Allen, Blanche Bates, Mrs Bates, and Margaret Anglin formed a Committee of Supplies of the California Relief Association headquartered in the Waldorf-Astoria in New York City. Already two traincar loads of clothes and supplies had been sent to the victims. All the theater companies across the continent were giving benefit performances for the survivors. Rankin canceled the engagements scheduled for Hamilton and London, Ontario, and took the company to the Montauk Theatre, Brooklyn, for a week. On the company's first night, April 30, it donated the proceeds from *Magda* to the San Francisco relief effort.[350]

Anxiously awaiting word of the fate of their properties, O'Neil and Rankin opened at the Hollis Theatre in Boston for an indefinite run. As Rebekka West in *Rosmersholm*, O'Neil appeared to one critic to be "a survival from a past generation of acting. She does not impersonate, she does not seek to project and develop a character, as the fine-fibred actresses of our time seem to do. She illustrates emotions as the players of an older day used to picture them....In fact, the subtleties and suggestion of modern psychological acting would probably baffle and weary [her audiences] as much as Miss O'Neil's forthright playing of the obvious gives them pleasure."[351] The *Boston Transcript* wrote: "Because she has no intellectual or imaginative grasp upon character, no innate or practised sense of impersonation, no faculty for subtlety, suggestion, or psychological evolution and contrast, she fails in parts like Magda, or Hedda, or Rebekka West."[352] This was not a New York critic writing, but a critic in the very city that had sung her praises. She and Rankin sensed a tide of ill fate moving towards them. They dropped *Rosmersholm* from her repertoire.[353]

The company comprised the same actors as had set out from the West Coast, which spoke of a remarkable cohesiveness and Rankin's good stewardship. *The Fires of St John* was the most popular of the plays; still being pursued by Swickard and the Boston publisher Luce, Rankin claimed that he was using a translation by Otto Von Klock, in which the characters' names were different; for example, Rankin's role of Brauer was now called Vogelreuter.

The news that all of O'Neil's equipment stored in San Francisco had been destroyed reached them at the close of their second week. The loss was in the many thousands of dollars, and it meant that the world tour had to be abandoned. Rankin hoped that the old-time thriller *Oliver Twist* would bring in badly needed funds, but the play seemed woefully old-fashioned when its blood-and-thunder style was compared to the modern version by the visiting English actor, Herbert Beerbohm-Tree, who had recently played Boston.

Rankin's happy dreams of wealth from his world tour and of the mystery and excitement such a tour would bring became a nightmare as he reflected on the money gone up in smoke. O'Neil's admirers arranged for a testimonial, at which there was a large audience. O'Neil declared bankruptcy the next day to protect certain of her interests.[354]

D.W. Griffith, having made a considerable sum for the first time in his life, left the company in Boston. He sent for his girlfriend in San Francisco to come east to marry him, which she did. The two looked for work on the New York stage and, by chance and necessity, drifted into the New York movie industry, then thought to be far inferior to the stage. According to one critic, Griffith "escaped" the theater by going into film and thereby went from "autobiographical parable to formula fiction." The film enabled him to avoid confronting his personal fears which as a stage actor he had to face when probing deep into himself. Yet he was a compulsive theatergoer, hired stage actors in his films, and created his best films from stage plays such as *Judith of Bethulia*.[355]

O'Neil had to keep the dream of traveling in the Far East alive with the hopes of new financing for it in order to sustain her spirit through her tiring one-night stands in New England and Maine. The O'Neil company won praise from the critics and attracted large houses by performing in only three plays—*Magda*, *Hedda Gabler*, and *The Fires of St John*—until it closed the season on June 8. By now, the unflappable Rankin had arranged to overcome the setback presented by the earthquake. O'Neil signed with Jackson and Reed, syndicate adherents who owned a chain of theaters in New England, to manage her company for the next three years. Ira Jackson promised to provide her with a first-rate company, new scenery, and new costumes for her plays. Jackson and Reed also bought the interests of Secor and Blair, who were to finance O'Neil's trip to the Orient. Rankin remained as overall director, but he was getting too old to be stage director. For the next season, he intended that the company play through the West and embark from San Francisco for the Orient.[356]

Rankin and O'Neil did not spend the summer at Tyngsboro because a creditor had a judgment against them for $200 for providing the estate with shrubberies. O'Neil began spending her summers in Paris. To her, Paris was like the old San Francisco. "There's a little studio I know hidden away in the heart of Paris where two clever Americans live," she said. She also rented a cottage near Giverney, where she would paint with friends, unmarried women like herself. In the meantime, Erlanger got the rights to Sardou's *The Sorceress* for O'Neil. Mrs Patrick Campbell had sprained an ankle, it was reported, and could not continue with her production of the play.

1906–1907: The Last Chance

O'Neil's new company included Martha Mayo as leading lady, and Isabel O'Madigan, among others. Both O'Madigan and Mayo went on to long careers on stage. Mayo said her experience with O'Neil, during which she played Lady Sneerwell in *The School for Scandal* and other roles, was one of her happiest. Mayo, who was like O'Neil in height, grace, and the manner of her gestures, thought the star a very great woman, whose performances as Queen Elizabeth and in the Ibsen plays were masterpieces. She credited Rankin with noticing the actors who wanted to learn and spending time and effort teaching them. "He saw that I was very ambitious," she said, "and took great pains with me and gave me many priceless pearls in the art of acting."[357]

In mid-October, in Norwich, Connecticut, Rankin first presented *The Sorceress*. Audiences packed the house and gave O'Neil many curtain calls. Said to be Sardou's best play, *The Sorceress* tells of a Moorish woman, Zoraya, played by O'Neil, and her unfortunate lover, both of whom come before the Inquisition in early-sixteenth-century Spain. It was inevitable that O'Neil would be compared to Mrs Patrick Campbell, who had been touring in the play, and to Sarah Bernhardt, for whom Sardou wrote it. "At the tribunal she has not the fine composure of Bernhardt or Mrs. Patrick Campbell," wrote a critic, "nor the suppressed emotion of either, and in the scene with the Don as she confesses to witchcraft to save him, the voices of the two at the top of their lungs suggest a wild beast's rage as the curtain goes down."[358] O'Neil's acting was indifferent and dispassionate in the first two acts but built up to a crescendo when Zoraya appeared before the Inquisition. Rankin, who played Cardinal Ximenes, "is very clever if a trifle suggestive at times of the justice shop."[359] Martha Mayo's pathetic rendering of the terrified young peasant woman, Manuela, shone forth from a cast of forty.

Management spent lavishly on scenery and costumes and succeeded in giving the atmosphere of Spain under the Inquisition. Everyone expected the play to be a moneymaker. It was the company's main presentation from then on, with *Magda* performed now and then for variety. In Montreal, a critic saw great progress in O'Neil, who had not played there since the early days of her career. Rankin was not ideal physically for the cardinal, in the critic's view, but he made his character consistent.[360] At Springfield, Illinois, the company was two hours late in performing because the scenery had been held up by a train wreck. There were 1,200 in the audience; only a few had cashed in their tickets. O'Neil came before the curtain and thanked the audience for its patience—"one of the finest compliments ever paid to an actor." For the evening performance, there was a record attendance of 2,500, with all seats sold and many patrons standing.[361]

Regardless of the critics, audiences felt compelled to see *The Sorceress*. "A voluptuous creature of great size and some beauty of face with a voice big and deep as a man's, she makes an impressive figure," wrote a critic. She was a fleshy sorceress, dressed in robes of barbarous splendor "and rather more arm and shoulder exposure than is absolutely necessary to accentuate the barbarian age."[362]

The company headed back to New England still pleasing large audiences, generally playing *The Sorceress*, and adding *Magda* for matinees and second nights. By New Year's Day 1907, the company was playing in Lowell, Massachusetts, the birthplace of O'Neil's father, the very man whose controlling conduct at home had given birth to the rebel woman, whom O'Neil had been portraying on stage for years now. After touring Maine, the O'Neil company cut west through New York, Ohio, Illinois, and Kentucky on its way to the West Coast to go on its long-awaited trip to India, China, and Japan. The audiences were large and reportedly pleased, but the productions were expensive, and Jackson and Reed left the company a small amount to cover operating expenses. The managers replaced actors who left the company with poor actors, a sign that they were getting ready to abandon it.

Because the company carried the equipment for just two plays, it had to present both plays twice on stands longer than two nights. This may have affected box office receipts. In February 1907, in Kansas City, Missouri, the company had its scenery attached when Rankin could not pay $150 to the theater.[363] Jackson and Reed wired the money to Rankin and advised him to close the company. Aside from breaking their contract, the managers were backing away from their promise to finance a tour to the Orient. Where had all the profits gone?

O'Neil, disappointed once again, relied on Rankin's ingenuity and fighting spirit. He persuaded two local investors to study the accounts, travel to Denver with the company, and finance it for the rest of its route to San Francisco. In Salt Lake City, a critic remarked, "it is little short of professional criminality to surround an artist of the attainments of Miss O'Neil with a company of such manifest incompetence."[364] Jackson and Reed had not been putting money back into the production and had hired actors on the cheap in order to pocket more profit. Rankin had to accept whatever he could get to keep the company solvent and moving. "McKee Rankin, on whom the infirmities of age have swiftly stolen the past few years," wrote a critic, "came near being himself several times last night in the role of Col. Schwartze, which he has ever played as no other actor. In that he is still wonderfully effective in spots. But it is evident that the day cannot be far distant when even the 'spots' will have to be eliminated."[365] Another critic referred to him as "the sturdy old wheel-horse of the dramatic West."[366]

The harshness of winter touring, rising early to catch trains from cold and drafty stations, and looking after the problems of a very large cast with the added difficulty of having to train novices and amateurs to do their roles as well as they possibly could, had taken a toll on Rankin. He had great staying power and will, but the forces against him for so long a time were getting the better of him. His determination had affected O'Neil. "All I desire is to command serious attention," she told a reporter. "What I hope to do I cannot tell to you. I cannot even talk about it. I shall only keep on working and I shall never give up."[367]

The company entrained for San Francisco, where it played *The Sorceress* for two weeks from March 5, 1907. Then, abandoning the remainder of its scheduled stops northward, it disbanded. Very low on funds when entering San Francisco—"in a chronic state of bust," to use Rankin's description of himself—Rankin and O'Neil seemed to have reached their nadir. Suddenly, to quote Rankin's favorite Dickens character, Harold Skimpole, "something turned up." To cover the nonpayment of taxes on Tyngsboro, two Boston lawyers were preparing to sell off two lots from the estate, the best spots on the Merrimac River, and, having lost in court to a creditor over the bushes he had supplied to Tyngsboro, Rankin and O'Neil were actually able to pay him.[368] Their sudden solvency came from Charles Dillingham, a theatrical manager allied to the syndicate. Dillingham had contracted with Mrs Leslie Carter to play the starring role in a new play, *Cleo*, which was adapted from the same source used for *L'Article 47*, in which Rankin had played opposite Clara Morris in 1875. The playwright brought an injunction against Dillingham and Carter, who had changed the script in ways he disapproved, and the court upheld his challenge. Carter then quarreled with Dillingham over the new play, all of which prompted Dillingham to look for another strong emotional actress. Nance O'Neil was the only other actress who could play the role. A critic, who called O'Neil "theatric combustion incarnate," warned that the play represented O'Neil's last chance for her artistic life.[369] She desperately needed a good play and financial backing to get out of the endless touring rut, which accounted for her readiness to take on a work that had been a matter of contention in the courts. Moreover, Rankin was given the role of General Bouligney, in which he was required only for the first act, and O'Neil was able to bring her old companion Clara Thompson Bracy into the cast. The sensationalism of the original play had been refashioned to suit the modern taste for the milder, sophisticated style.

Rankin and O'Neil left immediately for New York City to begin rehearsals. After three weeks, the play opened in Atlantic City on April 18. O'Neil was reported to have made a profound impression as Cleo, and Dillingham predicted it would be one of the most successful productions of the year. When the company opened in Boston on April 22, however, the play was condemned by some as clumsy and obtuse. O'Neil had splendid seconds but bad quarter-hours in a role given ridiculously high-flown, long-winded, and unnatural speeches. "It was not her fault that she failed," wrote a critic.[370] Nevertheless, her last chance to come into Broadway triumphant in a big role seemed lost. *Cleo* closed "temporarily" on May 2 with the verdict of "mock heroics with slow music" as an epitaph.[371]

Undaunted, and still depending on Rankin's indomitable optimism, O'Neil, who said that she could have been crushed a thousand times if it were not for Rankin, joined the Henry Bishop Players at Ye Liberty Playhouse in Oakland, California. Bishop had started the stock company in 1904 and followed a policy of a new play every week, which he maintained for eleven years. Ye Liberty Playhouse resumed operations a month after the earthquake and, being the one theater available for entertainment, was filled to capacity with those wanting comic diversion. Henry Bishop, quiet and mild-mannered, was an opponent of the Theater Trust. He reinvested his profits in his theater and seemed ready to risk everything for good drama. Because his theater seated 2,000 and he refused to advertise in the papers, it was impossible to fill it nine times a week. Eventually, it lost money. By 1909, it was costing $10,000 a month to operate.[372]

O'Neil opened a six-week season on May 20, 1907, in *Magda*. All the productions were under "the personal direction" of Rankin. In the second week, O'Neil played *The Sorceress* and followed it on successive weeks with the other plays in her repertoire. By the fourth week, audiences began to fall off, and the admission price was lowered to $1, at which it stayed for years. The large number of performances demanded from O'Neil in these emotional roles exhausted her. Possibly also with a sense of despair, she went directly to her retreat at Tyngsboro in July. She refused to go to Portland, Oregon, in early September to begin touring in Charles Dillingham's production of Pinero's *His House in Order*, without more rest. Andrew Robson, however, accepted a role in the play and left the O'Neil company.

O'Neil spent a restful summer at Tyngsboro with her friend Edna Snell and her menagerie of pets. Rankin still lived with her and ran her business interests, although he must have doubted at times his usefulness when he saw his grandiose plans destroyed by fate and when he delivered her into the hands of unscrupulous managers. He used the summer to reassess the ways in which they could climb out of the pit in which they found themselves. One way was to write a play.

1907–1908: Vaudeville—Where the Money Is

To relieve O'Neil from the exhausting work of full-length tragedies and yet make an income, Rankin adapted a one-act play from *The Jewess*. It required five actors: O'Neil as Leah, Rankin as Farmer Lorenz, Clara Bracy as Dame Von Groetchen, Dallas Anderson as the romantic lover Joseph, and Edna Snell as Lena. Robert Grau and William Lykens, theatrical agents, who booked a tour in the Keith and Proctor theaters in vaudeville, took 5 percent of O'Neil's weekly earnings of $1,200 to $1,500; another 5 percent was taken by the United Booking Office.[373] Beginning at the Grand Theatre in Pittsburgh for a week in late September 1907, the playlet became instantly popular, owing to O'Neil's "enthralling magnetism."[374] Rankin appeared only for a moment in the introductory lines of the sketch, but, according to a reviewer, he was theoretically onstage the whole time as the words used were his own.

O'Neil mentioned the continuing presence of Clara Bracy in her company when she told a reporter: "Isn't it a strange coincidence that Miss Clara Bracy, who played with us in Australia the last time we were there, was brought over by Mr. Dillingham for my starting engagement under him [meaning *Cleo*], and now that we have temporarily abandoned that, Miss Bracy is with me in this little Broadway offering."[375] Bracy had been with O'Neil since her first world tour. Why should O'Neil seek to conceal this fact? O'Neil needed a confidante, an older woman, to offer her advice and emotional support. O'Neil's emotional temperament was subject to breakdown, which was a good reason for Rankin's constant companionship, and he must have recognized that she needed a woman who could be a steadying influence. Her enemies, of course, leveled accusations of lesbianism against her, and this may have put her on the defensive concerning Bracy.[376]

By mid-October, the group had a two-week stint in Boston vaudeville. A critic wrote: "That they (the audience) seemed to want it (this tragic sort of stuff) was evidenced in the enthusiasm displayed yesterday at the close of the sketch."[377] As the group worked their way through the Orpheum Theatre Circuit westward, O'Neil suffered sudden fatigue, both physical and emotional. She disappeared on her way to Los Angeles. After five days, the managers of the Orpheum Syndicate worriedly offered a reward to anyone who could find her. It developed that Rankin had come from the north with her to Paso Robles Hot Springs, north of Los Angeles, where O'Neil rested.[378]

The preceding year, O'Neil had expressed her dissatisfaction with playing *The Jewess*: she thought she was capable of better things. How much worse must it have been playing a sketch from the play sandwiched between vaudeville acts! O'Neil must have reached a crisis point in her life where the criticisms of Rankin's management of her career began to pierce the rosy delusion she had created as protection. The long hours of rehearsals, constant travel, and intense dedication to her art, to the deprivation of friendships and even love in her life, sometimes brought her to despair. Years later, she admitted that she often wished she had not become an actress because it was such hard work. "The public little realizes the long hours of rehearsing, of studying, of trying on clothes, buying shoes, having pictures made," she said. "All that glitters isn't gold, and even the brightest career must have hours of despondency."[379] If all that hard work appeared to be taking her in the wrong direction or no place at all, how much greater was her despondency! Yet it was clear to all that Rankin had her interests at heart and was her best promoter. A reporter meeting him at this time said that he was a big chap with the manners of old-time chivalry that had the effect of making women quite content and happy when he was around.

When O'Neil appeared in *The Jewess* sketch in Los Angeles in mid-December, she feared tittering from the "Gods" or gallery, but she played the part so sincerely that she was a success. A signal honor boosted her confidence by recognizing her excellence in classical drama. She was asked to perform as Parthenia in *Ingomar* at the Greek Theatre at the university at Berkeley in December. Only two other actresses had been so honored: Bernhardt in Racine's *Phedra* and Maude Adams in Rostand's *L'Aiglon*.

As she was regaining her confidence, a New York magazine, *Vanity Fair*, aimed a blow at her and gratuitously added seven years to Rankin's age:

> Mrs. McKee Rankin, a splendid artiste and a wife and mother of the finest fibre, has been compelled to take a benefit, and Nance O'Neil is to become a "star" again in the near future. Doesn't that sort of thing appeal to your sense of humor? Or does it simply enrage and disgust you?...If ever a woman has

earned a crown of immortality by clean living, self-sacrifice, self-abnegation and silent suffering, it is this latest recipient of loving regard. Mr. McKee Rankin, did you ask? Oh, he is still hiking around the country with Nance O'Neil whose admiration is not lessened by the fact that he is grizzled and paunchy and nearly seventy."[380]

Kate Blanchard's testimonial at the Broadway Theatre on December 12, 1907, was organized by a number of prominent actors, including Ethel Barrymore. An afternoon of performance from various stars, ranging from Nazimova to Victor Herbert, raised $7,500 for Blanchard, who, it appeared, would never be able to act again.[381]

In mid-February 1908, when the O'Neil group reached Chicago, O'Neil was hailed as an actress of uncommon ability and of a robustness of figure and voice in keeping with the spirit of the ideal tragedian. She "created a highly favorable impression, despite the glaring faults of the vehicle which McKee Rankin has provided for her plunge into the domain of tabloid drama," wrote a critic. He added that O'Neil was destined to become a tragedian of unusual power with her beauty, magnetism, and experience, "once she cuts loose from the Rankin apron strings which now are weighting her down and impeding her progress to ultimate fame." He described Rankin's Farmer Lorenz as "the merest phantom of the Rankin of thirty years ago when he was a matinee idol. His voice was hoarse and his lines scarcely audible."[382] At Cleveland, the group played a scene from *Macbeth*, upon which a reporter commented: "She was sandwiched in between an English music hall player—an amusing little cuss—and two negro comedians. The atmosphere was frivolous, if not foolish. Yet she hadn't been on the stage for a moment before she gripped the audience. She made it appreciate the solemnity of the occasion, she made it realize the agony, the remorse, that sent Lady Macbeth to public confession of her crime. The people sat spellbound. They never released their tenseness of interest till the curtain fell, and then they broke into vociferous applause."[383]

Rankin kept O'Neil going with the hope of doing a great modern drama. It was in her words "a gem. I feel confident of its success." The play was *Agnes*, written by Gladys Drew under the pseudonym George Cameron. Rankin and Sidney Drew were "whipping it into shape." "I am counting very much on this new play of mine, 'Agnes,'" she said. "It's so simple and so strong. A modern emotional play that deals with elemental things in a big elemental way."[384]

When the group, reduced to four, reached New York City in March, O'Neil still hypnotized the audience in breathless attention as she enacted a scene from *The Jewess*, where Leah witnesses the wedding of the man who had cast her off for another woman.[385] After two weeks, the troupe set out touring the vaudeville houses to the west again.

Still attacking Rankin, the press lamented the artistic passing of O'Neil. It blamed

> her mistaken loyalty to the hoary-headed old Svengali, who hypnotized her in her fresh young days....Several of the best managers in America have been willing to take Nance O'Neil in hand and try to do something for her, but they could not stand for Rankin, whose protested notes, unsatisfied judgments and dishonored obligations would paper the new tunnel from Battery Park to Brooklyn City Hall. One whose moral sense is wholly blunted does not appeal commercially as a valuable asset when managers are taking stock of a woman star.[386]

O'Neil, constantly touring cross country in vaudeville and dreaming of the one great play that could bring her back to the legitimate theater, must have read this criticism and winced at its possible truth yet deeply sympathized with Rankin, who, like the fat boy at school, endured these barbs. Should she have wanted to break free of Rankin, she had to be certain that some other manager really wanted her. She had experienced only his guidance and control for many years, which, as her critics said, kept her emotionally tied to him. Yet no matter how sincerely she assured Rankin of her devotion to him, a part of her mind must have been looking for a way to free herself.

In mid-May 1908, O'Neil returned to Ye Liberty Playhouse in Oakland, California, and performed plays from her repertoire for seven weeks.[387] Rankin took his usual roles in these plays and directed the actors. In mid-June, the company presented Gladys Drew's *Agnes* for the first time.

Gladys Drew was developing into quite a playwright. The prediction by a critic, after seeing the Sidney Drews in *That Girl from Mexico* in 1892, that "the Drews will succeed anywhere," appeared to be correct. Gladys discovered that she was a good comedy writer for the stage, and, together with Sidney, she acted many of her sketches in vaudeville. They traveled widely, including to Australia, where they had a series of triumphs. While in London, England, at the Tivoli Theatre, they became great favorites and were noted for revolutionizing the method of playing sketches in music halls.

Her play *Agnes* challenged O'Neil to develop the character of a modern woman. Urged on by a selfish, designing mother, Agnes Belgradin marries a man of wealth whom she hates. Three days into their honeymoon, their yacht is struck by an ocean liner and the rich husband, Geoffrey, apparently drowns despite Agnes's attempt to save him. Two months later, Agnes chances upon the letters she had written before her marriage to the man she really loved and his replies, which she had not seen, in her mother's old trunk. Realizing the perfidy of her mother, Agnes is interrupted by the visit of her true love and they are reunited. Five years later, with a child and her husband, now a famous brain surgeon, Agnes is confronted by the return of Geoffrey, who, rescued by French fishermen, has lost his memory of what went before the collision and cannot recognize her. Geoffrey wants her husband, the specialist, to cure him. Agnes wrestles with the problem confronting her if the operation is successful. Geoffrey dies on the operating table, thus eliminating her problem.

Reflecting on O'Neil's great emotional power, a critic considered the play well adapted to her talents. "Her acting is marked by a restraint, as a rule, which makes it the more forceful," he wrote. The play was called an "unmistakable success."[388] Rankin immediately commissioned E.E. Rice to secure a New York engagement. Rice was the manager of the 1870s who combined the form and pattern of old English burlesque with the talent and originality of comic opera to try to stem the frankly sexual exhibitions that were vulgarizing the theater. The 1880s and 1890s were not receptive to delicate parody or airy fantasy, and Rice fell victim to the brash, nude spectacles set up by inelegant dancers and posturing chorines. He knew the theater world well, however, and may have been a business party through the years to Rankin's musical productions, to which only allusions have been made.[389]

The O'Neil company opened in Los Angeles with a new cast to a crowded house in *Magda* in July and continued to San Francisco for a three-week engagement at the American Theatre, where L.R. Stockwell, who had become deaf and no longer able to act, was co-manager.[390] They also presented *The Sorceress*, which had thirty-one speaking parts. Its many supers had to be moved about the stage as soldiers or in crowds of citizens. After over three decades of directing huge casts, Rankin was so experienced that it had become second nature to him. That he no longer filled the demanding role of the cardinal in addition to directing and managing may be forgiven him—he was now sixty-five years old. Rankin reduced the company for its brief western tour, keeping only *Magda* and *Fires* in its repertoire.

A young man, recently graduated from the University of California, found his first job as a show manager for O'Neil at this time and recalled reaching the theater in Virginia City, then a city of 40,000 people, which had standing room only for *Magda*. The audience, wild with enthusiasm, gave O'Neil eight curtain calls. The young manager went behind the scenes to Rankin who, he thought, had played a great death scene. "It is you the audience is applauding. They want you to take a bow," he said. Rankin sighed: "Miss O'Neil is young. She enjoys applause. I am too old. I don't care anymore."[391]

1908: *Agnes* and the Shubert Imbroglio

It was a tired Rankin and an expectant O'Neil who came to New York City in September 1908 to hire a cast for the East Coast production of *Agnes*. To finance the play Rankin probably used the money he had gained from the recent sale of the Tyngsboro estate. By choosing actors of some acclaim in the city, he hoped to win the favor of New York critics and audiences. Adeline Wheatcroft came out of retirement to play the avaricious mother; Cuyler Hastings, as the husband, and Robert Drouet, as the brain surgeon, were prominent on the New York stage; Winifred Voorhees was known for her comedy work; Herbert Fortier had a minor role. It was a big gamble.

Like a bothersome fly, Swickard and the Luce publishing company, which had been granted an indictment by a San Francisco court, had Rankin and O'Neil arrested in New York City for infringing the copyright of *The Fires of St John* because Rankin supposedly planned to present the play in New York in October. Rankin insisted that there was no copyright in America on the play. His daughter Phyllis came up with the $1,000 bail, allowing the company to proceed to Lowell, Massachusetts.[392]

At first, *Agnes* was well received, but, when it came to New York City, the play got mixed reviews. One critic called it a strong drama—"a real theater play, filled to the brim with acting, emotion, soul harrowing situations, unexpected denouements and all the other features of the true and tried drama."[393] Another saw it as "trash...a lurid melodrama of the cheapest sort."[394] Still another wrote, "A well-balanced cast failed to raise the play above mediocrity" and added that O'Neil "lacks the force of intellectuality. Her efforts are inspired by feeling and not by understanding. Mrs Fiske, our greatest emotional actress, is an example of the purely intellectual endowment triumphant over every other capability."[395] This charge of lack of intellect was the new weapon in the hands of the independent producers. The *New York World* deplored O'Neil's waste of talent, which it attributed to the "grossest mismanagement....It may not be too late, even now, for Miss O'Neil to be aroused to a realization of her mistakes and to redeem herself in a profession, which she ought to adorn."[396]

This persistent insistence that Rankin was ruining O'Neil could no longer be attributed just to the agenda of the syndicate; Rankin's reputation for avoiding paying his debts and for a growing carelessness in conducting his companies as he became weakened by alcohol and the lack of challenge of vaudeville seemed to substantiate the allegations. Although he was aware of his decline, he was mentally unable to overcome his addiction and reform himself, and he refused to recognize the effect he was having on O'Neil's career, not least because she was his meal ticket. It was ironic that the man who had fought hard against commercialization and for good drama for the people was unable to see that his careless attitude to other people's money had coarsened him as surely as the new entrepreneur had coarsened the theater. Yet, in his favor, there is no question that his enemies used the threat of imprisonment for debt to harass him and that some of the charges against him were exaggerated, unscrupulous, and motivated by competitors. There is also no question that for much of the time throughout his career he was insolvent, but the theater was his life, and he could create it only through his own will and energy. He relied on financial backers and had to accept the bills when those backers deserted him. The accumulation of pressures, both artistic and financial, and his physical degeneration, of which critics often reminded him, wore him down as he entered late middle age and suffered the consequent self-doubts and depressions.

Rankin's difficulties were exemplified by the Shuberts' approach to the New York production of *Agnes*. The Shuberts had contracted the play for a six-week engagement in New York, backed out and left Rankin to produce it, then stepped back in when it seemed to be a success and when Rankin was in need of financing to continue. They signed O'Neil to a five-year contract and allowed Rankin to remain as stage manager. When the New York engagement closed after two weeks and went on tour, they made Rankin bear the expenses of the week in Washington, DC, and replaced the leading men with actors at less salary. The brothers' objective was to squeeze as much mileage out of the company at the least cost.[397] Rankin's subsequent dealings with the Shubert brothers demonstrated the manipulative instincts of theater managers, against which acting companies were as powerless as victims. The Shuberts approved of E.E. Rice's program for selling tickets and directed him to sell 3,000 tickets to schools in Pittsburgh, the next stop. But when Rice suggested that they get a great play in rehearsal as soon as possible because, while *Agnes* was good, it was a waste of time for so fine an *artiste*, the Shuberts sent an experienced manager, Victor Harmon, to manage the company from its last day in Washington. They refused to pay Rice's salary in Washington after Harmon took over, and, fearing that Rice had Rankin's welfare at heart, they sent him to the towns ahead.[398] Rice, at least, was able to fix O'Neil's salary at $250 per week and Rankin's at $100 per week. O'Neil was to have an interest in the profits and was to be handled as a star and furnished with a stateroom or parlor-car seats and a maid. The Shuberts told Harmon to ignore all bills prior to October 26, the date the company opened in Pittsburgh. They instructed Harmon to pressure the actors to take smaller salaries, although Rankin had already agreed to their salaries. "We want to make money, but we will not if any leakages occur," J.W. Jacobs, general manager for the Shuberts, wrote. "All salaries should be chopped by $10."[399]

Having suffered heavy losses the past four weeks, to raise the money to pay his debts Rankin offered to sell the Shuberts all his theatrical properties and costumes for the plays in which O'Neil appeared. Rice advised the Shuberts to pay Rankin $1,000 as a loan, adjusted when they bought the scenery to his plays. Otherwise, Rankin was unable to pay salaries in full and deliver the company over to Harmon clear of debts. If he could not pay his actors, the negative rumors would hurt the star and the organization.[400] The Shuberts, again divining that Rice was too sympathetic to Rankin for their purposes, terminated him and henceforth depended on Victor Harmon, whose reports to the New York office provide a graphic picture of this tour. Before the Shuberts' instructions not to advance money to Rankin reached him, Harmon lent Rankin and O'Neil the money to pay their hotel bills and clear Washington. Lee Shubert, who lent Rankin $250 over the telephone, instructed Harmon to take the money out of O'Neil and Rankin's salaries. J.W. Jacobs telegrammed to Harmon, "I know very well the kind of people you are forced to deal with."[401]

Harmon successfully pressured three actors to take a reduction in salary, but four were stalling and one refused. He complained that it was more difficult to get salary reductions on the road than it was in New York because once on the road the actors got independent. He fired one actor and doubled another in his role, saving $50. One actor would not take a cut as she carried a maid or hired one in each town and already worked for $25 less than usual. When the Shuberts wanted the cast to take half-salary for the week before the federal election, Harmon feared "a howl." Because the cast would see that fewer people attended the theater during election period, Harmon should have no difficulty in reducing salaries, the Shuberts thought, but, the next day, they advised him not to press the half-salary too hard as it was the first time that O'Neil's actors had been on contract. "If they do it willingly, all well and good." The following day, they contradicted themselves and insisted that Harmon press all the actors, except Rankin and O'Neil, to go on half-salary.[402]

Harmon complained that one of the new actors had a bad stomach and was getting worse. He was in pain all the time and in debt. Rankin gave him $60 for clothes. When Harmon replaced him, he had to advance money to the replacement. The company's sinking fund of $3,000 established by the Shuberts was dwindling rapidly. In addition, the new advance man, replacing Rice, tried to get money from Rankin for the advance man's sleeper from New York to Pittsburgh. Rankin paid in protest.

In Wheeling, West Virginia, the receipts for the first night were $79. "It does beat anything I have ever known, and is enough to make a man ill," wrote Harmon. "It almost seems as if it was impossible for any attraction to play to such a business—but if you could have been here and seen the excitement on the streets you would have wondered at it....I do sincerely hope that this bad business will end in the near future."[403] The Shuberts replied that Harmon could "paper" the house a little—that is, give out some free passes—but not to keep it up.

Harmon prevailed on everyone but three in the company to take half-salary for election week. He considered Clara Bracy, Paul Scardon, and Herbert Fortier replaceable because they refused to take salary cuts and used their "old crony" relationships with O'Neil to stand firm.

The scenery for *The Fires of St John* arrived in Philadelphia with doors missing and the rusty ceiling rotting away. Rather than bring the company to New York City, the Shuberts changed the company's route to follow the *Gay White Way*, a popular musical revue by Ludwig Englander, but, refusing to hire the two railway cars required to carry the actors and scenery to Kansas City, they left the scenery behind in Philadelphia so as to take one car and save the cost of twenty-five extra tickets. To pay the hotel bills in Philadelphia, the Shuberts sent Rankin a week's advance salary ($350) for O'Neil and himself, which they would pay back at $100 a week. When the check went to the wrong person and came to Rankin three hours late, Rankin was "wild and insulting."[404]

Hearing that his old companion De Wolf Hopper, a musical comedian, would soon be taking a company on the road, Harmon declared his stay with O'Neil to be temporary and waited impatiently to manage the Hopper company. His attitude to the O'Neil company grew more severe. He reported that Rankin did not know his lines or where he was at. He was so fat that he could not act for he could hardly move. "His voice is so covered with fat and whisky he is not intelligible. He's been drinking, but, as he is a great patron of liquor at most times, it is strange that even this would make him so bad," he wrote. "This proposition is hopeless. I don't think this combination could make a dollar. Mr. Rankin is over his usefulness and reliability and I think Miss O'Neil is past hers too."[405]

By refusing to pay a salary to O'Neil's maid, the Shuberts had made Rankin and O'Neil "savage" to Harmon. "I am polite in transactions but firm when bulldozed," Harmon wrote. "Mr. Rankin tried to get me on his staff so that I would be his minion and if he wanted it, to work against the interests of those who employ me."[406] When Rankin and O'Neil tried to impress him with their importance, he considered them "first and last the Champion long distance, short distance, and for all time 'Kickers' that I have ever known in the thirty years I have been in the business, and it has become a nasty, disagreeable proposition, an absolutely unbusinesslike proposition."[407] Rankin was hardly ever onstage during a performance and spent his time at the neighboring saloon "getting tanked up until it is time to take her home." Rehearsals were halfhearted and lax. Rankin reportedly said to the properties man as he cuffed the scenery with his foot, "To hell with Harmon, that cheap skate!" To which Harmon made the comment: "If Rankin abuses me to my face, I won't stand for it for a minute. I won't stand for abuse from a man who is four-flushing and has nothing to say about the business of the Company."[408] Harmon advised the Shuberts to do no more plays with Rankin as stage manager because he was down and out, without energy, could no longer play a part with effect, and could not take many one-night stands.

From the foregoing, it is clear that Rankin and the company thought that Harmon had brought these draconian measures into the company and that the Shuberts were unaware of what was happening. This was what the Shuberts wanted. A final paragraph in Harmon's letter, however, reveals an uneasiness on Harmon's part that he may have overstepped his bounds. A railway man, an old friend of Rankin's, had become "abusive," according to Harmon, when told to leave the pass Rankin had given him to be approved by Harmon. This challenge to Rankin's authority, which, in effect, was a humiliation, infuriated Rankin and O'Neil. Undoubtedly, it was out of fear of what Rankin would say to the Shuberts that caused Harmon to write his damning report on him. Harmon closed his letter with the news that he got all the properties on one railcar.

O'Neil had wired the Shuberts for money to buy costumes because there were none outside of those for *Agnes* and *Fires*. The Shuberts thought the expense would be $350, but, when it rose to $600, they instructed Harmon to present only *Agnes* and *Fires* and abandon *Magda* and *Hedda Gabler*. Business for *Agnes* was absurdly poor—"discouraging."[409]

Rankin had been reacting to the pressures from the head office by showing his displeasure personally to Harmon, but, faced with the cancellation of two plays, he now was trying to be friendly. "He is trying to square himself for his past nasty manner to me and all the Company,"

Harmon wrote. "His breath was not of the nature of a 'violet' either."[410] O'Neil quarreled with Rankin as she had heard complaints from the company through her close friends Clara Bracy and Peg Bloodgood: reductions in salary, after signing contracts with Rankin promising a particular salary; refusal to purchase costumes; the canceling of half the repertoire, which endangered the very jobs of the actors because there were fewer roles to play; all these grievances were directed at Rankin, who was powerless to correct them. Rankin, in a fit of concern, planned to travel to New York City to complain to the Shuberts, but thought better of that idea. Rankin knew his vulnerability but pretended to the company, and particularly to O'Neil, that he was still in charge. Harmon called it "four-flushing."

The Shuberts informed Harmon in no uncertain terms that he was their man and need fear nothing from O'Neil and Rankin. If Rankin left the company, Harmon was to deduct the time from his salary. If he came to New York, that would be the end of him. Rankin and O'Neil worked under contract and had no rights. "If you want to break their contract, I don't mind," wrote J.W. Jacobs, the Shuberts' manager of the New York office. "Collect all outstanding so if crash comes we will be protected."[411]

Harmon began to weigh in against Clara Bracy, calling her a "troublemaker," "a bad influence on O'Neil," and "the institutor of many of the Kicks." By "Kicks" Harmon meant objections to his cutbacks in the company. Harmon claimed that Rankin agreed that the company could do without Bracy and save $50 a week by having Peg Bloodgood take over Bracy's part as the mother in *Agnes*. Rankin thought Bracy was influencing O'Neil against him. The Shuberts fired Bracy and regretted that they had to pay Bracy's train fare back to New York City as called for in her contract. Next, Harmon suggested cutting Herbert Fortier because he was just Rankin's understudy in *Fires* and his role in *Agnes* could be taken by Rankin. The change could save $60 weekly.[412]

In spite of the chaos and backbiting, the critics were encouraging. In Philadelphia *Agnes* was judged to have "strong dramatic action," and O'Neil's acting was a "more balanced study of light and shade instead of the one pitch she used to use."[413] Harmon, however, reported when the company reached Cincinnati in mid-December: "Playing in that kind of play ['Fires'] and before small audiences has robbed the company members and the Star of a certain amount of spirit in performance. They live in a continued air of depression."[414] Harmon was exaggerating. The Cincinnati critics thought both plays were well acted, but that *Agnes* was better because it was more thoroughly understood by the company. "Its superficial incidents permitted a certain graceful and pleasing execution which made them more palatable."[415] The key was repression. O'Neil "carries the whole play with her foot safely pressed upon the brake."[416] Considering the internal dissension, the company's sangfroid on stage was remarkable.

The big news was that Rankin and O'Neil had quarreled so violently that O'Neil spoke to him only on business and went to a separate hotel for the first time when the company arrived in St Louis. The Shuberts were incredulous about the dissension between the two and thought it was why they were now nice to Harmon. "It seems impossible," wrote Jacobs. "Let me know what you find out."[417]

The cause of the quarrel, Harmon reported, was O'Neil's belief that Rankin was responsible for getting her dear friend Clara Bracy out of the company. "Rankin was not the means of getting Bracy out of the company," Harmon remarked, "but he probably four-flushed about it and was given credit for it."[418] Rankin began to regret it and sent O'Neil letters every day but could not fix the break between them. "O'Neil is as queer a woman as I have ever known in this business," Harmon added, "but I don't see how any woman could stand for an old 'Soak' like Rankin about them. Rankin spends all his money on Champagne and Rum—drank two bottles of Champagne after we arrived here [Cincinnati] before breakfast, Sunday morning. I have little regard for them as performers or individuals."[419]

The head office responded to Harmon's revelations about Rankin by ordering Harmon to close the O'Neil company in Buffalo on January 3, 1909, and to give the company one week's notice: "Keep this to yourself," he was told.[420] He would leave Cincinnati on Monday, December 21, with the company and arrive in Buffalo in the evening, rest the company until it opened with *Agnes* on Christmas day, and transfer the sinking fund for the O'Neil company to the Hopper company in Brooklyn, to which he was to be sent.

Harmon's pleasure at going to the Hopper company was undermined when O'Neil continued on the train past Buffalo on to New York to see the Shubert head office without telling anyone. She cabled Harmon that she had seen Jacobs and would be returning only on Thursday night. "Her conduct is discourteous and unprofessional," Harmon complained. "Rankin, I know, is a sort of 'knave' and will resort to almost anything to try to gain his ends, but in a different line, she is about the limit too." He suspected that O'Neil was spending the days before Christmas with Clara Bracy.

> Whatever the trouble between Rankin and Miss O'Neil is, I don't know all of it, and bad as Rankin may be, I think that the lady presses him a good close second and he is now getting his reward from her for a long period of devotion to her interests,

whether good or bad. It is the usual outcome when the woman thinks that she can't get any more. I feel quite sure that her main reason for going on to New York was just to see Mrs. Bracy, who was discharged from the Company, and I have seen enough since I have been with the Company to show me that Mrs. Bracy is a bad old cat.[421]

The significance of O'Neil's visit to head office was that she, not Rankin, was now managing the company.

Harmon rescheduled the eight-day engagement in Buffalo to four performances without explanation. Since it was the Christmas holidays, large audiences witnessed *Agnes* in Buffalo.[422] For the two performances of *The Fires of St John* the next day, Saturday, December 26, 1908, the last time that Rankin and O'Neil shared a stage, O'Neil performed brilliantly and "McKee Rankin as the bluff, old farmer Vogelreuter," wrote the critic, "gave a most artistic and ideal portrayal of this unctuous role."[423]

The Shuberts instructed Harmon to post a notice after the Saturday-evening performance that the company had closed and to pay the actors half-salary since they worked for only half the week. If the actors argued that they were entitled to another week's salary since a week's notice of termination was mandatory, Harmon was to send them to the head office, where the problem would be adjusted. O'Neil had agreed to these arrangements, Jacobs wrote. Harmon was to take an I.O.U. from O'Neil for a loan of $50 and deduct the cost of her stateroom traveling to Buffalo ($7) from her salary. Presumably the Shuberts paid the train fares for the cast back to New York City. It must have been a gloomy ride in a railway car, rife with suspicion, recrimination, and a sense of betrayal. Rankin may have been hopeful that he could patch up his disagreement with O'Neil and continue as they had been; he might have taken comfort in the legal power of his agreement with O'Neil that ran to 1914. Yet he was being ignored and treated as if he no longer mattered. His excessive drinking weakened his judgment and voided any energetic response.

Once in New York, O'Neil announced to the media that she had withdrawn the power of attorney from Rankin and was awaiting assignment by the Shuberts to a production that would not include Rankin. She had a five-year contract with the Shuberts, whereas Rankin's connection to the Shuberts was only through O'Neil as her manager. For her first season, the Shuberts paid her $250 weekly and one-third of the profits, and for the second season she was to receive 40 percent of the profits. The Shuberts refused to pay her a salary for the weeks remaining in the second season. Both parties had the option of continuing the contract for three years.[424]

Given that the Shuberts were at a loss where to star her for the moment, O'Neil went to San Francisco in the third week in January 1909, where, it was reported, "the California newspapers are in a state of incoherent enthusiasm" over her arrival.[425] O'Neil had to borrow money to live. The Shuberts suggested that she play vaudeville and advanced her $600, which she had to pay back from her vaudeville earnings before June 1, 1909.

1909: Larkin Bunce, Belasco, and *The Lily*

Rankin was unemployed. A note he wrote to Augustus Thomas, the playwright, in mid-February 1909 from the Hotel Cadillac in New York City, revealed a chastened man: "Is it possible to have a little chat with you? I have something to put before you that I think will possibly be worth your while. I am stopping at this hotel and at present my time is all my own—so I can call upon you at any time you fix."[426] Since Rankin spent much of his time in his last years writing short plays, presumably he had an idea for a drama on which he wanted Thomas, a close friend of the Sydney Drews, to collaborate.

Rankin co-authored a play with the young Oakland dramatist Henry Kirk at this time, which very probably was the "something" that he wanted Thomas to see. Entitled *Invasion*, it described a Japanese invasion of California, not an uncommon fear in the early twentieth century. The first act concerned a family quarrel over whether a Japanese American can be loyal to America. In the second act, a character announces a surprise Japanese invasion:

> Two fast cruisers with fifteen hundred infantry and arms, ammunition, clothing and supplies for fifteen thousand more landed in the Hawaiian Islands yesterday, defeated the battalion of regular troops, marines and the National Guard Regiment there, at the same time sinking the Revenue cutter and small gunboat, all that represented our navy. The Japanese General in command called all ex-soldiers of the Japanese population to the colors. There are forty-five thousand Japanese in the Hawaiian Islands and I can tell you every one of them knew a month ahead just what he was to do and where he was to report![427]

The Japanese flotilla escapes detection by sailing a few miles north of the established sailing routes and captures the Presidio in San Francisco. The gloomy third and last act portrays a harsh Japanese military occupation of the western seaboard. The play was never staged.

Rankin may have been hoping that O'Neil would tire of her vaudeville sketch and seek him out. In case she did not, he and his lawyer, Henry Kowalski, notorious as an heir hunter who tracked down heirs to estates for large commissions, planned to take a case of a breached contract to the courts. Rankin remained in New York into the summer until the producer William Brady hired him for the role of Larkin Bunce in a new comedy, *Cameo Kirby*, in August. It had been tried out that spring with Dustin Farnum, a popular young actor, playing Eugene Kirby, a card-sharp gambler on a Mississippi steamboat out of New Orleans. Kirby, nicknamed "Cameo," is shot in the lung by a gambler, and, after a long convalescence, he returns to avenge himself. His faithful friend, Larkin Bunce, is also a professional gambler. With Falstaffian touches of "mastodonic humor"[428] Bunce helps Kirby plan to escape a dangerous situation, which includes Kirby's infatuation with a young lady.

Farnum and Rankin made personal hits, and the play was a roaring success. Rankin as the obese old sport, who trains with Cameo, did a superb piece of character work with great humor. Some even called it the best role of his career. In San Francisco, both Rankin and Farnum were called before the curtain at the close to make speeches, and in Los Angeles, the *Examiner* called Rankin "irresistibly funny....Miss O'Neil may miss him as a manager but the public is indebted for the return of one of the best comedians."[429]

Playing one-night stands, the company toured the Northwest and eastward on a route that Rankin had traveled so many times in his life. The company played the week of December 6 in Buffalo and headed south through New York State. Rankin bowed out before it opened in New York City on December 20 because, by then, O'Neil was involved in a legal battle for her independence, and Rankin had to prepare to put forward his claims upon her in competition with the other managers.

O'Neil had been touring in a sketch entitled *$1000 Reward*, in which she played a woman in a cabin in Arizona waiting for the return of her train-robbing husband. Paul Scardon played the deputy sheriff pursuing her husband.[430] In the Midwest, the Orpheum Circuit employed her for its theaters for thirty weeks. O'Neil now seemed to get high praise wherever she went as "the highest salaried star that vaudeville has taken from the legitimate."[431] "Probably not one of the women who have been rivals in this line of endeavor would dare turn from the Camilles and the La Toscas to what Miss O'Neil has."[432] Formerly, she was degrading her talent in vaudeville with Rankin; now she was courageous in vaudeville without him. O'Neil—a great believer in the spiritual and supernatural forces, to the point of experiencing ghosts in a country house in New England—

divined an intervention that would revive her career. Just after she broke with Rankin, she attended the Belasco Theatre in New York and said to a friend in the lobby: "I don't even know Mr. Belasco, but I have a feeling that some time I shall be connected with all this."[433]

O'Neil spent the summer in Nottingham, England, preparing to tour in vaudeville in a playlet she was bringing from England. The Shuberts had done nothing to get a play for her. Suddenly, she received a telegram from David Belasco asking simply: "When do you come to New York?" She replied, "Immediately!"[434] Belasco wanted to produce a play from the French entitled *The Lily* and needed four actors who looked alike to play members of the De Maigny family. As he read the script, he thought of Nance O'Neil for the part of Odette, the older, spinster sister, and was delighted to see that she resembled the actor cast for the father, Charles Cartwright. He hired Julia Dean, a good-looking talented young girl, for the younger sister, and Alfred Hickman, a bright young man who was playing in one of his companies.

O'Neil left for New York, was met at the steamer, deposited her belongings at a hotel, and went to the theater. Belasco entered with the script and asked her to read the third act. The scene mounted and mounted, taking her breath away. Tears streamed down her face. Belasco, enjoying her amazement and emotion, had tears in his eyes.

The cast rehearsed in the downstairs rehearsal room. At lunch, O'Neil was given the honor of sitting next to Belasco. She chose two drab dresses as costumes and had to show them to Belasco and a co-producer. She was outwardly calm but inwardly seething with excitement and nervousness. The co-producer was complimentary, but Belasco was quiet. Fearing he did not like her choices, she heard him call, excitedly, "Where's Nance O'Neil? Have you seen her make-up?"[435] The previous summer in Paris, something had prompted O'Neil to pick up old-fashioned earrings of filigree washed with gold, although she knew she would not wear them. They were perfect for Odette and pleased the fastidious Belasco.

O'Neil admired Belasco's attention to detail. He spent a day devoted to light cues, which he worked out with his electrical effects assistant. "He never fussed anyone or intruded his personality. When he saw actors were on the right lines, he let them go ahead, undisturbed," she said. "Such a blessing! Such an important quality in a director! to allow an actor to develop the character he is acting."[436] She may have been indirectly criticizing Rankin, who had demonstrated to actors the development of character that he wanted them to follow.

The Shuberts, now awakened to O'Neil's potential, renewed their contractual rights, telling her to report for rehearsals of *The Secret Woman* in a role that, they claimed, only O'Neil could play satisfactorily. They obtained a court order preventing her from rehearsing with Belasco. Against this, Belasco's lawyers argued that actors should not be prevented from going onstage, that they must be guaranteed more than a weekly payment, that they must have the right to appear. Moreover, O'Neil had the right to abrogate the Shubert contract because the Shuberts contravened it by giving her a role of which she did not approve in a play of which she had not even heard. The justice vacated the injunction on this last point, saying that the Shuberts had not kept the contract and thereby forfeited the right to relief. In addition, the master of the rolls, the Appeals Court judge who has charge of the rolls and patents in England, had recently ruled that actors would lose their standing in the amusement world if not allowed to appear in a play of their choice, and this decision influenced the American judge.

Shortly thereafter, on December 6, 1909, Belasco opened *The Lily* in Washington, DC, where it was an instant success as "an idyllic sex tragedy, without the love triangle."[437] The play was called a triumph for O'Neil, who was billed first, although not as the star. The story concerns a puritanical, selfish martinet, who forces his elder daughter, Odette, to renounce her suitor and become his own housekeeper, but when he interferes in the life of his younger daughter, Odette initiates a passionate rebellion. Since O'Neil had been playing rebellious women in the problem plays of the time, she was easily identified with the role. (A "lily" in Parisian slang was a girl forced to remain celibate.)

While the play was in Pittsburgh for the week of December 13, Rankin filed for an injunction in New York City on the grounds that O'Neil was still under contract to him and owed half of her earnings to him. "I gave up fifteen years of my life and a large fortune to making her an actress. I took her when she was penniless," Rankin said. Claiming that he was ready to present her in a play, he deplored the fact that Belasco had made her a stock actress and injured her position as a star.[438] With Rankin she made $26,000 annually, but when she refused his management she made $6,000 a year. Rankin was willing to make an out-of-court settlement with Belasco, much like the settlement Belasco made with pork-packing millionaire Fairbanks in his suit over Mrs Leslie Carter after Belasco, just as Rankin at this time, had devoted his career to developing an actress and demanded compensation. When Belasco made an offer, Rankin rejected it as too small. Rankin promised sensational revelations during the court proceedings.

The Lily opened at the Stuyvesant Theatre in New York City on Monday, December 23, 1909. O'Neil, as was customary with her before opening night, spent the day in bed, alone, going over her part and thinking of the movements of the play. She got to the theater to find a red carpet passing from the entrance door to the stage. Belasco, pacing back stage, patted her shoulder in a complimentary gesture and mentioned that the whole world of art and fashion was out front. Adding to her nervousness, a deputy sheriff forced his way into her dressing room to serve her papers from Rankin enjoining her appearance. "Oh, this is dreadful!" she cried. Both her and Belasco's legal advisers persuaded Rankin's lawyers to let the play go on. Rankin had said that he bore no animosity towards her, but it was reported that, barred from the theater, he was in a bare little room at the Hotel Cadillac sick in body, mind, and heart. He could scarcely believe her ingratitude.

The reviews filed by Rankin's major enemies among the critics, including Acton Davies of the *New York Evening News* and Alan Dale of the *New York American*, announced O'Neil's triumph. Wrote Davies:

> Wearing a make-up which deprived her of every shred of physical beauty until almost the end of the third act, she had to stand by, a mere grim, stately, tender-hearted spinster in the background, watching Charles Cartwright playing the role of her selfish old roué of a father give a performance which Coquelin himself could scarcely have excelled....But suddenly, in defence of her sister, Odette de Maigney, the old maid, the household drudge burst into flame. In a scene of denunciation lasting for almost ten minutes, the woman laid her soul bare. It was a speech typifying the sorrows of all womanhood, the cry of a woman who had been deprived of her two natural birthrights—love and maternity. It was a great speech, devoid of all trace of theatricalism, rendered for the most part in a conversational tone, but as Miss O'Neil rendered it, it stirred and touched that audience as no words spoken by a player have in many a long day.[439]

The paternalism so dominant in the plays when Rankin began his career had been vanquished now near the end of it.

After the ovation on the ringing down of the curtain, Belasco stepped forward to acknowledge his play's success, but the audience literally drove him off the stage to make way for O'Neil. She received a record thirty-six curtain calls.

Underlying the passionate acclaim was public sympathy for her struggle for freedom from Rankin, which, in a subtle way, affected Rankin's attempt to get a temporary injunction from the Supreme Court of Brooklyn at the end of December. O'Neil's lawyers furnished the judge with scores of affidavits from theater managers testifying to Rankin's loss of standing and influence. It was because O'Neil could not get suitable engagements under Rankin that she was forced to seek new management, they argued. The judge, without looking at Rankin's papers, refused the injunction and declined to set a date for a trial. Nothing further of the case appeared in the papers. If an out-of-court settlement was reached, it was not announced.

Nance O'Neil (left) as Odette De Maigny with Julia Dean as her younger sister in David Belasco's production of *The Lily*, New York, 1909.

Rankin deserved to lose his case. He did sacrifice a lot of himself in imagination, intellect, effort, and care to create Nance O'Neil, but he gained enormously from his investment, not the least of which was seeing the beauty and power of his creation. He used his magnetism, theater power, and financial management to control O'Neil much longer than needed; despite his pleas that he could find no managers for her, in reality, he was reluctant to give up his control over her. Part of this was owing to his vision of great art, which differed greatly from the profit-centered theatrical entrepreneurs and the sentimental Belasco who were his rivals. Another part was owing to his deep attachment to the woman and the excitement and earning power that she commanded. Subtly, without his being aware of it, he gave up his career to hers. Thus, the greater she became, the less respect he had for himself and the more precipitous was his decline into alcohol, gluttony, and self-pity. By sharply rejecting him, O'Neil made him aware of what he had become. Of course, she made the decision for herself, and it came to her like a revelation, in which she saw her years with Rankin cast in a different light. Her only reasonable option was to take up with Belasco. That she loved Rankin at one time is unquestionable. Rankin, as Amy Leslie wrote, awakened deep emotions in women.[440] Moreover, he had devoted his considerable ambitions and energies to her, caring for her in one of the most difficult times of her life, and nurturing her career thereafter.

Rankin had a dream that was larger than O'Neil and himself as actors, and for a long time he imbued O'Neil with that dream. He wanted to return the theater to the period of his youth, when a major object of actors was to instruct the public through their art and effect social change. Through O'Neil he had advanced the cause of women's liberty, such that O'Neil was honored by many groups for her portrayal of the spirited woman rebelling against her bondage. O'Neil's role as the spinster Odette seemed to be a culmination of many of her rebel roles with Rankin, and, at the same time, it symbolized to the public her breaking free of the bonds in which Rankin, alias Svengali, had kept her for so long.

Later in January 1910, when *The Lily* was in Cleveland, a local critic began the praise for Belasco that several periodicals echoed: "Belasco saw the great talent of the girl hidden in the rubbish heap of her stage method....He put a curb on her emotionalism and made her walk sedately where once she had galloped of her own free will. It was the finest bit of lion-taming that the modern stage has known."[441] "She demonstrated," wrote the critic for the *New York Times*, "that her gift for the theater amounted to genius, and lacked only the hand to guide and fashion and advise."[442]

O'Neil, however, was becoming disillusioned with Belasco. She complained that he had set her name with the other cast members, despite her great success and despite his promises to make her a star. Belasco went to Cleveland to talk with O'Neil. He asked a Broadway actress to prepare for the part of Odette and assured O'Neil that he was making every effort to star her in a play if she would be patient until he could find the right vehicle.[443] O'Neil was aware of her vulnerability. From that moment, she always made it a point to praise Belasco and vow her devotion to this "stage genius." Her confidence in him seemed supreme.

O'Neil felt that she had changed. "I believed in the old adage that 'straight is the line of duty and curved is the line of beauty: follow the first and thou shalt see the other ever following thee,'" she told a reporter. "And now I have just changed it right about-face. If a person gives up everything worthwhile—love—their work will never reach the highest because they cease to live in harmony."[444] To symbolize her new persona as distinct from her previous reliance on Rankin, she asked her friends to call her "Diane," which was the nickname given Agnes in the play *Agnes*.

Belasco did not star her in a play. He made inquiries about the Kelley music in a project to mount *Macbeth* with O'Neil as Lady Macbeth, but it did not come to fruition. Was he simply in the game of winning her from Rankin, as so many managers had been trying to do for years, and then putting her aside as expendable? Or did he doubt her abilities for the kind of sentimental play that he favored? Or were no plays of consequence being written? A Boston critic wrote that the problem with O'Neil was the refining of her coarse power. Her failure in psychological parts of contemporary drama, except in their flaring moments, according to him, was owing to her lack of imagination to penetrate or finesse to execute them.[445] Possibly Belasco agreed.[446] Although Belasco had joined with Fiske and other independents in January 1908, in late 1909 he and Fiske were cooperating with the Theater Syndicate. O'Neil understood that she would not be seen on the stage again if she did not toe the line. Her praises of Belasco from this point sounded extreme, and she carried his autographed photos on tour with her to display in her hotel rooms. It appears that Belasco and the syndicate did finally marginalize her, as Rankin warned they would. Belasco kept O'Neil in expectation of starring in a play that he would produce until she must have realized that it would never happen, although she continued her fulsome praises of Belasco for years to come.

O'Neil said that her first year in *The Lily* was wonderful, her second year was less pleasant, and her third year was unendurable. Finally, she left the cast. Martha Mayo played Odette in a second touring company sent out in May 1911 by Belasco, who had eight major companies on the road. "The play got on my nerves," O'Neil said.[447] Still under contract to Belasco, O'Neil received her salary although she was idle; in her second year of idleness, she broke with Belasco, who let her go.

Before Mayo took over the role of Odette, Martha Mayo and Isabel O'Madigan spoke with a reporter about the art of acting. "Miss O'Neil is the coldest woman: she seems to keep her real self apart and away from everyone and everybody," O'Madigan said, recalling their time in her company. "She will never kiss her lover on the lips; it's always on the cheek or forehead. Now, these little details are necessary to art. I saw her in 'The Lily.' She's just the same as McKee Rankin taught her. Belasco hasn't changed her one particle, and I don't really believe she can do big things without Rankin."[448]

O'Neil, however, had great roles yet to come. Her future lay not with Belasco, but rather with an actor who played her young brother in *The Lily*—Alfred Hickman. Hickman was an English actor who originated the role of Little Billie in *Trilby* for the American stage. He married Blanche Walsh, who had played Trilby in that production in 1896 and went on to star in Belasco's plays. After O'Neil left *The Lily*, Hickman became her manager. He directed and acted with her in vaudeville during the theater year and in modern plays in summer stock. After Blanche Walsh died in 1915, he married O'Neil in 1917.

ACT V

Rankin on the Rebound

1909–1911: Lionel, Doris, and Mac

When Rankin was acting in *Cameo Kirby* on the West Coast in October 1909, he became acquainted with a young playwright, Er Lawshé, who had worked for years as drama critic on the *Louisville Courier-Journal*, and agreed to produce two of his plays: *The Woman of It*, a modern play of New York life in which Rankin planned to feature his new California protégée, Betsy Bourke, and *Down South*.[1] Nothing more was heard of the ventures, or of Betsy Bourke, possibly because Rankin, whose reputation was badly damaged by the adverse publicity he received in his fight with David Belasco over Nance O'Neil, could not find backers. That he should have had a protégée so soon after losing O'Neil does speak to his determination to continue.

Rankin had family obligations. His daughter Doris and her husband, Lionel Barrymore, were back from almost four years in Paris. They had been supported partly by Lionel's sister, Ethel, but since she had married, she was no longer able to send them money. Rankin sent Lionel to D.W. Griffith, who was making films with the Biograph Company on Fourteenth

---

Notes are on pages 492-94.

Street in New York.[2] Griffith hired Lionel for a minor role in the film *Friends* and paid him $15 a day and $25 a script, which Griffith encouraged him to write.[3] All the films were made in the hard sunlight at Fort Lee, New Jersey. An old Pathé camera that cranked from the back was run by sprockets and bicycle chains as an instrument of art for the first time. The future of the film was very uncertain, and actors still considered only stage work as real acting.

The legitimate theater, however, was being quietly undermined by the advent of the film industry and the growing popularity of grand opera. Unknown to the public, $10 million was invested in opera houses in medium-sized cities. In 1909, people saw the talking picture on the horizon and were predicting that grand opera would be heard in the movies. At the same time, the film was pushing vaudeville towards extinction, competing for the 5- and 10-cent admission. Vaudeville tried raising its prices to compete with the legitimate theater, which charged over a dollar, a competition it could not win.

Phyllis Rankin and her husband, Harry Davenport, had done sketches in vaudeville from time to time, and now Phyllis wrote a sketch called *The Jail Bird* for herself, Lionel, and Rankin to present. They tried it out at Mount Vernon, New York, in mid-January 1910, and then took it to Wilmington, Delaware. The interest centered on the portrayal of the ex-con, Philip Garth, who had just been released after twenty-four years in Sing Sing. Rankin's acting as Garth was so powerful and convincing that, in comparison, Lionel and Phyllis seemed "mere callow amateurs."[4]

When they reached New York City, critics condemned *The Jail Bird* as a hopeless morass of stagy talk and false theatricals, thus forcing Lionel to substitute a sketch of his own, *The White Slaver*, in which he played an Italian coal teamster, Doris Rankin played his sister forced into prostitution, and Rankin, who owned her, was the petty political boss profiting by the white slave traffic.[5] The scene was a dreary room cheaply furnished. It began in misery and ended in murder. A reporter commented: "The title role of 'The White Slaver' will be played by Doris Rankin, Phyllis Rankin probably having concluded she is better fitted for musical comedy than for emotional roles." It opened in Atlantic City on February 13, 1910, to an appreciative audience, and the threesome signed contracts with various vaudeville houses for one-week stands. They were paid $750 as a troupe a week for two shows daily for seven days.[6]

The White Slaver proved a success, and all three actors won praise from the very demanding vaudeville audiences.[7] They toured through New England and over to the western Orpheum circuit, appearing in Spokane, Washington, in October 1910, and gradually wound their way back eastwards. To play one sketch twice a day for over a year took perseverance, although they did mix in other sketches such as *Confusion* to break the monotony. Nevertheless, it served as a means to rehabilitate the disgraced Rankin, who must have been humiliated and deeply depressed by the antagonism shown him by the theater community and his public disgrace over the O'Neil affair.

Doris Rankin, actress and daughter of McKee Rankin and Mabel Bert. She was married to Lionel Barrymore.

When the Rankin-Rankin-Barrymore troupe played its closing engagement of *The White Slaver* in vaudeville in New Orleans for the week of March 6, 1911, Rankin celebrated fifty years upon the stage. Actually it was fifty-one years, but he had been working so hard he had forgotten to celebrate earlier. A worn-out and forgotten matinee idol, whose beauty had become grossness, his illegitimate daughter and his penniless son-in-law raised glasses in toast to his undoubted talents and irrepressible determination.

Doris Rankin was a born actress. She was encouraged by her father, who said that there was no calling where a girl with talent could do better than on the stage. Much later, in 1918, she won national acclaim playing opposite her husband on Broadway in *The Copperhead*, both as the gray-haired wife of the Confederate sympathizer and his sixteen-year old granddaughter. Barrymore's role as the copperhead also established him. The opening-night audience cheered him for fifteen minutes, which was considered the greatest ovation for an individual in the history of the American theater.

With his vaudeville earnings, Rankin purchased Er Lawshé's play *Peace on Earth*, which, he said, was to shape the destiny of his son-in-law Lionel Barrymore. The play portrayed the folks and scenes in the Kentucky mountains and centered on a feud between the Gilberts and the Sanders. Rankin played Reuben Gilbert, a robust and genial Kentucky sheriff.[8] Klaw and Erlanger produced it at the Belasco Theatre stock company in Los Angeles.

Lawshé wrote to Rankin from New York City: "You'll do more for this play than Denman Thompson ever did with 'The Old Homestead' at the outset, and it is going to be your steady work for just so long as you want to remain in harness. When you become Reuben Gilbert you are going to be rejuvenated over your own wonderful personality and vitality. It was McKee Rankin who gave me my inspiration for Reuben and you are Reuben," Lawshé continued in the vein of giving Rankin confidence. He predicted that the play would be on Broadway the next season when Rankin would be tipping Peter at the Hotel Cadillac as well as spending a few dollars "on what Peter brings you." Lawshé had dreamed for years of writing a play for which Rankin would rehearse the actors, and now it was a reality after his struggles in adversity. When the play opened on March 27, he predicted that all talk about Rankin being "the last rattle out of the box" would be seen as nonsense. "Once they turn the spotlight on you as Reuben Gilbert, it is a downright cinch that you will live to be successfully sued on your ninetieth birthday for bastardy. You've been rolling ones and twos of late years, but now you'll throw double sixes every time."[9]

The local critic called the play bucolic, aimed at storytelling rather than climax building. The characters "don't work up any very terrific intensity," but they did represent "wholesomeness, sweetness, and rugged honesty." As for Rankin, he was better than his part:

> Mr. Rankin has a real character, and gives it such creation as the author might not get from any other living actor. For the distinctive worth of McKee Rankin lies in the fact that while he is a veteran of veterans, he has discarded—as veterans usually will not do—such methods as have fallen into disuse, and has kept absolutely down to date in every particular of the art of acting. As a result, he presents not only the resources of the intelligent player of today, but practically all of the good points of the great old character actors of twenty-five and thirty years ago. Mr. Rankin's humorous, lovable, bluff, hearty and intensely virile sheriff must be seen to be appreciated. It is an adroitly rounded piece of acting which cannot be accurately described.[10]

The cast was large. Doris, Lionel, and Frank Keenan starred along with Rankin. The play's popularity kept it on the boards for a second week.[11] Rankin, Lawshé, and manager John Blackwood went to Chicago to complete the details for the production of *Peace on Earth* at the Blackstone Theatre from May 28 indefinitely, but the theater was dark from that date, which indicated that the production was canceled at the last moment, possibly over fears that it would fail in Chicago.[12]

Rankin did indeed return to the Hotel Cadillac in New York and filled in at the syndicate offices for Mark Klaw, who went to Europe. In an affectionate letter to Phyllis, whom he still called Pixie, Rankin asked her to let him know where she was going after the season closed as he expected to be free in July after Klaw returned. Rankin, who reduced *Peace on Earth* to a vaudeville sketch, expected to open it in Chicago in late August. "You might put in four or five weeks with me in the part of Zeke—a great comedy character part," he told her. "Management will give you $200 for the part." But she intended to give up acting for at least a year to look after her children's education.[13]

While employed in the syndicate office, Rankin reworked a Sudermann play, *California*, and in mid-July went to the Auditorium Theatre in Los Angeles to stage it. He gave himself the role of a Confederate veteran with a wife, a spoiled daughter, and an enterprising adopted daughter, Kate, whose mysterious past life and strong love interest are the themes of the drama. He added a young San Franciscan businessman, an enthusiastic reverend from Boston, and an old prospector, Alex McKee, known as 49, who came across the plains from Michigan in a wagon train. Clearly, Rankin's uncle was again the inspiration for this last character. From Sandy McGee in *The Danites* and Old '49 in *'49*, Rankin introduced him to a new generation, to whom those earlier plays were either distant memories or entirely unknown. George Osbourne played 49. The critic declared the play to be "shaky and uncertain." Rankin had adapted it from so many sources, he said, that its patchwork was evident. Germans could not be transplanted to California easily, and the American characters such as Colonel Elmer Johnson, Sallie Sloan, and '49, though well played, did not fit in. Rankin's bluff, breezy comedy style as the colonel was successful, as were the stage settings, but to no avail.[14]

By presenting this play, Rankin deserted the Rankin stock company, which opened in Atlantic City on the day he opened in *California*. Sidney, Gladys, Doris, and Lionel, and Sidney and Gladys's son S. Rankin Drew,[15] and others formed the company and did a series of one-act comedies such as *The Yellow Dragon*, *The White Slaver*, *The Counsellor for the Defense*, and *Bob Acres*, the last being a playlet derived from Sheridan's *The Rivals* by Sidney Drew. They enjoyed a large business from "pleased" audiences, but some must have been miffed that Rankin would abandon an organization that, with him, might have given them work for some time.

Stopping to play his vaudeville sketch in Chicago, Rankin returned to New York to appear on September 3 in a new George Cameron playlet, *As Others See Us*. Excellent as an irascible, deaf old man who regains his hearing, unbeknownst to those about him, he hears his daughter, cook, and farmhands criticize him while writing the opposite on a slate for him to read.[16] Like Gladys, Rankin's talents for writing dramatic situations were perfectly suited to the vaudeville circuit, and Rankin sold a number of his one-act plays to the Orpheum Theatre Syndicate. He adapted short plays from the German and French, including *Above the Law* from the French of Brieux, and wrote *The Wages of Sin* and *Betsey and I Are Out*. The Orpheum company proudly announced the plays as "written by a prominent dramatist who is now contributing solely to the Orpheum's producing department."[17]

Rankin also worked on perfecting his invention of a rotary safety razor and massage roller, which he had asked a machinist in New York to fashion for him. The work was slow, from 1908 to 1913, for which the machinist wanted $74, but the electric razor worked. The machinist advised Rankin that he would need a great deal of capital to exploit it and should try the firms in the field. Phyllis took over the job of finding a manufacturer.[18]

1911–1913: Margaret Drew and the West

Kate Blanchard, having recovered from her invalidism, was always ready to accept her husband back, but she knew that the stage was his sole interest. For that reason, she prepared herself to act beside him once again. Making her debut in vaudeville as a widow who is embarrassed by a mechanical mannequin, she received good reviews, aside from a critic who admonished her for taking a role below her talents. While waiting to stage Rankin's vaudeville production of *Peace on Earth*, in which Lionel and Doris would play their parts, and possibly other members of the family would have roles, she took an apartment in the Hotel Belleclaire in New York.[19] Theatrical managers and friends of the Rankins sent McKee and Kate letters and telegrams of encouragement. Although McKee regarded her with affection and would have found pleasure in her company once again, it was dire necessity that brought them together in the hope that a production featuring them both could attract large audiences. In the meantime, Rankin appeared in vaudeville with Lionel and Doris in the sketch *Bill Sykes*, which Rankin wrote. The brutal pimp had become one of Rankin's greatest stage creations. "Rankin had a richly mellow gift," Amy Leslie wrote, "for portrayal of the rugged, sonorous old men of worth and the distinguished middle aged dignitary with powerful tyrannies and refinement of cruelties. His Bill Sikes reeked with bloody realism and a kind of bandit humor which sent shudders to the spine."[20] On December 14, 1911, he spent a few hours away from the apartment he shared with Blanchard. When he returned he found her dead. Preparing to take a bath, she had stepped into the tub and suffered a heart attack.

Amy Leslie eulogized her as "one of the most remarkable women the stage ever produced, merely as a woman."[21] A letter from Roxbury, Connecticut, appearing in the *New York Telegram,* recalled all the members of the cast of the *Cinderella* production of 1867 in Boston, who now were dead, and added Kitty Blanchard to the list—"the pretty, dashing, gay, piquante, bewitching Prince Poppetti and Carline, who died at the age of seventy. Can it be possible I ask you men who saw this dashing soubrette, when she was all that I have named—can it be possible that time has run so fast, that it seems as if it were but last week? Seventy! Died, and alone, in a bath tub, by some odd failure of the heart to do its duty for a minute or two until she could have called for help. Oh, yes, we who saw Kitty Blanchard in those days will never forget her, never."[22] Rankin undoubtedly shared the same sentiments, but he may have been criticized by members of his family for being absent when she died. Could he not have remained with her on returning from his tour instead of pursuing theater business? Whatever the reason, from this point he never acted again with a member of his immediate family.

Shortly thereafter, Rankin was reported as "directing" the film *The Danites* in two reels for the Selig Polyscope Theatre Company in San Francisco. There were numerous film companies and all were looking for good scripts, but the Selig Company was by far the best. "In point of big achievements," wrote the *New York Dramatic Mirror,* "in which time, money and elaborate preparation are unspared, no company in the world can match Selig."[23] Its policy was to hire producers or directors who had written their own scripts. Actually, Francis W. Boggs, as head of Selig's West Coast studio, produced numerous well-known stage plays with associated writers and actors used for publicity purposes. Rankin was probably paid as a consultant. Hobart Bosworth, who, in the mid-1880s, had played minor roles in Rankin's combination company in San Francisco, wrote the scenario. Earlier, Bosworth wrote the scenario for *'49* and directed it as a one-reeler, which was released by Selig in September 1911.[24] *The Danites* was announced for early release as an important film for over a month before the first part was screened on February 19, 1912, and the second on February 20. "McKee Rankin never more clearly revealed his complete mastery of the art of dramaturgy than in this standard play constructed and elaborated for the screen by the noted author-actor," wrote a reviewer. "It moves forward steadily and irresistibly, setting before the audience the essential scenes of the essential struggle."[25] Either Rankin or Bosworth had made changes, such as showing the father and son of the Williams family being murdered by the Danites. The actress playing Nancy Williams/Billy Piper (actors in films were not mentioned by name) "sharply projected" her character with "admirable acting."[26] Rankin could not help but remember scenes with Kitty Blanchard during the years when the play made them household names. He had acted in it well over 2,000 times.

By the time of the film's release, Rankin was on the road in a vaudeville sketch of *Oliver Twist*, a revision of his *Bill Sykes* to accommodate just two actors, himself as Bill and Margaret Drew as Nancy. This actress from the Drew family entered Rankin's life as a good companion at a time when he was the most lonely and the most vulnerable. Her relationship to him is mysterious. The *New York Times* mentioned parenthetically after her name that she was Sidney Drew's daughter.[27] The family made much of S. Rankin Drew, the son, but never spoke of a daughter, except once when Nance O'Neil told of Gladys giving her a dress for the role of Agnes in *Agnes*, which Gladys said had been worn by her daughter in a theatrical performance.[28] Margaret appeared as early as September 1902 as La Caprice, a music hall singer, in *Hearts Aflame* at the Bijou in New York. This meant that she must have been born in the mid-1880s, at least, and would not have been Gladys's daughter as Gladys was married only in 1889. Could she have been Sidney's daughter from an earlier relationship? Very likely.[29]

Rankin and Margaret Drew's tour in *Oliver Twist*, beginning on January 22, 1912, at the Hudson Theatre's Union Hall in New York, took them over the Orpheum circuit. The *New York Telegram* wrote: "If McKee Rankin's Bill Sykes is of the old school surely that is the school that should live forever, for acting that means make-up as well as recitation, where the actor really acts the character instead of being the type in his off-stage life."[30] The *Fort Wayne Journal* of May 19 reported that the performers were just as popular at the end as they were at the beginning of the week. The brief stints on stage and the one-week rather than one-night stands suited Rankin. He found the time to write short plays, which he scribbled on the back of hotel notepaper, as he had done for years. Of course, Margaret Drew was not Nance O'Neil, yet Rankin must have felt that he was helping her to improve. After O'Neil left him, he had spent much of his time training and encouraging his family, figuring, no doubt, that they would not desert him as O'Neil had done. Certainly Margaret stayed with him for as long as she could.[31]

When Rankin was in San Francisco in March 1912, the district attorney, on the advice of the U.S. attorney general, quashed the criminal indictment sought against Rankin and O'Neil for supposedly infringing the copyright of *The Fires of St John*. The long nuisance suit was over, and Rankin was proven to be right about the copyright.[32] This severed the last connection between these two great actors of their day. Rankin may have taken time to assess his life, although Amy Leslie's statement that he never had a moment to himself indicates that he did not brood over it. He was now the most experienced actor onstage, having changed his style with the times but retained the best from the past. Unfortunately, his services were no longer in demand: the impresarios that he knew were gone, as were his old friends, his reputation was sullied, and his energies were lower than at any time. Still, he yearned to experience once again the excitement and the glory that he could bring to a young actress. To this end, he and Margaret Drew continued in vaudeville into the summer of 1912, when he formed a company and opened in Seattle, Washington, on September 1 for a week in *Magda*. Margaret was Magda and he was Colonel Schwartze, by now a famous role that drew people to the theater more than the play itself. A large audience assembled on short notice and was pleased by the acting of Rankin's capable company. The following week, he presented *Peace on Earth*, and added actors to the company to fill all the roles. For *The Typhoon*, his adaptation from the Hungarian of a drama about a Japanese diplomat who strangles his French lover, the players had just three days of preparation. This would have been sufficient in the old days, but, in 1912, they were weak in their lines and lost the effect of the play. "If audiences went to theaters to see how well a piece could be played under almost insurmountable difficulties," wrote a critic sarcastically, "last night's performance would be well worth while."[33] Undaunted, Rankin kept the play in his repertoire and set forth on the road. He had to show in court that the copyright treaty between Hungary and the United States was flawed and allowed for productions other than the version played by Walker Whiteside, who had tried to have the courts stop other productions. His ability to get around barriers had not been diminished with age.

In October, Rankin began a series of plays at the Mason Theatre in Los Angeles with *Magda*. His perfect portrayal of Colonel Schwartze was given with a minimum of acting. "He has always seemed to me to be in the ranks of genius," wrote a critic. "He does not have to flop about a stage and make faces and do physical culture stunts of gesticulation in order to portray; with no apparent effort he 'characterizes'; and that, after all, is the actor's business....While you have to hate Schwartze because he is Schwartze, you develop an ardent affection and respect for the artist who plays him."[34]

Margaret could not exhibit the hidden pathos of Magda in the early scenes, but "in spite of herself, and in spite of the natural disadvantage of a colorless personality, her enthusiasm and sincerity won a splendid victory for her at the end."[35] Assuredly, this was a tribute to Rankin's coaching. Was he trying to prove that he actually could create another great actress? And was he still reacting to O'Neil's abrupt termination of their relationship? If so, he must have been pleased to read that, in *The Fires of St John*, the role of Marika was better fitted to Margaret Drew's personality and the production deserved the same amount of appreciation as the one Rankin presented with O'Neil some years earlier. When Drew played Helèna Laroche, who wins the love of a Japanese diplomat on an important mission for his government in Paris in *Typhoon*, a critic called the play "a tragedy of compelling power, of subtle and intense interest."[36] Many subsidiary parts were filled by Japanese actors, whom Rankin rehearsed. Rankin took a small part.

Caricature of McKee Rankin and Margaret Drew in *Magda*, Mason Theatre, Los Angeles, 1912. Courtesy of the Billy Rose Theatre Collection, New York Public Library.

The actor Howard Lindsay, who in the mid-twentieth century became known for playing *Life with Father* on Broadway for 3,224 consecutive performances, met up with Rankin at this time. He had been making minor films, and, discouraged that his scenes were always cut, he joined Rankin's company as actor, stage manager, and, because he carried a typewriter, press agent. Rankin, he said, was "a falling star who had damned near reached the earth."[37] Their first stop was in Reno, Nevada, then a town six blocks long. Rankin presented *Oliver Twist*, *Magda*, *The Fires of St John*, *A Kentucky Colonel*, *The Bachelor's Baby*, and whatever plays the actors may have had in their trunks, such as *The Thief* and *Paid in Full*, for which Rankin did not pay royalties. Lindsay would type out the parts from any scripts found. Virginia City was dying then, and the company stayed for one night. In Goldfield, which was one-third inhabited, it stayed a week.

Lindsay gave an amusing picture of Margaret Drew:

> She...had a wall eye. One eye looked at you and the other eye circled around. She always seemed to be trying to think of the next line which she wasn't very good at remembering. In fact she was so bad a study we had to prompt her....Finally we got a little tired of this. We got together and formed a sort of cabal and said we would not help her from now on. The word was: beginning with tonight's performance nobody helps her out; nobody prompts her. Well, that performance was "The Thief" which opened in a scene between her and me. The rest of the cast were in the wings watching to see whether I was going to help her or not. But I'd given my word. At the end of one of my lines, or, I believe it was a half-line, and it was her cue, she didn't say anything. I just sat and waited. Her wall eye went around and around for what seemed to me two minutes. Possibly it was no more than thirty seconds—a long time on the stage. Then suddenly, she thought of her next words. She pointed her finger at me and said, "Don't interrupt!"

The troupe stopped at Tonapah, Nevada which had the last working dancehall. The miners, mostly Poles and Czechs, paid five cents a dance, and, if the women were so inclined, they took them upstairs. None of the actors were paid, but their hotel rooms and laundry were paid for. When the troupe reached Reno, Rankin got some bad news. He had been negotiating with the Spreckels family, the sugar barons, to back a tour of the troupe to Honolulu. Now he received the news that they were withdrawing their support.

The company manager always directed the actors to the cheapest hotels; Rankin and Drew went to the best hotels and shared a room to save money. In Fresno, where they played in early January 1913, the actors rebelled against this treatment and registered in the best hotel after Rankin had gone upstairs. As they sat in the dining room that night, Rankin came down and saw them as he came through the door. The look on his face told them that they were through. Rankin closed the tour immediately. Margaret Drew played in Seattle for the rest of January, while Rankin raised the capital for another theatrical venture in San Francisco.

Rankin formed a new stock company with Margaret Drew as his leading lady and opened at the American Theatre in San Francisco on February 1, 1913. Intending to give a new play every week, he began with *Typhoon*. Whiteside's version had recently run at another theater, but Rankin's version was found to be more audacious, which attracted playgoers. "In subsequent plays, requiring less perfection of detail and demanding less of minor players, we predict strikingly good productions," wrote the local critic. "Rankin brings experience, knowledge of the San Francisco theater, great intelligence, and an enthusiasm that remains as keen as ever. He chiefly needs an audience."[38]

For the second week, Rankin presented *A Kain-tucky Feud*, which was a new title for Lawshé's *Peace on Earth*, with himself as the old sheriff Reuben Gilbert, and Margaret Drew as an emotional Kentucky girl, Doris Rankin's role in the first production. For the third week, the theater announced *A Wife's Secret*. Thereafter, the newspapers stopped noticing its productions because it was a repertory company with frequent changes of bill.[39] Margaret Drew went to Spokane in April as leading lady at the American Theatre stock company.[40] Rankin remained as stage director in San Francisco and gave private acting lessons. He could not help reflecting on his change in fortune when he saw that Mabel Bert was enjoying a popular run in the city in a comedy with veteran comedian William H. Crane. "Mabel Bert's impersonation of the housekeeper was a study in placidity which refused to be rippled," wrote a critic, "storm and blow over it as the Senator would. If some of her gowns were more demanding than the part demanded, the audience reaped the benefit."[41]

Joaquin Miller, who had been living on the heights of Oakland as an honored poet, died. As if he were clearing up the record now that the contentious playwright had left the scene, Rankin gave a series of interviews that spring to the *San Francisco Examiner* about the writing of *The Danites* and his early western experiences in his acting career.[42]

Rankin persuaded one of his students, Mrs A.W. Scott, the wife of the wealthy commissioner of the Panama-Pacific Exposition then running in San Francisco, to star onstage. He rehearsed her in *Magda* and *Mary Magdalene*. The pressure upon her to carry off such difficult parts before San Francisco society was immense. Maeterlinck's *Mary Magdalene* was a poetic drama, "strange and powerful,"[43] a dramatic recital of a redeemed woman's refusal to debase herself again, although it would save the life of Christ, to whom she owed her redemption. The productions were to raise money for the Happy Day Home for orphans, which rented the Tivoli Theatre for a week. Many of the children attended the matinee performances on Wednesday and Saturday as a reminder to the audience of where the proceeds would go.

Rankin knew that the society ladies would turn out to see one of their own and that he had to impress them with Scott's gowns. For a scene in the first act of *Mary Magdalene*, Scott wore a gown made of 6,000 peacock feathers, each one separately jeweled and all blended together in a wizardry of iridescent colour. As Magda in *Magda*, she wore Parisian gowns said to be of "unusual beauty and originality."[44]

The week opened with *Magda*, in which Scott "leaped to a high professional level." The audience "of starched bosoms and flashing shoulders, top-hatted and aigretted, and limousined" gave her curtain call after curtain call. She played a Magda of richness and beauty never before seen in San Francisco.[45] The critics applauded her stunning gowns. A separate newspaper piece described the gowns of the ladies of the audience, giving as many society names as could be squeezed into the column. As Colonel Schwartze, Rankin "in his ancient role won an enormous individual success and captured a liberal segment of the show."[46] The next night as Mary Magdalene, Scott was acclaimed as even better than as Magda. The role of Mary was deeper and offered more of a challenge, which she met perfectly. Rankin took the part of Silanus, professor and patron, wrapped in a toga and "majestically mantled."[47] Rankin's emphasis on beautiful gowns was clever because Maeterlinck's *Mary Magdalene* was more of a pageant than a play, in which the playwright's poetic thoughts did not make good drama.

The company played in Oakland for a week and then in Los Angeles. "If she is not the most beautiful woman on the American stage," wrote a critic, "she is one of the loveliest, and she is a superb actress as well."[48] The company presented both plays to audiences in San Diego and then disbanded. Scott's romance with the theater may have been satisfied because she did not appear on stage again.

Early in November, Rankin agreed to direct and produce for a recently organized motion picture combination, the Western Moving Picture Company.[49] Based in Fresno, it intended to specialize in feature films. Rankin was happy with his decision to concentrate on films. He felt that he had been subconsciously working towards the film all his life and had found his true métier at last. In 1877, his play *The Danites* had been called photographic realism. His later development of Saxe-Meiningen stage principles, such as realistic scenery, special lighting, and crowd direction, paved the way for the realism of the motion picture. Rankin advocated melodrama for sustaining dramatic interest, which was a strong element in the silent film. Other stage directors such as David Belasco and Steele Mackaye contributed to the advent of film by promoting acting of a restrained naturalism, creating sliding stages to create pictorial illusion, and using mechanical stages to adjust the size of the stage picture. Scenic artists had been creating panoramic views for decades and thereby unwittingly preparing audiences for motion picture scenery.[50]

Judith of Bethulia is considered a prime example of the transition from stage to film. When Rankin produced it in 1906, a critic called it "a series of picturesque essays."[51] Nance O'Neil's promptbook described Rankin's technique of implying a surging mass of humanity at the eastern gate of Bethulia by employing a number of supernumeraries being held back by two spearmen and the sound of voices offstage. D.W. Griffith remembered Rankin's direction from when he played in it, which influenced him when he made his film of it in 1912.[52]

Rankin engaged a first-class group of actors in San Francisco for his new film company, but as there was no explanation of the method by which the company would market its films, it is probable that it did not get off the ground. Film companies bought their own chain of theaters in which to show their releases. Klaw and Erlanger, for instance, had entered the movie business by taking over movie houses. The Western Moving Picture Company may not have counted on sufficient capital to compete against numerous competitors in this way. It was likely that the theater entrepreneurs once again thwarted Rankin, possibly with a trump card.

1914: Death

Rankin felt that he was too old to tour again. Even Dustin Farnum, a much younger man, announced that he was "weary of the stage." Moreover, Rankin's colleagues of the stage from the early years were dead or dying, which must have affected him. May Howard, the beautiful young actress with whom he had shared many stages in his young days, died in January in sad circumstances. She had had a happy second marriage to an English actor with whom she toured the world and was received by English royalty. When he died, she came to live with her sister in Shelbyville, Ohio. She developed bronchitis and a morphine habit. When her sister died, she was taken in by the widow of the town's mayor who died eventually, leaving her dependent on charity for room and board. Becoming unhinged, May was kept in the town jail for safety, where she died with a confused mass of mementos and photos around her.[53]

Many of the actors whose brief biographies appeared in the dramatic newspapers had got their start in one of Rankin's companies. He had touched many lives, and, despite the bad press engineered by his enemies, the acting profession regarded him with affection and gratitude. His financial woes were common among theater folk and understood by them all.

When his daughter Gladys Drew died of cancer on January 9, 1914, Rankin left immediately for New York City. Gladys's last five months were "a positive martyrdom."[54] Traveling by train, he must have thought of the trip westward in 1870 when Gladys was a baby and of the uncertain future ahead of them. Her accomplishments had delighted him, but now her death, at an early age, cutting short her promise, regardless of his preparedness for the event, depressed him as he entered the gray, wintry city. Rankin stayed to witness a silent tribute to his daughter on February 7. A month later, "the whole film world," the directors, producers, actors and financiers, attended the Vitagraph Theatre in New York to see the first item, a five-act drama, *A Million Bid*, adapted by "George Cameron" for film from "his" play *Agnes*. "The scenes of 'A Million Bid' were so many and varied and the reproduction of natural scenes was so used to reinforce and realize the fiction of the story," wrote a reviewer, "that one is inclined to ask where will the development of this new theatrical entertainment end?"[55]

Rankin valued his independence of living and action, despite being emotionally tied to his children. By February 14, he was back in San Francisco. A postcard stamped on that date was addressed to him at the Continental Hotel in the city from an unknown source. On the back of the card was a sketch of an old gentleman with pince-nez and the words "Dear W—— This here guy was in here to see you. Wheelan."[56] "W" must have thought that the penciled likeness would give Rankin a laugh. It was the last likeness to be made of him.

A month later, about mid-March, Rankin suddenly fell ill. He had been contemplating acting for a brief engagement, but when his doctor attributed his decline to old age, and he realized that he would have to forego his project, he grew steadily weaker and was confined to his hotel room. For some time he had suffered from poor blood circulation. He collapsed in his hotel on April 11. His doctor said that although his condition was critical he was not suffering pain to a marked

The last picture, 1914.

degree. He took little food. Phyllis came from New York to nurse him. He died on April 17, 1914, "as a result of kidney trouble of long standing," as a newspaper worded it, which was a euphemism for cirrhosis of the liver.[57]

Amy Leslie found it significant that he should die in San Francisco:

> That McKee Rankin should have drifted in his vigorous dotage, his poverty and his last battle for the stage back to California, where the most thrilling of his romances, the greatest of his works for the stage and his most picturesque tableaux of life were enacted, seemed rather a curious coincidence, for, though he was Canadian born, his best attempts and years belong to the history of the theater of San Francisco in its spangled, sentimental, brilliantly progressive and influential era of fifty years ago.[58]

Phyllis accompanied Rankin's body by train to New York City, where services were held by the rector of the St Stephen's Protestant Episcopal Church in a house on West Fifty-first Street. Ethel Barrymore was expected to attend the funeral but did not appear. Among those present were John Sherman, Edward Rice, Margaret Drew, Harry C. McKee (a cousin), Phyllis Rankin and Harry Davenport, Doris Rankin Barrymore, Sidney Drew, Jr, Arthur Davenport, Charles Canfield, and George Stephens, who had been in his companies in the early days. Sidney Drew and Lionel Barrymore may have been engaged in film work and unable to attend. A large floral tribute came from the actors' Lambs Club. Rankin was interred at Mt Kisco cemetery in Kensico, New York.

One of the obituaries mourning the passing of a great histrionic artist emphasized Rankin's insistent versatility and suggested that because he was so remarkably successful in a great variety of roles that his claim to greatness was diluted by the very variety of his accomplishments. "The dramatic historian of the future will recount the achievements of Belasco, Frohman and a score of others, who prominently figure in theatrical accomplishments of the past and present, but above them all he will indite the name of the wholesouled and gallant, artistic and unconquerable hero of the stage— McKee Rankin."[59] Amy Leslie made a more realistic assessment:

> Things never did turn out for McKee Rankin, though he was a sinister and plucky gambler in the art upon which he shed much luster and spent much chagrin. He should have been chronicled one of America's most decorative and valuable dramatic assets through the fifty years of his trump card acting and

splendid labors in tumultuous adventures in untrodden fields and forests of the stage and its literature. There is no man so picturesque today, no man so capable, no man so brilliant and probably no man of such startling genius who will leave so little to commend him to posterity. Somehow he always stacked the cards against himself and overplayed the game.[60]

Appendixes

Appendix A

Progeny

Rankin's grandson Arthur Davenport, who was present at his funeral, took the name Arthur Rankin for his stage career. Names were easy for him to carry or cast off. The first son of Phyllis Rankin, he felt much of the affection that his mother did for the venerable old actor. Thus it was not surprising that he settled on the name as his own. He had a long and successful career in films. During the First World War, he served with a British tank corps and later with the U.S. Marines, from which he was given a medical discharge.

While recovering in a London hospital, Arthur looked up to see a stranger approach his bed with great interest. The stranger introduced himself as his father, Harry Gibbs; dumbstruck, Arthur learned that the man he thought was his father, Harry Davenport, was actually his stepfather. That Gibbs had not made himself known before this moment and yet must have watched his son from afar was a testament to extremely rare forbearance. It had been his

---

Notes are on pages 494-95.

so-called social inferiority that lay at the root of his marital problems, and this had been no fault of his own. Phyllis had made a happy marriage with Davenport, and, with the encouragement of her mother, had consigned Gibbs to oblivion. But the world after the Great War was distinctly different from the world before it. Possibly this difference gave Harry Gibbs the courage to come forward and then step back again into the unknown.

Too old to enlist for the Second World War, Arthur prevailed upon President Franklin Roosevelt to arrange for him to be a combat correspondent and photographer with the Marine Corps. He was badly wounded in the Bougainville campaign, which eventually led to his death in 1947.

The other grandson present at McKee Rankin's funeral, S. Rankin Drew, seemed destined for a brilliant career. On the advice of his uncle, Lionel Barrymore, he went into film as an actor, writer, and director. He worked with the Vitagraph Company and directed and starred in several films opposite Anita Stewart, a favorite of the day. Before the death of his mother, Gladys, she dictated to her son a story suggested by the Bible, "Thou Art the Man," dealing with David, Bathsheba, and Uriah. He directed the film version of the story, dedicating it to his mother. It placed him, by all reports, in the highest ranks of his profession. On December 2, 1914, his playlet *What the Moon Saw*, in which he played the principal role supported by his father, demonstrated a quick change of action that "made Broadway sit up and gasp."[1] In November 1916, he joined the Metro-Rolfe studios, where his father and Lionel and Ethel Barrymore were employed. His last important release was *The Girl from Philippa* in February 1917. The United States entered the First World War on April 6, 1917. On April 27, Sidney Drew arranged to pay a recruit $500 and to pay the boy's mother $50 a week for the duration of the war.[2] When S. Rankin Drew discovered that he was barred from enlisting for some inexplicable technicality, he sailed for France in May to enlist in the aviation school of the French army. Sidney Drew, who dearly loved his son, could only watch with dismay and hope. On May 19, 1918, while flying reconnaissance over enemy lines, Corporal Drew went missing. His grave was found later, marked by a rude cross at Arbillières, France. He was the first American actor to be killed in the war. The actors' branch of the American Legion is dedicated to his memory.

S. Rankin Drew wrote descriptive letters to his father, which his stepmother published after the war as *The Life and Letters of Sidney Rankin Drew*. "The son was an indefatigable but deliberate worker and every story, every play he wrote or every manuscript he adapted for the screen, was created, thrashed out or built anew with his father as his confidant and adviser," she wrote in the preface.[3] Sidney Drew remarried in 1914 to twenty-four-year-old Lucille McVey, a concert singer and recitationist. Together they formed a film company and made wholesome comedies starring themselves as Henry and Polly. Sidney was hit hard by his son's death, and within the year he was struck by a fatal heart attack while playing in Detroit with his wife. He was fifty-four. Lucille McVey Drew continued in films as one of the first female comedians. She died at the age of thirty-five in 1925.

Phyllis Rankin Davenport starred in many plays with her husband, Harry Davenport. Phyllis closed her career in 1924 with *The Cradle Song*, in which her husband, her two daughters, and her eldest son had roles. She died in November 1934. Harry Davenport tried his luck in Hollywood and, fortunately, met an old actor friend, then a film director, on the street shortly after he arrived. He had supporting roles in over a hundred films, including *Gone with the Wind*, *The Hunchback of Notre Dame*, and Frank Capra's *You Can't Take It With You*, in which Lionel Barrymore also appeared. He died in 1949 at eighty-three.[4]

Phyllis's second son, Edward (Ned) Davenport III, made his stage debut in 1933 in *Move On, Sister*. He pursued a long career of bit parts before becoming a cameraman in Hollywood. He died in December 1969 some months after his twenty-one-year-old son died. His daughter, Phyllis Davenport, starred as a six-year-old in the television film *The Man Who Came for Christmas*, in 1950. This may have been the last appearance in film and theater of a descendant of McKee Rankin.

Lionel and Doris Rankin Barrymore arrived in Los Angeles after their vaudeville experience with Rankin and located Lionel's old employer D.W. Griffith, who said that he did not hire stage stars. Lionel said that he was not a star, had just two dollars, and was afraid that even they were phony. Griffith paid him $25 a day and $10 a rehearsal. Doris Rankin played in films but spent more time acting on the Broadway stage, in stock companies, and in the leading cities of the world, at one time costarring with Ethel Barrymore. Doris and Lionel apparently had two daughters, but only one was alive when they divorced in 1922. Doris was awarded custody, which, because the girl must have been an adult by then, implies that she was unable to care for herself. Doris had another daughter by her second husband, a retired English army captain who wrote vaudeville acts and ran an inn in Virginia. Doris died in 1946.

Lionel Barrymore married again and carried on acting in and directing films. He directed Nance O'Neil in films. After "talkies" appeared in the late 1920s, he pioneered the adaptation of stage plays for talking films with *The Lion and the Mouse*. Like many stage actors, including his siblings John and Ethel, he made a successful transition from silent to sound films, appearing in such classics as *Grand Hotel* and *It's a Wonderful Life*.

O'Neil was considered a perfect actress for the silent screen, recreating many of her famous stage roles. Her feelings towards film were not reciprocal. "Can you imagine a live human being, full of emotion, trying to express her feelings behind a sheet of plate glass?" she asked. "That is the effect the movies had on me."[5] She continued to star in many plays until after the Second World War. Her greatest achievements were in Spanish plays, which her friend John Garrett Underhill translated for her. *The Passion Flower* by Benavente became her greatest success. As Raimunda, who shoots her faithless husband, she did 187 performances in New York in 1920 and toured from coast to coast for 869 performances. It was her production, and she used the same design for the costumes as did the Spanish actress who created the role in Madrid. The Spaniards considered it as authentically Spanish as if she were acting in Spain. One of her supporting actors was Clara Bracy.

When her husband, Alfred Hickman, died suddenly in 1931, Nance got rid of her possessions and lived the remainder of her life in the Gorham Hotel in New York opposite the entrance of the City Center for the Performing Arts. She still attracted ardent admirers. In 1946, when she was in a poor play, *Crescendo*, on Broadway, she received a note from O.Z. Hall:

> I'm sorry your show was such an awful turkey, but we have no great producers now as we used to have. The cheap gamblers and racketeers have taken over the theater as they have everything else. There never was so much cheapness in the world as now. The Mike Todds and Billy Roses are only despicable things, but they run things, with the aid of a lot of subsidized columnists. They should all bow to an artist like you, but they all go for a lot of ex-waitresses and stupid movie "actresses." They are the danger of the time.[6]

Later in the year, O'Neil toured Canadian cities as Queen Margaret in Shakespeare's *Richard III*, with Jose Ferrer in the title role. It was her last stage appearance. She was often noticed attending the ballets and plays at the City Center through the early 1960s and was reported to be working on an autobiography.[7] In 1965, she died in the Actor's Home in New Jersey at age ninety, having outlived all her starring contemporaries, save for Frances Starr, with whom she was friends in New York, both being still devoted to the memory of David Belasco.

Margaret Drew, the leading actress with the American Theatre stock company, played in Billings, Montana, where she was "a favorite with playgoers," in January 1917.[8] She disappeared from the stage about this time, perhaps a victim of the influenza epidemic, perhaps retiring from the stage, which offered her no more than a nomadic existence in small towns of the Northwest. Necrologies of actors cover only a small number of those who strutted their hour upon the stage; tens of thousands like Margaret Drew and Agnes Ranken, regardless of their prominence, fade unrecorded into oblivion.

Mabel Bert is also among the unrecorded. In May 1915, she acted in *Daddy Long Legs* on Broadway in New York. She was alive when Forrest Robinson, her husband, died in 1924. As she was about ten years older than Nance O'Neil, she may have lived until the Second World War. Whether she was ever in contact with her daughter, Doris, after she left her with Rankin at the age of four is unknown. The heartaches of the actor's life offstage are what help make the performances onstage so real, or so they say.

Appendix B

Plays by McKee Rankin

Collections where copies of the plays may be found are indicated at the end of an entry. The following abbreviation is used: Shields—Shields Library, University of California, Davis. The dates refer to the year of copyright.

1870   *Rip Van Winkle; or, The Legend of Sleepy Hollow*, a domestic drama in three acts, adapted and arranged from Washington Irving's legend of the same name (c. September 21).

   Nannie; or, The Dutch Orphans, an original sensational drama in four acts (c. September 21).

1877   *The Danites; or, The Heart of the Sierras*, an idyllic drama in five acts, by Joaquin Miller. Actually arranged by Rankin with dialogue by P.A. Fitzgerald (c. September 6). British Library; Shields; Billy Rose Theatre Collection. In 1887 Rankin revised the play into *The New Danites*.

1878   *'49*, an American drama in five acts, by Joaquin Miller. After a scenario by Rankin and rewritten by Rankin, J.H. Barnes, and A. Gordon and later revised by Leonard Grover (c. December 5). Rankin's scenario in Shields.

1882   *The Metropolis*, a drama of New York life in five acts and seven tableaux, by Leonard Grover and Rankin (c. December 5). Possibly played in Los Angeles, California, as *The Great Metropolis* in 1894.

The Indians, a poetic American drama in four acts by L.C. Fletcher (c. November 2), actually by Fletcher and Rankin. The first version of *The Americans*, in four acts, by Rankin and Fletcher, produced in 1883.

1883   *Wife and Child*, an emotional society play in five acts, by Rankin and F.G. Maeder (c. May 25).

1884   *Gabriel Conroy*, in four acts. Rankin supervised and totally revised an adaptation for the stage from Bret Harte's novel.

The Golden Giant, a drama in five acts, by Clay Greene and Rankin (c. April 1884).

1885   *Allan Dale*, in four acts, adapted to the stage by Rankin from a novel by Admiral David D. Porter.

1887   *Old London*, a drama, embodying incidents from Ainsworth's novels and other sources with original effects and situations, by Rankin and F.G. Maeder (c. April 13). It was kept in Rankin's repertoire but no performance has been found.

1888   *The Runaway Wife*, a domestic play in five acts, by Rankin and F.G. Maeder (c. Aug. 4). Billy Rose Theatre Collection.

1889   *The Skirmish Line*, a play by McKee Rankin and F.G. Maeder (c. April 12).

The Canuck, a play of French-Canadian life in four acts, by Rankin and F.G. Maeder. With additions to the character of Jean-Baptiste Cadeaux by George Cameron Rankin; George Rankin claimed to have written the play completely, but called it *The Habitant*; in 1900 he published a novel, *The Border Canuck* (c. Aug. 7).

1891   *Abraham Lincoln*, a historical drama in four acts and seven tableaux. The Huntington Library, San Marino; Shields.

1892   *A Kentucky Colonel*, in four acts, adapted by Rankin from a novel by Opie Reid.

1893   *The Grandfather's Clock*, an American comedy drama in three acts (c. May 22).

The Baxters, a comedy-drama in three acts. Set at President Garfield's old home in northern Ohio. First produced at Bartley

McCullum's Summer Theatre, Peake's Island, Portland, Maine, on August 7, 1893; on February 5, 1894, at the Bijou Theatre, Brooklyn. Since both *The Grandfather's Clock* and *The Baxters* were written for the comedian Charles Cowles at about the same time, they may be the same play. Cowles retitled the play *A Country Merchant* and toured for several years in it.

1896 *True to Life*, a drama in four acts; first called *Judge Not*.

1897 *The French Ball*, a local New York sketch in one act (c. June 22). Rare Books and Special Collections Division, Library of Congress.

1902 *The Counsel for the Defense*, a comedy-drama in one act, arranged by Rankin and embellished by W. Robyn (c. October 9). Microform Reading Room, Library of Congress.

1909 *Invasion*, a dramatic composition in three acts, by Rankin and Henry Kirke (c. March 8).

1911 *California*, a four-act drama based on a play by Hermann Sudermann.

1912 *Wages of Sin*, one-act play.

Above the Law, one-act thriller adopted from the French of Brieux.
Betsey and I Are Out, a vaudeville sketch.
The Betrothal Waltz, a motion-picture script. Shields.
The Milkman's Daughter, in one act. Shields.

1913 *Home and Abroad*, a play in one act, by Rankin and Cramer (c. May 24). Shields.

Fortune's Fool, a sketch in one act adapted from the French by Rankin. Harvard University Library (date uncertain).

Notes

Prologue

1 Some sources wrongly refer to Rankin's birthdate as 1841, derived from some obituaries that first made the mistake. The Canada West Census for 1851, taken after February, gives his age as eight, which verifies his birth year as 1844. There is an early mention of McKee as a child in a letter to Mary Rankin from Mary's sister, Arabella, in Erin, a small town north of Toronto. Arabella, looking after McKee while Mary was traveling in Quebec with the colonel, referred to him as "Attie," a nickname that the colonel continued to use throughout his life. "Attie is very well but rather troublesome," Arabella wrote. "He has not made friends yet with the new girl so that I am obliged to have him with me all the time. He is getting much stronger, though his leg is still bent a little but am in hopes that he will soon outgrow it." For Arabella, the big news came in letters from Sandwich and Windsor "all full of gossip and any number of flirtations going on, especially among the married ladies." ALS, Arabella to Mary Rankin, Erin, CW [n.d.], Colonel Arthur Rankin Papers, Ontario Archives.
2 "A Party of North American Indians in Manchester," *Manchester Guardian*, November 11, 1843.
3 English papers began criticizing both Rankin and Catlin for exploiting the Native people for profit. Rankin carried on showcasing the Indians in their dances, the chase, and social customs until Cadotte, it was said wrongly, resented Rankin's disapproval of his marriage and fomented dissension among the Indians, which compelled Rankin to take them home. This rumor was later used in the form of Rankin's alleged dying confession in a scurrilous pamphlet attacking Rankin when he ran for political office in 1857. "The Last Speech and Dying Confession of Arthur Rankin," broadside, inserted after 041235, Rankin Papers, National Archives of Canada, Ottawa. Closer to the truth is an account by the novelist John Richardson, who met "the celebrated" Cadotte (or Cadot, as Richardson called him) in October 1848 on a ship taking presents to Native peoples at Port Sarnia. Cadotte told him of the hypocrisy he encountered in England after his marriage but offered no criticism of Rankin, whose partner he became after Catlin's departure. "A Trip to Walpole Island and Port Sarnia in the Year of 1848," *Copway's American Indian* (New York), July 10, 1851, reprinted in David Beasley, ed., *Major John Richardson's Short Stories* (Penticton, BC: Theytus, 1985).
4 "A Busy Life: The Remarkable Career of Arthur Rankin," *Detroit News*, March 13, 1993.

5 "An Adventure in Canada," in *A Short History and Description of the Ojibbeway Indians Now on a Visit to England* (London: [Vizetelly Bros.,] 1844).
6 One historical source claims that Thomas's son Alexander was born in Ireland (George F. Macdonald, "Tells Story of Col. Alexander McKee," *Amherstburg Echo*, August 1, 1966); another claims that he was born in 1748 in America (Elma E Gray, *Wilderness Christians* [Toronto: Macmillan, 1956], 167). His descendants thought he was a half-breed like his brothers. The Indians called him White Elk. He died on January 5, 1799.
7 A painting of the second Alexander, Colonel Alexander McKee, whose exploits as a Loyalist were a source of pride to the family, found its way through the generations to Catherine Davenport of Hollywood, who offered it for sale in 1947. This Alexander purportedly links McKee Rankin to the Shawnee Chief Tecumseh, who led the Indian forces against the American Generals Sullivan, Wayne, and Harrison until his death at the Battle of the Thames in 1814. A story told to Mary by her father concerns Captain Thomas, the son of the first Alexander, who, when camped at his hunting cabin on Bigg Island in the Ohio River, awakened one stormy night in January 1743 to the impassioned warnings of a Shawnee girl, who told him of a plot of some Indians to kill him and take his trading goods. They escaped with only guns, knives, a hatchet, some food, and blankets before the Indians attacked. Mary Rankin's father identified her as Tecumseh's sister Tecumapease. She was said to be the mother of Alexander. But 1743 seems too early for Tecumseh's sister to be marrying, as Tecumseh was born in 1768. The mistake, if such it was, was an honest one because the family believed that Alexander had been born in 1735, after the McKees' arrival in America. Possibly the Shawnee woman who married Thomas was Tecumseh's aunt, Tecumsapah. As for the Shawnee woman whom the second Alexander married in 1769, she could have been Tecumapease, an older sister of the great chief. The first son of Alexander and Tecumapease was Mary's grandfather Thomas, a half-breed and chief. He leased all of Pelee Island in Lake Erie from the Indians from 1788 to 1815, when Mary's father, Alexander, took it over until he sold it in 1823, the year before Mary was born. Thomas married Therese Askin, daughter of the fur trader John Askin and aunt to John Richardson, Canada's first novelist, so that Mary was related through her grandmother to the Richardsons. Thus, in turn, in some odd fluke of history, Arthur McKee Rankin, Canada's first actor of note, was related to Canada's first novelist, both of whom had Indian backgrounds. Richardson's grandfather and McKee Rankin's great-grandfather was John Askin. John Richardson mentioned in his narration of *The War of 1812* that Tecumseh was fond of the large ostrich feather given to him by a relative in the Windsor area. That relative may well have been Thomas McKee, the son of Tecumseh's sister.
8 Temple Orme, *University College London–Alphabetical and Chronological Register for 1831-1891* (London: H. Walton Lawrence, 1892).
9 H.J.K. Usher, *An Angel without Wings: The History of University College School, 1830-1890* (London: University College School, 1981).
10 A.H. Young, *The Roll of Pupils of Upper Canada College* (Kingston, 1917).
11 John Ross Robertson, the Toronto newspaper editor and historian, was a fellow student. Robertson wrote to McKee's daughter of his association with her father at school when she was buying her grandfather's house, Thornfield, in 1910, bringing it back into the family as it were. Robertson wanted to write an article on its history.
12 John Carboy, "Theatrical Reminiscences: A.M. Rankin," clipping file, Pusey Library, Harvard University.
13 Ibid.
14 *Rochester Union and Advertiser*, April 13, 1860.
15 Lord Say, oppressor of the people, killed Jack's father and drove Jack into exile. Jack and his men capture London, forcing the king to flee, and Jack fatally stabs Lord Say, who manages to cut Jack with a poisoned dagger. Cade's wife, crazed by an attack upon her by Lord Clifford, whom she murders in self-defense, appears on the scene to die moments before Jack, who cries, "The bondman is avenged, my country free!" Neafie's characterization of Jack was "one of the most consummate pieces of art the stage can boast of," according to the Rochester paper. *Rochester Union and Advertiser*, January 9, 1860.
16 Carboy, "Theatrical Reminiscences."
17 *Rochester Union and Advertiser*, January 9, 1860. Review of Neafie's performance.
18 *Rochester Union and Advertiser*, April 26, 1860.
19 *Syracuse Post Standard*, April 17, 1914.
20 Obituary, *Dramatic Mirror*, April 22, 1914.
21 Mrs Haller, unfaithful and long separated from her husband, refuses to marry the Baron de Steinfort. A stranger comes to the castle where she is staying and woos her successfully. The "stranger" turns out to be her husband, with whom she is reluctant to reunite, but she is persuaded by their children.
22 *Cincinnati Daily Commercial*, March 14, 1863.

Act One
Repertory Theater

1. There was another actor in the company bound for fame—Mrs G.H Gilbert. She played old ladies. A dancer in England, she migrated to America with her husband, who was also an actor, and played secondary roles until she discovered that her plain looks and natural comic ability suited her for the old lady line of business. Augustin Daly brought out her talents in New York City in the years to come. Her husband, as stage manager for Wood's, has the distinction of starting Rankin on his career.
2. Impoverished aristocrats will lose their lands unless the son marries the wealthy Ann Chute, but the son is secretly married to Eily O'Connor, a poor maiden known as the Colleen Bawn for her fair hair. Myles, who loves Eily, has a large role in bringing the plot to a happy conclusion.
3. Rankin mentioned that he moved to Pike's after a brief stay at Wood's. One can only speculate as to when he made the move. A review in the *Cincinnati Daily Inquirer* for March 16, 1863, of the young star Charlotte Thompson, playing Julia in Sheridan Knowles's *The Hunchback* at Pike's, reported, "The Clifford of the evening, a promising young actor, was out of his depth." The actor was new, presumably not a member of the company, and remained anonymous owing to the respect of the reviewer for a novice, but this Sir Clifford may have been Rankin on loan for the evening. I suggest that when Nickerson became stage manager at Pike's on March 11, he saw Rankin's letter asking for employment, knew of him through his daughter and the Rankin family, and asked Gilbert, stage manager at Wood's to give him a try. Nickerson liked what he saw in Rankin on March 13, gave him a guest appearance at the more respectable Pike's the following night, and returned him to Wood's for more seasoning under Billy Florence before taking him on as a cast member at the end of March. This is sheer speculation and leans heavily on the assumption that it was Nickerson who was behind Rankin's hiring for the professional stage. I speculate that Rankin stayed for just the one performance of *The Hunchback* because he was not listed in the cast of Thompson's next play, *Little Barefoot*, which ran for a few days.
4. The playbills, information about the companies at Pike's and Wood's, and so on, are at the City Archives in Cincinnati.
5. *Cincinnati Daily Commercial*, May 16, 1863.
6. Ibid., March 7, 1863.
7. Ibid.
8. Carboy, "Theatrical Reminiscences: A.M. Rankin," clipping in Pusey Library, Harvard University.
9. Helen Damico, "The Stage History of Werner," *Nineteenth Century Theatre Research* 3, 2 (1935).
10. Playbill, May 16, 1863.
11. *Cincinnati Daily Commercial*, May 13, 1863.
12. Davenport played William, a comic, witty, frolicsome hearty. He returns home after three years at sea to find his wife, Susan, being wooed by Doggrass, who has told her that William is dead. William throws them out of his house, but later when Captain Crosstree tries to carry Susan off, William, unaware that the man is his captain, wounds him. William is condemned to hang. Just as the noose is being adjusted and the tearful Susan has given up hope, Captain Crosstree, recovered and repentant, saves him by a technicality. Crosstree had signed William's discharge before the incident, which meant that when William struck him, William was no longer in the navy.
13. *Cincinnati Daily Commercial*, January 9, 1864.
14. Rankin is listed as boarding at Clifton House in *Williams' Cincinnati Directory for year commencing June, 1863* (Cincinnati: Williams and Co., 1863).
15. *Call Boy* (San Francisco), October 4, 1903, in Robinson-Locke Collection NAFR+V.371, Billy Rose Theatre Collection, New York Public Library (NYPL).
16. *Cincinnati Daily Commercial*, September 7, 1863.
17. *New York Clipper*, October 10, 1863. In the company also was Ed Marble, comedian.
18. All across the North, young men, including actors, were being swept up by the draft. Others fled to Canada. The Indianapolis paper called the draft dodgers Copperheads and Butternuts and blamed them for rampant crime in the city. In mid-July, troops killed and wounded hundreds of protesters in the draft riots in New York, Troy, and Boston.
19. *Indianapolis Daily Evening Gazette*, September 29, 1963.
20. Ibid., October 6-7, 1863.
21. The plot of *The Woman in White*: Sir Percival Clyde tries to acquire the wealth of his wife, Laura. With the help of Count Fosco, he buries a demented woman who resembles Laura, claims she is Laura, and commits Laura to an insane asylum. His scheme is exposed, Fosco is murdered by a secret society, and Laura is free to marry again.
22. *Indianapolis Daily Evening Gazette*, November 6, 1863.
23. Ibid, November 12, 1863. On his last night, Neafie, as Brutus in Shakespeare's *Julius Caesar*, received unexpected condemnation from the local critic: "His declamation is that of an old fashioned Methodist circuit-rider. His acting is not easy or natural. His step is not stately or graceful. He walks as though he were measuring distances." Neafie replied that after eighteen years perfecting the part, he gave the best Brutus of his career, one that reflected the proud Roman, unbending in

dignity, measured in expression, and purely declamatory in oratory. It was a clear sign that the gap between the intentions of the actor and the expectations of the critic was widening.

24 *Our American Cousin* had been chosen as a fill-in by Laura Keene for her New York theater until another production was ready. The nonsensical plot concerns Asa Trenchard from Vermont, who visits Trenchard Manor in England in time to save Sir Edward Trenchard from ruin and his daughter from a forced marriage to the unjust steward. To keep his cousin Mary from poverty, Asa burns the will that leaves their grandfather's fortune to himself, and he withholds a bottle of hair dye until its influential owner promises to make the Admiralty do something for the sailor who loves another cousin.

25 A New York newsboy who is really a young girl of the streets, Capitola Black, is rescued by the kindhearted Major Warfield, who takes her to his Virginia home. Counterfeiters learn that she is an heiress, kidnap her for black Donald and Colonel Le Noir, from whom she rescues herself and others. Warfield's old slave, Wool, became the most interesting character.

26 *Indianapolis Daily State Sentinel*, December 21, 1863. J.B. Roberts, regarded by critics of his day as a first-class actor, has escaped notice by historians of the drama.

27 *Indianapolis Daily Evening Gazette*, December 26, 1863.

28 *Indianapolis Daily Sentinel*, January 7, 1864. "Deborah" was to become "Leah" in a later version.

29 *Indianapolis Daily Evening Gazette*, February 2, 1864.

30 Ibid., February 8, 1864.

31 *The Dead Heart* concerns the love of sculptor Robert Landry for Catherine Duval, who is taken from him by the Count of St Valery. Landry, imprisoned in the Bastille, is freed when it falls but sacrifices himself for Catherine's son, who is about to be guillotined.

32 *Clipper*, April 16, 1864. His second wife, Miss Phillips, an actress with the company, and their two young children, had to depend on Miss Phillips's earning power. A letter to the editor from Nickinson's son from his first marriage claimed that Nickinson never divorced his mother, who was living in Canada.

33 Ibid., May 21, 1864.

34 *National Unionist* (Lexington), April 15, 1864.

35 Ibid., April 22, 1864.

36 William Winter, *Life and Art of Joseph Jefferson* (New York: Macmillan, 1894), p. 120.

37 *National Unionist*, April 29, 1864.

38 From the time of its appearance in 1863, *The Ticket-of-Leave Man* was a hit in Britain and the United States. The hero, Bob Brierly, is a greenhorn from Lancashire who is befriended by counterfeiters in London and used as a fall guy until he is caught passing a bogus bill. Sent to prison for three years, he keeps a grip on himself through the help of letters from a poor seamstress who knows he is an innocent country boy. When he is released, she gets him a job through her employer, but the counterfeiters locate him, and, when he refuses to help rob his employer's safe, they denounce him as a ticket-of-leave man—that is, a paroled prisoner. Both he and his girlfriend are sacked on their wedding day. In an East End music hall, Bob manages to get work in a gang of laborers but is denounced again and approached to help rob his former employer. He pretends to agree but writes a note to the employer to warn him, at which time the detective Hawkshaw, who has been trailing the gang and who sent him to prison, appears behind him, reads the note, and volunteers to deliver it. The gang is taken in a desperate fight in which Bob is slightly wounded, and, in the embrace of his faithful girl, he administers a well-deserved rebuke to his employer for firing him.

39 *National Unionist*, May 3 and 6, 1864.

40 Ibid.

41 Ibid., May 13, 1864.

42 *Clipper*, May 21, 1864.

43 Ibid., June 18, 1864.

44 *New York Dramatic Mirror*, December 11, 1897. Mirror Interviews.

45 Mrs McKee Rankin, "The Dancing Girl," *American Magazine*, January 1908, 262-66.

46 *Cincinnati Daily Inquirer*, July 8, 1863.

47 *Clipper*, August 22, 1863. "We were then favored with a grand Spanish dance by Miss Kitty Blanchard which was encored," wrote a reporter.

48 Mrs McKee Rankin, "The News of Lincoln's Death, including two stories of John Wilkes Booth," *American Magazine*, January 1909, 259-62.

49 Despite his stage passion, or perhaps because of it, Wilkes Booth was a great favorite with the ladies. Of medium height, he had a good figure, a slight frame, very long and bushy jet-black hair, and a heavy black moustache. When talking, he inclined his head forward, and his voice was musically full and rich, with a rare compass and modulation. His face seemed to talk with the audience, his eyes expressing tenderness and love, malice and hate, pleasure and sorrow, as perfectly as the language he uttered or the tone conveyed. He had a clever perception of characters, and audiences found the transition of his moods "absolutely electrifying" (*Clipper*, April 22, 1865). In 1861, he was having affairs with an actress formerly with the Park Theatre in Brooklyn, with another at Mrs John Wood's Olympic Theatre in New York, and with a popular equestrian actress, when he was shot at by one of the women, the ball hitting him in the hand and causing him considerable pain for some time. After touring for the 1863-64 season, he gave up the stage to devote his time to investing in oil, although he later made a few appearances prior to his assassination of President Lincoln.

50 *New York Dramatic Mirror*, Mirror Interviews. December 11, 1897.
51 *Clipper*, June 18, 1864.
52 *National Unionist* (Lexington, KY), July 15, 1864.
53 Ibid., July 26, 1864.
54 Ibid., August 9, 1864.
55 *Clipper*, July 1, 1865.
56 *Louisville Daily Press*, June 27, 1865.
57 Mrs McKee Rankin, "When Sherman Marched Down to the Sea," *American Magazine*, December 1897.
58 Her own mother was said to be octoroon.
59 ALS, W.S. Wolfe, Garmi, IL, to Mrs McKee Rankin, December 23, 1908, in Rankin Papers, Shields Library, University of California at Davis.
60 *Clipper*, August 5, 1865.
61 Ibid., October 16, 1865.
62 *Montreal Herald*, August 4, 1864.
63 "A Busy Life: The Remarkable Career of Arthur Rankin," *Detroit News*, March 13, 1993.
64 *Montreal Herald*, August 5, 1864.
65 *Detroit Free Press*, September 1, 1864.
66 This was Rankin's first time as the twins, and it is an appropriate place to illustrate the manner in which both brothers appear on stage at the same time. After Fabian di Franchi kills the Duke to avenge his brother's death, the ghost of Louis di Franchi rises gradually through the earth to place his hand on Fabian's shoulder. The stage technique was called the Corsican Trap. The process required that two ledges rise gently from the mezzanine below the stage. The Corsican brother stood on a circular stand inserted between the ledges and above him at stage level was an oval opening or aperture edged with black bristles and fixed in a traveling plank, similar to rolled window shutters. Both the aperture and the stand worked off the same drum: when the drum drew the stand up the inclined plane, it simultaneously opened the apertures. Separate from the aperture was the Corsican Trap, which was concealed behind a tree on stage with the actor's second or stand-in. After Fabian kills the Duke, he walks behind the tree, drops into the trap, and steps onto the circular stand of the ghost machine. As he rises into view, the ghost of Louis, the stand-in, pretending to be Fabian, steps from behind the tree with his face covered, and it appears that Louis has returned as a ghost to comfort his brother, Fabian.
67 *Detroit Free Press*, September 6, 1864.
68 Ibid., September 14, 1864.
69 *Evening Chronicle* (Pittsburgh), September 27, 1864.
70 President Lincoln and Vice-President Johnson, attending a mass convention in Pittsburgh, may have seen Rankin's performances and met the young man whose father Lincoln had commissioned to raise a regiment of Lancers.
71 *Pittsburgh Commercial*, October 5, 1864.
72 *Clipper*, October 22, 1864.
73 *Pittsburgh Dispatch*; *Pittsburgh Commercial*; *Pittsburgh Evening Chronicle*, all November 3, 1864.
74 G.C.M., "Another, but Welcome, Invader," *British Realm*, July 1902. After tracking down most of Rankin's hours spent upon the stage, I have found just one performance as Othello. Could such praise be merited on the basis of one performance? Could Miln have seen it, an unheralded appearance by a neophyte in a Pittsburgh theater in 1864? Could its power have been so great that it was the subject of wonder throughout the acting profession of the day? There are some months in his early career which have evaded me, in which Rankin could have starred as Othello. Many times have I wished that the waters would reletter this deed and give us a description of his characterization of the role. As for Rankin's Macbeth, its record is indelible because of the attention that his productions attracted.
75 Spies were neglected by the government and shown no official gratitude; female spies for the North, whom the Union forces found languishing in Shelbyville prison waiting to be executed, were removed to Nashville, where they remained destitute as wards of public charity.
76 *Clipper*, December 17[?], 1864. Rankin played Brierly on November 30.
77 The other great Camille, Mrs D.P. Bowers, in a different approach, brought out the finer lights and shadows of the character with rare delicacy yet with so much dramatic verve that her portrayal of the unhappy woman was refined and artistic without being weakened by affectation. She eschewed Heron's show of abandon but kept the sense of it absorbed in the character, which made the key scenes with the father and her death very effective. Of the near-greats in the role, Jean Davenport interpreted Camille too grandly and showed a reckless, dissipated woman struggling to emerge from degradation without showing that degradation; Clara Morris, who was at this time struggling to find her way in stock in Cleveland, eventually was to play Camille opposite Rankin with a *force majeure* controlling her actions.
78 *Clipper*, January 12, 1865. Rankin's last role in Pittsburgh was as George Harris in *Uncle Tom's Cabin*, which ran for the week of December 25, 1864.
79 "McKee Rankin; Another Great Artist Who Was Born in These Parts," *Detroit Evening News*, November 20, 1877.

80 Ibid.
81 H.P. Phelps, *Players of a Century; A Record of the Albany Stage* (New York: Benjamin Blom, 1972 [c.1880]). Part of Rankin's problem was that he was replacing a popular actor. The *Albany Evening Journal* (20 January 1865) reported that "Mr. Meldrum's reappearance after an absence of two nights brought down the house."
82 Playbills for all productions at the Howard Athenaeum featuring Rankin are in the Rare Book Room of the Boston Public Library.
83 *Eastern Argus* (Portland, ME), April 8, 1865.
84 *Clipper*, May 13, 1865.
85 McKee Rankin, "The Story of J. Wilkes Booth's Wardrobe. An account of what became of Booth's clothes," 1909. Lincoln Collection, Misc., 1909. Chicago Public Library.
86 See T.P. Slattery, *The Assassination of D'Arcy McGee* (Toronto: Doubleday, 1968).
87 John Wilkes Booth had aided in the capture and execution of John Brown, the militant abolitionist, and had tried to involve an actor friend in a plot to capture the heads of government while they were at the theater and take them to Richmond. Booth admitted that from 50 to 100 men were in the conspiracy. Busy with his investments in oil and Maryland real estate, and with planning the conspiracy, Booth had little time for acting. He appeared on stage rarely: once the year before in *Julius Caesar*, with his two actor brothers to raise money for the monument to Shakespeare in Central Park in New York, and in Washington at a benefit for John McCullough. According to a story told by the actor Otis Skinner in later years, it was McCullough to whom he entrusted his trunk of costumes while McCullough was touring in Canada, and it was to Rankin that Edwin Booth turned several years later to retrieve it when the general suspicion of actors had abated. The story was incorrect, and Rankin tried to correct it, but his reminiscence recorded by Henry Kirk was not published.
88 *Clipper*, April 29, 1865.
89 Ibid., February 27, 1864, 403.
90 Bruce McConachie, *Melodramatic Formations: American Theatre and Society, 1820-1870* (Iowa City: University of Iowa, 1992).
91 *Clipper*, June 7, 1873. In the year following this Boston visit in 1865, Sensation accidentally got its hind legs over the rope across the entrance to its stall and, lying down with its halter under its neck, was unable to raise itself and choked to death. Hudson got another horse, which she reared and trained. This horse, Black Bess, stood 15 hands, 3 inches, and weighed 800 pounds. Bess suffered many mishaps over the years, some of them resulting in fairly serious injuries. In early 1873 in San Francisco, the horse's fall resulted in a broken arm and four cracked ribs for Hudson. However, in May of that year, while performing *Mazeppa* at the Grand Opera House in St Louis, Black Bess lost her footing and fell to the stage while Hudson was bound to her back. Bess broke her spinal column and died; Leo Hudson lingered for three weeks before dying of hemorrhaging in the lungs.
92 *Autobiographical Sketch of Mrs. John Drew* (New York: Scribner's, 1899), 114; See James Kotsilibas-Davis, *Great Times, Good Times: The Odyssey of Maurice Barrymore* (New York: Doubleday, 1977).
93 Ethel Barrymore, *Memories* (New York: Harper, 1955), 8.
94 J.H. Barnes in his reminiscences in the *Stage* (London) said that Mrs Drew was a born humorist and a wonderful companion and friend, as mentioned in the *Chicago Record Herald*, April 19, 1914.
95 Robson grew up in Baltimore, Maryland, with the actors Edwin Booth, John S. Clarke, James Talbot, and Theodore Hamilton, who formed a theater in a barn, where they put on plays. As a twelve-year-old, Robson played tragic roles with the same squeaky voice that made those roles impossible for him as an adult.
96 Playbills for performances at the Arch Street Theatre, 1865. Six are in the Drama Collection, Free Library of Philadelphia.
97 *Clipper*, September 9, 1865.
98 *The Press* (Philadelphia), September 4, 1865.
99 There were four great actors in the Wallack family. Two of them were flourishing in Rankin's time: James William Wallack, Jr, (1818-73), who toured with E.L. Davenport and was a mentor for Rankin and was the son of the actor Henry Walack; and Lester Wallack (1819-88), whose figure was tall and straight, and whose appearance was graceful and distinguished, with piercing black eyes, jet-black hair, shapely limbs, and small extremities, was the son of Henry's younger brother James, also an actor.
100 Rankin, "The Story of J. Wilkes Booth's Wardrobe."
101 Charles Dickens depicted Mrs Lander as the Infant Phenomenon in *Nicholas Nickleby*.
102 *The Press*, October 9, 1865.
103 Furthermore, Lander had enormous competition from another Philadelphia theater, where Mr and Mrs Charles Kean were making their last American tour before retiring from the stage. Charles Kean, who had none of the brilliance and erratic spark of his father, Edmund, covered his defects and shortcomings with consummate tact and skill so that his acting, like that of Macready, was always effective and often brilliant. "A man of great talent, judgment and perseverance," said *The Press*, "almost a man of genius." But he was beginning to lose his memory. One critic found his voice deficient in power and range and deplored his utterance whereby he confused consonants such as in "He poisoned hib in the garded."

104 In *The Fairy Circle, or, Con O'Carolan's Dream*, Robert O'Neil was an Irish patriot, one of the brave but unsuccessful contenders for liberty in 1798 when the Irish rebelled against England at the cost of 150,000 Irish and 20,000 English lives. He believed that if a person fell asleep within the charmed precincts of a Fairy Circle, he or she would dream of the whereabouts of buried treasure. On the other hand, if a person had too strong a desire for wealth, good people would turn against that person. Barney Williams played Con O'Carolan, whose foster brother O'Neil is being pursued as a rebel and is betrayed by his guardian, Blake, who covets his lands. Ellen, Blake's daughter, loves O'Neil and warns him of her father's treachery. Con dreams of a fight between Blake and O'Neil through the magical presence of the Fairy King and awakens with a bag of gold, which, it turns out, Blake had stolen from an English general, but which magically came into Con's possession. O'Neil saves the general's life, and the general saves O'Neil from being hanged by Blake.

105 W.B. Bernard wrote *St Mary's Eve, or, A Solway Story* for Celeste in 1855. It was her first great dramatic speaking part. In the play, Madeleine, the sister of Major Wentworth, a Jacobite, played by Rankin, is wooed by the young farmer Robert Vaughan. The period is 1745, the time of the Jacobite uprising in Scotland, and Major Wentworth is saved from hanging only by the efforts of Madeleine to win a reprieve of his sentence from General Carlisle. The scene in which she rides against time to bring the reprieve to her brother's captors and is intercepted by the smuggler Barty Sharp has the wild romantic air about it, especially when Madeleine disarms the smuggler by flirting with him, takes his gun, and kills him when he tries to stop her. *The French Spy*, also written for Celeste to give her pantomimic gifts full expression as she transformed herself into three different characters and danced as the wild Arab boy, featured Rankin as Colonel Bernelle, the man she loved and came to North Africa to be near. Mute since the age of eight, when her parents and brother were chased by a corsair's ship and murdered before her, Mathilde was enslaved, escaped, and came under Bernelle's protection. As Henri, the cadet, she prevents Mohammed, the leader of the Arabs, from shooting Bernelle. When Bernelle is captured, she infiltrates the Arab camp as an Arab boy and, with an arrow, shoots instructions from Bernelle into the French fortifications. Just as she is found out and Colonel Bernelle is about to be executed, there is a huge explosion and the French Legion storms the Arab position to rescue them. Throughout the play, at dramatic moments, the actors froze as in a picture, which audiences loved, and then continued the action. Celeste, although "over sixty," was praised by the papers for being buxom and comely and looking half her age. She was poetry in motion, "not mere rapidity of movement but that expressive and graceful action which is almost a substitute for spoken language" (*The Press* [Philadelphia], December 3, 1865). The public, however, did not come, and the houses were meagre. People knew that it had been thirty-eight years since Celeste appeared in Philadelphia. The young and dynamic Lucille Western was compelling competition at another theater.

At the close of her last week, Rankin supported Celeste by playing the Chevalier de Torquerolles in an adaptation from the French, *The House on the Bridge of Notre Dame*, in which Celeste played the dual roles of Ernest de la Garde, a young officer, and Zambaro, a gypsy. The play is a melange of relationships and surprising revelations. Rankin played the villainous Chevalier, a roué and schemer, whose character must again have called upon his talent for portraying earthy and threatening figures. Ernest de la Garde is the illegitimate son of the Count of Torquerolles; Zamboro, the gypsy, is the countess's illegitimate son. The dying count wants Ernest to marry Adeline and inherit his wealth, which he knows his younger brother the chevalier covets, but Ernest appears to have met with foul play, thanks to the chevalier. When Ernest appears unexpectedly, he marries another woman Melanie and someone called Florian marries Adeline. The chevalier must have been affronted at his brother favoring the illegitimate Ernest and disgusted at discovering another illegitimate nephew was a gypsy. Audiences did not seem to mind that both brothers were played by one woman, but did mind that she was a sixty-something Celeste! Business was poor during Celeste's run.

106 Job Armroyd loves his wife, Nelly, who is secretly being courted by the rich villain, Gilbert Featherstone. Job is heartbroken when she runs away to London with Gilbert. After months, he tracks down Gilbert and finds that Nelly has sunk to low levels under Gilbert's treachery. But Job spares Gilbert's life, and leaves him to his conscience for having destroyed a happy family. The dying Nelly asks Tilly Dragglethorpe to bring her to Job and begs his forgiveness. Job forgives her for leaving him in a rueful ending. The dialect Rankin had to use throughout the play in the major role went like this: "Sing away lass! I always said thee was the prettiest singer in the country. But, I say, Nelly, Tilly Dragglethorpe ha' been cuttin' wood wi' my razor. She be as bad as Tom Wiggle's gal, who opened oysters wi' his; but, bless ye, Tom were so soft muzzled that he never knowed it til he were told o' it."

107 *The Press*, January 23, 1866.

108 Just as Marlon Brando, for example, in mid-twentieth-century cinema affected a crude image that suited the characters he portrayed.

109 Gennaro, the illegitimate son of Lucretia but ignorant of his mother's identity, is a military adventurer in the service of Venice early in the sixteenth century. Lucretia does what she can to protect him and loves him from a distance, but he rejects her because of her reputation as a poisoner. When she poisons her enemies, Gennaro takes the poisoned wine by mistake. She has an antidote and gives it to him. When he finds that she has poisoned men he thought were his friends, he stabs her, only then discovering that he has killed his own mother.

110 In *Evadne*, Colonna's sister, Evadne, wishes to marry Vincento, but the king's treacherous adviser, Ludovico, instructs Olivia, Vincento's friend, to persuade Vincento, whom she loves, that Evadne is unfaithful. When Vincento repels Evadne, Colonna challenges him and believes he kills him. In prison, Colonna is given a dagger by Ludovico to kill the king, whom, he says, has lecherous designs on Evadne. Intercepted by Evadne and persuaded to bid the king to see her, Colonna hears Evadne show the king the statue of their father and recount their father's loyalty and generosity to the king. The king and Evadne hide while Colonna tells Ludovico that he has done his bidding and killed the king. Ludovico reveals his true self and, triumphant in his villainy, summons the guards to kill Colonna. The king steps out, Ludovico rushes at him with a dagger, but the loyal Colonna stabs Ludovico first. Vincento, very much alive, and having heard a confession of duplicity from Olivia, steps forth to pledge his love for Evadne. This was fairly typical of the well-made play and kept the audience enthralled through its twists and turns and enamoured of its majestic blank verse.

In *Love, or, The Countess and the Serf*, the countess falls in love with the serf Huon and is torn between pride of her lineage and passion for the man. The foil to the countess is another member of the duke's household, Catherine, who often ventures forth dressed as a man. When the duke insists that Huon sign a paper declaring his willingness to marry Catherine, Huon refuses because he does not love her. The duke gives Huon time to sign or die. Only when the countess tells Huon, out of his love for her, to sign, does he do so, but then he flees. He becomes a member of the empress's household and rises quickly as her favorite. When Huon returns to the duke's home with the empress, the empress and the countess quarrel over Huon. The empress has annulled Huon's marriage to Catherine, but the countess reveals that her name is Catherine and she is Huon's real wife, a state of affairs that Huon readily agrees with. Meanwhile the other Catherine, who is to duel with Sir Rupert, who loves her and does not recognize her disguised as a man, is suddenly confronted with her as a woman, and they agree to marry. At one point the countess tells Huon that although he has been ennobled by the empress, the blood of a serf is in his veins, to which Huon replies: "Madam! men's natures are / Their blood; they have no other, high or low"—a democratic sentiment for the time.

111 In the play *Ion*, the title character is a foundling youth who is protected by Medon, the high priest of the Temple of Apollo at Argus. Ctesiphon stabs King Adastrus to death to avenge his father's death. The role of the youthful Ion, who wins a place in society, was favored by actresses whose range was limited and whose beauty could be shown to advantage in male attire. Two decades after Rankin appeared in the play it was in the repertoire of Mary Anderson, whose fame was based on her beauty and her polished but controlled style. Ion nobly kills himself in order to expiate the regicide and dispel a plague from the city.

112 *The Press*, February 13, 1866.

113 Rankin appeared for Dillon's Friday-night benefit as Icilius, who is in love with Virginia, the daughter of the centurion Virginius in Sheridan Knowles's blank-verse tragedy *Virginius*. The noble soldier Virginius was a favorite role for Forrest and John McCullough, particularly for the latter, whose tall, muscular presence, heroic air, and broad style gave a dignity to the role beyond what others could attain. The young Icilius and his older friend Virginius opposed the oppressive rule of the Decemvirs in Rome. Senator Appius Claudius claims that Virginius's daughter is his slave by virtue of being the daughter of another of his slaves. When Claudius seems to be winning his case in the corrupted court of opinion, Virginius slays his beloved daughter. Virginius goes mad and later encounters Claudius in a prison cell. His mad scene and his violent killing of Claudius captured the sympathies of the time, such that the essayist William Hazlitt called it the best acting tragedy of the modern stage.

In the afterpiece Rankin played Athos in *The King's Musketeers* to Dillon as D'Artagnan, Marlowe as Aramis, and Everham as Porthos. Dillon was breaking the theater code by asking the leading man to support him, but Rankin's ability obviously improved the performances and made acting with him enjoyable.

The following Monday, Rankin played the prodigal Wellborn in Massinger's comedy, *A New Way to Pay Old Debts*. Dillon was Sir Giles Overreach, the extortioner. Was there ever such a cruel dissembler as Overreach? His type, who forced innocents into bankruptcy and made them practically his slaves, was common enough in the early decades of the new capitalism which was destroying the landed gentry, though perhaps not so outspoken in their pleasure at their cleverness. The audiences delighted in the trap that the impoverished Wellborn, one of Overreach's tenant victims, laid for him with the help of Lady Allworth. The greed and insensitivity of the character could with no effort be applied to the masters of industry in today's late capitalism. This timelessness, along with its tightly constructed plot, is why the play has become a classic. An entertaining comedy, its undertones are grim and saturnine.

Waiting for the Verdict, or, Falsely Accused brought the audience once again back to the dispossession of the gentry by evil manipulators of the law and criminal forgeries by so-called men of virtue. Rankin played Jasper Roseblade, the farming son of Jonathan, who had lent money to a friend and, failing to get it back, reduced the family to poverty. Harassed and tricked by a land extortioner, Jasper intends to kill him, but finds that the man has been killed by someone unknown. Jasper is tried for murder and convicted by a jury. Fortunately, the real killer is exposed by his underling, and the Roseblades are saved from beggary. The role gave Rankin full range to develop the honest rustic whose faith in justice is painfully shaken. Benevolent Providence came in to play at the end, but it was a near thing for poor Jasper.

Rankin played Laertes in *Hamlet*. He played just once with Lawrence Barrett, as the Duke of Richmond to Barrett's Richard of Gloucester in *Richard III*.
114 *The Press*, May 6, 1866.
115 *The Streets of New York* had run for three weeks in New York City. It was a potboiler of the lowest sort, which Boucicault altered to suit particular locales and ran under different titles: *The Poor of New York*, *The Streets of London*, *The Streets of Liverpool*, *The Streets of Philadelphia*, and *The Money Panic of '57*. Because Rankin eventually played the starring role of Badger in it, and since Rankin's friend, Frank Mayo, would tour for years as Badger, a brief analysis will provide a glimpse at what thrilled the public. *The Streets of New York* is a complicated plot about a lost fortune and lovers parted by cruel circumstances, spiced with broad Dickensian humor and a spectacular scene of a burning tenement (spectacular scenes being a necessity in a Boucicault formula). Boucicault used every staple of popular theater—virtue in distress, noble magnanimity, sinister unscrupulousness, a rousing fight, a scrap of paper that will make all come right, a feast, a wedding, the moderate but not original novelty of dual action on a divided stage, and an appropriately platitudinous moral that was calculated to offend no segment of any audience anywhere. All is extremely theatrical rather than real, traditional rather than individual, hackneyed rather than original. The evil financier grinds down the poor, and the poor are long-suffering, selfless, clean, honest, God-fearing folk whose emotions are phrased in conventional stock terms.
116 Orlando is pursued by his murderous older brother and defeats Charles the Wrestler. His servant, Adam, at one time played by William Shakespeare, called him "my sweet master" for putting Adam's welfare before his own.
117 *The Press*, May 27, 1866.
118 Ibid., May 30, 1866. Among the plays in which Rankin supported Mrs Drew at this time was *Agnes de Vere*, in which he played Alfred de Vere to her Agnes. Alfred de Vere is one of the stage's great hypocrites and more real than the usual villain because his characterization is well-rounded and close to the truth. Alfred is Agnes's doctor. He secretly marries her and gives her a daughter even though she is supposed to marry Edward, a good man who loves her and who has the respect of her father. Agnes tells the truth about her marriage, is banned by her father, and discovers that her husband is having an affair with a courtesan, Lydia. At a fancy dress ball she poses as Lydia and elicits the confession from Alfred that he dislikes his wife. Beside herself with grief and anger and hiding when Lydia appears, she shoots to kill Alfred but wounds Lydia and escapes. Back home, she welcomes Alfred and Lydia, ostensibly a relative on a visit, and gives them poisoned chocolate. Alfred drinks it and dies, and so does Agnes, who, in her last words, charges Edward, the village curate, to care for her daughter. The play shocked audiences, who saw Alfred through the loving eyes of Agnes until he reveals his real character to her at the ball.
119 Mordaunt acted heavies. He got his break when watching Matilda Heron in *The Colleen Bawn* at Niblo's Gardens. The actor playing Hardress Cregan had to leave after the second act to see his wounded brother, who was dying in the hospital. Without having acted the part, Mordaunt glanced over the script and with his retentive memory finished the play to praise from the audience and management.
120 Although the *New York Clipper* reported that Rankin would open for a summer engagement at the Chestnut Street Theatre in *The Ice Witch* on July 22, this performance did not take place. Instead, the play opened on July 23 at the Olympic Theatre in New York with the Webb sisters, Mark Smith, and a good company assembled by Leonard Grover, but not with Rankin. Despite the heat of the summer, the play drew large houses for well over a month, helped, no doubt, by its ice-bound setting in the Scandinavian Sea.
121 The Theatre Museum, London, England, kindly tried to find records of Rankin's visit, but in vain. The *Brooklyn Eagle* (April 18, 1914), however, refers to Rankin's experience on the London stage when mentioning his role in *The Hunchback* in New York in 1867: "[He] had a little experience on the London stage." Kate and Ellen Terry were starring at the London Olympic, but, in the few extant playbills for the season, Rankin does not appear.
122 Playbills for this summer season are in the Rare Book Room, Boston Public Library.
123 On Saturday, September 1, in the matinee, the company produced a comedy adapted from the French, *The Serious Family*. Rankin played the outspoken, outrageous, convention-breaking Captain Maguire, who, returning from service in India, drops in for a stay at the home of his old friend Charles Torrens. In Maguire's absence, the once libertine Torrens has become a conventional family man controlled by his wife, who in turn is controlled by her mother, Lady Creamly, and her hypocritical political friend, Aminadab Sleek. In the end, Maguire, with help from the charming widow Delmaine, frees Charles from his bondage and convinces his wife to devote herself to Charles rather than to her mother. Davenport took a rest from this play, but James Lewis as Aminadab Sleek and Fanny Davenport as Mrs Torrens ably supported Rankin. In the evening Rankin was Macduff to Davenport's Macbeth.
124 *Clipper*, September 1, 1866.
125 Rankin was supporting the great Falstaff of the nineteenth century, James H. Hackett, then sixty-six and beginning to lose his fire, though not his art.
126 "The Stage in New York, by an Englishman," London *Times*, August 21, 1867; September 2, 1867; September 3, 1867; October 1, 1867; October 3, 1867; October 9, 1867; October 11, 1867; October 22, 1867. The article includes the description of the theaters.

127 *Clipper*, September 29, 1866.
128 Ibid., October 5, 1866.
129 Clipping of a published letter from Frank Carlos Griffith, Roxbury, December 16, 1911. Billy Rose Theatre Collection, NYPL.
130 *Clipper*, October 6, 1866.
131 Its first scene opens in a Manchester inn, where the manufacturing owners are discussing the workers' strike. A union delegation headed by Noah Learoyd, played by Wheatleigh, appears and gives terms for ending the strike. Refused and starving, the workers decide to burn down the mills. They draw lots, and the task falls to Noah. Noah's daughter Jane, who had been in love with Jem Starkie, foreman of the engineers, played by Vandenhoff, and at one time with the Irish sailor Johnny Reilly, has switched her affections to Radley, an owner who has been instrumental in denying the workers' demands. When Radley is threatened on the street, Jane hides him in her house, and he overhears the plot to burn the mills. He has three men arrested but spares Noah. When Jane goes to meet Radley, Noah follows her, overhears Radley mock her at the suggestion of marriage, and shoots him. Jem Starkie is suspected of the murder. Only Reilly, whom he accompanied on the road to his ship in Liverpool at the time of the shooting, can save him. Jane, to whom Noah has confessed killing Radley, gets the lawyer Moneypenny to telegraph to the mouth of the Mersey River to intercept Reilly's ship. This is followed by the telegraph scene and Reilly arrives in court in time to exonerate Jem Starkie.
132 *Clipper*, December 15, 1866.
133 *St. Louis Globe Democrat*, December 24, 1866.
134 The play, also known as *Flowers of the Forest*, had a complicated plot centered on crime and intrigue involving an aristocratic family and a band of gypsies. Knichen, a sort of human spirit of the forest, steals everything and lends a lighter touch to the gypsy personality, which, although carefree when on its own, is deeply antagonistic to all non-gypsies, who are the cause of their continuous sufferings.
135 In Buckstone's *Green Bushes*, Rankin played Wild Murdmen (a variation on Wild Murtogh of the original script), a horse thief who speaks with an Irish brogue that became known as stage Irish: "Tare on owns who's that? What Master George and is it yourself now? faix I thought it was one of the boys that had been jairing at me, and it's a marcy my switch didn't come in contact with your iligant frontispiece."
136 ALS, McKee Rankin to D.M. Waller, 246 Bridge St., Brooklyn, January 2, 1867, Pusey Library, Harvard University.
137 *Clipper*, March 16, 1867.
138 Rankin, "The Story of J. Wilkes Booth's Wardrobe." It can only be speculated, however, that Hill must have had the trunk delivered to his residence and turned it over to Edwin Booth after the fire, if we are to believe the story told by the actor Otis Skinner. Skinner said that Booth, at a later date, in the dead of night in the basement of his New York theater with a faithful employee, spent some emotional hours inspecting and throwing into the furnace his brother's magnificent costumes. Otis Skinner, *Footlights and Spotlights* (Indianapolis: Bobbs-Merrill, 1924), 179.
139 *Cincinnati Tribune*, March 29, 1896.
140 *Clipper*, June 22, 1867.
141 Dion Boucicault, "The Decline of the Drama," *North American Review* 125 (September 1877): 235-45; "Early Days of a Dramatist," *North American Review* 58 (May 1889): 584-93.
142 Charles Dickens was in the United States giving readings in 1867, but his main goal was to secure an international copyright for literary works. As far as plays were concerned, international copyright became effective only in 1890.
143 *Clipper*, September 22, 1866.
144 Ibid.
145 Ibid., June 1, 1867.
146 Ibid.
147 As Nat Goodwin wrote twenty years later (Ibid., December 15, 1886), "We are living in a commercial era...[in which] art is subservient to the dollar."
148 *Clipper*, July 6, 1867.
149 *New York Times*, July 9, 1867.
150 Ibid., July 11, 1867.
151 In *Adrienne, the Actress*, which Dean presented on July 17, Rankin revived his role of Maurice, Count de Saxe. As Adrienne Lecouvrier, who moves like a ray of sunshine through the licentious court, Dean approached the famous declamatory scene with poetic fervor. Before the brilliant company in the salon of the princess who, unknown to her, is her rival in love, Adrienne, stirred by the princess's cruelty, recites a passage from *Phedre*, giving a stroke to the heart of the sinner. The great French actress Rachel began the tradition of reciting it with wild declamatory business, but the modern view was that the scene should be undemonstrative, which was the manner in which the young Sarah Bernhardt gave it in her examination for entrance into the Académie Française.

In Knowles's *The Love Chase*, in which two comically complicated chases finally pair an old baronet with a widow and the baronet's daughter with a young sportsman, Julia Dean played the widow and Rankin the young sportsman. Dean saved other plays for her third and last week. In *The*

Lady of Lyons Rankin played his old role of Claude Melnotte. A new play of five acts, *Griseldis*, translated from the German and adapted from one of Chaucer's *Canterbury Tales* and Boccaccio's *Decameron*, retells the story of Patient Grisell. Julia Dean gave an earnest picture of moral purity, ideal womanly character, and self-sacrificing fortitude. Rankin's role was not mentioned. In blank verse, the play was a dragged-out affair, and, according to the critic, represented a perilous act by entrusting poetic drama to the actors of that day. Hattie Thorpe, who was playing the queen, walked out of the theater and left another actress and the prompter to get through the part as best they could. In *Medea*, Dean was Medea to Rankin's Jason, and in the elder Colman's comedy *The Jealous Wife*, Dean acted Mrs Oakley, who suspects her husband of having an affair with Lady Freelove. Rankin had been versed by Mrs Drew in the role of Colonel Freelove.

152 *Clipper*, June 15, 1867. Rankin advertised again in the issues for July 13 and July 20, 1867.
153 "Ours" is the name of a British regiment. When war is declared in the Crimea, all of the principals enlist. In Act Three a snowstorm swirls about their cabin where Hugh Chalcotte has a leg wound and from where Lord Shendryn and Angus McCallister go to the front. The women arrive, nurse Hugh, and greet the returning Angus with love. All misunderstandings are resolved.
154 *Clipper*, September 7, 1867.
155 Ibid., August 31, 1867.
156 *Cleveland Leader*, September 24, 1867.
157 Ibid., September 27, 1867.
158 Ibid., October 4, 1867.
159 Ibid.
160 *Clipper*, October 19, 1867.
161 In *Caste*, the son of a marquise proves by devotion to the instinctively well-bred daughter of a common drunk that social class is no barrier to marriage.
162 *Clipper*, October 26, 1867.
163 Ibid., December 14, 1867.
164 Fred Maeder was a good eccentric and light comedian who began writing melodramas with astonishing frequency. His father, J.C. Maeder, had been a well-known musician who trained the voice of the young Charlotte Cushman and became her guardian; Fred's mother was a famous actress, Clara Fisher. Chevalier Balthazar discovers a relationship between his older brother, the Count de Rougeville, and the wife of a local magistrate and tries to blackmail him. The count leaves all his money to his lover and flees the country. Balthazar poisons her wine to get his hands on his brother's fortune, but the count returns unexpectedly and, drinking the poisoned wine by accident, makes the chevalier promise to protect her after his death. Pike, it will be recalled, was the same whisky trader in whose theater in Cincinnati Rankin acted as a neophyte. Pike had rebuilt the Cincinnati Opera House after it had burnt down and then had built the imposing building in New York that had the largest stage in the country.
165 *New York Times*, May 27, 1868.
166 *Clipper*, June 20, 1868.
167 Letter from Frank Carlos Griffith, Roxbury, December 16, 1911, in Kitty Blanchard Clippings, Billy Rose Theatre Collection, NYPL.
168 *New York Times*, June 11, 1868.
169 Joseph F. Daly, *The Life of Augustin Daly* (New York: Macmillan, 1917).
170 *New York Times*, August 10, 1868.
171 "Tragedy in a Theatre," ibid., August 25, 1868.
172 When Lingard transferred his company to the Academy of Music in Brooklyn, Rankin was in the company and performed with Raymond in *All That Glitters* and *A Day after the Wedding* for Lingard's farewell benefit on October 19. See Odell, *Annals of the New York Stage*. Under Academy of Music, Brooklyn.
173 *Clipper*, September 19, 1868.
174 Ibid., November 28, 1868. George Medhurst committed forgery and, to escape blackmailers, changes his name to Hayward, becomes a cabman, and marries a poor girl. His friend Chumley, who will buy forged papers for Medhurst from the villain Bellingham, is saved from the railway tracks, where he has been bound, by Old Tom, who turns out to be the long-lost father of Medhurst's wife.
175 *Chicago Tribune*, December 9, 1868. The cast-off son of the Countess Montrevide, Vyvan returns as a sea captain, visits Eveline, ward of the countess, whom he loves, and discovers that he is the countess's son. The countess favors her second son by another marriage and refuses at first to acknowledge Vyvan. Both sons love the same woman, and in a quarrel Vyvan falls over a cliff. Eveline wanders about like an Ophelia and the countess is filled with remorse as the second son is to be tried for murder. Then Vyvan turns up and all is resolved happily.
176 *Chicago Tribune*, December 15, 1868.
177 Howard, who had lost her parents in the Civil War, ran the blockade and began acting in 1861 at Wood's in Cincinnati. She played juvenile leads in touring companies through Ohio and Indiana before joining stock in Philadelphia. She is not to be confused with the burlesque actress of the same name.
178 *Chicago Tribune*, January 17, 1869.
179 *Clipper*, March 17, 1869.

180 *Chicago Tribune*, March 10, 1869.
181 Ibid., March 13, 1869.
182 Ibid., March 22, 1869.
183 After discovering that the boy is wealthy, a count searches for the son he disowned as a baby. His notary, Andre, discovers that the duke, who the count thinks is the boy's real father, wants the young count to marry his daughter to prove that the countess was misjudged by her husband. Andre murders the old count and arranges for a nobody, Joseph, played by Rankin, to pass as the young count. Meanwhile Andre discovers that the real young count is a painter in Paris in love with a woman called the Queen of Hearts. Andre plots with Rocambols, also played by Rankin, to lure the real count to an island and kill him, but Rocambols scuttles the boat to drown Andre and the count to get the estates of the old count. Throughout the action there appear the Knaves of the Pack, a band of counterfeiters and robbers in Paris. A chilling scene takes place when Andre, having escaped drowning with the young count, discovers Rocambols living in a cave with a woman whom he thinks is the Queen of Hearts, but who is really Rocambols's mother. Andre seals the cave shut. Rocambols is found with a card of the Knave of Spades pinned to his breast on which is written the name of his killer. Together with his mother, who survived, the card leads to Andre's arrest before he can collect the fortunes that he expected to control. Rankin also played a third role, possibly one of the Knaves of the Pack, but, according to the critic, he "was perceptibly ill at ease from having so little to say or do during the first half of the play, though he subsequently found a little more scope for action."
184 *Clipper*, April 24, 1869. Another critic called it one of the most elegant plays put on stage, but faulted the doubling of the father and son characters. "Rankin's peculiarities of action are such that a concealment of identity with him is well-nigh impossible. The result was that at one time he was a prematurely young father, and at another, a prematurely old son, and the double role lacked the force of contrasts. Some of the scenes, however, he played with remarkably good taste, especially the pretty love scene at the piano, in which he makes known his attachment for the coquette, Lady Clara—a scene which he gave with unusual dignity and a very clear conception of a very embarrassing situation. Stage love-making is not the most grateful task, but his success in it was evinced by the fact that he carried the sympathies of the audience with him."*Chicago Tribune*, April 13, 1869.
185 Ibid., April 26, 1869.
186 Ibid., May 31, 1869.
187 Ibid., June 7, 1869.
188 *Clipper*, June 26, 1869.
189 ALS, McKee Rankin, Chicago, June 7, 1869, to Colonel Brown, New York. Pusey Library, Harvard University. Brown obliged.

Act Two
Stardom

1 *Clipper*, July 5, 1869.
2 Ibid., July 17, 1869.
3 Ibid.
4 *New York Times*, June 22, 1869. Blanchard was called by the critic dashing and "a decorous proficient in all nimble-footed and dexterous vocal artifices."
5 Amy Leslie, "McKee Rankin Goes Home for Last Trip," *Chicago News*, May 2, 1914.
6 L. Clarke Davis, "Among the Comedians," *Atlantic Monthly*, June 1867, 751-52.
7 W.G. Pike, the same manager in whose company Rankin had worked in Portland, Maine, had put together a good company for Rankin to handle.
8 *Clipper*, October 9, 1869.
9 *Hamilton Spectator*, November 23, 1869.
10 Ibid., November 26, 1869.
11 *Montreal Herald and Daily Commercial Gazette*, December 6, 1869.
12 According to the paper, his unexpected departure was caused "by the illness of his intended mother-in-law." Ibid., December 10, 1869.
13 *Boston Sunday Times*, December 12, 1869.
14 It was well known that traveling troupes were often left stranded in midwestern towns or in some out-of-the-way settlement by managers who skipped with the proceeds during the night. If stranded actors had relatives to send them money, they could get back home; otherwise, they would be left to team up with other actors to try to eke their way by performances from town to town until they could reach a city where they might find employment in the local company. Actors who had not been paid could not pay for their room and board, which accounts for their bad reputation for sneaking out of windows in the dead of night or putting on all their clothes and walking out in the daytime.
15 *Clipper*, January 15, 1870. James A. Herne played Bill Sykes.
16 *New York Times*, February 15, 1870.
17 Ibid., February 16, 1870.
18 Kate Field, *Charles Albert Fechter* (Boston, 1882), 98, 102.
19 *Clipper*, March 19, 1870.

20 Ibid., April 9, 1870.
21 The play concerns the murder of Quintana by a Spanish planter as Quintana is about to depart for France with his gold in search of his grandson, Leon. The planter tries to kill Quintana's adopted daughter, Olivia, played by Lydia Thompson, but she escapes. Disguised as a Creole boy, she persuades a pirate crew that she has killed Olivia, and she joins the crew. She learns that the murderous planter has assumed the name of Quintana and plans to find and murder Leon. At an inn in France she overhears a plot to lure Leon to the inn and kill him as he leaves in second place behind one of the conspirators. Olivia, dressed as a man, leaves before the others, thus marking the conspirator as the second man, who is shot; Leon, as the third man, escapes. Olivia accuses the planter of murder, discovers she is of noble birth, and is made happy by Leon.
22 For instance, James Lewis ran into trouble at the Continental Theatre when the manager refused to pay him because he had gagged, that is, he said "Kiss me for Phoebe" at two evening performances and a matinee. Lewis was suing on the grounds that only at first-class theaters were there rules against gagging, and the penalty was a fixed one, not discretionary. Moreover, his gags were generally popular, and he had never been reproved by management.
23 *Clipper*, June 18, 1870. The plot: Because employment is hard to find, Arnold joins the navy, but before embarking, he tries to get food for a starving child. A benevolent man, St Clair, gives him money, which saves the child from death, but a villain, Silas Jarrett, steals Arnold's tools, commits robbery, and leaves the tools to implicate Arnold. Arnold is sentenced to the Dartmoor Quarries before St Clair discovers that Silas is the real culprit. Silas escapes capture. St Clair becomes embroiled in financial difficulties, but in the end Silas is captured, Arnold released, and St Clair pardoned for financial mistakes. Rankin was praised for a good piece of acting, "for as the mechanic and the gentleman, he was correct, not overacting either."
24 William C. Hudson, "Between the Lines," *Brooklyn Eagle*, March 20, 1914.
25 *New York Times*, September 8, 1870.
26 Daly's company was interesting and capable of playing other than lines of business. Fanny Davenport played Lady Gay Spanker in *London Assurance* for the first time at age nineteen with Daly and became the best Lady Gay of her time. She had great self-possession, blooming health, and a splendid presence. The burlesque performer James Lewis now played everything. Agnes Ethel, a pupil of Matilda Heron, came to prominence under Daly. She was slender, with candid eyes, flowing auburn hair, an oval face, and features lit up by an expression of childish appeal. Her low voice had a penetrating quality. Daly hired veteran actors such as William Davidge, who appeared in revivals of old comedies and modern burlesque; George Holland, a much-loved comedian; Mrs G.H. Gilbert; and Mrs Chanfrau. He also added actors who had leading roles at Lester Wallack's Theatre, such as Clara Jennings and J.B. Peck. Daniel Harkins stage-managed as well as acted for Daly. The remarkable resonance of his voice made his speaking of Shakespeare's lines delightful to hear. Joseph F. Daly, *The Life of Augustin Daly* (New York: Macmillan, 1917).
27 Clara Morris, *Life on the Stage* (London: Isbister, 1902).
28 "Rambles around New York, by Muggins," *Sporting Times and Theatrical News*, October 22, 1870. Rankin's impatience to be on the road may be measured by the fact that he had engaged his company to open in St Louis on October 24, when the baby was barely two weeks old and Kitty was recovering. The announcement of Gladys Rankin's birth was in the *Clipper*, Oct. 15, 1870, under "Report (of amusements) for Oct. 10."
29 Would one leave on an arduous trip to the West under primitive traveling conditions with a newborn baby or wait for at least four months after its birth? A story in the papers about the murder of several actors by Indians near the Hastings Pass en route for Austin, Texas, must have given Rankin pause as he would be traveling with his wife, a baby daughter, and his mother-in-law. The actors were minstrels traveling in minstrel coaches and one of them was carrying $30,000 for their expenses along the way. Whatever second thoughts Rankin had, they were dispelled by a later report from one of the minstrels who said that they had a pleasant journey across the continent from Omaha, saw some Indians who were harmless, enjoyed the grand scenery, and opened in San Francisco to a full house after turning away 2,000 people. Their first night's receipts were $1,900 in gold coins, which was what they collected for their first five days, before the take fell to $700 a night. Rankin needed no other persuasion.
30 *Clipper*, November 5, 1870.
31 Ibid., November 26, 1870.
32 Ibid.
33 The following night at a benefit for Blanchard, the company played Dickens's *Dot, or, The Cricket on the Hearth*, with Blanchard as Dot and Rankin as Caleb Plummer. W.H. Whalley played John Perrybingle. Rankin followed it with *A Regular Fix*, in which he made a tour de force as Hugh de Brass, the gambling debtor. The audience for this was larger than for *Nicholas Nickleby*, and it was so for the same play at the Saturday matinee as well. On Saturday evening, the company did *Oliver Twist* and left for Omaha.
34 "McKee Rankin Tells of Old Days on the Stage and of Early Stars," *San Francisco Examiner*, May 18, 1913, 48.
35 *Clipper*, January 7, 1871.
36 Ibid., January 14, 1871.

37 Ibid., February 18, 1871. John Dunn left for Australia at this point.
38 "McKee Rankin Tells of Old Days"; "When McKee Rankin Played the Pueblo," *New York Telegraph*, April 9, 1911. Rankin's company included Kitty Blanchard, Fannie Young, Fannie Gibson, Susie Soule, Mrs Sinclair, W.H. Powers, Harry Sinclair, Frank Rea, Harry Colton, J. King, and F. Cleaves.
39 "When McKee Rankin Played the Pueblo."
40 Ibid.
41 *Clipper,* March 11, 1871. For the historical record, the company included Kitty Blanchard, Maggie Moore, Mrs Harry Sinclair, Alicia Mandeville, William Barry, Harry Sinclair, Harry Colton, George Hinckley, Charles Thornton, and W.H. Powers.
42 "McKee Rankin Tells of Old Days."
43 "McKee Rankin Tells of Plays before the Early Mormons' Rigid Censorship Placed over Drama by Brigham Young," *San Francisco Examiner,* June 15, 1913, 42.
44 Most prominent among these Danites were John D. Lee, Bill Hickman, Orin Rockwell, Eph Hanks, and Hezekiah Carter, desperate and determined men who regarded all they did as the solemn dictate of Brigham Young and the Mormon Church.
45 "McKee Rankin Veteran Scion of Stage Tells of Pioneer Days," *San Francisco Examiner,* July 6, 1913, 39. The businessmen were Joslin of the famous jewelry store, Joslin and Park, which used the beautiful moss agate specimens of Colorado and Wyoming, and Josephs, who ran a stationery and rare-book store in Cheyenne.
46 "McKee Rankin Veteran Scion."
47 "When McKee Rankin Played the Pueblo."
48 "McKee Rankin Veteran Scion."
49 *Clipper,* July 22, 1871. Rankin played Chalcotte "in a careful and conscientious manner." *Clipper,* July 29, 1871. Wyndham, who had been a doctor in the Civil War, won recognition for his acting in Wallack's New York repertory company. Within a short time, he was to become famous as an actor-manager in London, England. For the moment, he had been called to New York to take on a role, and Rankin received a cordial welcome when he took his place.
50 *Clipper,* September 30, 1871.
51 *Clipper,* October 21, 1871.
52 In St Louis also were the Jane Combs Company, in which Jane starred in her old repertoire of *The Lady of Lyons, The School for Scandal,* and *Romeo and Juliet,* and Matilda Heron, whose age and avoirdupois tended to detract from her charm. *Clipper,* December 2, 1871. Heron had been absent from the stage for two years and now appeared extremely nervous, fumbling with her hair, stroking her brow, and muttering unintelligibly in the old play *Naomi.* After Act I, she told the boisterous people to leave the theater, and, after the play, she came forward to thank Ben De Bar for giving her a chance as a pauper to regain her legs again. "My heart is in my soul, and my soul is with my God. I don't care a fig for the world, and I am just as happy as a big sunflower," and she danced offstage waving her arms in a wild manner. It was devastating to see a great actress reduced to penury and near madness. Heron eked out a living teaching acting in New York but became a pitiable sight in later years. Only the success of her daughter Bijou on the stage brightened her final days.
53 *Clipper,* November 25, 1871.
54 *Clipper,* December 23, 1871.
55 *Clipper,* February 3, 1872 The reconstruction comprised advancing the stage six feet into the auditorium, replacing the old scenery, hanging a new drop curtain, renovating and painting the front of the house, replacing the old, stiff-backed benches with soft-cushioned chairs, fixing up the aisles with oil cloth and new carpeting to deaden the footfalls of latecomers, adding gas fixtures, and putting up hangings and accessory paraphernalia.
56 *The Bouquet Programme* (St Louis Times, n.d.).
57 *Clipper,* February 10, 1872. Gerald Goodwin inherits £100,000 but loses it through fraud and along the way earns the envy and finally the friendship of Pennythorne and others.
58 *Clipper,* February 17, 1872.
59 *Clipper,* March 2, 1872.
60 *Clipper,* April 6, 1872.
61 *Clipper,* April 20, 1872.
62 The plot of *The Bells*: A young gendarme in the village has become intrigued by tales of a murder, and Mathias encourages him to marry his daughter in the hopes that the rich dowry from the money he has stolen will make the gendarme forget the case. The news that a mesmerist can force out hidden truths unhinges Mathias. He dreams that he has been taken to court, mesmerized, and made to tell the true story. The shock of his nightmare kills him. Rankin, playing Mathias, brought his own interpretation to the role, somewhere between Irving's passion and Wallack's introspection. Meagre audiences appeared for Rankin's production owing to the bleakness of its theme.
63 Elsewhere, Rankin's theater friends were busy. May Howard joined with Owen Marlowe, J.C. Williamson, and the long-time California player Walter Leman to reorganize John McCullough's old company in the San Francisco California Theatre. In Rochester, New York., Frank Mayo was alternating with Frank Murdock in the great roles of Shakespeare to acclaim and introduced a new play, *Davy Crockett,* in which he was to make a fortune. Edwin Forrest died about the same time, prompting long eulogies in the newspapers. In his last appearances, Forrest had been laughed at for

Notes

his old style of heroic acting and often had found theaters just half full. Later in the year, Robert Craig died of brain fever and Mrs John Drew with her Arch Street Theatre company held a benefit for his widow and children. Craig had been at Arch Street from just after Rankin left in 1866 to May 1871, and, as has been suggested, may have fathered Sidney Drew. James Kotsilibas-Davis, in *Great Times, Good Times: The Odyssey of Maurice Barrymore* (New York: Doubleday, 1977), writes that Craig abruptly asked to leave Mrs Drew's company soon after Mrs Drew went for a rest in the country. He stayed until May 1871, however. See obit. *Clipper*, December 21, 1872.

64 *Clipper*, December 7, 1872. Touring actors and troupes not only had to settle all the details of staging their plays in the scores of stops they made in a season, they also had to follow a protocol that William Shakespeare mentioned in *Hamlet*: they had to "extend the usual courtesies to city officials" in each town when they arrived. In October, W.H. Lingard was made to pay a license fee of $25 instead of the usual $5 in Toledo, because he had arrived too late to pay his courtesies.
65 *Cincinnati Daily Times*, February 11, 1873.
66 *Cincinnati Daily Gazette*, February 11, 1873.
67 *Clipper*, April 12, 1873.
68 Ibid., April 26, 1873.
69 Ibid., May 24, 1873.
70 Ibid., June 7, 1873.
71 David P. Botsford, "The History of Bois Blanc Island," *Ontario History* 47, 3 (1955):138.
72 ALS, McKee Rankin, Detroit, to Augustin Daly, Fifth Avenue Theatre, June 6, 1873, Folger Shakespeare Library. Washington, DC.
73 Playbill, Rare Book Room, Boston Public Library.
74 Ibid.
75 *Clipper*, July 5, 1873.
76 Ibid., August 16, 1873. The Rankins may have taken roles in the productions at the New Orleans Academy of Music.
77 Dion Boucicault took over Lester Wallack's theater in New York for the summer season and produced and starred in his dramatization of Henri Murger's *Scènes de la Vie de Bohème*, entitled *Mimi*, with himself in the role of the enamored poet Maurice and Katherine Rogers as the doomed mistress, Mimi. It became apparent that Boucicault was helping to give international exposure to his mistress, Katherine Rogers.
78 Kate Ryan, *Old Boston Museum Days* (Boston: Little Brown, 1915).
79 *New York Times*, September 8, 1873.
80 *Arrah-na-Pogue* (*Arrah of the Kiss*) takes place in County Wicklow in the Rising of 1798. Like Boucicault's two other "Irish" plays, *The Colleen Bawn* and *The Shaughran*, this one has two pairs of lovers balanced one against the other: Beamish MacCoul, serving with the Irish rebels, and Fanny Power on one side, and Shaun the Post and Beamish's sister, Arrah Meelish, on the other. The Rankins as Beamish and Arrah were praised for the production.
81 Ida Vernon as quoted in Pat Ryan, Jr, "A.M. Palmer, Producer: A Study of Management, Dramaturgy, and Stagecraft in the American Theatre, 1872-1896" (PhD diss., Value University, 1959).
82 Ibid.
83 While quite young, Eytinge had starred with Davenport and Wallack, but, after her marriage, she went to Europe and Asia for a few years and encountered difficulty in returning to the American stage. Daly took her on, and she began to climb back to stardom. This role established her once again.
84 Odell, *Annals of the New York Stage* (New York: Columbia University Press, 1927-49), 15v.
85 Ryan, "A.M. Palmer."
86 Clara Morris, *Life on the Stage*, 389.
87 *Clipper*, June 6, 1874; *Spirit of the Times*, May 30, 1874.
88 *Chicago Tribune*, July 24, 1877. Morris's strange, emotional, and magnetic nature was combined with genius and culture. She was self-taught and conversant with books and art. Small and thin, with flat features like those of the Sphinx—lips unusually thick, wonderful deep gray eyes full of thought and expression—she had a sonorous, heart-stirring voice, notwithstanding a Yankee twang, that no one could resist. She could make an audience feel the force and truth of pathos as no other actress. Morris played *Camille* from May 14 to June 5, and repeated it in charity performances from June 8 to 11, during which, in conjunction with performances given concurrently at other New York houses, it raised $27,000 for the poor. *Led Astray* was brought back for June 6, 1874, and replayed from June 12 to the matinee of the 13th, *Camille* being played between these times and for the last time on the evening of the 13th, for which the theater was decorated with flowers; souvenir programs on satin and a bouquet of flowers were given to each woman in the audience. A benefit to Claude Burroughs, a good supporting actor with the company, on the 15th, marked the last full performance of *Led Astray*.
89 *Clipper*, July 4, 1874. The scenic painter at the theater, Richard Marston, mounted the play sumptuously and won exclamations of wonder for the setting of the last act, representing one of the principal hotels at Long Branch on the New Jersey shore with the grounds and view of the ocean, the moon's rays rippling on the water.
90 *Clipper*, July 4, 1874.

91 ALS, Kitty Blanchard to Augustin Daly, March 14, 1875, Folger Shakespeare Library.
92 *The Arcadian* (New York), September 24, 1874. The unhealthy tendency of the French stage has never been more clearly evinced. Not only is the heroine a wife unable to rest satisfied till she has gained the love of the husband of her dearest friend, but she must spend her spare time in leading four other men to believe that they may have the honor of eloping with her. When her schemes are exposed, and she is ruined by the passion against which she has never really struggled, she turns to suicide.
93 *New York Times*, September 22, 1874.
94 Ryan, "A.M. Palmer."
95 *New York Spirit of the Times*, September 26, 1874. "[Among the men] the chief honors are secured by Mr. Rankin. If he could only get rid of a certain slouching walk, he would bid fair to become one of our best 'leading men.' A good course of drilling and some fencing lessons would, we believe, accomplish the desired result." *Arcadian*, September 24, 1874.
96 Rankin would have remembered Charlotte Thompson (who played Jane Eyre) at Pike's Opera House in Cincinnati when he was an inexperienced novice. Earlier, in the closing weeks of the summer, Charlotte Thompson played *Jane Eyre* at the theater. Despite its popularity, after three weeks it had to give way to *The Sphinx*.
97 *New York Tribune*, October 29, 1874.
98 Ibid., October 26, 1874. "Now, as always, Miss Cushman's Lady Macbeth was seen to be marvelous for lurid lights of horror, and for the perfect embodiment—mental, spiritual, and physical—of conditions of tragic passion. Her figure towering above Macbeth and pointing beyond him to the coming Duncan, who 'must be provided for,' or crouching against the door-post of the chamber in which the midnight murder is afoot, is awful beyond the power of words to describe, and it can never pass from the memory of the living who have seen it, or from the most glowing page of the annals of our drama....All the old points were made, and made with superb spontaneity and perfect precision; and the unity of the personation was as fixed as that of the diamond, giving all colours and keeping one form."

Rankin would have been just as interested in Vandenhoff's portrayal of Macbeth because Macbeth was a Shakespearean role that Rankin thought he could play. Vandenhoff's art sprang from the intellect rather than from the soul and lacked that glow of inspiration that alone can cause spontaneity. His tone of polished culture and bland modern refinement was not consonant with the haunted, harrowed, fiend-driven chieftain. But his Macbeth was Shakespearean in that he was massive, majestic, royal with imaginative splendor, and awful with the ravages of a most afflicting anguish. The critic wrote: "Macbeth is a man of noble mind, splendid imagination, tender heart, indomitable valor, and imperial individuality, and he is seized, possessed, dragged down, and despoiled by those dark and tremendous forces of evil which contend with goodness throughout the essence of universal life. The crimes that he commits are not the crimes of a cruel man but of a man whose nature has been inverted, polluted and partly crazed. The torturers of remorse begin to tear his heart even before he smites the King; and afterward, his life is a horrible delirium. Flecked here and there with clear moments of settled misery and pathetic dejection—upon a lonely and awful eminence of evil." *New York Tribune*, October 29, 1874.
99 Ibid., November 9, 1874.
100 *New York Times*, November 17, 1874, 4.
101 *The Arcadian*, November 26, 1874.
102 Preface to George Lovell's *Love's Sacrifice, or, The Rival Merchants*, 1842. Playscript on microfiche. *Modern Standard Drama*, ed. Epes Sargent (New York: Berford, 1846-48), 2.
103 A critic lauded Rankin as: "making rapid strides towards the very front rank of our leading men. The loose dress and slightly stooping gait of Matthew Elmore tended to conceal the heaviness and awkwardness of movement which to a considerable extent mars his acting when appearing in modern dress. His make up was excellent, and he never for a moment forgot the age of the character he was representing, even when called upon for the strongest display of passion. At times Mr. Rankin showed great power, but he failed somewhat in his description of the murder. This, one of the finest points of the piece, should elicit more from the actor than any previous situation, and Mr. Rankin failed therein, not because he did not then act as well as before, but because he had not kept a reserve force as should lift this situation above the level of the remainder of the play." *The Arcadian*, December 7, 1874.
104 Mrs McKee Rankin, "Behind the Scenes with 'The Two Orphans'," *Theatre Magazine*, May 1910, 157.
105 *New York Times*, December 23, 1874.
106 Ryan, "A.M. Palmer," op. cit.
107 *The Arcadian*, December 24, 1874.
108 *Clipper*, February 13, 1875.
109 Robert Grau, *Forty Years' Observations of Music and the Drama* (New York: Broadway Publishing, 1909), 314-15.
110 Mrs McKee Rankin, "Behind the Scenes with 'The Two Orphans'."
111 *The Arcadian*, February 27, 1873. Another sign of the theater as a growing business was the rise of actors' agents. A comedian, Charles Parsloe, opened the first dramatic agency in 1857, and James Connor started the first agency for all branches of the theatrical business in 1860. When Frank Rivers, the owner of melodeons, began his agency in the mid-sixties, McKee Rankin enlisted but

switched to Corbyn and Wall in 1867, as that agency began drawing actors to it with more liberal terms, and when Colonel Brown left his post as dramatic editor of the *Clipper* in 1871 to start an agency, Rankin switched to him. By 1873, two agencies had the lion's share of business: Brown's on Fourth Street near University Place, who took on all branches of the theater, and Morris Simmonds, one-time treasurer at Pike's Opera House, Cincinnati, who had commodious rooms on Broadway. Managers came from far-flung American cities in July of every year to consult these astute men, who charged them about $50 a year. Agents charged stars a percentage of their receipts and they received a percentage of the salaries of stock company players, which was secured by order of the manager. In July 1875, an actors' exchange was established in Union Square, where a telegraphic communicator showed the demands for artists in all parts of the country, the ruling rates of pay, and the prices of board and lodging in all areas. *The Arcadian*, July 10, 1875, 7.

112 Ibid., May 22, 1875.
113 Odell, *Annals of the New York Stage*.
114 *Clipper*, June 26, 1875. Kitty was ill for the last performances, and her place was taken by her understudy. She again approached Daly for employment for the next season, but in vain.
115 Gerald Bordman, *American Theatre: A Chronicle of Comedy and Drama, 1869-1914* (New York: Oxford University Press, 1994), 45.
116 John Ranken Towse, *Sixty Years of the Theater* (New York: Funk and Wagnall, 1916); Garff B. Wilson, *A History of American Acting* (Westport, CT: Greenwood, 1980); Edward Mauman, *The Old Stock Company School of Acting* (Boston: 1945).
117 Junius Booth, Sr, together with the light comedian William Rufus Blake and the tragedian Edmund Kean were considered the great actors of the first half of the century. In their histrionics there was little difference between the excesses of the imagination and the freaks of a madman. Junius Brutus Booth, Sr, had the best intellect of the three. He spoke six languages and acted successfully in Racine plays at the French Theatre in New Orleans, then considered the Paris of the United States. He had a classical education, had learned printing, studied law, served as a midshipman in the British Navy, and was a wonderful conversationalist, able to talk on the occult and any religion, all of which he held sacred. With him, acting was an independent art, not a mere combination of oratory with scenic display. His absolute identity with the character he was playing had never been exceeded in any era. His voice was said to have transcended music and portrayed the beauty, truth, and power of which the human voice was capable. Later in life, his nose was broken, which, said James Murdoch, gave his voice an unfortunate nasal twang. He bequeathed some of his acting talent to three of his sons, although his youngest, Joe, who was enamored of the stage, was hopeless as an actor. Junius Booth, Sr's, attention to detail, his unlimited industry, and his refusal to stand on dignity were characteristics of his actor sons. To differentiate him from two important actors, Thomas Cooper and Edwin Forrest, the story is told of his dressing up for the small part of Almagro in *Pizzaro* within ten minutes when the actor playing the part failed to arrive. The others would have considered it beneath their dignity. Walter M. Leman, *Memories of an Old Actor* (San Francisco: 1886).
118 "Charles R. Thorne, Jr.," MWEZ+13,635, Billy Rose Theatre Collection, New York Public Library (hereafter NYPL).
119 *Clipper*, August 21, 1875.
120 Her mother had endeared herself to all persons she met and had made many friends in the theatrical profession. *Clipper*, August 14, 1875.
121 *Clipper*, September 4, 1875.
122 Ryan, "A.M. Palmer."
123 *Clipper*, December 18, 1875.
124 Meanwhile, Palmer had a profitable engagement of *The Two Orphans* in Boston with Claxton and Wilkins and brought a revival to New York City at the Union Square Theatre late in 1876. This New York revival was the occasion for a great tragedy. The play had to be temporarily transferred to the Brooklyn Theatre and was due to return on December 9. On December 5, 1876, the Brooklyn Theatre caught fire. Several of the cast, including Claude Burroughs, were killed in the flames. In total, 295 people perished. Frederic Robinson, who was acting Rankin's role of the brutal Jacques Frochard, and James O'Neil (father of the playwright Eugene), who played Mackay's role of the cripple Pierre, were among the cast that escaped. Palmer sold the play to Claxton for $1,000. By the late 1880s, Kate Claxton had earned $150,000 touring it. For an all-star production in 1904, Palmer had to get Claxton's permission.
125 *Clipper*, April 8, 1876. Rankin undoubtedly had seen Charles Fechter in the role, for it was one of Fechter's masterpieces. When Fechter first entered as Lagardere, he hurled himself into a group of ruffians, scattering them like a bombshell, and then in a flash, he stood with naked rapier in the center of the stage, with his military cloak on his left arm, ready for attack from any quarter. Such panache proclaimed him a hero of romance, equal to any hazard and preordained to triumph. Rankin had played Carrickfergus when in Indianapolis with Riley.
126 E.F. Thorne, a brother of Charles, Jr, played the Duke Gonzagues, and Charles H. Morton, who tried all aspects of theater, including management, was Carrickfergus, friend of Lagardere.
127 *Clipper*, May 13, 1876.
128 Ibid., January 18, 1879.
129 Ibid., October 2, 1876.

130 "McKee Rankin Taps Fund of Memories; Actor Tells How 'The Danites' Came to Be Written from Old Tales," *San Francisco Examiner*, July 27, 1913, 58.
131 Ibid.
132 The story was by John Habberton, well known for his novel *Helen's Babies*. Rankin may never have known who the author was, because he mentioned that years later when playing in London he was approached backstage during an interval by a shabbily dressed man who claimed to have written it. Rankin gave him a ticket for the best seat and told him to come to see him after the performance when they could work out compensation over dinner, but he never saw the man again.
133 To show how successful the Chestnut Street Theatre's production was, it should be compared to Daly's production in New York, which ran for only five weeks before touring. The Philadelphia production ran for 174 performances to November 18, 1876—about twenty-one weeks. Aside from Rankin, the only cast member of star stature was George Holland. The first-night audience augured success: the parquet was overflowing, and the upper tiers held an audience remarkable for its repectability and distinguished appearance, as if it were an opera night. Daly's New York production, by the way, included two newly arrived English actors who were to have an impact on America and an association with Rankin: Jeffreys Lewis and Maurice Barrymore.
134 *Clipper*, August 21, 1876. *Our Boys* concerns a conflict between a son, Charles Middlewick, and his crude but good-natured tradesman father, Perkyn Middlewick. Charles and the son of a snobbish aristocrat, Talbot Champneys, meet and become friends on a tour of Europe but return home to find that their fathers have planned marriages for them, coincidentally, to the very girls that the other man's son loves. The sons rebel; the fathers throw them out; the sons scrape out a living in a London garret until the eventual reconciliation.
135 *Clipper*, November 11, 1876.
136 "'The Danites' Author," *The Press* (Philadelphia), October 7, 1881, 1.
137 Aside from the evidence of playbills reflecting Blanchard's change in status, there is a handwritten note in the Mss. Room, Columbia University Library, that supports this claim and Rankin's relationship to Caroline Henri. The note was not signed. See "Blanchard, Kitty. Biographical Sketch (Phila?)," 2 p. The note makes reference to Gladys Rankin as "never a dutiful daughter as she is a Rankin and they are a restless tribe."
138 *Clipper*, November 27, 1876.
139 *Our Boarding House* deals with a wronged woman, Beatrice Mannheim, a music teacher residing at the Bon Ton Boarding House in Chicago, who is told by Fioretti, a new boarder, that her marriage was a sham and her child illegitimate. Many of the boarders are outraged and demand she leave, but she finds a staunch defender in Walter Dalrymple. At the last moment, a New York detective arrives to announce that her marriage was legal and her husband has died, leaving her an heiress. He arrests Fioretti. Beatrice agrees to marry Walter. Two characters, Colonel Elevator, an impecunious speculator always dreaming of making a killing on the commodities market, and Professor Gregarious Gillypod, determined, after seventeen failures, to invent a flying machine, are feuding boarders.
140 *Clipper*, March 12, 1877. The lead character, Mrs Elizabeth Victoria Stark, played brilliantly by Mrs Phillips, believes that the world is made of those who squeeze others like a lemon or are squeezed. She tries to marry off her son and daughter as lemons to other lemons, but events conspire against her. Her son's lawyer, a consummate lemon-squeezer, turns Mrs Stark's stratagems inside out, in which he has help from Mrs Stark, who, mistakenly believing that two men are in love with her, vacillates in choosing between them.
141 *The Press* (Philadelphia), April 10, 1877.
142 Leonard Ashley, in preface Cibber. *She Would and She Would Not* (1702), 1989. In *The Kind Imposter* Hypolita turns down her suitor, Don Philip, and then, when he goes to Madrid to marry another girl, follows him in disguise. Don Philip prepares to marry Rosara, but she is being courted by Octavio, who, to prevent her marriage, takes the disguise of a friar. Intrigues develop rapidly, assisted by the clever servant Trappantio. Hypolita appears wearing breeches as a young gallant, claims to be Don Philip, duels with the real Don Philip, and marries Rosara. She promises to have the marriage annulled only if Rosara marries Octavio. Rosara's father agrees, Hypolita reveals her identity, and Don Philip embraces her with expressions of ecstasy.
143 Set in contemporary Paris, *Slander* concerns a young Corsican, Blanche Marino, who becomes engaged to a viscount and thus suffers the enmity of his nephew and heir. This nephew hires a thief, Hector Despard, to pose as a nobleman in order to claim Blanche was his lover, and ruin her in the eyes of the viscount. As a result, Blanche is spurned by the viscount and deserted by her brother, Joseph. Hector abducts Blanche to a den of thieves, from which her brother rescues her but still believes her guilty. Joseph wants to kill Hector and learns from him the plot to dishonor his sister. When Blanche attempts suicide, Joseph rescues her. With the truth coming out, the viscount drives out his nephew and Blanche is restored to the viscount.
144 "McKee Rankin Taps Fund of Memories." Although this interview took place in 1913, it is basically the same as a report in the *Detroit Evening News*, November 22, 1877, "Miller and Rankin: How the First Made a Poem, and the Second Reduced It to a Play," which must have come from Rankin, who was playing *The Danites* in Detroit at the time. The latter account, however, has Miller turning up in Philadelphia unexpectedly with a bulky role of manuscript that Rankin found practically use-

less but turned it over to Fitzgerald after "trimm[ing] it off and cut[ting] it down." Fitzgerald's widow mentioned that the play was first produced at the Walnut Street Theatre in the spring of 1877. If so, it was just a one-time experiment done to secure backers.
145 "The Star Course," *North American* (Philadelphia), April 17, 1877, 4.
146 Signed by Miller, Boston Mall, March 26, 1878. Shields Library, University of California at Davis.
147 "Joaquin Miller in Court," *New York Dramatic Mirror* (hereafter *NYDM*), October 15, 1881, 7.
148 Bertram in *Quits* was an important role but secondary to a comically befuddled Yankee who alternately hinders and helps in the pursuit of justice. After saving a young woman from death by a runaway horse, Bertram woos her successfully until his long-lost mother appears and asks him to go away because she wants to marry the woman's father. He is about to ship out for India when all is resolved happily and there is a double marriage. In *Married in Haste*, two young painters marry and alienate the groom's uncle by their haste. The bride's father has suffered reversals in business and cannot help them. Moreover, the groom is jealous of the bride for being able to sell her paintings and refuses to allow her to sell more, thus reducing them to poverty. Their quarreling is resolved by a friendly man-about-town, Gibson Greene.
149 *North American Review*, May 26, 1877.
150 "Mr. McKee Rankin as 'Macbeth'," *The Press*, May 28, 1877, 2.
151 Ibid.
152 "Miss Pomeroy's reading," commented the *North American*, "was faulty in the extreme." "Miss Pomeroy," said another critic, "has genius, but it is as a comedienne, not as a tragedienne." May 26, 1877. Her Lady Macbeth lacked "intensity." Louise Pomeroy, however, had been professional for less than a year and had been enduring the fury of her husband, who had given her an opera house as a wedding gift to keep her from acting. He was now divorcing her for disobeying him.
153 *Chicago Tribune*, May 29, 1877.
154 Ibid., June 17, 1877.
155 ALS, Joaquin Miller, Boston, n.d. to Mrs Rankin, Huntington Library.
156 *New York Times*, August 23, 1877. "Much that is obscure and tedious." Nevertheless, the reviewer was impressed by the acting.
157 *New York Daily Tribune*, August 24, 1877.
158 Juanita Brooks, *The Mountain Meadows Massacre* (Norman: University of Oklahoma Press, 1962).
159 "The Danites: Betrayal and Murder; Orin Porter Rockwell, The Great Danite Chief," n.p., n.d. 4-page pamphlet, Billy Rose Theatre Collection, NYPL.
160 *Clipper*, September 1, 1877.
161 Ibid., August 25, 1877.
162 *American Theater 1880* (Cincinnati), No. 4, p. 403, Billy Rose Theatre Collection, NYPL.
163 "Actresses in Trousers," *Chicago Tribune*, December 30, 1888, NBLA+ American Theatre 1880, Rose Theatre Collection, NYPL.
164 Ibid.
165 The previous January, at the age of only thirty-four, Lucille Western had died of pneumonia after carrying a high fever the night before while playing the role of Nancy.
166 Levi Damon Phillips, "Arthur McKee Rankin's Touring Production of Joaquin Miller's *The Danites*" (PhD diss., University of California at Davis, 1981), p.43. All of the financial information and touring routes for *The Danites* from 1877 to 1881 (except for the play's tour in the British Isles) I have taken from this source. Dr Phillips used Rankin's account books covering his American tour of the play, which are in the Shields Library at Davis. His account books for the first two years have miraculously survived to give a picture of his earnings. Although I researched Rankin's papers at Davis, I did not see them. On 11 October, the Rankins appeared in an afternoon benefit performance for the widow of Edwin Adams, the much-loved actor who had died from causes relating to alcohol. Ailing, Adams had attended several benefits in a long, agonizing good-bye from San Francisco to New York, in which his many friends took part. Nonetheless, after his death his widow was still impoverished. The benefit included Rankin and Blanchard in scenes from *The Danites*. Rankin also played Armand Duval opposite Clara Morris as Marguerite Gautier in the fourth act of *Camille*. A storm of applause greeted Clara Morris, who played her part with intensity and deep emotion. Rankin was manly, vigorous, and effective as Armand, making their scenes the dramatic event of the afternoon.
167 *American Theatre 1880*, NBLA+v.1-, Billy Rose Theatre Collection, NYPL.
168 *Clipper*, October 21, 1877.
169 During this Brooklyn appearance, Rankin gave a benefit performance for the Custer Memorial Fund. He played Mr Rochester opposite Clara Morris as Jane Eyre at Wallack's Theatre in New York. It was Clara Morris's first appearance in the role. Although the run of *The Danites* was disappointing in terms of numbers, it brought the company good publicity. The Brooklyn paper declared that it was the best company the city had seen for many years.
170 *Detroit Evening News*, November 14, 1877.
171 *Clipper*, February 9, 1878.
172 *New York Times*, February 13 and 16, 1878, p.1, col. 6.
173 *Clipper*, March 23, 1878.
174 Ibid.

175 Phillips, "Arthur McKee Rankin's Touring Production," 68.
176 *Clipper*, May 25, 1878.
177 Ibid., June 15, 1878.
178 The Fitzgerald family was elated when the widow was interviewed in 1880 because her husband's authorship of the play had been revealed at last by Rankin. Actually Rankin had told a reporter for the *Detroit Evening News* in 1877 that Fitzgerald was the author. *Detroit Evening News*, November 22, 1877.
179 John Scott McElaney, "The Professional Theater in San Francisco, 1880-1889" (PhD diss., Stanford University, 1972).
180 Bruce C. McConachie, *Melodramatic Formations: American Theatre and Society, 1820-1870* (Iowa City: University of Iowa Press, 1972).
181 David G. Schaal, "Rehearsal-Direction Practices and Actor-Director Relationships in the American Theater from the Hallams to Actors' Equity" (PhD diss., University of Illinois, 1956).
182 Phillips, "Arthur McKee Rankin's Touring Production," 80. Haverly was forty years old in 1878. He began his theatrical career in 1875 with a theater in Chicago, where he put on new plays, burlesques, minstrel shows, and highlighted popular stars. He was a great risk-taker, which made him the leading impresario, but his personal characteristics belied this. He had a modest demeanor and a retiring manner and was scrupulously polite. His slight figure of medium height was activated by a nervous temperament, however, that made his movements quick, his gray eyes keen, and his mouth decisive. Rankin was to discover that he would also make a vicious enemy.
183 Gardiner appears in David Beasley's *Who Really Invented the Automobile* (Simcoe, ON: Davus Publishing, 1997) as the financial backer of Leon Serpollet, who built and raced his steam car in France in 1900.
184 *Clipper*, September 7, 1878. Both Maggie Arlington as Captain Tommy and Emma Marble, the daughter of Rankin's comedian friend Ed Marble and granddaughter of the great actor William Warren, were praised for their admirable makeup and thorough identification with their characters.
185 *New York Times*, September 8, 1878. p. 7, col. 4.
186 *Clipper*, October 5, 1878. The company played on Sunday evening, as it had done on previous visits to Chicago. The practice in Chicago had begun with charity performances on Sundays, which evolved into an extension of the theatrical week. Haverly promoted Sunday performances at first but soon realized that the actors became exhausted without one day of rest. The practice of Sunday shows had been an old one in New Orleans and had spread to other cities by the late 1870s because of the better class of European immigrants who used the ballot box to effect changes in the religious laws. In the eastern cities, however, the civic leaders strictly enforced the ban on theatricals on Sunday. Although box office returns were high on Sundays, Rankin rarely played that day because there was no noticeable financial advantage to the actors; yet managers did realize a substantial financial gain, of which he, as a manager, took advantage on occasion. On the other hand, some star actors such as Jefferson refused to appear on Saturdays, let alone Sundays, because the effort was too draining when taken in the context of constant touring for ten months of the year, and sometimes longer.
187 *New York Times*, January 14, 1879, p. 7, col. 4.
188 *NYDM*, February 1, 1879.
189 Ibid., April 5, 1879.
190 Ibid., July 5, 1879. Set in California, *My Partner*, as was generally acknowledged, owed much of its inspiration to *The Danites* and was declared by the *Mirror* to be far superior to it. *My Partner*, which toured for six years, made Aldrich rich and famous. That the interviews were fictional is suggested by the reporter's referring repeatedly to the Detroit River as the St Lawrence River, a mistake that no one who had visited the area would make.
191 *NYDM*, August 23, 1879.
192 "Death of Mrs. Charles Henri," *Clipper*, October 1879, 214.
193 *NYDM*, October 4, 1879.
194 Ibid., December 6, 1879.
195 Ibid., January 10, 1880.
196 "Cora Tanner," Clipping, Billy Rose Theatre Collection, NYPL.
197 *NYDM*, February 28, 1880; *Chicago Tribune*, February 22, 1880, p. 7, col. 1.
198 The report from Pittsburgh claimed that the play had deteriorated under Rankin's careless hand, and the company was mediocre; *NYDM*, March 27, 1880. In Providence, however, the company was called excellent, the acting fine, the mountings elegant, the scenery and mechanical effects unequaled in the history of the Providence Theatre. The houses were crowded. *NYDM*, April 3, 1880.
199 The actors going to England were Bill Sheridan as the Parson, E.M. Holland as the Judge, Harry Hawk as Washee Washee, P.A. Anderson as Stubbs, J.G. Peakes as Grasshopper Jake, Matt Lingham as Bill Hickman, George Waldron as Hezekiah Carter, J. Richardson as Sam (who had played the small role from the start), Little Bell as Georgie Williams, Isabel Waldron as Sallie Sloan, and Emma Marble as Henrietta Dickson. The actress Rankin chose to play the Widder was Genevieve Rogers, but Cora Tanner was substituted for her at the last moment. William and Harry Lee, Jerry Stevens, Lin Hurst, and Lillian Cleves Clark also went with the company. In this second company, Sid Ellis played Sandy McGee. He looked the part, but his voice was too husky and dis-

Notes 463

agreeable. Bertha Welby as Nancy Williams and Billy Piper looked amateurish and could not wear men's clothes well. Charles Chapelle, however, was a hit as the Parson, creating applause by his strong impersonation wherever they played. Gertie Johnson was successful as the Widder, Budworth's Washee was very funny, and Ben Maginley, who now managed the company, gave an "immense" performance as the Judge.

200 Mrs Bateman quit the stage to write successful plays such as *Self*, *Geraldine*, and *Evangeline*, in which her daughter Kate starred. The family then went to London and ran the Lyceum Theatre. When the father died, Henry Irving assisted Mrs Bateman with the management and eventually purchased her interest, which freed her to reconstruct the Sadler's Wells.
201 *The Stage* (London), May 1, 1880.
202 *The Theatre* (London), June 1, 1880, 354.
203 *Times* (London), April 28, 1880. A letter from J. Palgrave Simpson, known today for his anthology of poetry, to Mrs Bateman was a good omen. He thought the piece was generally well acted. "Mr. Rankin's style was all my fastidious judgment could have desired—at once eminently natural and effective—replete with the noblest variations of intimation—and sympathetic in the highest degree. Mrs. Rankin, too, was both forcible and touching and sweetly graceful." Blanchard preserved the letter. ALS, J. Palgrave Simpson to Mrs Bateman, London, May 14, 1880, Shields Library.
204 "McKee Rankin Taps Fund of Memories."
205 Ibid.
206 *Clipper*, July 19, 1879.
207 ALS, A. McKee Rankin, Liverpool, to Joaquin Miller, September 28, 1880. Huntington Library.
208 ALS, McKee Rankin, Liverpool, to Morris Simmonds, New York, September 19, 1880, Pusey Library, Harvard University.
209 A Liverpool theater had produced at the close of July a two-act drama *The Danites, or, Life in the Golden Gulch*, by a minor author who was using the same characters and situations to profit from the publicity. His placing of the time of the play as early as 1818 demonstrated the author's lack of knowledge on the subject. Later, it toured England under the title *The Golden Gulch*.
210 "Joaquin Miller in Court," *NYDM*, October 15, 1881, 7.
211 Miller wrote a number of plays, but he was a poor dramatist. His most recent effort was excoriated in Cincinnati: "The luxuriant genius of Joaquin Miller found vent at the Grand Opera House on Monday in 'Mexico'—one of the most pitiable, puerile and most inherently worthless pieces of dramatic claptrap which has encumbered the stage of that popular theater for some time. Whatever pretensions as a dramatist Miller may have had are quite offset by this production. It evidences anew the assertion so often made that the 'Danites' owes its vitality more to the cunning hand of poor, dead Fitzgerald than to the efforts of Miller." His faults were "bombast and trite jokes" and "no pretense of construction as the piece and the characters wander to and fro on the stage without apparent reason." *Cincinnati Commercial*, February 1879, citing *NYDM*.
212 *Manchester Guardian*, October 5, 1880.
213 ALS, McKee Rankin, Glasgow, to Morris Simmonds, New York, October 19, November 26, 1880, Pusey Library.
214 *NYDM*, December 25, 1880. "McKee Rankin arrived at the Union Square Hotel with his wife and children on Wednesday afternoon. Andrew Dam, Jr. met him with open arms, hand in hand they tripped gaily to the mysterious little apartment presided over by the 'Doctor' at the back of the cafe. Rankin looks as ruggedly handsome as ever."
215 Kate Rankin to C.W. Stuart, New York, December 30, 1880, Malone Papers, NYPL. Tom Maguire was probably there. Maguire's luck had changed. After surviving the depression of 1873, a local financial panic in 1875, and another catastrophic downturn in 1877, he had an irreversible setback in 1879 when he produced Salmi Morse's *Passion Play* at his San Francisco Opera House. It was one of the most notable stage events of the day. Actors were added to his company from the Baldwin Theatre; there were eighty singers and a full chorus; James O'Neill played Christus, Kate Denin played Herodotus, William Seymour was the stage director, and David Belasco was the prompter. Much of the audience, overcome by the beauty and religious fervor of the performance, knelt and prayed throughout whole scenes. Members of the cast felt uplifted, forswore worldly habits and thought of the hereafter. But the city fathers considered the play blasphemous, closed it, and prosecuted Maguire. He was now in New York City, where he had been recently arrested for pirating plays.
216 Note (n.p., n.d.) in Rankin papers, Shields Library.
217 *Clipper*, March 5, 1881.
218 St Louis *Post-Dispatch*, April 9, 1881. In Chicago for eight nights and two matinees, *The Danites* made $7,000. *NYDM*, April 2, 1881.
219 Kate Rankin to Clinton Stuart, April 15, 1881, Malone Papers, NYPL.
220 *Detroit Free Press*, June 31, 1881, p. 3, col. 1.
221 The term derived from the fashionable Delmonico's restaurant in New York City. "Delmonico's cafe on Fifth Avenue presents a gay and animated scene every Saturday night after the close of the theaters. The innumerable tables are surrounded by parties of well-dressed men of all nationalities, dining, smoking, talking. The French garçons rush frantically about with decanters of whisky, sherry, or brandy, and all is noise and confusion, the figures of men being dimly discernible through the heavy cloud of segar and cigarette smoke which fills the room." *Stage*, March 12, 1870, MWEZ+n.c.

12,228, Billy Rose Theatre Collection, NYPL. Before April 1862, Delmonico's was at the corner of Chambers Street and Broadway, with elegant rooms where countless masked balls were held. General Winfield Scott lived over the restaurant. After 1876, Delmonico's moved from Fifth Ave and Fourteenth Street to Fifth Ave and Twenty-sixth Street. It is now an exclusive restaurant far uptown on Beaver Street.

222 *NYDM*, September 24, 1881.
223 *Clipper*, September 24, 1881.
224 According to Barnes in his memoirs, Rankin made an excellent William, but Blanchard could not compare with Mrs Kendal as Susan. Ballet and the spirited country dancing by the principal actors added to the entertainment but could not enthuse the audience, who gave just one encore. J.H. Barnes, "Forty Years Ago," *NYDM*, March 11, 1914.
225 "Joaquin Miller in Court."
226 Rankin later claimed that after he had received the play from Miller in 1878 he rewrote the first act, changed the plot, and finished it on his return from England in 1880.
227 New York *Spirit of the Times*, Ocober 8, 1881.
228 *New York Sun*, October 12, 1881.
229 Ibid., October 14, 1881. *NYDM* carried charges and counter-charges at this time, but the best statement was "Two Sides of a Story," *NYDM*, October 8, 1881, 7. Later the *New York Times* called Miller "a most positive fraud," and Ambrose Bierce, the short-story writer, called Miller "the greatest liar this country has ever produced....He cannot or will not tell the truth." Miller replied: "I am not a liar. I simply exaggerate the truth." Quoted in *NYDM*, October 8, 1881. M.M. Marberry, *Splendid Poseur: Joaquin Miller—American Poet* (New York: Crowell, 1953), 252.
230 New York *Spirit of the Times*, October 22, 1881. "He will also be obliged to give bonds, as a native of Canada, to secure costs to Messrs. Miller and Wheeler in the civil suits with which he has threatened them."
231 *Chicago Tribune*, November 13, 1881.
232 Ibid., November 7, 1881, 19.
233 Barnes, "Forty Years Ago." A satirical article on *The Danites* noted the points that gratified the audience: the kicking of Washee Washee by Sandy, closely followed by the word "damme" uttered by Washee, and the expression "infernal cuss." Rankin seemed to play to this low strain in the audience because whenever poetry followed plain talk, he held up his hand as if to say, "Hear ye, the Hon. Sandy McGee will now be delivered of a high-strung and poetical utterance." The orchestra would give a little snarl, "like a cat whose tail has been trodden on, for the purpose of letting folks know that there are breakers ahead." The critic recommended that Rankin do less snickering, especially in the courtship scene, which was originally invented for the Yankee in love, and that Blanchard do less spasmodic shrieking and wailing. Nevertheless, he had to admit that the two plays throbbed with manly force and genuine raptures of sincere and wholesome emotion preaching the virtues of honesty, independence of character, kindliness of nature, generosity, and trust in God, which uplifted audiences. *Chicago Tribune*, November 16, 1881.
234 "That Rank Rankin," *NYDM*, November 19, 1881, 7.
235 *Chicago Tribune*, November 7, 1881.
236 *Cleveland Leader*, December 6, 1881.
237 *Chicago Tribune*, June 4, 1882. Although copyrighted, the play appears not to have been produced. It had five acts and seven tableaux and dealt with life in New York City. An item by a critic favorable to Rankin appeared in the press. Someone had told customs officials at Amherstburg that Rankin was bringing in a set of silverware and a mysterious basket on his steam yacht. The officials, eagerly anticipating appropriating three-quarters of the valuation they would receive, stopped his boat but discovered that the silverware was from Canada and the basket contained a watermelon. *NYDM*, August 5, 1882, 5.
238 *NYDM*, August 19, 1882.
239 Rankin's version of *The Danites* may be found in the Rankin Papers, Shields Library, and in the Billy Rose Theatre Collection. There is also a counterfeit version in the Billy Rose Theatre Collection. Meanwhile, Joaquin Miller had published his version of the play as *The Danites in the Sierras* and arranged for a production to tour Germany. It is quite different from Rankin's play, which has five acts and fifteen characters to Miller's four acts and eleven characters. The widow schoolteacher in Rankin's play becomes a missionary in Miller's. The poignancy of Nancy Williams/Billy Piper's unrequited love for Sandy McGee in Rankin's play is absent from Miller's, in which the Danites kill the widow by mistaking her for Nancy, and Nancy marries Sandy. The Danites have a small role in Rankin's play and a larger role in Miller's, in which they behave like terrorists. Rankin's play has short speeches, poetic thoughts, and dramatic tension, whereas Miller's is long-winded, undramatic, and unfocused.
240 *Clipper*, October 14, 1882.
241 At this time it was reported that Leonard Grover was writing a play, *Dominique Payard*, with which the Rankins expected to open the Park Theatre in Boston the next season. But like *The Metropolis* this play was never produced. *Clipper*, December 2, 1882.
242 *Chicago Tribune*, April 15, 1883.
243 James Woodfield, *English Theatre in Transition, 1881-1914* (London: Croom Helm, 1984).

244 *Clipper*, October 1, 1881.
245 Ibid., April 21, 1883.
246 *Chicago Tribune*, July 4, 1883.
247 *Clipper*, July 22, 1883. Plot of *The Americans*: The drama opens twenty-five years after Rex's adoption. Rex is an intelligent and educated gentlemen moving in the best society. He falls in love with his foster sister but dares not reveal his feelings. A lobbyist, Leach, who is in love with the same girl, arranges for a German, posing as an Indian agent, to defraud the government and enrich Leach. Meanwhile a Sioux interpreter visiting General Sterling recognizes Rex as his son, the twin brother of his militant son, Red Feather. A peace commission, which includes the general and Rex, arrives in Indian country and is about to be massacred by the Indians under Red Feather when more troops arrive to prevent it. Rex discovers the fraud that Leach and his German agent have perpetrated, but Red Feather, incited by Leach to kill Rex, is shot by a picket when invading the camp and, dying, reveals that Leach poisoned his mind against Rex, who, he now learns, is his brother. In the meantime, the girl has been made to marry the wealthy Leach by her father. Desperate for Rex to save her, she sends him the prearranged signal of an arrowhead. Finally, Rex arrives to denounce Leach and rescue the girl. The play had been tried out earlier in some eastern towns.
248 *Clipper*, July 22, 1883.
249 The Rankins gave the mortgage to Andrew Dam and Sons. See *Dramatic Times*, October 27, 1883. The same Andrew Dam met the Rankins as they disembarked in New York from their tour of the British Isles, which leads to speculation that Dam was a financial backer for some of Rankin's projects. For the seating, see the *Clipper*, September 8, 1883.
250 Harry Miner, a manager who later would have business relations with Rankin, took over the People's Theatre on the East Side not far from Rankin's theater. It also had been a variety theater and, like Rankin, Miner would have to educate the neighborhood to dramatic fare. His problem was greater because there still was a variety house close to him. Moreover, both his and Rankin's theaters were located upon the line of elevated railway.
251 The play was by a Scottish playwright and had been a quasi-failure in London. Cazauran of the Union Square Company remade it into a drama, in which Rankin played Christian Christianson, who courts Priscilla Sefton but discovers that Richard Orchardson, who had promised to marry his sister Kate, was also courting Priscilla. Christianson pursues the villain Orchardson to the Arctic, where he swears he will kill him for betraying Kate's innocent love. Priscilla and her suitors are on board a steamer that Orchardson tries to set afire. In the ensuing confusion, they do not notice an iceberg approaching, and, when it hits, the ship sinks. The three are stranded on an ice floe from which Christianson, in a mighty struggle with Orchardson, hurls his rival into the sea. A rescued Orchardson is chastened by his experience. He reforms and marries Kate while Christianson weds Priscilla. The attraction of the play was its scenery. The tableau vivant of the first act showed the participants in a May Day festival pausing in their sports beneath shady trees beyond which stretched a beautiful landscape. The second act featured the imposing residence of the Orchardson's in a magnificent display of architectural painting. The first scene of the third act was the deck of a vessel, which was closed off by the lowering of an ice scene instead of a drop curtain, which, when raised, revealed a vessel caught in huge masses of ice. A desolate island of ice held the stage for the fourth act, and the interior of a village church appeared in the fifth. Each change of scene aroused the audience to enthusiastic calls for the scenic artist, who frequently appeared to acknowledge its appreciation.
252 *Dramatic Times*, December 1, 1883.
253 Ibid., November 10, 1883.
254 Ibid., January 26, 1884. "The play," said the critic, "may be cut down and made to go, but if so it will require all the wit and ingenuity of McKee Rankin (no mean dramatist himself) to do it." *Gabriel Conroy* was about a party of immigrants lost in the Sierras and running short of food as winter sets in. Rankin played the title character, a high-minded but slow-mannered miner. Blanchard played one of his two sisters, the rollicking Olly. There was a large role for a gambler, Jack Hamlin, whom Frederic Bryton played as a warmhearted fellow, winning the sympathy and admiration of the audience. A critic suggested that it was annoying for the stars to be overshadowed by Bryton, who was called before the curtain several times while the stars were ignored. He added that to achieve success on the road, Rankin had to play the gambler or cut out the part. Best of all, he should shelve the play.
255 *NYDM*, February 23, 1884.
256 *Clipper*, May 24, 1884.
257 *NYDM*, September 13, 1884.
258 *Clipper*, December 13, 1884.
259 To gain some cash from the usually profitable Christmas holiday week, Rankin gathered a company to play *The Danites* at the Brooklyn Academy of Music, but aside from Christmas night, the receipts were poor, possibly because the Rankins were not in it. They had been booked for Fall River, Massachusetts, on New Year's Day, 1885, but had to cancel.
260 M.B. Leavitt, *Fifty Years in Theatrical Management* (New York: Broadway, 1912), 483.
261 *Chicago Tribune*, February 3, 1885.
262 "The Stage and Its People," *NYDM*, February 14, 1885, 10.
263 *NYDM*, February 14, 1885.

264 *The Wasp*, February 28, 1885. "McKee Rankin's impersonation of the old miner is a character-study of such unusual merit that one vainly seeks for a fitting comparison upon the American stage....The excellence of the other people engaged in this play is evident from the fact that each is so strongly effective beside the masterly performance of Mr. McKee Rankin."
265 *NYDM*, March 14, 1885.
266 *Daily Examiner* (San Francisco), February 24, 1885.
267 *NYDM*, March 14, 1885, Advertisement quoting reviews in San Francisco newspapers.
268 The very successful star cast began with Theodore Hamilton, who portrayed an amiable old wreck as an excellent foil to his less light-headed companion. J.J. Wallace was dry and fussy playing the traditional old stage lawyer, and his occasional displays of temper were "dear" to the audience, particularly to the gallery. Frank Mordaunt, playing the old black man, Ned, acted with hearty goodwill. Dan Harkins as the young Dennison and Charles Edmunds as the villain were slightly perfunctory and mechanical because they assumed the parts on short notice when Joe Holland failed to arrive. Alma Stuart Stanley made a striking Mississippi.
269 Ibid., March 5, 1885.
270 *Daily Examiner*, February 26, 1885, advertisement.
271 Hamilton played the Parson, Mordaunt was the Judge, Harkins and Wallace were the Danites, Alma Stanley played Captain Tommy, and from the East there arrived Emma Marble and Joe Holland to take up their usual parts of Bunker Hill and Limber Tim.
272 *Daily Examiner*, March 8, 1885.
273 Leavitt, *Fifty Years*, 482.
274 *Daily Examiner*, March 24, 1885.
275 Leavitt, *Fifty Years*, 482.
276 *Clipper*, May 2, 1885. Since the 1850s, theater companies had found appreciative audiences in these territories. The early theaters were mere upstairs halls with rough platform stages bare of wings and scenery. George Waldron, who had traveled with Rankin in *The Danites*, had managed the first opera house in Portland, Oregon, and brought in such actors as George Chapman, Lotta, Charles Kean, and Ellen Tree. In 1863, he imported Julia Dean Hayne, whose charm attracted the locals for thirty-nine nights, a record for the area.
277 John Scott McElaney, *The Professional Theater in San Francisco, 1880-1889* (Stanford: Stanford University Press, 1972).
278 *NYDM*, July 11, 1885.
279 *Daily Examiner*, June 21, 1885. Marie, a child of aristocrats brought up among peasants, seeks work in Paris and falls into the power of an evil woman. A young lieutenant rescues her, takes her to his mother's home, and falls in love with her. Meanwhile some noblemen discover that she is really the daughter of the Countess of Launnay, earnestly played by Jean Clara Walters. Flachon offers to restore Marie to the countess for terms, but Baron de Guerin, played quietly and effectively by Dan Harkins, foils him and persuades him to join with him in killing Marie and taking her inheritance. The good lieutenant, however, returns Marie to her mother, marries her, and exposes the villains, who are imprisoned.
280 *Daily Examiner*, June 21, 1885.
281 Ibid.,
282 The following facts were gleaned from articles in the *NYDM*, "Scene Painting in America," January 23, March 6, 1886.
283 In contrast to Italian and French designers, who lay canvases on the floor to paint, which was fatiguing to the assistant artists and unsatisfactory because the artist could not see the effect of his work, American scenic painters prepared the model to scale as they intended it to appear on stage. The stage carpenter made pieces of scenery from the model and placed them on a forty-foot frame, which was raised or lowered by means of a windlass through a slit in the floor so that the artist stood in front of the work without fatigue to judge its progress. Sometimes the frame was attached to a wall and the artist stood on a moveable platform that worked like an elevator with pulleys and counterweights. The artist marked off the larger canvas in an equal number of squares and copied the small model by drawing the picture square by square. Soon an artist introduced the idea of a number of stock mixed tints into which a few primitive colors were compounded, instead of mixing an infinite variety of tints.
284 *Daily Examiner*, June 30, 1885.
285 Ibid., July 5, 1885.
286 Ibid., June 28, 1885.
287 *NYDM*, July 25, 1885.
288 Ibid., July 25, 1885.
289 Obituary, ibid., June 12, 1886. Born on Lazina Island off the coast of Italy, Mazzanovich came to the United States at age twelve. When sixteen, he served as a bugler in the United States Army, where he met an army surgeon who was a good artist and gave him his first and only lessons in art. At age nineteen, Mazzanovich was a carriage painter in San Francisco and then apprenticed at the California Theatre.
290 *Clipper*, July 25 1885.
291 Augustin Daly and his company were playing for the summer season at the Bush Street Theatre. He had declared a policy of a "No Free List," which meant no free passes for critics and others, which

San Franciscan critics would undermine by having their friends buy up seats in the small theater and reporting business as poor when their friends failed to turn up. He registered a success, nevertheless, and, according to a critic, gave the citizens a dramatic treat to which they were not accustomed. As Daly departed for the East in late August, he gave Rankin permission to produce his plays in the West. Another friend of Rankin's, George C. Miln, the clergyman who had recently made a success on the stage, selected Sing Sing as the place to open the new season, an apparently strange choice until one considers that he had, quite literally, a captive audience. *NYDM*, August 1, 1885.
292 *Daily Examiner*, August 9, 1885.
293 Apparently, the play was written to suit scenery that had been painted up for a railway advertising scheme and that was too good to be lost. The original play, called *The Living Age*, had been a failure, and so it was rewritten to provide hairbreadth escapes and violent deaths. In *The Power of Money*, a train is wrecked to facilitate robbery and murder; a victim is choked, robbed, stabbed, and smothered; a character is imprisoned on a false charge of murder; a woman is almost abducted; a man is drugged in an underground den and left with two others, one fatally wounded, to drown. Frank Mordaunt played twins who are the heroes. J.J. Wallace was the heavy villain. Wallace engages in hand-to-hand combat with each of the twins and dies of a knife thrust. The seemingly dead twin, who had been stabbed and thrown over a precipice, rises up in the best of health and shakes hands all around, not unlike the hero of a Hollywood movie. The new ingenue Helen Rand made an agreeable young heroine. Beatrice Lyster, an English operatic soubrette from Australia, was said to be out of harmony with the company, seeming to belong to a different dramatic atmosphere, but another critic declared her a success in her American debut.
294 *Daily Examiner*, August 23, 1885.
295 Ibid.
296 Ibid., August 30, 1885.
297 It was Joseph Jefferson who arranged for Holland's burial when the New York Church of Atonement on Madison and Twenty-eighth Street refused to bury him because he was an actor. Its minister suggested that Jefferson try the little church around the corner, which became the nickname "the little church around the corner" for the Church of the Transfiguration on East Twenty-ninth Street, still patronized by the acting profession out of gratitude.
298 At the Shields Library, University of California at Davis.
299 Amelia danced and sang on Boston stages but did not attain the fame of her two sisters, Jane, afterwards Mrs Vernon, who was the first old woman on the New York stage, and Clara, afterwards Mrs Gaspard Maeder.
300 *NYDM*, July 17, 1886.
301 Montreuil, by the king's favor, gains the hand of Mignonne's mother, who dares not confess her previous secret marriage to the "prisoner for life." But Montreuil knows her secret and makes her life hell for sixteen years while the count lives in the dungeon of the castle in which his wife is made to suffer. Mignonne has grown into beautiful womanhood believing she is the daughter of Mme Marguerita, the sister of her old nurse. When she is loved by the young Count de Boisy, the young man's father tries to marry her to a steward's son but is prevented by Marguerita, and when Mignonne overhears telling the real story of her birth. Inspired instantly with the desire to free her unknown father, Mignonne goes to seek him out. She gains the post of a jailer in his prison after disguising herself as a mute boy and effects his rescue. The king, touched by her heroic conduct, pardons the count and punishes Montreuil. The Count and Countess de Valnay are reunited, and Mignonne is wedded to the young Count de Boissy. Harkins as the villain, dressed in the rich manner of the age, expressed all the stately insincerity and unscrupulousness of the times in his manner. Isabel Morris as the Countess de Valney proved she was capable of filling any role well. J.J. Wallace as Jacques, the mute idiot, reprised his success in the role in the first New York production and gave a strong performance of pantomime, especially with Mignonne wherein his attempt to assassinate her is prevented and he is killed by the avalanche.
302 *Daily Examiner*, September 13, 1885.
303 *NYDM*, September 12, 1885.
304 *Clipper*, October 24, 1885.
305 On October 9, the Rankins gave a performance of '49 as a benefit for Jay Rial, who was leaving the organization. Joseph Redding, the musical composer, became co-manager with Rankin. Redding was an attorney, one of the state fisheries commissioners, Rankin's chum, and, according to a critic, "a very attractive gentleman." The main purpose of his role with the theater, however, was to help with the music for *Macbeth*, which already was touted as one of the great compositions of the century.
306 *Daily Examiner*, October 25, 1885.
307 Alfred A. Wheeler, "Macbeth with Kelley's Music," *Overland Monthly*, February 1886, 185-94.
308 Maurice R. King, "Edgar Stillman Kelley: American Composer, Author, Teacher" (PhD diss., Florida State University, 1970). Kelley had migrated from his Wisconsin home to San Francisco after his mother's death, taught music, played the church organ, and studied Chinese scales, which he heard in Chinese tearooms and theaters. German musical thought dominated American music, owing to the German immigration, and Kelley was influenced by it, despite the liberating nationalistic trends and the new impressionism, which attracted other composers.
309 *Daily Examiner*, November 1, 1885.

310 *NYDM*, November 14, 1885.
311 "He has 'plucked out the heart of its mystery' and has set it forth in the music as the art of the painter finds and lays bare the soul of his model in the pictured face." Ibid., November 8, 1885.
312 Ibid.
313 Wheeler, "Macbeth with Kelley's Music," 187.
314 *Daily Examiner*, November 3, 1885.
315 Ibid., November 8, 1885.
316 Wheeler, "Macbeth with Kelley's Music," 188.
317 Ibid.
318 *Daily Examiner*, November 15, 1886.
319 Wheeler, "Macbeth with Kelley's Music."
320 *NYDM*, December 5, 1885. Nate Salisbury was a well-known comedian.
321 C.B. Bishop was Joshua Joab Jinks, insurance solicitor for the company of which Mordaunt played the president and Harkins played the chief clerk. The Harkins character becomes president of the Great Pacific Line and a notorious bank wrecker in the main play. Gentleman Jimmy, the most celebrated tough of the Bowery, played by Frank Wright, was in makeup and manner true to life. Emma Marble, the shepherdess of the fold in the prologue, becomes Mrs Patience O'Flynn, landlady of a Grand Street tenement and wife of an alderman who trades in liquor, in the main play. In the prologue, Frederic de Belleville played the medical examiner, who adopts the title of "Colonel" in the main play.
322 *Daily Examiner*, November 29, 1885.
323 *NYDM*, December 12, 1885. The Wall Street financiers, the men about town, and the society belles of Fifth Avenue impersonated in the play were a great attraction to a curious public. Again Mazzanovich produced dazzling scenery of New York: a Wall Street bank during the panic, the interior of the slum of the Shepherd's Fold, a Fifth Avenue dinner party during which a safe is burgled by the owner, a tenement house wedding on Grand Avenue, a beautiful view of the Palisades on the Hudson River. The playwright, Gunter, worked continuously to shorten the play during its two-week run, improving it greatly so that it was ready to open in New York. The houses were crowded.
324 It concerned twins who are abducted in the prologue and brought up separately. Twenty years later in the play, one of the twins is Allan Dare, a New York detective who has been trained in London and Paris. He wants to capture Robert, Le Diable, leader of a gang of robbers who outwit the poorly organized New York police force. Unknown to Allan, his twin brother is Robert, Le Diable. Harkins played a banker; Wallace, a castaway; and Mordaunt made a brief appearance in the prologue. A new member of the company, George Osbourne, played an eccentric Jewish character.
325 Isabelle Morris was tempted to join them but went to her brother, who was acting in London. Ellie Wilton went to New York, possibly to marry. The Rankins gave her a benefit at their theater on a Wednesday matinee. She played Campbell's *Separation*, and the Rankins did the last act of *A Prisoner for Life*. It was a large and flowery farewell. Adele Waters returned from New York to rejoin the company. The New York papers reported that Alma Stuart Stanley had lost her voice. Redding left for New York to negotiate with eastern managers for a New York production of *Macbeth* with Kelley's music, which Rankin was eager to do. Elsewhere in San Francisco, Louis Aldrich's company, in which Sidney Drew was acting, disbanded after it had been a failure everywhere but in Chicago.
326 *Daily Examiner*, December 27, 1885. Mordaunt had a significant success as Bottom, which role would have gone to Bishop had he remained with the company. He gave a realistic piece of acting as a self-assertive, narrow-minded ignoramus. Wallace played the timid tailor Starveling. Wright, Ray (particularly good as Snug, the joiner), and Osbourne added to the dramatic impression with good rustic models of the "hard-handed men of Athens." De Belleville, playing Theseus, Duke of Athens, and Mabel Bert, playing Hermia, suited their picturesque costumes particularly well, according to a critic, and suggested Greek calm and Athenian beauty more than the others. The critic admitted that Adele Waters was beautiful as Helena but looked modern, whereas Bert's grave, lovely face and deep eyes fitted a past age better than the brisk, flippant, wide-awake one of the present.
327 *Daily Examiner*, January 5, 1886.
328 Mordaunt was the Parson, Harkins and Wallace were again the avenging Danites, Osbourne was the Judge, Mabel Bert played Huldah Brown, Adele Waters was Captain Tommy, and Emma Marble was Bunker Hill. Alphonso played Washee Washee, while the Rankins filled their usual roles.
329 *Daily Examiner*, January 19, 1886.
330 *NYDM*, January 30, 1886.
331 A critic amusingly portrayed the affection in which Harkins was held by San Franciscans: "He made a very impressive salient character of the Arch-deacon of Notre Dame, and managed in some unaccountable manner to express an intensity of passion in the measured, metallic, and inflectionless tones which never desert him. This almost preternatural stiffness is startlingly shown when he is thrown from the tower by the devoted Quasimodo; he shoots through the air with every appearance of a ramrod in priestly garb—as if his voice had been knocked down his throat and straightened him out beyond all chance of collapse. Yet so thoroughly reliable and intelligent is this actor in all that he does, that one almost comes to regard this unchanging monotony of speech and manner with the gentle indulgence that we accord to the rather engaging, because characteristic, foible of a friend." *San Franciscan*, January 23, 1886.

Notes 469

332 Mordaunt as Clopin, King of the Gypsies, the huge, lusty despot who lacks a conscience, did a rare piece of acting. Osbourne was completely medieval in his conception of Gringoire, the poet, and made his scene in the Cour des Miracles a triumph; he could have made it a buffoon's effort instead of a curious and grotesque piece of comedy. Holland as Captain Phoebus and Adele Waters as Fleur de Lys were among the cast that made their characters seem to step out of the pages of the Hugo novel. Harkins fractured a small bone in his wrist when he fell heavily, and he finished the run with his arm in a sling. Fair-sized crowds kept the play on the boards for two weeks.

333 *Daily Examiner*, February 7, 1886.

334 *San Franciscan*, February 20, 1886.

335 *NYDM*, February 20, 1886.

336 *The Argonaut* (San Francisco), February 20, 1886.

337 All the acting was strong. Holland was so perfectly villainous "of the out-and-out radical school" that he awakened a new appreciation for his abilities. "In the strong scene where retribution overtakes him," wrote a critic, "he displayed a power which astonished even those who believe in his varied abilities." With the specious front of a church elder, he dealt the insidious poison Iago-like to Rankin's country Othello. Harkins was a surprise as the gypsy ruffian, Tom Lattiker, because his characteristic measured speech and unbendingness had given way to the most real and natural ruffian possible. Adele Waters as Polly Chibbles performed so well in the inviting little part that "the whole audience wished to kiss her ruby lips"—or perhaps the critic was projecting his own wish on a larger stage. *NYDM*, February 23, 1886. The rest of the cast included Mordaunt as the landlord of the Crooked Billet; Wallace as the evil land agent; H.Z. Bosworth, who had been with the company almost from the start, as Mad Willy; C.G. Ray and C.G. Greene, who were with the company just as long; Mrs F.M. Bates, Trella Foltz, Emma Marble, Fanny Young, long familiar with Rankin's direction; and child actors such as Annie Lockhart and Ruby Illidge.

338 *NYDM*, March 20, 1886.

339 McKee Rankin to Macgrady, February 17, 1886. Harry Ransom Humanities Research Center, University. of Texas, Austin.

340 *Daily Examiner*, March 7, 1886.

341 *San Franciscan*, March 13, 1886.

342 *Daily Examiner*, March 14, 1886.

343 For Genvieve Ward's second week, the company produced *Jane Shore*, starring Ward and Vernon. Monday opening night was a benefit for the Native Sons of the Golden West, who packed the theater; the falling off was only slight the next night, which showed that the attendance was owing to the intrinsic excellence of the performance. Although Ward was too old for Jane, she brought out the gentle, womanly side to give an emotional portrayal rather than the traditional intellectual one. Vernon made a strongly dramatic part of Henry Shore and compelled the audience to respect the man who could not forgive and to honor him when he did. Mabel Bert was an effective Queen Elizabeth, except that, as an angry, indignant queen, she tended to looked simply cross. Mordaunt played John Grist with so much lusty life, burly strength, and good humor that he formed a cheery spot of brightness amid the sombre gloom of the play's atmosphere. The company made a good profit. Rankin turned to comedy. The company, which was not known for its light comedy, was challenged by W.S. Gilbert's *Engaged*. C.B. Bishop, whose company had floundered in the Northwest, rejoined Rankin's company to play the central role of Cheviot Hill. Although Bishop won the lion's share of applause on the opening night, a critic later claimed that he lacked the graceful, subtle, quietly humorous qualities that the part required. Among the other performers, Blanchard made a charming Belinda Traherne, and Gilbert's keen satire and wit made the evening enjoyable, thus attracting larger and larger houses during its run of a week. The play made money.

344 They played *Pavements of Paris* from April 12 to 15, 1886, *Frou-Frou* on the 16th and the matinee on the 17th, and *Led Astray* on the 17th. Susie Williams took the lead roles in *Frou-Frou* and *Led Astray*.

345 Rankin had found another beautiful debutante to introduce to the stage as Diana Vernon in *Rob Roy*. Mary Sullivan of Oakland was the daughter of General Sullivan and niece of the poet Algernon Sullivan. She had a rich soprano voice. Mordaunt reveled as Rob Roy MacGregor with his earnestness and sincerity and was the chief success. Mrs Bates as Helen MacGregor was girlish, with her long hair and short dress, a far cry from the Amazonian impression she usually made. C.B. Bishop as Baillie Nichol Jarvie perfected the Scotch burr in his speech and the good-humored tone of the weaver's simple nature. Holland played Francis Osbaldistone.

346 *Daily Examiner*, April 25, 1886. "The wonder is," wrote another critic, "that the same gifted lady who has represented with so unequaled a charm, the soft, sweet womanliness of a Priscilla Sefton could be transformed into the reckless, rollicking idol of the London cracksmen and nightmare of the London constabulary. But, even as Mrs. Rankin strides about the stage as the gallant ex-apprentice, there rises in the memory a certain handsome 'dark little devil' called 'Albertine,' who years and years ago used to stamp her little heels and rattle her spurs around the stage of the old Forrest Theatre in Sacramento as the dashing highwayman, to the unbounded and demonstrative delight of the gallery gods and the bold volunteer firemen—the men all in love with the fascinating actress, and the women with the irresistible 'Jack Sheppard'." Considering the play with its "strong, simple lines and its dates and epochs like an illustrated biography in old print," the critic wondered at the

simplicity of his forefathers and mused at the thoughts of Jack Sheppard's first audience seeing modern stage appliances swing Jack's prison walls around until the adventurous Jack was revealed dangling from his cell blankets on the other side. "Melodrama," he wrote, "should live with its unfailing moral set in marvelous scenery and its long line of character parts for ambitious young actors." *San Franciscan*, April 17, 1886.

347 Ibid., May 1, 1886. Reed's popularity brought a temporary embarrassment to the theater. The Retail Shoemakers' League arranged for a benefit performance to raise funds for a boycott and insisted that Reed take part. Reed declined, saying he was under contract to appear at the California Theatre, whereupon the Shoemakers boycotted the theater, which, fortunately, did not affect attendance. The last scene of *The Field of the Cloth of Gold*, the tournament, pitted the female Samson, Mlle Jaugarine, mistress of the sword and knife and dressed in a jaguar skin, against Xavier Orlofsky, former fencing instructor to the Black Hussars. Jaugarine's sudden, graceful, strong movements in swordplay, as if she could mow down the American Army in some twenty minutes, helped fill the theater. The largest and gayest audience for a long time appeared on the first night and reappeared every night for two weeks to bring in a large profit. Rankin and his musicians added new numbers to keep up the interest, and Mabel Bert recited the poem "Ostler Joe" during the second week. *San Franciscan*, May 10, 1886.

348 *The Argonaut*, May 1, 1886.

349 Bishop played Ali Baba; Charley Reed was the ferocious cutthroat Hassarac; Kitty played Ganem, the son of Ali Baba; Adele Waters was the robber chief, Abdalla, in which role she wore tights for the first time, self-consciously; Osbourne was the Indian chief Geronimo; J.J. Wallace was Ali's wife, Cogia Baba; Holland was the genteel burglar, Mirza; and Mabel Bert played the slave, Morgiana.

350 Rankin, Harkins, Wallace, and Mordaunt were regarded as heavies, while the younger members, such as Joe Holland and Mabel Bert, were not trained sufficiently for their roles in *Sappho*. Holland played the young lover, Jean Gaussin; Mabel, called the best soubrette in the country, was Irene Vasson. Harkins played a general.

351 Salvini presented a challenge to other actors because his powerful presence and voice dominated the action. In their second performance of *Othello*, Booth as Othello was drunk and fell to the floor. *Morning Call*, May 16, 1886.

352 *Morning Call* (San Francisco), May 30, 1886, quotes the Chicago *News Letter* of May 22, 1886.

353 William Ralen James, "Clay Meredith Greene (1850-1933): A Case Study of an American Journeyman Playwright" (PhD diss., University of Iowa, 1969). According to the *Morning Call* (June 6, 1886), the play was "distinct from any thing in the Frontier Way that went before." Greene's record had been undistinguished, and he was not considered higher than a journeyman writer. His play about Louis Riel, which opened in Winnipeg, had not been successful. Others of his plays were beginning to meet with success, however, and just as he seemed to be on the threshold of recognition, his only daughter, a lovely girl of twelve years to whom he was passionately devoted, died. He was back in San Francisco for her funeral and handed the completed script of *The Golden Giant* to Rankin. Rankin liked it and asked Greene to supervise its staging.

An actor who had taken part in almost every Rankin production in San Francisco, usually playing minor roles, was C.G. Greene. He may have been a brother of Clay M. Greene, the playwright. The actors in the minor roles seemed never, or rarely, to be mentioned in the reviews, although their parts were well done and they contributed, particularly in Rankin's system, to the overall impression of a production. One of Rankin's actors deserves special mention. E.N. Thayer played older men in a number of the productions. No doubt he was the son of the great old man of the same name who had been in the Arch Street Theatre companies from the days of John and Louisa Drew in the 1850s. Another was H.Z. Bosworth, who played many demanding roles in the company but did not win recognition from the critics or, apparently, from the public. These minor actors brought excellent character studies to the productions, but, by their dedication to the stock company concept, never allowed themselves to stand out from their fellows. Suffice it to say that without them, Rankin's company would have failed.

354 *NYDM*, June 12, 1886. The gambler, played by Osbourne, had as much fascination in this version as in the earlier one. Rankin's best scene as Alex was in his argument with his gambling friend, Mason. In a scene set in New York City, Adele Waters played an amusing and convincing Mrs Vanderpol, a leader of fashion.

355 It was a full program as well. The Rankins, Osbourne, Harkins, Wallace, Ray, Mabel Bert, and Mrs Bates played the first act of *The Golden Giant*. Helen Conklin did a specialty routine. The actors named above were joined by Emma Marble and Adele Waters for the third act of *The Danites*. Clay Greene recited a poem. Charley Reed and another comic did the "Oratory Act." The evening closed with the fifth act of *'49*.

356 *NYDM*, June 26, 1886.

357 Clipping of advertisement, Detroit Public Library.

358 Wallace played his crippled brother, Pierre. Picard, the role made famous by Stuart Robson, was filled by C.B. Bishop. The handsome Chevalier de Vaudray, for which Charley Thorne, Jr, had been particularly fitted, was taken by Joe Holland. The terrible La Frochard was played by Fanny Young.

359 Adele Waters was praised for her role as Peg Stark, an outcast. Mordaunt gave "a most enjoyable study" as a heroic gambler, and Harkins and Ray were believable as road agents. Hardee Kirkland, who now was getting parts in every play, was the vigilante.
360 *NYDM*, July 3, 1886.
361 A local naval man gave Greene some good suggestions, such as when two men depart to seek help, they kneel in prayer on the ice. A moving moment was the death of the faithful guide and hunter, the Alaskan Alexy, played by Charles Ray. The rescue scene was an exact reproduction of the dramatic rescue of Commodore Greeley, the explorer, and his crew. Ibid., July 10, 1886.
362 The California Theatre was the first on the West Coast to experiment with electric lighting—briefly, in 1879.
363 The Eden Musée was erected as a temple of art in 1883 on West Twenty-third Street between Fifth and Sixth Avenues in a long building of French Renaissance architecture, which still stands. In its halls and rooms, it grouped wax figures. In the vestibule were a pickpocket, a policeman, and a lady lacing her shoe. Napoleon and Josephine stood in the entrance hall, Romeo and Juliet were on the balcony, the rulers of the world stood in a grouping, as did the world's great musicians, artists, actors, and so on. There were scenes of General Lee's surrender at the Appomattox Courthouse, General Custer's last stand, General Washington crossing the Delaware, the Chicago anarchists, Charlotte Corday in prison, and so on. The historical accuracy was good, as evidenced in the figure of the defeated gladiator holding up the index finger of his right hand for mercy. The spectators were shown granting mercy by holding up their right hands with their fingers covering their thumbs or refusing mercy by stretching out an arm with the hand wide open and thumb down.
364 Rankin had purchased the rights to *Glaucus*, a version of the *The Last Days of Pompeii*, from Lawrence Barrett when Barrett was in San Francisco. Although Rankin was playing the old Louisa Medina's 1835 version, he had to be careful of other actors' claims on the play.
365 Her real name was Carrie Walker; she was the daughter of an Oakland millionaire.
366 *NYDM*, August 7, 1886.
367 Ibid., August 7, 1886.
368 Amy Leslie, "McKee Rankin Goes Home for Last Trip." *Chicago News*, May 2, 1914.

Act Three
Obsession

1 *New York Dramatic Mirror* (hereafter *NYDM*), September 11, 1886.
2 The best was at the Opera House, where Edwin Booth, after an absence from Chicago of five years, was playing in *Hamlet*, *The Merchant of Venice*, *Macbeth*, *Richard III*, *Richelieu*, and so on. Booth made $25,000 the first week. When ticket sales opened, hundreds of men stood in three lines for over a block. At times the jam was so great that the street was blockaded.
3 *NYDM*, December 11, 1886.
4 *Clipper*, November 2, 1886.
5 *Toronto Globe*, November 24, 1886. W.H. Lytell, who had played the Judge in the original Broadway production, assumed the role again. Hardee Kirkland was now playing the demanding role of the Parson, and Mrs Bates had taken over the role of the Widder. A critic called Rankin's Sandy McGee "one of the finest dramatic pictures known to the American stage." When the company played '49 for the latter part of the week for the first time in Toronto, the critic rated it higher than *The Danites*, predicting that Old '49 would be more memorable than Sandy. *Toronto Globe*, November 26, 1886.
6 *NYDM*, December 25, 1886.
7 Library of Congress, Copyright Office, *Dramatic Compositions Copyrighted in the United States, 1870-1916* (Washington, DC: U.S. Government Printing Office, 1918), in 2 vols.
8 *NYDM*, January 29, 1887. Kitty Blanchard was still living in Detroit then, as revealed by a letter announcing that she was sending the scripts of *L'Article 47* and *Madeline Morel* to Augustin Daly at his request. She located them among Rankin's promptbooks. ALS, Kate Rankin to Augustin Daly, January 8, 1887, Folger Shakespeare Library, Washington, DC. Years earlier, Daly had produced these plays with Clara Morris as the star, and McKee Rankin supported Clara Morris in *L'Article 47* in 1875. That Daly knew that Rankin had both scripts indicates that Rankin acted in *Madeline Morel* as well, although there is no record of this.
9 Clay Greene, "Memoirs," unpublished ms, Santa Clara University Library, Santa Clara, California.
10 Greene arrived in New York in September 1886, and revised *Under the Polar Star* with Belasco. He fell ill, went to Florida to recuperate, and returned as Rankin made a contract with Frohman. Greene wanted to find an actor to fit his idea of the gambler Jack Mason. Frohman asked him to see a young man acting in one of his productions whom Greene recognized at once as perfect for the part. Thus, Robert Hilliard became a member of the Rankin company, outshone Rankin in the play, and, on the strength of his performance, became a leading man on the stage for many years.
11 The *New York Dramatic Mirror* and the *Clipper* briefly mentioned Mabel as giving a "particularly effective" performance as Billy Piper, referred to her as "the Frisco favorite," and complimented Rankin for looking better without his beard. *Clipper*, February 19, 1887.

12 *NYDM*, February 19, 1887. Giddy Gusher was a friend of Blanchard's and visited her home on occasion.
13 *Clipper*, March 12, 1887. Of the remaining cast just Charles Greene and Robert Murray had been with the company in San Francisco.
14 *NYDM*, April 2, 1887.
15 Ibid., April 16, 1887; *Sunday Herald*, April 6, 1887.
16 *Theatre* (New York), April 18, 1887, 98-99. A description in *Theatre* of the incantation scene gives one a good idea of its power: "Every instrument or group of instruments and each voice is given a distinct theme which they individually carry through to the end of the piece. The light airy movement of the smaller spirits (sopranos) answered in imitation by others (altos), these in turn called by hobgoblins and bogies (tenors and basses); again the female chorus, with their original song, while triangle, tamborine, xylophone, etc., added one by one with its own rhythm, are all so blended until at last all the choruses, with the full orchestra, resolve and mingle with the cauldron of sound, giving fourteen different themes and rhythms and twenty-seven distinct voice progressions."
17 The competition was Sarah Bernhardt, who was playing the last engagement of a fourteen-month tour under Henry Abbey, of which the most profitable stops were in South and Central America. Abbey and his partners had made over $100,000.
18 *Cleveland Leader*, September 27, 1887.
19 *Brooklyn Eagle*, November 30, 1887.
20 Ibid.
21 When in Cleveland in March, the company was hailed as "excellent." Mabel's Nancy and Billy showed her to be "an emotional actress of fine ability," and she won the sympathies of the audience and the main honors with Rankin. Fred Maeder played the Parson well, and Odell Williams as the Judge kept the audience in good humor. Dandy Jim, a gambler and one of the new characters in the reconstructed play, was played by Oscar Eagle. The Widder was played to perfection by Blanche Mortimer.
22 *NYDM*, May 12, 1888.
23 Ibid., January 14, 1888.
24 Maeder and John Jack were veteran actors. W.C. Holden had played in Rankin's company in Denver years earlier. Orrin Johnson and James Allen were newer names, but Johnson was being hailed as a rising star. Robert Murray had remained with Rankin since the California Theatre stock company days and was content to fill minor roles.
25 *Chicago Tribune*, August 19 and 26, 1888.
26 "The plot has much of freshness and originality," wrote the *Clipper*. "It abounds in powerful and artistic situations, and it is developed in dialogue that is always graceful and natural, and at times eloquent in passionate expression, whether of love and confidence or bitterness....There is an underplot in which a Boston drummer and Ada's piquant little sister furnish a good deal of fun, while comic Negro servants, a colorful quartet of jubilee singers and one or two minor characters are introduced with admirable effect....The dialogue is bright, fresh and strong with some brilliantly eloquent passages, which are introduced in a perfectly easy, natural way, without a shadow of anything like straining after effect." *Clipper*, December 23, 1888.
27 Ibid.
28 Ibid., December 8, 1888.
29 *Cleveland Leader*, February 11, 1889.
30 *NYDM*, March 9, 1889.
31 ALS, McKee Rankin, Hotel Bennett, Binghamton, NY, to Charley, March 19, 1889, Pusey Library, Harvard University.
32 *NYDM*, October 6, 1888, 10.
33 Amy Leslie, "McKee Rankin Goes Home for Last Trip," *Chicago News*, May 2, 1914.
34 George Odell, *Annals of the New York Stage* (New York: Columbia University Press, 1927-49).
35 *NYDM*, April 13, 1889.
36 Ibid., July 27, 1889.
37 *Clipper*, September 9, 1889.
38 Ibid., September 21, 1889.
39 The spelling was soon to be changed. In this early version, a French-Canadian farmer, Jean-Baptiste Cadeaux, and his daughter Angelique visit a farmer friend, Cyrus Stebbins, in Vermont. Stebbins's son Tom, a Wall Street broker, induces Angelique to elope with him to New York City. Tom is arrested for bigamy, and his wife points out to Angelique the wrong she is doing to her father. Persuaded to return to Canada, Angelique is angrily rejected by Jean-Baptiste at first, but then welcomed back. A burglar caught on their farm confesses that he is a friend of Tom, whom Angelique loves, and reveals the history of the young man's wife. Financial difficulties and the threatened loss of his farm beset Cyrus Stebbins, but he is saved by Jean-Baptiste. There is a happy ending for all. Cyrus Stebbins, played by L.R. Stockwell, an experienced actor, was quaint and natural. Angelique was essayed by Nellie Buckley but needed further study. The role of the sport caught burgling the farm became as interesting as Jean-Baptiste in the hands of E.J. Buckley. Fanny Young played the long-suffering wife well and gave an entertaining song and dance at the Christmas supper. The treatment was light and agreeable. Songs and dances, French-Canadian customs, and the sudden rise in "Red Gulch" oil stock on the New York Exchange added to the interest.

Notes

40 "'The Canuck': Interesting History of A Well Known Play," *Evening Record* (Windsor, ON), April 4, 1893.
41 Including towns like Oregon City, Corvallis, and Independence, and in Washington Territory towns such as Walla Walla, Colfax, Port Gamble, and Spokane Falls.
42 *Clipper*, December 21, 1889.
43 *NYDM*, January 11, 1890.
44 "'The Canuck': Interesting History."
45 It concerned Sara Lyons, who was abandoned in New York City with her young daughter by her husband, who has taken up with a French adventuress. The play may have pleased Blanchard because of the nearness of the theme to her real life, from her viewpoint. Sara surprises her husband and mistress in Paris but, turning the tables on her, they brand her as an impostor, take away her baby girl, and have her imprisoned. Ten years later, Sara, now a thief who steals in order to get the money to pursue the woman who has her child, finally catches up to her only to be thrown back into prison. But here she meets her lost child also in prison, and together they escape. Sara injures herself fatally in a fall and dies in the arms of her daughter. The play had many of Blanchard's friends in the cast. Frank Mordaunt played an old duke; George Osbourne was Marcus Geldheimer, a Jewish banker; Joe Holland was a French villain; Robert Hilliard played a sympathetic young American; and Ida Vernon was a duchess. An old friend who had been absent from the stage for some years, Mrs John Chamberlain, returned in the role of the French adventuress, although she acted too melodramatically for the modern taste. Chamberlain was actually Emily Thorne. The critic wondered how Blanchard could have played such a bad role in such a bad play. *NYDM*, June 28, 1890.
46 *New York Times*, July 29, 1890, p. 5, col. 4. The cast was good, except for Wilton Lackaye, who was "out of place" as a low sport and thief. Clarence Arper, who had been praised in that role, now played one of the new characters Rankin had added. Rankin's dialect was good, but one had to listen closely to understand him. Jennie Yeamans accompanied Mabel Bert singing "Down on the Farm" on the autoharp. Bert made the most of her role as Angelique.
47 *Clipper*, September 27, 1890; *New York Times*, September 26, 1890, p. 8, col. 1.
48 *New York Times*, October 1, 1890, p. 8, col. 3.
49 Ibid.
50 *Cleveland Leader*, December 12, 1890.
51 Ibid.
52 McKee Rankin, Kimballs, Atlanta, to Colonel Brown, March 3, 1891, Pusey Library, Harvard University.
53 *Evening Post* (San Francisco), September 20, 1893.
54 In the meantime, Blanchard had joined with Kate Claxton in early February to play their old parts of the twins in a revival of *The Two Orphans* at the New York Grand Opera House. She contracted to tour in Claxton's company, playing several dramas. She was with Claxton in *Cruel London* at the People's Theatre in mid-March and opened in Brooklyn in that play when Rankin opened at Niblo's Gardens at the end of the month.
55 *Clipper*, April 4, 1891.
56 *New York Dramatic News*, 11 April 1891.
57 *Clipper*, April 18, 1891.
58 Obituary, *Clipper*, November 18, 1890.
59 The *Pittsburgh Leader* gave a description of the action: "The whole work deals most tenderly with the memory of Lincoln, and also with that of Wilkes Booth, who is depicted in his real character of an earnest, over-zealous, intensely imbued fanatic, who was no more responsible for his action than some other men whose deeds of blood have won them honor and the love of patriotic citizens instead of the contempt which, through mistaken zeal, covers the memory of this brilliant, but ill-starred young man. The first act introduces Lincoln, Seward, Welles, Stanton and Chief Justice Chase in an informal cabinet meeting following a reception at the White house. They are discussing, of course, the great events of the day, the war and its progress. The characters are all drawn to life and the personality of each one of these historical men is strongly outlined. An incident of the scene illustrates particularly the wonderful kind-heartedness of Lincoln and also his sense of dry humor. The conspiracy at Mrs. Surratt's house is briefly shown, and there is introduced the love incident of the plot, in the appearance of two women, both of whom deeply love young 'Booth.' In the fourth act, after the failure of the conspirators to carry off Lincoln, occur the inaugural ceremonies, in which the oath of office is administered. In this sense the immortal 'Lincoln' utters the memorable words, 'Malice towards none and charity for all.' Then follows a beautiful domestic scene between the 'President,' his wife and children, and then the eventful scene at Ford's Opera House, in which the executive box is accurately reproduced. The shooting occurs and 'Booth' escapes. The last part of the act discloses the interior of 'Garrett's' barn, where Booth was shot by his pursuers and there is shown the final tragedy of the great historical drama." *Pittsburgh Leader*, September 29, 1891.
60 *NYDM*, July 18, 1891.
61 *Clipper*, September 12, 1891.
62 Program, *Abraham Lincoln*, Huntington Library, San Marino, California.
63 See playscript, Shields Library, University of California at Davis, California, and in the Huntington Library.
64 Program, *Abraham Lincoln*, Huntington Library.

65 *Clipper*, September 19, 1891.
66 *New York Dramatic News*, September 19, 1991, 12.
67 In 1909, a producer asked Rankin for a copy of the play, and Rankin obliged. Then in 1918, Elmer Grandin, in reply to another interested producer, sent a list of the cities in which the play was produced. The producer kept this letter, together with Rankin's manuscript of the play, which he had apparently received from the first producer. This was some months before the production of *Abraham Lincoln* by John Drinkwater, director of the Birmingham Repertory Theatre in Birmingham, England. Drinkwater's play was a rather stiff portrayal of Lincoln, with emphasis on the "malice toward none" aspect of his personality. It was written to inform the British about the Americans, who had helped them win the First World War. In this patriotic guise, it was acceptable in the United States, and it stimulated an American response a few years later with Robert Sherwood's *Abe Lincoln in Illinois*, in which Drinkwater's saintly young Lincoln became a folk hero. Rankin's Lincoln, on the other hand, gives us a very human character caught in the political meshes of civil war. Unlike Drinkwater's play, it develops the character of John Wilkes Booth and allows us to follow the plotting of the conspirators, beginning with the second act, which opens in Mrs Surratt's house.
68 *NYDM*, October 31, 1891; *Clipper*, November 14, 1891. Rankin left just before the birth of his first grandson, who was christened Sidney Rankin Drew at the Little Church around the Corner in November. Kitty Blanchard and Mrs John Drew were present. Phyllis had joined Rankin's company and would stay with it until December 1891.
69 M.B. Leavitt, *Fifty Years in Theatrical Management* (New York: Broadway, 1912). Amelia Bingham and her husband, therefore, came under Lee's management. Lee falsely informed the Binghams that the company had disbanded, which, a few weeks later, led to the husband assaulting the traveling manager of the company early in the morning in the train station of Duluth, Minnesota, after he discovered the truth. Bingham demanded full payment of their salaries. Rankin, who had entrained for San Francisco immediately after closing, stepped into the argument from a distance and arranged for both Binghams to rejoin the company under Lee's management in return for Rankin's recommendation that Amelia was an actress of promise. *NYDM*, April 23, 1892.
70 *San Francisco Evening Post*, September 20, 1893.
71 *NYDM*, February 13, 1892.
72 *Clipper*, March 19, 1892
73 *NYDM*, March 19, 1892.
74 *Clipper*, March 26, 1892.
75 Ibid., May 7, 1892.
76 *NYDM*, July 21, 1892.
77 Ibid., August 27, 1892.
78 Ibid., January 2, 1893.
79 *New York Dramatic News*, January 30, 1893.
80 "'The Canuck': Interesting History."
81 "Bill Of Sale: Arthur Rankin to Arthur McKee Rankin, 17th July, 1893." Shields Library.
82 "'The Canuck': Interesting History."
83 "'The Canuck': George and McKee Rankin Have a Fall Out," *Evening Record* (Windsor, ON), March 16, 1893.
84 *Clipper*, July 15, 1893.
85 Blanchard and Phyllis had bit parts in the one-act curtain-raisers for these plays.
86 *NYDM*, May 6, 1893.
87 Ibid., May 20, 1893.
88 James Kotsilibas-Davis, *Great Times, Good Times: The Odyssey of Maurice Barrymore* (New York: Doubleday, 1977).
89 *New York Times*, May 30, 1893.
90 The death of Edwin Booth on June 7, although expected, cast a pall over the profession. Booth had been ill for four years and had lain for some time practically unconscious in his apartment at the Players' Club on Gramercy Square. "The light of intelligence will never again shine from the burning eyes," wrote a commentator before his death, "that flashed their tragic rays upon the public during the wonderful career of triumphs that is now but a memory." *NYDM*, May 20, 1893.
91 *Clipper*, August 19, 1893.
92 *NYDM*, July 29, 1893, 9.
93 McKee Rankin, Los Angeles, to Augustus Thomas, September 9, 1893. Loyola University Archives, Chicago, Illinois. Rankin obviously wanted to prove that with an all-American cast he could make *Arizona* successful in Britain.
94 *San Francisco Examiner*, September 19[?], 1893.
95 *NYDM*, October 7, 1893.
96 *San Francisco Evening Post*, September 20, 1893.
97 *Evening News*, September 20, 1893.
98 *NYDM*, October 21, 1893.
99 Ibid., October 28, 1893.
100 *Evening Bulletin*, October 17, 1893.

101 Meanwhile Mrs Drew continued towards the East Coast with a company that included Sidney, Gladys, H.D. Gibbs, Mr and Mrs George Osbourne, and Lionel Barrymore. Osbourne replaced Rankin as Sir Anthony in *The Rivals*, and an accommodation was made for his wife by restoring the role of Julia Melville. The company stopped in Kansas City for a week and then made almost a month of one-night stands to Chicago, where it played two weeks from November 21. It was in Chicago that Sidney touched his half-brother John for enough money to take the company on to its next stop. The amazing thing, aside from the company's determination to continue on a losing proposition, was that Mrs John Drew, at seventy-three, danced the hornpipe at the close of Act 2 of *The Road to Ruin* as if she were a fraction of her age. Eventually, the company opened in New York City on Christmas Day 1893.
102 *NYDM*, November 4, 1893.
103 Clement's background suited him for German-accented comic roles. He was born Clement Laird Wollingham von Geiger, the son of a German actor. During the 1848 revolution, he fled to America, fought in the Union Army in the Civil War, studied law in Illinois and at Heidelberg, then went on the stage in 1884 as Clay Clement. He received good Shakespearean training under Daniel Bandman and was taught fencing by an Italian swordsman. "Clay Clement," Clippings, NAFR+ 72 Ser. 1 p.1-45, Billy Rose Theatre Collection, New York Public Library (hereafter NYPL).
104 *San Francisco Examiner*, October 30, 1893.
105 *NYDM*, November 11, 1893.
106 Ibid., November 14, 1893.
107 Ibid., December 30, 1893.
108 "In a Reminiscent Vein," *The Foyer*, December 1910, 10.
109 *Boston Transcript*, February 27, 1904. Clipping in Locke-Robinson no. 371, V.1, Billy Rose Theatre Collection, NYPL.
110 "How Nance O'Neil Learned to Act," *Boston Transcript*, February 27, 1904.
111 *Los Angeles Times*, January 12, 1894.
112 In the play, Eben Baxter's son Tom is employed by his father's old schoolmaster, John Loring, now a prosperous merchant in the South. Loring's daughter, Phyllis, and Tom fall in love and become engaged, but Robert Lee Glass, a young lawyer, covets Phyllis's prospective fortune and forges Tom's name on a note for $15,000, creating evidence implicating Tom. Glass tells Loring, who changes his will to stipulate that Phyllis must marry Glass or lose her inheritance. Loring dies brokenhearted. Eben Baxter, as his executor, brings home a fortune in cash, which is mistakenly sold as a package of cornmeal by his wife. His son, Tom Baxter, distraught over the false charge of forgery, flees to the West and is thought to have taken the money. In Tom's absence, Glass's villainy is found out and Tom returns to marry Phyllis. *Brooklyn Daily Eagle*, February 6, 1894, 5. Cowles continued touring successfully in *A Country Merchant* for several years, usually throughout New England and into the Middle States as far as Cleveland, Ohio, where, as a native son, he always received a warm welcome. Ill health forced him to retire from the stage, and some years later he was killed in an automobile accident.
113 Obituary, *NYDM*, May 5, 1894. Waters's father was a San Francisco banker; it seemed that her family had disowned her for going on the stage.
114 It included scenes from plays being acted in the city; songs and dances by popular performers; the Rankins in a scene from *The Canuck*; Leonard Grover, Jr, imitating famous actors; a singer in a scene from *Our Boarding House*, with Rankin in his original role of Joseph Fioretti; and Thomas Edison's new invention of Bradley and Camp's auditorium phonograph in a grand concert program. It went with the greatest éclat—mirth, melody, high kicking, and general all-round delight. Rankin's appearance in *The Canuck*, said a reviewer, was worth the price of admission. *Los Angeles Times*, January 23, 1894.
115 Ibid., February 18, 1894. An Irish comedian, Dan Creelan, played Judge Wise with a rich brogue, which the audience found innovative and very amusing.
116 A news wire report from Atlanta, March 16, 1894, reported that Phyllis "brought sorrow to her friends by marrying the property man of the company." *Evening Record* (Windsor, ON), March 16, 1894.
117 "Phyllis Rankin Weds," *Evening Record* (Windsor, ON), March 16, 1894.
118 Peter Robinson, "A Leading Actress," *San Francisco Chronicle* [n.d.], O'Neil Scrapbooks MWE2+nc 17, 839, Billy Rose Theatre Collection, NYPL.
119 The Burbank, alone among the theaters to remain open in Los Angeles for the next two weeks, went "on its peaceful and prosperous way, drawing crowded houses with a class of plays that appeal to the sentiments of those playgoers who like the stage presentation, which is full of stir and movement." *NYDM*, May 19[?], 1894. In recent weeks, the only big star to appear in Los Angeles was the phenomenal Madame Modjeska. An actress in Poland, she came without a word of English as a refugee to San Francisco, and, with the help of a drama teacher, learned the roles of Adrienne Lacouvoeur and Marguerite Gautier. McCullough, fascinated by her refined movements and speech and her handsome figure, gave her a chance on the California stage. The audiences forgot her accent when she seized their heartstrings and made them feel only what she felt. The young Gertrude Lamson undoubtedly witnessed her performances at this time, especially in *Magda*, which Modjeska introduced to America from the German.

120 *NYDM*, May 12, 1894.
121 *Clipper*, June 9, 1894.
122 Ethel Barrymore, *Memories* (New York: Harper, 1955).
123 Sydney Drew lived up to Kitty Blanchard's expectations of a philanderer and undependable young man. A reporter from the *New York Herald*, called to the Campbell Hotel, was confronted by an agitated Gladys Drew with a four-year-old boy in her arms and a lanky youth, John, at her heels. "Cheeks pallid, black eyes snapping dangerously, she talked rapidly in a choked voice to the lanky youth whose face was a mixture of perplexity and misery," went the report. Then she turned to the reporter and said, "Now you will help me to break into that room. I must have evidence. My married life is at an end, and I have left my unfaithful husband for good and all." The reporter explained that he was not a detective. Blanchard, who had arrived on the scene, moaned as Gladys Drew cried in anguish: "That boy, Barrymore, told me that the *Herald* employed a large staff of skilled detectives just for such emergencies—to climb through basements, to break into rooms, and that. Now what shall I do?" Blanchard interjected: "My daughter is terribly excited. In my absence from home she has allowed herself to be led by suspicions into a rash move." She slipped an arm around her trembling daughter's waist. "Young Barrymore, a relative of ours," said Blanchard as she glared with righteous indignation at the door, on the outside of which the young man in question was at that moment standing. "He is hardly the proper individual to manage a serious thing of this kind. He has made a terrible mistake in calling you. I know that you are blameless in the matter but promise me to publish nothing, tonight, at least, about the trouble." Taking a room across from the room where Sidney's voice was last heard, mother, daughter and several interested ladies listened and scouted through darkened hallways. When the reporter interviewed Sidney, he found him an object of nervousness and anxiety: "This is terrible. It will be a fearful sorrow to my venerable mother. Of course my wife has left me—acted hastily. Suspicions grossly exaggerated the facts. I can only hope she will listen to reason." It was great melodrama, and, true to its genre, ended in a conciliatory embrace. *New York Herald*, August 7, 1894.
124 *Clipper*, June 23, 1894. Rankin concluded his "absentee" engagement at the Burbank in Los Angeles with *The Two Orphans*, in which Osbourne took the lead for his third and last week of standing in for him.
125 *Butte Daily Mirror*, June 14, 1894.
126 *NYDM*, September 8, 1894.
127 Grant Wallace, "A First Impression of Nance O'Neil," O'Neil Scrapbook MWEZ+n.c.19,872. Billy Rose Theatre Collection, NYPL. When she was four, she had her first experience of the theater: when Phineas Fogg in *Eighty Days around the World* saved a train from being derailed by Indians, she convulsed the audience by jumping out of her seat and crying joyfully, "O, Phineas Fogg has saved the ladies." When growing up in San Francisco, she went to see the great drama then available. She saw Sarah Bernhardt many times, also Duse, Rejane, and Henry Irving. When she was a student at the Snell Seminary in Oakland, she would sneak out to watch melodramas like *The Still Alarm* and entertain the girls with quotations from the plays. Once she ran away from school over Thanksgiving to watch one of her idols, Tommaso Salvini, and sat in terror lest someone would come in who knew her.
128 While Rankin's company wandered in one- and two-night stands throughout the frontier towns of the Northwest, Blanchard supported Richard Mansfield in a series of modern plays through the 1894-95 season. She played Catherine Petkoff in Bernard Shaw's *Arms and the Man*, Madame de Targy in *A Parisian Romance*, the Duchess of Leamington in *Beau Brummell*, and the supporting roles in *The Scarlet Letter*, *Prince Karl*, *Dr Jekyll and Mr Hyde*, *The King of Peru*, and others.
129 Nance O'Neil, "One-Night Stands of America," *Harpers Weekly*, December 23, 1910, 23.
130 *NYDM*, April 13, 1895.
131 *Clipper*, March 9, 1895.
132 *New York Tribune*, March 2, 1895.
133 Frank Sheridan, "Picking Up a Few Strands," *Carmelite*, April [?], Clipping, O'Neil Scrapbook, MWEZ+n.c. 19,877, Billy Rose Theatre Collection, NYPL. Frank Sheridan remembered this Rankin company years later. "McKee Rankin was one of the great figures of the stage in his day," he wrote. "He was big in everything—actor, playwright, director, manager, and theater builder. Even today his Macbeth stands apart from all. His Bill Sykes was on a par with that other great actor, James A. Herne. His Schwartze in *Magda* was a creation that the critics of this country, Australia, and England stamped as tremendous. [Rankin's creation of the unforgiving father Schwartze was still a few years off.] Our company was strengthened by Mr. and Mrs. Drew—she was as great a comedienne as her husband was a comedian. He had no peer in eccentric comedy. A tall slip of a girl, Nance O'Neil, made you forget everything but her when in dramatic scenes....She and Blanche Walsh were the greatest dramatic actors I ever played with."
134 Billie and Trilby love one another but are thwarted when Svengali steals Trilby away. Only by accident do Billie, Taffy, another of Trilby's Paris friends, and others see Trilby sing in Paris and rescue her.
135 *NYDM*, May 25, 1895.
136 Rankin, tiring of managing on the road and eager to escape from financial troubles, wrote to Augustin Daly asking for a position in his company for the next season. Daly did not hire him. McKee Rankin to Augustin Daly, July 12, 1895, Folger Shakespeare Library.

137 *NYDM*, August 24, 1895.
138 Ibid., September 28, 1895.
139 Alfred Ayres, *Acting and Actors, Elocution and Elocutionists: A Book about Theater Folk and Theater Art* (New York: Appleton, 1894), 105-18. Critic and actor Alfred Ayres, who was given much space for his opinions by Harrison Fiske, the editor of the *New York Dramatic Mirror*, roundly attacked Rankin for his enunciation and word emphasis while he played Macbeth, while admitting that he and Rankin had opposing views about the matter. Rankin's view was upheld by Henry Miner, who established the Fifth Avenue Theatre School of Acting in 1893, which excluded elocution and the Delsarte System and taught only natural acting and American plays. The school was run by Charles Leonard Fletcher, the playwright and uncle to Lydia Coyne Fletcher.
140 *NYDM*, November 16, 1895.
141 *New York Transcript*, October 22, 1895.
142 "Corbett at Rehearsal," *NYDM*, November 30, 1895, 3. Rankin's direction ensured that *A Naval Cadet* met with great success wherever it went. Over Christmas, the company played in Providence, Rhode Island. The local critic commented on the easy and graceful style of Corbett's acting, which showed a marked improvement since he had played there the year before. The company gave two performances on Christmas Day and broke the attendance records for the theater. In Boston over the New Year, the cast opened by singing "Columbia" to an enthusiastic audience, which, the critic noted, could not have been contained on the Boston Common. On New Year's Day, hundreds had to be turned away. Passing through New York State, the company played in Philadelphia, Baltimore, Chicago, Pittsburgh, Cincinnati, and several other cities on its way to the last week of the season to standing room only in Kansas City.
143 *NYDM*, February 16, 1896.

Act Four
The Reign of Nance O'Neil

1 Clipping, article on hypnotism practiced by Rankin, in *MWEZ+n.c. 16,139, Billy Rose Theatre Collection, NYPL.
2 Mayo had improved his fortunes to some extent after he ran into his old friend Mark Twain on Fourth Avenue in New York on a cold, drizzly day in February 1894. It was said that Mayo's characterization of his Davy Crockett was fashioned after Joe Goodman, his journalist friend in San Francisco, from which he derived the sweet, wholesome, lovable qualities, and after their mutual friend Twain, from whom he derived the quaint and humorous side of Crockett. He asked Twain for permission to dramatize his novel *Pudd'n Head Wilson*, to which Twain readily assented. The dramatization was a huge success when it opened in New York in March 1895. In the company were Edgar L. Davenport and Harry Davenport, sons of E.L. Davenport. Rankin must have missed his friend, who was, very like him, an amusing conversationalist.
3 Rankin implied by a letter he wrote to Augustin Daly from Albany at this time that he was not content with doing his stock repertoire. James Lewis, the comedian who had acted in Daly's company for years, had just died of heart disease, and Rankin asked if he could fill his roles in the Shakespearean plays Daly was planning to produce in nearby towns, particularly in *Henry IV* and as the clown Touchstone in *As You Like It*. "I have made quite a study of both parts," he wrote. Daly, however, chose Edwin Stevens, who was playing in another production in Daly's Theatre, to replace Lewis. The old comedian Mark Smith, who was still strutting the boards, replaced Stevens at Daly's Theatre. Although Rankin's abilities to play in these Shakespearean roles could not be dismissed, his fame as a star and perhaps his notoriety would have decided Daly against him as unacceptable to fit into his tight ensemble system. McKee Rankin, Albany, NY, to Augustin Daly, September 20, 1896. Folger Shakespeare Library, Washington, DC.
4 While he was playing in *A Naval Cadet* in Baltimore in January, the press noted that Ed Marble was writing a drama to star Rankin for the next season under Brady's management. Possibly Rankin did the mapping out of the play and relied on Marble for the dialogue, as was his custom. Marble was long past his acting prime, and as a friend from Rankin's Boston Theatre days, he may have benefited from Rankin's wish to help him financially.
5 *New York Sun*, December 8, 1896.
6 Vaudeville was a disciplined form of acting. There was little reciprocity between the actor and the audience. The actor stood alone doing his or her stunt without the collaboration that art requires, which was why he or she felt emptied and exhausted after twenty minutes. Elbert Hubbard, a writer and actor who did a successful act in vaudeville, wrote: "In vaudeville you must be blended by the actinic ray of personality: otherwise you are flat, stale and unprofitable." Consecutiveness was the prime ingredient because there were two performances a day every day of the week. "It isn't the audience you are afraid of," he wrote, "it is yourself." Elbert Hubbard, *In the Spotlight* (East Aurora, NY: Roycrofters, 1917).
7 *New York Dramatic Mirror* (hereafter *NYDM*), December 20, 1896.
8 Set in the Mexican War, just before the Battle of Buena Vista, *Captain Impudence* concerns a woman prisoner on parole in the American camp—a hot-tempered Mexican who is in love with the American captain but plots revenge when she sees him courting an American girl, Lucretia Bugg,

the daughter of the camp's major. Rankin as Major Hannibal Bugg in a comic romance with a feisty widow, Mrs Trigg, played by Amelia Bingham, made an entertaining subplot.
9 "'Captain Impudence' at the American Theatre," *New York Times*, January 5, 1897, p. 7, col. 1. The appearance of *The Woman in Black* in New York City on January 25, 1897, after a season of touring, required Rankin's directorial attentions again for a brief tune-up. The combination of a corrupt millionaire and a corrupt political boss in a cynical bid for political power was beginning to bore audiences. The play remained a week and reappeared during the season at combination houses on tour. Rankin's attention was also needed for *Straight from the Heart*, which opened in New York a day late on January 26 because its scenery became lost in transit from Philadelphia. Rankin's steady directorial presence, by the way, was being missed in the *Naval Cadet* company. The show was late in reaching Detroit, and the scenery could not be set up in time. Moreover, the blowing of the steam whistle, which was effective in the love scene in the third act, had to be replaced by a house whistle, which failed to blow and caused Jim Corbett to miss his cue. As the curtain fell "Gentleman Jim" raced to the stage manager, calling him names, picking him up by the shoulders, shaking him and knocking him with his fist onto his back ten feet away. The stage manager charged Corbett with assault. *Clipper*, January 16, 1897.
10 *Clipper*, December 26, 1896.
11 James L. Ford, *Forty Odd Years in the Literary Shop* (New York: Dutton, 1921).
12 *Clipper*, February 14, 1897.
13 *NYDM*, January 2, 1897.
14 "O'Neil Discusses Her Art," *Toledo Daily Blade*, March 25, 1897.
15 *St Louis Dispatch*, April 26, 1897.
16 *Weekly Standard*, March 20, 1897.
17 *Clipper*, May 29, 1897. The cast included Frank Sheridan as Parson Godfrey, Charles Willard as Judge Wise, John Ince, Jr, as Stubbs, Annie Leonard as Huldah Brown, and Helen Lee as Sally Sloan or Captain Tommy.
18 As reported in *San Francisco Examiner*, January 25, 1904.
19 "Memo for McKee Rankin in re Zan McKee and The Desert Lake Mining location," George C. Rankin, Chatham, ON, September 15, 1897. Shields Library, University of California at Davis. The electric railway project called upon George's political persuasiveness in the provincial legislature to win passage for a bill incorporating the railway as a subsidiary of the Desert Mines and Portlock harbor, which was intended to carry the iron ore between the mines and the harbor and by extension to the Canadian Pacific Railway.
20 *The McKee Rankin School of Acting* (New York: Stock Company of the Murray Hill Theatre, n.d.), Harvard University Library.
21 *Clipper*, September 4, 1897. Rankin had a new cast of actors and retained some superb character actors from his previous tour, including John Ince, Jr, Charles Crosby, J.B. Cooper, and Annie Leonard.
22 *New York Journal*, September 5, 1897.
23 *Clipper*, September 18, 1897.
24 *New York Journal*, September 17, 1897.
25 "Rankin Surprised the Metropolitan with the success of East Lynne...." Clipping in Robinson-Locke Collection, NAFR+371, v.1, Billy Rose Theatre Collection, NYPL.
26 *Clipper*, October 2, 1897.
27 O'Neil received a few notes from an armchair critic known as a financier of the theater and amateur thespian who suggested that O'Neil was hindered by the others in the cast not knowing their lines in *Camille*, and added that she wept too much in the last scene and should give it more lightness. In J.V. Prichard's *Claire and the Ironmaster*, O'Neil carried her scenes with dignity and grace in the role of Claire. Rankin introduced a new actress, Mary White Hall, who had an emphatic success. Obviously, she had come out of his school.
28 "Rankin Surprised the Metropolitan with the success of East Lynne...." Clipping in Robinson-Locke Collection, NAFR+371, v.1, Billy Rose Theatre Collection, NYPL.
29 *New York Journal*, November 21, 1897.
30 "Notes of the Theatres," *New York Journal*, December 24, 1897.
31 F.F. Proctor/H. Brunelle to McKee Rankin, Nance O'Neil & Co., including Andrew Robson, New York, January 4, 1898. Harry Ransom Humanities Research Center, University of Texas, Austin, TX. The colleagues were Ed Lamb, Andrew Robson, Thomas Tuther, and Courtney Barnes. They agreed to appear nowhere else in New York City during their engagement with Proctor and continue indefinitely at the same terms and conditions upon Proctor giving Rankin two weeks' notice.
32 Her father was John Allen, a well-known ballet dancing-master who toured with his three daughters under the billing of the Allen Sisters. His eldest daughter was Louise Allen, who, before she was out of her teens, was a star actor. Ricca Allen, a character actress, played the maid Wilson in *The New East Lynne* at the start of the tour. By the time the company reached Boston she was playing Lady Mountsevern.
33 *Clipper*, February 19, 1898.
34 Ibid., February 26, 1898.
35 Rose Eytinge played the Parisian concierge, Madame Vinard. Of the eccentric characters, Robson played the Laird, Alex McCallister; Herbert Carr, a star actor in Indianapolis and a strapping big fel-

low with a jolly round face, was Taffy; Burwell Cutler was Little Billie. Mrs Bagot, Little Billie's mother, was played by Mrs John T. Raymond, widowed now for some years. Other character parts were played by Rankin's regulars, such as Thomas Tuther, Charles Crosby, and H.A. Weaver. Ricca Allen was the grisette Angela.

36 Jack Barrymore to Mrs Rankin, Springfield, MA, April 6, 1898, Rankin Papers, University of California at Davis.
37 "A Visit to East Lynne," [n.p.] April 1898. Clipping in Harry Ransom Humanities Research Center.
38 *Clipper*, May 7, 1898.
39 Nance O'Neil to Mr Albaugh, July 22, 1898, New York Library, Players Club. The second week of the engagement was devoted to a new play, *Charles O'Malley*, an adaptation from Charles Lover's novel in which Wilton Lackaye played the lead. Just two members of Rankin's company joined him: Alice Evans and Edward Lamb. Rankin gave the remainder of the company a week's rest. He was conscious of giving O'Neil a break now and then from the grind of rehearsals and from her challenging, emotion-draining performances. Lackaye, sensing a success, left Rankin's company and went on the road starring in his new play for the season. Rankin hired H.G. Carleton for the company's Buffalo and Philadelphia engagements to fill the serious absence of Lackaye.
40 On May 23, 1898, Rankin's company was playing at the Chestnut Street Theatre in Philadelphia for the supplementary summer season. Lionel Barrymore was filling minor roles such as Lorimer in *Trilby* and as Richard Hare, the blustering country gentleman, in *East Lynne*. Another young actor, Ben (Frank) Butler, who joined the company roomed with Lionel and, after work, repaired with him to the bars for intellectual fraternization. "He was a tall man," wrote Barrymore, "almost handsome, who would have been obese if he had had enough to eat." Butler left acting to become a theater critic, and criticized Barrymore's acting. Decades later, Barrymore evened the score good-naturedly in an autobiography.
41 Weaver had come to the United States from England in 1842 with his actor parents. Having a genial and gracious manner, a deep, pleasing voice, superior mental attainments, and a rare acting ability, he had played many important roles, but his highest achievement was as Iago to Tommaso Salvini's Othello. He made a fine Sir Toby Belch in Shakespeare's *Twelfth Night*, and his Adam in *As You Like It* was a masterpiece. He had hired Rankin in Lexington near the start of his career.
42 Lionel Barrymore, *We Barrymores* (New York: Appleton-Century-Crofts, 1971), 49.
43 Ibid., 48.
44 Nance O'Neil to Mr Albaugh, July 22, 1898, New York Library, Players Club.
45 Otto Heller, *Studies in Modern German Literature* (Boston: Ginn, 1905), 52-53.
46 Grace MacCurrier, "Sudermann's Women" (M.A. thesis, University of Chicago, 1920), 25. The original German version has Magda killing herself at the end, but it displeased English audiences, who preferred that Schwartze die of mental shock.
47 Barrymore, *We Barrymores,* 48.
48 Clipping, 1899, Minnesota[?] in Robinson-Locke Collection, NYPL.
49 Nance O'Neil to Mr Albaugh, August 16, 1898, New York Library, Players Club.
50 *Clipper*, September 3, 1898.
51 Nance O'Neil to Mr Albaugh, September 6, 1898, New York Library, Players Club.
52 Another point also was helpful to Rankin. Lederer's translation was of the play used by Madame Modjeska in the United States in 1892, but in 1895 another translation appeared, which, in Rankin's opinion, better preserved the German atmosphere. By then Modjeska's contract had expired and Rankin was presenting the new version.
53 *San Francisco Bulletin*, September 20, 1898.
54 Ibid., September [?], 1898, O'Neil Scrapbook MWEZ+n.c. 19,875, Billy Rose Theatre Collection, NYPL.
55 Helen Dare, *San Francisco Examiner*, September [?], 1898, O'Neil Scrapbook MWEZ+n.c. 19,875.
56 *The Age* (Melbourne), August 27, 1900, O'Neil Scrapbook MWEZ+n.c. 19,875, Billy Rose Theatre Collection, NYPL.
57 *San Francisco Examiner*, September 1898. A critic described O'Neil's Nancy Sykes as an unhappy woman of the London slums with a slender vein of pure goodness glinting through her depravity. "Did you see her in her brassiness come on in her housemaid frock, twirling the key on her finger, for all the world like a feather girl in Petticoat Lane? Did you see her defy old Fagin, and cower before Bill Sykes in fear and slavish love, like a beaten dog licking his master's foot? Did you see her mother little Oliver and crawl on in her dying agony with that awful, husky, blood-choked cry to the brute lover, 'Don't leave me to die alone, Bill!'?" "O'Neil as Nancy Sykes," *San Francisco Call*, September 30, 1898.
58 "Miss O'Neil as Camille," *San Francisco Call*, October 8, 1898.
59 Ibid.
60 On hearing the flattering words about herself in Shakespeare's *Henry VIII*, Elizabeth orders its production. She dictates two letters at once, and, when her marriage is proposed, she threatens to prorogue Parliament if the subject is discussed. By the third act, the problems between Spain and England are dealt with, and she pardons Maria Lambouro, her would-be assassin, while condemning her lover Lord Essex to be executed. The fourth act concerns her affair with Essex,

Bacon's skulduggery, Essex's execution, and Elizabeth's misery. The fifth act has Elizabeth on her deathbed bequeathing the crown to James of Scotland, but, when she hears the people shouting his name, she dies in anger and thus provides a very powerful scene.

61 Quoted in *Pacific Commercial Advertiser* (Honolulu), November 24, 1898.
62 *San Franciscan Bulletin*, September 20, 1898. "Oakland held its breath for one long minute last night," wrote the critic about *The Jewess*, "then burst into a perfect storm of applause as Nance O'Neil came wild and hunted, down through the forest to the feet of her savior, the priest, pursued by a maddened mob. And Oakland realized in that one brief moment how great was the woman before them, the Oakland girl whom prejudice had tried to keep from the footlights while fate blindly willed that there and no where else should she go." Quoted in *Pacific Commercial Advertiser* (Honolulu), November 17, 1898.
63 *Minneapolis Tribune*, October 12, 1898.
64 "The Playhouses," *Los Angeles Times*, October 25, 1898. This critic gave the best idea of her ability to shift from one emotion to another: "Daughter of a crushed and despised race, the rich, tropic nature of Leah flames up in a mighty love for one who is of the creed of her oppressors. Her wild defiance of the threatening mob, which she faces with the mien of a lioness at bay, melts into unfathomable depths of tenderness when she meets her lover in the forest. Then, after he has cast her off, comes the maddened anguish of appeal which breaks down the pride that is her only armor against the world. After this is the blackness of despair, and then the cyclone of frenzied hatred in which she calls upon the God of her fathers to curse him and all that he holds dear. Last of all, the pitiful hunger of mother-love which grips her at the sight of her child, and draws the iron from her tortured soul, has in it much of the sublime." Herbert Carr played Leah's lover, Joseph, with the force and physique to harmonize his part with Leah. H.A. Weaver as Father Lorenz did the best artistic work in the play, especially when he commissions Nathan to bribe Leah to go away.
65 *Los Angeles Times*, October 26, 1898. Owing to the illness of an actor, Rankin played de Varville, Armand's rival for Camille, in which he lacked the polish of the bon vivant that rehearsal would have given him. It had been years since he had played the role. *True to Life*, however, was considered "a mass of cheap, flashy melodrama, without one redeeming feature." *Los Angeles Times*, October 27, 1898. In *Ingomar*, O'Neil was the incarnation of Greek womanhood, "so exquisitely fresh and natural" she was beyond criticism. *Los Angeles Times*, October 28, 1898. Weaver was the vindictive, sneaking old miser, Polydor, and L.J. Plumer was good as the timid but boastful armorer Myron, while Mrs McVicker gave a good performance as the fussy mother of Parthenia. Rankin's leading man, Herbert Carr, who had made an ideal Ingomar with his superb physique, later astounded the audience as Fagin. "How Mr. Carr shrunk into the semblance of that stooping, slinking old villain in his tattered dressing gown, is known only to himself, but he did it. The Fagin of Dickens was before one, with his evil eyes and oily speech, given with Fagin's own accent. In the scene where he glides around the room behind the unconscious Nancy, his claws extended to seize her, he looks a devil incarnate." O'Neil was unrecognizable as the dark-browed, coarsely handsome Nancy Sykes as she did her best acting. "Her portrayal of the hapless girl hardened, reckless, yet with much womanly tenderness at the bottom of her seared heart, is wonderfully strong." *Los Angeles Times*, October 30, 1898.
66 Aside from O'Neil and Rankin, the important parts were played by some of the actors who had come west with Rankin and by new additions. Herbert Carr, H.A. Weaver, George Trimble, Ricca Allen, Gertrude Foster, and Mrs Horace McVicker and her daughter Affie had the roles that they enacted from the first presentation. Horace McVicker was still managing the company. Lionel Barrymore relinquished his role of Max to Leslie Morosco of the Los Angeles theatrical company family. It seems that Barrymore had left the company in San Francisco.
67 *Pacific Commercial Advertiser*, November 28, 1898.
68 Ibid. In *The Jewess*, O'Neil kept the audience spellbound. "Few women would care to possess the reserve force or the irresistible magnetism of Nance O'Neil," wrote the critic. "It would be dangerous to peace of mind. It would be oppressive and heavy and stabbing."
69 Ibid., November 21, 1898.
70 Ibid., November 28, 1898.
71 *Town Talk* (San Francisco), December 31, 1898.
72 Ibid.
73 "Famous Playhouses, Part 2," *History of the San Francisco Theatre* (San Francisco: U.S. Works Progress Administration, 1939) vol. XVI, 196.
74 Haverly committed suicide, leaving his wife impoverished. She carted a heavy basket of facial creams for sale up the back staircases of theaters for her remaining years.
75 *Minneapolis Tribune*, March 19, 1899.
76 Quoted from *Saturday Evening Post* in *Minneapolis Tribune*, February 25, 1899.
77 *Minneapolis Tribune*, April 3, 1899.
78 *Sunday Oregonian*, March 26, 1899.
79 *NYDM*, April 22 [?], 1899.
80 "McKee Rankin: The Captain Cook of the Drama," *Sunday Telegraph* (New York), October 12, 1902. Frank Butler, writing as a reporter, recalled the O'Neil company that included Charles Compton, Lionel Barrymore ("at that time the worst actor that ever showed up one hour and twenty

Notes

minutes late for rehearsal"), Ricca Allen, Henry Weaver, Sr, and a good comedian to play in *Trilby* as Taffy (by whom Butler meant himself).
81 Clipping, [n.d.], Robinson-Locke Collection, NYPL.
82 *Morning Telegraph*, July 10, 1899.
83 Clipping [n.d.], Phyllis Rankin file, Billy Rose Theatre Collection, NYPL.
84 Clipping [n.d.] in Kitty Blanchard clipping file, Billy Rose Theatre Collection, NYPL.
85 "Charlotte Thompson Chats with Nance O'Neil," *Dramatic Review*, October 14, 1899.
86 Clipping, July 13, 1899, Robinson-Locke Collection, NYPL.
87 Clipping, August 18, 1899, ibid.
88 "McKee Rankin Talks to M. Phister," September 11, 1899. Clipping [n.d.], McKee Rankin file, Billy Rose Theatre Collection, NYPL.
89 *Clipper*, September 30, 1899.
90 *Oregonian* (Portland), September 15, 1899.
91 *News Letter* (San Francisco), October 21, 1899. Another critic wrote that in the present theatrical waste, O'Neil was as "refreshing as the shadows of a rock in a weary land." She was never boring because she made the audience believe in her. *Argonaut* (San Francisco), October 15, 1899.
92 *San Francisco Call*, October 12, 1899. On Thursday afternoon of the second week, Rankin presented a new play, *The Shadow*, by Dr Paul Lindau, a local writer, which it played, unhappily for the playwright, just this once. The company was giving *A School for Scandal* for the evenings of that week.
93 "McKee Rankin Apologizes to Mr. Flannery," *San Francisco Examiner*, November 12, 1899.
94 *Los Angeles Times*, December 24, 1899.
95 Ibid., October 8, 1899.
96 Ibid., December 15, 1899. Unexpectedly, a Los Angeles critic turned on *Oliver Twist*, which he called a waste of time. Horrifying, it did not instruct or entertain, even though it was presented with tremendous force, realism, and varied touches of genius. Rankin as the most besotted and bestial of stage characters, Bill Sykes, by his masterful makeup became the "ideal." Ibid., December 19, 1899.
97 Ibid., December 30, 1899.
98 *Clipper*, January 27, 1899; *San Francisco Call*, December 13, 1889.
99 *Sydney Morning Herald*, March 6, 1900.
100 "Desmond on Australia," Locke-Robinson Collection, NAFR+v. 366, NYPL
101 Grant Wallace, "A First Impression of Nance O'Neil," *San Francisco Bulletin*, December 1, 1902.
102 *Sydney Morning Mail*, March 12, 1900, p. 5.
103 Ibid., March 26, 1900. Barton Hill showed a gentle pathos as Triplet, which, said the critic, would keep his memory green for years to come in Australia. In Hill's hands, the needy author in a rusty black suit revealed a man of gentle refinement, innocent vanity, and poignant suffering. All the cast were shown to greater advantage than formerly: Clay Clement gave Sir Charles Pomander an imperturbable self-possession to cover his exquisite feeling of defeat; Charles Canfield was too rough and deliberate as Ernest Vane but sincere in his lovemaking; Inez Bensuson played Mabel Vane with care and considerable feeling; George Becks dressed Colly Cibber sumptuously with a fine old face beneath a wig of snowy curls and played the great actor-manager of an earlier century with breadth, dignity, and humor; H. Overton was a glutinous Quin; George Majeroni assumed a falsetto for the simpering Soaper; Clara Bracy was maliciously witty as Mrs Clive; Atholwood was a rugged Burdock. W. Bernard as Snarl, C. Field as Calander, Ricca Allen as Mrs Triplet, and two pretty children completed the cast.
104 *Sydney Morning Herald*, April 16, 1900.
105 Ibid.
106 Ibid.
107 Ibid., April 30, 1900.
108 Ibid., May 21, 1900.
109 Ibid., May 28, 1900.
110 *Melbourne Age*, June 14, 1900.
111 *Melbourne Argus*, June 4, 1900.
112 *The Sun* (Melbourne), July 27, 1900.
113 *Sydney Morning Herald*, November 2, 1900. Thomas Kingston realized exactly one's preconceived ideas of Lovborg. His fine delivery created a marvelous imagery about the child. Harry Plimmer as Assessor Brack threw a light veil of mannerism over determination. Joseph Carne gave Tesman a certain refinement. Josephine Thynne as Thea Elvsted made the audience feel the sweetness, directness, and innocent charm of a timid, love-lost woman. Mrs Henry Bracy gave a sympathetic portrayal of the beautiful and refreshing Aunt Julia, the antithesis of Hedda. Ricca Allen played Bertha discreetly.
114 *Sydney Morning Herald*, August 4, 1900.
115 *Adelaide Register*, September 3, 1900. It was Nance's voice that remained with the critic: "God-given—expresses all—full, round, vibrant, ringing voice, soft and velvety in tenderness, full of tears in anguish, clamant in intensity, cutting and scornful in satire, and lashing in rage and passion."
116 *Advertiser* (Adelaide), September 17, 1900.

117 *Sydney Morning Herald*, October 22, 1900.
118 Ibid.
119 Ibid., October 1, 1900.
120 Ibid., October 15, 1900.
121 Ibid.
122 Ibid., November 3, 1900.
123 Ibid., November 5, 1900.
124 Ibid., November 19, 1900.
125 Ibid.
126 Ibid., December 10, 1900.
127 *Toronto Evening Telegram*, June 27, 1946. Papakura told O'Neil that Maori literature was so eloquent it was hard to find English words. I could not find their correspondence. Some of Maggie Papakura's letters are in the Pitt Rivers Museum, Oxford, England. Her *The Old Time Maori* was republished in 1986 by the New Women's Press in Auckland, New Zealand, and has a biographical introduction by Ngahuia Te Awekotuku, who reportedly is writing Papakura, biography. Papakura lived from 1872 to 1930.
128 *New Zealand Sporting and Dramatic News,* January 10, 1901.
129 William A. Brady, New York, to McKee Rankin, Sydney, NSW, March 30, 1901. Harry Ransom Humanities Research Center.
130 *Table Talk* (Melbourne), April 25, 1901.
131 Wallace, "A First Impression."
132 Nance did not play Hamlet until August 1924—at the Greek open-air theater in Berkeley, California. According to one observer, she made the young Dane seem more like a sensitive and charming girl than a stubborn prince. She portrayed him as in full possession of his faculties and at all times capable of using them to avenge a wrong. "It seemed that the finer subtleties were lacking," wrote a critic. "All those soliloquies were too much hurried, closed informally, with a lightness and lack of meditation." Yet the general tenor of the performance was excellent. She gave Fechter's medallion and Hamlet costume to the Museum of the City of New York.
133 McKee Rankin to J. Duke Murray, O'Neil Scrapbook, MWEZ+n.c. 17,839, Billy Rose Theatre Collection, NYPL.
134 Thomas Kingston, Cyril Knightly, Reginald Daltry, George Becks, Walter Raynham (who also was stage manager), Benson North, Percy Brough, A. Tullett, J.H. Hood, F. Phillips, Bessie Thompson, Ricca Allen, Lena Brasch, and Laura Hanley. The other actors from Australia and New Zealand elected to remain behind.
135 *Cape Times*, August 30, 1901.
136 Clipping, San Francisco, November 27, 1902, in MWEZ+n.c. 19,822, Billy Rose Theatre Collection, NYPL.
137 *Durban Mercury Times*, September 14, 1901.
138 "Sass vs. Wheeler," *Cape Argus*, September 26, 1901.
139 *Durban Mercury Times*, September 14, 1901. Another critic wrote: "Her fine presence, splendid voice, and an absence of that *calinerie* with which Duse, Bernhardt, and others 'woo' across the footlights are among the qualities which bring O'Neil to the front rank of powerful actresses." *South African Review,* September 20, 1901.
140 *Cape Times*, September 24, 1901.
141 Ibid.
142 *Cape Argus*, October 3, 1901.
143 *Cape Times*, October 14, 1901.
144 Ibid., October 22, 1901.
145 Ibid.
146 *Cape Argus*, October 3, 1901.
147 *Diamond Fields Advertiser* (Kimberley), November 7, 1901.
148 Ibid., November 21, 1901.
149 ALS, McKee Rankin to George Becks, November 23, 1901. Mss. Room, Columbia University Library, New York. When he returned to America, Becks joined Kate Claxton in her ever-touring production of *The Two Orphans*. He died in May 1904, willing his extensive library, which included hundreds of promptbooks, to the New York Public Library.
150 *Natal Mercury,* December 16, 1901.
151 Nance, with a couple of friends, took a carriage tour of the town and were astonished when the driver charged 13,000 reis. Fortunately, it did not mean bankruptcy as the equivalent amounted to £2.
152 *National Magazine,* March 1, 1905.
153 Helen Fitzgerald Sanders, "Nance O'Neil, Her Travels and Her Art," *Overland Monthly,* October 1906, 212-20.
154 *Minneapolis Times,* May 18, 1903.
155 *Pittsburgh Post*, May 14, 1909.
156 See clippings in Nance O'Neil Scrapbook MWEZ+n.c. 17,839, Billy Rose Theatre Collection, NYPL.

Notes

157 The Gatti brothers, Agostino and Stephano, had invested a fortune made in restaurants into the theater business. *Morning Telegraph,* September 23, 1902.
158 See clippings in Nance O'Neil Scrapbook MWEZ+n.c. 17,839, Billy Rose Theatre Collection, NYPL.
159 *Sunday Sun,* September 28, 1902.
160 *Clipper,* August 30, 1902. The cast comprised Ethel Warwick as Marie, the younger sister; Mrs Bracy as Augusta Schwartze, the stepmother; Ricca Allen as the aunt Franziska; Cyril Keightley as Max, the nephew; Thomas Kingston as Pastor Hefferdingt; Herbert Carr, who must have been brought to London for the part, as Dr von Keller; Reginald Daltry as Major-General Von Klebs; Benson North as Beckmann; Bessie Thompson as Mrs Von Klebs; Claire Cavendish as Mrs Justice Ellrich; Dorothy Humbert as Mrs Schumann; Evelyn Martheze as Theresa, the maid; Nance as Magda; and Rankin as Colonel Schwartze.
161 *Stage* (London), September 4, 1902.
162 *NYDM,* September 20, 1902.
163 *Sydney Morning Herald,* October 11, 1902.
164 *Stage Staff Journal,* September 1902, 232.
165 G.C.M., "Another, but Welcome, Invader," *British Realm,* July 1902.
166 Herman Vezin to McKee Rankin, September 7, 1902, O'Neil Scrapbook MWEZ+n.c. 19,872, Billy Rose Theatre Collection, NYPL. An American observer wrote: "She has a habit of turning her back on the audience, a habit which, although well meant as a part of a system aiming at realism of movement, is yet at times irritating or at all events monotonous," *NYDM,* September 20, 1902.
167 "A New Tragedienne," *British Realm,* October 1902, 259. This was Crichton Miln, who did his best to counteract the negative English bias.
168 Clipping, September 17, 1902, in Nance O'Neil Scrapbook, MWEZ+n.c. 19,872, Billy Rose Theatre Collection, NYPL.
169 Clipping, September 1902, in Robinson-Locke Collection NAFR+371, Billy Rose Theatre Collection, NYPL.
170 *Stage Staff Journal,* September 1902, 69.
171 Clipping, September 1902, in Robinson-Locke Collection, NYPL.
172 *Evening Post,* September 27, 1902.
173 Clipping, September 1902, in Robinson-Locke Collection, NYPL.
174 "Nance O'Neil and Her Critics," *San Francisco Call,* September 25, 1898.
175 Belasco wrote *The Heart of Maryland* in one of Mrs Carter's rooms and persevered with her through hard times until his play got the backing to appear in October 1895. Carter was the sensation of the season, and her reputation as "the Queen of Drama" was made. Henceforth, she and Belasco became rich on the successes of the plays that he wrote and she enacted. But there were criticisms of Belasco's methods: Carter's every word, every inflection of her voice, every movement was said to be made by Belasco, hence her style was artificial.
176 *Portland Evening Telegram,* October 8, 1910.
177 "The Great Theatrical Syndicate," *American Magazine,* October 1904, 581-92.
178 *Sydney Morning Herald,* October 11, 1902.
179 "Last of the Broadway Alphabet for Tots," *Morning Telegraph* (New York), November 22, 1902.
180 Ratcliffe was as forceful offstage as on. He had spent six months in the penitentiary on Blackwell's Island for beating his wife because his dinner was cold. Another woman claiming to be his wife divorced him. His ex-wife's father, who was prominent in society, made it impossible for him to get a Broadway engagement, and he was suing William Brady for letting him out of the cast of a play without reason. Rankin hired him as a good actor on the West Coast, where his ex-father-in-law would have no influence.
181 Clipping, December 19, 1902, San Francisco, in Robinson-Locke Collection, NYPL.
182 *San Francisco Examiner,* December 23, 1902.
183 *San Francisco Call,* December 30, 1902.
184 *NYDM,* January 31, 1903.
185 Ibid., February 7, 1903.
186 Ibid., February 14, 1903.
187 Ibid.
188 "Nance O'Neil Scores Again in Ibsen's play," *San Francisco Call,* February 6, 1903.
189 *NYDM,* March 21, 1903.
190 *San Francisco Examiner,* February 16, 1903.
191 *San Francisco Call,* February 16, 1903.
192 *Clipper,* January 21, 1903.
193 *San Francisco Bulletin,* March 3, 1903.
194 *San Francisco Examiner,* February 16, 1903.
195 Wallace, "A First Impression."
196 Ibid.
197 *NYDM,* February 28, 1903.
198 *Deseret Evening News,* April 9, 1903.
199 Amy Leslie, "McKee Rankin Goes Home for Last Trip," *Chicago News,* May 2, 1914.

200 The *Sacramento Evening Bee* called O'Neil's *Elizabeth, Queen of England* a somber play with horror at its core. "The vain, cruel, capricious woman was pictured with superb strength. All of Nance O'Neil's fire blazed forth. Modjeska's bursts of passion in *Mary Stuart* were impotent compared with O'Neil. Yet also there were subtle shadings. Nance knows that it is with the tragic she must win lasting fame." The death scene was "awful in its intensity, ghastly, dreadful. Her voice was a mockery of full commanding tones of a Queen in the bloom of her power." *Evening Bee*, March 4, 1903.
201 *Province* (Vancouver), Clipping, in Nance O'Neil Scrapbook MWEZ+n.c. 19,872, Billy Rose Theatre Collection, NYPL.
202 *Daily News* (Denver), April 15, 1903.
203 *Milwaukee Free Press*, May 17, 1903.
204 Ibid.
205 *Minneapolis Times*, May 25, 1903.
206 U.S. Works Progress Administration, *History of the San Francisco Theatre*, vol. XVI. Pt. 3. "Theatre Republic."
207 *San Francisco Chronicle*, June 8, 1903.
208 "Agreement with L.R. Stockwell, San Francisco, June 9, 1903." Harry Ransom Humanities Research Center.
209 See ibid.
210 *San Francisco Call*, June 23, 1903.
211 Ratcliffe's Scarpia seemed slight against O'Neil's Tosca but was informed with a small, cynical, epicurean cruelty. Millward acted Cavaradossi with natural manliness and easy grace while demonstrating a great improvement in his stage work since he came under Rankin's direction. Carr depicted Schiarrone as the "mildest that ever tortured man." Agnes Rankin was noted for playing a pretty and clever boy, Gennarino, and Ricca Allen was praised for her role as the queen. The torture scene was drawn with "splendid strength." The audiences were large and gave O'Neil many curtain calls.
212 *San Francisco Chronicle*, June 30, 1903. For the latter part of the week, the company was supposed to play an adaptation of Hawthorne's *The Scarlet Letter*, which a young Australian had written for O'Neil, but Rankin must have decided against presenting it after the cast rehearsed it.
213 *San Francisco Chronicle*, July 14, 1903.
214 *San Francisco Examiner*, January 14, 1903.
215 *NYDM*, August 1, 1903.
216 *Sunset Magazine*, clipping in Nance O'Neil Scrapbook MWEZ+n.c. 19,872, Billy Rose Theatre Collection, NYPL. The banished duke was played by Herbert Carr; Jacques, Orlando's pessimistic brother, was played by Charles Millward; and Adam, the gentle old servant, was played by George Bosworth, an actor who had a long relationship with Rankin's companies on the West Coast and had filled countless roles for him. Audrey, the country wench, was played well by Ricca Allen. Agnes Rankin played the shepherdess, Phoebe.
217 *Sunset Magazine*, August 1903.
218 *NYDM*, August 13, 1903.
219 "New York Managers Lost a Treasure in Nance O'Neil," *Morning Telegraph* (Boston), April 4, 1904.
220 Ibid.
221 Ibid.
222 *Minneapolis Tribune*, October 4, 1903.
223 Quoted in obituary of Amy Leslie, July 4, 1939, in Nance O'Neil Scrapbook MWEZ+n.c.19,879, Billy Rose Theatre Collection, NYPL.
224 John Barrymore, *Confessions of an Actor* (Indianapolis: Bobbs-Merrill, 1926).
225 *Minneapolis Tribue*, October 4, 1903.
226 "Rankin's success at Metropolitan...." clipping (n.d.) in Robinson-Locke Collection, NYPL.
227 *NYDM*, December 5, 1903.
228 *San Francisco Call*, December 19, 1903.
229 "A New Trilby on Stage," clipping, December 12, 1903, in O'Neil Scrapbook MWEZ+n.c. 19,875, Billy Rose Theatre Collection, NYPL.
230 "Trilby and Svengali in Real Life!" *Sunday American* (Chicago), December 13, 1903.
231 Clipping, in 8-MWEZ+n.c. 16,139, Billy Rose Theatre Collection, NYPL.
232 "Is Nance Another Trilby?" *Hawaiian Star*, December 12, 1903.
233 Sam Shubert to McKee Rankin, New York, December 5, 1903. Harry Ransom Humanities Research Center.
234 Clipping, Mrs Leslie Carter, "What My Career Means to Me," C+L Brown Collection, Billy Rose Theatre Collection, NYPL.
235 Lise-Lone Marker, *David Belasco: Naturalism in the American Theatre* (Princeton: Princeton University Press, 1975).
236 "In the Wilds of Algoma: Geo. C. Rankin, Well Known Canadian Author, Is Still on Earth," clipping [n.p., n.d.] from Chatham (ON) Public Library. "He recently wrote a strong testimonial for the prohibitionists, setting himself up as a startling example of rum ruin."
237 "Death of G.C. Rankin," *Evening Record* (Windsor), January 7, 1903.
238 See *Boston Globe*, January 1-4, 7, 1904. The Iroquois Theatre fire on New Year's Eve is associated with the heroic efforts of the comedian Frank Faye, who tried to keep the audience from stamped-

ing by remaining onstage. The ineptitude and negligence of the theater managers and city officials have been forgotten. The previous summer, thirty Chicago theaters were found to be firetraps and in violation of fire ordinances, but the city council struck out some provisions of a new fire code as unjust to property owners. The eleven emergency exits from the theater were all padlocked. Because the fire started when a linen curtain came in contact with a hot and inadequately protected floodlight, the fire curtain should have been lowered to prevent the flames from being swept into the orchestra. The fire curtain got stuck on a stage mechanism so that a draft, caused by the opening of the rear stage doors, swept the deadly gas fumes and flames into the main body of the theater. The man whose sole duty was to look after the asbestos fire curtain was shopping at a nearby hardware store. There was no fire alarm box in the theater, as was required by law. The alarm was given from a box two blocks away. The automatic skylights over the stage, which should have created a flue through which the flames and smoke could be drawn out, did not open. The theater employees panicked. None of them had been given instructions in case of fire. The stage ventilation could have saved hundreds of lives if opened, but the man who was supposed to operate it was never told that it was his responsibility. Most of the victims were in the first and second balconies. Of the 591 people who were killed, most through suffocation or from being trampled, 588 were in the two balconies; only three were killed on the first floor. The ordinance that required that galleries above the ground floor have separate stairways to the street had been ignored. The response of the Chicago authorities was panic-driven. They arrested all the members of the Bluebeard Company, which was performing at the theater, on a charge of manslaughter and set bail at $5,000 for each person. An attorney acting for Klaw and Erlanger guaranteed the return of the members of the company if they were allowed to leave the city. All the 234 public halls in Chicago were closed. This action brought unemployment to 15,000 theater workers who were made destitute. Representatives of the theaters asked the city council to open the lower floors of certain playhouses to relieve the financial distress. There was no attempt made to prosecute the theater owners even though the ordinance requiring each balcony to have a separate stairway to the street was disobeyed.

239 Clipping, January 11, 1904, O'Neil Scrapbook MWEZ+n.c. 19,872, Billy Rose Theatre Collection, NYPL.
240 Clipping, Nance O'Neil Scrapbook, beginning 1904, MWEZ+n.c. 19,872, Billy Rose Theatre Collection, NYPL.
241 *Boston Globe*, January 12, 1904.
242 Ibid. Blanche Stoddard made a strong Marie, the ingenuous sister of Magda, who electrified the scene when she affects to see her sister alighting from a carriage (offstage) after an absence of seventeen years. Ratcliffe played the pastor with dignity, discretion, and feeling. Ricca Allen amused the audience with her portrayal of a meddlesome and narrow-minded aunt.
243 Rankin took no role, but the support of George Staley as Tesman, Mrs Brooke as the maid, Bertha, and Ricca Allen as Aunt Julia were admirably acted.
244 *Boston Globe*, January 16, 1904.
245 Ibid., January 22, 1904.
246 "The Fires of St. John: Erotic Theme of the Drama Exploited with Daring Frankness," *Boston Globe*, January 22, 1904.
247 *Morning Telegraph* (Boston), April 4, 1904.
248 *Boston Sunday Globe*, February 14, 1904.
249 *Boston Globe*, January 24, 1904.
250 "Nance O'Neil at Tremont," *Boston Globe*, January 24, 1904.
251 *Boston Evening Transcript*, January 23, 1904.
252 *Boston Globe*, February 5, 1904. In the first two acts, O'Neil suggested, more delicately than any other actress, the progressive nature of Marguerite's disease. The scene at the close of the second act was original. She sits alone in a darkened room absorbed in the thoughts of her new happiness, which made a wonderfully impressive picture for theatergoers. The third act brought out O'Neil's great powers. Her interview with the older Duval excelled in the simulation of grief and despair. It was "a triumph such as could be attained only by a tragedienne of genuine genius. Her writing of the farewell letter to Armand and her parting scene with him is appealingly pathetic and moved yesterday's audience to such a tribute of tears as have rarely been paid to sorrows on the stage," wrote a critic. "When she meets Armand and is cruelly humiliated, she gives further evidence of her extraordinary powers of sustained emotional force, and the scene is made superbly effective without once resorting to the sensational ranting that customarily occurs in this situation. The closing scene is pitifully pathetic. There has never been a death scene acted on the stage that seemed more real, but many of the conventionally harrowing details are omitted and with most artistic results." Ibid.
253 *Boston Post*, February 26, 1904.
254 *Boston Globe*, February 12, 1904.
255 "The Editor's Club by H.C." *Literary World*, February 1904.
256 *Portland Sunday Telegram*, February 7, 1904.
257 *The Press*, February 8, 1904.
258 *Boston Herald*, February 19, 1904
259 *Boston Globe*, March 1, 1904.
260 *Boston Post*, February 16, 1904.

261 John D. Barry, "'Fires of St. John' and Nance O'Neil," [n.d.] clipping in Robinson-Locke Collection, no. 37, v. 1, Billy Rose Theatre Collection, NYPL.
262 Ibid.
263 *Boston Herald*, March 18, 1904. O'Neil gave a spectacular performance as Meg Merrilies. The play is half over before Meg appears, and she has just four brief scenes, but it was her character that kept the play from being shelved and made it a "towering success." The play, mostly talk, with little action, is a strange mixture of burlesque, romance, music, broad farce, and tragedy. "In the weird stage moonlight, with long white hair, thin and disheveled, falling over her drooping shoulders and framing a tanned, dried, wrinkled face, from which two great eyes stared owl-like; with bent form wrapped in a brown, weather-faded, red-lined garment held in place by a leathern belt strap with steel buckle, and leaning heavily upon a forked stick, O'Neil...presented an ideal picture of the supposed mad gypsy queen of Scott's romance—the witch of Ellangowan."
264 Blanche Stoddard clipping, November 26, 1904, in Robinson-Locke Collection 2173, NYPL.
265 Clipping, October 27, 1905, in E.J. Ratcliffe file, Billy Rose Theatre Collection, NYPL.
266 Robert Sullivan, "Library Lamps: Nance O'Neil at Close Range Behind the Scenes," *The Republic* [n.d.], Nance O'Neil Scrapbook MWEZ+n.c. 19,872, Billy Rose Theatre Collection, NYPL.
267 *Boston Herald*, March 25, 1904.
268 *Boston Globe*, April 2, 1904.
269 "New York Managers Lost a Treasure."
270 *Worcester Daily Telegram*, April 10, 1904.
271 *Boston Evening Transcript*, April 20, 1904.
272 Robert Sullivan.
273 *Boston Globe*, April 29, 1904.
274 In Nance O'Neil papers, Harry Ransom Humanities Research Center.
275 *NYDM*, December 5, 1903.
276 Herne, who collaborated with Belasco in writing sentimental drama, now turned to realism that dramatized the human qualities of everyday people in the 1890s, for which he was celebrated in dramatic circles. Realism being unprofitable, however, he ended his career with sentimental domestic comedy like *Shore Acres*, which brought him a beautiful estate on Long Island to mark his success. He died in 1901.
277 Frank Spiering, *Lizzie* (New York: Random House, 1984). See chs 17 and 18. See also Sharon Pollock's play *Blood Relations*.
278 Victoria Lincoln, "What Ever Became of Lizzie Borden?" October 1967, Clipping in Nance O'Neil Clippings file, Billy Rose Theatre Collection, NYPL.
279 Ricca Allen to Nance O'Neil, January 29, 1905, Harry Ransom Humanities Research Center.
280 McKee Rankin to Thomas B. Aldrich, [n.d.], Judith of Bethulia Papers, Temple University Library, Philadelphia, PA.
281 Ibid.
282 Schoeffel engaged a new supporting cast for O'Neil. Over the summer, the actors of O'Neil's old company needed work because they could not afford a summer-long layoff. Rankin was solicitous in helping his actors to find jobs; he wrote to the actor William Seymour on August 3 to recommend Walter Cluxton. "He is a capital young actor and a gentleman. He played George in 'The Fires of St John' better than E.J. Ratcliffe who was the original in the English." Only Ricca Allen remained from the previous company. Charles Dalton was now the leading man. Charles Millward was back in the company. Louis Massen, Joseph Wheelock, J.B. Coughlan, and George Friend were all veteran actors whose presence raised the level of the company. W.L. Thorne was from the youngest generation of the Thorne acting family. Gertrude Binley, the leading woman, was a society girl from Brookline, Massachusetts, who, showing great promise in amateur acting, now found herself a leading professional. McKee Rankin, O'Neil Manor, Tyngsboro, MA, to Willie Seymour, August 3, 1904. Princeton University Library.
283 See "Manuscript Changes and Additions for 'Judith of Bethulia'," Judith of Bethulia Papers, Temple University Library.
284 *Boston Evening Record*, October 11, 1904.
285 Charles Dalton played the Assyrian general, Holofernes, who lays siege to Bethulia on the orders of King Nebuchadnezzar; Charles Millward played Holofernes's slave Bagoas, who becomes enthralled by Judith's charms and furnishes her with a soporific drug to slip into his master's wine; Arthur Sawyer was Archior, the Ammonite, whom Holofernes has sent among the Israelites of Bethulia as punishment, and who loves Judith and follows her in her perilous expedition into the Assyrian camp. Gertrude Binley played Marah, Judith's handmaiden, and Ricca Allen was Arazel, the chief dancer to Holofernes. Briefly, the play opens with the news that the Assyrians have given the starving, plague-ridden Bethulians five days in which to surrender. Inspired by a vision, Judith goes into the enemy camp, attracts Holofernes by her beauty, and, drugging him, cuts off his head, which she brings back to the Israelites. Before she slays him, Judith struggles with herself, for she is attracted to Holofernes's manly beauty, but, praying for strength, she does the deed.
286 Thomas Aldrich to Edmund [?], November 21, 1904, Judith of Bethulia Papers, Temple University Library.
287 *NYDM*, October 29, 1904.

288 "The Blight of Nance O'Neil," *New York Age*, October 15, 1904.
289 *New York World*, November 22, 1904; *New York Evening Post*, November 22, 1904.
290 *New York Evening World*, November 25, 1904.
291 *New York Evening Sun*, November 23, 1904.
292 "A True Christmas Story," *New York American*, clipping in Robinson-Locke Collection, NYPL.
293 Clipping in Robinson-Locke Collection, NYPL
294 It is interesting to note that Hearst did his best to ruin Orson Welles, after Welles had made his famous movie about Hearst, *Citizen Kane*. Welles was a sort of latter-day theater maverick in the style of Rankin, but this was much later in Hearst's increasingly egotistical life.
295 *New York Evening Mail*, November 30, 1904.
296 *Theatre Magazine*, January 1905.
297 *Evening Post*, December 6, 1904.
298 *Theatre Magazine*, January 1905.
299 *NYDM*, November 21, 1904.
300 Thomas Aldrich to Edmund [?], November 30, 1904, Judith of Bethulia Papers, Temple University Library. The "Winter" to whom Aldrich was referring was William Winter, the dean of drama critics, who wrote for the *New York Tribune*. Fellow critics criticized Winter for hating the moral plays of Ibsen and Shaw and ridiculed his "overwrought invective." Winter's comments on O'Neil's plays ran true to form. Magda was "a disreputable female—art should not force morality." *The Fires of St John* was full of "licentious passions and lewd conduct." He called *Judith of Bethulia*, however, "a step in the right direction, equally for the public and the actress." Charles Millward as Bagoas was the most accomplished actor, he said, and the exhoratory manner of Charles Dalton was right for Holofernes. "Miss O'Neil's performance of Judith, coming after her dreary displays of inefficiency as Magda, Gabler, and Calamity Jane, was, however, a surprise—because it evinced imagination, intuitive insight, and a considerable faculty of sustained impersonation." *New York Tribune*, December 6, 1904, p. 7, col. 1. Other critics wrote that O'Neil's performance as Judith fell below her previous performances at Daly's Theatre.
301 *Evening Mail*, December 12, 1904.
302 Clipping [n.p., n.d.], Robinson-Locke Collection, NYPL. The *Toldeo Blade* quickly responded that O'Neil was wrong to answer her New York critics and concluded: "She undoubtedly has talent and unlimited ambition, but she has had very bad training with McKee Rankin, and she lacks much of the finesse of the successful actress of today." *Toledo Blade*, December 30, 1904.
303 *Theatre Magazine*, January 1905.
304 *NYDM*, June 1, 1905.
305 News of her intention to take Aldrich's play to Australia reached an Australian playwright who had given Rankin a playscript on the subject. The playwright accused Aldrich of stealing his script and warned Rankin that he would prevent him from presenting the play in Australia. Rankin replied: "So far as your play is concerned, you seem to have forgotten that I furnished you with a copy of Giacommetti's play of 'Judith' and that you had simply arranged some of the language using the same names for the cast of characters—and on the strength of this you propose to prevent anybody on Earth from using this material in the apocrypha." He warned that nothing could dissuade O'Neil from doing the play in Australia. "Don't be stupid or vindictive," he added, "there's nothing in it." McKee Rankin to Mr Mills, Boston, April 29, 1905. Harry Ransom Humanities Research Center. See "Agreement with Samuel Alfred Mills, December 19, 1900," also in the Center.
306 *Clipper*, April 29, 1905.
307 *NYDM*, May 6, 1905.
308 "The 'Lady Macbeth' of Nance O'Neil," *New York Times*, April 26, 1905.
309 McKee Rankin to the editor of the *New York Times*, [n.d.], Harry Ransom Humanities Research Center.
310 "Nance O'Neil and the Mantle of Cushman," *Theatre Magazine*, March 1905.
311 "The Great Theatrical Syndicate," *Leslie's Monthly Magazine*, July 1905, p. 331.
312 McKee Rankin to Abe Erlanger, Worcester, MA, May 7, 1905, Shubert Archives, NYC. The theatrical news related at length the death of Joseph Jefferson, which came shortly after the death of Madame Janauschek. Rankin must have read Jefferson's obituaries with thoughts of the past and his long-forgotten achievements. More than ever, he depended on O'Neil to keep him relevant in the profession and keen to do battle with the naysayers. A minor item recorded the serious illness of Mrs McKee Rankin at the New York home of her daughter, Mrs Harry Davenport.
313 "Nance O'Neil and Pier Drama Star," clipping, May 25, 1905, Robinson-Locke Collection, NYPL.
314 Glendinning had had a successful career in the British Isles, playing for many seasons in Dublin, Liverpool, and other provincial cities before joining the Kendals on the London stage. He had accompanied the Kendals on their first tour of America and stayed to support such stars as Clara Morris and Olga Nethersole. Jane Marbury, whose real name was Louise Sturgis Jones, had toured the small towns of Michigan at age sixteen in 1884. She was supposed to have been paid $5 a week with board, but invariably her companies disbanded in some isolated spot and left her broke. Those were the days when stage footlights comprised three kerosene lamps and actors' parts were written in longhand on foolscap and actors memorized them while traveling from one stop to the next. The hotel rooms were poor, the baths worse, but the meals were home-cooked and good. Marbury

worked her way up the ladder and began supporting Sarah Bernhardt, Richard Mansfield, John Drew, and Minnie Fiske. Margaret (Peggy) Bloodgood belonged to a well-known acting family whose most famous member, Clara Bloodgood, was a star and in whose company Kate Rankin had acted. Clara committed suicide while on the road. Peggy Bloodgood rose no higher than a good supporting actress. She became close friends with Nance O'Neil, shared a cottage in France with her and another "bachelor girl," and stayed in the O'Neil company for two or three years.

315 Jim Williamson had recruited an interesting group of actors for the company. Gaston Mervale was a strong supporting actor. Harry Overton, who had played in her earlier tour, joined the company. Mario Majeroni, who had played with the company briefly on its first visit, left the Williamson stock companies to support O'Neil. Maurice Nodin, Dallas Cairns, C.M. Berkeley, and the others were favorites with Australian audiences.
316 *Daily Telegraph* (Melbourne), June 24, 1905.
317 *Evening Post* (New York), August 22, 1905, quoting the *Ventura* (Melbourne).
318 Mrs Henry Bracy again played the mother as frivolous, George Friend was the card-playing general, Majeroni was the nervous professor, Andrew Robson played von Keller as superficially pious, and Glendinning was too matter-of-fact as Pastor Hefferdingt.
319 *Sydney Morning Herald*, September 4, 1905.
320 Ibid., September 29, 1905. O'Neil "carried all before her by the quiet intensity of her grief as the Calamity Child. And what a part it is! It opens with a sigh and ends in a moan, as the slowly-descending curtain shuts from view the suffering woman, the fires of whose heart were extinguished by her fast-flowing tears."
321 Ibid., September 11, 1905.
322 An Australian playwright, who had furnished Rankin with his playscript of *Judith*, caused trouble through the press, which decided Williamson against the production of *Judith of Bethulia* in Australia.
323 *Sydney Morning Herald*, August 28, 1905.
324 Ibid.
325 Ibid., September 29, 1905, p. 6.
326 McKee Rankin to Abe Erlanger, Menzies Hotel, Melbourne, July 29, 1905, Shubert Archives. All correspondence between Rankin and the Theatrical Trust mentioned hereafter may be found in the Shubert Archives.
327 McKee Rankin to Abe Erlanger, San Francisco, January 1, 1906.
328 Nance O'Neil to McKee Rankin, October 31, 1905, Harry Ransom Humanities Research Center.
329 *San Francisco Call*, December 3, 1905, 19.
330 Ibid.
331 Mrs Bracy, resuming her maiden name, Clara Thompson, played Mrs Brauer; Robson was George Van Harten, Brauer's nephew; Glendinning was Pastor Haffner; Jane Marbury played Gertrude; Ricca Allen was the gypsy mother; Peg Bloodgood was Katie: and George Friend played Paul.
332 "Rankin and O'Neil Arrested Monday for Infringing Copyright," *New York Sun*, September 23, 1908.
333 Russell Merritt, "Rescued from a Perilous Nest: D.W. Griffith's Escape from Theatre into Film," *Cinema Journal*, Fall 1981, 2ff.
334 In O'Neil's company, Griffith played the cunning Judge Brack in *Hedda Gabler*, Lieutenant Borso in *Monna Vanna*, Ulrich Brendel in Ibsen's *Rosmersholm*, Banquo in *Macbeth*, Pastor Hefferdingt in *Magda*, and the pastor in *The Fires of St John*. Ironically, Griffith admired the introspective and understated style of Minnie Fiske, who was leading the theater away from the emotional style represented by O'Neil, but as O'Neil had brought more repression into her style of late, which some critics regretted, he was not critical of her. His experience with the O'Neil company represented the high point of his acting career, for which Rankin was largely responsible.
335 *San Francisco Evening Post*, December 18, 1905.
336 The besiegers want Giovanna, or Vanna, to come to them to petition for the city's salvation. Vanna crosses over to meet Prinzivalle, who commands the siege, and finds that he remembers her from his boyhood and loved her for all the years he spent in captivity in Africa. For guaranteeing his safety when she brings him back to Pisa, Vanna ensures the breaking off of the siege. She protects him from the wrath of her husband, Guido.
337 *San Francisco Examiner*, December 26, 1905, 4.
338 Ibid.
339 Clipping, Boston, February 15, 1905. Robinson-Locke Collection, NYPL.
340 Letter to O'Neil from [?], January 21, 1906, in Nance O'Neil Scrapbook MWEZ+n.c. 19,881, Billy Rose Theatre Collection, NYPL.
341 Nance O'Neil to McKee Rankin, January 29, 1906, Harry Ransom Humanities Research Center.
342 *Los Angeles Times*, January 30, 1906.
343 *Los Angeles Examiner*, January 26, 1906.
344 My thanks to Carol Bacon, director of the Littlefield Library, Tyngsboro, MA, for this information.
345 Carlos K. McClatchy, "A Wonderful Actress in a Very Repulsive Play," *Evening Bee* (Sacramento), January 25, 1906.
346 The rest of the cast comprised Andrew Robson as John Rosmer, the retired clergyman and owner of Rosmersholm; George Majeroni as Rector Kroll, Rosmer's conservative brother-in-law; Lawrence

Griffith as the romantic wanderer Ulrich Brendel; Paul Scardon as Peter Morgensgard; Clara Thompson as the housekeeper Madame Helseth.
347 *NYDM*, April 28, 1906.
348 Agnes Ranken's leading man at the Central Stock Theatre was Herschel Mayall, six feet tall, handsome, and aristocratic looking. In an interview with a Pittsburgh newspaper three years later, he left a harrowing account of his experiences during the quake. He was hurled from his bed and slammed in the back by a folding bed, which broke a rib. He got out of the room and met the other occupants of the house in the lower hallway unable to open the door of the swaying building because it was leaning over on a thirty-degree angle. He grabbed a fire ax and chopped down the door. The street had sunk three feet. After assisting the others from the building and seeing the women to a safe place, he went back to his room and dressed in a pair of light trousers, a sweater, and a straw hat. The silence in the streets was appalling. The people were awed and occasionally broke into whispered prayers. When daylight came, he went to the theater because all his earthly belongings, including his wardrobe of sixteen years on stage, were in his dressing room. "I found it guarded by firemen and policemen," he said. "They would not let me through the ropes, the chief, whom I knew quite well, saying that sparks and great blazing pieces of wood had been falling on the room for some time. I begged of him to let me enter the building but he said if I attempted to do so I would be placed under arrest. I was about to dash through the line when there was a whiff and a roar and the whole theater collapsed and was enveloped in flames. Then I turned to the chief and thanked him for having saved my life." With his broken rib, which caused him excruciating pain, he went to the General Hospital, where he remained four days and watched the city "being licked up by fire." Mayall was given permission by the mayor to carry a revolver to fight off looters who attacked the citizens. Eventually, Mayall left for Salt Lake City, and by October 1906 was acting again in Cincinnati, although his nerves remained in a terrible state for years. It took some years for the city to return to normal and for its theaters to reopen. The many unemployed actors, however, were available for the new film industry that was beginning to build studios on the West Coast. "Wants No More Quakes in His Life," *Pittsburgh Gazette*, December 5, 1909.
349 In Nance O'Neil Scrapbook MWEZ+n.c. 19,875, Billy Rose Theatre Collection, NYPL. The Central and Alhambra were owned by Belasco and Mayer, as was the Alcazar. The Central was a combination drama and vaudeville house under H.W. Bishop; the Alcazar had one of the best stock companies and was managed by E.D. Price; the Alhambra was a melodrama house devoted to sensational productions at popular prices. The *San Francisco Theatre Guide* for 1905 welcomed Agnes Ranken's return to the Central Theatre for the summer months: "Miss Agnes Rankin who will be recalled with pleasant memories by a host of friends has been specially engaged to play the part of June [in *Blue Jeans*] the leading role. She has all the fire, dash and winsome beauty that are essential for a successful portrayal of the role, and combined with wide experience and a notable histrionic talent, Miss Rankin should find a congenial opportunity for the exploitation of her talent." Agnes acted in the O'Neil company on the West Coast in 1906 before joining the Alhambra company. *San Francisco Theatre Guide*, July 22, 1905.
350 *Brooklyn Eagle*, May 1, 1906.
351 Clipping, "Rebekka West in Ibsen's *Rosmersholm*, May 8, 1906." Robinson-Locke Collection, NAFR+v 371, Billy Rose Theatre Collection, NYPL.
352 *Boston Transcript*, May 8, 1906.
353 O'Neil told the press that she intended to include in her repertory a new play, *The Story of the Golden Fleece*, which a young playwright from Oakland, Henry Kirk, wrote for her after following O'Neil's company about New England the previous spring to observe her acting. Due the next week, Rankin had to stage the moneymaking *Oliver Twist* in its stead.
354 Clipping, June 2, 1906, in Robinson-Locke Collection, NYPL.
355 Russell Merritt, "Rescued from a Perilous Nest: D.W. Griffith's Escape from Theatre into Film." *Cinema Journal* 21, 1 (Fall 1981).
356 Clipping, June 26, 1906, in Robinson-Locke Collection, NYPL.
357 *Portland Sun Telegram*, May 30, 1915. The company opened the season with *Macbeth* in Hartford, Connecticut, on Labor Day, in a matinee performance that stretched to 6 o'clock. The critic called it little better than a dress rehearsal, in which the actors were uncertain of their lines. The same went for *Elizabeth, Queen of England*, presented the second night. Moreover, the public was tired of these old plays and would have preferred *Magda* and *The Fires of St John*. The company gave the same two plays at the Hyperion Theatre in New Haven, Connecticut, where the audience was small but enthusiastic. "It is not too much to say," wrote the local critic, "that Miss O'Neil is without peer, as far as natural endowment goes, for the position of leading tragedienne of her time in the English speaking countries." Clipping, September 6, 1906, in Nance O'Neil Scrapbook MWEZ+n.c. 19,875, Billy Rose Theatre Collection, NYPL. The company continued through Massachusetts in one- and two-night stands. In Portland, Maine, it began alternating *The School for Scandal* with *Elizabeth*.
358 *Daily News* (Denver, CO), February 19, 1907.
359 Ibid.
360 *NYDM*, October 27, 1907.
361 *Springfield Union*, November 30, 1906.

362 *Daily News* (Denver), February 19, 1907.
363 Clipping, Kansas City, February 17, 1907. Robinson-Locke Collection, NYPL.
364 Clipping, March 1, 1907. Martha Mayo, MWEZ+n.c. 23, 123, Billy Rose Theatre Collection, NYPL.
365 Ibid.
366 *NYDM*, March 2, 1907.
367 *National Magazine*, March 1, 1905.
368 Clipping, Worcester, MA, March 23, 1907. Robinson-Locke Collection, NYPL.
369 *Cleveland Leader,* March 16, 1907.
370 Clipping, April 30, 1907. Robinson-Locke Collection, NYPL.
371 *Hartford Courant*, April 24, 1907.
372 William C. Wente, "The Oakland Theatre, 1890–1915" (PhD diss., Stanford University, 1965).
373 Clipping, September 28, 1907. Robinson-Locke Collection, NYPL.
374 Clipping, Pittsburgh, September 27, 1907. Robinson-Locke Collection, NYPL.
375 *Pittsburgh Sun*, October 1, 1907.
376 In November 1910, O'Neil appeared in *The Impostor* in New York and brought Clara T. Bracy to the footlights. "Nance O'Neil picked me up in Australia," explained Clara Bracy. "Not at all," Nance replied, giving her a girlish hug. "She adopted me and I've found a Polish word that exactly describes her. It's manusma, my mother."
377 Clipping, Boston, October 15, 1907, Robinson-Locke Collection, NYPL.
378 *Los Angeles Examiner,* December 8, 1907.
379 *Sunday Globe* (Boston), January 27, 1946.
380 *Vanity Fair*, December 27, 1907.
381 Augustus Thomas, the playwright, spoke of Blanchard's long and prominent career on stage while she listened from her wheelchair. Some of the stars then playing on Broadway contributed scenes from their plays, including Nazimova in *The Doll's House*. Victor Herbert and his orchestra provided the music, and actors sang selections from *The Merry Widow*. Pretty girls selling programs and candy raised $600. Ethel Barrymore, Maude Adams, and Tony Pastor each paid $100 for a seat. "Mrs Rankin's Testimonial," clipping file on Mrs McKee Rankin, Pusey Library, Harvard University. A spokesperson for the organizers of a fund for Blanchard, crippled by Bright's disease, pointedly stated that her husband had yet to forward a donation. Rankin replied in an open letter that he had given her $65,000 at their separation, "all I had in the world." "I have since contributed whenever I have been able to do so, which I can prove by telegraph and express receipts, and I sincerely wish I was in a position to do so now," he added. Clipping, February 15[?], 1907, McKee Rankin file, Billy Rose Theatre Collection, NYPL. Rankin refers to an accusatory letter in the issue of *NYDM* for February 8, 1907
382 *Show World*, February 22, 1908.
383 *Cleveland Leader,* February 28, 1908.
384 Ibid.
385 *Variety,* March 14, 1908.
386 *Vanity Fair*, May 29, 1908.
387 The company performed Henry Kirk's *The Story of the Golden Fleece* the week of the 24th so that at last Kirk was able to see his play in action.
388 Clipping, June 16, 1908, in Robinson-Locke Collection, NYPL.
389 Rankin invested in musicals and good drama, but I have not come across particular references, just general statements. Both Michael B. Leavitt and E.E. Rice might be sources for discovering them. Leavitt had a penchant for replacing male actors with female performers and started the first standard burlesque show, in contradistinction to Rice, who, trying to meld the allure of legs from Lydia Thompson-type burlesque to satirical lyrics and real talent, found it a losing proposition in the 1880s. No doubt Rankin favored Rice's efforts and earned Leavitt's sympathy. See Irving Zeidman, *The American Burlesque Show* (New York; Hawthorne, 1967).
390 The theater, built in 1907, had 1,600 seats, was fireproof, and boasted all the modern conveniences of the city's first modern playhouse. Every seat had a sweeping view of the stage.
391 Eugene Fritz to Nance O'Neil, September 9, 1945, telling of a letter he wrote to the *San Francisco Chronicle*, in which it was recently published. O'Neil Scrapbook MWEZ+19,880, Billy Rose Theatre Collection, NYPL.
392 *New York World,* September 22, 1908.
393 Clipping, "Nance O'Neil as Sad Agnes," October 6, 1908, O'Neil Clippings, Billy Rose Theatre Collection, NYPL.
394 *New York Evening Post*, October 6, 1908.
395 *Toledo Blade*, October 24, 1908.
396 *New York World*, October 17, 1908.
397 E.E. Rice to Lee Shubert, June 30, 1908. Edward E. Rice RIA-RIC 1908-09, Shubert Archives. O'Neil would get 50 percent of the first $4,000 and 60 percent on all over that sum per week, and "get the very best results with the least possible cost." J.W. Jacobs to E.E. Rice, October 19, 1908, Shubert Archives.
398 E.E. Rice to Jake and Lee Shubert, October 19, 1908, ibid.
399 J.W. Jacobs to Victor Harmon, October 20, 1908, ibid.

Notes 491

400 E.E. Rice to J.W. Jacobs, October 23, 1908, ibid.
401 J.W. Jacobs to Victor Harmon, October 27, 1908, ibid.
402 J.W. Jacobs to Victor Harmon, October 31, 1908, ibid. O'Neil's concern was for the poor notices she was receiving, not for the squeeze being put on the company. "It has been my lot to inspire strong friendships and bitter enemies, high praise and almost cruel criticism," she told a reporter. "Perhaps I should be equally grateful for both. Unjust criticism is the hardest thing in the world, but if it will arouse one's fighting spirit, I suppose even it has a good end. Fighting spirit is only another word for will, and will is the greatest power in the world. Enthusiasm is the most intoxicating delight. To experience it is to be well paid for the spell of the dumps which is bound to follow. Still, it is wearing, and I think I sometimes envy the person who keeps an even tenor on his way." *Pittsburgh Gazette*, October 25, 1908.
403 Victor Harmon to J.W. Jacobs, Wheeling, WV, November 3, 1908, Shubert Archives.
404 Victor Harmon to J.W. Jacobs, Kansas City, MO, November 29, 1908, ibid.
405 Victor Harmon to J.W. Jacobs, November 20, 1908, ibid.
406 Ibid.
407 Victor Harmon to J.W. Jacobs, Kansas City, MO, November 29, 1908, Shubert Archives.
408 Ibid.
409 O'Neil received word that all her belongings at Tyngsboro were snatched up in a frenzy at an auction that brought her $5,000, about three-quarters of the actual value. Her cat basket, for instance, went for $3.25. Clipping, Boston, November 19, 1908. Robinson-Locke Collection, NYPL. "Any small thing likely to have been intimately used by Miss O'Neil was eagerly sought."
410 Victor Harmon to J.W. Jacobs, November 30, 1908, Shubert Archives.
411 J.W. Jacobs to Victor Harmon, December 3, 1908, ibid.
412 Victor Harmon to J.W. Jacobs, St Louis, December 9, 1908, ibid.
413 *Philadelphia Times*, November 21, 1908.
414 J.W. Jacobs to Victor Harmon, December 14, 1908, Shubert Archives.
415 *Cincinnati Enquirer*, December 20, 1908.
416 Clipping, Cincinnati, December 14, 1908, in Robinson-Locke Collection, NYPL. "[That] O'Neil let the other players talk to a stated spot in the back of her neck, rather than to her face...seems unreal."
417 J.W. Jacobs to Victor Harmon, December 11, 1908, Shubert Archives.
418 J.W. Jacobs to Victor Harmon, December 17, 1908, ibid.
419 Victor Harmon to J.W. Jacobs, December 17, 1908, ibid.
420 J.W. Jacobs to Victor Harmon, December 19, 1908, ibid.
421 Victor Harmon to J.W. Jacobs, Buffalo, December 23, 1908, ibid.
422 *Buffalo Courier*, December 26, 1908.
423 Ibid., December 27, 1908.
424 Clipping, November 19, 1909, Robinson-Locke Collection, NYPL.
425 Clipping, January 23, 1909, Robinson-Locke Collection, NYPL.
426 McKee Rankin to Augustus Thomas, February 16, 1909, Loyola University Archives, Chicago.
427 *Invasion* is preserved on microfilm according to copyright law in the Library of Congress, Washington, DC. Copyrighted plays from the nineteenth century were either thrown away by library staff, according to one staff informant, or not sent to the library, as only titles were required, according to a printed source.
428 "The man is irresistibly funny," *Los Angeles Examiner*, September 14, 1909.
429 Clipping, September 14, 1909. McKee Rankin Clippings file, Billy Rose Theatre Collection, NYPL.
430 *Boston Transcript*, May 30, 1909.
431 *Pittsburgh Leader*, May 9, 1909.
432 *New York Telegram*, March 17, 1909.
433 "A Talk with Nance O'Neil," *Inter Ocean*, January 9, 1910.
434 Ibid.
435 Clipping "The Lily" in O'Neil Scrapbook MWEZ+n.c. 19,875, Billy Rose Theatre Collection, NYPL.
436 Ibid.
437 Clipping, December 2, 1909. Robinson-Locke Collection, NYPL.
438 *New York Review*, December 19, 1909.
439 *New York Evening News*, December 24, 1909.
440 His quality for deep and lasting friendship was reflected in a letter to him from an English actor, Lal Brough, who emotionally expressed what Rankin's friendship meant to him. Rankin kept the letter with his personal effects. ALS, Shields Library. University of California at Davis.
441 *Cleveland Leader*, January 22, 1910.
442 Quoted from the *New York Times* in *Actor Chat Scrapbook*, March 1910. Clipping in Robinson-Locke Collection, NYPL.
443 *New York Review*, January 30, 1910. Amelia Gardiner was being readied for the part.
444 *Toledo Blade*, February 10, 1911.
445 *Boston Transcript*, October 13, 1910.
446 Belasco did allow her to star in the occasional single performance that did not interfere with *The Lily*.
447 John Colton, "Work, Truth, Charity—What Else Is There?" *Minneapolis News*, April 25, 1914.
448 "Behind the Scenes," *Kansas City Post*, September 28, 1910.

Act Five
Rankin on the Rebound

1. *New York Dramatic Mirror* (hereafter *NYDM*), January 1, 1910.
2. Clipping, *New York American*, n.d., quoting John Barrymore on Lionel. Harry Ransom Humanities Research Center. University of Texas, Austin, TX.
3. "Lionel Barrymore Celebrates 64th Birthday and 50th Anniversary as an Actor," *Austin American*, April 30, ?, clipping in Harry Ransom Humanities Research Center.
4. Clipping, [n.d.], article by Robert Speare, Rankin Clipping File, Billy Rose Theatre Collection, NYPL.
5. *Variety*, February 10, 1910.
6. See Agreement of Percy Williams, Greater New York Circuit, and Lionel Barrymore, McKee Rankin, and Doris Rankin; also agreement of Edward F. Albee with McKee Rankin, L. Barrymore, and D. Rankin for Keiths in Providence, RI, Harry Ransom Humanities Research Center.
7. *NYDM*, March 5, 1910. A Chicago critic, noting how easily Rankin caught and held the close interest of the audience, urged him to find a play and return to the legitimate theater, where he was badly needed.
8. A post office robbery is investigated by a federal inspector who falls in love with Reuben's daughter Mary. The robber is discovered to be Sanders's son. Moreover, Reuben is found to be courting Sanders's sister.
9. Er Lawshé to McKee Rankin, New York, March 8, 1911. Harry Ransom Humanities Research Center.
10. *Los Angeles Times*, March 28, 1911.
11. An interview with Rankin reminiscing about his early days in Los Angeles appeared in the *Los Angeles Times*. The reporter portrayed him as a whirlwind as a stage director, which he preferred to any other vocation. "He has not only the energy and the magnetism, but the absolute enthusiasm of a man of thirty years." *Los Angeles Times*, March 26, 1911.
12. Ethel Barrymore was starring in a series of her plays at the Blackstone and expected to stay there until 24 June. She had drawn large houses, so *Peace on Earth* would have to be postponed or sent to another theater. The arrangements, which would have had to be diplomatic in such a case, resulted in Ethel closing on May 27.
13. McKee Rankin to Pixie Rankin, New York, June 2, 1911, McKee Rankin papers, Shields Library, University of California at Davis. Phyllis and Harry Davenport, owing to Phyllis's good business sense, were rich. She bought the Rankin homestead Thornfield at Sandwich and began restoring it. Remembering romping there as a girl, she told the local reporter, "Buying this Windsor property was a matter of sentiment with me....But I think it is also a shrewd business investment. With the passage of the reciprocity treaty all the border towns are bound to become prosperous." "Prominent Actress Prefers Home Life to the Stage," *Evening Record* (Windsor, ON), July 25, 1911.
14. *Los Angeles Times*, July 11, 1911.
15. S. Rankin Drew had made his debut at age nineteen in his father's company at the Plaza Music Hall in New York. The critics predicted a brilliant career for him. He resembled McKee Rankin and had inherited his love for literary work. Anxious that he not be an actor, his parents had sent him to military school, but the talent in him demanded expression. The play *A Man with a Past* concerned a bridegroom whose bride wanted to relish his notorious past, which he did not have but borrowed from his roguish young brother. Sidney, Sr, played the bridegroom, and Sidney, Jr, was his young brother. Junior was excellent. Gladys wrote a majority of her husband's scripts and still acted in them with him. *Out There*, which she wrote early in 1910, became a successful comedy vehicle for the couple. Late in 1910, her play *Billy*, or *Billy's Tombstones*, a farce in three acts, was presented at Daly's Theater in New York. Sidney Drew played the football hero, Billy Hargreave; Gladys played his sister, Alice; and S. Rankin Drew played Sam Eustace. It was the hit of the season, but when the Shuberts took it on the road, Gladys tried to stop it because they had cut back on the parts. Sidney quarreled with the leading lady and left the production. Amends were made, the Shuberts hired the full complement of cast, and the Drews toured with it well into 1911.
16. *Variety*, September 9, 1911, 16. At the close of December 1911, the Sidney Drew Company did a new one-act farce by Gladys, *Stalled*, in New York. A young man on his way to be married is stalled in his disabled auto in the deep mud of a country road. A justice of the peace marries the couple as they urge the bridegroom's doltish younger brother to get the auto running for them to get away before the girl's irate father appears. The critics said it was well written, the acting was of a high order, and the action never lagged. Sidney Drew carried the heaviest burden as he gave almost a monologue depicting a man who was having trouble getting married. His brother, played by S. Rankin Drew, had forgotten everything that his brother had wanted him to do. Lionel Barrymore as the excited justice of the peace was said to be wasting his talents in such a small role. Doris was sweet and charming as the girl.
17. NAFR+v. 253, p. 81, Billy Rose Theatre Collection, NYPL.
18. McKee Rankin to Pixie Rankin, New York, June 2, 1911. Rankin papers, Shields Library. She tried but failed.

19 A playwright wrote *Made to Order* for her. It had three characters: a widow played by Blanchard, her male admirer, and a mannequin The widow was robbed, and, since she reported on the fashions for newspapers, she decided to install a mechanical mannequin in her apartment while she attends a reception, leaving the impression that someone is home. Her admirer spots the mannequin through the window and thinks it is another man. Jealous, he goes to her apartment to accuse her of infidelity, when the dummy falls from its hook in the closet and walks into the room. The widow returns him to the closet, but the dummy keeps breaking free. Once, by mistake, she locks her suitor in the closet. After the dummy runs down and is carried out as a corpse, she releases her suitor from the closet and reconciles with him. Blanchard acted with great humor, but the critic called the piece totally unworthy of her powers. Clipping, June 1911, clipping file on McKee Rankin, Pusey Library, Harvard University.
20 Amy Leslie, "McKee Rankin Goes Home for Last Trip," *Chicago News*, May 2, 1914.
21 Amy Leslie, ibid.
22 Clipping, Frank Carlos Griffith, Roxbury, December 16, 1911, in Blanchard, Kitty, clipping file, Billy Rose Theatre Collection, NYPL.
23 *NYDM*, January 31, 1912.
24 I am indebted to Bob Birchard for bringing Boggs's and Bosworth's contributions in these films to my attention. *The Danites* was one of the earliest two-reelers and was originally to be shown in two sittings on one evening. Mr Birchard will publish an article on the subject with a photo of Rankin and Boggs. H.Z. Bosworth later played small parts in Augustin Daly's companies and appeared in the major cities of Europe. Daly destroyed his confidence so much that when he applied for a bit part with Julia Marlowe, she gave him the leads in Shakespearian plays. He became a Broadway star until tuberculosis forced him to retire to Arizona. The advent of film allowed him to live out of doors and continue acting. He wrote 112 scenarios for Selig's, many from Jack London stories, and produced 84 of them. See Richard Willis, *Movie Pictorial*, July 4, 1914.
25 *NYDM*, March 6, 1912.
26 Ibid.
27 Clipping about McKee Rankin funeral services in McKee Rankin clipping file, Billy Rose Theatre Collection, NYPL.
28 For Nance O'Neil's reference see the *Chicago Tribune*, April 18, 1909. The visitor, who witnessed Kate Blanchard's New Year's Eve party when Gladys rushed in with an infant in her arms to symbolize the birth of the New Year, likely mistook Phyllis's infant daughter for Gladys's child. See James L. Ford, *Forty Odd Years in the Literary Shop* (New York: Dutton, 1921).
29 Margaret Drew's stage career on Broadway had faltered. *Vanity Fair* predicted in January 1908 that she would be heard from some day: "All the Drews seem to draw." Then, in April, it asked, "Whatever Happened to Margaret Drew?" Margaret had been touring as the leading lady with the Paul Gilmore company in *The Mummy and the Humming Bird* for 1904 and 1905. In 1909, she played opposite Gilmore in *The Third Degree* in the role of Mrs Howard Jeffries for a year of touring.
30 *New York Telegraph*, January 22, 1912.
31 "George Cameron" wrote more one-act plays for the members of the Rankin family. For instance, *A Still Voice* opened at Keith and Proctor's Theater in New York on March 5, 1912, as a feature in the vaudeville bill. A millionaire industrialist-financier, played by Sidney Drew, objects to the prospective marriage of his daughter, played by Doris Rankin, to the son of a banker, played by S. Rankin Drew. He ruins the young man's family. From behind the scenes are spoken the words of Christ about rich men having difficulty getting to heaven; guilt-ridden, he becomes a broken man. Gladys staged her plays, wrote sketches for the movies, and joined Sidney in the films he made for the Kalem company, which were called Metro-Drew films.
32 Nance O'Neil starred in the play that summer of 1912 with the Lindsay Morison Stock Company in Boston. It was thought to be a coup to have won O'Neil's services, which entailed her giving up her summer vacation and breaking her contract with Belasco. During rehearsals in early July, she was described as "big, blonde and splendid, directing, advising, helping, acting, reading, suggesting, striding here and there about the stage with big, swift movements that are part of her personality—full of nervous energy and enthusiasm. She's red-blonde with brilliant eyes, violet blue, heavy, rather languorous lids and lashes, and red gold hair of amazing softness." *Boston Record*, July 5, 1912. From the tired look she brought from acting *The Lily*, O'Neil suddenly was reborn and enacted all her old repertoire that summer. In September, she was asked to fill in for another actress, who had fallen ill, in the title part of the play *Thais*. She saw the play for the first time on Friday, shut herself up all day Saturday, rehearsed on Sunday, and gave a splendid performance on Monday. "Now that it is all over," she said, "I know that I could not do it again. Well, perhaps I could, but I wouldn't have the courage to try." Clipping, [n.d.], Rare Book Room, Boston Public Library.
33 "The McKee Rankin Company in 'The Typhoon,'" *Seattle Post Intelligencer*, September 17, 1912, p. 5, col. 5.
34 Another critic gave a harsher verdict by stating that the properties were inadequate and that some of the actors impeded rather than advanced the action. Still, "the genius of McKee Rankin, tremendously virile, though full of years, and electric with the dramatic spark which should belong only to early youth," lit the play like "the flame of a torch in a dark place." *Los Angeles Times*, October 20, 1912.
35 Ibid.

36 Ibid., October 29, 1912.
37 "Reminiscence by Howard Lindsay Playing in Road Company about 1812." *Players' Bulletin*, spring 1965.
38 *San Francisco Examiner*, February 19, 1913.
39 In late June a report to the *New York Dramatic Mirror* commented on the American Theater: "This 10-20-30 house is having many 'ins' and 'outs,' besides 'ups' and 'downs.' Nothing seems to go. It is too far up Market Street."
40 Clipping, Spokane, April 2, 1913, in Margaret Drew clipping file, Billy Rose Theatre Collection, NYPL.
41 "The Senator Keeps House." *San Francisco Examiner*, February 25, 1913.
42 That same week, Nance O'Neil's sister, Lillian Lamson, arrived from Australia. She and her husband, the actor William Desmond, who later became a daredevil star in scores of films, had gone to Australia in 1910 and met with great success. They planned to tour the world, but Lillian, in preparing to leave for Egypt, fell down the stairs and injured her leg. Since the Australian surgeons could not mend it, the Desmonds returned to California. Lillian remained an invalid until she died in 1917. *San Francisco Examiner*, February 21, 1913.
43 Ibid., September 17, 1913.
44 Ibid., September 12, 1913.
45 Ibid., September 16, 1913.
46 Ibid.
47 Ibid., September 17, 1913.
48 *Los Angeles Times*, September 29, 1913.
49 *NYDM*, November 12, 1913. McKee Rankin clipping file, Billy Rose Theatre Collection, NYPL.
50 See A. Nicholas Vardac, *Stage to Screen: Theatrical Method from Garrick to Griffith* (New York: Blom, 1949).
51 Ashton Stevens in *San Francisco Examiner*, January 7, 1906.
52 He used more than 1,000 people and 300 horsemen. He concentrated on four kinds of scenes: the relationship between Judith and Holofernes, the wooing of Naomie by Nathan, the streets of Bethulia massed with people in sluggish movement, and the assault on Bethulia, with camp and battle scenes interpolated to unify the continuity. The romance of Nathan and Naomie gave the film an emotional significance that wound throughout the spectacle and made it superior to the chase melodramas so common at the time. A complete musical score to the action made it distinctive from the stereotyped music of other films. The film of four reels was released in 1914 by Biograph, and, owing to its cost of $32,000, led to Griffith's resignation from the company. If Rankin's film *The Danites*, which was released early in 1912, could be found and studied, it might prove to be the pioneer film linking the stage to the screen and might be shown to have affected Griffith's direction.
53 Obituary, *NYDM*, January 29, 1913, p. 13.
54 Obituary, Gladys Drew, *NYDM*, January 14, 1913.
55 Clipping, Robinson-Locke Collection, NAFR+Ser. 3, v. 377, Billy Rose Theatre Collection, NYPL.
56 In possession of the author, a gift from Peter Rankin, stepson of Arthur Rankin, who was Phyllis's son and McKee Rankin's grandson.
57 *NYDM*, April 22, 1914.
58 "McKee Rankin Goes Home for Last Trip," *Chicago News*, May 2, 1914.
59 Quoted by Levi Phillips in "Arthur McKee Rankin's Touring Production of Joaquin Miller's 'The Danites'." PhD diss., University of California at Davis, 1981, from an unidentified magazine article in the Shields Library.
60 Amy Leslie, "McKee Rankin Goes Home for Last Trip."

Appendix A
Progeny

1 *Motion Picture Magazine*, July 1915. The magazine sketched a profile of S. Rankin Drew to 1915. Ten years earlier, he had toured with his parents from the Atlantic to the Pacific, from the Gulf of Mexico to the prairies of Canada in his father's companies. He thought that *The Island of Regeneration* was his best film so far. In April 1916, his five-reel film *The Vital Question* was released.
2 Note of agreement, April 27, 1917. Harry Ransom Humanities Research Center University of Texas, Austin.
3 *Life and Letters of Sidney Rankin Drew*, edited by Mrs Sidney Drew [Lucille McVey Drew] (New York: Cheltenham Press, 1921).
4 Harry Davenport was in good shape. He jitterbugged with Merle Oberon in *The Cowboy and the Lady* when he was well into his seventies.
5 "O'Neil in 'The Wanderer',." August 1, 1919, clipping, Harry Ransom Humanities Research Center. She also said, "I think I may claim to being the first actress to discover that sincerity is the most important thing on the screen just as it is in real life and on the stage. The screen, however, is quicker to detect hypocrisy and what I may term, for want of a better word, 'feeling,' than is the speaking stage." Clipping, November 16, 1915, "'A Woman's Past' Fox Film," Robinson-Locke Collection,

Notes

Billy Rose Theatre Collection, New York Public Library. Nance O'Neil became interested in motion pictures after seeing Herbert Brenon's three-reel *Robespierre* in May 1912. She asked him to film her in her two favorite roles: the sleepwalking scene in *Macbeth* and the curse scene from *Leah*, which he did the same day. She began making films between stage appearances and eventually made a great many, including the talking picture *His Glorious Night* in 1929, directed by Lionel Barrymore, in which the ill-fated John Gilbert was exposed as having a high-pitched voice.

6 O.Z. Hall to Nance O'Neil, New York, April 18, 1946. O'Neil Scrapbook MWEZ+ 19,880, Billy Rose Theatre Collection, NYPL.

7 O'Neil wrote to Ward Morehouse that she had finished the chapter on *The Lily*, which meant that she had covered her period with Rankin. In 1959 she wrote to Arthur Row that "if I ever get to the point of really getting my book in order" she would send it to a Mr Meade, apparently a literary agent. She sent Meade's address to Clara Blandick, an actress friend, who had finished a book of memoirs. I have searched for O'Neil's ms and for her diaries in vain. If anyone knows who this Mr Meade was, perhaps he might be the clue leading to the discovery of these two manuscripts so important to theatrical history.

8 Clipping, February 3, 1917, Margaret Drew clipping file, Billy Rose Theatre Collection, NYPL.

Select Bibliography

Many newspapers were consulted for the periods in which Rankin performed in those cities and regions that they covered; they may be found in the notes.

Archival

Billy Rose Theatre Collection, New York Public Library: Clipping files under Rankin, McKee; Blanchard, Kitty; and O'Neil, Nance. Portfolio in the Players Collection (MWEZ+n.c. 13,547).

O'Neil clippings (MWEZ+n.c. 16,139). Billy Rose Theatre Collection, New York Public Library.

O'Neil Scrapbooks, Billy Rose Theatre Collection, New York Public Library. (MWEZ+n.c. 19,872 (1902–03); 19,873 (Sept. 1901–Jan. 1902); 19,874 (1917–22); 19,875 (clippings); 19,876 (1922–25); 19,877 (ca. 1928); 19,878 (1925–29); 19,879 (1935–39); 19,880 (1940s); 19,881 (letters); 19,882 (1950s); 19,883 (1960s and other dates); 19,884 (Eliza O'Neil playbills).

Ontario Archives, Toronto. Colonel Arthur Rankin Papers

Performing Arts Department, Shields Library, University of California, Davis. McKee Rankin Papers, plays and account ledgers of *The Danites*.

Robinson-Locke Scrapbook [Collection], Billy Rose Theatre Collection, New York Public Library. (NAFR+no. 371, no. 372).

Newspapers

New York Clipper, 1853-1924.
New York Dramatic Mirror, 1879-1922.

Books and Articles
McKee Rankin

Beasley, David. "McKee Rankin: The Actor as Playwright." *Theatre History in Canada* 10, 2 (1989): 115-31.

———. "The Nance O'Neil Company and the Shuberts in 1908." *The Passing Show: Newsletter of the Shubert Archive* 14, 1 (1992): 2-8.

———. "An Unconquerable Hero of the Stage: McKee Rankin." *Bulletin of Research in the Humanities* 7, 4 (1986–87): 515-42.

Fyles, Vanderheyden. "An Apollo of Long Ago: The Story of McKee Rankin, a Matinee Idol of Our Parents' Day." *Green Book* 12 (July 1914): 39-42.

Dictionary of American Biography, "McKee Rankin."

Obituary, *New York Dramatic Mirror*, 22 April 1914.

Phillips, Levi Damon. "Arthur McKee Rankin's *The Danites*, 1877–1881: Prime Example of the American Touring Process." *Theatre Survey* 25, 2 (1984): 225-47.

———. "Arthur McKee Rankin's Touring Production of Joaquin Miller's *The Danites*." PhD diss., University of California, Davis, 1981.

Kitty Blanchard

Grey, Mabel. "A Notable Theatrical Family: The Rankins—Old and Young." Clipping, [n.p., n.d.], Museum of the City of New York.

"Kitty Blanchard to Have Benefit." *New York Telegram*, 21 November 1907.

"Mirror Interviews: Kitty Blanchard." *New York Dramatic Mirror*, 11 December 1897, p. 23.

Nance O'Neil

Shee, Maureen A. "Nance O'Neil: Power and Passion of the Modern American Stage." *Theatre Studies* 21 (1974–75): 61-68.

The Theatre

Bernheim, Alfred L. *The Business of the Theatre*. New York: Actors Equity, 1932.

Bordman, Gerald. *American Theatre: A Chronicle of Comedy and Drama, 1869–1914*. New York: Oxford University Press, 1994.

Burge, James C. *Lines of Business: Casting Practice and Policy in the American Theatre, 1752–1899*. New York: Lang, 1986.

Daly, Joseph F. *The Life of Augustin Daly*. New York: Macmillan, 1917.

Ellis, James, ed. and comp. *English Drama of the Nineteenth Century: An Index and Finding Guide*. New Canaan, CT: Readex, 1985.

Fawkes, Richard. *Dion Boucicault*. London: Quartet Books, 1979.

Select Bibliography

Herne, James E. "Old Stock Days in the Theatre." *Arena* (September 1892): 401ff.

Hixon, Don L., and Don A. Hennessee. *Nineteenth Century American Drama: A Finding Guide*. Metchuen, NJ: Scarecrow Press, 1977.

Hollingworth, Gerelyn. "Legitimate Theatre in St Louis, 1870–1879." *Missouri Historical Review* (April 1975): 260ff.

Leavitt, Michael B. *Fifty Years in Theatrical Management*. New York: Broadway Publishing, 1912.

McConachie, Bruce C. *Melodramatic Formations: American Theatre and Society, 1820–1870*. Iowa City: University of Iowa Press, 1992.

McElaney, John Scott. "The Professional Theatre in San Francisco, 1880–1889." PhD diss., Stanford University, 1972.

Morris, Clara. *Life on the Stage: My Personal Experiences and Recollections*. London: Isbister, 1902.

Odell, George Clinton Densmore. *Annals of the New York Stage*. 15 volumes. New York: Columbia University Press, 1927-1949.

Reynolds, Ernest. *Early Victorian Drama, 1830–1870*. New York: Blum, 1936.

Ryan, Kate. *Old Boston Museum Days*. Boston: Little, Brown, 1915.

Ryan, Patrick Martin, Jr. "A.M. Palmer, Producer: A Study of Management, Dramaturgy and Stagecraft in the American Theatre, 1872–1896." PhD diss., Yale University, 1959.

Towse, John Ranken. *Sixty Years of the Theatre*. New York: Funk and Wagnall, 1916.

Vardac, A. Nicholas. *Stage to Screen: Theatrical Method from Garrick to Griffith*. New York: Blom, 1968.

Warde, Frederick. *Fifty Years of Make Believe*. New York: International Press Syndicate, 1920.

Woodfield, James. *English Theatre in Transition, 1881–1914*. London: Croom Helm, 1984.

Index

Please note that the Notes are not indexed. Of the plays only those of special significance and certain of Rankin's roles are indexed. You may wish to use "Rankin's Roles," a chronological listing of McKee Rankin's roles with play and theater, which will be found on the Web site of Wilfrid Laurier University Press, in conjunction with the text. This could lead you to the footnotes in the text that will take you to plot and character and other information in the Notes.

'49, genesis of, 171-72; new version, 180; payment to Miller, 176; plot, 177-78
A Romance of the Sierras, 146
Abbey, Henry, 169-70
Abraham Lincoln, 261-63; innovation of Rankin, 262
Academy of Music Theatre, New Orleans, 121
Academy of Music, Albany, NY, 43
Academy of Music, Brooklyn, NY, 68
Academy of Music, Cleveland, OH, 77
acting in Chicago, 84
acting manager, 69

acting style: Delsarte, 135, 358; elocutionary, 135, 216; imaginative pictorialization, 8; intellectual school, 135; letting of acting alone school, 51; living the roles, 135; middle ground, 134-35; natural, 22, 159; old demonstrative style, 248; old English, 91, 159; rant, 22; robustious, 8; seductive gentleness, 135-36; speaking at the audience, 47, 139 acting, essence of, 341, decadent, 347, psychological, 389
Actor's Art Union, 57

actor-manager, duties of, 76; versus entrepreneurial managers, 180
actors' masquerade ball, 208
actresses, male companions of, 26
Adams, Annie, 105
Adams, Edwin, 29-30, 41, 53, 253
Adams, Maude, 105
Adelphi Theatre, London, 331, 334
advance man, 153, 159, 165
Agnes: plot, 398-99; criticism, 400
Ah Gow, *see* Alphonso
Ah Wung Sing, 241
Aiken, Fred, 85
Aiken, George L., 19, 142
Aimée, Mlle, 152
Albaugh, John, 23, 33, 35, 39-40, 156, 295-96
Albough's Lafayette Square Opera House, Washington, DC, 295
Alcazar Theatre, San Francisco, 235, 254, 272, 275, 341
Aldrich, Louis, 151, 154, 160, 163, 207,
Aldrich, Thomas Bailey, 359, 367, 370-74; views on O'Neil, 371, 374
Alexander, George, 326
Alhambra Theatre, San Francisco, 103, 344, 388
Ali Tookh, 237-38
Allan Dare: in New York, 243-44; in San Francisco, 219-20
Allen, Ricca, 294, 313, 330, 348, 357, 367-69, 377, 379-80, 383, 386, 389
Alphonso, 195, 237
American Dramatic Protective Association, 193
American Theatre Company, 218, 428, 438
American Theatre, New York, 288
American Theatre, San Francisco, 399
Americans, The: plot, 184
Anderson, Dallas, 395
Anderson, Mary, 337, 348, 355
Anglin, Margaret, 384, 389
Antoine of Theatre Libre, 315
Antoinette, Marie, 325

Apollo Theatre, Lexington, KY, 30-31
Arch St Theatre, Philadelphia, 41, 43, 49-61, 141, 161, 166, 182, 269; almost bankrupt, 265
Archer, William, 332-33
Ashley, Leonard, 145
Ashton, Harold, 383
Astor Opera House riot, 9
Athenaeum, Detroit, MI, 40
Atheneaum Theatre, Wheeling, WV, 51
attitudes to theater, American vs English, 64
Aubrey, Ida, 196
audience, importance of, 348
audience manager, 69
audience participation, 25
Auditorium Theatre, Los Angeles, 421
Augier, Emile, 183

Baby Elberts, 140
Bachelor's Baby, The: O'Neil creates role of Geraldine, 282
Baker, Lewis, 64
Baker, T.B., 137, 139
Baldwin Theatre, San Francisco, 157, 196, 198, 220, 223, 225, 230, 232, 271, 303
Bancroft, Mrs: her version of *Masks and Faces* (*Peg Woffington*), 314
Bannock, poet, 168
Barnes, J.H., 176, 179
Barnum's New Museum, New York, 63
Baron von Hoenstauffen, 274
Barras, Charles, 26
Barrett, Lawrence, 58, 196, 230
Barrett, Viola, 39
Barrett, Wilson, 337
Barry, Eleanor, 264
Barry, Sheil, 122
Barrymore, Ethel, 270, 278-79, 289, 336, 367-68, 384, 417, 432, 436-37
Barrymore, John, 270, 295, 321, 367, 437; debut, 348-49
Barrymore, Lionel, 270, 283, 295-96, 298, 336, 351, 367-68, 417-22,

Index

432, 436-38; marries Doris Rankin, 367
Barrymore, Maurice, 65, 269, 271, 321; death, 368; description of, 207
Bartley McCullum's Summer Theatre, Peake's Island, ME, 270
Bateman, Mrs H.L., 166, 170
Bates, Blanche, 273, 353, 389
Bates, Mrs F.M., 210, 273-74, 389
Baxters, The, 268, 270-71; opens in Brooklyn, NY, 276; retitled *A Country Merchant*, 270
Becks, George, 309, 313, 325, 328
Belasco Theatre, New York, 410
Belasco, David, 157, 195, 197, 207-208, 232, 334, 341, 352-54, 363, 378, 410-15, 417, 429, 432, 438; concept different from Rankin, 353; despair over theater, 352
Belasco, Ike, 195
Belle of New York, The; 484th performance, 307; leaving New York for London, 294-95
Belleville, Frederic de, 213, 217; as Robert in *Allan Dare*, 219
Bellew, Kyrle, 320
Benavente, Jacinto, 438
benefit, 87, 98, for earthquake victims, 389; for Rankin as manager, 192
Berkeley, Little Ollie, 242
Bernhardt, Sarah, 169-70, 308, 318, 331-32, 338, 358, 360, 363, 365, 382, 392; her interpretation of *Magda*, 297; Rankin's impressions of, 170
Bert, Fred, 197
Bert, Mabel, 208-11, 214, 217, 219, 222-28, 230-33, 235, 237-41, 245-47, 250, 252-56, 262-66, 268, 337, 367, 428, 439; as Billy Piper in *The Danites*, 239; as Lady Macbeth, 245; baby girl, 244; crisis of conscience, 260; description of, 232; double role in *Hoodman Blind*, 224; leaves Rankin, 263; marriage, 273; praise from Rankin, 259-60; pregnant, 241

Beveridge, J.D., 183-84
Beverly, painter, 200
Bey, Mauriette, 330
Bijou Theatre, New York, 257
Bingham, Amelia, 263
Biograph Company, 417
Bishop, C.B., 157, 198-99, 202, 206, 209-10, 220, 228, 230, 233, 322, 340; without equal in low comedy parts of Shakespeare, 214
Bishop, C.J., 206, 220, 227
Black Crook, The, 72-73; scenery of, 200-201
Black Eyed Susan, introduced the domestic story, 30
Blackwood Theatre, Chicago, 420
Blackwood, John 420
Blaisdell, John W., 85-86, 156
Blake, Mrs W.R., 31, 152
Blanchard, Kitty, 33-38, 61-62, 64, 80-81, 90-91, 93, 101, 238-44, 250-51, 257, 288, 396-97, 424; adrift, 204; as Billy Piper in *The Danites*, 151; as Capitola Black for General Sherman's troops, 37; as Bessie in *The Golden Giant*, 231; as Bet in *The Golden Giant Mine*, 247; as Carrots in *'49*, 178; as Earl Darnley, 228; as Jack Sheppard, 227-28; as Nancy in *Oliver Twist*, 152, 223, 272; as Oberon in *A Midsummer Night's Dream*, 220-21; as Sappho in *Sappho*, 229; as Susan in *William and Susan*, 205-206; changes name to Kate Blanchard-Rankin, 265; changes name to Kate Rankin, 250; compared to Maggie Mitchell, 36; copyrighted *The Danites*, 146; death, 422-23; description of, 144; gains alimony, 265; her temper, 173-74; idol of Harvard men, 81; illness, 181-82, 203; in male attire, 151; marriage to Rankin, 94-95; photographer, 337; produces *The Baxters*, 271; reconciliation with Rankin, 268; reflections on *The Two Orphans*, 132-33;

rejoins Rankin's company, 272-77; returns to New York, 277; serves Rankin with separation papers, 258; sketch against Rankin, 288-89; stage partner with Rankin established, 111; stars in standard comedies, 225-26; testimonial, 397; threatens suit, 175; tours with her company of relatives, 278
Blanchard, Mrs [Gladys], 33-34, 95, 102, 110; death, 136
Bloodgood, Margaret [Peg], 379, 405
Bodworth, Frank, 164
Boer War, benefit for soldiers, 327-28
Boggs, Francis W., 423
Bois Blanc Island, 120, 163, 175, 181, 190, 195, 230, 238, 290; sale of, 231
booking, 160, 382
Booth's Theatre, New York, 128, 136, 152, 162, 186
Booth, Agnes, 357
Booth, Edwin, 20, 30, 35, 45-47, 59, 61, 66, 68, 212, 213, 229, 261, 269, 309, 358
Booth, John Wilkes, 24, 35, 44-46, 53, 59, 68, 261-62
Booth, Junius Brutus, 135
Booth, Junius Brutus, Jr, 35, 46, 61, 102, 357
Booth, Junius Brutus, III, 283
Booth, Sidney
Borden, Emma, 368-69
Borden, Lizzie, 368-69
Boston Athenaeum, Boston, 121
Boston Museum, Boston, 97, 283
Boston Theatre, 154, 156, 207
Bosworth, Hobart Z., 210, 423
Boucicault, Dion, 24, 65, 70-71, 121-123, 125, 199, 201; innovations, 71, 83; personality of, 122
Bourke, Betsy, 417
Bowdoin College, 33
Bowers, G. Vining, 39, 152, 154, 157, 158
Bowers, Mrs D.P., 99, 301, 309, 345
Bowery Theatre, New York, 25, 99
Bracy, Clara Thompson, 316, 325, 330, 371, 377, 379, 381, 383, 394-95, 403, 405-407, 438
Brady, William, 283-84, 324, 409
Broadhead, Colonel, 12
Broadway Theatre, New York, 63, 74-75, 78, 80-82, 149, 152
Brook and Dickson, 176, 179-80
Brooklyn Theatre, Brooklyn, NY, 60, 62
Brougham, John, 145
Brown, Colonel Thomas Alston, 88, 101, 149, 259
Brunell, Mr, 299
Bryant, Dan, 134
Bryton, Frederick, 186, 189-90
Buchanan, McKean, 42
Buchanan, Virginia, 42
Burbank Theatre, Los Angeles, 277-78, 301, 304
Burke, Charles, 91, 123, 309
Burleigh, John, 245
burlesque, 72
Burroughs, Claude, 68, 133
Bush St Theatre, San Francisco, 194, 198, 263
Byron, Henry, J, 147, 229
Byron, George Gordon, Lord, 22

Cadotte, Albert, 2
Caldwell, Billy, 5
California circuit, 158
California Theatre Company, 199, 206, 337
California Theatre, San Francisco, 103, 196-99, 213, 220, 223, 224, 303-305, 310; Hayman gains control, 197; most thoroughly appreciative audience, 214
California, plot, 421
Cameron, George. *See* Rankin, Mary Gladys
Camille: comparison of stars as Marguerite Gautier, 358-59
Campbell, Bartley, 159, 164, 204, 255; his *My Partner*, 163
Campbell, Mrs Patrick, 297-98, 307, 331, 363, 378, 382, 391
Campion, Anna, 113, 116, 117
can-can, introduction of, 79

Index

Canfield, Charles, 313, 432
Canuck, The: authorship, 247, 254, 256-57, 260, 267-68
Captain Impudence: Rankin directs, 288
Carden, James, 171
Carr, Herbert, 339
Carter, Mrs Leslie, 334, 341, 353-54, 363, 375, 393
Cartwright, Charles, 410
Castle Square Garden, Boston, 363
Catlin, George, 1-2
Cazauran, A.R., 124
Celeste, Madame Celine, 55, 58-59
Chanfrau, Frank, 24, 27, 58, death 191
Chapelle, Charles, 173
Charles St Theatre, New Orleans, 67
Charlie Collins Cafe, 159
Chatham Theatre, New York, 186
Chicago fire, 113
Chiltrain, Charles, dramatist, 224
Chinese-American actor, 195
Christy's minstrels, 63
Cibber, Colly, 21, 145
Clark, George, 69, 99
Clarke, John S., 46, 59
Clarke, Lillian, 169
Claxton, Kate, 131, 132, 188-90
Clement, Clay, 272, 310-14; description of, 274
Cleveland Theatre, Chicago, 348-49
Cleveland, Grover, 193
Cleveland, W.S., 347-51, 354
Clifton, Marion, 136
Cluer, Miss, 90
Clunie Opera House, Sacramento, CA, 214
Cody, Bill, 261
Cogswell, W.J., 152
Colleen Bawn, The: Myles na Coppaleen vs Danny Mann, 122
Collins, John, 93
Collins, Wilkie, 26
Colonial Theatre, Boston, 361-62, 366
Columbia Theatre, Boston, 352
Columbia Theatre, San Francisco, 299
Committee of Supplies of the California Relief Association, 389

Conklin, Helen, 209, 228-29
Continental Theatre, Boston, 60-62
Continental Theatre, Philadelphia, 34
Conway, Sarah Crocker, 99
Cooke, George Frederick, 69
Cooke, Jay, 123
Coolbrith, Ida, 157
Coombs, Jane, 12, 29, 253
Cooper, Fred, 277
copyright, 70, 83, 314
Coquelin, Constant, 135, 289, 308
Corbett, Jim, 283-84, 346, 382
Corbyn and Wall, 75
Corcoran, Katharine, 157
Cordray Theatre, Portland, OR, 309; most successful venue, 305
Cornwall, Duke and Duchess, 325
Corsican Brothers, The: masculine superiority, 40; plot, 31
cost of productions, 350
Couldock, Charles, 18
Couldock, Eliza, 18
Counsel for the Defense: one-act adapted from *The Long Strike*, 287, 290
Covent Garden, London, England, 69
Cowles, Charles, 256, 259-61, 270, 276, 288
Crabtree, Lotta, 24, 68
Craig, Robert, 50
Crane, William, 145, 148, 428
Criterion Theatre, Chicago, 187
critics, payments to, 133, 166
Crockett, Davy, 169, 264
Cromer, Lord and Lady, 330
Crosbie, W.C., 255
Crosby Opera House, Chicago, 66, 79, 83-85, 93,
Currie, W., 259
Curtis, Frank, 185-87, 190, 305
Curtis, M.B., 188
Cushman, Charlotte, 71, 128, 142, 152, 245, 298-99, 309, 363
Cushman, Pauline, 42
Cutler, Burwell, 294

D'Ennery and Cormon, playwrights, 130
Dale, Alan, 292, 372, 412

Dalton, Charles, 363, 374, 379
Daly's Theatre, New York, 372
Daly, Augustine, 75, 80-81, 90, 96, 100-101, 121, 123-24, 127, 133, 134, 145, 159, 183, 210, 291, 309
Danites, Mormon police, 108, 148
Davenant, Sir William, 212
Davenport, Arthur (Gibbs), 295, 432. *See also* Rankin, Arthur (Davenport)
Davenport, E.L., 19-23, 30, 61-62, 121, 190, 308
Davenport, Edgar, 190
Davenport, Edward (Ned), 437
Davenport, Fanny, 61, 99, 152, 344
Davenport, Harry, 308, 336, 367, 418, 432, 435-37
Davenport, Phyllis, 437
Davey, Tom, 159
Davies, Acton, 372-73, 412
De Bar's Opera House, St Louis, MO, 102, 117, 138
De Bar, Ben, 102
Dean, Julia, 75, 84, 410
Deanys, 31
Dearborn St Theatre, Chicago, 85
debutantes, 193
Deering Hall, Portland, ME, 44
Delaney, Patrick, 141, 155, 161
Delmonico crowd, 175
Delmore, Ralph, 243-44
Denin, Kate, 44, 99
Denvil, Rachel, 8
Desert Lake mining, 290
Dickens, Charles, 96, 273, 275, 325
Dickens, Charles, Jr, 168
Dillingham, Charles, 393-95
Dillon, Charles, 58
Dillon, John, 86
Dixon, Edson, 269
Dockstader's Minstrels, 357
Don Cesar de Bazin: as melodrama, 26-27
Donaldson, W.A., 89
Donaldson, W.C., 173
Doré, Gustave, 217
Drake, Samuel, 31
Drew, Georgie, 49, 207, 269-70

Drew, John, Jr, 49, 133, 207, 266, 268, 279, 336, 368
Drew, John, Sr, 33, 49
Drew, Louisa, 49
Drew, Lucille McVey, 437
Drew, Margaret, 424-28, 432, 438-39
Drew, Mrs John (Louisa Lane), 24, 41, 49-60, 165, 182, 207, 265-66, 268-72
Drew, Mrs Sidney (Gladys). *See* Rankin, Mary Gladys
Drew, Sidney Rankin, Jr, 265, 421, 424, 432, 436-37
Drew, Sidney "Uncle Googan," 50, 207-208, 253, 265-66, 269, 278, 289, 367, 397-98, 408, 424, 432, 436-37; death, 437
Drew-Rankin company, 265; combination, 271-72
Drouet, Robert, 400
Drummond, W.H., 354
Drury Lane, London, England, 69
Duclos, Madame, dressmaker, 331
Duff, James C., 146
Duff, John, 31
Duff, Mary, 31
Duffield Theatre, Nashville, TN, 35
Dumas, Alexandre, fils, 26
Dumas, Alexandre, Sr, 97
DuMaurier, George, 281
Dunn, John "Rascal Jack," 98, 102-103
Dunning, Alice, 83
Duplessis, Marie, 315
Duse, Eleanora, 298, 318, 331-32, 359, 363

economic crises, 193, 328, 342, 354
Eddy, Edward, 10-11, 29
Eden Musée, 233-34
Edmunds, Charles, 193, 199
Edwards, George, 331
Edwin, Lina, 99
Eldridge, Lillie, 152
Elliott, Maxine, 384
Elliston, 135
Ellsler, John, 77
Emerson, Adelaide, 233, 244
Emmett, Joe, 83

Empire Theatre, New York, 336
Englander, Ludwig, 403
English, Jane, 292
entrepreneur-manager class, 137
Erin A'Chorra, mishmash, 226
Erlanger, Abe, 335, 340, 343, 352, 378, 382, 387, 391, 430
Ethel, Agnes, 124
Eustache Baudin: character nurtured by nature, 87
Evesson, Isabelle, 186
evolution in stagecraft, 13
Eytinge, Rose, 125-26, 131, 134, 152, 293; her play *That Lass o' Lowrie*, 295

Fairchild, Florence, 102
Fairchild, Marie, 102
farce, nineteenth-century, 124
Farnum, Dustin, 409, 430
Farren, Mrs, 20ff, 66
Fechter, Charles, 96-97, 184, 325; compared to Edwin Booth, 96
Ferrer, Jose, 438
Field of the Cloth of Gold: burlesque cross-dressing, 222-29
File (Fyles), Frankin, 145, 335
film industry, 418
fin de siecle worldliness, 311
Fires of St John, The: plot, 356-57; suit quashed, 424
First Family of the Sierras, The, 142
Fisher, Amelia, 207
Fiske, Harrison Grey, 305, 352, 378, 387, 415
Fiske, Minnie Maddern, 305-306, 361, 372-75, 400
Fitch, Clyde, 367
Fitzgerald, Alexander, 152, 164
Fitzgerald, Mrs P.A., 144, 158
Fitzgerald, P.A., 51-52: writing *The Danites*, 143
Fitzwilliam Island, 267
Fletcher, Lydia Coyne, 184, 282
Flood, 106
Florence, Mrs William (Malvina), 15-16
Florence, William, 15-16, 70, 78-79, 169, 284; death, 266

Ford's Opera House, Baltimore, MD, 241
Ford's Theatre, Washington, DC, 44
Forepaugh's Theatre, Philadelphia, 287
Forrest, Edwin, 8, 24, 29-30, 41, 56, 68, 122, 309
Fortier, Herbert, 249, 400, 403
Fox, George, 186
Foy, Eddie, 284
Free Joe, 249
French Theatre, New York, 63
French, Samuel, 137
Friend, George, 379
Frohman Syndicate, 303, 335
Frohman, Charles, 197, 239-40, 243, 273, 304, 337, 353, 432
Frohman, Daniel, 304
Frohman, Gustave, 304
Fuller, Barney, 280
Furbish Fifth Avenue Combination Company, 137
Furbish, Charles, 137
Furness, scholar, 147

Gabriel Conroy: construction of, 188-89
Gaekwar of Baroda, 326, 331
Gaiety Theatre, London, 169
gallery patrons, 198-99
Gardiner, Charles, 160, 163, 173
Garfield, President James, 176
Garrick Theatre, Chicago, 354
Garson, Count, 169
Gatti Theatrical Syndicate, 331
Gay White Way, 403
Gayle, Future, 249
Germaine, R., 269
Giacommetti, Paolo, 301
Gibbs, Henry D., 269, 277-78, 307-308, 435-36
Gilan, Ada, 126
Gilbert, Mrs G.H., 82
Gilbert, W.S., 124, 227
Gillette, William, 27
Gilman, Ada, 152
Girty Brothers, 5
Glendinning, John, 379
Globe Theatre, Boston, 154; burnt, 120

Globe Theatre, London, 168
Golden Giant, The, plot, 230-31
Golden, Martin, 30, 32
Goldthwaite, Dora, 152, 154, 156
Gordon, Archibald, 177-78, 261-62, 265
Gotthold, J. Newton, 89
Grand Opera House, San Francisco, 198-99, 209, 338-39, 384
Grand Opera House, Toronto, 156
Grandin, Elmer, 261-63
Granger, Maude, 126, 132
Grau, Robert, 132, 395
Great Metropolis, The: Rankin wrote and directed, 278
Great Triple Alliance, 102
Green, Charles, 210
Greene, Clay, 208, 230, 232, 270
Greenwood, Grace, 168
Grieves, painter, 200
Griffith, Lawrence (D.W.), 384-85, 387-88, 417-18, 430, 437; goes into film, 390
Griswold Opera House, Troy, NY, 68
Grover's Theatre, Washington, DC, 65
Grover, Leonard, 65, 69, 73-74, 137, 177, 180-81, 199, 277
Grundy, Sidney, 266
Gunter, A.C., 219
Gusher, Giddy, 252

Hall, O.Z., 438
Halley, Richard, 192
Hamilton, Baldy, 195
Hamilton, Theodore, 66, 192, 194, 209
Hammerstein Opera House, Harlem, NY, 270
Harkins, Dan, 82, 169, 192, 208-10, 213, 226-27, 233, 242; as Emir Mohammed in contrast to Rankin in *The Veteran*, 202; as Macbeth, 216
Harkins, W.S., 283
Harmon, Victor, 401-407
Harris, Lin, 172
Harrison, Maude, 278
Hart, Josh, 163

Harte, Bret, 142; his and Mark Twain's *Hop Sing*, 155
Hastings, Cuyler, 400
Hauptmann, Gerhart, 353
Haverly's Fourteenth St Theatre, New York, 176
Haverly, Bert, 209
Haverly, Colonel Jack "Colonial Jack," 159-60, 162, 173, 175-76, 179, 304; quarrel with Rankin, 163
Hawaii, 302-303; plague, 312
Hawk, Harry, 45, 167
Hayman, Al, 196-97, 220, 230, 232, 235, 271, 303, 335
Hearst, William Randolph, 373, 386
Held, Anna, 288
Henderson, William, 40
Henri, Charles, 51-52
Henri, Mrs Charles (Caroline), 51-52, 62, 63, 78, 79, 81, 94, 144; death, 165; marriage to Rankin, 60
Henry Bishop Players, 394
Her Majesty's Theatre, Sydney, 319
Herald Square Theatre, New York, 340, 372
Herbert, Victor, 397
Herne, James A., 89, 135, 152, 157, 192, 269, 367
Herne, John, 152
Heron, Bijou, 192
Heron, Matilda, 42, 152, 192; as Camille, 42
Hickman, Alfred, 410, 415, 438
Hickok, Wild Bill, 110
high-class drama, undermining of, 69
Hill, Barton, 68, 309, 313-15; his version of *Camille*, 310, 314-15, 358; as Triplet in *Peg Woffington*, 312
Hill, Caroline, 183
Hilliard, Robert, 241, 291
Hilton, W.H., 83
Hind, T.J., 39
Hogan, Little Alice, 35
Holcroft, Thomas, 270
Holland, E.M., 174, 288-89
Holland, George, 176, 207
Holland, J.J., 176, 204, 206-207, 217-18, 223, 233, 270, 288-89, 291

Index

Holliday St Theatre, Baltimore, MD, 155
Hollis Theatre, Boston, 363, 366, 382, 389
Holmes, Oliver Wendell, Sr, 154
Holt, Clarence, 272
Honey Moon, The: popularity of, 29
Hood, Thomas, 6
Hoodman Blind: plot, 223
Hooley's Opera House, Chicago, 112, 183
Hooley's Theatre, Brooklyn, NY, 99
Hopper, De Wolf, 355, 403, 406
Hosmer, Jean, 57-58
House of Lords, hotel, 68
Howard Athenaeum, Boston, 44, 64
Howard, Bronson, 159
Howard, May, 51, 61, 79, 84-88, 90, 103; death, 430
Hudson Theatre's Union Hall, New York, 424
Hudson, Leo, 49
Hudson, William, 100
Hughes, Jack, 110
Hunter, Bessie, 160
hypnotism. *See* mesmerism

Ibsen, Henrik, 159, 297, 320, 335, 339, 353, 388
Ilidge, Ruby, 220
Ince, Hohn, 269
independent theater producers, 305, 375, 378, 387, 415
Invasion: plot, 408
Irving, Henry, 117, 212, 331
Irving, Washington, 92
Italian school of dancing, 151

Jack Sheppard, 227-28; working class hero, 48
Jack, John, 82, 183
Jackson and Reed, 390, 392-93
Jackson, Hart, 130, 132
Jackson, Ira, 390
Jacobs, J.W., 402, 405-406
James, Henry, 359
James, Louis, 59
Janauschek, Fanny, 158, 205, 207, 209

Jefferson, Joseph, 63, 64, 135, 182, 185-86, 194, 207, 289, 309; as Rip Van Winkle, 91-92
Jeffreys, Ida, 152
Jeffries, James J., pugilist, 346
Jewess, The: in London, 307; money-maker, 338; Rankin's version of *Leah*, 299
job actors, 159
John W. Luce and Company, 384, 389, 400
Johnson, Ben, 145
Johnson, Hank, 204
Jones, Inigo, 200
Jordan, Mabel, 152, 154
Judge Not: Rankin adapted from the German, 286-87
Judith of Bethulia, 371, 373, 385, 430; Rankin's suggestions to Aldrich, 370
Judith: 1st time in English, 339
Justice, Bessie, 181

Kamekamela III, 303
Kanuck, The. See Canuck, The
Kate Davenport (Gibbs), 288
Kawananakoa, Prince David, 303
Kean, Edmund, 29-30, 212
Keenan, Frank, 364, 420
Keene, Laura, 71
Keith and Proctor theaters, 395
Keith Theatre circuit, 290
Kelley, Edgar Stillman, 211-12, 214, 242
Kelly, J.D., 121
Kelsey, Herbert, 183
Kemble, Charles, 135
Kendal, W.H., Mr and Mrs, 176, 183, 206, 265
Kentucky Colonel, The: adapted by Rankin, 265
Kenwyn, Cora, 313
Key, Thomas Hewitt, 5
Khedival Opera House, Cairo, 329-30
King of Diamonds, The: plot, 203
Kingston, Thomas, 314-16, 322-23, 329
Kiralfy Ballet, 220
Kirk, Henry, 408

Kirkland, Hardie, 227
Kitchener, Lord, 329
Kitty Blanchard Burlesque Troupe, 120
Klaw, Marc, 335, 378, 382, 387, 420-21, 430
Klock, Otto Von, 389
Knight, Mr and Mrs George S., 187
Kotzebue, August, von, 12, 25
Kowalski, Henry, 409

Lackaye, Wilton, 291, 294
Lady Inger of Ostrat: bears O'Neil's philosophy, 324-25; largest audience for Ibsen play, 340
Lambouro, Maria, 315
Lamson, Gertrude, 273-82; first stage appearance, 273. *See also* O'Neil, Nance
Lamson, Lizzie, 273, 284
Lander, Mrs F.W., 54
Langrish, Jack, 110
Langtry, Lily, 196
Laura Keene's Company, 44
Law and Order Leagues, 237
Lawshé, Er, 417-20
Leah, the Forsaken: racial division, 66-67
Leavitt, M.B., 192-97, 263-64, 280, 333
Led Astray: famous production, 125
Lederer, Emanuel, 299, 326
Lee, Bishop John D., 150, 177
Lee, Henry (Harry), 169, 263-64
Leffingwell, Myron, 262
Leland Opera House, Albany, NY, 156
Leslie, Amy, 91, 234, 252, 341, 348, 413, 422-23, 425, 432
Levy, Becky, 249
Levy, Benjamin A., 387
Lewis, James, 61
Lewis, Jeffreys, 279
lighting: coal lamps, 111; electric, 186, 233; gas, 9; oil lamps, 9
Lily, The: background, 410; New York opening, 411-12
Lincoln, Abraham, 11, 261-62; assassination, 44-46, 262

Lincoln, Robert, 263
Lincoln, Victoria, 368
Lindsay, Howard, 426-27
lines of business, 8, 30, 123
Lingard, William Horace, 82, 385
Lingham, Matthew, 19, 23, 113, 167
Little Belle, 167-68
Little Mamie, 140, 152
Lloyd, Colonel, 82
Lock, Matthew, 212
Logan, Olive, 87, 119
London Assurance: box set, 12-13
Long Strike, The: plot, 65-66
Longfellow, Henry Wadsworth, 154, 358
Lord Dundreary, 27, 208
Los Angeles Theatre, Los Angeles, 276
Louisville Theatre, Louisville, KY, 36
Lourenco Marques, 329
Lowell, James Russell, 168, 358
Ludlow St jail, 149
Lyceum Theatre, Denver, 278, 281
Lyceum Theatre, London, 331, 333
Lyceum Theatre, New York, 337
Lykens, William, 395
Lytell, W.H., 151

Macauley, Barney, 30, 32
Macbeth: in Brooklyn, 245-46; innovations of Rankin, 148, 364-65; music for, 211-14; production at Niblo's Garden, 244-45; Rankin's direction of, 214-16; Rankin's San Francisco production, 211-18; realism of, 213; souvenir edition, 321; supernumeraries for, 214, 244-45
Macdonald, John A., 4, 168
Macdonald, John Sanfield, 11
MacKay, Steele, 135
Mackay, Frank, 51-52, 98, 126, 131, 132, 136, 143, 145
Mackay, John, 106
Mackaye, Steele, 429
Macready, William Charles, 8, 22, 47
Madison Square Theatre Company, 253
Maeder, Fred, 80, 185, 221, 239, 247, 249, 251, 254; death, 261

Magda: plot, 297; as protest against tyranny of convention, 310; O'Neil in London in, 332
Maginly, Ben, 164
Maguire, Tom, 79, 102, 104, 157
Majeroni, George, 313, 384
Majeroni, Mario, 384
Managers' and Stars' Agency, 160
Manhattan Theatre, New York, 372
Mansfield, Richard, 135, 187-88, 288
Marble, Ed, 120
Marble, Emma, 204, 207, 210
Marbury, Jane, 379-80, 386
Marlowe, Julia, 268, 355
Marlowe, Owen, 7, 43, 51, 142
Marston, Richard, 201
Martin, Luke, 183, 242
Mary Magdalene, 428-29
Mason Theatre, Los Angeles, 425
Masonic Temple, Louisville, KY, 38
matinees, 52
Matthews, Charles, 24, 60
Mayall, Herschel, 338-39, 388
Mayhew, Katie, 112, 114, 117, 120
Mayo, Frank, 61, 169, 263-64, 292; death, 285-86; experiments with ensemble playing, 183
Mayo, Martha, 391, 415
Mazzanovitch, John, 204, 208-209, 213, 217, 220, 224; death, 230; ill, 221; retirement, 225; returns, 223
McCullough, John, 29, 103, 144, 196, 199, 206, 230, 253; death, 218
McGee, D'Arcy, 46
McHenry, Carrie, 102, 118
McKee Rankin combination company, 139-40
McKee Rankin Comedy Company, 113, 118
McKee Rankin School of Acting, 291, 293
McKee, Alexander "Sandy," 171, 195, 290
McKee, Alexander, 4
McKee, Captain Thomas, 4
McKee, Colonel Alexander, 4-5
McKee, Frank, 346

McKee, Thomas, 5
McKee, Thomas, manager, 238, 246, 251
McVicker's Theatre, Chicago, 77, 84, 93, 148, 270
McVicker, Horace, 296, 334
McVicker, Mrs, 296
McWade, Robert, 112, 262
Meade, James, 163
Meech, Wellington, 8
melodeons, 34
melodrama and villainy, 71
melodrama of moral reform, 48
melodrama, French, 71
Mendelssohn, Felix, 212, 220-21
Mendum, Georgie, 367
Menken, Adah Isaacs, 17, 84
Merced Theatre, Los Angeles, 104
Mervale, Gaston, 380-81
mesmerism, 286, 350-51
Mestayer, Louis, 160
Metro-Rolfe studios, 436
Metropolitan House Cafe, 68
Metropolitan Theatre, Denver, 255
Metropolitan Theatre, Indianapolis, IN, 24
Metropolitan Theatre, Minneapolis, 296
Metropolitan Theatre, Rochester, NY, 7-8
Michels, Madame Ivan, 137, 139
Midsummer Night's Dream, A: harmonized direction, 220-21
Miller, Joaquin, 142, 148, 154, 167, 170-73, 191; death, 428; description of, 146; paid in full for *The Danites*, 173
Millward, Charles, 337-38, 379
Miln, George Crichton, 41, 332
Miner, Harry, 242-45, 260, 335
Mischler circuit, 180
Mitchell, Maggie, 16, 24, 253
Mitchell, Mary, 16, 39-40
Mitchell's Olympic, New York, 114
mobility of actors, 30
Moçambique town, 329
Modjeska, Madame Helene, 298, 311, 358, 385
Monna Vanna: problem play, 385

monopoly on western theaters, 303
Montauk Theatre, Brooklyn, 389
Montfort, 135
Moody, William Vaughn, 164
Mooney's minstrels, 32
Moore, Maggie, 171
Mordaunt, Frank, 60, 191-92, 202, 205, 209-11, 233, 235, 310: as Macbeth, 217
Moriacchi, Madame, 104
Mormon Theatre, Salt Lake City, 108-109, 193
Morosco Theatre, San Francisco, 264
Morosco-Burbank Theatre, Los Angeles, 311
Morris, Clara, 77, 101, 124-27, 133, 186, 190-91, 355, 359; as Cora in *Article 47*, 134
Morris, Isabelle, 199, 204, 210
Morrison, Charlotte Nickinson, 156
Morrison, Lewis, 183-84, 196
Morton, C.H., 99, 169, 171
Morton, Frank, 354
Mountain Meadows Massacre, 108, 150, 177
Mullaly, W.S., 221
Mundy, Colonel Marc, 37
Murdoch, James, 56
Murdock, James, 30, 58
Murphy, Joe, 43, 60
Murphy, Joseph, 191
Murray Hill Theatre, New York, 287, 289, 291-93, 372
Museum Theatre. *See* Wood's Museum, Philadelphia
Musgrove, partner to Williamson, 317
Myer's Opera House, Chicago, 120
Myers, Louise, 61
Myers, Louise, 61
Myers, Mary, 138-39

Naiad Queen: extravaganza, 19
Nance O'Neil company, 310, 342, 344-45, 375-76, 384-93
Nanny, or, The Dutch Orphans, 102
Napoleon II, 303
National Theatre, Cincinnati, OH, 23, 34, 76

National Theatre, Philadelphia, 33
National Union of Theatrical Employees, 333
Naval Cadet, A: Rankin directs, 283-84
Nazimova, 397
Neafie, John Andrew Jackson, "Mr," 8, 9-10, 26-27
Nethersole, Olga, 359
New Chestnut St Theatre, Philadelphia, 57, 121, 143, 146, 147, 235, 263
New Danites, The: by Rankin, 245
New East Lynne, The: revised by Rankin, 294-95
New Market Frye's Opera House, Portland, OR, 197
New Sadler's Wells, 166-70
New Walnut St Theatre, Philadelphia, 46
New York Clipper, 30
New York Dramatic Mirror, The, 162
New York Dramatic News, The, 163
New York Theatre, New York, 63, 64, 81
Niblo's Garden, New York, 63, 72, 79, 83, 98, 121, 181, 243, 260
Nickinson, John, 6-7, 16-17, 19, 23, 85, 98; death, 30
Nickinson, Virginia (Mrs Marlowe), 6, 283, 285, 309
Nightingales, 6
Ninth St Theatre, Tacoma, WA, 280
Nixon, 335, 378
Nodier, Charles, 281
Notice to Quit, 192-93
Notre Dame: production of, 222-23
Novelty Theatre, Brooklyn, NY, 162
Nunnemacher's Opera House, Milwaukee, WI, 112

O'Brien, 106
O'Madigan, Isabelle, 391, 415
O'Neil, Eliza, 280
O'Neil, James, 172
O'Neil, Nance, 424; 1st London appearance, 306-308; as Elizabeth in *Elizabeth, Queen of England*, 301, 327; as Fedora in

Index

Fedora, 344-45; as Floria Tosca in *La Tosca*, 319; as Hedda in *Hedda Gabler*, 317-18, 339, 356; as Lady Inger of Ostrat, 340; as Lady Macbeth, 338, 364, 377, 385, 387; first time, 312; in Australia, 322; as Magda in *Magda*, 310; as Marguerite Gautier in *Camille*, 300-301, 310, 315, 359; as Marie Antoinette in *Marie Antoinette*, 381; as Marie in *The Fires of St John*, 356; as Nancy in *Oliver Twist*, 300; as Odette in *The Lily*, 412; as Rebekka West in *Rosmersholm*, 387-88; as Rosalind in *As You Like It*, 345-46; as Zoraya in *The Sorceress*, 392; attack on O'Neil, 309, 396-97; attacked by New York critics, 371-75; caught and compromised, 304; changes name from Gertrude Lamson, 282; compared to Mary Anderson, 358; comparison to Bernhardt, 338; death, 438; defends Rankin, 305; description of, 279-80, 342, 359-60; desperate for a manager, 346; failure as Juliet in *Romeo and Juliet*, 345; following among women, 317, 357, 369; her voice, 301, 357, 361-62; illness, 285-86; impact on San Francisco, 299-300; in London, 307-308, 330-33; in sketch *$1000 Reward*, 409; in Spanish plays, 438; loyalty to Rankin, 398; O'Neil as Parthenia in *Ingomar, the Barbarian*, 300; O'Neil's intelligence, 311; opening night in Boston, 355; plans world tour, 387; point of despair, 396; preference for classical drama, 375; profit, 340, 363, 382; quarrel and split with Rankin, 406-407; reception in Melbourne, 379; reception in Sydney, 314; refinement of roles, 311; success in Boston, 359-60; training under Rankin, 289, 341; view of films, 438; views on Belasco, 410; writes to Rankin, 383, 386

O'Neil-Rankin company, 310
Ohio-Michigan circuit, 155
Ojibwa Indians, 1-2
Old Bowery, The, New York, 63
Old Heads and Young Hearts: upholstery school, 52
Old London: play by Rankin, 239
Oldfield, Nance, 282, 308
Oliver Twist: intricacies of, 349-50; Rankin's version, 302-303
Olivier, Laurence, 349
Olympic Music Hall, Philadelphia, 34
Olympic Theatre, London, England, 60, 137
Olympic Theatre, New York, 63, 65, 67
Olympic Theatre, St Louis, MO, 66, 113
Opera House, Columbus, OH, 38
Opera House, Honolulu, 302
Opera House, Port Elizabeth, SA, 329
opera bouffe, 69, 72
Oregon circuit, 254
Orpheum circuit, 348, 409, 418
Orpheum Theatre Syndicate, 422
Osbourne, George, 208, 227-28, 264, 272, 278, 421
Owens, John E., 24, 84
Oxenford, John, 138

Palmer, Alfred Marshall (Harry), 123-26, 130-38, 145, 235
panic of 1873, 137, 196
Papakura, Maggie, 323
paper the house, 403
Park St Theatre, Brooklyn, NY, 99
Park Theatre, Boston, 283
Park Theatre, Brooklyn, NY, 121, 180
Park Theatre, New York, 57, 63
Parkes, A.L., 113
Parrott, John, Jr, 212
Parselle, John, 123, 188
Parsloe, Charles T., 142, 155, 163, 263; example of the importance of stage business, 161
Pasadena Opera House, Pasadena, CA, 276
Pastor, Tony, 34, 192
payment of actors, 8, 29, 52, 133, 153, 268, 402-403, 427

Peace on Earth, 419
Perley, Frank, 343, 346
Phillips, Watts, 80
Pico, 104
Pierce, Frank, 136
Piercy, Sam, 137
Pike's (Grand) Opera House, New York, 80, 89, 98, 152, 160, 166, 173, 377
Pike's Dramatic Company, 93-94
Pike's Opera House, Cincinnati, OH, 16-17, 19, 21, 23-24
Pinero, Arthur, 302
Piper's Opera House, Virginia City, 105, 107, 157
Piper, John, 105, 157
piracy of plays, 139, 156
Pittsburgh Theatre, Pittsburgh, OH, 40-41
Pixley, Annie, 157
plays, paucity of good, 347
Plimmer, Harry, 314, 320, 336
Plympton, Eben, 268-70
Ponisi, Madame Elizabeth, 56-57, 122
Porter, Admiral, 219, 243-44
Potter, Mrs, 320
Potter, Paul, 281
Powell, Lord Baden, 328
Powers, William H., 104-109
Pratt, Harry, 152
Preaner, Mr, 298
Price, E.D., 199, 206, 218, 235
Price, Fanny, 78, 156
Princess Louise, 165
Princess Theatre, London, 331
Proctor's 23rd Street Theatre, New York, 348
Proctor's Theatre, New York, 294
Proctor's Theatre, Newark, NJ, 348
Proctor, Joseph, 28, 29
Providence Opera House, Providence, RI, 183
Provost, Mary, 23, 26
Pulitzer, Joseph, 175

quick studies, 28, 298

Ralston, 103
Rand, Helen, 205
Randolph, Eva, 173, 174
Ranken, Agnes. *See* Rankin, Agnes
Rankin's Comedy Theatre, St Louis, MO, 114-118
Rankin's cooperative stock company: members, 192, 210; change of direction, 225; demise, 234; excellence recognized continent-wide, 224; strongest organization, 196; terms, 192
Rankin's Third Avenue Theatre, 185-92, 250, female ushers of, 190
Rankin, Agnes, 341-43, 386, 388, 439; Rankin's daughter, 341
Rankin, Arthur (Davenport), 435-36
Rankin, Arthur McKee: alcohol abuse, 320, 351, 401, 403; amateur acting, 6-7; as '49 in *'49*, 178; as Adam Bashford in *The Lonely Man of the Ocean*, 48; as Badger in *The Streets of New York*, 78; as Bill Sykes in *Oliver Twist*, 272-73, 302, 316, 422, 424; as Bob Brierly in *The Ticket-of-Leave Man*, 32, 40; as Brauer in *The Fires of St John*, 380; as Captain Henri de Lagardere in *The Duke's Motto*, 140; as Colonel Schwartze in *Magda*, 345, 355, 374, 380, 393, 425; as Count de Valnay in *A Prisoner for Life*, 208-209; as Elliot Gray in *Rosedale*, 78; as Fagin in *Oliver Twist*, 74, 78, 152; as George Henley, 7; as Georges de Lesparre in *Led Astray*, 125; as Giuseppi Fioretti in *Our Boarding House*, 144, 148; as Hugh Chalcourt in *Ours*, 76-77; as Iago in *Othello*, 62; as Jack Yeulett in *Hoodman Blind*, 223-24; as Jacques Frochard in *The Two Orphans*, 131-32; as Jean-Baptiste Cadeaux in *The Canuck*, 254, 258; as Johnny Reilly in *The Long Strike*, 65; as Larkin Bunce in *Cameo Kirby*, 409; as Littleton Coke in *Old Heads and Young Hearts*, 52-53; as Macbeth in *Macbeth*, 28, 147-48, 216, 321-

22; as Othello in *Othello*, 41; as Poyntz in *School*, 85; as Quasimodo in *Notre Dame*, 223; as Randolph Chandoce in *Led Astray*, 204; as Reuben Gilbert in *Peace on Earth*, 420; as Rip in *Rip Van Winkle*, 94, 118-19; as Sandy McGee in *The Danites*, 150-51; as Savigny in *The Sphinx*, 127-28; as Shoulders in *The King of Diamonds*, 203; as Sir Charles Pomander in *Masks and Faces*, 54; as Sir Peter Teazle in *A School for Scandal*, 320-21; as stage manager, 93, 272, 292, 363, 374; as The Stranger in *Dot*, 68; as Vicomte de Flachon in *The Pavements of Paris*, 199-200; as walking gentleman, 12, 21-22; as Wool in *The Hidden Hand*, 27, 31; athleticism, 48; bankruptcy, 119, 258, 357; birth, 1; charged with hypnotizing O'Neil, 350-51; civil servant, 11; commission in the Union Army, 12; compared to Salvini, 194, 223; considered hopeless in business, 154, 192; constructing *The Danites*, 142-43; cracking under pressure, 165-66; creates new kind of hero, 136; criticized for old style of acting, 248, 371; criticizes modern style, 341; crudity, 57; death 432; defends O'Neil, 377-78; description of, 234, 351, 383-84; directs film *The Danites*, 423; education, 5, 17; encourages playwrights to travel with his companies, 159; failure to repay loans, 369-70, 401; failure, 43, 76, 267; first professional appearance in Canada, 38-39; first professional experience, 8; harassment for debt, 162, 401; his beard, 168, 172; his mastery at staging, 200; his production policy, 202; his talent directing children, 219; his theater boycotted, 274; horsemanship, 6; illegal retention of a manuscript, 306; illness, 275; in musical burlesque, 64; inherits from his father, 267; knight of the parlor, 80; learns art of make-up, 17; lectures on the theater, 367; legal actions, 155-56, 165, 166, 179-80, 232, 242, 251, 255, 257-58, 261, 265, 267, 274, 280-81, 350, 376, 379, 384, 390, 400, 412-13; marriage to Caroline Henri, 60; marriage to Kitty Blanchard, 94; nervous breakdown, 255-56; not a moment to himself, 252; opinion on acting, 289, 342, 346-47, 384; pantaloon hero, 75; pays alimony to Blanchard, 265; phenomenal in vaudeville, 287; potential of, 133-34; promotional talent, 306; public quarrel with Blanchard, 252; quarrel with Cleveland, 349-50; quarrel with George, 256; ranks first among Canadian actors, 94; razor, 422; re-writing *Dark Days*, 210; salary at the Union Square Company in 1883, 187; settled long-standing debts, 311; social person, 61; sued by Blanchard, 258; sues Joaquin Miller, 178; thoughts on melodrama, 26, 347; tutor of acting, 133; versatility, 53, 67, 196; vigilance over O'Neil, 325; weight problem, 188, 295; writes one-act plays, 422

Rankin, Colonel Arthur, 1-7, 10, 38-39, 184, 190, 256, 290; background, 2; death, 267; rescue of runaway slave, 2-4; showmanship, 2

Rankin, Doris, 253, 266, 268, 272, 274, 277-78, 417-22, 428, 439; birth, 244; death, 437; marries Lionel Barrymore, 367; national acclaim, 419

Rankin, George Cameron, 46, 114, 117, 184, 238-39, 247, 256, 290; birth, 4; death, 354; sues McKee, 267

Rankin, Mary Gladys "Dido," 101-102, 107-108, 111, 127, 152,

208, 221, 265-66, 269-72, 277-79, 289, 367, 397-98, 421, 424; death 431; debut of, 252; elopes, 253; starts career as playwright (George Cameron), 367
Rankin, Mary McKee, 1, 10, 11, 12, 38, 184, 267; death, 190
Rankin, Phyllis "Pixie," 208, 221, 263, 265, 269, 272-77, 288-89, 348, 367, 418, 421, 432, 435-37; birth, 127; death, 437; debut, 257; elopes, 277-78; marriage to Harry Davenport, 308; stars as Fifi Fricot in *The Belle of New York*, 294-95; toast of London, 307-308
Rankin-Drew combination, 281-83
Rankin-Lewis company, 279
Rankin-Rankin-Barrymore troupe, 419
Ratcliffe, E.J., 337-38, 347, 349-50, 361-62, 365-66, 369
Ray, Charles G., 209-10
Ray, Charley, 208, 233
Raymond, John T., 83, 103, 208
Raymond, Mrs John T., 294
Reade, Charles, 281
Redding, Joseph, 207, 220
Rede, Percy, 183
Reed, Charley, 228-30
Rehan, Ada, 133
Rent Day, The: new type of villain, 18 respectability in the theater, 25
Rial, Jay, 197, 199, 202, 204, 226
Rial, Louise, 205
Rialto, 68, 123, 159
Rice, E.E., 399, 401-402, 432
Rich, Isaac, 242
Riel Rebellion, 4
Riggold, B.T., 152
Rigle, Emily, 183, 188
Riley, W.H., 24-26, 28-30
Ring, Jimmy, 283
Ring, Julia, 283
Rip Van Winkle: endorsed humane values, 92; Rankin tours with only, 118-19
Ristori, 63, 197, 301, 325, 339
Rivals, The: vehicle for Drew-Rankin company, 268-71

Rivers, Frank, 34, 65, 75
Road to Ruin, The: reworked by Mrs Drew, 270
Robert Macaire: advances the concept of the working class hero, 48
Roberts, David, 200
Roberts, J.B., 28
Robertson, Tom, 75, 77; innovation, 71-72, 83; quest for realism, 76, 116
Robinson, Forrest, 273, 367, 439
Robson, Andrew, 292-94, 379
Robson, Stuart, 51-52, 69, 99, 119-120, 142, 144-45, 148, 172, 383, 395
Robyns, Mr and Mrs William, 348
Rockwell, Orin, 150
Rogers, Ben, 103
Rogers, Katherine, 122
Roosevelt, President Franklin, 436
Rose, Billy, 438
Ross, Fred, 269
Royal Lyceum, Hamilton, ON, 6
Royal Lyceum, Toronto, ON, 6, 38
Royal Opera House, Toronto, 164
Runaway Wife, The, 246; plot, 248-49
Rushton, Lucy, 59
Russell, Townsend, 249
Ryan, Belvil, 69, 113, 126
Ryan, Sam, 44

Salisbury Troubadors, 188
Salisbury, Charles, 357, 361, 365, 369
Salisbury, Nate, 218
Salvini, Signor Tommaso, 41, 229; mental power of, 223
San Francisco earthquake, 388-89
San Francisco in the 1880s, 198-99
San Gabriel mission, 105
Sardou, Victorien, 27, 71, 183, 319, 382
Savoy Theatre, New York, 336
Saxe-Meiningen company, 182-83
Saxe-Meiningen, George II, Duke of, 182-83, 203, 353
Scardon, Paul, 384-85, 403, 409
scenery: borders, 153; flats, 153; flipper, 153; history of, 200-201; led to public appreciation of art, 201;

scenic painter, 200; shipping of, 153; wings, 153
Schoeffel, John, 242, 357, 361-63, 365-66, 371-72, 376, 379, 384
Schoolteacher at Bottle Flat, 142
Scott, Mrs A.W., 428
Scott, Sir Walter, 112
Scott-Siddons, Mary Francis, 100-101
Scribe, Eugene, 71, 183
seating at New York theaters, 185
Secor and Blair, 390
Selig Polyscope Theatre Company, 423
Selwyn company, 90, 93, 97
Selwyn's Theatre, Boston, 95, 98, 120
Selwyn, John, 95, 98
Sensation, horse, 49
Seward, William, 46
Shaftesbury Theatre, London, 307
Shakespeare, William, 353; anniversary of death, 147
Shaw, George Bernard, 27, 288, 353, 370
Sheehan, manager, 383
Shelly, P.B., 280
Sheridan, Frank, 281
Sheridan, J.F., 101
Sheridan, Richard Brinsley, 229
Sheridan, W.E. (Bill), 66, 89, 164, 167, 171, 179
Sherman, General William T., 36-37
Sherman, John, 213, 432
Shirley, Lizzie, 118
Shook and Collier, 190
Shubert Brothers, 352, 378, 401-408, 410-11
Shubert, Lee, 402
Shubert, Sam, 352
Simmonds and Brown, 170-71, 175
Skimpole, Harold, Dickens' character, 275, 393
Skinner, Otis, 354
Skirmish Line, The: plot, 249-50
Smith, Billy, 275
Smith, Joseph, 149-50
Smith, Mark, 64, 117
Snell, Edna, 395
snide cast, 157
Sorceress, The: Sardou's best play, 391

Sothern, E.A., 27, 208, 253
Sothern, Sam, 208
Sound country circuit, 197
Spreckels, Adolphe, 302, 427
St Clair, Sally, 25-26
St. Marc: power of tableaux, 22
stage manager, 69
Stair and Havlin theaters, 352
Standard Theatre, London, 170
Standard Theatre, New York, 186
Standard Theatre, San Francisco, 198
Stanfield, Clarkson, 200
Stanley, Alma Stuart, 194, 199, 202, 205
Stanley, Charles, 113, 241
Stark, James, 47
Starr, Frances, 353, 438
stars chose the plays, 42
Stephens, George, 432
Sterling, George, 157
Sterling, Harriet, 294
Stevens, Ashton, 300, 334, 345
Stevenson, Charles, 188-89
Stevenson, Robert Louis, 313
Stewart, Anita, 436
Stockwell, L.R., 264, 302, 338, 340, 343-44, 346, 386, 399
Stoddard, Blanche, 338, 345, 357, 362-63
Stoddart, Belle, 266
Stoddart, J.H., 65, 67, 188
Straight from the Heart: Rankin directs, 286
Stranger, The: message of, 12
Sudermann, Hermann, 384, 388; reveals the human heart, 297
Sullivan, Arthur, 227
Sullivan, Robert, 364
summer seasons in Canada, 38
Sunday performances, 237
Sutro Heights, San Francisco, 345-46
Swain, Carrie, 208
Swickard, Charles, 384, 389, 400
Sylvester, Louise, 51, 102

Talbin, painter, 200
Tanner, Cora, 166, 169, 187
Tecumapease, 5
Tennyson, Alfred, 168

Tennyson, Lord Hallam, 318
Terry, Ellen, 282
That Girl From Mexico: fame for the Sidney Drews, 265
Thayer, E.N., 210
The Danites, 146, 148-175; 2nd American company, 167; 2nd English company, 171; American company for England, 167; anti-Mormon, 195; challenge to middle-class hegemony, 164; expenses in England, 170; film of, 423; improvement in, 160; opening of, 149; payment for, 146; plot, 149-50; realism of, 164; run of, 175; terms for American theaters, 171; without the Parson, 181
theater: abbreviated combination company, 154; actors' theatre, 180; average run of, 162; burlesque as satire, 64; burlesque as spectacle, 72; combination company, 71, 153; combination system, 69-70; on the wane, 182; rise of, 158; commercialization of, 74, 180, 203, 234; decline of, 158; democratic change in, 9; disadvantages of combination system, 184-85; documentary, 262; ensemble playing and theatrical reform, 182; long runs, 95; naturalism, 258; paternal melodrama, 9; problem drama, 234, 311; realism, 71, 262; repertory, 84, 98, 184, 224, 234, 268, 291, 428; Saxe-Meiningen, 182-83, 211, 429; stage naturalism, 183; star system, 69; stock company, 24, 70-71, 291-93, 336, 347; loss of, 158; revival of, 182; local stock, 334-35; theatrical middlemen, 180; to educate the public, 42, 87, 414; upholstery school, 52
theater agent, 70; mistreatment by, 180
theatre attendance, slump in, 202-203
theatre circuits, 160
theater fire, 354-55
theater manager, 70, 401

theater trains, 161
Theatre Comique, New York, 82-83
Theatre des Varieties, New York, 63
Theatre Republic, San Francisco, fire, 434-44
Theatre Royal, Montreal, 39, 94
Theatre Royale, Adelaide, 318
Theatre Royale, Sydney, 313
Theater Syndicate, 304, 305-306, 334-336, 340, 343, 352, 362, 374, 387, 415; in trouble, 378; new ideology, 335
Theatrical Managers' Association of America, 159
theatrical families, inter-relationships, 207
Thomas, Augustus, 271, 408
Thompson's Theatrical Exchange, 335
Thompson, Denman, 419
Thompson, Lydia, 97-98
Thorne, Charles, Jr, 100-101, 103, 124-126, 132-137, 172, 183; death, 136; style, 135-36
Thorne, Charles, Sr, 44, 103, 207
Thorne, Emily, 28, 289
Throne, Charles, Jr, 83
Ticket-of-Leave Man, The: protests injustice, 32; Rankin fights Florence in, 284
Tilton, E.L., 51-52, 89, 188
Todd, Mike, 438
Tool, John, 168
touring, discomforts of, 193, 376, 393
Tree, Herbert Beerbohm, 308
Tremont Theatre, Boston, 357, 361-62
Trilby, Rankin's version, 281,
troupe manager, 69
True, Loring Blanchard, 33
Tupper, Colin, 168
Tupper, Sir Charles, 168
Tuttle, Zoe, 208
Two Men of Sandy Bar: influence on Rankin, 142
Two Orphans, The: most successful play, 129-39; plot, 130-31; profit, 131
Tyngsboro, 367, 386-87, 390, 393-95, 400

Index

Ulmer, Lizzie May, 182
Ulrich, Lenore, 353
Under the Polar Star: naval pageant, 233
Underhill, John Garrett, 438
Undine, 79
Union Square company, 129, 187-88
Union Square Theatre, New York, 123-29, 184, 187-90, 201
United Booking Office, 395
University College School, 5
Upper Canada College, 6
utility, 8

Vanbrugh, Sir John, 200
Vandenhoff, Charles, 65, 95, 99, 136-39, death, 257
Vandenhoff, George, 128
vaudeville, 287, 290, 348, 352, 395-98, 408, 418, 425; performance times, 294
Verne, Jules, 233
Vernon, W.H., 226
Vestris, Madame, 13, 51
Vestvali, Felicia, 47-48
Veteran, The: Rankin's stage management of, 201; scenery of, 201
Vezin Herman, 332
Victoria Theatre, Victoria, BC, 197
vigilantes, 104, 106-107
Vitagraph Company, 436
Vitagraph Theatre, New York, 431
Voegtlin, William, 201, 204

Waite, Annie, 118
Walcot, Charles M., 98
Walcot, Mrs Charles M., 98
Walcott, Ernest, 281
Waldron, George B., 152, 154, 165; praise for the Danite Carter, 168
Waldron, Isabelle, 174
Wall Street Bandit, A: plot, 218-19; profit from, 219
Wall's Dramatic Agency, 164
Wallace, J.J., 192, 209-11, 218-19, 226-27, 233; played every male part in *Macbeth*, 214
Wallack's New York company, 183

Wallack's Theatre, New York, 55, 63, 73, 192, 204, 223
Wallack, Fanny, 152
Wallack, J.H., 137
Wallack, J.W., 19-23, 74, 117; death, 120
Wallack, Lester, 70, 98, 126, 135, 202
Waller, D.M., 28, 58, 67
Waller, Emma, 28, 41, 58, 66, 309; acting style, 28
Walnut St Theatre, Philadelphia, 141, 147
Walsh, Blanche, 286, 415
Walter, Master, 118
Walters, Jean Clara, 199
Warbrick, Alfred, 323
Ward, Genevieve, 226-27
Ward, James, 65, 69, 142
Ward, Thomas, 197
Warren, William, 135, 207
Waters, Adele, 202, 205, 226-27, 232, 235, 239; death, 276-77
Weaver, Henry A., 30, 61, 296
Webb, Ada, 39
Webb, Emma, 39
Weber and Fields, 352
Weber and fields, 287-88
well-made play, 71, 183
Wellington Opera House, Wellington, New Zealand, 382
Western drama, death of, 186
Western Moving Picture Company, 429-30
Western, Helen, 16, 47, 84
Western, Lucille, 16, 66-67, 74-75, 89-91, 95, 152, 253, 292; as Nancy in *Oliver Twist*, 89-90
Whalley, W.H., 103
Wheatcroft, Adeline, 400
Wheelan, 431
Wheeler, Andrew C., 177-78, 215-16
Wheeling Opera House, Toledo, OH, 118
White Slaver, The, 418
Whiteside, Walker, 425
Whitman, 61
Whittier, John Greenleaf, 154

Wicked World, The: satirizing the romantic hero, 124
Wife and Child: plot, 221. See also *The Runaway Wife*
Wilder, Marshall, 289
Wilkins, Marie, 89, 99, 126, 132, 136
Wilkins, painter, 233
Williams, L., 169
Williams, Mr and Mrs Barney, 54-55
Williams, Susie, 220, 227, 232-33
Williamsburg Opera House, Williamsburg, NY, 79
Williamson, J.C. "Jim," 171, 366, 308, 313-14, 317, 319-21, 331, 361, 378, 381
Willow Copse, The: influence on the stage, 18
Wills, W.G., 206
Wilton, Elie, 204-205, 210; as Lady Macbeth, 213, 217
Windsor Theatre, New York, 173, 181, 261
Windsor Town Hall, Windsor, ON, 40
Winter Garden, New York, 63, 68
Woffington, Peg, 28, 308
Woman in Black, A: Rankin directs, 286
Wood's Museum, Chicago, 84, 93
Wood's Museum, Philadelphia, 139, 141, 145
Wood's Theatre, Cincinnati, OH, 12, 15, 23
Wood's Theatre, Louisville, KY, 23, 32-33, 36
Wood, George, 38
Woodthorpe, Edith, 228-29
Woodthorpe, Georgia, 277
Woodyard Hall, New Albany, IN, 38
Woorhees, Winifred, 400
Worrell sisters, Sophia, Irene and Jennie, 93
Wright, Frank, 202, 205, 210
Wyndham, Charles, 112, 352

Ye Liberty Playhouse, Oakland, CA, 394, 398
Young Men's Hall, Detroit, 39
young girls play boys, 242
Young, Brigham, 108-109
Young, Fanny, 64-65

Zavistowski troupe, 19
Zimmerman, 335, 378
Zola, Emile, 183, 194